The Mitterrand years (1981–1995) in France sa\
business and its relationships to government. *From State to Market?* details the French government's policies toward business, which went from nationalization to privatization, deregulation, and ever-increasing European integration, bringing with them the move from a *dirigiste,* or state-directed, economy to a more market-oriented one. It illuminates the statist policymaking processes in which the *dirigiste* or "heroic" policies formulated without business input have given way to more everyday policies based on a growing consensus between business and government.

Professor Schmidt profiles the players, the interpenetrating elite of top business and government officials who share a common state educational history and career track and who, as the beneficiaries of the all-pervasive culture of the state, have managed not only to maintain their hold in the ministries but also to colonize industry. These changes in policies and processes, if not players, contributed to the revitalization of the economy and the restructuring of capital.

While lending new insights into French industrial policy and providing new empirical evidence based on interviews with over forty top business and government officials, *From State to Market?* sets French state–society relations in comparative perspective with a new theoretical framework that contrasts the pluralist model of the United States and the corporatist model of the smaller European countries and Germany with France's statist model, also characteristic of Japan and Great Britain. Professor Schmidt concludes, moreover, that the changes resulting from the impact of European integration and the dismantling of the *dirigiste* state have generated a crisis for France's statist model of policymaking.

FROM STATE TO MARKET?

FROM STATE TO MARKET?

The transformation of French business and government

VIVIEN A. SCHMIDT

University of Massachusetts

Published by the Press Syndicate of the University of Cambridge
The Pitt Building, Trumpington Street, Cambridge CB2 1RP
40 West 20th Street, New York, NY 10011-4211, USA
10 Stamford Road, Oakleigh, Melbourne 3166, Australia

First published 1996

Printed in the United States of America

Library of Congress Cataloging-in-Publication Data
Schmidt, Vivien Ann, 1949–
From state to market? : the transformation of French business and
government / Vivien A. Schmidt.
p. cm.
Includes index.
ISBN 0-521-49742-6 – ISBN 0-521-55553-1 (pbk.)
1. Industrial policy – France. 2. France – Politics and
government – 1981– 3. Industrial management – France. 4. Public
officers – France – Interviews. I. Title.
HD3616.F83S36 1996
338.944 – dc20 95-32609
CIP

A catalog record for this book is available from the British Library.

ISBN 0-521-49742-6 Hardback
ISBN 0-521-55553-1 Paperback

Contents

Contents

Contents

Contents

Preface

The Mitterand years (1981–1995) saw the transformation of French business and government. This book describes that transformation and discusses why it occurred, how it was accomplished, and by whom, by considering the policies, processes, and players in industrial policymaking and their impact on business. More specifically, the book details the governmental policies toward business, policies that shifted from nationalization to privatization, deregulation, and ever-increasing European integration, bringing with them the move from a *dirigiste,* or state-directed, economy to a more market-oriented one. It illuminates the "statist" policymaking processes that, although always less *dirigiste* than traditionally assumed because the "heroic" policies formulated without business input were generally adapted at the implementation stage to business needs, became even less *dirigiste* as the heroic gave way to more everyday policies based on a growing consensus between business and government. It profiles the players, the interpenetrating elite of top business and government officials who share a common state educational history and career track and who, as the beneficiaries of the all-pervasive culture of the state, have managed not only to maintain their hold in the ministries despite ostensibly hostile governments of the left and the right but also, as the state has retreated, to colonize industry. Finally, it shows how these changes in policies and processes, if not players, contributed to the revitalization of the economy and the restructuring of capital, with industry rationalized, internationalized, and now owned and controlled by a mixture of public and private financial and industrial concerns; to the improvement of the business environment, through the rehabilitation of business and an end to economic ideology; and to the reform of French managerial practice, with closer labor–management relations, less centralization of decision-making, and the beginnings of change in management recruitment and promotion systems.

The book also offers a new way of thinking about French government and business that sets it into comparative context, arguing not only against views that see France as anomalous because of failure to emulate pluralist or corporatist polities but also against views that see it as the epitome of the strong state. In so doing, it revives an old term, "statist," but infuses it with new meaning as a pattern of policymaking shaped by history, culture, and institutions, which may appear strong from certain vantage points and weak from others. The book outlines this "statist" model of French policymaking, compares it to similar patterns in Japan and Great Britain, and contrasts it with the pluralist pattern of the United States and the corporatist patterns of the smaller European democracies and Germany. Finally, it explores the impact on this model of changes in the substance of French policymaking during the Mitterrand years, especially regarding business and its relationship to government, and points to an impending crisis in this model of democracy, in particular as a result of the pressures of European integration.

Major research for this book began in 1991, when I held a Fullbright Senior Research Scholar Award in Paris. Between February and July 1991, I interviewed over forty top business executives and government officials in industries and ministries. In subsequent yearly visits, I interviewed several more. On the government side, the list includes Roger Fauroux, Minister of Industry under Prime Minister Rocard, and his top two assistants, José Bidegain, in charge of special projects for the Minister, and Jean-Pierre Jouyet, cabinet director of the Minister; Dominique Strauss-Kahn, Minister of Industry under Prime Ministers Edith Cresson and Pierre Bérégovoy; Louis Gallois, at the time of the interview chief executive of SNECMA, the defense contractor, and now head of Aérospatiale, but formerly Director-General of Industry under Ministers of Industry Jean-Pierre Chevènement, Laurent Fabius, Edith Cresson, and Alain Madelin; and Jacques Maisonrouge, former Director-General of Industry under Madelin and, before that, head of IBM World Trade. In addition, I interviewed a number of senior civil servants in the Ministry of Industry and the Ministry of Finance who must remain nameless.

On the business side, to mention but a few, the list includes top managers of nationalized and/or privatized financial concerns such as André Lévy-Lang, president of Paribas; Daniel Lebègue, at the time of the interview Director-General of the BNP and former director of the Treasury; Jean Peyrelevade, currently head of the bank Crédit Lyonnais and formerly head of Suez, but at the time of the interview head of the insurer UAP; and Jean Deflassieux, former head of the Crédit Lyonnais. Among top managers of nationalized and/or privatized industrial concerns, the list includes Jean-Louis Beffa, CEO of Saint-Gobain; Jean Gandois, now head of the CNPF but at the time head of Péchiney; Louis Schweitzer, number one at Renault but number two at the time of the interview;

Francis Lorentz, at the time head of Bull; François de Wissocq, a director of Elf-Aquitaine and former CEO of Cogema; and Jean Grenier, head of Eutelsat and a former top director at France Télécom. Private enterprise was also represented by Bernard Laplace, former head of Ciments Français, the cement manufacturer; Jean-Louis Descours, head of Groupe André, the shoe and clothing retailer; Maisonrouge of IBM, as mentioned above; and a top manager of Lyonnaise des Eaux-Dumez. In addition, those interviewed included several chief economists or strategists of major banks – Jean-Paul Betbèze at the Crédit Lyonnais, Michèle Debonneuil at Indosuez, Bruno Boudrouille of the Caisse des Dépôts – and a number of lesser directors of major corporations who wished to remain anonymous (at Alcatel-Alsthom, France Télécom, EDF). There were also a few management consultants and heads of business associations, such as Michel Drancourt of the Business Institute.

The interviews themselves were fascinating as a window into the "corridors of power" and the people who inhabit them. To begin with, simply getting the interviews was a lesson in French social relations: Only by having a contact who was a good friend or an important acquaintance of the person to be interviewed was it possible to get an appointment. On this score, I am indebted to a numbers of friends and friends of friends, but especially to Dominique Strauss-Kahn (at the time head of the finance and budget committee in the National Assembly), whose assistance proved invaluable for obtaining a number of the interviews.

The interviews themselves were fascinating not only for what they yielded in terms of insights into French government and business, but also in terms of what they revealed personally about this "ruling class." First of all, top business and government leaders are a diverse lot. It is impossible to make any generalizations as to their looks or their manner. They come in all shapes, forms, and attire, although within the limits of being for the most part white, male, and in suits.

Looks are quite varied. Many of the men are short and slender. One is very big, and dwarfs the others. Most are not very stylishly dressed. Only one banker wore what one might have expected: a dark blue Yves Saint Laurent (or equivalent) suit. The women, by contrast, wore fashionable clothing: one in a muted blue silk Daniel Hechter suit, another in a bright blue-purple suit with a white silk blouse and pearl necklace and earrings. Much more colorful than their American counterparts, and consciously so, they were not, as one of them made a point of saying, one of those sad American business women in their sad business suits.

The interaction itself was also extremely varied. One seemed a bit nervous at first, and eager to please. Another stared back after each question, in an almost defiant manner. Some were reticent. Others were chatty: one barely let me get a word in edgewise; another kept me for three hours and twenty minutes relating current French industrial policy to the Merovingians and the Carolingians, and to other important moments in French history. Two of the older business leaders had a funny habit of pulling up their socks many times during the interview. Another had a not so funny habit of illustrating his points with explicit sexual references.

On matters not related to the interview, most steered clear of speaking of family matters (in direct contrast with the typical American pattern). Although most were married and with children, only the women and two of the older men mentioned having offspring. And in keeping with the French tradition of keeping private life separate from public, almost no one mentioned his or her spouse, even though some had prominent ones.

Only one or two sat behind their desks for the interviews. Most sat at the ubiquitous round table with the same set of black (or in one case red) leather chairs, or at the same black (or in one case grey) leather sofa with two side armchairs and the low dark glass coffee table. Truly, the CEOs don't have much imagination when it comes to furnishings. Although the offices were well appointed, with good-quality furniture and the like, they were for the most part not very interesting. Those at the Défense were particularly sterile. There was no Italian furniture here, nor Louis XV, for that matter, with the exception of one or two CEOs who had inherited age-old offices in the center of Paris, and the ministers, of course.

Although the furniture varied little, remaining essentially modern, top-of-the-line fare, the size of the offices varied a great deal. The best, of course, were the corner offices at the Défense, where the large desks seemed way off in the distance. But there was no predicting the size. The office of number three at a big state-owned company at the Défense, with a large picture window overlooking Paris, dwarfed number two's office at a big state-owned, centrally located bank, even though they had the exact same leather sofa, black for the one, grey for the other. Most impressive in the banker's case was the hallway leading to the office, a slowly curving corridor all paneled in dark wood and rimmed by cream plush carpets and white ceilings, seeming to go on forever with doors every couple of feet, minus names or numbers, anonymous, so that I found myself wondering as I wandered through, following the *huissier*, how anyone could find the office he or she worked in.

Neither of these offices, however, could hold a candle to the waiting room of one of the old *banques d'affaires*, an enormous atrium seemingly four stories high, with windows at the upper levels and the walls all in white marble, and what could have been Louis XV or XVI furniture on enormous oriental rugs. Other waiting areas were not as impressive, although sometimes one thing or another struck a note, like the soft pink walls and doors, rimmed in red, with blue plush carpets in the entrance hall of one of the large insurance companies. In one case, most attractive was the elevator of the old Napoleon III building, with its red carpet, red velvet walls, and little glass doors that closed behind the black metal-grilled elevator door.

The individuals who inhabit the corridors of power, in short, are not an extravagant lot, and their surroundings reflect this. Although they are happy to work in grand spaces when these are the legacies of history, they do not try to re-create past glories in modern office buildings. For the most part, these are individuals who have arrived where they are on the basis of merit, and know it, although they do not flaunt it. They are the products of an elite, state educational system that from a very early age declared them "the best and the brightest." They are the ones who have spurred the changes in France that have brought the modernization of both business and government. They are also a rather nice bunch of people.

I thank them wholeheartedly for the interviews, since much depended on the willingness of these very busy individuals to give up some of their precious time. I would also like to thank the Fulbright Foundation for the Senior Research Scholar Award, held from February to July 1991, that enabled me to conduct a large part of the interviews. Additional thanks go to a Healey Grant from the University of Massachusetts that enabled me to engage in follow-up research, in particular on the impact of European integration on France.

I owe much to certain institutions and individuals who facilitated my stay in France: to the University of Paris X, Nanterre, where I was a visiting professor in March 1991, and Professor Michel Basex, who arranged my stay; to the University of Paris V, where I was a visiting professor in November–December 1992, and Professor Michèle Voisset; and to the Maison Suger, which provided lodging in 1992. Thanks also to Marie-Louise Antoni, who very generously allowed me to use the files of the *Nouvel Economiste*. Back in the United States, Stanley Hoffman and the Center for European Studies, as always, provided a congenial environment in which to pursue my research during my sabbatical leave in 1992.

Professional colleagues also deserve mention for helpful comments on early drafts presented as papers at meetings. Particular thanks go to Martin Schain, John Keeler, Amy Mazur, David Wilsford, and Frank Baumgartner, who participated on panels at APSA meetings in 1991 and 1992, the latter of which focused on the statist pattern of policymaking; to Anthony Daley, whose conference at Wesleyan University in April 1992 enabled me to fine-tune some of the issues related to the changes in business and its relationship to government, and to participants at the conference such as George Ross and Mark Kesselman; to Alfred Diamant; and to Peter Katzenstein and Alberta Sbragia for comments on a paper presented at the 1993 APSA meetings on the implications of European integration for France.

In addition, I would like to thank the reviewers of the manuscript for Cambridge University Press, Yves Mény and one anonymous reviewer, whose insightful suggestions have certainly made this a better book. And of course, I cannot forget my editor, Alex Holzman, whose encouragement and interest remained constant throughout. Finally, thanks to my family, friends, and students, all of whom must have gotten very tired of hearing about France by the end of this.

Introduction: From state to market?

In 1981, on the eve of François Mitterrand's accession to the presidency, France's economic outlook appeared grim. The economic miracle of the postwar period, the *trente glorieuses,* or glorious thirty years of economic expansion, had ended. The economy had been particularly hard hit by the oil shocks of the seventies, and seemed unable to regain its balance. Much of big business was either in the red or barely breaking even, and looked like an easy target for foreign acquisition. The government appeared to be overseeing the deindustrialization of an economy which it regulated heavily through controls over prices, wages, foreign exchange, and so forth. Public attitudes toward business were quite negative, while business–labor relations remained adversarial. In short, the country seemed to be grinding to a halt economically, ready to be torn asunder politically, and descending into a highly ideological set of conflicts, with the Communists seemingly at the gates, given the electoral alliance of the left.

By the end of the decade, all this had changed. France was riding the crest of economic success. Most of its major industries were making large profits, and using those profits to expand worldwide. Over the course of the eighties, businesses had modernized and internationalized. Ideological battles appeared a thing of the past, with the Communists in particular in total retreat. The hidebound Bourse had been transformed into an up-to-date stock market and the economy largely deregulated. Labor–management relations had become more cooperative while business had been rehabilitated, with the heads of the major banks and industries having become the darlings of the media. Although many problems still remained, as the French have always been the first to note, the economy had nonetheless made an amazing recovery. And even the subsequent slide into recession in the early nineties could not negate the changes.

Introduction

How was this transformation of French business accomplished? Not as economists might have expected, by following traditional formulae which ordinarily demand governmental stability, predictability in economic policies, a steady opening up to market mechanisms, diminution of the size of the state, and reduction of ideological conflict and ideologically motivated initiatives. On the contrary, since 1981 France has seen wide swings in governmental ideology – from Socialists on the left bringing in "more state" to neoliberals on the right calling for "less state" – and wide swings in policy. There were back-and-forths in industrial policy, with extensive nationalization under the government of Pierre Mauroy in 1982, succeeded by privatization by the government of Jacques Chirac as of 1986, followed by a policy of "*ni-ni*," or neither privatization nor nationalization, as of 1988 under the government of Michel Rocard, which was followed by the post-*ni-ni* period of 1991 under the governments of Edith Cresson and Pierre Bérégovoy, which allowed privatization up to 49%, and finally complete privatization again as of 1993 under the government of Edouard Balladur. There was an abrupt switch in macroeconomic policy, from an initial inflationary, countercyclical approach and a focus on reconquering the domestic market as of 1981 to a program of economic austerity and subsequent support for internationalization beginning in 1983. And there were continuing changes in rules governing business and the economy as a result of the countdown to 1992 and the creation of a single market for the European Community.

With all these disruptions and drastic turnabouts in policy, one might have expected the French economy to founder. It did not. Why? When asked this question, an overwhelming majority of French business executives interviewed by the author responded that the industrial policies of nationalization and privatization had little to do with economic recovery in either a positive or a negative way. The bankers and Treasury officials, for the most part, credited governmental macroeconomic policy, deregulation, and business internationalization. The industrialists added to this an emphasis on the modernization of business, and their own leadership. Only Ministry of Industry officials, past or present, saw industrial policy focused on the microeconomic level as of importance, even though they also agreed that macroeconomic policies were necessary to the economic recovery.

The answer, however, is that it was all this and much more. For recovery also depended upon the underlying stability in the practices and interrelations of business and government which served to offset the tur-

2

bulence on the surface. French economic recovery has much to do with the fact that while the radical shifts in industrial policy created a climate for change, permitting a reevaluation of French attitudes and policies toward business, they at the same time did not seriously challenge the traditional relationship between government and business, their internal operational processes, or their management recruitment and decision-making practices. Moreover, these constancies in patterns of industrial policymaking and management effectively moderated the potentially disastrous impact of the wide swings in ideologically inspired industrial policy represented by nationalization and privatization, at the same time that they may have intensified the effects of more modest policies aimed at deregulation and Europeanization.

Among the continuing practices and interrelationships which served to moderate excessive interventionism and to intensify modest interventions, probably the most important was successive governments' continued adherence to France's traditional "statist" model of policymaking, which ensures that while governments may take heroic action at the policy formulation stage, without much consultation with societal groups, at the implementation stage societal groups have their say. In the industrial policy process, this meant that although business had little input into the formulation of the heroic policies, announced with great fanfare, of nationalization, privatization, and the *ni-ni*, in the implementation of these policies business more often than not got its way, either through mutual accommodation or downright co-optation, with only occasional confrontation.

In addition, the successive governments did nothing to alter the long-standing pattern of interaction between ministries and nationalized industries, where governments tended to respect the traditional managerial autonomy of public enterprises and to name graduates of the ENA (École Nationale d' Administration) or X (École Polytechnique) to head them. Most significantly perhaps, given their strong ideological commitments, neither the Socialists nor the neoliberals sought to alter the traditional profile of the CEO by appointing, for example, union activists or self-made entrepreneurs, or expected the new heads to infuse the firm with the government's stated political values, whether socialist egalitarianism or neoliberal laissez-faire.

This is not to suggest, however, that continuities in policymaking processes therefore in some sense either cancel out changes in institutions or give the lie to shifts in ideology. On the contrary, the shifts in ideology were significant not only as inspiration for governmental initiatives, but also in their indirect effects on societal values. Until the eighties, France as a culture was basically hostile to business. Nationalization and privatization together ended much of this, serving as a way of chasing away ideological demons. With nationalization, the Socialists in some sense exorcised the old ghosts, enabling the entire society to come to see business no longer as exploiter but as "creator of riches." With privatization, by contrast, the neoliberals chased away the new ghosts, if one is permitted to speak in such a way of Thatcherism and Reaganism, demonstrating that privatization was not the panacea anticipated, and that, public or private, business is business.

Moreover, very real changes have occurred in business, which has rationalized and internationalized itself appreciably, and in government, which has reduced its purview, if not its size, through deregulation. Much of this resulted not only from changes in leadership in business and government, but also from European integration, which served as a challenge to business and a spur for government to move from a state-directed economy to a more market oriented one.

Overall, the Mitterrand years saw a revitalization of the economy, with many important indicators suggesting that, however far France has yet to go, it has already come very far indeed. Ironically, the French Socialists, having entered office vowing to establish a socialist economy, ended up creating a more modern, capitalist one. This period saw the restructuring of industry, both in terms of firm activities and of their ownership and control; the renewal of the managerial elite, with a younger and more dynamic although no less elite leadership; and the reform of managerial practice, with closer labor–management relations, more management participation, less centralization of top management decision-making, and the beginnings of change in management recruitment and promotion systems.

Business that had been tightly controlled and facing inward at the beginning of the Mitterrand years had loosened up and turned outward by the end, combining and acquiring with abandon both inside and outside of France. The economy that had been in decline in the previous decade, leaving French businesses vulnerable to foreign takeover, had been revitalized, making it possible for French businesses to take over foreign concerns. Industry that had been undercapitalized, horizontally diversified, and increasingly in the red, was recapitalized, vertically integrated, and for the most part increasingly in the black. Finally, and perhaps most importantly for the future of industry, firms that had been part of the "protected capitalism" of the past, having been controlled by a *noyau dur* or hard core of private industrial investors, have become part of what one might call today's "dynamic capitalism," in which ownership and control are truly mixed, with nationalized and privatized, public and private firms controlling one another through participation in the *noyaux durs,* and with banks for the first time also participating, such that the French model of industrial capital structure has begun to look something like the German model of banking–industry partnership.

Management practice also underwent a major transformation. The heads of business who had been autocratic and paternalistic in management style, overly centralizing in their decision-making, distant and mistrustful in their relations with labor, and often conservative and behind-the-times in their management, changed: They became more dynamic in management practice, introducing modern management techniques; closer to labor and less distant from the personnel; less autocratic and somewhat less centralizing. Their profile, however, remained remarkably similar to that of their predecessors. The new heads were from upper-middle-class families, received an elite education at one of the *grandes écoles,* became members of an elite civil service corps, had extensive state service, including experience in a ministerial cabinet, and had comparatively brief business careers begun at the top. This elite recruitment and promotion system, although guaranteeing that well-qualified individuals head French firms, nevertheless has a negative impact on the corporation, since it blocks access to top positions, thus lowering morale and undervaluing business achievement. But this, too, is beginning to change as firms seek to diversify their recruitment in response to the modernization and internationalization of business.

The Mitterrand years, in short, brought significant attitudinal and institutional changes to business and government. The kinds of changes brought about by privatization, deregulation, and Europeanization, moreover, have served to modernize French government and its relationship to business without significantly altering the ongoing patterns of policymaking, business–government relations, and management practice.

Although these ongoing patterns served the country well through a period of great ideological and institutional upheaval, whether they will continue to do so in the future remains to be seen, given the challenges of the new Europe. Even with the changes in industry resulting from restructuring, privatization, and deregulation, certain structural and cultural impediments to competitiveness remain. In business, the elite recruitment and promotion system that served as a stabilizing force through the disruptions of the eighties tends to eliminate much talent, and may not be adapted to the needs of the twenty-first century, at the same time that the centralized managerial decision-making processes which reduce flexibility and responsiveness may not be changing fast enough for an increasingly global economy. In government, the statist model of policymaking may no longer be adapted to a situation in which business has become increasingly independent of national governments as a result of European integration and business internationalization.

As it is, the statist model itself is already showing signs of strain. Faith in the state's leadership capacity has been shaken not only as a result of its inability to solve economic problems related to unemployment and slow growth, but also by the scandals that raise questions about the competence and honesty of upper-level civil servants (e.g., the tainted blood affair). This, together with the enlargement of the private sector and the concomitant retreat of the public, has meant that the best and the brightest are no longer as attracted to civil service careers, even if they are still likely to attend the elite schools that train for such careers. Finally, as if this were not enough, European integration has diminished state autonomy in the formulation of policy at the same time that it has undermined state authority not only through its promotion of regional decentralization and economic deregulation but also through EC-level policymaking which allows business access to policy formulation, thus making it in some sense a partner of national government at the supranational level. In addition, and perhaps most significantly for the French model of democracy, the European regulatory model has reduced state flexibility in the implementation of policy, leaving societal interests other than business with less possibility for accommodation or co-optation, and therefore little recourse other than confrontation.

Whatever the future holds, however, the Mitterrand years have shown that radical policy changes are often only surface changes, with cultural norms, institutional patterns, and old systems of interrelationships much more tenacious than one might suppose. At a time when much of the world, but in particular Eastern Europe and the successor states of the Soviet Union, is experimenting with radical industrial policy changes, France provides an enlightening case. It suggests that however much governments seek to break completely with the past, traditional patterns remain as constraints. The genius (or luck) of successive French governments was to recognize how to use those constraints to their advantage, adapting the ideology to pre-existing cultural patterns and institutions as well as to changing circumstances, and thereby successfully managing the transition from a state-led economy to a more market-oriented one.

This case also demonstrates that there is no single formula for liberalizing the economy or loosening the relationship between business and government. Each country must find its own way. Often, ideologies and policies that appear throwbacks to the past, as did those of the Socialists in 1981, nevertheless serve as a vehicle for change. Nationalization in France provided the opportunity for a radical restructuring of French capital that previous governments, let alone the private sector, had been unable to accomplish. This interlude served as a catalyst for change – but it could only be an interlude. It has become increasingly clear that countries no longer have the option of charting their own economic course and bucking international forces for very long. The increasing internationaliz-ation of trade and the globalization of business, along with increasing capital mobility, have drastically limited government flexibility in this domain. European economic integration represents an added constraint for France, as for other members of the European Union. Nonetheless, within these limits, significant political leeway remains. Although France in short order found that it had to switch macroeconomic policies and to privatize and deregulate, it did it in a manner in keeping with its own policymaking traditions. What appeared as a radical break was in fact often more simply an improvement on previous arrangements, as in the case of privatization that created *noyaux durs* of shareholders made up of public and private industries and banks.

All such change demands significant political will, and the ability to carry through, given that any reform ordinarily requires bucking en-trenched interests that often have close ties to government, if they are not themselves part of the government. On this score, a statist pattern of policymaking has its benefits, whatever its other drawbacks, since govern-ments with a clear majority can in fact put through their policies quickly and with minimal interference. Institutional arrangements, however, are only one element in ensuring success. No amount of political will is enough if economic trends go against you. The Socialists painfully found this out with their initial neo-Keynesian project. Subsequent governments until the early nineties had the good fortune to be instituting changes when the economy was on the upswing.

Economic climate, institutional arrangements, political will, and adaptability to traditional patterns, in short, all contribute to the success of modernization efforts. Success, however, inevitably breeds as many problems as failure, albeit of a different order. In the case of France, economic modernization has undermined the very model of policymak-ing through which the reform was accomplished. France's statist model of policymaking itself now requires radical reform. But for this, a new gov-ernment with a new mandate for political modernization will be required, one that speaks to a new state–society relationship that is nevertheless built on the old.

THE APPROACH OF THIS STUDY

This study examines both government policymaking and business prac-tice in order to illuminate the liberalization of France under Mitterand's presidency. To look at one without the other, whether by offering a purely political-scientific study of the formulation and implementation of gov-ernment industrial policies or a purely economic study of the manage-ment strategies and structures of business within an increasingly competitive, international environment, is not enough. Industrial policy cannot be properly evaluated without an examination of its impact on business, while business's performance cannot be sufficiently understood without an eye to government policy. And these are the issues that often fall between the cracks. To explain the success of the French economy, one must consider how both the state and industry have been transformed through an examination of the changing policies, processes, and players. Part II focuses on the policies of succeeding governments toward business from the pre—World War II era through the Mitterrand years, and from the building of the *dirigiste* state to its dismantling. Part III examines the processes of policymaking, first the structure of decision-making in the ministries, then the interrelationships between ministries and the EU, and finally the policy processes that link ministries and industries. Part IV considers the players in the policymaking process, first offering a profile of administrative and managerial elites and then seeking to explain elite dominance in terms of the culture of the state. Part V, finally, explores the impact on business of the changing governmental policies and ongoing processes during the Mitterrand years, discussing the revitalization of the economy, the restructuring of French capital, the reform of certain aspects of managerial practice, and the lack of significant change in the managerial recruitment system.

Part I, by contrast, develops the theoretical structure within which to understand France in comparative perspective. It argues that the public policy models of the political science literature, whether pluralist, corporatist, state-centered, or policy community—oriented, fail to deal with France adequately, and that instead a "statist" model best works for France, as it does for Japan and Great Britain to a lesser extent.

Talking of a statist pattern, however, is intended as a corrective to, rather than a substitute for, the debates pitting pluralists, corporatists, and state-centered theorists against one another. Rather than applying any one model of the political system to all polities, or rejecting all models altogether in favor of an approach that privileges policy communities, Part I concludes that certain countries, because of culture, history, and institutions, may be better explained by one or another of three patterns of policymaking: pluralist, corporatist, or statist. In epistemological terms, the approach is therefore more historical than systemic, not only because of its objects of explanation, which are the institutions, processes, and events of polities rather than the structures, functions, and goals of political systems, but also because of its relationship to previous explanations. For instead of an attempt to create a new model to replace all others by systemizing different facts in different ways, the approach represents an effort to build upon previous concepts and problems and, thereby, to cast new light on the generally agreed-upon facts.[1] As such, it builds more on Stephen Toulmin than on Thomas Kuhn in a philosophy of science sense, because the progress it represents comes less from a revolutionary break with the past, where concepts, problems, methods, and goals are transformed all at the same time, such that there can be little or no understanding from one paradigm to the next, than from an evolutionary shift, where some concepts, problems, and goals may change while others continue, and where whatever the disagreements, understanding among those favoring rival concepts, problems, or goals nonetheless remains.[2]

What is more, if Dryzek is right to suggest that in political science, research traditions change in response to external conditions rather than internal contradictions, as in science, then we can probably offer further justification for this particular approach by reference to current events.[3] At a time when culture and history are playing havoc with social scientists' models and predictions, when states have been dissolving before our very eyes, and when ideological worldviews no longer confront one another as opposing monoliths, it is quite clear that previous models which systematize governments according to a single set of static organizational structures and functions, whether pluralist, corporatist, or state-centered, cannot deal adequately with the constant flux. But although it might therefore be tempting in response to throw out all efforts to organize this reality, and resort instead to some sort of post-modernist pastiche that sees a mixing of styles of policymaking, this goes too far. For although much has been changing dramatically, for example, as governments in

---

[1]For the justification of systemic explanation, see: Robert T. Causey, "Structural Explanations in Social Science," in *Scientific Discovery, Logic, and Rationality*, ed. Thomas Nickles (Dordrecht: Reidel, 1980); Dorothy Emmet, *Function, Purpose and Powers* (Philadelphia: Temple University Press, 1972). For the historical, see: Raymond Martin, "Beyond Positivism: A Research Program for Philosophy of History," *Philosophy of Science* vol. 48, no. 1 (March 1981); W. H. Walsh, "Colligatory Concepts in History" in *The Philosophy of History*, ed. Patrick Gardiner (London: Oxford University Press, 1974); and William Dray, *Philosophy of History* (Englewood Cliffs, NJ: Prentice-Hall, 1965). On the differences between the two models of explanation, see: Vivien A. Schmidt, "Four Approaches to Science and Their Implications for Organizational Theory and Research," *Knowledge* vol. 9, no. 1 (September 1987).

[2]Stephen Toulmin, *Human Understanding* (Princeton: Princeton University Press, 1972); and Thomas Kuhn, *The Structure of Scientific Revolutions*, 2nd ed. (Chicago: University of Chicago Press, 1970). For comparisons of the two approaches, see: Vivien A. Schmidt, "Four Models of Explanation," *Methodology and Science* vol. 21, no. 3 (1988); and idem, "The Historical Approach to Philosophy of Science: Toulmin in Perspective," *Metaphilosophy* vol. 19, no. 3 (July–October 1988).

[3]John S. Dryzek and Stephen T. Leonard, "History and Discipline in Political Science," *American Political Science Review* vol. 82, no. 4 (December 1988); and John S. Dryzek, "The Progress of Political Science," *Journal of Politics* vol. 48 (1986).

Eastern Europe shed authoritarian structures for more democratic ones and those in Western Europe add a new, European layer of regulation, there are nevertheless continuities, with traditional political institutions and long-standing political processes persisting even in the new environment, along with cultural identities and collective histories. By recasting the old models as patterns of policymaking and then by relating them to particular countries, this more historical approach is better able to take account of these continuities along with the changes brought about by the new realities.

As such, the approach taken in this book is part of the "new institutionalism" in political science, where institutions, themselves shaped by history, are seen to shape politics.[4] Of the various kinds of new institutionalism, the approach of this book comes closest to the historical institutionalist. Thus, rather than depicting institutions primarily as static entities – either structuring the rules of the game that help determine actors' political behavior, as in game theory and rational choice modeling,[5] or setting the organizational roles and routines that set the limits of the political system, as in organizational theory[6] – it takes institutions as historically evolving entities, the products of ongoing political processes and particular events.[7] The explanations that emerge from such an approach are more historical in method, focused on tracing the evolution of institutions, on characterizing political processes and "colligating" events through classificatory and developmental concepts,[8] than the systematizing methods of organizational theory or the lawlike techniques of game theory and rational choice modeling.

The book, however, does not limit itself to a historical institutionalist account of the Mitterand years. Such an approach, focusing on the development of institutions and process and the impact of events, would risk depicting a world without people, where individuals are subsumed un-

[4]See the discussion by Robert Putnam, *Making Democracy Work: Civic Traditions in Modern Italy* (Princeton: Princeton University Press, 1993), pp. 7–8.

[5]For this approach, see, for example: Terry M. Moe, "Political Institutions: The Neglected Side of the Story," *Journal of Law, Economics, and Organization* vol. 6 (1990), pp. 213–253; Kenneth Shepsle, "Studying Institutions: Some Lessons from the Rational Choice Approach," *Journal of Theoretical Politics*, vol. 1 (1989); Elinor Ostrom, "An Agenda for the Study of Institutions," *Public Choice* vol. 48 (1986), pp. 3–25.

[6]For this approach, see in particular James G. March and Johan P. Olsen, *Rediscovering Institutions: The Organizational Basis of Politics* (New York: Free Press, 1989).

[7]For examples, see: Peter Hall, *Governing the Economy: The Politics of State Intervention in Britain and France* (New York: Oxford University Press, 1986); Stephen Skowronek, *Building of a New American State* (New York: Cambridge University Press, 1982).

[8]See: Walsh, "Colligatory Concepts"; and Dray, *Philosophy of History*.

der group classifications, where individual actions are grouped collectively in organizational processes, and where individuals' reasons and motives are understood primarily in terms of ideological justifications or cultural predispositions. Although such classifications are clearly necessary to explanations of overall patterns of interaction, to focus on these alone would sacrifice the richness of particular human experience on the altar of political-scientific generalization. And unnecessarily so, since individuals' understandings of their own experiences are a valuable complement to the more general categorizations. Institutions cannot be fully understood apart from the actors who give them life, acting in them and on them. With this in mind, this book adds to the historical institutionalist approach an interpretive one that seeks to explain individuals' reasons and intentions by reference to cultural rules, that finds justification in ordinary language analysis and phenomenology,[9] and that takes the social context very seriously indeed.[10] Therefore, in addition to the normal sources, that is, French and American scholarly literature, newspaper accounts, statistical and macroeconomic data, and archival material, this study uses the results of in-depth interviews with top officials in business and government to explore the reasons and rules that inform their action within the French institutional context.

THE INTERVIEWS

Relying in part on over forty interviews with major business and government actors of the Mitterrand years, the book also takes a close look at the attitudes and interrelationships of bankers, industrialists, politicians, and civil servants, and at how these affected industrial policymaking and business–government relations. This is by no means a scientific sample, although it is representative. The interviews with top government and business officials encompassed Ministry of Industry officials (including two ministers) and top managers (numbers one, two, or three) of major public, private, privatized, and nationalized firms in heavy and light industry, in the energy sector, in electronics and high technology, and in retailing, as well as in banking and insurance. There were also a handful of management consultants and heads of business associations.

The interviews themselves were long and loosely constructed (averaging one to one and a half hours, although a couple lasted as long as three and a half); most were taped, with permission to quote granted in almost

---

[9]See: Peter Winch, *The Idea of a Social Science* (London: Routledge and Kegan Paul, 1970); and Alfred Schutz, *The Phenomenology of the Social World* (Chicago: Northwestern University Press, 1967).

[10]On the importance of the social context as an added, and often forgotten, component of an institutionalist approach, see: Putnam, *Making Democracy Work*.

all instances. Because these individuals are for the most part used to speaking in front of the camera, and speaking their minds, the veil of anonymity would most likely have done little to affect their level of frankness.

Some might be suspicious of this as "happy talk,"[11] or in the French *"langue de bois,"* comments for public consumption that paint a too favorable picture of France and the speakers themselves. I did not find this to be the case – if anything, the French were harsher on themselves than they might have been. In the interviews, they tended to be quite straight-forward and honest. But even if they were engaging in clichés or "happy talk," it is talk that is shared by an entire group, thereby making it interesting at least as a social datum, if not as a true reflection of reality. Moreover, by setting out what people say against what they do – for example, by testing elite pronouncements about industry against its per-formance, or their views of elite recruitment against their actions – we can gain valuable insights into French rhetoric and reality. The format of the interviews themselves allowed for the exploration of seeming contra-dictions not only between what the subjects said and what actually went on, but also between the views of different individuals. This proved most fruitful in the areas of interministerial relations and ministry–industry relations.

The major questions asked of those in government focused on their views of the internal operational processes of government; their experi-ence of the relations between ministers, civil servants, and businesspeo-ple, especially through the changing political agendas of succeeding gov-ernments; and their take on the changes in the competitiveness of business. For those in business, in addition to these questions, they were asked specifically about their views of the impact on business of govern-ment policies of nationalization, privatization, and deregulation; their experiences of government involvement with industry; and their own take on the changes in management practice and recruitment.

Although the interviews constitute only a small part of the research for this study, they were nevertheless an invaluable part of it, serving to set much into context and enabling major players in French business and government to speak for themselves. This, added to profiles of the players' educational and career histories, to accounts of their participation in the processes of policymaking, to descriptions of the policies that they formu-lated and implemented, and to evaluations of their performance in busi-ness and government, should provide a complete picture of the evolution of French business and government in the Mitterand years.

---

[11]George Ross, comment at the conference "Labor and the Left in France: A Decade of Mitterrand" (Wesleyan University, April 11–12, 1992).

PART I

France in comparative perspective

I

Between state and society

The French would probably find it rather surprising that American political scientists have only relatively recently rediscovered the "state." The
French have used it as an explanatory concept since even before Louis
XIV claimed to be it; and certainly neither the public nor political scientists could imagine doing without the term. And yet in the United States
from the fifties to the late seventies, the very word disappeared almost
entirely from the vocabulary of mainstream American political scientists,
rejected out of hand as too vague and unscientific to warrant use as an
explanatory concept, as well as too burdened with ideological and mythic
trappings.[1] These political scientists preferred instead to talk about the
"political system" in which societal interests constrain government action, either in a pluralist fashion, where a full range of interests have
access to policy formulation,[2] or in a corporatist manner, where only
certain organized interests have privileged access to both policy formulation and implementation.[3] The result, as their critics have argued begin-

[1]See the discussion of the reasons for the abandonment of the term in Timothy
Mitchell, "The Limits of the State: Beyond Statist Approaches and Their Critics,"
American Political Science Review vol. 85, no. 1 (March 1991), pp. 78–81.

[2]For pluralist approaches, see: Robert Dahl, *Who Governs* (New Haven: Yale University Press, 1961); David Truman, *The Governmental Process* (New York: Knopf,
1951). For neopluralists, see: Theodore Lowi, *The End of Liberalism: Ideology, Policy,
and the Crisis of Public Authority* (New York: W. W. Norton, 1969); James Q. Wilson,
ed., *The Politics of Regulation* (Chicago: Chicago University Press, 1980).

[3]For corporatist approaches, see: Philippe C. Schmitter, "Reflections on Where the
Theory of Neo-Corporatism Has Gone and Where the Praxis of Neo-Corporatism
May Be Going," in *Patterns of Corporatist Policy-Making,* eds. Gerhard Lehmbruch
and Philippe C. Schmitter (Beverly Hills, CA: Sage Publications, 1982); Philippe
Schmitter, "Neo-Corporatism and the State," in *The Political Economy of Corporatism,* ed. Wyn Grant (New York: St. Martin's, 1985); Philippe C. Schmitter, "Corporatism Is Dead! Long Live Corporatism," *Government and Opposition* vol. 24, no. 1
(winter 1989); Gerhard Lehmbruch, "Neo-Corporatism in Comparative Perspective,"
in *Patterns of Corporatist Policy-Making,* ed. Lehmbruch and Schmitter; Alan Cawson, *Corporatism and Political Theory* (Oxford: Basil Blackwell, 1986).

ning in the late seventies, is a society-centered view of political life which denies any primary role to governmental institutions and/or decision-makers. These state-centered critics contend, instead, that the state has to be considered as an autonomous, independent agent.[4] But as such, according to the defenders of mainstream political science, they have turned the state into a metaphysical entity.[5]

How, then, to deal with France? No account of it can possibly do without the concept of the state, embedded as it is in the cultural fabric and the history, and embodied as it is in the institutions and in the seemingly autonomous action of decision-makers, and decision-making organizations. Even American political scientists who apply pluralist or corporatist analyses tacitly acknowledge that France conforms fully to neither pattern; but they find it wanting as a result.[6] Recent discussions of the "strong state" go some way toward righting the balance, but they bring with them other problems. Finally, although those political scientists who have rejected pluralist, corporatist, and state-centered models as too confining in order to talk of "policy communities" that include state and society in the political system have managed to avoid many of the problems that flow from these categorizations, they themselves risk not taking institutional differences seriously enough.[7]

The result is that in much of the comparative political science literature, France gets short shrift. Unlike the United States, it is a country

[4]See, for example, Theda Skocpol, *States and Social Revolutions: A Comparative Analysis of France, Russia, and China* (Cambridge: Cambridge University Press, 1979); Alfred Stepan, *State and Society: Peru in Comparative Perspective* (Princeton: Princeton University Press, 1978); Theda Skocpol, "Bringing the State Back In," in *Bringing the State Back In*, ed. Peter Evans, Dietrich Rueschemeyer, and Theda Skocpol (Cambridge: Cambridge University Press, 1985); Eric Nordlinger, *On the Autonomy of the Democratic State* (Cambridge, MA: Harvard University Press, 1981); and Stephen D. Krasner, *Defending the National Interest: Raw Materials Investment and U.S. Foreign Policy* (Princeton: Princeton University Press, 1978).

[5]David Easton, "The Political System Besieged by the State," *Political Theory* vol. 9 (1987), p. 316; Gabriel Almond, *A Discipline Divided* (Newbury Park, CA: Sage, 1990). For an epistemological discussion of these debates, see: Vivien Schmidt, "Evaluating the State–Society Debates: Lessons from the Philosophy of Science." Paper prepared for presentation at the XVIth World Congress of the International Political Science Association, Berlin, August 21–25, 1994.

[6]Frank L. Wilson, *Interest Group Politics in France* (New York: Cambridge University Press, 1987); Lehmbruch, "Neo-Corporatism"; T. J. Pempel and K. Tsunekawa, "Corporatism without Labor? The Japanese Anomaly," in *Trends Toward Capitalist Intermediation*, ed. Philippe C. Schmitter and Gerhard Lehmbruch (Beverly Hills, CA: Sage Publications, 1979).

[7]Jack Hayward, "The Policy Community Approach to Industrial Policy," in *Comparative Political Dynamics*, ed. Dankwart A. Rustow and Kenneth Paul Erickson (New York: Harper Collins, 1991), pp. 381–407. Interestingly enough, the main examples that Hayward uses are France and Great Britain, both of which fit the "statist" pattern I elaborate.

where the state is and has long been a central concept, where the executive is strong, the legislature weak, and the bureaucracy predominant, and where interest group politics and lobbying are often seen as illegitimate (all much like Japan and Great Britain to a lesser extent). Because of this, American pluralists have had a tendency to imply that France is somehow less than democratic, as a case of "limited pluralism." France does not do much better with the corporatists, since in its long history of a close, cooperative relationship between business and government, government remains predominant in the formulation of policy, while labor is excluded altogether. In consequence, corporatists see the country overall as at best a case of "weak corporatism" (although they find pockets of corporatism in certain sectors), unlike in the smaller European democracies and Germany, where business, labor, and government are all coequals in the formulation and implementation of policies. Even the state-centered theorists, despite their more approbatory characterization of France as having a "strong state" which acts as an independent, autonomous agent, do not provide the full picture, since there is much "weakness" in the French state, given actions that are not always independently formulated and that, even when they are, may be reversed at the implementation stage. Finally, the policy-community approach, which seeks to avoid the excesses of pluralist, corporatist, and state-centered models by paying as much attention to the processes linking state and society as to the politics that make one or the other side appear paramount, also leaves France at a disadvantage. Because this approach applies best to France and Great Britain, but purports to apply universally, it underestimates the importance of the institutions that serve to differentiate France and Great Britain as well as Japan from countries that conform more to pluralist or corporatist patterns.

THE LIMITS OF THE PLURALIST APPROACH

The state as the French conceive of it has never had a place in pluralist accounts of the political system, in which policymaking is the outcome of a decentralized system of bargaining in which organized interest groups exert pressure on government officials.[8] This may be why most country specialists who work on France have continued in the more institutionalist tradition which enables them to focus on the role of the state and its

---

[8]Although in neopluralist accounts such as those of Lowi (*Liberal Tradition*) and Wilson (*Politics of Regulation*), the institutions of the state are brought back in as the framework in which interest groups and government officials interact, the account remains more pluralist and, therefore, society-centered rather than state-centered to the extent that its emphasis is on the societal constraints to governmental action.

bureaucracy,[9] despite the primacy of pluralist analysis in mainstream American political science. And it may also be why pluralist analyses of France are relatively rare, and for the most part carried out by Americans.

The American-centeredness of pluralist studies was remarked on quite early, albeit inadvertently, by Henry Ehrmann when, in noting the dearth of non-American interest group studies at the beginning of his 1957 book on the activities of business groups, he commented that studies such as his on France have "often been described abroad as the single most important contribution American political scientists have furnished of late."[10] This was a contribution the French may have appreciated, but they did not emulate. Outside of Jean Meynaud's work in the late fifties and early sixties, there have been no comprehensive French studies of interest groups, and no American ones either until that of Frank L. Wilson in 1987.[11]

Moreover, whenever pluralist analysis has been applied to France, it has generally underscored its limitations, emphasizing the comparative weakness of interest group politics and seeming to imply that France is somehow less democratic because less responsive to pluralist interests. Ehrmann himself made no claims that pluralism was the predominant pattern in the Fourth Republic, despite the fact that interest groups were indeed a major influence on Parliament during that time.[12] What is more, in his later discussion of the Fifth Republic, Ehrmann remarked on the independence of the government with regard to major decisions, and its deliberate refusal even to consider, let alone respond to, interest group pressures.[13]

More recently, Frank L. Wilson has suggested that France exhibits, at best, a limited pluralism, and agrees with Jack Hayward[14] that "organized interests in France are less likely to impede or even affect government action in France than in other western democracies; they are some-

[9]The literature is too vast to cite in its entirety, but for Europe, see: Mattei Dogan, ed., *The Mandarins of Western Europe* (New York: John Wiley, 1975); John Armstrong, *The European Administrative Elite* (Princeton: Princeton University Press, 1973); Ezra Suleiman, *Politics, Power, and Bureaucracy in France: The Administrative Elite* (Princeton: Princeton University Press, 1974).

[10]Henry Ehrmann, *Organized Business in France* (Princeton: Princeton University Press, 1957), p. x.

[11]Jean Meynaud, *Les groupes de pression en France* (Paris: Armand Colin, 1958); idem, *Nouvelles études sur les groupes de pression en France* (Paris: Armand Colin, 1962); Wilson, *Interest Group Politics*.

[12]He does suggest this elsewhere, however. See: Henry W. Ehrmann, "French Bureaucracy and Organized Interests," *Administrative Science Quarterly* vol. 5 (1961).

[13]Henry Ehrmann, "Bureaucracy and Interest Groups in Fifth Republic France," in *Faktoren der politischen Entscheidung*, ed. Ernst Fraenkel (Berlin: Gruyter, 1963), p. 278; cited in Almond, "Return to the State," p. 866.

[14]Jack Hayward, "Institutional Inertia and Political Impetus in France and Great Britain," *European Journal of Political Research* vol. 4 (1976): 341–359.

times more pressured groups than pressure groups."[15] Finally, although Hayward himself prefers an even more complex, pluralist description of state–group interaction as a "domestic hexagon of pluralist interests," he nevertheless recognizes that in France, however "plural" or fragmented the state and interest groups may be, state-related centers of power generally retain the upper hand, not only choosing those groups which are to be junior partners in the consultation process (and ignoring those which are not), but also resisting group pressures when the political centers of power so decide.[16] In short, however pluralist they may find France, all these scholars would probably agree in the final analysis with Stanley Hoffmann that "while the state has incited French society to change, French society has only rarely forced the state to change, and pressures for change internal to the state have been almost nonexistent."[17]

France, in fact, often gives the appearance of pluralist consultation because of its proliferation of government committees in which representatives of officially recognized groups are consulted frequently. But this occurs generally more in an effort to inform such groups of an already independently formulated policy and to persuade them of its validity, or to gather information where the government has not already formulated a policy, than to allow them actually to contribute to the formulation of policies (although this does occur in certain cases, as discussed below).[18] Illustrative of this is the remark of a representative of an employers' association in Wilson's study who commented that "Sometimes I feel that there are several ways to ignore the ideas of others: never consult them or consult them so often that they don't have time to really think out the problem."[19] The excessive consultation in France is nevertheless functional: as David Wilsford has noted, it represents a formal strategy to control interests at the same time that it "serves as a symbolic benefit that administrators use to forestall interest group opposition."[20]

[15]Frank Wilson, "French Interest Group Politics: Pluralist or Neocorporatist?" *American Political Science Review* vol. 77 (December 1983), p. 909.

[16]Jack Hayward, *The State and the Market Economy: Industrial Patriotism and Economic Intervention in France* (New York: New York University Press, 1986), pp. 39–55. In this domestic hexagon of pluralist interests, routine relations may involve "concerted politics" when there is consensus or "endemic conflict" when there is not, and crisis relations may be characterized by "domination" when state or group seeks to coerce the other or "institutional collapse" when it goes too far.

[17]Stanley Hoffmann, *Decline or Renewal? France since the 1930's* (New York: Viking Press, 1974), p. 454.

[18]Suleiman, *Politics, Power, and Bureaucracy,* pp. 316–340; Wilson, "French Interest Groups," pp. 900–902; Wilson, *Interest Group Politics.*

[19]Wilson, "French Interest Groups," p. 900.

[20]David Wilsford, "Tactical Advantages versus Administrative Heterogeneity: The Strengths and the Limits of the French State," *Comparative Political Studies* vol. 21, no. 1 (April 1988), p. 146.

Only in America, as Tocqueville pointed out over a century and a half ago,[21] is private interest representation and group associationalism so much the predominant and accepted pattern of societal organization that any notion of the public interest as something apart from this is submerged as a result. In France, by contrast, the public good is seen as something above the pressures of interest. Interest group pressures on government are therefore generally regarded as illegitimate and lobbying is seen as corruption (as distinguished from ongoing consultation with the "professional organizations" legitimized by central administrators because they are seen as representing group interests as opposed to private interest).[22] This has a long history, beginning with the fact that all intermediary bodies were outlawed for close to a century by the Le Chapelier law of 1791, which was rescinded in 1884, and that only the law of 1901 allowed interest groups to be formed without prior government authorization. Interest groups have traditionally been viewed, as Tocqueville noted in the 1830s, "as a weapon of war to be hastily improvised and used at once on the field of battle. . . . Its members regard legal measures as possible means, but they are never the only possible means of success."[23] This remains somewhat the case even today, although now it is more a question of taking to the streets than taking up arms. For most unrecognized groups, as well as for the legitimized ones unhappy with government decisions, active confrontation is often the only way to be heard.[24]

This state–society relationship, in which the state acts and society reacts, derives in large measure from France's long history of government centralization and insulation from the political community. As John Zysman explains it, "from the beginning the state was an instrument of centralizing power, created apart from the society, almost in opposition to it, and thus at least partially autonomous," which meant that "mass political movements had to adapt to existing government structures," by contrast with the United States where "the structures were created in an epoch of democratic mass politics."[25] Whereas in France, state power emerged before organized societal interests, in the United States the orga-

[21] Alexis de Tocqueville, *Democracy in America* (New York: Doubleday, 1969).

[22] See: Suleiman, *Politics, Power, and Bureaucracy*, pp. 337–340. Attempts to exert influence, of course, still occur, but the game is more subtle. See: José Frèches, *Voyage au centre du pouvoir* (Paris: Odile Jacob, 1989), and the discussion in Chapter 7.

[23] Tocqueville, *Democracy in America*, p. 193.

[24] See the discussion in Wilsford, "Tactical Advantages," pp. 152–156. On the French tradition of protest, see: Charles Tilly, *From Mobilization to Revolution* (Englewood Cliffs, NJ: Prentice-Hall, 1978).

[25] John Zysman, *Political Strategies for Industrial Order: State, Market, and Industry in France* (Berkeley: University of California Press, 1977), p. 194.

nization of state and society proceeded at about the same time, ensuring that society would have a larger, legitimate place in the formal institutions and processes of the polity.

It is for this historical reason, among others, that only in the United States, and perhaps Great Britain, would it be possible to excise "state" from the political science vocabulary, and not risk irrelevance. In France, as in many other European countries, the state is a concept that so pervades ordinary discourse and political practice that social scientists ignore the term at their own peril.[26] This is because, as Kenneth Dyson put it, "the idea of the state forms part of the considerations that groups have in mind when determining where their interests lie and what types of conduct will appeal to decision-makers and the public."[27] In France, the word had already been established as a fundamental legal concept by the early seventeenth century, while by the eighteenth century it had become a common political term throughout continental Europe, reflecting the need to find a way of justifying the often abrupt and seldom consensual extension of public activity by sovereigns who had behind them an administration and an army.[28] In England, on the contrary, "state" as a term never took hold, with the preferred words being at first "realm, body politic, and commonwealth," and later "kingdom, country, people, nation, and government," reflecting "the gradual extension of public activity, legitimated by Parliament and local government," which therefore did not require justification "by reference to the notion of an autonomous state acting to realize certain inherent purposes."[29] It may be no accident, therefore, as Dyson suggests, that Marx's "preoccupation with the idea of the state receded, after leaving a 'state conscious' Europe for Britain," where he focused instead on the capitalist mode of production.[30]

Even without a state tradition, however, the British "state," meaning the executive power, has historically been accorded a great deal of power. As Andrew Shonfield noted, the British in the nineteenth century "pursued with evangelical vigor" the limitation of the sphere of government "while recognizing the need to maintain the strength of an irreducible hard core of governmental power."[31] And this remains to this day, so

[26]For how important the term is to the French understanding of the polity, see: Georges Burdeau, *L'état* (Paris: Seuil, 1970). See also the discussion in Chapter 12.
[27]Kenneth J. F. Dyson, *The State Tradition in Western Europe* (New York: Oxford University Press, 1980), p. 3.
[28]Ibid., pp. 25–36.
[29]Ibid., pp. 36–44.
[30]Ibid., pp. 104–105.
[31]Andrew Shonfield, *Modern Capitalism: The Changing Balance of Public and Private Power* (Oxford: Oxford University Press, 1965), p. 386.

much so that parliamentarians in England "take it as an axiom that the country ought to have a strong executive."[32] Margaret Thatcher, in other words, was no accident.

Thus, although prior to Thatcher there were those who related Britain's economic decline to the "pluralistic stagnation" resulting from the "new group politics" in the sixties and seventies,[33] that decline can just as readily be related to the power of misguided governments that pursued policies that consistently sacrificed the domestic economy to the pursuit of renewed world power.[34] Interest group pressure is one thing, effectiveness another. And in Great Britain, it is the executive that has the power to listen or not.

But whereas this axiomatic acceptance of a strong executive is based on an unwritten constitution and on evolving tradition in Great Britain, in France of the Fifth Republic, which was in reaction against the parliamentary paralysis of the Fourth Republic, nothing was left to chance: When the Fifth Republic was created, the executive power gained both certain structural assets which privileged the government over Parliament and the constitutional weapons which enabled it to combat specific problems.[35] Tightened conditions for votes of censure, shorter parliamentary sessions, expanded decree powers for government, government control over the parliamentary agenda, drastic curtailment of the powers of parliamentary committees, and strengthened government control over the budget all provided the government with the structural assets that the government needed to avoid being blocked in its programs by parliamentary opposition or paralysis.[36] In addition, various parliamentary mechanisms provided the government with the weapons to ensure that its bills, or *projets de lois,* would become laws with a minimum of parliamentary inter-

[32]Ibid., p. 392.

[33]Samuel Beer, *British Politics in the Collectivist Age,* rev. ed. (New York: Random House, 1969), ch. 12.

[34]Stephen Blank, "Britain: The Politics of Foreign Economic Policy, the Domestic Economy, and the Problem of Pluralistic Stagnation," in *Between Power and Plenty: Foreign Policies of Advanced Industrial States,* ed. Peter J. Katzenstein (Madison: University of Wisconsin Press, 1978).

[35]John T. S. Keeler, "Patterns of Policymaking in the French Fifth Republic: Strong Governments, Cycles of Reform and Political Malaise," in *Ideas and Ideals: Essays on Politics in Honor of Stanley Hoffmann,* ed. Linda Miller and Michael Smith (Boulder: Westview Press, forthcoming).

[36]Ibid. See also Stanley Hoffmann, "The French Constitution of 1958: The Final Text and Its Prospects," *American Political Science Review* June 1959; Philip Williams, *Crisis and Compromise: Politics in the Fourth Republic* (New York: Doubleday, 1966); Vincent Wright, *The Government and Politics of France,* 3d ed. (New York: Holmes and Meier, 1989), pp. 136–139; William Safran, *The French Polity* (New York: Longman, 1991), pp. 168–172.

ference. These include: Article 45.2, the declaration of urgency, which allows waiver of the second reading of a bill; Article 38, which enables Parliament to authorize government to legislate through ordinances for a limited time in a given domain; Article 44.3, the *vote bloqué* or package vote, which allows the government to require a single vote on all or parts of a bill, without amendments other than those proposed or accepted by it; Article 45.4, which allows the government to circumvent an obstructionist Senate by enabling the National Assembly, in which it necessarily has a majority, to pass the bill in question when a joint parliamentary committee cannot come to agreement; and Article 49.3, the "guillotine," which enables the government to pass a bill without a vote by making it an issue of confidence which can therefore only be defeated, along with the government, by a motion of censure. The result is that while the overall number of bills (*projets de lois*) per year to become laws dropped by an average of close to half in the Fifth Republic by contrast with the Fourth (84.5 vs. 153.9), and the laws promulgated per year on average dropped to over half (95.6 vs. 219.1),[37] the coherence and significance of the laws rose immeasurably. The Fifth Republic was not characterized by the stalemate of the Fourth in most domains.

Even without the constitutional advantages that France has, or the unwritten tradition that favors a strong executive in Great Britain, though, governments can prevail as long as parties are highly disciplined and hold a commanding majority. By contrast, when party strength declines, then having the constitutional mechanisms at one's command to use as needed is very important. Governments during the Fifth Republic until 1986 did not need the weapons that the constitution provided them, even if they often used them. The stability of the majority was such that by the early 1970s, Maurice Duverger could remark that these weapons "no longer battled anything but ghosts."[38] But the Chirac government of 1986–1988, which had a thin majority and an opposition member as president, found them quite handy. The government's average use per month of Article 44.3, which was directed mostly at members of the government's own majority, who might otherwise seek to introduce amendments that would impinge on the "coherence" of the text, and Article 49.3, which sought to prevent opposition members and dissident majority members from unraveling a favored piece of legislation, was well above any previous level. The increased recourse to such mechanisms was matched by Rocard's government, which only had a relative majority, and

[37]Keeler, "Patterns of Policymaking."
[38]Maurice Duverger, *La Monarchie Républicaine* (Paris: Robert Laffont, 1974), p. 175. See also Keeler, "Patterns of Policymaking."

had to count on abstentions from the Communist Party or the Centrist UDF for their measures to pass. These "weapons of the weak," as Keeler put them, made up for the weak majority of the Fifth Republic governments beginning in 1986, enabling them to be as heroic in their policymaking as previous governments.[39]

Even where a majority is strong, however, such constitutional weapons may prove necessary where the opposition dominates one of the two parliamentary chambers, as was the case of the conservative-dominated Senate in France under the Socialists since 1981. The Socialist government's recourse to Article 45.4 for one-fourth of all bills between 1981 and 1985, by contrast with the recourse to 45.4 for only 3% of all previous bills during the Fifth Republic, bespeaks the great usefulness of this measure.[40] The British clearly discovered the importance of such capability years before, in the early years of the century when it threatened to pack the House of Lords if it did not bow to the will of the Commons. Consider what a difference it would make in the United States, if the House of Representatives were able to pass its bills over Senate opposition when a joint conference committee failed to reach a compromise – and how with just this sort of constitutional measure the Senate could be reduced to the equivalent of the House of Lords in Great Britain or the Sénat in France. Even with such a change, however, the executive in the United States would still not have the power of the executive in France, because the Congress would still be a transformative legislature, by contrast with the arena legislature that is Parliament, which is more a forum for the discussion of government legislation than a locus of debate and generation of new legislation.[41]

In France, in effect, governments throughout the Fifth Republic have had the ability to take unilateral action, without the kinds of constraints that interest group politics or a strong legislature might impose. In the industrial-policy arena, however, this kind of independent action was possible even without the formal institutional assets afforded the state during the Fifth Republic, and is related primarily to France's bureaucratic tradition.

There is a long list of scholars who have detailed the French state's capacity for intervention in the industrial-policy sphere. Some preference the role of ideas, relating the rise of the interventionist state to the per-

[39]Keeler, "Patterns of Policymaking." Note that Keeler borrowed the term from James Scott, *Weapons of the Weak: Everyday Forms of Peasant Resistance* (New Haven: Yale University Press, 1985), who in turn borrowed it from Robert Michels.

[40]Keeler, "Patterns of Policymaking."

[41]For the differences between arena and transformative legislatures, see: Wilsford, "Tactical Advantages."

ceived need for modernization;[42] others underline the cultural bases for France's planning abilities by contrast with Great Britain[43] or France's institutional characteristics;[44] yet others credit the government's policy instruments and the policy networks of officials from private firms, state enterprises, and administrative bureaus for France's state-led financial, trade, and energy policies, by contrast with America's more society-centered one;[45] and others relate the state's capacity to the bureaucracy's insulation from competing actors.[46] But whether scholars preference ideas, culture, organizational processes, or institutions in their explanation of France's interventionist history in industry, they all accord a central role to the bureaucracy. And rightly so.

In France, the state's interventionist tradition, its *colbertisme, dirigisme,* or *volontarisme* in the industrial-policy arena as in others, owes much to its strong, independent administrative bureaucracy, which has a tradition going back at least as far as Napoleon, and which is imbued with a sense of the state.[47] It is peopled, moreover, by an elite corps of highly skilled, technically trained civil servants who, with their *corporatisme,* or corporate self-consciousness reinforced by their attendance at the same elite state educational institutions and their membership in the prestigious *grands corps* of civil servants, take a leadership role in public policymaking, with little risk of capture of the kind Grant McConnell describes for the United States.[48] It is this civil service that had the vision as well as the leadership capacity to change its own role from protector of the social order in the Third Republic to promoter of modernization in the Fourth and Fifth Republics.[49]

The French are by no means the only polity with a strong bureaucracy, however. Japan is the most comparable case, with a similarly close business–government relationship, albeit one that is more seamless and consensual than in France. Thus, whether one emphasizes state control,

[42]Richard Kuisel, *Capitalism and the State in Modern France* (New York: Cambridge University Press, 1981).
[43]Hayward, "Institutional Inertia."
[44]Hall, *Governing the Economy.*
[45]Peter Katzenstein, "International Relations and Domestic Structures," *International Organization* vol. 30 (winter 1976), p. 43.
[46]John Zysman, *Governments, Markets, Growth: Financial Systems and the Politics of Industrial Change* (Ithaca, NY: Cornell University Press, 1983), p. 300. See also: Shonfield, *Modern Capitalism.*
[47]For an excellent, brief summary, see the discussion in Dyson, *State Tradition,* pp. 233–226.
[48]Grant McConnell, *Private Power and American Democracy* (New York: Vintage, 1970). On the French administrative elite, see: Suleiman, *Politics, Power, and Bureaucracy.* See also the discussion in Chapter 10.
[49]See Chapter 3.

by characterizing the Japanese business–government relationship as one of "administrative guidance,"[50] or business, by characterizing it as one of "reciprocal consent" in which "firms give the state jurisdiction over markets in return for their continuing control of those markets,"[51] the overall industrial policymaking process in Japan is more of an everyday one of continuous consultation and negotiation than in France, where heroic governmental policies formulated absent consultation with business are generally implemented in accommodation with or even co-optation by business. The differences between the two countries are related not only to culture – since France as a culture is much more conflictual than Japan – but also to the level of organization of societal interests, with Japanese business much more organized and cohesive than French, not only through trade and peak associations, but also through the *keiretsus* and the semipermanent linkages between large firms and their smaller subcontractors.[52]

In any event, whatever the differences between France and Japan, the closeness of the business–government relationship is facilitated by similarities in civil service recruitment patterns and career histories.[53] Where French civil servants attend the National School of Administration (ENA) or Polytechnique, Japanese civil servants are graduated from Tokyo University. Where France has *pantouflage*, the practice of higher-level civil servants moving back and forth from administrative posts into top positions in politics and business, at the head of public or private corporations and banks, Japan has *amakudari*, where retired MITI and Ministry of Finance officials move into top positions in politics or business, at the head of public corporations and banks or on the boards of private ones.

But even Great Britain, although minus the concept of the state, nevertheless has a civil service that, despite its cloak of neutrality and its lack of back and forth, can exercise leadership.[54] Hugh Heclo's account of income maintenance policies in twentieth-century Britain as well as Sweden suggests that "the activist civil service role is a pervasive policy phenomenon" even in Britain, despite its emphasis on a neutral civil service, for "British administrative consultations with outsiders have seemed more often aimed at persuading interest groups than reconciling

[50]See: Chalmers Johnson, *MITI and the Japanese Miracle* (Stanford: Stanford University Press, 1982).

[51]Richard Samuels, *The Business of the Japanese State: Energy Markets in Comparative and Historical Perspective* (Ithaca, NY: Cornell University Press, 1987), p. x.

[52]See T. J. Pempel, "Japanese Foreign Economic Policies: The Domestic Bases for International Behavior," in *Between Power and Plenty*, ed. P. Katzenstein.

[53]B. C. Koh, *Japan's Administrative Elite* (Berkeley: University of California Press, 1989). See the discussion in Chapter 15.

[54]Hugh Heclo, *Modern Social Politics in Britain and Sweden* (New Haven: Yale University Press, 1974), p. 303.

their positive pressures."[55] Moreover, whatever its role in policy formulation, it is preeminent in policy implementation, so much so that, as Heclo and Wildavsky observed, "The government may agree all to quickly, before the major implications of the policy are understood or the affected interests realize what is about to happen to them, leaving all concerned agape and aghast as the machine implements the policy with its usual splendid impartiality, that is, with equal harm all around."[56]

In Great Britain, however, despite its powerful executive and strong bureaucracy, other factors militate against a strong (or at least successful) governmental role in the industrial-policy arena. Unlike France or Japan, Great Britain has traditionally had "an abiding prejudice which sees it as the natural business of government to react – not to act," in particular with regard to business.[57] This has not stopped governments from intermittently seeking to intervene in the industrial sphere, in particular the conservatives in the fifties or sixties and labor in the seventies, but it has negatively affected their likelihood of success (compare, for example, British by contrast with French industrial policy in the sixties).[58]

This cultural prejudice, together with the early rise of an industry able to generate its own sources of capital and compete worldwide, has meant that the private sector in Great Britain has historically benefited from comparatively little government interference, and that when there has been "interference," it has not worked very well. The contrast with France is telling, given its long history of cooperation between business and government, where a strong leadership role has always been accepted for the state, stretching back to Louis XIV and his minister Colbert. The same, moreover, can also be said for Japan, where state interventionism has its roots in the Tokugawa period (1603–1868). What is more, in both countries, the long tradition of state intervention served to ensure public acceptance of the more recent, postwar histories, where the scarcity of private capital, the lack of competitiveness of business, and the perceived backwardness of the capitalists led government to take a leadership role in the promotion of economic development.[59]

The difference between Great Britain and France in particular are illus-

---

[55]Ibid.
[56]Hugh Heclo and Aaron Wildavsky, *The Private Government of Public Money* (Berkeley and Los Angeles: University of California Press, 1974), p. 12.
[57]Shonfield, *Modern Capitalism*, p. 386.
[58]Ibid.
[59]On Japan, see for example: Richard Boyd, "Government–Industry Relations in Japan: Access, Communication, and Competitive Collaboration," in *Comparative Government–Industry Relations: Western Europe, the United States, and Japan,* ed. Stephen Wilks and Maurice Wright (Oxford: Clarendon Press, 1987), pp. 67–68. On France, see for example: Tom Kemp, *Economic Forces in French History* (London: Denis Dobson, 1971); Zysman, *Political Strategies.*

trated by the different options the government is assumed to have with regard to economic policymaking. Whereas in Great Britain the debate on government intervention in the economy allows for two choices, state control or the free market, in France there are three choices, *faire* (where the state does), *faire faire* (where the state incites others to do), and *laissez faire* (where the state leaves it to the private sector – which is not necessarily to say the free market, since it may allow for private market-circumventing arrangements).[60]

Even absent the cultural prejudices and the history, however, Great Britain would have found it much harder to intervene successfully in the economy. This is because, where the system of capital allocation is based on highly developed capital markets, as it is in Great Britain as well as the United States, the state has limited tools to intervene, by contrast with France and Japan, where capital has been channeled through the banks, thereby allowing the state to ration credit to banks and channel capital to targeted sectors.[61] In fact, had France and Japan not benefited from this system and the policy instruments that follow from it, no amount of vision or leadership capacity would have enabled these countries' civil services to succeed in the modernization of their economies.

Nevertheless, although Britain's "statism" may therefore appear negligible by comparison with that of France or Japan, it is still great, in particular when compared to the United States. In the United States, the founders, both very British in their philosophical conception of the public authority and deeply suspicious of strong central government, deliberately weakened public power by creating a decentralized set of political institutions which ensured against the development of a state similar to those on the Continent or in Great Britain.[62] This did not, however, in the early years preclude a business–government relationship similar to that of France; but by the late nineteenth century, the British pattern came to the fore. The rise of big business before big government in the United States, together with the triumph of a radical laissez-faire ideology (just as it was being attenuated in Great Britain[63]), conspired to ensure to this day that an active U.S. industrial policy would be seen as legitimate only in times of crisis, as during the New Deal era, or where external threat was at issue, that is, during wartime or in defense policy.

It is the weakness of the phenomena of "stateness" in the United States,

[60]John Zysman, "The French State in the International Economy," in *From Power to Plenty*, ed. P. Katzenstein, p. 269.

[61]Zysman, *Governments, Markets, and Growth*. On the role of the Bank of Japan in particular, see: Pempel, "Japanese Foreign Economic Policy," pp. 152–153.

[62]For a full discussion, see: Skowronek, *Building a New American State*.

[63]For the history, see: Shonfield, *Modern Capitalism*, pp. 298–329. See also: David Vogel, "Why Businessmen Distrust their State: The Political Consciousness of American Corporate Executives," *British Journal of Political Science* vol. 8 (1978), pp. 45–78.

then, that enabled political scientists to eschew the concept.[64] And yet, even in the United States, the concept, if not the word, has remained part of the discourse, at least insofar as Americans blame "the government" for all the ills of the moment. Moreover, in the foreign policy arena, the term itself has always been part of the language, witness the "State Department" and "Secretary of State."[65] The executive has since the founding had significant powers to formulate foreign policy independently, with relatively little interference from Congress or outside interest groups – so much so that its "statist" powers rival those of foreign states. Graham Allison's account of the Cuban missile crisis is the classic illustration of this.[66]

Ordinary discourse, then, along with history, cultural values, organizational processes, and institutional arrangements, all combine to suggest that even if pluralist approaches appropriately account for the American domestic policy formulation process, they do not either for the foreign policy arena or other countries – in particular for France, Japan, and even Great Britain.

THE LIMITS OF THE CORPORATIST APPROACH

The corporatist approach, which applies most appropriately to the smaller European democracies and Germany, is no better adapted to France than the pluralist. In corporatist polities, organized interests remain central to the policy process, but the political system is restricted to those groups that participate not only in the formulation of policy but also in its implementation as "an integral part of administration."[67] The state, in this context, is at best "an amorphous complex of agencies with ill-defined boundaries, performing a great variety of not very distinctive functions," co-equal with the organized interests with which it interacts, and striving for accommodation with an egalitarian style and collegiality in decision-making.[68]

Corporatism has been identified most closely with the small European democracies such as the Netherlands, Sweden, Austria, and Germany to a lesser extent.[69] Democratic corporatism in these countries is charac-

[64]See: J. P. Nettl, "The State as a Conceptual Variable," *World Politics* vol. 20 (1968).
[65]Dyson, *State Tradition*, pp. 38–39.
[66]Graham Allison, *Essence of Decision: Explaining the Cuban Missile Crisis* (Boston: Little Brown, 1971).
[67]Cawson, *Corporatism*, p. 37.
[68]Schmitter, "Neo-Corporatism and the State," p. 33.
[69]Peter J. Katzenstein, *Small States in World Markets* (Ithaca, NY: Cornell University Press, 1985); Arend Lijphart, *The Politics of Accommodation: Pluralism and Democracy in the Netherlands,* 2d ed. (Berkeley: University of California Press, 1975); N. Elder, *Modern Sweden* (Oxford: Pergamon Press, 1970); K. Steiner, *Politics in*

terized by an ideology of social partnership; by relatively centralized and concentrated interest groups – peak associations exercising power over a relatively compliant base; and by bargaining between government and organized interests that is voluntary, informal, and continuous.[70] The bargaining itself, moreover, is tripartite, meaning that it occurs between state agencies, business, and labor, with the last two represented by peak organizations; and it often even supersedes the independent role of Parliament, as in the case of Austria.[71]

This kind of macrocorporatism, which is often identified with particular polities, defines a systemwide organization of interests where peak associations aggregate on a broad class basis and negotiate major socioeconomic issues.[72] Many polities do not fit this pattern; but this has not stopped some from urging, nevertheless, that corporatism be seen as "an axis of development" where "political systems can be more or less corporatist, more or less advanced in the process of corporatization, depending on the degree to which public status is attributed to organized interest groups."[73] Although this may indeed be useful for the purposes of comparison, the result is that corporatists run a risk similar to that of the pluralists: By essentially defining countries by what they lack, corporatists end up implying that those polities that do not conform to the ideal pattern are somehow less desirable, and that no other pattern may hold sway.[74]

For example, Great Britain, once described in positive terms as corporatist by J. Winkler, who could not have anticipated Thatcher's ability to muster the powers of the state to destroy Labor's shaky corporatist set of interrelations,[75] is now seen either "as a case of medium (on the bor-

Austria (Boston: Little Brown, 1972); Kenneth Dyson, *Party, State, and Bureaucracy in West Germany* (Beverly Hills, CA: Sage Publications, 1977); and J. Steiner, *Amicable Agreement vs. Majority Rule* (Chapel Hill, NC: University of North Carolina Press, 1974).

[70]Katzenstein, *Small States*, pp. 32–33.

[71]B. Marin, "Organizing Interests by Interest Associations: Organizational Prerequisites of Cooperation in Austria," *International Political Science Review* vol. 4 (1983), pp. 197–216. This has begun to change, however, with the crisis of the eighties which has strengthened the role of Parliament and of political parties. See: Peter Gerlich, Edgar Grande, and Wolfgang Müller, "Corporatism in Crisis: Stability and Change of Social Partnership in Austria," *Political Studies* vol. 36, no. 2 (1988).

[72]Katzenstein, *Small States*, p. 72.

[73]Claus Offe, "The Attribution of Public Status to Interest Groups: Observations on the West German Case," in *Organizing Interests in Western Europe*, ed. Suzanne Berger (Cambridge: Cambridge University Press, 1981).

[74]Although Offe is himself highly critical of corporatism and may not be guilty of this, his remarks nevertheless lend themselves and may lead others to this interpretation.

[75]J. T. Winkler, "Corporatism," *European Journal of Sociology* vol. 17, no. 1 (1976).

derline to weak) corporatism,"[76] or as "corporate pluralism" (not quite corporatism, but not really pluralism), with a near-corporatism only in the war years, and intermittent corporatist episodes thereafter.[77] Moreover, Japan has been given a "corporatist reading,"[78] despite the central role it reserves for the state. And although France on the purely corporatist scale has never been described as anything other than "weak corporatism"[79] (to do any more would be a bit like having the tail wag the dog, given corporatism's ideal-typical fit with the small European democracies), France has nevertheless along with Japan been on occasion more strongly qualified as "corporatism without labor."[80]

France, needless to say, does not fit the ideal corporatist pattern. Organized interests generally are extremely weak and ideologically fragmented by comparison with both pluralist and corporatist countries. Labor, with its fragmented, ideologically divided unions, has been traditionally weak and getting weaker,[81] in particular at the plant level where the Socialists' reforms intended to increase workplace democracy only further reduced the unions' power.[82] Moreover, labor remains what Hayward has called a "policy community outsider."[83] It has been "conspicuous by its absence"

[76]Lehmbruch, "Neo-Corporatism," p. 21.

[77]R. K. Middlemas, *Politics in Industrial Society: The Experience of the British System since 1911* (London: André Deutsch, 1979). Cawson defines corporate pluralism as the case where, although the "corporate sphere" of groups has greater access to government than those in the "pluralist sphere," the corporate groups' role "falls short of being an instrument of implementation through their capacity for self-regulation," while "competitive groups can exert, at least in the short term when issues are alive, considerable influence upon policy by campaigns and mobilisation." *Corporatism and Political Theory*, p. 42.

[78]Ronald Dore, *Flexible Rigidities* (Stanford, CA: Stanford University Press, 1987).

[79]Gerhard Lehmbruch, "Introduction: Neo-Corporatism in Comparative Perspective," in *Patterns of Corporatist Policy-Making*, ed. Lehmbruch and Schmitter, pp. 22–23.

[80]Pempel and Tsunekawa, "Corporatism without Labor?" pp. 9–10.

[81]French unions as of the mid to late eighties represented only 10% of potential members, down from around 30% in the late seventies and 50% just after World War II, and far below current levels for so-called corporatist countries like Sweden, at 83%, and West Germany, at 43%, and even Japan, at 28%, and the United States, at 18%. Henry W. Ehrmann and Martin Schain, *Politics in France*, 5th ed. (New York: Harper Collins, 1992), pp. 176–177. The figures are taken from *Le Monde*, December 5, 1989.

[82]On the impact of the Auroux laws, see: Mark Kesselman, "The New Shape of French Industrial Relations: Ce n'est plus la même chose," in *Policymaking in France: From de Gaulle to Mitterand*, ed. Paul Godt (London: Pinter, 1989); and Duncan Gallie, "Les lois Auroux: The Reform of French Industrial Relations?" in *Economic Policy-Making under the Mitterrand Presidency 1981–1984*, ed. Howard Machin and Vincent Wright (London: Frances Pinter, 1985). On labor at the plant level more generally, see: W. Rand Smith, *Crisis in the French Labor Movement: A Grassroots Perspective* (New York: St. Martin's Press, 1988).

[83]Hayward, *The State and the Market Economy*, pp. 56–67. See also: A. Cox and

in industrial policy[84] and has tended to play a minor role even in collective bargaining, with the government generally imposing its views in wage negotiations even under the Socialists.[85] What is more, although the main employers' association, the CNPF, has greater access than labor, in particular because governments have ordinarily delegated industrial relations to business, it has comparatively little organizational clout in policy formulation (although its members may be influential as individuals on the basis of their status and position) – except where its analyses mesh with those of the government, as in the turnabout in Socialist macroeconomic policies in the early eighties.[86]

In addition, although France, like the ideal-typical corporatist country, Austria, has a small elite, it does not lead to a corporatism in which there are close and personal linkages between interest groups, parties, and the governmental system, where senior representatives of corporatist interest groups are also members of top party bodies and of Parliament.[87] Rather, it leads to *corporatisme,* because in France the ties that bind involve primarily government and business officials.

Nevertheless, there is no doubt that France has had a history of interest in corporatism, with theorists from the extreme right and the left in the last century joined by the more moderate right in this one expounding the virtues of cooperative interest representation, but with little significant political impact other than in the Vichy period.[88] Moreover, de Gaulle has been the only democratic leader to take corporatism seriously enough to seek to institute it in the regions, which became administrative units with a quasi-corporatist structure in the early sixties, and in the Senate, which he proposed to turn into a corporatist chamber linked to newly enfranchised corporatist regional assemblies in his reform of 1969, which failed in referendum.[89] The regions, however, were never really corpora-

Jack Hayward, "The Inapplicability of the Corporatist Model in Britain and France: The Case of Labor," *International Political Science Review* vol. 77 (1983), pp. 217–240.

[84]Hayward, *The State and the Market Economy,* p. 63.

[85]George Ross, "Labor and the Left in Power: Commissions, Omissions, and Unintended Consequences," in *The French Socialists in Power, 1981–1986,* ed. Patrick McCarthy (New York: Greenwood Press, 1987); Martin Schain, "Corporatism and Industrial Relations in France," in *French Politics and Public Policy,* ed. Philip Cerny and Martin Schain (New York: St. Martin's, 1980); Gérard Adam, *Le pouvoir syndical* (Paris: Dunod, 1983).

[86]Henri Weber, *Le parti des patrons: Le CNPF (1946–1986)* (Paris: Seuil, 1986).

[87]Gerlich, Grande, and Müller, "Corporatism in Crisis."

[88]For the theory, see: Matthew Elbow, *French Corporative Theory, 1789–1948* (New York: Octagon Books, 1966). For its place in the debates on decentralization, see: Vivien A. Schmidt, *Democratizing France: The Political and Administrative History of Decentralization* (New York: Cambridge University Press, 1990), pp. 53–54, 66, 78.

[89]Schmidt, *Democratizing France,* pp. 78–79, 88–91.

tist in practice; and as de Gaulle's successors progressively increased their functions and powers, they became less and less corporatist in organization, to culminate with their enfranchisement as representative assemblies under the Socialists (within a statist pattern of policymaking).[90]

In France, in brief, the role of the state has historically remained paramount, despite momentary flirtations with corporatism. This has not been the case with either Germany or the smaller European democracies, where the state plays a more co-equal role with organized interests. In Germany, this is a relatively recent phenomenon: the state does not lead the economy in large measure because it was discredited as a result of Nazism and World War II. Unlike in Japan, where the state was able to reestablish its traditional leadership despite the wartime experience, in Germany, the banks moved in to fill the vacuum, thus in some sense reclaiming their historic role in financing the rise of industry. At the same time, moreover, one could argue that propitious institutional arrangements, including postwar success in creating decentralized governmental institutions and centralized, sectorwide unions – combined with the failure to destroy the centralized power of the large firms and banks that had fueled Hitler's war machine – helped consecrate the corporatist pattern of tripartite bargaining. That pattern, however, remains unstable by comparison with the smaller European countries, where more centralized governmental institutions and more cohesive peak associations ensure smoother and often more successful bargaining.

In the smaller democracies, democratic corporatism is the product of a longer historical evolution. It begins with the fact that the smaller European states did not experience the revolutionary breaks which larger countries such as France underwent, and continues with the corporatist compromise of the 1930s against a background of depression, fascism, and World War II. This, together with certain structural elements encompassing social organization, political makeup, and industrial strategy, provided the political foundation for the democratic corporatism that was to follow.[91]

Culture, however, is also an important variable. Austria, for example, which has maintained a stable corporatism long after others showed signs of breakdown as a result of the economic crisis of the eighties, was ripe for a corporatist social partnership. This stems from a historical pattern of negotiating compromises which goes back to the Hapsburg empire, and

[90]Ibid., pp. 92–95, 115, 121, 128, 140.
[91]Katzenstein, *Small States*, pp. 138, 149. The structural elements include "a weak landed nobility, relatively strong urban interests, and a divided Right; a moderate left; no revolutionary break with the past; and a willingness to share power among political parties as illustrated by the adoption of proportional representation," and industrial strategies, focused on export specialization. Ibid., pp. 189–190.

attitudes which correspond to agrarian and pre-industrial values, including the "acceptance of authority, taking one's place within clientele relationships and search for personal security within rather intimate social groups . . . the fear of risk and acceptance even of material losses as long as stable conditions are guaranteed in principle."[92] But while cultural predispositions such as these, according to Shonfield, may have made Austria the ideal-typical but probably therefore not generalizable case of corporatism, contrary predispositions in Britain denied it the benefit of corporatism in its planning and incomes policies, primarily because of the culture's difficulty in mingling public and private in the economic sphere.[93] Corporatism, in other words, would stand as a betrayal to the philosophical birthplace of liberalism and laissez-faire capitalism.

History and culture, in effect, are as necessary to the growth of corporatism as political institutions and social organization. To extend the corporatist concept to polities that barely fit the pattern, therefore, is to risk misunderstanding those polities as well as misusing the concept. Schmitter himself rejects any corporatist label for Japan with the statement, also applicable to other countries, that "corporatism – with or without a qualifying prefix or adjective – cannot be all things to all people. It should not be pushed or stretched to explain away particular cases."[94] Rather, for these particular cases that fit neither the corporatist nor pluralist pattern, what is missing is another, noncorporatist label.

But instead of a new, noncorporatist label, some corporatist scholars have in recent years come up with two other kinds of corporatism: mesocorporatism, consisting of sectoral policies on economic or social questions where bargaining may be bipartite (ordinarily state and business interests) rather than tripartite (with labor); and microcorporatism, where bargaining takes place between state actors and individual firms, without the benefit of intermediating interests. Often, countries which have failed the macrocorporatist test pass the meso and micro tests. Thus, despite the fact that most corporatists deny that the United States can be corporatist, given its federal structure and weak peak organizations,[95] Cawson sees evidence of corporatism in "the sectoral and professional

---

[92]Gerlich, Grande, and Müller, "Corporatism in Crisis," p. 215.

[93]Shonfield, *Modern Capitalism*, pp. 194, 160. Schmitter, who credits Shonfield with having paternal rights to the concept of corporatism, overlooks the cultural point Shonfield is making with both of these cases in order to use them as examples of inconsistencies in his thinking (in "Corporatism Is Dead!").

[94]Schmitter, "Corporatism Is Dead!" p. 60.

[95]Robert H. Salisbury, "Why No Corporatism in America?" in *Trends in Corporatist Intermediation*, ed. Schmitter and Lehmbruch; and Graham Wilson, "Why Is There No Corporatism in the United States?" in *Patterns of Corporatist Policy-Making*, ed. Lehmbruch and Schmitter.

organizations and relationships with public agencies," as Milward and Francisco have described it.[96] Cawson even sees it in France, not only in the bipartite relationship between the state and the farmers in the agricultural sector, as Keeler has elaborated it,[97] but also in the planning area.

In agriculture, the relationship between farmers and the state, although bipartite, did indeed appear to exhibit a corporatist pattern, where peak organizations represent the farmers and negotiate for them with the state. It is a pattern that was at its height from the time de Gaulle successfully instituted it in the late sixties to the time the Socialists arrived in power in the early eighties. When the Socialists sought to alter the pattern, by including new, more left-leaning farm groups (under then-Minister of Agriculture Edith Cresson), however, the relationship broke down as the farmers took to the streets and marketplaces to protest what they saw as illegitimate government action. Government's capitulation to the farmers' pressures, by replacing Cresson with Rocard as Minister of Agriculture, only delayed the day of reckoning, because this "politics of decorporatization," in Keeler's words,[98] continued as the French government bowed to the European Union's farm policy and the demands of the GATT negotiations (even though there was some last-minute posturing).

Given this, the question which comes to mind now, as it did to Frank Wilson as early as 1983, is: Is this, then, a corporatist pattern of negotiation? Wilson answered this question in the negative by insisting that "In France, the government clearly controls the use of corporatist forms,"[99] and preferring instead to label the pattern of negotiation one of limited pluralism, as discussed above. But this is just another way of saying that the government for the most part also controls the use of pluralist forms, by being able to structure its relations with interest groups, to listen or not, as Wilson himself makes clear,[100] and to legitimize and subsidize or not, as Keeler contends in his critique of Wilson.[101] In France, the state

[96]Cawson, *Corporatism and Political Theory,* p. 106. H. B. Milward and R. A. Francisco, "Subsystem Politics and Corporatism in the United States," *Policy and Politics* vol. 11 (1983), pp. 273–293.

[97]Cawson, *Corporatism;* John Keeler, *The Politics of Neocorporatism in France: Farmers, the State, and Agricultural Policy-Making in the Fifth Republic* (New York: Oxford University Press, 1987). Jack Hayward notes that Cawson himself is hard put to find good examples of mesocorporatism outside the dairy industry, or agriculture more generally. "Policy Community Approach," p. 384.

[98]Keeler, *Politics of Neocorporatism.*

[99]Wilson, "French Interest Group Politics," p. 909.

[100]Ibid.; and Wilson, *Interest Group Politics.*

[101]John T. S. Keeler, "Situating France on the Pluralism–Corporatism Continuum: A Critique of and Alternative to the Wilson Perspective," *Comparative Politics,* vol. 18 (January 1985), pp. 232–233.

remains in control (as Wilson has more recently acknowledged),[102] to alter the form and content of interest representation, whether corporatist or pluralist, as it wishes – even though, for obvious reasons, it cannot control societal response, especially in the case of the best-organized societal interests such as the teachers as well as the farmers.

Thus, there is some question as to whether mesocorporatism fully explains what goes on in isolated sectors of noncorporatist polities. There is even more question for microcorporatism's claim to account for state–firm relationships. Because of the absence of the involvement of interest organizations at the peak or sectoral levels, corporatists such as Streeck do not include this in their definition of corporatism – for them, firm-level negotiation represents a breakdown of the model.[103] Cawson, however, argues nonetheless that microcorporatism can be found in French industrial policy with the planning contracts in which firms agree to certain investment and employment strategies in exchange for economic assistance. He sees it as a form of corporatism because, although the state has greater autonomy than in a pluralist case of agency capture, it still depends upon the firm to implement the policy.[104] But this misses the point of the planning contracts, given that it is the state which has already formulated the policy, by setting the priorities for funding or the principles for restructuring, before it begins negotiations with individual firms (even if, for the most part, the firms get their way within the framework established by the government in the implementation phase); and it misunderstands the personalistic nature of the interaction between state, meaning top bureaucrats, and firm, meaning CEOs. To see firms as "interest aggregating bodies" which "intermediate between state and society" is to assume that CEOs act as representatives of the firm's employees, rather than, say, of the firm's shareholders, or of themselves, as embodiments of the firm. Moreover, to imply that state bureaucrats are co-equals with business managers in this process is to underestimate the relative independence of government actors and the complex interaction that occurs in planning and industrial policy between state officials and CEOs. In short, planning in France is not corporatist, because the state remains paramount.

This is also the case in the banking arena, despite William Coleman's argument, following Cawson, that banking meets all of the requirements of

[102]Frank L. Wilson, "Groups Politics in a Strong State." Paper prepared for delivery at the Annual Meeting of the American Political Science Association (Atlanta, August 31–September 3, 1989).

[103]Wolfgang Streeck, "Neo-Corporatist Industrial Relations and the Economic Crisis in West Germany, 1973–1982," in *Order and Conflict in Contemporary Capitalism: Studies in the Political Economy of Western European Nations*, ed., J. Goldthorpe (Oxford: Oxford University Press, 1984).

[104]Cawson, *Corporatism*, pp. 120–121.

mesocorporatism. To begin with, Coleman himself acknowledges the predominant role of the state in organizing the banking community; in setting up the mesocorporatist relationship where banking interests, however disorganized, are responsible for policy formulation and implementation along with the state; and in reforming that relationship, e.g., with the 1984 *loi bancaire,* where the state designed a law that put it in a stronger position than before through a switch from unanimity to majority decision-making. Finally, the differentiation between state and banking-policy community is itself more difficult to make in France than in more truly corporatist polities, given the fact that virtually all banks were public under the Socialists, and most top bankers products of the same state educational institutions as the Treasury bureau that oversaw them. Given this, instead of mesocorporatism, one could as profitably discuss the level of autonomy afforded public banks by the state, or the amount of co-optation as opposed to accommodation or confrontation in the state–banking relationship, whether this involved public or private banks.[105]

Even French academics, in recent years, have begun applying the corporatist label to certain aspects of state–society relations in France, although they place this within a model that is basically statist in overall pattern of policymaking. Pierre Muller, for example, defines the relationship the state sets up with societal groups as corporatist, whether these groups are external to the administration, such as the farmers, or internal, such as the engineers of the *grands corps* in the energy or telecommunications areas, because these groups, however fragmented, are the sole interlocutors with the state. This, as Muller admits, is "corporatisme à la française," meaning a sectoral corporatism which has "the effect of increasing in a considerable way the role of the administrative elite in creating coherent public policy."[106] But then, this is really simply another way of acknowledging that the French "corporatist" relationship is really a statist one, given that government decision-makers are the key players in organizing the state–society relationship, even if as often as not societal actors get their way.

One of the major problems with the corporatist approach as it applies to noncorporatist polities at the macro, meso, or micro level, in sum, is that, much like the pluralist approach, it leaves too little room for independent state agency. Although as principal co-actors with corporatist interests, as Alfred Diamant remarks, government actors are no longer

[105]William D. Coleman, "Reforming Corporatism: The French Banking Policy Community, 1941–1990," *West European Politics* vol. 16, no. 2 (April 1993), pp. 122–143.

[106]Pierre Muller, "Entre le local et l'Europe: La crise du Modèle français de politiques publiques," *Revue Française de Science Politique* vol. 42, no. 2 (April 1992), p. 279–280.

the "captured," pliant tools of pluralist interests or the "automata exe-
cuting orders on behalf of the ruling class" of the neo-Marxists, they have
still not been accorded separate standing as "additional actors in the
interplay of groups," something which the more traditional, comparative
institutionalists who focused on the role of the state and its bureaucracy
have.[107] In part in response to this, as well as to the problems of pluralism, certain theorists began privileging the state's role and insisting that
government officials are not simply additional actors, but autonomous
ones as well. This state-centered approach, too, however, encounters
problems.

THE LIMITS OF THE STATE-CENTERED APPROACH

The state-centered approach, on the surface at least, would appear to
have been devised with France in mind. The state, instead of being at best
one element in the political system, whether pluralist or corporatist,
became an independent, autonomous agent. As such, it was seen as an
active agent rather than a passive entity, and a force in its own right rather
than a set of institutions with no apparent purpose.[108]

It is interesting to note that among the earliest state-centered theorists,
while all condemned pluralism in general, most offered specific counter-
examples only in comparative settings and in the American foreign policy
arena, places where the state as such has conceptually and historically
played significant roles. For instance, in Eric Nordlinger's major exposi-
tion of state-centered theory, the bulk of the cases cited in demonstration
of state autonomy are in foreign countries or in American foreign policy,
with the lone domestic policy example focused on local government.[109]
Moreover, it is probably telling that one of the main exponents of the
state-centered approach, Theda Skocpol, developed her analysis through
work on France, Russia, and China, countries with decidedly "statist"
public authorities, and that Alfred Stepan developed his while studying a
Latin American country.[110] In addition, it is surely no accident that the
first major American-focused exponent of the state-centered approach,
Stephen Krasner, developed his analysis through a case study of foreign
trade policy, itself in one of the most "statist" areas of American policymaking.[111] For in foreign policy and international relations, the con-

[107]Alfred Diamant, "Bureaucracy and Public Policy in Neocorporatist Settings,"
Comparative Politics, vol. 14, no. 1 (October 1981).
[108]Skocpol, "Bringing State Back In"; Nordlinger, *Autonomy of Democratic State;*
and Krasner, *Defending the National Interest.*
[109]Nordlinger, *Democratic State.*
[110]Skocpol, *States and Social Revolutions;* Stepan, *State and Society.*
[111]Krasner, *Defending the National Interest.*

cept of the state has always been central, and government actors and institutions have traditionally been seen as key players, minimally constrained by societal pressures.

This is not to say, however, that state-centered theorists cannot or do not apply their state-centered analyses to U.S. domestic policy. But when Skocpol turned to the United States, her choice of the New Deal era bespeaks a moment when the depth of the economic crisis in American society conspired to allow the United States to overcome its fragmentation, and to appear more "statist" than at any other time in American history other than, perhaps, Johnson's Great Society.[112] A state-centered approach, in fact, often appears most apt when focused on moments of crisis which have a tendency to strengthen the role of the executive; and this is especially the case with external threat, whether military or economic.[113] Thus, when John Ikenberry analyzes oil policy in state-centered fashion, he takes an area that is not only on the cusp between foreign and domestic policy, but one in which, because of the atmosphere of crisis as well as the international dimensions of the problem, the executive was able to expand its capacities beyond the traditional limits.[114]

Even in the domestic policymaking process, however, it is possible to make a case for the independence of government decision-makers – by focusing on the implementation process. Certainly the Reagan era, with its informal deregulation of the social policy arena through the appointment of agency heads who crippled the enforcement of regulations by returning large portions of their budgets, as did Anne Burford Gorsuch when head of the Environmental Protection Agency, or by not hearing cases, as did Clarence Thomas when head of the Equal Employment Opportunity Commission, suggests a good deal of administrative discretion.[115] And this continued in the Bush era, for example, with the delay in the application of environmental rules by Vice-President Quayle's Competitiveness Panel.

The state, then, can be seen as having independent power even in the domestic policy arena, although the case for such independence is more

[112]Theda Skocpol, "Political Response to Capitalist Crisis: Neo Marxist Theories of the State and the Case of the New Deal," *Politics and Society* vol. 10 (1981) pp. 155–201.
[113]In the case of war, see: Franz Schurmann, *The Logic of World Order* (New York: Pantheon, 1974).
[114]John G. Ikenberry, *Reasons of State* (New York: Cambridge University Press, 1989).
[115]This "executive" deregulation, by contrast with legislative or judicial, may very well be the shortest-lived, since a new president and/or new appointees can reverse the policies, but it is still an example of the autonomy of state actors. See: Vivien Schmidt, "La dérégulation aux États Unis," *Revue Française d'Administration Publique* no. 41 (January–March 1987): 115–127.

convincingly made in the foreign policy area, where there are many fewer institutional as well as societal constraints, and in foreign countries. And it is here that France has finally gotten its due.

France has in recent years been portrayed as the ideal-typical strong state, insulated from the political community and centralizing enough to ensure it at least partial autonomy,[116] with institutions which provide it with "tactical advantages" that enable it to take independent action[117] and to manifest a policy style notable for its capacity not merely to initiate far-sighted planning efforts but also to impose them where it deems necessary.[118] The French themselves, of course, have traditionally portrayed state–society relations in this way, primarily as a system in which the state remains central, dominating the political agenda and monopolizing the construction of the populace's worldview, organizing and controlling societal interests, and taking charge of the implementation of public policies, thereby devaluing the role of local elected officials.[119] And yet, even studies of France, where the state is generally accepted as strong, encounter problems keeping the boundaries between state and society clearly delineated, due to the state's many "weaknesses."

Although the state is for the most part able to formulate policy independently, absent most societal constraints, it cannot implement such policy independently. Much depends upon the willingness of societal interests to go along with government policy. In the industrial policy area in particular, as attention in recent years has shifted from policy formulation to policy implementation, most scholars have detailed the relative independence of industry from state control. Similarly, in center–periphery relations, even before the decentralization reforms of the eighties, scholars traced the informal circuits of power that enabled local elected officials to have much

[116]Zysman, *Political Strategies*, p. 194.

[117]Wilsford, "Tactical Advantages." Wilsford enumerates these as: a strong independent executive with proposal and decree powers that even allow it to impose its programs without debate in the National Assembly if it so chooses; a weak or "arena" legislature which does the majority government's bidding; an active, homogeneously trained bureaucracy with strong ministerial direction; a judiciary with limited powers and little tradition of judicial review; and ideologically fragmented, societal interests.

[118]Jack Hayward, "Mobilising Private Interests in the Service of Public Ambitions: The Salient Element in the Dual French Policy Style?" in *Public Styles in Western Europe*, ed. J. Richardson (London: Allen and Unwin, 1982), p. 116. See also Peter Hall, who attributes the French state's strength to its ideal typical "étatism," which is derived from the state's cohesiveness, its insulation from the demands of other societal actors, its ability to speak for the public interest, and its capability to implement policy over the objections of social groups if necessary. *Governing the Economy*, pp. 164–165.

[119]See the summary description of this model by Muller, "Entre le local et l'Europe," pp. 275–276. See also: Bertrand Badie and Pierre Birnbaum, *Sociologie de l'état* (Paris: Grasset, 1979).

more influence in policy implementation than the law allowed or the rhetoric admitted.[120] Moreover, as many scholars have pointed out, the image of the strong state hides great fragmentation because of rivalries both between ministries involved in implementing major policies and within ministries.[121]

Finally, there are certain areas where the allegedly "strong" French state is very "weak" even in the policy formulation process, allowing private interests to share in it, if not to dominate it. This was true of agriculture between the early sixties and early eighties (discussed above) and education, the only policy area where organized interests actually sit on official ministerial committees (in the granting of tenure, promotion, etc.). In both cases, the government allowed organized interests for the most part to get their way, either by helping to shape policies (as did the farmers between the late sixties and early eighties)[122] or to block them (generally the pattern of the teachers)[123] – even if a determined minister with presidential backing can always take unilateral action, and has, albeit often with uncertain results.

This weakness of the strong state has also been the case with the *notaires,* where Suleiman in his study condemns the use of the terms "strong" and "weak" state as "not entirely logical."[124] He prefers instead to talk about the administrative pluralism of France's centralized or unitary state in order to make the point that "centralized structures which allow for the concentration of jurisdictions in an arm of the state often do not prevent but rather facilitate the takeover of the state by a private group," allowing the private group to use public power for private gain.[125]

Even where private groups are not allowed in, however, there are instances when governments cannot impose their policies. For the presence of an elite, independent administrative bureaucracy, one of the characteristic sources of state strength, as we have already seen in the earlier discussion contrasting France with the more pluralist United States, can under certain circumstances also ensure state weakness. Thus, although ministries are often real political forces for innovative change if they so choose, as were the Ministry of Finance with macroeconomic policy in the eighties, or the Planning Commission in the

---

[120]For a discussion of the range of views, see: Schmidt, *Democratizing France.*

[121]Suleiman, *Power, Politics, and Bureaucracy,* pp. 137–154.

[122]Keeler, *Politics of Neocorporatism.*

[123]John Ambler, "Neocorporatism and the Politics of French Education" *Politics* vol. 8, no. 3 (July 1, 1985).

[124]Ezra N. Suleiman, *Private Power and Centralization in France: The Notaires and the State* (Princeton: Princeton University Press, 1987), p. 27.

[125]Ibid., p. 17.

postwar period until the early sixties,[126] they can just as easily be a drag on change, and even scuttle any chance of innovation, if they so choose. Certain powerful ministries, in particular those which are dominated by a single corps (e.g., the Ministry of Finance, the stronghold of the graduates of the ENA) or closely linked to a single, centrally organized interest group (e.g., the National Education Ministry, to the centrally organized teachers' union) can exercise veto power over proposed governmental changes and are often impervious to governmental political pressures for policy changes.

Thus, where society-centered theorists could be criticized for underdetermining the role of the state, state-centered theorists could be criticized for in some sense "overdetermining" the state's role, as well as for implicitly praising "strong" states, by contrast with the "weak" ones. How, then, to deal appropriately with the balance between state and society, without assuming that we must choose between state- or society-centered approaches, that is, between concentrating on government decision-makers and decision-making organizations on the one hand for their independence of action, or on organized interests, pluralist or corporatist, on the other hand for their constraints on policy and on policy-makers? In recent years, the policy-community approach has sought to resolve this problem by insisting that both state and society need to be put together into a single discussion of the process of policymaking.

THE LIMITS OF THE POLICY-COMMUNITY APPROACH

Policy-community analysts reject the separation between state and society as misleading because they privilege either government decision-makers and decision-making bodies, as do state-centered theorists, or societal interests, as do pluralists and corporatists. Instead, they prefer an approach that considers the interactions of state and societal agents as part of systems or communities of policymakers, and which focuses on the complex networks of relationships between particular governmental decision-making bodies on the one hand and the particular societal interests they regulate on the other.[127] The policy community, as a result, is sectorized in special subsystems "based on the functional interdependence between fragmented public administration and its sponsored private subgovernments."[128]

[126]See Jean-Louis Quermonne, *L'appareil administratif de l'état* (Paris: Seuil, 1991).
[127]See, for example, Hayward, "Policy Community Approach"; Maurice Wright, "Policy Community, Policy Networks and Comparative Industrial Policy, *Political Studies* vol. 36, no. 4 (December 1988).
[128]Hayward, "Policy Community Approach," p. 381.

As such, policy-community analysts avoid the confusions inherent in talking of the weakness of strong states or the strength of weak ones, and the exaggerations that come from seeing either state actors imposing policies on society or societal groups manipulating government in their own interest above all else. In fact, instead of concentrating on the politics alone, which may make state or societal actors appear predominant, they consider the policies first, insisting that politics follow from the policies and not vice-versa, because policy problems much more than societal or state actors' choices determine the resulting decisions, or policy outputs. In other words, rather than state actors or societal interests developing their policies and then imposing them on the other, "policy communities will develop around particular programs, ministries, or policies."[129]

Cultural values, moreover, are a significant component of these policy systems, defining the norms that govern their functioning. These values are to be found in the regulatory norms and the legitimizing rhetoric which inform the communities' policies, and which represent the standards by which such policies will be evaluated.[130] Thus, for example, in France, the major regulatory norm in the industrial policy area prior to World War II was preserving socioeconomic stability, whereas in the postwar period there was a shift to promoting modernization, with the substitution of competitiveness for protectionism. This in turn entailed a move away from the emphasis on protecting small business to that of encouraging the growth of large-scale business. But because of the subsidiary norm of solidarity, the painful adjustment process was managed "with a modicum of good order."[131] In Britain, by contrast, the regulatory norms represent less an overarching goal for the system than a prescription about behavior or the rules of the game, which include mutual confidence, a certain accepted amount of state intervention, informal consulting, secrecy and confidentiality, and so forth.[132]

Leadership in these communities, in addition, may be by state or society, whether by "modernizing elite agents within the administration" or "change agents from organized interests."[133] For France, as we have already seen, the administrative agents of change are the products of the ENA and the Polytechnique. Even in France, however, change has been promoted by societal interests, for example, the telecommunications en-

[129]Gary P. Freeman, "National Styles and Policy Sectors: Explaining Structural Variation," *Journal of Public Policy* vol. 5 (October 1985), pp. 484–485.

[130]Hayward, "Policy Community Approach," p. 384.

[131]Ibid., p. 386. See also: Bruno Jobert and Pierre Muller, *L'état en action* (Paris: Presses Universitaires de France, 1987).

[132]Wright, "Policy Community"; and Hayward, "Policy Community Approach," p. 386.

[133]Hayward, "Policy Community Approach," p. 390.

gineers who sought to modernize the French telephone system or the more left-leaning farm leaders of the CNJA.[134]

Policymaking, in short, is an ongoing process that arises out of a particular policy problem or set of problems around which a system or policy community emerges made up of the networks of interrelationships in which leadership may be exercised by state or societal interests according to norms set by the values of the culture as a whole. Most policy-community analysts see this approach as a replacement for pluralist, corporatist, and state-centered approaches. And yet, the approach itself applies successfully primarily to Great Britain and France, countries for which neither the pluralist nor the corporatist approach works very well, and for which the state-centered approach, while more adequate, nevertheless runs into problems as detailed above. This primacy of Great Britain and France comes out most dramatically in a review essay by Jack Hayward on the policy-community approach to industrial policy, where he notes that for "a focus on policy communities, we must turn to European scholars who are accustomed to a more tightly structured pluralism than is usually found in North America."[135] This is because in the United States, instead of essentially closed policy communities, we find the "issues networks" described by Hugh Heclo.[136] The European scholars cited by Hayward tend to focus on Britain[137] or France alone.[138] The only other example considered is that of West Germany in the industrial policy area, which when discussed in policy-community terms provides a stark contrast with France because of the weaker government leadership capability and the greater permeability to opposing interests.[139] Thus, although the policy-community approach purports to apply to all policy areas, regardless of polity, it in fact applies best to countries such as France and Great Britain, where policies are the product of a relatively

---

[134]Jobert and Muller, *L' état en action* – examples cited by Hayward, "Policy Community Approach," pp. 390–391.

[135]Hayward, "Policy Community Approach," p. 392.

[136]Hugh Heclo, "Issue Networks and the Executive Establishment," in *The New American Political System,* ed. Anthony King (Washington, DC: American Enterprise Institute, 1978).

[137]Specifically, Jeremy J. Richardson and A. Grant Jordan, *Governing Under Pressure: The Policy Process in a Post-Parliamentary Democracy* (Oxford: Robertson, 1979); A. Grant Jordan, "Iron Triangles, Woolly Corporatism and Elastic Images of the Policy Process," *Journal of Public Policy,* vol. 1, no. 1 (February 1981); Brian W. Hogwood, *From Crisis to Complacency? Shaping Public Policy in Britain* (New York: Oxford University Press, 1987).

[138]Specifically, Hayward, *State and Market Economy;* N. J. D. Lucas, *Energy in France: Planning, Politics, and Policy* (London: Europa Publications, 1979).

[139]As elaborated by Kenneth Dyson, "West Germany: The Search for a Rationalist Consensus," in *Policy Styles in Western Europe,* ed. Jeremy Richardson (London: 1982).

close relationship between state administrators and societal interests organized in communities sharing common values imposed by the culture, in which sometimes state administrators take the lead, and other times societal interests.

The problem with this approach, then, just as with the other approaches, is that it risks implying that those polities that do not conform to the ideal pattern are somehow less desirable. This is not to suggest, though, that policy-community analysts are wrong to argue that polities should be considered in terms of their policies rather than their politics alone, or that both sides of the state–society equation should be examined. The problem for policy-community analysts is that, in preferring policy over politics, they still risk neglecting the institutions that underlie both, and that serve to differentiate polities, regardless of their politics or policies.

To give institutions their due within the context of the policy-community approach, however, would entail abandoning any pretense of explaining all polities according to a single definition of the policy process, and acknowledging that the approach as it is currently outlined applies ideally only to France and Great Britain. To expand the policy-community approach beyond this by taking account of institutional differences would make it lose its special organizational characteristics, leaving us only with the insight (albeit an important one) that, instead of focusing on the structures of the state or society alone, we should also consider the processes by which state and society interact in making policy.

CONCLUSION

Such an insight is the key to the approach I outline below, in which considerations of politics, policy, and institutions are wrapped up all together in a discussion of the different patterns of policymaking in different polities. Such an approach is relatively straightforward for the pluralist pattern of policymaking of the United States and the corporatist pattern of the smaller European democracies and Germany, which have been thoroughly explored both in terms of their political structures and their policy processes. But this has not been the case for the "statist" pattern of policymaking of countries such as Great Britain, Japan, and France, the ideal-typical case considered below, where comparatively little general theorizing has been done.

2

The statist pattern of policymaking

In the political science literature, France has generally been treated as an anomaly, a country with revolts and revolutions rather than the peaceable representation of interests, and an authoritative imposition of policy rather than pluralist consultation of the kind found in the United States or corporatist concertation characteristic of the smaller European democracies and Germany. As a result, France has at best been characterized as having "limited pluralism" or "weak corporatism." It is only lately that the state has been brought back in, and France has been able to take its place among "strong" states, by contrast with such "weak" states as the United States. But this over-"states" the case, given that there is much weakness even in France's strong state. The policy-community approach seeks to remedy this by rejecting the emphasis on politics that seems to demand the definitional separation of state and society for one on policy, and by blurring the lines between state and society. Even here, however, the lack of adequate attention to underlying institutions is problematic.

In what follows, I argue that the most appropriate analysis for France is one that refers to its "statist" pattern of policymaking, also the pattern in Japan and to a lesser extent in Great Britain, by contrast with the pluralist pattern predominant in the United States (with the exception of the more "statist" foreign policy arena), and the corporatist pattern present in the smaller European democracies and, to a lesser extent, Germany. As such, my approach builds on the state-centered while modifying its definition to include weakness as much as strength and limiting its applicability to those polities that best fit this modified state-centered pattern.

The term "statist" has been used before for France, albeit with a somewhat different content. France has time and again been characterized as "state capitalism,"[1] or more simply as "statism,"[2] one of three dominant

[1]Jack Hayward, *The One and Indivisible French Republic* (New York: Norton, 1973).
[2]Katzenstein, *Small States.*

forms of contemporary capitalism (the other two being liberalism and corporatism). Moreover, *étatisme* has historically been part of the vocabulary used to describe the predominantly interventionist or *dirigiste* role of the French state in the economy, and France's "statist" tradition has time and again been used to characterize a polity in which the state has been characterized as "strong" and autonomous.[3] None of these definitions conveys the full meaning of "statist" as used herein, where it refers to a pattern of policymaking shaped by history, culture, and institutions, which may appear strong from certain vantage points, in particular at the formulation stage of policymaking, and weak from others, primarily at the implementation stage.

In the statist pattern, government decision-makers and decision-making organizations take a leadership role in policymaking and have primary control over structuring the "state–society relationship," meaning that they are for the most part able to dictate the pattern of interest representation and to resist the pressures of interests, whether organized or not, where they choose. This is generally the case because in the statist pattern typical of polities such as Japan and France, state structures tend to be centralized, with governments afforded tactical advantages through particular institutional arrangements and organizational processes, ordinarily a powerful executive backed by a majority party and/or a strong bureaucracy, which tend to be legitimized by history and reinforced by culture. In these polities, the state predominates, although the degrees of societal centralization do affect the stability of the state–society interaction, with the higher the degree of societal centralization, the more stable the polity. This is epitomized in the political economic sphere, where France exhibits less stability than Japan because the former's societal interests are more decentralized than those of the latter. The pattern is quite different in a pluralist polity such as the United States, where a decentralized state combines with a decentralized society; or in corporatist polities, whether a stable one such as that of Austria, where a centralized state combines with a centralized society, or a less stable one, as in Germany, where a decentralized state combines with a centralized society (see Figure 2.1).[4]

A statist polity, as a result, is one in which government has the power and authority to take unilateral action at the policy formulation stage, without prior consultation with those most interested in the policy. This

[3]Peter J. Katzenstein, "Introduction," *Between Power and Plenty*, ed. Katzenstein.
[4]Peter Katzenstein offers a similar model of state–society relations divided along organizational lines of centralization and decentralization, but he does not include the added institutional dimension here of pluralist, statist, and corporatist. See: "Conclusion: Domestic Structures and Strategies of Foreign Economic Policy," in *Between Power and Plenty*.

SOCIETAL ORGANIZATION

		decentralized	centralized
STATE	decentralized	pluralist (U.S.A.)	less stable corporatist (Germany)
ORGANIZATION	centralized	less stable statist (France and U.K.)	more stable corporatist (small European democracies) more stable statist (Japan)

Figure 2.1. The effect of state and societal organization on policymaking patterns.

contrasts directly with both pluralist polities, in which societal interests are involved primarily in the formulation of policy, and corporatist ones, in which certain privileged interests, mainly business and labor, are involved in policy formulation and implementation, and where in both cases governments have neither the power nor the authority to take such unilateral action. As such, this approach represents a corrective to the state-centered approach, which focuses primarily on the independence of state action in all countries without sufficient attention to societal interests, by considering the interaction of state and society in specific countries and finding that the independence of policymakers at the formulation stage tends to be offset by their dependence upon societal interests at the implementation stage. As such, it also goes one better than the policy-community approach, which blurs the line between state and society so much as to fail to differentiate between formulation and implementation stages.

Although in statist polities the state has the ability to impose, the affected interests have the ability to resist. Thus, even if statist governments may take unilateral action at the formulation stage, in particular if it involves "heroic" (to borrow a term from Hayward)[5] policies central to their agenda, they do generally consult with the most affected parties at the implementation stage. And here, the result may be the politics of accommodation, co-optation, or confrontation. What is more, where the policies are more everyday ones, accommodation or co-optation may begin already at the formulation stage, and private interests may hold sway. Governments, after all, can choose to use the tools

[5]Hayward, "Mobilising Private Interests." Hayward uses the term to connote primarily a policy style. Here, however, the term also refers to policies governments see as central to their agenda.

at their disposal or not. And this may be dictated by their electoral mandate, the personality and/or vision of the leaders, the size of their majority, the sense of crisis in the society that may appear to demand heroic plans, and so forth.

Thus, instead of using the term "statist" to connote an ideal-typically strong and centralized state, imposing its will on a seemingly docile public which only occasionally objects through protest, I use it to define a polity in which the so-called strength of governmental decision-makers intent on putting through heroic policies is often offset by their apparent weakness when engaging in everyday policies or faced with organized opposition or disorganized protest. After all, if our understanding of the pluralist pattern can encompass not only the ideal version where organized interests democratically balance one another out at the formulation stage but also the corruption of the process through capture of regulatory agencies, then surely the statist pattern can have bound up in its characterization not only the ideal but also the all too real. In fact, by identifying a statist pattern with heroic and everyday policies at the formulation stage and the politics of accommodation, co-optation, and confrontation at the implementation stage, I am seeking to avoid the language of strength and weakness altogether. Such terms are too fraught with bias, either seeming to applaud France as a "strong state" by contrast with the United States' "weak state," or to denigrate it, by implying that France is characterized by a certain authoritarianism at the formulation stage, a kind of incompetence at the implementation stage. The statist pattern in France is simply a different kind of democracy from the pluralist kind found in the United States or the corporatist kind found in Germany. It is Jacobin in its ideal at the formulation stage, as democratically elected governments fulfill the desires of the people directly, thus embodying Rousseau's General Will, without the intermediation of interests or the "mischief of faction," as a French transposition of Madison might put it. But it is Girondist in its implementation, decentralized and responsive, ensuring that the General Will does not drift too far from the particular one.

France, in short, has been characterized by a pattern of policymaking where heroic policies at the formulation stage have been tempered by the politics of accommodation, co-optation, or confrontation. In recent years, however, this traditional pattern has been jeopardized. In the eighties, governments of the left and the right engaged in heroic policymaking that effectively stripped the state of many of the very policy instruments that had enabled it to direct the economy and the society in *dirigiste* manner. Europeanization has decreased government independence in decision-making; deregulation and privatization have diminished government power over business; and decentralization has diminished the power the state has traditionally had over the periphery.

Although these changes have not radically altered the statist pattern of policymaking, they may very well have served to precipitate a crisis in it.

FORMULATING STATIST POLICY

Statist policy formulation runs the gamut from heroic policies, characterized by unilateral governmental action with little or no prior consultation, to everyday ones. In this latter case, private interests may play a major role in policy formulation, so much so that the lines between formulation and implementation blur; and although government decision-makers remain dominant as the organizing and/or initiating force, policymaking is basically cooperative, and involves a coordination between state and societal interests. Heroic and everyday policies are found in every policy area, although some areas are characteristically more one or the other. Thus, in France, educational and agricultural policy tend to be dominated by everyday policymaking, with the periodic attempts at heroic policymaking generally doomed to failure, primarily because of the historical strength and cultural importance of these well-organized interests. Industrial policy, by contrast, has historically been the ideal-typical area for heroic policymaking, with its acme being in the early to mid eighties as the policies of nationalization, privatization, and deregulation provided for radical change in the structure of French capitalism. In the late eighties to the present, however, the everyday has come to the fore, having produced equally important changes.

Heroic policies

In France, with its statist pattern of policymaking, governments with solid majorities and "vision" are generally able to move ahead swiftly to fulfill their campaign promises with "heroic" programs in which government leadership remains paramount and consultation is often minimal.[6] No presidents or prime ministers in pluralist or corporatist polities can possibly fulfill their campaign promises to the voters so fully (whether the voters like it or not) or so rapidly, given the demand for prior consultation with the affected interests, unless the country is in grave crisis.[7] As a

---

[6]Ultimate success in a government's policies also depends upon the size of the mandate and the sense of crisis in the society, which may determine the "window" for reform. See John T. S. Keeler, "Opening the Window for Reform: Mandates, Crises and Extraordinary Policymaking," *Comparative Political Studies* (1992).

[7]One primary difference between a pluralist polity such as the United States and France's statist pattern is that in the United States, as John W. Kingdon explains, "The president may be able to dominate and even determine the policy agenda, but is unable to dominate the alternatives that are seriously considered, and is unable to determine the final outcome." *Agendas, Alternatives, and Public Policies* (New York: Harper

result, problems that may find swift resolution in France may fester where no consensus has been reached, as they have in the United States in terms of health care policy.

By the same token, however, the very precipitousness of the policy formulation process means that some of the more thoroughgoing reforms that require painstaking and time-consuming deliberation never get done; while the sometimes radical nature of the reforms may cause serious problems that require more legislation to undo. Moreover, where heroic policies are unlikely because the government lacks a clear majority, confidence in its leadership, and/or vision, then having a statist pattern of policymaking may be the worst of the three patterns for a polity in need of reform or facing a crisis, because the government alone is responsible not only for implementing policy but also for initiating and inspiring it.

Perhaps the most spectacular recent examples of heroic statist policymaking are in the industrial policy arena: nationalization and privatization in France under the Mauroy and Chirac governments, respectively, and privatization in Great Britain under Thatcher. In all three cases, governments with clear majorities fulfilled their campaign promises to bring about significant changes in industry without prior consultation with those most affected by the policies. In France, there was no prior consultation for the nationalizations of industry, which left the state owning thirteen of the twenty largest firms in France and a controlling share in many other French companies, or for the nationalizations of all but a few family-owned banks, which gave it control of over 96% of deposits.[8] The neoliberals' privatization program was similarly unilateral and precipitous as it denationalized such symbols of state authority as the national television station, TF1, the industrial giant Saint Gobain, and the bank Société Générale, halting only as a result of the stock market crash of October 1987, with the program 40% completed. However, while claiming to end state *dirigisme* and to set up a "people's capitalism," the neoliberals were highly interventionist as they picked the *noyau dur,* or hard core, of investors (including state-owned banks) to hold a controlling interest in the newly privatized firms and not very populist in their capitalism as they provided for no representation of small, individual shareholders on the boards of directors.[9]

The Thatcher government's privatization program was more radical than the French, which it had to some degree inspired. Not only did it sell all shares freely on the market, but it also sold off public housing and utilities in addition to nationalized industries in the face of much opposi-

Collins, 1984), p. 26. In France, the president or prime minister dominates throughout.
[8]See Chapter 4.   [9]See Chapter 5.

tion, in particular in the cases of gas and water. That in France, privatization was a centrally controlled, highly regulated affair, whereas in England, laissez-faire ruled, bespeaks the very different histories and philos-
ophies of the two countries with regard to economic policymaking in
general. Moreover, that the Socialists nationalized at a time when the rest
of the world had already turned to privatization reflects the long history
of acceptance of nationalization as a solution to economic problems.

One need not have a long history of extensive nationalization, however,
to have heroic industrial policies in which the government takes a major
leadership role with regard to industry, nor one where governments may
take so little account of those most affected by their policies at the formulation stage. Planning in France (in particular in the early postwar years)
and in Japan are cases where private interests became an integral part of
the policymaking process – but where government officials retained the
initiative in determining the overall objectives of the plan and in organizing the implementation of the planning process. In Japan, however, planning was less *"dirigiste"* than in France because the medium-term (three
to five years) and long-term (five to ten years) plans were not binding
either on the private sector or on government, and were seen less as
authoritative directives than as general forecasts which outlined concrete
near-term goals within a long-term vision of future directions for industry.[10] In the postwar years, when planning was the primary instrument
for industrial policymaking in France, Japan had already elaborated a
whole series of industrial policies.

In France, planning was particularly heroic from the mid to late 1940s
at the outset of the Fourth Republic until the early 1960s in the first years
of the Fifth Republic.[11] Even though the Fourth Republic had anything
but statist institutional arrangements, given its weak executive and transformative legislature, highly permeable to interest group pressures, heroic
industrial policymaking obtained nevertheless not simply because of a
shared commitment to the idea of planning but also because the financial
resources and institutional independence of the bureaucracy were both
assured. Thus, although the Fourth Republic resembled the Third in its
parliamentary paralysis – with no clear majority and little leadership – it
did nevertheless have vision with regard to industrial policy, and civil
servants capable both of initiating policy and of mobilizing the necessary
forces to carry it through.

[10]See Daniel Okimoto, *Between Miti and the Market: Japanese Industrial Policy for
High Technology* (Stanford, CA: Stanford University Press, 1989), p. 24; and Stephen S.
Cohen, *Modern Capitalist Planning; The French Model* (Berkeley: University of California Press, 1977), parts I–IV.
[11]See the discussions in Chapters 3 and 9. For an excellent summary of French
planning, see: Hall, *Governing the Economy*, pp. 139–191.

The statist pattern of policymaking

As time went on, however, planning became less effective, more ambitious, and more politicized; it was ultimately more heroic in rhetoric than reality. And as planning declined as a focus for heroic policies in the economic sphere, industrial policy came to the fore, with planning as an adjunct to it. Under de Gaulle, economic planning was combined with the heroic policy of encouraging concentration among companies in order to create "national champions." Under Giscard d'Estaing, planning was subordinated to the government's official industrial policy, the *politique de créneaux*, which sought to create leaders in particular sectors of the international economy, and to its unofficial policy of bailing out companies on the verge of bankruptcy, which effectively substituted a policy of support for "lame ducks" for that of national champions.[12]

Under the Socialists between 1981 and 1986, planning also took a back seat to industrial policy, which was focused primarily on the massive restructuring of the nationalized enterprises through the *politique de filières*. Through this heroic policy, the Socialists reorganized the nationalized industries into vertically integrated firms, recapitalized them, and streamlined their operations, eliminating jobs and closing obsolete plants where necessary.[13] As a result, the Socialists performed in an organized manner in a few short years what a decade of takeovers and acquisitions did in the United States; and they did this with less waste, more rationality, and fewer attendant problems with employee morale and productivity.

The benefits of the heroic capabilities of the statist model of industrial policymaking here cannot be exaggerated. In *Made in America*, the authors (among them French scholar Suzanne Berger) argue that economic success depends less on the mode of industrial policymaking, whether it be typical of Japan, Germany, or France, than on the fact of cooperation between business and government, which the United States in particular lacks.[14] But surely there is more to it than this. France in the eighties required a massive restructuring of industry that neither Germany nor Japan did to begin to reach appropriate size and competitiveness. It was able to succeed in this because of the heroism of its statist policymaking, combined with its cultural openness to nationalization and its institu-

---

[12]Suzanne Berger, "Lame Ducks and National Champions: Industrial Policy in the Fifth Republic," in *The Impact of the Fifth Republic on France,* ed. William G. Andrews and Stanley Hoffman (Albany: SUNY Press, 1981), p. 160. For a discussion of the particular cases, see: Elie Cohen, *L'état brancardier: Politiques du déclin industriel (1974–1984)* (Paris: Calmann-Lévy, 1989).

[13]See Chapter 4. See also: Schmidt, "Industrial Management."

[14]Michael L. Dertouzos, Richard K. Lester, Robert M. Solow, et al., *Made in America: Regaining the Productive Edge* (Cambridge, MA: MIT Press, 1989), pp. 108–112.

tional strengths, in particular its elite civil service.[15] In the United States, the pluralist model alone makes any such coordinated action except in times of extreme crisis highly unlikely, not to mention the institutional and cultural impediments which make the extension of the state difficult.

Heroism was also evident in the deregulatory policies that the Socialists began and subsequent right- and left-wing governments continued, as well as in the push toward European integration.[16] These heroic policies include not only the "Great U-turn" in macroeconomic policy of 1983, when the Socialists switched from Keynesian expansionism to liberal austerity with strict monetary policies and tight budgets but also the opening of the financial markets, the lifting of price controls, the abrogation of most barriers to competition, and all of the measures required by the European Union in terms of the opening of borders, standardization of products, and so forth. Ironically enough, these heroic policies ultimately undermined French governments' ability to engage in the kind of heroism traditionally associated with French industrial policymaking, that is, *dirigisme*, because they had essentially given away the state's macroeconomic independence along with the microeconomic policy instruments that governments had traditionally used to gain compliance from business.

This heroic dismantling of heroic capability was equally true of the decentralization reforms of 1982 through 1986 in France, where the Socialists overcame 200 years of endless debates and failed initiatives to redefine the role of the state in the periphery by transferring state powers, functions, and funds to newly enfranchised and/or empowered local governments.[17] Unlike Socialist nationalization, however, the policy formulation process for decentralization did involve much consultation; but it was still in no way pluralist. The government firmly controlled the process; and although there was some compromise on a range of issues in response to civil service pressure, in particular on the division of health and social services, there was little on the major ones – for example, on the abolition of the prefect's *tutelle*.[18] The result, moreover, was the creation of a heroic statist pattern of policymaking at the local level which mirrored that at the

[15]One could, of course, also argue that it was because of France's statist model, which had enabled it to keep such a stranglehold over the economy through controls over prices, wages, exchange rates, credit, and so forth, that heroic action had become so necessary.

[16]For details, see Chapters 4, 5, and 6.

[17]Schmidt, *Democratizing France;* idem, "Unblocking Society by Decree: The Impact of Governmental Decentralization in France," *Comparative Politics* vol. 22, no. 4 (July 1990), pp. 459–481; idem, "Decentralization: A Revolutionary Reform," in *The French Socialists in Power, 1981–1986,* ed. Patrick McCarthy (Westport, CT: Greenwood Press, 1987).

[18]Schmidt, *Democratizing France,* pp. 126, 112.

national level, where strong executives and capable civil servants are able to formulate policies without significant input from local organized interests. Although the decentralization reforms increased local democracy, it is a particularly statist one where, although local government has been brought closer to the people and local leaders have become more responsible and responsive, local decision-making remains mostly in the hands of local decision-makers rather than being based, as in a more pluralist model, on local interest group activity and citizen participation.[19]

The contrast with Great Britain is significant. While France decentralized in a heroic manner, Britain recentralized. Thatcher's weakening of local government authorities, epitomized by the fights over the Greater London Council, over local education (with the policy of allowing for local opting out), and the poll tax, in different ways represent her ability to reassert central governmental control over policymaking that had increasingly been left to the locality, and where traditionally there had always been a great deal of participatory democracy. That she lost her job in part over the poll tax (although the precipitating event was her opposition to the European Community), suggests that it is dangerous for leaders to push heroic policies too far when they lack full support from their own party.

Even where a government is able successfully to impose heroic policies, however, unanticipated problems can often result. After all, heroic policies based on targeted state action are not always a panacea. They can lead to great waste if they are based on miscalculation or on insufficient internal resources or are simply overtaken by events. For example, the Socialists' nationalization of industries and banks at 100% rather than at 51% led to headaches of a kind that the country is still in the process of undoing.[20] Moreover, in the sixties and seventies, the Plan Calcul in France, one of de Gaulle's initiatives, was an unmitigated disaster, while the Concorde, although a technological success, was a financial failure. In the eighties, the sectoral plans for the textile, wood, and machine tool industries were also failures. Such problems are not limited to France, however. In Japan, MITI's ambitious plans for the petrochemical industry also turned into a costly mistake when the first oil crisis hit.[21]

Everyday policies

Heroic policies are not the only kinds in statist policymaking. Statist polities also have everyday policies that may or may not be peripheral to a

[19]Schmidt, "Industrial Management"; and idem, *Democratizing France,* pp. 289–309.
[20]See Chapter 4.　[21]Okimoto, *Between Miti and the Market,* pp. 5–6.

government's plans. Here, private interests may have a great deal more influence in the policy formulation process. For Suleiman, such everyday policies constitute the bulk of policymaking in France, by contrast with heroic or what he calls "pure state policies," which he dismisses a bit too quickly as a rarity.[22] For even if relatively rare, their presence or absence has been the focus of most attention when judging a government's success or failure.

The everyday, quiet and often unannounced policies, however, are often every bit as important as the heroic ones. Probably the best recent example of this has been in France in the industrial policy area since 1988, when everyday policies based on a growing consensus between government and business effectively replaced the heroic policies of the past.[23] Mitterand's heroic policy of the *ni-ni*, or neither nationalization nor privatization, was essentially undermined by the everyday policy that began as a way of responding to the demands of capital-starved public corporations for additional investment funds and strategic alliances by allowing them to trade shares in one another, with foreign companies, and ultimately with private concerns (after 1991), and became a way of restructuring French capitalism. State ownership and control became more and more indirect, as nationalized and privatized, public and private financial and industrial concerns increasingly owned and controlled one another, in a manner akin to the German model of banking–industry partnership. Thus, when the right returned to office in 1993, its privatization initiatives, heroic in 1986, had become everyday affairs.

Most everyday policies, however, do not result in major changes in state–society relations; and they generally entail a great deal more consultation. Often, they are peripheral to the government's agenda, so that their prospects for passage as laws are minimal; and if they are passed at all, they will do little to solve major problems. This was primarily the case with the decentralization bills of the conservative Fifth Republic after de Gaulle, which tended to die after much debate or to end up in a weak and basically insignificant reform.[24]

Where the peripheral everyday policies succeed, moreover, it is for the most part because they are in the interests of those most affected by the reform, as in the case of the *notaires,* who actually proposed their own reform.[25] The danger here is similar to that of clientelistic relationships everywhere, and to captured agencies in the United States, where civil servants outside of the limelight or without the benefit of countervailing

---

[22]Suleiman, *Private Power and Centralization,* p. 235.   [23]See Chapter 6.
[24]Schmidt, *Democratizing France,* pp. 93–104.
[25]Suleiman, *Private Power and Centralization,* p. 255.

pressures end up acting in the interests of those whom they oversee rather than in the public interest.[26]

But whether the relationship goes as far as capture or not with everyday policies, the main distinguishing characteristic is that there is generally much more consultation than with heroic ones. Already in the 1950s, Henry Ehrmann had noted that in cases where an industry and its associated ministry shared authority in the making and implementing of policy, the authority along with much of the work moved from ministry to industry in such a way that decisions were essentially reached by industry and ordinarily given ministerial approval.[27] More recently, this has been the case with the farmers between the late sixties and the early eighties and in education (as noted above). Where policy formulation and implementation blur, as it may with everyday policies, private interests most often hold sway – and, in the terms of state-centered theorists, the strong state is at its weakest.

In these cases, everyday policymaking may look more corporatist or pluralist on the surface than statist. But such policymaking nevertheless remains definitionally part of a statist pattern because the government retains the upper hand, to invite outside interests in, or to freeze them out. This has certainly been true of the agricultural sector, where the left-wing farm groups frozen out of the bargaining process under the conservatives were brought in under the Socialists. And it remains true of business even today, because even though policymaking is now more consensual, government always has the capability of engaging in unilateral action. This is not, in other words, the relatively stable corporatist relationship one finds in the smaller European democracies or in Germany to a lesser extent, where government is a co-equal with business and labor. Nor is it the pluralist relationship of the United States, where government does not have the power to legitimize and delegitimize interests in quite this way, or to choose with whom to consult. It does not even mirror the relatively stable statist pattern of Japan's business–government relationship, where the centralization of business interests makes for a more consensual interaction with ministry officials, such that the state can impose less.

In France, consultation at the formulation stage for everyday policies as much as for heroic policies generally occurs only when the interests affected are organized in professional associations and legitimized by the bureaucracy. By contrast, where the interests are disorganized and not perceived by government as important for any ongoing consultation process, as with the students in the education sector and patients in the

---

[26]On capture theory, see: McConnell, *Private Power and Democracy.*
[27]Ehrmann, *Organized Business,* p. 262.

health area, government action is always unilateral, and consultation almost never occurs at the formulation stage. Moreover, for these least organized groups, it also may not occur at the implementation stage. By contrast, those groups formally consulted but with little impact at the formulation stage may have great influence in the implementation stage.

IMPLEMENTING STATIST POLICY

However much the state commands, those affected do not necessarily obey. The state is not really able to govern by decree because, as Shonfield noted already in the sixties, "The system will not function unless private organizations give their willing collaboration to the pursuit of public purposes. What is therefore required is the opposite of a bully state – rather a wheeling and dealing type of public authority constantly seeking out allies, probing and maneuvering for the active consensus."[28] Whereas in the pluralist pattern this occurs at the policy formulation stage, and in the corporatist pattern at both policy formulation and implementation stages, in the statist pattern with heroic policies it occurs for the most part at the implementation stage alone. After all, while the state may seek to impose its will, the affected parties can and do effectively resist. In the statist pattern of policymaking, such resistance may lead to accommodation, co-optation, or confrontation. Much depends upon the centrality of the policy to the government, its strategy, the policy's potential impact on the most affected interests, and these interests' level of access, upset, and organization. Only in an authoritarian statist polity could an unelected government not only formulate policy unilaterally but also impose it unilaterally, without attention to societal response.

Responsiveness to society at the implementation stage in statist policymaking is facilitated by the administrative nature of the state, where civil servants have wide latitude in interpreting the law, and even making exceptions to it when they see fit. This is in stark contrast to the pluralist pattern of policymaking, where the regulatory nature of the implementation process denies civil servants much latitude, and where making exceptions to the rules is regarded as illegitimate. In France, the relationship between formulation and implementation was captured years ago in Tocqueville's oft-repeated phrase: "the law is rigid, but the application is flexible." This means that laws formulated absent societal input can be adapted in the implementation process, ensuring that societal interests can be heard, but giving civil servants the discretionary power to listen or not.

[28]Shonfield, *Modern Capitalism*, p. 389.

The statist pattern of policymaking

The politics of confrontation

The politics of confrontation obtain when neither accommodation nor co-optation is possible, either because the government or the affected interests are unwilling to compromise. Where confrontation occurs with groups that play a regular role in the implementation process, the state may or may not capitulate. Where the state capitulates, all reverts to the politics of accommodation or co-optation. Where it does not capitulate, the confrontation may then go outside the regular political channels. By contrast, for affected groups that remain outside of the policy process, confrontation through extra-governmental means are the only ones open to them. This has been true for Japan in the case of organized labor and the left,[29] as it has for a variety of groups in France.

In France, sometimes extra-governmental confrontation occurs because the groups, although highly organized, simply cannot get their way by any other means, as in the case of the French farmers before and after the quasi-corporatist period between the late sixties and the early eighties, as well as during the GATT negotiations. Other times, it is because they are in competition with stronger groups more favored by the state in negotiations, as has traditionally been the case with French labor. Yet other times, it is because they are highly disorganized on an everyday basis, and therefore unable to be certified by the state as worthy of negotiation except during their mobilization, if then. In France, this has especially been the case with the students who have been time and again quickly mobilized and highly organized in their protests against successive attempts to reform the university (although in a number of instances the highly organized faculty also mixed in), most notably in the neoliberal government's 1986 initiative to liberalize the universities (by allowing individual universities to select their students and to seek outside funding from private sources). But it was also apparent with the 1984 dispute precipitated by the Socialist government over diminishing state support for private education, which brought in a wider group of protesters (primarily on the right) intent on saving private schools,[30] as well as more recently, in January 1994, with the attempt to increase state support for private education by the Balladur government (by allowing municipalities to fund private education beyond the traditional ceiling of 10%), which also brought in a wider group of protesters (primarily on the left) intent on saving the public schools.

One need not go so far as to say that rioting is a national sport,[31]

---

[29]Pempel, "Foreign Economic Policy," pp. 154–155.

[30]See John S. Ambler, "Educational Pluralism in the French Fifth Republic," in *Searching for the New France,* ed. James F. Hollifield and George Ross (New York: Routledge, 1991), pp. 193–220.

[31]Alain Peyrefitte, *The Trouble with France* (New York: Knopf, 1981), p. 263.

moreover, to recognize that confrontation, peaceable or violent, is very much a part of the policy process, as a last recourse in response to the lack of meaningful prior consultation.[32] But although confrontation may be effective as a negative action, in order to get the government to abandon a policy initiative, it can do little positively to get a desired reform put through, mainly because the government can wait out the protest with a "feather quilt strategy," whereby it cushions the blows without responding to the demands.[33] Only where groups are already involved in the policymaking process as legitimate interlocutors, even if only formally at the formulation stage with heroic policies, may confrontation yield results. This has been particularly true in the industrial policy area, where governments have often capitulated to CEOs of major firms who have threatened to resign if a given policy that affects their firm is not reversed. Just as often, however, the government refuses to capitulate, which sometimes leads to the resignation of the CEO, as in the case of Jean Gandois of Péchiney in 1983, or their nonrenewal, as with Albin Chalandon of Elf-Aquitaine the same year.

One of the most serious problems for France in recent years is that major reform initiatives have been dropped over and over again in response to protest. The high schools and universities, in desperate need of reform, have yet to experience any serious overhaul that truly addresses their problems. Moreover, whenever innovative proposals for dealing with issues of productivity in the workplace meet the resistance of public employees, the government backs off. This was as true for the Chirac government with the 1986 strike of the SNCF against linking pay to merit rather than seniority, which then spread to much of the public sector, as it was for the Balladur government in November 1993 in response to the strike by Air France workers against the proposed restructuring plan. In the face of protest, the result is often governmental impotence.[34]

The politics of accommodation and co-optation

The politics of accommodation and co-optation appear in all policy areas. They particularly epitomized center–periphery relations through-

[32]There are many in recent years who have examined protest as part of normal political exchange, e.g., W. Gamson, *The Strategy of Protest* (Homewood, IL: Dorsey, 1975); Charles Tilly, *From Mobilization to Revolution* (Englewood Cliffs, NJ: Prentice-Hall, 1978); Sidney Tarrow, *Democracy and Disorder: Protest and Politics in Italy, 1965–1975* (Oxford: Oxford University Press, 1988); Wilson, "French Interest Groups," pp. 906–907.

[33]Suzanne Berger, *Peasants Against Politics: Rural Organizations in Brittany, 1911–1967* (Cambridge, MA: Harvard University Press, 1972).

[34]See Denis Olivennes and Nicolas Baverez, *L'impuissance publique* (Paris: Calmann-Lévy, 1989). See also Michel Crozier, *État modeste, état moderne* (Paris: Fayard, 1987).

out the Fifth Republic up until the Socialists' reforms. Although the laws and the rhetoric described a highly centralized, formal system in which the center dictated to the periphery, local government was in fact highly decentralized in an informal system of mutual accommodation between prefects and local notables which insulated both from local pressures and central control.[35] Moreover, whenever the central government sought to break this "complicity," for example, with de Gaulle's regional reforms of 1964, local elected officials managed nevertheless to co-opt the process, in this case by "colonizing" the new regional units once they realized they couldn't stop them.[36]

The politics of accommodation and co-optation are also much in evidence in France in the industrial policy and planning area. Even in the early years, when the French model of planning was synonymous with strong state interventionism, it was much less *dirigiste,* or able to impose its will, than commonly assumed. And as time went on, as planning gave way to industrial policy, there are those who suggested that industrial policy had in many areas even become tantamount to an industrialists' policy.[37]

Accommodation and co-optation in the implementation of industrial planning and policy are facilitated not only by state fragmentation, which allows businesses to play off one ministry against another, but also by the personalistic nature of ministry—industry relations, where high-level government officials and top managers tend to negotiate on major firm-related issues. Because *corporatisme* is often at play here, given that a majority of top managers share with top officials old school ties, membership in a prestigious civil service corps, and government experience, CEOs in both public and private sectors have significant leverage.[38] But even where *corporatisme* is not at issue, CEOs carry great weight as a result of their positions at the head of the relatively small number of large firms and their technical expertise. By the same token, however, government officials also have great power to persuade, not simply by their elite status but also by their specialized knowledge; their institutional clout – administrative and financial; and their ability to appeal to business heads' patriotism, that is, their willingness to act in the public interest.

[35]Schmidt, *Democratizing France,* chs. 6 and 7. See also: Pierre Grémion, *Le pouvoir périphérique* (Paris: Seuil, 1976).

[36]Schmidt, *Democratizing France,* pp. 82–83. See also: Yves Mény, *Centralisation et décentralisation dans le débat politique français* (Paris: Librairie Générale de Droit et de Jurisprudence, 1974), p. 323.

[37]Hayward, *State and Market Economy,* p. 230; Michel Bauer and Elie Cohen, "Le politique, l'administratif, et l'exercice du pouvoir industriel," *Sociologie du Travail* no. 27 (March 1985), p. 139.

[38]See Chapters 11 and 12; and Michel Bauer and Bénédicte Mourot, *Les 200: Comment devient-on un grand patron?* (Paris: Seuil, 1987).

This pattern of industrial policymaking depends upon the fact that only a small number of high-powered individuals are involved from business and government. A similar pattern obtains in Japan in the economic policy arena for similar reasons. The pattern is also reproduced to a large extent in the American foreign economic policy arena where, as Krasner describes it, public officials find it easier to exercise leadership when dealing with the managers of a relatively small number of large, diversified corporations, than a large number of small ones, because they can more effectively make appeal to their own superior knowledge and to managers' national loyalties or individual desires for status and privilege.[39] It is also important to note, however, that appeals to patriotism only go so far. In the United States, business heads often tap into the pluralist system by appealing to Congress in efforts to resist the pressures of civil servants in the foreign trade arena. In Japan, despite the historic role of the state, big business nevertheless "successfully resisted attempts to subordinate profits to patriotism."[40] And in France, business heads typically seek allies in other ministries or try to sway the Prime Minister or even the President, when unhappy with a proposed policy.

In France, as in Japan and even the United States in the foreign trade area, the small number of actors involved in the process ensures that as much depends upon the individuals themselves, related to their leadership style and political power, as it does on the policies they promote or resist. Thus, in France, while strong business leaders with good political connections can often write their own tickets, as was the case with Pierre Dreyfus at the head of Renault in the sixties and seventies, strong ministers with political clout can similarly get business heads to go along with heroic government policies – witness the relatively smooth sailing of Ministers of Industry during the restructuring process such as Dreyfus (again) and Fabius by contrast with Jean-Pierre Chevènement, who simply offended.[41]

Thus, while government plays the leadership role in industrial policy formulation, there is often a good deal of mutual accommodation between government's objectives and business's needs at the implementation stage. Sometimes, that accommodation may even go so far as to modify the heroic policy, as with nationalization under the Socialists, which was early on diminished through the government's turning a blind eye to the "illegal" floating of nonvoting shares and the sale of subsidiaries. Other times, the accommodation may lead to a new policy initiative, as in the case of the policy of the *ni-ni* between 1988 and 1991, when increasing

---

[39]Krasner, *Defending the National Interest*, pp. 75–82.

[40]Barrington Moore, *Social Origins of Dictatorship and Democracy* (Boston: Beacon Press, 1966), p. 301.

[41]See Chapter 7.

numbers of special exemptions were granted allowing shares in the nationalized firms to be acquired by foreign companies, until the policy itself had to be formally redefined. It is here in particular that we can see a blurring of the lines between formulation and implementation, with the everyday politics of accommodation turning into everyday policymaking.

Perhaps the best example of mutual accommodation is the industrial planning process from the mid forties to the early sixties, which was tantamount to a "conspiracy to plan" between senior civil servants and senior managers of big business, bypassing politicians and labor. Although the relationship was cooperative, it was not corporatist: while business benefited greatly through public investments, the planners also held certain trump cards not only because they controlled the content of the plan but also because they had a variety of institutional mechanisms to ensure that business "voluntarily" followed their recommendations.[42]

The contrast with Britain under the Conservatives, who consciously sought to imitate the French model, is telling. Not only were the institutional mechanisms to "encourage" compliance missing to a large extent, but also the civil servants remained junior partners, professional planners were kept outside the governmental machine, and interest groups were mostly in charge,[43] thus beginning and ending with a "pluralistic paralysis."[44] The British cultural aversion to government intervention in business presumably got in the way of the Conservatives' intellectual recognition of the need for strong government action to foster growth.

In France too, however, as planning became softer and heroic in rhetoric alone, government led less, and accommodation began to look more and more like co-optation.[45] The Sixth Plan looked like a classic case of capture as the policy recommendations of the CNPF, the main employers' association, oriented the final product. Co-optation was apparent in sectoral planning, too, for example, in the case of steel, where a "corporatist-style collusion" developed in which the main industry trade association organized, mediated, and monitored compliance in place of the government. Co-optation to this degree, however, was not necessary for other sectors of industry also to get their way. This was as true for private firms such as Thomson and CGE, where the state took the risks while the enterprises disposed of the profits, as it was for public enterprises in sectors such as energy, where the oil companies traded on their expertise. In these cases as in many others such as nuclear energy, armaments, and aerospace, however, by contrast with steel, computers, and the Concorde (in financial

---

[42]See Chapters 3 and 9.   [43]Shonfield, *Modern Capitalism*, pp. 151–163.
[44]Jack Hayward, "National Aptitudes for Planning in Britain, France, and Italy," *Government and Opposition* vol. 9, no. 4 (1973), p. 407.
[45]See Chapter 9.

terms), although the relationship was also characterized by co-optation, it was for the most part effective in terms of policy outcomes.

Little changed in this relationship with the advent of Socialist nationalization, moreover, except during the restructuring process.[46] But even during this process, ministries exercised varying degrees of control over industries with varying effects on ministry–industry relations, while it left internal decisions up to the firm. Despite a high degree of interventionism with a declining industry such as steel, mutual accommodation was at play. By contrast, a similar degree of interventionism in the case of Saint-Gobain led to confrontation. In the case of other, healthier industries such as aerospace or electronics that were less out of line with government industrial policy, ministries were less interventionist, and tended to respond to the desires of the industry. Finally, co-optation was the key with respect to internationally competitive companies such as the pharmaceuticals giant Rhône-Poulenc, where the Ministry of Industry was essentially liberal in its policy. In this last case, however, as with all companies with "social products," whether in the competitive or noncompetitive sector, freedom in setting its own industrial and investment strategies was limited by the Ministry of Finance's imposition of price controls, and no amount of confrontation could change this. Recent reforms, however, have diminished this kind of nitpicking control for companies in the noncompetitive sector such as EDF, the electric power company, and France Télécom, although not as yet for those in the social service sector, such as the pharmaceutical companies.

In recent years, a whole variety of factors that result from government policies favoring privatization, deregulation, and Europeanization, have progressively altered the relationship between ministry and industry. First of all, privatization has diminished the number of companies subject to close ministry scrutiny. Second, deregulation has stripped governments of the policy instruments they had in the past used to gain business compliance with their policies, in particular through price and exchange controls, competition policy, and sectoral rules governing business. Third, financial deregulation has opened up new, nongovernmental sources of financing and decreased governmental control over the allocation of credit at the same time that austerity budgets have deprived governments of the money that they traditionally used to influence business. Finally, the new structure of capital ownership and control, where public and private industrial and financial concerns own and control one another, has left ministries with much less direct influence over industry. In fact, even with regard to the ministries' oversight function over the nationalized enterprises, opportunities for confrontation have diminished significantly, and

[46]See Chapter 9.

co-optation tends to be the order of the day. Only when a firm is losing money, and therefore has to go to the government for capital grants, may accommodation or even confrontation occur, as have been the cases with Bull and Air France during the Balladur government. But even here, government intervention tends to limit itself to the appointment of a new CEO.

In short, government policies through the Mitterrand years have reduced current and future governments' ability to influence business, not only because government no longer has the regulatory or financial tools to "persuade" business to do as it wishes, but also because business needs government less for guidance or support as a result of the new competitive environment and the opening up of nongovernmental sources of financing.[47] The result is a loosening of the ties that bind business to government, with government at best exerting indirect control over business: in part through its more supply-side macroeconomic policies and microeconomic incentives, and in part through its colonization of business by way of state-trained, former civil servants at the head of major French banks and industries, whether public or private, nationalized or privatized.[48]

Heroic policymaking is not dead, however. There is just a lot less of it; and what there is of it is rarely successful because of the increased independence of business and the decreased power of government. Prime Minister Cresson certainly found this out in the case of an initiative to create an electronics-to-nuclear energy superfirm as did Prime Minister Balladur with a similar merger attempt.[49]

In short, business has become more independent of government and more interdependent instead as a result of the policies, heroic and everyday, of French governments during Mitterrand's presidency. Parallel changes have taken place in local government.

Local governments have also become more independent of the central government and more interdependent as a result of the heroic decentralization reforms of the eighties. Subnational units now have their own sources of financing and their own clearly delineated powers and responsibilities. Although French local governments do not have legislative assemblies, as Italian and Spanish ones do, and thus cannot create their own laws, they nevertheless have gained a tremendous amount of autonomy by comparison with the past, when the prefect's *tutelle,* or powers of oversight, over the communes and executive powers in the departments and regions left them with little independence of action. Now, mayors have primary responsibility for such things as local land-use planning,

---

[47]See Chapter 7.   [48]See Chapters 10 and 11.   [49]See Chapter 6.

municipal services, and elementary schools; departmental council presidents exercise the prefect's former powers with regard to social services and middle schools; and regional council presidents have gained new powers and resources with regard to local economic development and high schools. Moreover, given their often overlapping functions and needs for coordination, the actions of local elected officials have become increasingly complementary with one another as well as with the French governmental administrators and European officials in a full range of their areas of activity.[50]

Throughout Mitterand's presidency, then, the statist pattern of policymaking remained dominant even as the state reduced its purview through the decentralization of government and the deregulation of the economy. Put another way, the French state has altered its form of intervention, but not the fact of intervention. And it has modernized its state–society relations without significantly altering its model of state–society relations. This would probably have been sufficient had it not been for European integration which, at the same time that it has been a major spur for such change, has also served to undermine the model itself.

EUROPEAN INTEGRATION AND THE CRISIS OF THE STATIST MODEL OF POLICYMAKING

Over the course of the eighties and into the nineties, European integration has had a growing impact on the statist model of policymaking at both the formulation and implementation stages. This impact has been recognized by all and sundry as having diminished French governments' autonomy and impinged on national sovereignty. However, most have failed to see that it also strikes at the very basis of the French conception of democracy as embodied in the statist pattern of policymaking.

The primacy of the European Union in policy formulation, which has become more and more significant as the Single European Act was followed by the Maastricht Treaty, in the first place means that French governments have lost their traditional independence of decision-making. Decisions that were formulated unilaterally in the past are now made at the EU level in consultation with member states. Moreover, societal interests that were always excluded from the policy formulation process at the national level find that they have access at the EU level. Big businesses in particular now find themselves the privileged interlocutors of the European Union Commission, and partners rather than supplicants of French ministries in the lobbying efforts of the nation. In addition, region-

---

[50]See Schmidt, *Democratizing France*.

al governments, only recently given significant powers of their own, find that they have a direct relationship with the EU unmediated by the national government. Other interests, however, such as labor and consumer groups, having been slow to organize themselves effectively at the EU level, have much less access or impact.[51]

At the implementation stage, the EU regulatory model (which bears great resemblance to the pluralist pattern at the implementation stage) has also altered the traditional relationship by decreasing the ability of the state to engage in the politics of accommodation by granting exceptions to the rules. Although this will not affect big business much, given its access to EU-level policy formulation and its increasing independence from government, it is likely to affect other societal interests that have little access to policy formulation at either the EU or national level. For once they lose their ability to influence policy at the implementation stage through accommodation or co-optation, their only recourse will be confrontation.[52] This has clearly already been true for the farmers with respect to the GATT.

The result of this is that France's statist pattern of policymaking has been undermined, and with it a model of democracy in which representative governments formulated policies independently but implemented them in consultation with the most affected interests. For now, much policy formulation is in the hands of the EU, which also suffers from a "democratic deficit," while the new regulatory form of policy implementation is barely permeable to societal interests.

In giving all of this up, however, the French thought to gain a lot more: not only greater control over its macroeconomic environment via the European Monetary System but also a larger arena for its industrial policies. Neither has panned out, at least for the moment. Although the French did manage to bring down inflation and create a healthier environment for business after 1983, the problems with the EMS beginning in 1992 suggest that this may only have been a successful remedy for times of prosperity. Similarly, moreover, the EU's industrial policy initiatives of the past, which led the French to believe that what they had given up at the national level they could dominate at the supranational level, have not continued into the nineties, as the EU has rejected a variety of French-supported projects. In short, although the European Union has the ability to institute heroic industrial policies, it is infused with the British reluctance to intervene in business.

European integration, together with the retreat of the state with regard to interventionist industrial policymaking and the decentralization of lo-

[51]See Chapter 8.   [52]Ibid.

cal government, has precipitated a crisis for the French state. The French themselves have acknowledged this crisis, as demonstrated by the proliferation of conferences on the future of the state beginning in 1991.[53] For most, the major issue is the relationship of the French state to democracy. For some, the main problem is that of the increasing powers of the executive, reinforced by the EU, next to the declining powers of Parliament and the regular civil service in the central ministries.[54] For others, the problem is in the declining power of the French state more generally, as the EU has decreased the power of the French state from above, while decentralization has represented an attack from below. But whatever the complaints, all readily admit that the French state is in trouble.

CONCLUSION

The current crisis of France's statist model of policymaking, brought about in large measure by European integration, should not take away from an appreciation of its accomplishments under Mitterand's presidency. France during this time has effectively liberalized its business–government relationship and democratized its center–periphery relations. Moreover, there are still many parts of the statist model of policymaking that remain intact, primarily in areas where businesses remain sheltered from European competition, or have not yet been affected by European integration.

The French experience may therefore serve as a lesson to all polities with a statist pattern of policymaking, and in particular to Japan, where the liberalization of its business–government relationship, despite pressures from the international community, and the democratization of its center–periphery relations, despite internal pressures, have yet to be accomplished. For France's experience suggests that in statist polities – where institutional arrangements, organizational processes, culture, and history conspire to ensure that change can only come from above – as the old formulae slowly crumble, government decision-makers must have the vision and leadership capacity to introduce new formulae. Where they do not, the paralysis can be devastating to a country, as it was in the mid to late seventies in France. And this may very well be the case for Japan today, as the government's inability to exercise much leadership in the

---

[53] See for example René Lenoir and Jacques Lesourne, *Où va l'état?* (Paris: LeMonde Editions, 1992), a conference held in 1991 presided over by Edith Cresson and sponsored by *Le Monde* and the ENA; or *Quel avenir pour l'état?* (Paris: La Documentation Française, 1993), a conference held in 1992 made up primarily of upper-level civil servants and elected officials, including former ministers (e.g., Marceau Long, vice-president of the Conseil d'État; André Chandernagor, former minister and honorary president of the Cour des Comptes; Anicet le Pors, former minister and Councilor of State; Laurent Fabius; Michel Rocard; and so forth).

[54] See the article in *Le Monde*, March 28, 1995, on the "presidentialization" of the French political system.

face of increasing economic problems related to foreign trade, unemployment, and high consumer prices, as well as the social problems related to high-level corruption and a lack of local democracy, are beginning to take their toll.

In pluralist countries such as the United States or quasi-corporatist ones such as Germany, one could argue that the dangers from a lack of government initiative are not quite as great as in statist polities, because leadership can continue to be exercised in the private sector or in combination with the public sector. However, we have already seen that in pluralist polities in moments of great crisis, as in the United States during the New Deal era, only a quasi-statist pattern manages, if not to pull the economy entirely out of its downward spiral, at least to keep the polity from falling apart: muddling through is not enough. Similarly, moreover, in times of crisis, the very element that makes the corporatist pattern so attractive, cooperation, may break down, at which point quasi-statist patterns may also come into play.

Statist action, however, is not always a panacea. In countries where the pattern is ingrained, too much state control can stifle economic development, as it did in France during the Third Republic. But too little leadership can be equally disastrous if the society cannot or does not take up the relay, as was the case with Thatcher's statist attempt to create the enterprise culture by getting government out of business and out of the business of directing business.

Statist, pluralist, and corporatist patterns of policymaking, finally, are not fixed in stone. They may change as a result of historical evolution or a major historical event, a cultural shift, a reorganization of economic or political processes, or a rearrangement of institutions. But for those countries that have exhibited patterns for a very long time, such as France and Japan with the statist pattern, the United States with the pluralist pattern, and the smaller European democracies with the corporatist pattern, the likelihood of major change is slim; although a breakdown in the pattern is always possible.[55] And this means that it is important to try to work within the pattern to attempt to overcome its limitations. For pluralist polities, this could mean finding extra-governmental structures to provide leadership – for example, using the pension funds in the stock market to ensure long-term planning for U.S. industry. For corporatist polities, this could entail having government extend the cooperation networks beyond business and labor to include other affected groups at both policy formulation and implementation stages, say, consumer groups, minorities, and the unemployed. And for statist polities, this would require

[55]For an examination of the problems of breakdown in patterns of policymaking, see: Vivien Schmidt, "The New World Order, Incorporated: The Rise of Business and the Decline of the Nation-State," *Daedalus* vol. 124, no. 2 (spring 1995).

finding ways to build in more democratic participation at the policy formulation stage – for example, with more everyday policymaking and real consultation with those groups already part of the process and new channels of communication open to those groups such as students and workers who find protest the only politics available to them. In the case of France in particular, given the new EU level of policymaking, it might also require ensuring that groups other than business have greater access to EU-level formulation. If such adjustments were to be made, the benefits and drawbacks of the various patterns would be minimized, but the overall patterns would nevertheless remain.

PART II

The changes in government policies toward business

3

Building the dirigiste *state (prior to 1981)*

Historically, the French state has always played a key role in managing the economy and in owning and/or controlling business, supported by strong, cohesive bureaucratic institutions and a culture receptive to government leadership in the economy. Indeed, the *étatisme* involved here has generated its own vocabulary: "*colbertisme*," indicating the first major state intervention by Colbert, and "*neo-colbertisme*," its modern equivalent; "*dirigisme*," first used positively to denote industrial policy in the Fourth and early Fifth Republics, now more negatively used to indicate excessive state intervention; and "*volontarisme*," the latest term in vogue among those who advocate a continued role for the state in industrial policy. From very early on, in other words, the French state has played the role of promoter of industry, in particular through state investment in private concerns, cooperative ventures, or state ownership.

For all this interventionist history, however, there has also been a countercurrent of liberalism,[1] and there have been periodic reactions against state interference in the market. Even in liberal times, though, the state continued to have a role to play. During the Third Republic in particular that role was one of protector of industry, limiting competition with the protective tariff and controlling the market by business arrangement and political action.[2] By contrast, the role of promoter came to the fore after World War II, with modernization and an opening to international markets replacing the focus on protecting the domestic market.

From the postwar period until the Mitterrand years, the state benefited from ever-expanding powers over industry, gaining policy instruments and public enterprises (either through acquisition or creation) that en-

[1]I use the term "liberalism" here in the European sense, to denote an economic focus on free market economics and laissez-faire capitalism, rather than in the American sense, to suggest a center-left political orientation.
[2]For a good summary, see: Zysman, *Political Strategies*. See also: Kemp, *Economic Forces*.

abled it to control business more and more. And yet, simultaneously, ever since the signing of the Treaty of Rome in 1957, membership in the European Community, with its "liberal" bias, has acted as a major spur for French governments to move away from a state-directed economy to one with a greater emphasis on the market. This has been a gradual but ineluctable process, one in which each action in conformity with EC policy has, taken together with other exogenous factors, so undermined the effectiveness of the traditional set of policies that it literally forced governments to adopt new EC-inspired policies which brought even greater market openness and a larger commitment to European integration. The conflict between the two competing strands of economic management policy, that is, of *dirigisme* and liberalism, came to a head in 1983, when the Socialist government, faced with a choice between abandoning major elements of its *dirigiste* policies or the European Community, decided in favor of the latter and, therefore, of liberalism.

The pressures of European integration which opened the domestic market to greater competition, however, were only one of a whole panoply of problems related to external economic constraints, such as the end to the fixed exchange rate system that had enabled French governments to correct payment deficits through devaluation, the impact of the two oil crises, and so forth, that had decreased French governments' ability to manage the economy effectively in the *dirigiste* manner they had perfected during the postwar period. These constraints undermined not only French governments' traditional macroeconomic tools for controlling the economy, e.g., the *encadrement du crédit,* or the system for rationing credit, but also their microeconomic tools, whether the national plans that no longer accurately forecast economic trends or the industrial policies that no longer adequately sorted out the most appropriate industrial investments.[3] By Giscard's presidency, the *trente glorieuses,* or thirty glorious years of economy prosperity, had ended, and with it faith in the state's economic leadership.

By the seventies, in fact, the national champions that had been the focus of de Gaulle's industrial policies had become lame ducks, more interested in catering to protected home markets than competing in the international economy. And government policymakers were no help. The special relationship between planners and big business, which had contributed to the strength of France's industrialization efforts in the Fourth Republic and the early Fifth because it excluded not only the business associations which would have constituted a drag on modernization but

[3]See Hall, *Governing the Economy;* Michael Loriaux, *France after Hegemony: International Change and Financial Reform* (Ithaca, NY: Cornell University Press, 1991).

also labor, had become a weakness. But big business and big government were at an impasse, and at a loss as to how to break it.

FROM PROTECTION TO PROMOTION IN STATE MANAGEMENT OF THE ECONOMY

The French tradition of *dirigisme* goes all the way back to Louis XIV and his minister Colbert, whose *colbertisme* was instrumental in encouraging the development of the armaments industry, glass, textiles, and so forth. During the July Monarchy (1830–1848) as well as the Second Empire (1851–1870), "*colbertisme*" described the cooperation between the "engineers" of the state and the entrepreneurs which led to the development of the railroads and the infrastructure of transport, the coal mines, and the steel industry. The Third Republic (1871–1940) continued in this tradition, although with much less vigor. Its innovation came in the area of the nationalization of public service enterprises related to communications and transportation, and included the PTT (Post, Telegraph, and Telephone Services – nationalized in 1899); the autonomous ports of Le Havre, Bordeaux, and Strasbourg (1920); the transatlantic ocean line company (1933); as well as Air France (1936) and the railroads (1937). In fact, whereas the Second Empire under Napoleon III, with its technocratic vision, promoted rapid growth, spurred on by large-scale urban renewal projects that included the rebuilding of Paris, Marseilles, and Le Havre in addition to the infrastructural investments, the Third Republic did not.

During the Third Republic, the state was more focused on maintaining the balance among social groups and protecting established interests than on promoting economic growth. Thus, it deliberately slowed down industrial growth when it threatened the groups that were at the foundation of the Third Republic, the "republican synthesis" made up of the shopkeepers and the peasants. Moreover, with the defeat of the Freycinet plan of 1882, coordinated government planning and investment such as that seen during the Second Empire were abandoned in favor of a more "liberal" view which favored the market and sought to limit the role of the state in managing the economy.[4] This liberalism, however, was not seen as at odds with the state's increasing role as protector, as it instituted protective tariffs and allowed for business arrangements that, beginning after World War I, limited competition through the formation of cartels, generally run by an industry's trade association, which often divided the market, set quotas for products, or limited members' productive capacity through

---

[4]See Kuisel, *Capitalism and the State*, ch. 1.

joint borrowing agreements.[5] Moreover, although certain aspects of the protector's role were largely abandoned after the French entry into the Common Market in the late fifties, in particular as regards the limitation of competition through trade barriers and market sharing, other aspects survived in certain sectors, including the cartels which, consecrated during the Vichy years as the instrument of industrial planning, continued into the Fifth Republic.[6]

It was really only after World War II that the economy became a central preoccupation of government, though, and that the state's role as protector was overshadowed by its role as promoter. This is when extensive national industrial planning, aided by the creation of a good-sized nationalized sector and underpinned by a new state-directed credit allocation system that ensured that "capital would be both strategic and cheap,"[7] came into its own. This *neo-colbertisme* or *dirigisme* was regarded as the only answer to the post–World War II economic crisis. Coordinated planning on a scale not seen before appeared to many the only way to bring about the massive economic modernization and industrialization required by a country that had suffered a lengthy occupation period, a war on its own territory, and shattered industries. Because of the inflationary tendencies of the economy and low business confidence resulting from business's collaborationist tendencies during the war, the government had to step in not only to guard against continued inflation but also to provide the inducements to business necessary to encourage it to invest in France and to help rebuild the economy. There were also "new men and the new French attitudes,"[8] new leaders who were less wed to the old republican synthesis of the Third Republic and in favor of the new *colbertisme* or *dirigisme*. In consequence, even if the government of the Fourth Republic was as *immobiliste* or politically at a stalemate as that of the Third Republic, its economic policies were not. The economic miracle of the Fourth Republic was created more from above than below. And it was largely the work of the state bureaucracy, which made the most of the positive international economic climate of the postwar period.

It is the state bureaucracy that, having for the most part taken the blame for helping to maintain the stalemate of the Third Republic by protecting the existing social order, can from the Fourth Republic on

[5]See: Ehrmann, *Organized Business,* pp. 368–380.
[6]There were still industrial cartel-like arrangements in the mid sixties. See: John H. McArthur and Bruce R. Scott, *Industrial Planning in France* (Cambridge, MA: Harvard Business School, 1969).
[7]Loriaux, *France after Hegemony,* p. 113. For the rationale behind the setting up of this credit allocation system, see: Kuisel, *Capitalism;* Loriaux, *France after Hegemony.*
[8]Charles P. Kindleberger, "The Postwar Resurgence of the French Economy," in *In Search of France,* ed. Stanley Hoffmann et al. (New York: Harper and Row, 1962), p. 165.

largely take the credit for changing that social order by pulling the rest of society forward in its quest for modernization, thereby ensuring, in Stanley Hoffmann's words, that "When the watchdog became a greyhound, those who had been holding the leash had to learn to run."[9] The result was that whereas the Third Republic had a "stalemated" pattern of policymaking which left the country industrially weak and unprepared to face the Nazi menace, the Fourth Republic, although also stalemated in many ways, was nonetheless in large measure responsible for launching the "economic miracle" of the *trente glorieuses* which was to end only thirty years later under the uninspired leadership of Giscard d'Estaing, who was unable to respond effectively to the worsening economic climate.

European integration was part and parcel of state planners' modernization project. Planners felt that only by being part of a larger Europe and participating in European programs such as Euratom could France move forward, despite their misgivings about the impact of European integration on French business, given the high social and wage costs that weighed heavily on production.[10] The liberalism represented by European integration, however, was balanced out by the *dirigisme* in evidence in government policies toward business, in particular with respect to the nationalizations and the national plan.

The Fourth Republic saw two kinds of nationalizations: ones involving enterprises regarded as providing basic public services that were essential for rebuilding France such as the large deposit banks, the large insurance companies (thirty in all), electric power and gas, as well as coal; and ones consisting either of confiscations of property controlled by the enemy and collaborators, as in the case of Renault, or of continuations of the nationalizations of the Vichy government as in the cases of the radio (ORTF) and of the oil companies (e.g., Petrol Aquitaine).[11] These nationalizations, together with the Monnet plan, gave the government considerable control over the economy.

The Monnet plan was essentially a "rational investment program" run by planners who, as "non-bureaucratic experts . . . coordinated and cajoled rather than commanded economic actors,"[12] and whose major pur-

---

[9]Hoffmann, *Decline or Renewal?* p. 450.

[10]At the time of the negotiations that followed the Conference of Messina in 1955, France was mainly interested in being part of Euratom, the common nuclear research program. To be part of this, it also accepted membership in the Common Market, despite misgivings. Pierre Gerbet, *La naissance du Marché Commun* (Brussels: Complexe, 1987).

[11]For a discussion of the nationalizations, see: Kuisel, *Capitalism,* pp. 202–203, 208–209; Claire Andrieu, Lucette Le Van, and Antoine Prost, eds., *Les nationalisations de la libération* (Paris: Presses de la Fondation Nationale des Sciences Politiques, 1987).

[12]Kuisel, *Capitalism,* p. 213.

pose was to encourage economic modernization and industrialization. Its success was related very much to the development of a shared commitment to the idea of planning and modernization that slowly gained ground through the thirties and the war years.[13] But it also depended upon the fact that financial resources and institutional independence were both assured when Parliament voluntarily gave away its power to the bureaucracy with a *loi-programme,* a "super budget" (as described in the Second Plan) which allowed the planners access to funds independently of the annual budget and, thereby, of the political forces of the moment.[14]

Planning was an unquestioned success between 1946 and 1963, when it had a clear set of goals, principally to end the economic chaos following the liberation, and a limited set of programs focused on restoring health to a small number of industries: steel, cement, farm tractors, fertilizers, transport services, energy, and automobiles.[15] Planning grew softer over the course of the conservative Fifth Republic, however.[16] As it became more and more a central part of governments' agendas, and as responsibility for policy formulation shifted from professional planners in the civil service to government ministers and their cabinets, planning decisions were increasingly based on political rather than economic calculations.[17]

Also conspiring to undermine planning were unforeseeable events such as the strikes of 1963, the student uprisings of May 1968, and the oil crisis of 1974. In addition, membership in the European Community, by mandating the end of tariff barriers and thereby opening France up to international competition, left the country vulnerable to economic conditions outside of the planners' control, such as downturns in neighboring European economies. As a result of the unpredictability of the international and domestic situation, planners faced increasing difficulties not only in forecasting but also in mobilizing the necessary forces, given the growing divisions in society and their own identification with the government.[18]

Finally, planning itself went from a relatively modest, technical opera-

---

[13]Ibid.   [14]Shonfield, *Modern Capitalism,* p. 130.

[15]For a brief but excellent summary of the history of planning and industrial policy, see: Henri Aujac, "An Introduction to French Industrial Policy," in *French Industrial Policy,* ed. William James Adams and Christian Stoffaës (Washington, DC: Brookings, 1986), pp. 13–35. For the lengthier, classic treatment of the early history, see: Cohen, *Modern Capitalist Planning.*

[16]Vera Lutz, *Central Planning for the Market Economy* (London: Longmans, 1969).

[17]For an excellent overview of the planning process, see: Saul Estrin and Peter Holmes, *French Planning in Theory and Practice* (London: George Allen & Unwin, 1983).

[18]Hayward, *State and Market Economy,* pp. 170, 174. See also: Estrin and Holmes, *French Planning,* p. 67–68.

tion with specific economic objectives to an elaborate operation focused on global resource planning, thereby ensuring that "as the Plans became more grandiose, they became more fragile."[19] Planning, in other words, became if anything more heroic in rhetoric – but less and less effective in reality, both as a predictor of the future and as an organizer of economic activity. And as planning declined as the favored instrument of government action, industrial policy came to the fore.

Under de Gaulle in the beginning of the Fifth Republic, national planning was combined with selective nationalizations and an industrial policy focused on creating "national champions" in an effort to improve the international competitiveness of French industry as a whole. This industrial policy sought to encourage greater industrial concentration and the formation of conglomerates in both public and private spheres in an attempt to find a solution to the inefficiencies of French industry that were becoming more and more apparent as France became increasingly subject to international competition. Thus, the nationalized sector was enlarged through the creation of public enterprises in growing sectors of the economy such as in the aerospace and computer industries, and rationalized through the reorganization into a single enterprise of a variety of long-nationalized companies, as in the case of Elf-Aquitaine. This process also involved restructuring through vertical integration – for example, in the acquisition of the Meridien Hotels by Air France and in the overseas operations of the oil companies and of Renault – and horizontal diversification – for example, in the case of Elf-Aquitaine, which went from oil-refining to petrochemicals to polymers to pharmaceuticals and even into perfumes (i.e., Roger et Gallet).[20] Moreover, at the same time that public enterprises were becoming larger and larger conglomerates, the government, as part of its industrial plan, was also encouraging private enterprises to enlarge horizontally and vertically with a variety of loans and subsidies in such areas as regional development, research, special aid to targeted sectors of the economy, restructurings, worker training and unemployment compensation, foreign commerce guarantees, and so forth.[21]

The government was also involved in a variety of multibillion franc infrastructural projects, the *"grands projets,"* that marshalled vast resources for sometimes ill-fated ventures. These included the Concorde, the France (ship company), the Roissy Airport, Fos, the New Towns, the Rhine-Rhône Canal, la Villette, and so on. And although the high costs

[19]Hall, *Governing the Economy,* p. 147.

[20]Marceau Long, "La diversification des entreprises publiques françaises," *Revue Française d'Administration Publique,* no. 15 (July–September 1980), pp. 504, 507.

[21]Bertrand Bellon, *Le pouvoir financier et l'industrie en France* (Paris: Seuil, 1980), pp. 156–157.

and the often low returns left many complaining about the creation of "white elephants," they were nevertheless an integral part of the heroic set of industrial policies that essentially saw the big as beautiful.[22]

In addition to being the objects of the national champion policy and participants in the *grand projets,* the nationalized enterprises played a special pilot role for the rest of industry as the vanguard of business. Because the private sector, made up of small and medium-sized family firms, was historically timid and lacking in entrepreneurialism, public sector enterprise took on an ever-increasing importance as innovator and engine for the economy. Renault, for example, set the standard for vacations, first a three-week vacation which the rest of industry soon followed, then a fourth week, this time over government objections; and it pioneered ongoing job training in 1970. At this same time, public service enterprises such as EDF, GDF, the SNCF, and the coal-mining industry introduced progressive contracts raising wages in line with the rate of inflation which were subsequently adopted by the rest of the public services and then by a number of private industries.[23] At a time when in the United States the saying was "What is good for General Motors is good for America," in France, in the words of one minister, it was "When Renault sneezes, all of France gets the shivers."[24]

Although the larger enterprises and large-scale projects were the main focus of state intervention, the smaller businesses were not entirely forgotten. De Gaulle along with subsequent governments sought to promote industrial concentration and encourage the creation of large conglomerates with virtual monopolistic or oligopolistic power without, however, jeopardizing the small and medium-sized enterprises (the SMEs). Thus, they continued to allow for cartels such as that of the electric cable manufacturers (encompassing CGE and PUK) begun in 1931 or permanent agreements between large companies and their smaller suppliers such as those negotiated by public enterprises with client firms selling cigarette paper (clients of Seita) or films (clients of ORTF). The *loi Royer* of 1973, which favored small shopkeepers by limiting the proliferation of supermarkets, was another example of the government seeking to protect small enterprises against the encroachments of larger ones.

In the seventies, in fact, the increasing reliance of the government on

[22]See the discussion in Stephen S. Cohen, "Informed Bewilderment: French Economic Strategy and the Crisis," in *France in the Troubled World Economy,* ed. Stephen S. Cohen and Peter A. Gourevitch (London: Butterworths, 1982), pp. 23–24.

[23]See: Daniel Derivry, "The Managers of Public Enterprises in France," in *The Mandarins of Western Europe,* ed. Mattei Dogan (New York: John Wiley, 1975), p. 212.

[24]Maurice Bokanowski during the debate on the 1963 budget in the National Assembly, *Journal Officiel, Débats* (January 10, 1963), p. 422 – cited in Derivry, "Managers of Public Enterprises," p. 212.

votes of shopkeepers, farmers, pensioners, and other declining social groups led it to limit planning in areas that might alienate this electorate, and to make small, medium-sized, and artisanal enterprises one of its priority programs in the Seventh Plan (not that allocating 816 million francs was nearly enough to right the weaknesses of the SMEs).[25] At the same time that the government saw its main role as promoter of industry, in other words, it continued with its traditional role as protector in certain sectors. The way in which the government conceived of the promotion of industry did change over time, however.

While national planning and selective nationalization remained central to de Gaulle's *dirigiste* economic policy, it did not continue as such under his successors. However soft planning had become under de Gaulle, the change was nothing compared to the seventies. With regard to the Sixth Plan of 1970 to 1975, Yves Ullmo recounts that "the state did not hesitate to intervene in sectors that were not mentioned in the Sixth Plan and in more traditional sectors, such as steel, aeronautics, and shipbuilding. In effect, the state persisted in a strategy of selective, *coup par coup* [day-to-day] intervention, even though this was less prominent than it had been earlier."[26] Moreover, plans were increasingly vague, in particular at the sectoral level, so much so that by the Seventh Plan in the case of steel, commentators could note that "Never was a report by the Steel Commission so succinct, vague and useless."[27]

Although a certain amount of *dirigisme* remained under Pompidou and Giscard d'Estaing, particular economic plans tended increasingly to be put aside whenever deemed expedient while nationalization was no longer considered much of an option. Even so, the economy was nevertheless becoming increasingly intermixed as nationalized firms became more and more heavily involved with private industry, either as partial owners or partners of joint ventures. Thus, the Caisse des Dépôts et Consignations held between 4 and 6% of the capital of most of the major corporations while IDI, the Institut de Développement Industriel, which initially was to take over companies in difficulty and then return them to the private sector once profitable, extended its role to that of financing private sector enterprises, for example, the 1977 acquisition of 18% of the capital of Nobel Bozel together with CCF (which acquired 37% of the capital). Moreover, public and private enterprises set up joint subsidiaries – for

[25]Hall, *Governing the Economy*, p. 177.
[26]Yves Ullmo, *La planification française* (Paris: Dunod, 1974), p. 350; René Mouriaux, "Trade Unions, Unemployment, and Regulation: 1962–1986," in *Searching for the New France*, ed. James F. Hollifield and George Ross (New York: Routledge, 1991), p. 181.
[27]Michel Freyssenet, *La sidérurgie française, 1945–79: L'histoire d'une faillite, Les solutions qui s'affrontent* (Paris: Salvelli, 1979), p. 181 – cited in Hayward, *State and the Market*, p. 89.

example, CEA with both PUK and Rothschild; Paribas with EMC, Elf-Aquitaine, and CDF; Elf with CFP, PUK, Rhône-Poulenc-Pricel, Suez, CGE, Lafarge, Wendel, Empain, Rothschild; EDF-GDF with Thomson, SGPM, Empain; CDF with Air Liquide; and EMC with Rhône-Poulenc-Pricel, PUK, SGPM, and Agache-Willot.[28] Most saw this intermixing as a kind of creeping nationalization, the result of day-to-day decisions rather than part of some overarching plan, although the Communist Party complained that the nationalized companies were being "privatized," as in the case of Elf.[29] The intermixing itself was very much in keeping with Giscard d'Estaing's overall approach to economic policymaking, since Giscard himself preferred to "manage the unforeseeable" rather than to plan.[30]

Throughout the seventies, in fact, planning had lost much of its importance due to the increasingly slow rate of economic growth and the decreasing resources available to allocate. Industrial policy, by contrast, came to be preferred.

Giscard d'Estaing's industrial policy, the *politique de créneaux*, provided loans and subsidies to industries with the potential for becoming leaders in particular sectors or "niches" of the international economy – for example, subway technology, offshore drilling equipment, electrical generators, telecommunications, aircraft, and arms. As it turns out, while this policy allowed French industry to gain in international competitiveness, it also caused it to lose a significant share of its domestic market (from the mid 1970s to 1981, foreign penetration in basic manufactured goods rose from 25% to close to 40%) and to waste a lot of money on products that couldn't sell and on firms that couldn't compete on the international market.

Moreover, Giscard's unofficial policy of rescuing companies on the verge of bankruptcy did little for the competitiveness of industry, since it substituted a policy of support for "lame ducks" for de Gaulle's "national champions."[31] Although the government claimed that its purpose was not "to save endangered species but to provide funds for their mutation,"[32] it was in fact more concerned with stemming the rising tide of unemployment than in reorganizing the firms themselves. Because its unwritten criteria for rescue had as much if not more to do with maintaining employment in distressed areas than ensuring that only competi-

[28]Bellon, *Pouvoir financier,* pp. 158–159.
[29]*Le Monde,* June 18, 1972 – cited in Harvey Feigenbaum, *The Politics of Public Enterprise: Oil and the French State* (Princeton: Princeton University Press, 1985), p. 30.
[30]Hayward, *State and the Market,* p. 170.
[31]Berger, "Lame Ducks and National Champions," p. 160.
[32]*Fortune,* April 9, 1978 – cited in Hall, *Governing the Economy,* p. 190.

tive firms with good chances of survival were helped, the entire process became highly political as conservative governments, seeing the rising fortunes of the left in the periphery, worried increasingly more about the effects of industrial failure on the voting booths than on the economy's competitiveness. The result is that declining firms tended to get the lion's share of government support. And although by 1979 Giscard also began seeking to designate and foster growth industries, it was too little too late.[33]

Deindustrialization and an end to Pompidou's *impératif industriel,* in short, really started with Giscard, who sought to discourage investment because he thought inflation resulted from it; and this was only helped along by Chirac who, as Prime Minister under Giscard, created the *taxe professionelle,* which put the tax burden on large industry.[34] Moreover, the traditional remedies for economic slowdowns no longer worked, despite the fact that in 1975 alone, public support for business (including public purchasing and direct aid) came to 126 billion francs, or 9% of the GDP of France.[35] Chirac's injection of 30 billion francs into the economy along with loans and subsidies to stimulate investment in areas hardest hit by the economic crisis failed, with inflation and unemployment worsening along with trade and the balance of payments deficits.

Finally, the somewhat neoliberal policies of Prime Minister Raymond Barre toward the end of Giscard's term, which involved introducing a mild economic austerity program combined with market liberalism, higher corporate profits, deregulation, and an emphasis on the entrepreneurial spirit, did little to revive the economy. Barre, recognizing that the traditional approach no longer worked in an increasingly internationalized economy, adopted many policies that were more liberal. With the Barre Plan of 1977, he tried unsuccessfully to impose some monetary rigor in an effort to replace the inflationary strategy of the past with one that emphasized the need for a strong currency and monetary stability as

[33] W. Rand Smith, "We Can Make the Ariane but We Can't Make Washing Machines: The State and Industrial Performance in Postwar France," in *Contemporary France: A Review of Interdisciplinary Studies,* ed. Jolyon Howorth and George Ross (London and New York: Pinter, 1989), p. 190.

[34] Philippe Alexandre and Roger Priouret, *Marianne et le pot de lait* (Paris: Grasset, 1983).

[35] Of this amount, 4.1 billion francs in subsidies and 334 million francs in loans were for targeted sectors, 149 million in subsidies and 8.6 billion francs in loans for restructuring. Most of the sectoral aid went to companies in the older sectors of industry, such as automobiles (1 billion francs for Peugeot); Denain Nord-Est Longwy and Wendel (0.6 billion), steel (1.3 billion), the mechanical industries and maritime transport (1.2 billion), and the chemical industry (1.3 billion). The restructuring aid went to naval construction (1.1 billion), to aeronautics (2 billion to Dassault, Snias, and SNECMA), and, for the smallest amount of all, to the computer industry (0.7 billion to CII and CGE). Bellon, *Pouvoir Financier,* pp. 156–158.

a basis for economic growth.[36] With the decision to join the European Monetary System in 1979, he sought to reduce inflation by pegging the franc to the Deutschmark. In addition, he removed price controls in some spheres for the first time in one hundred years; provided tax incentives to stimulate the purchase of shares (to encourage the growth of the financial markets and diminish dependence upon banks as a source of funds); and instituted development contracts that more directly tied state subsidies to market performance.[37] Moreover, an effort on the supply side was made to encourage the national champions to engage in "industrial redeployment," meaning that they were to rationalize production, streamline operations, and move into higher value-added export niches, primarily by reducing state aid, introducing competition into public procurement, and vitiating cheap labor strategies through a strong franc.[38] These liberal policies were not enough, however, to stem the rising unemployment or to stimulate the economy. But neither were the *dirigiste* policies in other areas.

The Barre government, after all, did not abandon traditional *dirigisme* completely. In addition to greater reliance on the market, industry was still receiving large subsidies.[39] In 1978, direct aid alone came to 20 billion francs or 2.7 % of the GDP.[40] Moreover, government procurement continued apace. In 1979, public purchases of goods and services through national and local governments along with public enterprises came to 7% of the GNP.[41]

The economy, reeling from the second oil crisis of 1979, probably needed stronger medicine than that prescribed by Barre, both in the direction of more *dirigisme* and greater austerity. But neither of these was possible so close to the next set of national elections in a climate in which the Socialists had reclaimed *dirigisme* for themselves.

[36]John Goodman, *Monetary Sovereignty: The Politics of Central Banking in Western Europe* (Ithaca, NY: Cornell University Press, 1992), p. 119.
[37]Peter A. Hall, "The State and the Market," in *Developments in French Politics*, ed. Peter A. Hall, Jack Hayward, and Howard Machin (New York: St. Martin's Press, 1990), p. 176.
[38]Jonah Levy, "Tocqueville's Revenge: The Decline of *Dirigisme* and Evolution of France's Political Economy," Ph.D. dissertation in political science, Massachusetts Institute of Technology (1993), p. 51; Christian Stoffaës, *La grande menace industrielle* (Paris: Calmann-Lévy, 1978).
[39]See the discussion in Chapter 9.
[40]In 1978, the 20 billion francs in direct aid encompassed these appropriations: sectoral aid, with 3 billion francs going to steel, 3 billion francs to aeronautics, 1 billion francs to computers, 1 billion francs to telecommunications, and 1.5 billion francs to shipbuilding; aid to industry in depressed regions, at 3 billion francs; aid for research and development, at 1 billion francs; and export subsidies, at 6 billion francs. Hall, *Governing the Economy*, pp. 190–191.
[41]Aujac, "Introduction," p. 25.

Building the dirigiste state (prior to 1981)

Barre's liberal macroeconomic policy, together with Giscard's industrial policy, led some to insist that economic liberalism had substituted itself for "statism," meaning *dirigisme,* in France after 1974. Giscard's industrial policymaking, however, was no less *dirigiste* than before: What appeared to be a rise of liberalism and a decline of *dirigisme* was more simply a reversal of policy up until 1978, where government action switched from one focused on promoting growing sectors and leaving declining sectors to the market to one which concentrated on rescuing the declining sectors and leaving rising sectors to the market.[42] Subsequently, however, Giscard corrected for this, thus making it clear that the difference from the past was not an end to interventionism, just a somewhat more selective interventionism.[43] In fact, although the state was beginning to dismantle its *dirigiste* controls in macroeconomic matters at this time, thereby promoting the deregulation of the economy, it was doing no such thing in the microeconomic sphere. And this continued between 1981 and 1986 under the Socialists, who deregulated the economy even as they nationalized and restructured industry.[44]

Moreover, even the dismantling of *dirigiste* controls in macroeconomic matters was not in itself a total surrender to market liberalism. Much the contrary, since it represented an attempt to take back control of an economy that could no longer be regulated as it had been in the past.[45] The "overdraft economy" of the postwar period, with its lax monetary policies linked to the state-administered credit-rationing system, had enabled companies to prosper despite a high level of indebtedness by allowing high rates of inflation that governments would periodically counter through aggressive devaluations against the dollar, which in turn would give French firms a temporary competitive advantage. However, this was possible only so long as the Bretton Woods system of fixed exchange rates was functioning. Its collapse in the early seventies made it impossible for France to continue to use its inflationary growth strategy as it had in the past, or to use periodic aggressive devaluation to adjust for inflation. By the late seventies, the government became convinced that nothing short of giving up some of France's independence in monetary policy by joining the European Monetary System would enable it to regain some control in the macroeconomic sphere. This also meant, however, limiting France's ability to devalue, since devaluation required approval by France's partners, and such approval was for relatively small currency adjustments that

[42]Berger, "Lame Ducks and National Champions," pp. 160–162.

[43]D. Green, "Strategic Management and the State: France," in *Industrial Crisis: A Comparative Study of the State and Industry* (Oxford: Martin Robertson, 1983), p. 167; and Smith, "We Can Make the Ariane," p. 190.

[44]Hall, "State and Market."

[45]See Loriaux, *France after Hegemony.*

did not cover the gap between French and German inflation rates. This in turn demanded anti-inflationary policies that included restrictive monetary policies and cutting budgets. In short, the government adopted neo-liberal economic policies less as a result of an all-out conversion to neo-liberal economic doctrine than out of a continued *dirigiste* spirit, in order not to lose all control in the macroeconomic sphere. The conversion was to come later for the conservatives, after their defeat at the polls in 1981 and as a reaction against the Socialists' initial expansionary policies.

FROM NATIONAL CHAMPIONS TO LAME DUCKS

By the late seventies, then, the kind of strong leadership of the economy that had characterized French government since the late forties seemed to have run its course. The *dirigiste* policies that had proven so successful in promoting rapid industrialization and modernization through the post-war period no longer seemed to work. Not only were the macroeconomic policies unable to function as they had, but the microeconomic policies that had encouraged the creation of national champions were no longer producing the same results. The merger of firms had not necessarily led to their greater productivity or growth because they often remained unwieldy, and still required a rationalization of their structures.[46]

The microeconomic policies themselves, moreover, were increasingly outdated. The focus of government decision-makers on big business to the detriment of the small, not only in terms of involvement in the planning process but also for access to subsidies and loans, was ultimately to have a negative effect on France's competitiveness. The national champions that had been the answer to the needs of the new consumer society, providing them with mass-produced goods at low prices, were becoming less and less competitive, while the small and medium-sized enterprises were less and less able to supply the national champions' needs. Policy-makers were at a loss to alter this trend, in part because of the politics of the moment, in part because of the very nature of industrial policymaking which privileged the relationship between ministry and large-scale industry. Absent input from any other groups, whether small-business associations or labor, state policymakers received none of the signals that might have alerted them to the fact that their strategies were increasingly outdated, and they felt none of the pressures that might have pushed them to pursue other ways of meeting the crisis.

A major problem for the planners was that the model of modernization that had served them so well in the past, the "Fordist" model based on mass production of low-cost, standard commodities by unskilled workers

[46]H. Aujac, director of the BIPE (Bureau d'Information et Prévision Économique) – cited by Zysman, *Political Strategies*, p. 8.

and dedicated equipment, was no longer well adapted to a situation in which competitive advantage was shifting to manufacturers able to produce specialized, high-quality goods (e.g., specialty steels), often in small, customized batches (e.g., machine tools); able to undertake continuous innovation (through computers); and able to target high value-added market niches.[47] Moreover, the macro- and microeconomic mechanisms that were on the demand side of this Fordist model – the social security system that stabilized the economy, the inflationary growth policies, and the system of wage indexation after 1968 that ensured that aggregate demand grew in tandem with productivity – had ceased to function appropriately. Increasing international competition, saturated markets, and discriminating consumers who more and more turned to foreign goods had thrown the Fordist system into crisis.[48]

In the face of this crisis, the planners stepped up their traditional approaches rather than change strategies. Thus, they continued to encourage mergers, assuming that the inefficiencies resulting from competition among many weak, small producers would be resolved through the creation of large producers. This, however, resulted only in the creation of larger and, if anything, more inefficient producers; and a government captive to these large "lame ducks," which were even more impervious to change than the smaller entities from which they had been created. A case in point is the machine tool industry where, instead of promoting the ability of the existing SMEs to produce customized, high-profit output with new computer-control technologies and workers whose skills were consistently upgraded through technological innovation, French policymakers pushed for their merger into large companies that went in for long runs of low-cost, standardized products with little innovation except for a few highly risky technological experiments, and with the deskilling or replacement of workers.[49]

---

[47]"Fordism" takes its name from the mass production system invented by Henry Ford. For a thorough account, see the explanations by the French "regulation school," in particular Robert Boyer, *The Regulation School: A Critical Introduction* (New York: Columbia University Press, 1990); Robert Boyer, "The Current Economic Crisis: Its Dynamics and Its Implications for France," in *The Mitterand Experiment: Continuity and Change in Modern France,* ed. George Ross et al. (Oxford: Polity Press, 1987); Alain Lipietz, "Governing the Economy in the Face of International Challenge: From National Developmentalism to National Crisis," in *Searching for the New France,* ed. James Hollifield and George Ross (New York: Routledge, 1991). For an excellent short summary of Fordism as applied to France, see Levy, "Tocqueville's Revenge," pp. 31–39.
[48]Levy, "Tocqueville's Revenge," pp. 34–35.
[49]Ibid., p. 49; and Jonathan Nicholas Ziegler, "Reshaping the Industrial Plant," in "The State and Technological Advance: Political Efforts for Industrial Change in France and the Federal Republic of Germany, 1972–1986," Ph.D. dissertation, Government Department, Harvard University, 1989.

Changes in government policies toward business

The French failure, here as elsewhere (e.g., textiles), stems not simply from bad strategy but the whole statist pattern of policymaking in the political economic sphere that excluded labor and made it impervious to change. Germany, by comparison, did extremely well because of its corporatist pattern of policymaking. The presence of the unions as partners in policymaking pushed companies to reskill rather than to deskill workers, and thereby to promote technological innovation, which in turn facilitated niche in place of mass production. Moreover, the participation of industry associations ensured that the smaller firms would not be forgotten, while the close interaction among academics, professionals, and unions ensured that the technology was well adapted to the needs of industry, and not "some planner's vision of the ideal 'factory of the future.'"[50]

While other countries such as Germany and Italy were responding in their own ways to the need for more skilled workers, flexible firms, and well-organized production networks of small and medium-sized enterprises, France, much like the United States, was following the old strategy focused on large firms, unskilled workers, and so forth, with industrial policies that increasingly favored rescuing declining industries rather than promoting growing ones.[51] The difference between the United States and France is that whereas major responsibility for the delayed adjustment in the United States can be laid at the feet of business alone, in France it had as much if not more to do with state policymakers who, given the choice, as Alain Lipietz saw it, between "audacity or getting bogged down" (*l'audace ou l'enlisement*), chose the latter.[52]

But why did they get bogged down? After all, it was not as if the above analysis of the problems and needs of modernizing industry was totally unknown. By the mid seventies, French policymakers themselves had commented on the need to switch gears, and to focus more on the SMEs and toward higher value-added output.[53] Public pronouncements in favor of a new approach, however, belied actions that favored the status quo and that delayed adjustment rather than promoted it. Aid continued to flow to the national champions, with only negligible amounts going to the SMEs. The politics that favored protection over promotion in the seventies, together with the ongoing ministry—industry relations that ensured increasing co-optation of ministries by industry, meant that, how-

[50]Levy, "Tocqueville's Revenge," pp. 49–50; and Ziegler, "Reshaping the Industrial Plant."

[51]See Michael Piore and Charles Sabel, *The Second Industrial Divide: Possibilities for Prosperity* (New York: Basic Books, 1984).

[52]Alain Lipietz, *L'audace ou l'enlisement: Sur les politiques économiques de la gauche* (Paris: La Découverte, 1984).

[53]See: Stoffaës, *Grande menace industrielle.*

ever good the intentions, state policymakers could not alter the patterns that they had themselves established.[54]

Moreover, the national champions themselves had become increasingly fat and lazy. They tended to be more interested in gaining large state contracts than in competing in the open market and in relying on public research and development or on licensing technologies from abroad than in investing their own monies. Rather than focus on exports, the strategy of their German competitors, they relied on the large, protected home market. In 1979, almost 60% of the 167 billion francs in public procurement went to Electricité de France (42 billion francs), the Ministry of Defense (36 billion francs), and the post and telephone system (20 billion francs).[55] But even where they did export, they did it in areas where government-to-government relations were a key factor, e.g., in weapons, trains, subways, nuclear plants, and so forth.[56]

Even the nationalized enterprises, touted as the leaders of industry through much of the early postwar period, were subject to increasing criticism. Commentators had time and again issued economic critiques focused on nationalized enterprises' technological adventurism, bad management, and structural defects, with their ensuing higher costs; and political critiques that saw the increasing politicization of top management along with that of the personnel as a threat to a liberal economy and society.[57]

On the economics of nationalized enterprises in particular, typical were views that condemned public enterprise's emphasis on technological prowess over sound finances, such as Antoine Pinay's criticism of the SNCF's "cult of the minute and disdain for the milliard,"[58] or the complaint of former president of the Comité Central des Houillères de France, Henri de Peyerimhoff, about public enterprises' general preference for "the spectacular and the expensive" over "the efficient and profitable."[59] Even more predominant, however, were the criticisms of public enterprise management that focused on the fact of state ownership, which made for complex rules that made it impossible for public managers to manage efficiently or to plan for the future, and which shielded them from the

---

[54]See Chapter 9.   [55]Aujac, "Introduction," p. 25.

[56]Levy, "Tocqueville's Revenge," pp. 50–51; Cohen, "Informed Bewilderment."

[57]Patrick Fridenson, "Atouts et limites de la modernisation par en haut: Les entreprises publiques face à leurs critiques (1944–1986)," in *Le capitalisme français 19e–20e siècle: Blocages et dynamismes d'une croissance,* ed. Patrick Fridenson and André Straus (Paris: Fayard, 1989), pp. 175–94.

[58]Association des amis de Louis Armand, *Louis Armand* (Paris: Charles Lavauzelle, 1986), p. 59 – cited in Fridenson, "Atouts et limites," p. 176.

[59]Henri de Peyerimhoff, *Souvenirs* (Montpellier: Carbonnerie-Copie, 1977), pp. 412, 415 – cited in Fridenson, "Atouts et limites," p. 176.

discipline of the market and encouraged them to increase the number of their employees, the size of their staffs, or even the size of the firm itself without reason and to the detriment of the state budget, which had to cover their deficits.[60] The performance problems, as the Nora report summarized them, resulted from the ambiguity of state objectives, the proliferation of its controls, and the suffocating nature of its supervision.[61]

Some of these criticisms were attenuated by the late fifties and early sixties, when nationalized enterprises took a more "commercial turn" and had also become leaders in the push toward modernization, in particular in terms of the management of production, distribution, and personnel.[62] By the mid to late sixties, though, some began questioning whether, however justifiable certain nationalizations might have been or continue to be, it was necessary to continue with all of them. After all, as the Nora report suggested, "it is useless for the State to stay so heavily engaged in certain sectors only because they needed its help decades ago. Although it would be harmful for the state not to give its support to those that need it today, it ought to put an end to it when this need ends."[63] For many firms, moreover, the very public intervention that brought the push toward concentration and competitiveness led them to demand full liberty of action and, therefore, an end to public intervention.[64] What they got, however, was not privatization, but increased autonomy. And this did little for their competitiveness.

The performance of the nationalized industries during the postwar period was mixed, and was related primarily to their positions in the national and international markets. Public service enterprises sheltered from international competition such as the railroads, the subways, electric energy, deposit banks, and insurance companies, where the State set the prices of their products and services, had difficulties related to their use of maximal growth in place of business strategy, and the lack of reality with regard to pricing. The problems for public service enterprises subject to international competition but sheltered from it nevertheless by national regulation and protectionism, such as air transport, atomic energy, oil, and aeronautics, came from products that did not meet international standards (e.g., television with 819 lines); products that could not make a profit, often the result of government interference, whether positive (e.g., government encouragement for the Concorde) or negative (e.g., government refusal to allow Air France to replace the Caravelle); and overinvest-

[60]Fridenson, "Atouts et limites," p. 176–177.
[61]Simon Nora Groupe de Travail du Comité Interministériel des Entreprises Publiques, *Rapport sur les entreprises publiques* (Paris: Documentation Française, 1967).
[62]Fridenson, "Atouts et limites," p. 184.   [63]Nora, *Rapport*, p. 32.
[64]Bellon, *Pouvoir financier*, p. 155.

ment (e.g., Elf's investment in oil refining because of access to easy financing). Finally, there were the few public enterprises open to international competition that had no other French competition, such as EMC, Charbonnages de France, SEITA (tobacco), Compagnie Générale des Messageries Maritimes, and CII (computers). All of these sought government protection, had high salary costs, and were doing middling to poorly. There were also those with other French competitors, such as Renault, which had been a model of top performance and autonomous management, and two chemical companies, one of which, CDF-Chimie, was a model of what not to do given the lack of coherent strategy, homogeneous structures, and escalating state intervention prior to 1981.[65]

In addition, state intervention with regard to public enterprise had been generally condemned as at best ineffective if not downright disastrous. The cases of CDF-Chimie and CII (Bull) are the most notable,[66] but there was also the Concorde, which was a technological success but a financial fiasco. In terms of public financing as well, the state was not a very generous shareholder, with the exceptions of Renault, which since 1963 had benefited from multiyear capital grants; of the planning contracts with EDF (1970) and ORTF (1971); and of the enterprise contracts with Charbonnages de France (1978), Air France (1978), SNCF (1979), and the Compagnie Générale Maritime (1979).[67]

All this might not have been so serious had French business not also experienced problems as a result of the drive toward European integration. These began primarily in the late sixties with the final removal of all protectionist barriers, which opened French business up to a competition for which it was basically unprepared. No longer able to rely on its traditional protectionism, France experienced first an increase in commercial exchanges and then, starting after 1970 but accelerating after 1976, direct foreign investment, in particular by American multinationals. Thus, while French businesses were still investing in the Third World, they found their own home markets invaded. Moreover, with the end to all tariff barriers, French companies discovered that they could no longer depend upon producing more; they had to produce more competitively, with better-quality goods at lower prices in order to meet the challenge of

[65]Fridenson, "Atouts et limites," pp. 180–182; Michel Sauzay, "Le rôle moteur du secteur public," in *Une politique industrielle pour la France,* ed. Ministère de la Recherche et de l'Industrie (Paris: Documentation Française, 1983); Taïeb Hafsi, *Entreprise publique et politique industrielle* (Paris: McGraw-Hill, 1984).

[66]See Elie Cohen and Michel Bauer, *Les grandes manoeuvres industrielles* (Paris: P. Belford, 1985) for the details.

[67]Jean-Pierre Anastossopoulos, *La stratégie des entreprises publiques* (Paris: Dalloz, 1980), pp. 113–114, 127–130, 135–136, 162–178; and Fridenson, "Atouts et limites," p. 183.

foreign manufacturers not only in foreign markets but also in the domestic market.[68]

French business, however, was doing little to meet that challenge. While the costs of salaried workers were going up, investment was going down: between 1974 and 1983, the rate of investment fell from 14% of the GDP to 12%. Although some of this can be blamed on external economic constraints such as the oil shocks of 1974 and 1979 and on internal political weaknesses such as the failure of governments to respond forcefully enough with adequate macroeconomic policies, the fault also rests with business.

French businesses in the seventies suffered from three handicaps by comparison with their European competitors: heavier debt loads, insufficient investment and research, and defensive reactions to the economic crisis. French business's level of indebtedness – resulting from past losses, long payment delays, high interest rates, and a preference for paying dividends rather than servicing their debt – was double that of the Germans (4% of added value by contrast with 2%).[69] Investment also suffered from the high debt load and from business's focus on dividends, while investment in research and development in particular experienced negative growth of −4% per year from 1968 to 1974 and zero growth from 1974 to 1981.[70] In addition, instead of reorienting their efforts toward growth sectors of industry, French governments increasingly focused their efforts on propping up the declining sectors.

Heavy industry was probably in the worst shape, primarily because key sectors such as steel, convinced that the problem was conjunctural rather than structural, had not taken the necessary steps to restructure or streamline operations.[71] Gone were the sixties, when steel had been hailed as an example of national success. By the seventies, the steel industry was in deep trouble. The steel industry's "haughty refusal to integrate vertically 'downstream'" with the lower status but more profitable, high-value manufactured products, rationalized by an out-of-date strategy based on an integrated crude steel complex instead of one which would have created a diversified industrial group (as the Germans were doing), explains a major part of its problems. And this was only made worse by

---

[68]See Hall, "The State and the Market." On foreign trade policy, see Helen V. Milner, *Resisting Protectionism: Global Industries and the Politics of International Trade* (Princeton: Princeton University Press, 1988).

[69]Dominique Bocquet and Philippe Delleur, *Génération Europe* (Paris: Editions François Bourin, 1989).

[70]Jean-Louis Levet, "Réindustrialiser la France," *Politique Industrielle* no. 19 (spring 1990), pp. 24–25.

[71]Hayward, *State and Market Economy*, pp. 92–93.

the slowing down of investments resulting from declining profits and a reliance on self-financing.[72] Instead of facing these problems head on, the steel industry consistently demanded, and received, subsidies from government to the tune of 100 billion francs in exchange for maintaining employment and not closing outdated plants.

Business, in short, was to be faulted for having failed to respond appropriately to the changes in the domestic economy resulting from European integration and the increasing internationalization of business more generally. Business was not the only one, however, to have failed to see the challenge posed by European integration and internationalization. French scholars were also relatively late at recognizing the potential effects of this on the French economy.[73] The French government was even later. Giscard d'Estaing's *politique de créneaux* was clearly unable to right the situation for business generally, even though it had been successful in creating industry leaders in certain sectors. In the meantime, it was becoming apparent to businesspeople and economists alike that another kind of strategy, a *politique de filières* focused on increasing the size of firms while integrating them vertically along lines of production, was the only way to ensure competitiveness.[74] But this demanded a kind of heroic policymaking that the conservative government would not, and could not, engage in, especially since it was the left that had claimed it as its own.

CONCLUSION

By the beginning of the eighties, the conservatives were at a loss as to what to do to solve "*la crise,*" the seemingly intractable economic crisis that had generated ever-growing levels of unemployment and ever-slowing rates of industrial growth. For the Socialists, the answer was relatively simple: to return to the *dirigisme* of the earlier, most heroic part of the postwar period and, through nationalization, to accomplish one of that period's last imperatives.

[72]Ibid.
[73]Only in the mid seventies did one see an explosion of literature on this. See, for example: Charles-Albert Michalet, *Le capitalisme mondial* (Paris: Presses Universitaires de France, 1976); Christian Palloix, *L'économie mondiale capitaliste et les firmes multinationales* (Paris: Maspero, 1975); Olivier Pastré, *La stratégie internationale des groupes financiers américains* (Paris: Economica, 1979).
[74]See the discussion in Bellon, *Pouvoir financier*, pp. 182–190.

4

From dirigisme *to disengagement*
(1981 to 1986)

When, in the March 1986 electoral campaign, the neoliberal conservatives accused the Socialists of increasing state *dirigisme,* or interventionism, they were not wrong with regard to the intentions of the Socialists. Taken together, the Socialists' reflationary macroeconomic policies, widescale nationalization program, and highly interventionist industrial policy containing a mandate to refinance and restructure the nationalized industries at least potentially gave the new government a *dirigiste* kind of control over the economy. Confronted in 1981 with the decreased competitiveness of French industry, the general slowdown in economic growth, the relatively high unemployment rate, as well as the aftereffects of the two oil crises and the general worldwide economic climate, the Socialist government of Mauroy felt that the economy was in need of heroic measures and a revival of the traditional state *dirigisme* that had proven so successful in the past.[1] Therefore, in direct opposition to Barre's neoliberalism and mild austerity program, and instead of instituting austerity measures as were most foreign governments in the face of recessionary pressures, the government engaged in a high degree of market interventionism along with economically expansionist policies focused on investing in industry. However, they remained committed to European integration and intent on remaining within the European Monetary System that the Barre government had joined in 1979. Within a very short time, that commitment led to a crisis for the Mauroy government, whose expansive macroeconomic policies and expensive microeconomic policies were totally out of step with those of fellow European Community mem-

---

[1]Peter A. Hall, "Socialism in One Country: Mitterrand and the Struggle to Define a New Economic Policy for France," in *Socialism, the State and Public Policy in France,* ed. P. Cerny and M. Schain (London: Frances Pinter, 1985); and André Delion and Michel Durupty, *Les nationalisations* (Paris: Economica, 1982).

bers. French exceptionalism could not last long in an increasingly interde-pendent, global economy and in an integrating Europe. By 1983, instead of the break with capitalism that the Socialists had promised in their economic projects from the forties through their victory in 1981 (al-though by the 1981 election campaign this break was admittedly primari-ly a campaign slogan, side by side with slogans promising to modernize capitalism and strengthen traditional values), the break was with social-ism, as was evident not only in the shift in policies but also in the rhetoric.

The decision to stay in the EMS brought "the Great U-turn" in macro-economic policy, as the Mauroy government instituted strict monetary policies and an economic austerity program that continued under the government of Laurent Fabius. The turnabout had significant conse-quences for the full range of the Socialists' policies, since there was no longer any money left to fund as needed the ambitious social projects and the generous industrial investments. This lack of resources therefore al-most guaranteed the further liberalization of the economy since, no long-er able to stimulate industry through demand, the Socialists had to turn to more supply-side measures to improve the competitiveness of French industry.

Even before the turnabout in macroeconomic policies, though, the pro-gressive disengagement of the state had begun with deregulatory policies and an easing of interventionism that only intensified under Fabius's leadership, spurred on by the pressures of European integration and the demands of the increasingly global economy. The Socialists passed a raft of measures that opened up the markets, encouraged competition, and loosened restrictions on business. At the same time, moreover, they al-lowed the nationalized enterprises greater autonomy, and even allowed some informal privatization.

The Socialists, having gained office espousing a break with capitalism, ended their first five-year legislative mandate having broken only with old-style French capitalism. Having begun with *dirigisme,* they ended up essentially embracing economic liberalism and promoting the disengage-ment of the state from the economy.[2] And having instituted "more state" through the increase in state ownership and control of French business in

---

[2]In some areas, however, the Socialists were not so "liberal," as with the law alleged to encourage greater pluralism in the press, but in fact intended to dismantle Robert Hersant's conservative press empire, which was largely overturned by the Constitu-tional Council, and as with the proposed *loi Savary* which sought to reform the state's relationship with private schools (primarily Catholic) and which Mitterrand had to withdraw in response to well-organized protests. See: Alain Savary, *En toute liberté* (Paris: Hachette, 1985); Pierre Daniel, *Question de liberté* (Paris: Desclée de Brouwer, 1986); Gérard Leclerc, *La bataille de l'école* (Paris: Denoël, 1985); and John Ambler, "Constraints on Policy Innovation in Education: Thatcher's Britain and Mitterrand's France," *Comparative Politics* 20 (October 1987).

1981, they shortly thereafter started the shift to "less state," beginning the process of denationalization and deregulation that subsequent governments of the right and the left were to take much farther.

All in all, the Socialists' tenure in office did not turn out badly. The change in macroeconomic policies as of 1983 put the economy back on track, while nationalization, despite dire initial predictions, had a salutary effect on business. Not only did it serve to preserve the industrial base from foreign acquisition, it also served to rationalize and recapitalize it, putting traditionally undercapitalized French industry back on its feet.

Equally importantly, however, nationalization, which made Socialists responsible for business, served to free them from the old ideological apparatus. Although the Socialists slowly but surely backed away from their most radical views of nationalization through the seventies, it was only once they controlled business that their rhetoric changed, with nationalization justified as a way of saving French firms from foreign takeover and no longer as a "break with capitalism"; with business described as "creator of riches" instead of exploiter; and with the CEO seen as friend rather than foe of labor and alone capable of liberating the productive energy of the society, benefiting everyone. The change in rhetoric, moreover, anticipated the change in policies. By 1983, the Socialist economic project, nurtured during the postwar period and formalized during the time of the Common Program of 1972, had been rejected both as ideology and policy. The *dirigiste* state, having been built up so diligently during the postwar period and in the first year or so of the Socialists' tenure in office, was on its way down, as the disengagement of the state became the heroic policy agenda of the Socialists after 1983.

THE SOCIALIST ECONOMIC PROJECT

Ever since the forties, French Socialists had been committed to nationalizing the means of production as a way of promoting economic efficiency and social justice, and to coordinating industrial development through some form of national planning. Already in 1944, the supporters of Pierre Mendès-France had outlined a program for nationalization that entailed acquiring a controlling interest (whether at 51% or even less) in major French firms.[3] The contemporary Socialists' specific projects, however, began with the 1972 Common Program, which was heavily influenced by the Communist Party, and focused on diminishing capitalist power.

In the Common Program of 1972, the proposed nationalization of the entire financial and banking sector and nine industrial groups, and the

[3]See Kuisel, *Capitalism,* p. 194.

acquisition of shares in many other major concerns in strategic sectors of the economy, were "to break the domination of big capital and to establish a new economic and social policy that departs from that carried out by big capital."[4] Planning, moreover, was to be a democratic process, extremely decentralized, going so far as having neighborhood committees that would be incorporated into a national plan covering all of the nation's economic activity voted by Parliament as the "decisive act of the legislature."

With the worsening of the economic crisis and the break with the Communists in 1977, however, the Socialists' views of nationalization and planning underwent some subtle changes, and for the first time they provided their own economic rationale for the nationalizations.[5] Although the general rhetoric was still one of rupture with the capitalist system and liberation of the worker from exploitation, the specific discussions of nationalization characterized it more conservatively as an instrument of industrial policy to combat the economic crisis in a manner different from that of the powers that were in place.[6] Thus, whereas for the Communists, the primary goal of nationalization remained one of diminishing if not eliminating the power of private capital, the Socialists now saw nationalization as an element of a mixed economy in which public enterprise would complement private enterprise rather than substitute for it, and make up for its failures rather than eliminate it. As Pierre Mauroy explained it, "we definitively accepted the market economy"; but, recognizing that the market economy has problems which demand counterweights, "you need two things: first, in the economic sphere, a public sector and a certain amount of planning; and second, in the social sphere, a solidarity policy which implies that the fruits and efforts of economic growth be redistributed equitably."[7]

Nationalization was therefore to be the *fer de lance,* the weapon of economic defense, that the Socialists would use to overcome the weaknesses of French capitalism, in particular those of industry. With nationalization would come, first and foremost, investment in industry, a major necessity, in the view of Alain Boublil, Mitterrand's future economic advisor, if they were to compensate for the weaknesses of a capitalism which disregarded industrial investment in favor of banking and property

[4]*Programme Commun de gouvernement du Parti Communiste et du Parti Socialiste* (Paris: Editions Sociales, 1972), p. 113.

[5]Alain Boublil, *Le soulèvement du sérail* (Paris: Albin Michel, 1990), pp. 30–32.

[6]See the discussion in: Jocelyne Barreau and Jean le Nay, "Du programme commun (1972) au programme électoral du PS (1981)" in *L'état entrepreneur: Nationalisation, gestions du secteur public concurrentiel, construction européenne (1982–1993),* ed. Jocelyne Barreau et al. (Paris: L'Harmattan, 1990), pp. 17–18.

[7]Cited in W. Rand Smith, "Nationalizations for What? Capitalist Power and Public Enterprise in Mitterrand's France," *Politics and Society* vol. 18, no. 1 (1990), p. 79.

interests.[8] Thus, there was also to be a National Investment Bank to facilitate such investment. That investment in turn was to bring a return to full employment and strong economic growth.

For nationalization to be successful, however, the Socialists were convinced that a major transformation of the means of production was in order. They felt that they needed to constitute a powerful and diversified industry, present in all sectors, that would satisfy the main needs of the internal market and diminish dependence on external markets, in particular in strategic areas such as electronics, computing, space, aeronautics, biotechnology, and so on.[9] For these strategic areas, sectoral plans were to be drafted that would act as blueprints for the restructuring of the nationalized industries in a given sector around a public enterprise that would be *chef de file*, or head of the line. This *politique de filières* was to be coordinated with a democratic planning instrument that would serve to substitute the "criterion of social utility" for that of oligarchical profit. Thus, although the market would remain to adjust supply and demand, the Plan was to become "the overall regulator of the economy," substituting therefore for the market as "the overall regulator of the capitalist economy," and determining, first and foremost, industrial investment.[10]

Even with planning, however, there were subtle differences from the past. In the 1980 *Projet Socialiste,* the planning itself was no longer to control all aspects of economic activity, although it remained the overall regulator of the economy. In this project, the "initiative of industrial economic agents" was to take over where the plan stopped, with "the spirit of enterprise" regaining its rights and the role of the market its utility.

Economics, however, was not the only justification for nationalization. Equally important was the social justification, which saw nationalization as a vehicle for societal change, bringing not only higher wages and fewer hours worked, but also *autogestion,* or worker control, with negotiated agreements between workers and management on work conditions, elections for employee directors on the board, and work councils that would discuss the planning contracts, working conditions, and so on.[11] The Common Program of 1972, using the language of "citizenship in the enterprise," anticipated establishing worker control over the organization and remuneration of labor and giving enterprise committees the power to oppose management decisions affecting hiring, firing, and work condi-

---

[8]Alain Boublil, *Le socialisme industriel* (Paris: Presses Universitaires de France, 1977).
[9]Report by Michel Charzat for the conference "Socialisme et Industrie," discussed in: Barreau and Le Nay, "Du Programme Commun," p. 22.
[10]See: Barreau and Le Nay, "Du Programme Commun," pp. 19–20, 22–23.
[11]Ibid., p. 24.

tions. Moreover, in the nationalized industries in particular, it proposed experiments with *autogestion,* for example, with the election of foremen and managers. By 1980, in the campaign platform *Projet Socialiste,* the election of managers had been dropped, but the rest remained. The platform proclaimed that *autogestion* was at the center of the Socialists' *"projet de société,"* or project for the society, insisting that, because *autogestion* cannot be decreed, "a dynamic of workers taking responsibility in enterprises" was to be encouraged by extending the democratization of power into plant and workplace councils.

Once the Socialists gained power, the discourse changed once again. In the parliamentary debates, although the commitment to nationalization remained – as Prime Minister Pierre Mauroy underlined its "fit with the temperament, the history, and the traditions of France" while Jean Le Garrec, Secretary of State charged with the extension of the public sector, took credit for fulfilling the unaccomplished imperatives of the postwar period[12] – its goals and rationale had changed yet again. There was no longer any talk of the break with capitalism, of the Plan as a regulatory mechanism of the market, of workers' control, or of a National Investment Bank. Instead, nationalization was portrayed only as a way of fighting the economic crisis and of promoting an ambitious and interventionist industrial policy within the context of a market economy.[13] Jacques Delors, the Finance Minister, insisted that the nationalizations must respond to the challenges of international competition while Laurent Fabius, Deputy Minister for the Budget, argued that the nationalizations were to increase employment and allow for a new industrial policy.[14] Thus, as Lionel Zinsou, one of Fabius's advisors, noted, "We went from the idea of a break with capitalism to the very different idea of a break with the failures of capitalism."[15]

During those first heady months of power, nationalization meant a great many things to a great many people – for example, the implementation of worker control, the elimination of private profit, the strengthening of the unions, or even the creation of "islands of socialism" in a "sea of capitalism" (although this passed once job eliminations and plant closings began).[16] But in fact it quickly became more simply the means to revive the economy, enabling the country to avoid a number of economic

[12]Jean Le Garrec, "L'enjeu véritable des nationalisations," *Le Monde,* Sept. 1, 1981.
[13]Barreau and Le Nay, "Du Programme Commun," pp. 51–52.
[14]Quoted in the Charzat Report annex, pp. 239–240, 249, 259 – cited in Barreau and Le Nay, "Du Programme Commun," pp. 39–41.
[15]Lionel Zinsou, *Le fer de lance* (Paris: Olivier Orban, 1985), p. 61.
[16]For a full discussion of the reasons for Socialist support of nationalization before their 1981 victory, see: Richard Holton, "Industrial Politics in France: Nationalisation under Mitterrand," *West European Politics* vol. 1, no. 1 (January 1986).

disasters that would have been caused by the bankruptcies or foreign acquisition of companies critical to France's industrial and technological base and necessary to its future growth and international competitiveness.[17] Within a relatively short span of time, the Socialists' rationale had gone from the postwar socialist one of expropriating the capitalists' means of production in order to put them more appropriately in the hands of a state under socialist tutelage to the more typically neoliberal one that understands nationalization solely in nationalist terms, as safeguarding the French means of production from almost certain takeover by foreign firms that would repatriate profits and ignore national concerns.[18] Symbolic of this shift was the replacement of J. Piette – the upper-level civil servant in charge of the *mission* to study the nationalizations during the monthlong first Mauroy government who, having come out of the SFIO and participated in the first nationalizations at Liberation, saw nationalization as a political combat against determined adversaries – by Jean Le Garrec during the longer-lived second Mauroy government. A former businessman who had spent twenty years working at IBM, Le Garrec saw the nationalizations solely as a means of combatting France's economic and social crisis, and was concerned to avoid any brutal or hasty measures that could traumatize the nationalized industries, thereby compromising the continuity so necessary to their health.[19]

Along with the Socialists' early move away from any left-leaning ideological interpretation of the nationalizations came their recognition that nationalization was to produce a stronger, but not necessarily more socialist, set of industrial and financial institutions. As Dominique Strauss-Kahn, Minister of Industry in the governments of Cresson and Bérégovoy, explains it, assuming that ownership per se, whether through nationalization or privatization, could lead to profound changes was wrong – these affected property rights, but not the structure of the economy or the strategies of CEOs. Nationalization had little effect on industries other than recapitalizing and rationalizing them as well as saving them from foreign takeover. When the CEOs did change, they followed the same policies, as much for the nationalizations as for the privatizations. Thus, as Strauss-Kahn concluded, the Socialists who said, "thanks to this, we

[17]Philippe Messine, "Nationalisations, dénationalisations," *Le Monde Diplomatique,* March 1986, p. 6.

[18]The neoliberals (in the Anglo-American sense of the term, that is, in the liberal tradition) have traditionally understood nationalization as a public compromise forged among competing groups in order to defend national interests against the threat posed by foreign investment. See Stuart Holland, "Europe's New Public Enterprises," in *Big Business and the State,* ed. R. Vernon (Cambridge, MA: Harvard University Press, 1974), pp. 25–44. See also the discussion in John R. Freeman, *Democracy and Markets: The Politics of Mixed Economies* (Ithaca, NY: Cornell, 1989), pp. 25–27.

[19]Barreau and Le Nay, "Du Programme Commun," pp. 27–29.

will have a strong economy," and the right that said, "because of that, the economy will collapse," were both wrong.[20]

Regardless of their ideological goals or rationales, in sum, the Socialists very soon after taking office began to speak of nationalization in more pragmatic economic terms, as a way of shoring up capitalism rather than destroying it. This is not the only part of the Socialists' economic project that changed almost immediately upon their arrival in power. Their promises with regard to planning and worker democracy were equally quickly abandoned.

To begin with, the Socialists went from the idea of the Plan as a guiding document to one that could be set aside whenever deemed expedient, as it had been in recent conservative governments. Michel Rocard's Interim Plan of 1981–1983 had no more impact than those of the previous decade: it was revised or put aside as changing economic circumstances demanded. For example, it called for the creation of 500,000 jobs; instead, 110,000 positions were lost in that time period alone.[21] The Ninth Plan (1984–1988), moreover, had even less the appearance of a plan than the interim one. It was significant more for the particular planning contracts between state and nationalized industries and between state and region, the latter of which were in fact important in the context of decentralization and the promotion of small and mid-sized firms.[22] In the eighties, in fact, national planning was virtually finished as anything more than an exercise. *Autogestion,* by comparison, was finished even before it started.

When they gained power, the Socialists left workers' control behind entirely. Although they did institute some form of worker democracy, this came over a year after the law on nationalization, and was a far cry from the radical empowerment of the workers that had been described in the pre-1981 literature of the Socialist Party. The Auroux laws of April 1982, applicable to all enterprises with over 200 employees, and the more rigorous law on the democratization of the public sector of July 1983, established worker participation through the institution of plantwide health and safety committees, the strengthening of the work councils, the creation of firmwide work councils, and the institution of direct negotiations with management, as well as, for the public enterprises, through seats on the *conseils d'administration* or boards of directors. Rather than bringing *autogestion,* which would have established worker control over

---

[20]Dominique Strauss-Kahn, Minister of Industry in the Cresson and Bérégovoy governments, formerly deputy in the National Assembly and head of the Finance Commission. Interview with author, Paris, May 16, 1991.

[21]Bela Belassa, "La politique industrielle Socialiste" *Commentaire* no. 30 (summer 1985), p. 587.

[22]See Schmidt, *Democratizing France.*

management, these laws contractualized the relations between management and labor.[23] *Autogestion* was not put into effect partially because of the fear by the Socialists of the Communist-controlled CGT, which was larger than the Socialist CFDT and the FO, and might therefore have come to dominate industry. The Socialists, after all, were in a relationship of "competitive pluralism" with the Communists, in which they attempted to contain and marginalize them as much as possible.[24] It was also the case that by the time the Socialists gained power, the *autogestion* movement was all but dead; and without any popular mobilization around the theme of establishing new power relations in the firm, the Socialists were unlikely to institute any changes in this area.

While *autogestion* was never adopted and planning set aside, the one thing that most thought immovable, the negative attitudes toward business that had fueled not only the *autogestion* movement but the entire nationalization program, did change. The Socialists relatively soon after taking office began to adopt a conciliatory approach toward business. Although in his first press conference on September 18, 1981, in Figeac, Mitterrand reiterated the traditional rhetoric of combatting "the wall of money" that had prevented reform in the past, he also noted that nationalization would make the economy just "a little more mixed" than before, and that if employers spent their profits on investments that created jobs, they would be exempt from the wealth tax.[25]

It did not take long after that for the Socialists to alter their entire rhetoric regarding business – even before, that is, they had changed their policies. Within the year, gone was the discussion of business as the exclusive domain of the capitalist class, out to enslave the proletariat and exploit its labor, keeping the surplus value, or profits, for itself, with the CEO in particular depicted as profiteer and enemy. In its place, the CEO had become an entrepreneur in the service of the public, making money to invest it in the future, not to exploit the worker. With this change in rhetoric, moreover, the Socialists managed to convince not only themselves, but the public at large.

As late as 1980, in the Socialist campaign literature, business was described as right-wing while the banks expressed the "diktat of big capital" and "devoured the substance of the country."[26] In September 1981, business heads still complained about the class conflict language of

[23]See Chapters 10 and 14.

[24]George Ross and Jane Jenson, "Pluralism and the Decline of Left Hegemony: The French Left in Power," *Politics and Society* vol. 14, no. 2 (1985): 147–183.

[25]*Le Monde*, Sept. 25–26, 1981.

[26]Alain Vernhoules, "Bilan du Septennat, l'alternance dans l'alternance," *Le Monde* special supplement; reprinted in *Le bilan économique des années Mitterrand*, ed. Alain Gélédan (Paris: Le Monde Editions, 1993), p. 54.

Socialist leaders, with one CEO noting that "Jospin wasn't just anyone and therefore it was annoying to hear him talk of the *patronat* as if it represented the enemy." They criticized the Socialists for considering the word "profit" an obscenity, insisting that "They must come to see that the first duty of a top manager is to ensure the company's *rentabilité*. The rest is either talk or ill-will. In both cases, it paralyzes us." And they wanted the government to take the lead in making it clear that "the heads of business are not pariahs, that they have a difficult job and that they should not be prevented from doing their job," that they are "the ones who make the economic engine run," who are in "the front lines of the battle of competition."[27] Little did they know how soon they were to have their wishes fulfilled, that they were to become the new heroes, so much so that one among them, at least, thought that it may even have gone a bit too far.[28]

By 1982, top managers themselves noted that the Socialists had begun the rehabilitation of business, with CEO after CEO echoing the same refrain, that from exploiter, business had become the "creator of riches."[29] As one Socialist banker put it, once business became "ours" rather than "theirs," it went from the exploiter, where profits went to the capitalists, to the "creator of riches," where it worked for the benefit of everyone.[30] This, of course, was a natural by-product of the nationalizations themselves, since how could the Socialists continue to see business as the exploiter if they themselves were in charge of it? Most importantly, however, the Socialists changed not only their own view of business, but that of the public at large. Many were those who noted a revolution in values, with the general acceptance that companies produce wealth and therefore jobs.[31] As another Socialist banker (and former ministerial cabinet member) explains it, the Socialists are responsible for the fact that "France that didn't like industry now does. . . . The French now see that the future is with business. Before the eighties, they still had a Marxist vision of entreprise, where profit meant that the company was making money off the backs of the workers. No more. And this is thanks to the

[27]"L'état et les chefs d'entreprises," *L'Observatoire de la Cofremca* no. 5 (1981). These views were expressed in a meeting in September 1981 with eight heads of major enterprises representing a wide range of sectors.
[28]This was the view of Jean-Louis Descours, CEO of Groupe André. Interview with author, Paris, May 2, 1991.
[29]In interviews with the author of over forty top officials in business and government between February and July 1991, this was the phrase used over and over again. And not one top official suggested otherwise.
[30]Jean Deflassieux, former CEO of Crédit Lyonnais. Interview with author, Paris, May 2, 1991.
[31]Comment by M. Vulliez, former head of HEC and head of the Paris Chamber of Commerce education department – cited in NEDO, *The Making of Managers*, Report on behalf of the MSC, NEDC, and BIM (London: NEDO, 1987), p. 73.

Socialists. The Socialists who had originally seen the *patrons* as adversaries took responsibility for the success of industry, perhaps because of nationalization. So they explained that it's good for the enterprise to make money, to invest. And this was a major cultural change. The conservatives could not do this."[32] The cultural change, moreover, encompassed not only more positive feelings for the heads of business, but also an acceptance of the entire panoply of Socialist measures that liberalized the economy in the effort to enable business to operate more efficiently.

Public opinion surveys confirm this. Public confidence in CEOs went from 44% in 1981 to 56% in 1985. Profit, from a negative concept in 1980 (for 39% of French as opposed to 37% for whom it was a positive term), had become a positive one as early as 1982, at 42% (vs. 33%).[33] The entrepreneurial spirit was also on the rise in the population, with more than one in three in 1984 claiming that they would be happy to head a business (with 18% seeing themselves as entirely capable of owning or starting a business; 18% as just about capable of doing so; 20% as somewhat able to; and 43% not at all). When compared to eight other European countries, France came in second, behind Spain, just ahead of Italy, and way ahead of the northern European countries.[34] Moreover, the public's view of business as exploiter had diminished significantly: Whereas in 1976, 42% of the population were convinced that the supermarket chain Carrefour enriched itself at the expense of the nation, only 26% felt that way in 1983. A similar decline occurred for BSN, the other large food purveyor (decreasing from 30% in 1976 to 19% in 1983), for Nestlé (33% to 22%), for Shell (46% to 29%), and for Hachette (29% to 21%).[35] Finally, already in 1983, the management consulting firm *Cofremca* had found a new realism in the population, such that 90% of those polled agreed either completely (61%) or for the most part (29%) that for the economy to get better, it was first necessary for French enterprises to become competitive, while 67% agreed (35% completely, 32% for the most part) that one must reduce controls and regulations on enterprises to facilitate their development and success.[36]

---

[32]Lebègue, interview with author.

[33]SOFRES, *L'état de l'opinion 1988* (Paris: Seuil, 1988), p. 31.

[34]"Nouvelles Brèves, 1984," *L'Observatoire de la Cofremca* no. 27 (1989).

[35]Ibid.

[36]Among these, the least favorably inclined were skilled workers (at 55%), while middle-level managers (61%), employees (63%), and unskilled workers (64%) were closer to the national average, although nothing like the small businesspeople, CEOs, liberal professionals, and upper-level managers, 70–90% of whom were in favor. Needless to say, adherents of the PC were the least in favor of this (at 36%), and the right the most (the RPR at 80% and the UDF at 82%), with the left in between (the PSU at 55%, PS at 56%, Ecologists at 63%, and others at 69%). "Le nouveau réalisme," *L'Observatoire de la Cofremca* no. 11 (1983).

The public's attitudes toward business were not the only things to change. Labor, too, confronted with a Socialist government and nationalized means of production, had to make an about face. With its own friends in power, it felt less able to strike than before, feeling bound to accept the government's urging to consider the good of the company and of the nation, despite government indifference to its demands for wage increases.[37]

The Socialists' change in rhetoric, in short, was quite successful, judging by its impact on the populace as a whole. In a very short time, it had served to convert a population from an attitude of long-standing hostility to business to one quite supportive of it. The result is that, in this area at least, French culture has become much more like those of Germany and Japan, which have never had cultures hostile to business, than like British culture, which, for all Thatcher's efforts, remains hostile. This is all the more ironic once we recall that the French Socialists had no such intention upon their triumphant ascension to power, by contrast with the British Conservatives, who came to power insisting that just such a transformation was their direct policy goal.

The Socialists' success in the rehabilitation of business, however, although welcomed by business and most on the right, was not greeted with unequivocal enthusiasm on the left. In the view of one Socialist banker, which echoes those of many disillusioned Socialists, the Socialists were all too successful, because

the Socialists rehabilitated not just the enterprise but the entrepreneur. They liberated profits, but they kept salaries down; they created an inheritance tax that was not applied equally because they were afraid that a tax paid by everyone would impede investment; instead, it punished widows on fixed incomes with apartments that had appreciated in value and allowed owners of businesses to escape on the grounds that an enterprise is an *outil de travail* or a means of production, in German, *das Kapital*. With this, the Socialists went too far. They abandoned socialism.[38]

The Socialists, in brief, were not only good propagandists for capitalism, they were also good capitalists. This was reflected not only in their policies toward the nationalized enterprises, through large-scale investment in the companies and, after an initial interventionist period, with a return to a respect for their traditional autonomy, but also in their macroeconomic policies. And here too, a change in rhetoric accompanied the switch from Keynesian expansionism to liberal austerity, with "industrial dynamism," "competitive technology," and "modernization" the new watchwords of the Socialist government. The switch itself, moreover, symbolized the demise of "two sterile myths," in the words of Alain

[37]*Le Monde*, September 28–29, 1986.   [38]Deflassieux, interview with author.

Vernhoules. First, it brought an end to the myth of the state able to do everything, including ensuring economic growth, industrial investment, and employment, and to regulate everything, from the length of the work week to the repartition of salaries. Thus, the budget was no longer seen as an all-powerful weapon able to stimulate or brake investment, nationalization was no longer the answer to the problems of production, and the enterprise, rather than the state, came to be seen as the place where wages are fixed, decisions for hiring or firing are to be made, and so on. Second, the switch put to rest the myth that the opening to the outside was a danger to French independence and autonomy of decision; it thereby acted as a spur to French competitiveness, consumer orientation, alliances with multinationals, and acceptance of international competition and international organizations, including the IMF and the EMS.[39] The year 1983, in other words, spelled the end of the socialist economic project both as ideology and as policy.

FROM KEYNESIAN EXPANSIONISM TO LIBERAL AUSTERITY IN STATE MANAGEMENT OF THE ECONOMY

The Socialists elected in 1981 blamed the crisis in state economic leadership on the abandonment of traditional *dirigisme* and of nationalization as an instrument for economic renewal. The Socialists' answer to the economic crisis, therefore, was a set of heroic policies that were to institute "more state" through expansionary, neo-Keynesian macroeconomic policies coupled with a strongly interventionist or *dirigiste* program of nationalization and restructuring of major industries and banks. In addition, they proceeded with a dazzling array of reforms that included the decentralization of local government,[40] the institution of innovative social policies, the reform of health care,[41] of housing, of the systems of justice and liberty,[42] of culture and communications, and so forth. Finally, they instituted a social spending program that was to revitalize the economy.

In their campaign, the Socialists had promised to revive the economy through a "redistributive Keynesianism" that would be countercyclical, enabling them to catch the next world economic recovery on the upswing while promoting both economic growth and social justice. The Socialists reasoned that an increase in revenue for those with the lowest wages and incomes would allow popular consumption to take off along with eco-

---

[39]Vernhoules, "Bilan du Septennat," pp. 54–55.
[40]See: Schmidt, *Democratizing France.*
[41]See: David Wilsford, *Doctors and the State* (Durham: Duke University Press, 1991).
[42]See: Alec Stone, *The Birth of Judicial Politics in France* (New York: Oxford, 1992).

nomic activity, thus creating new jobs and concomitantly reducing unemployment, increasing productive capacity and business revenues while lowering business's fixed costs, damping inflation while bringing in higher government revenues, and thereby reducing the deficit while increasing economic competitiveness.[43] To that end, the Socialists raised the minimum wage by 10% (from 15.20 francs to 16.72 francs per hour) and increased allowances to the elderly and the handicapped by 20% and those for family lodging by 50%. This cost 8 to 9 billion francs, to be paid for by a tax on the richest taxpayers and on the profits of the largest firms. In addition, they passed a wide range of pro-worker measures that included a reduced work week (of 39 hours, with the extra hour remaining in workers' paychecks), a fifth week of paid vacation, retirement at sixty, the hiring of another 100,000 public employees, manpower training programs, and various employment protection statutes. These, however, did little to stem rising unemployment, in particular because the reduction in the work week could not diminish unemployment as anticipated since employers lacked the wherewithal to hire extra workers for the hour lost since they were still paying workers for that hour. Moreover, these measures, too, were extremely expensive, and were financed by higher social insurance and corporate taxes as well as by a higher budget deficit.[44] In 1982, government spending increased by 27.6%, and 60,000 new civil service jobs were created.[45]

All of these policies proved to be expensive and highly inflationary. The nationalizations only contributed to this by severely depleting the coffers of the state at the same time that the private capital the nationalizations freed up was generally invested abroad, and not back in the economy. The nationalizations alone were to cost 51 billion francs, of which 28 billion francs were for the banks and financial concerns, 23 billion francs for the industrial firms.[46] Moreover, not only had the nationalizations been extremely expensive, but the nationalized industries were also racking up record losses, leading to record government investment, in particular in declining sectors such as steel and heavy industry (see Table 4.1). Bertrand Jacquillat, no friend of nationalization, estimated that in the first three years of nationalization, from 1981 to 1984, the public sector accumulated over 130 billion francs in losses. If one adds to this the subsidies

[43]Michel Beaud, *Le Monde*, December 30, 1982.

[44]Howard Machin and Vincent Wright, eds., *Economic Policy and Policy-Making under the Mitterand Presidency* (London: Pinter, 1985).

[45]*Le Monde, L'économie française: Mutations, 1975–1990* (Paris: Le Monde, 1989), p. 47.

[46]These are the figures given at the time (cf. *Le Monde, Bilan économique et social 1981,* January 15, 1982). Later figures provided are slightly lower, at around 45 billion.

Table 4.1. *A comparison of the financial results of and capital grants received by public industrial groups, in billions of francs*

Industrial Group	Accumulated Results (1981-1985)	Capital Grants Rec'd (1982-1986)
Sacilor	-25.30	16.30
Usinor	-25.00	16.10
Renault	-27.40	12.00
CDF-Chimie	-6.50	3.00
Péchiney[a]	-3.90	3.60
Bull	-2.80	3.70
CGCT	-2.30	2.00
Thomson[b]	-1.90	3.60
EMC	-0.60	0.50
SNECMA	-0.02	1.10
Matra	+0.40	0.70
Aérospatiale	+0.80	0.20
Dassault	+1.90	---
Saint-Gobain	+2.50	---
CGE[b]	+2.60	0.60
Rhône-Poulenc	+3.00	0.70

[a] Excepting capital grant to PCUK (3 billion francs)
[b] Excepting capital grant to Thomson-Telecommunications (1.1 billion francs)

Source: Michel Durupty, Les privatisations (Paris: Documentation Française, 1988), from Direction du Trésor, "Rapports d'activité des groupes," Journal Officiel, no. 786 (1986-1987).

received by public enterprises, the amount jumps to 320 billion francs.[47] Continued investment in these companies, a necessity if the nationalization program were to be a success, was a serious drain on the Treasury.

The result was that within a year, inflation was spiraling upward (from 13% to 14%) and the economy downward. Although industrial production grew in response to an increase in consumption, imports far outdistanced exports, as the high inflation rate decreased the competitiveness of French products compared to those of its competitors abroad. The trade deficit with Germany alone grew by 35% in 1981 and by 81% in the first quarter of 1982. Moreover, firms' net profit margins were eroding in the face of rising wage costs combined with the reduction of the work week, while firms' net savings fell to nearly zero in response to the high interest rates demanded by the international context and the need to defend the franc. In addition, despite Socialist initiatives, private investment had declined 12% in volume in 1981.[48] At the same time, unemployment had already gone above the 2 million mark and a huge budget deficit emerged, going from 0.4% of GDP in 1981 to 3% in 1982, along with a large social security deficit and a trade deficit that had increased from 56 billion francs to 93 billion francs.

[47]Bertrand Jacquillat, *Désétatiser* (Paris: R. Laffont, 1985).
[48]Lipietz, "Governing the Economy."

In that first year, the Socialists had done relatively little to try to counteract the inflationary spiral and the deterioration in the macroeconomic profile of the country that had started almost as soon as they were elected. Because they assumed, based on the OECD's faulty prediction, that the West would pull out of recession late in 1981 and that the United States would begin a reflationary policy, they delayed taking any steps that might have limited the damage. In truth, though, there was not much they could have done without a dramatic reversal in their policies, given the external constraints. These included France's dependence not only upon foreign sources of energy and other primary resources but also on numbers of industrial goods, which left France unable to stop the deteriorating balance of trade. France's membership in the EC and the EMS also played a role, reducing France's margins for maneuver at the same time that it increased competition for French business. The Socialists had in fact underestimated the impact of the opening of the European market and overestimated the ability of the nationalized enterprises to hold their own in competition.[49] Finally, pressures on the franc resulting from the exit of French capital, external imbalances, speculation, and the high interest rates in the United States left the government little choice other than to devalue the franc. Devaluation, however, was something Mitterrand refused to do early enough, despite a run on the franc and a drop in value of 7% compared to the pre-election rate; he declared that "You do not devalue the money of a country when that country has just placed confidence in you."[50]

By early October 1981, however, Mitterrand had little choice but to devalue (with a drop in value of the franc by 8.5% next to the Deutschmark), and Delors then declared a price freeze on basic products. This was too little too late. Inflation was already at 14%. Economic growth was at a standstill. And the government was unwilling to take any further measures, such as a "pause" in the highly inflationary policies which Jacques Delors called for in November 1981, and which elicited a rebuke from Mauroy. By mid April 1982, however, Delors had again called for a pause, which this time was greeted more seriously. The government announced another stopgap measure, a reduction in business taxes and social security contributions; it was concerned about the fact that the roughly $10 billion in new taxes and social costs had squeezed business profits and reduced industrial investment, to say nothing of the high interest rates designed to defend the franc and tame inflation.[51] By

[49]Louis Schweitzer, current CEO of Renault, councillor to Delors at the time. Interview with author, Paris, May 10, 1991.

[50]Philippe Bauchard, *La guerre des deux roses: Du rêve à la réalité, 1981–1985* (Paris: Grasset, 1986), p. 27. See also the discussion in: Northcutt, *Mitterrand*, p. 96.

[51]See the discussion in: Wayne Northcutt, *Mitterrand: A Political Biography* (New York: Holmes and Meier, 1992), p. 111.

June 1982, the government had imposed a wage and price freeze; in September it reduced welfare payments, and later still increased taxes. But as the economy continued to deteriorate, more drastic measures were called for.

Between June 1982 and March 1983, the Socialists agonized over whether to stay in the EMS, which meant reducing the budget deficit and deflating the economy, or to exit, and thereby sustain reflation by devaluing the franc and putting up protectionist barriers to imports in order to stabilize the trade deficit.[52] For some, only the discipline of the EMS would permit France to retain its place in global competition; for others, the only quick escape from the crisis was to get out of the Community environment with its impossibly high interest rates.[53] On one side of the debate was much of the Socialist Party, including some of Mitterrand's own councilors such as Jean Riboud, and the more doctrinaire Socialists, whether the Socialists from the old SFIO or Jean-Pierre Chevènement, leader of the Jacobin CERES, who favored withdrawing from the EMS, sharply devaluing the franc, and tightening exchange and trade controls. On the other side of the debate was Prime Minister Mauroy, unwilling to turn his back on Europe and convinced that the Socialists would lose power if they continued with their expansionist policies; Minister of Finance Jacques Delors, who had centrist credentials as a Social Catholic and as the architect of Jacques Chaban-Delmas's "New Society" program, and who from the first had warned of the dangers of the highly inflationary policies; and Presidential advisors such as Jacques Attali and Bianco, who maintained that any approach such as that recommended by Riboud and Chevènement would make the franc fall by 20 to 30%. In between the two groups were men such as Laurent Fabius, originally on the side of Riboud but who then came over to Delors's side, and Minister of Social Affairs Pierre Bérégovoy, who originally vehemently opposed the plan but who subsequently came to incarnate it.[54] The debate itself was an internal one, primarily involving party leaders, who only minimally consulted

[52]See: Hall, "State and Market," pp. 177–178; A. Fontaneau and P.-A. Muet, eds., *La gauche face à la crise* (Paris: Presse de la Fondation Nationale des Sciences Politiques, 1985); and David Cameron, "Exchange Rate Politics in France: The Regime-Defining Choices of the Mitterrand Presidency," in *The Mitterrand Era: Policy Alternatives and Political Mobilization in France,* ed. Anthony Daley (New York: Macmillan and NYU Press, forthcoming).

[53]Pierre Favier and Michel Martin-Roland, *La décennie Mitterrand,* vol. 1 (Paris: Seuil, 1990), p. 441.

[54]Lebègue, interview with author, April 26, 1991. He wrote the Plan Commun de la Gauche, was close to Chevènement in the CERES until he found him impossible, later joined Mauroy's cabinet, and later still became Director of the Treasury and then Director-General of the BNP.

with the larger party, let alone societal interests. Above all, it excluded the Communists, the Socialists' coalition partners.[55]

The problem, as Henri Weber explains it, was that already after one year, the Socialists were faced with a major dilemma: if they accepted reality, they had to renounce their socialist doctrine, and thus be plunged into ideological crisis; if they rejected reality and stayed with their ideology, they would lose politically.[56] In the end, President Mitterrand, having listened to both sides over a period of fifteen days, and almost no one else, decided in favor of reality, choosing Europe and the opening to the international market. With this decision, as Michael Loriaux argues, the Socialists gave away some of the state's independence in macroeconomic matters in order to regain control over the economy, and to "restore the state's power to exercise control over the evolution of fundamental monetary quantities: monetary growth, prices, credit, and the values of the currency."[57] Moreover, although the room for maneuver became smaller, as André Lévy-Lang, head of Paribas, remarked, it was all the more reason for the French government to play its role.[58]

In other words, heroic policymaking continued, but its content changed, with the disengagement of the state the manner in which the Socialist government sought to continue to manage the economy. Mitterrand as early as January 1983 prepared the way for this when he argued in contradistinction to 1981 that "Nothing obligates the state to multiply its laws or intervene at all moments, because it is not the only one to be able to respond to all needs. . . . In some circumstances, the state must know how to efface itself. This is, according to me, the basis for its authority and its efficacy: to be the solution of last resort once its action becomes clearly indispensable."[59]

In March 1983, along with the third devaluation of the franc, the Mauroy government undertook the "Great U-turn" in macroeconomic policymaking, introducing the *politique de rigueur,* a quite severe economic austerity program, in an attempt to reverse the serious losses in the nationalized sector, to damp inflation, and to reduce the deficit without, however, discouraging business growth and industrial investment. While the government imposed a 1% surtax, a 10% obligatory loan from the taxable incomes of the 8 million richest taxpayers, and froze the state budget at 20 billion francs, it promised to impose no new taxes on

[55]See Bauchard, *Guerre des deux roses.*

[56]Henri Weber, at the time member of the cabinet of Laurent Fabius (the former Prime Minister who was leader of the Socialist Party and deputy in the National Assembly), subsequently in charge of the Socialist Party newspaper *Vendredi.* Interview with author, Paris, March 13, 1991.

[57]Loriaux, *France after Hegemony,* p. 270.   [58]Lévy-Lang, interview with author.
[59]*Le Monde,* January 6, 1983.

business, to lower business social costs, and to ease rules regulating business, in particular layoff restrictions. Moreover, it had to cut back public spending, scale back aid to industry, in particular to the nationalized industries, and allow more bankruptcies. It also had to cut back on its social policies and avoid wage increases, since bringing down inflation of necessity took the place of bringing down unemployment rates or bringing up workers' salaries.

Finally, absent the resources that its inflationary policies had allowed it, the government was no longer able to stimulate industry through demand using its traditional policy instruments. It therefore had to improve the competitiveness of French firms through more supply side measures. This had actually started even before the Great U-turn of 1983, in 1982 with the deindexation of salaries on prices, and the January 1983 law on savings (the Delors Act), which allowed the introduction of new debenture shares in investment certificates, and the creation of a "second market" for unlisted securities, which enabled SMEs to gain access to equity markets in February 1983.

The liberalization only accelerated under Prime Minister Fabius, who put an emphasis on profit and faith in the market, spurred on by necessity, by the pressures of Europe, by the pressures of business, and by his own ministers. In particular Pierre Bérégovoy, who, as Finance Minister, underwent a conversion along with most of the Socialist Party in 1983, pushed hard for greater freedom for the economy. As of 1984, the Socialists put through measures encouraging competition in the banking system (the Bank Act), relaxing regulations in the financial markets, authorizing many new financial instruments, loosening controls over exchange rates, partially eliminating price controls, and reducing a variety of business taxes, including the *prélèvements obligatoires,* or payroll taxes, and the tax on revenues. In the capital markets in particular, as of December 1985 they established a commercial paper market, which enabled companies to raise capital directly from the public, and in February 1986, Bérégovoy inaugurated a futures market, the MATIF (Marché à Terme des Instruments Financiers). The result of all this, as Alain Vernhoules noted, with only slight exaggeration on his part, as he himself admitted, was that "the French financial system managed to achieve as much progress with the left in three years as it had in the previous twenty-five."[60]

Finally, in 1985 the Socialists even went so far as to consider a law on competition which, though never passed, was to have reinforced antitrust measures and loosened restrictions on competition. In particular, it was to have specified which kinds of price-fixing agreements and tying arrangements were legal; to have loosened restrictions imposed by the *loi*

[60]Vernhoules, "Bilan du Septennat," p. 54.

Royer of December 27, 1973, which benefited the small shopkeeper to the detriment of the large; and to have reinforced the law pertaining to market concentration by making a 20% (rather than a 40%) market share the level at which mergers would have to be justified on the basis of lowering prices, increasing productivity or competition, and improving employment or the balance of trade.

Even without this last measure, however, the Socialists had already done much to alter the environment for business. The opening of the markets under the Mauroy and Fabius governments enabled business to gain new nongovernmental sources of financing, including stocks, money market funds, mutual funds, negotiable certificates of deposit issued by banks, and treasury bills issued by companies along with negotiable treasury bonds, thus diminishing business's dependence upon government for subsidies and its vulnerability to government pressure. Equally importantly, however, it also enabled business to diminish its dependence upon the banks. Whereas in 1978, business financing from nonbanking sources came to only 30.7% of that of financial institutions (54.1 billion francs coming primarily from the stock market by contrast with 176 billion francs from financial institutions), by 1985 it had jumped to 60.6% (with 226.5 billion francs coming from nonbanking sources and 373.5 billion from financial institutions), and by 1986 to 153.6% (with 340.4 billion to 221.5 billion).[61] Between 1984 and 1986 alone, the share of external financing provided to industry by banks had dropped from 58.6% to 33.7%.[62] For the first time, as a result, the banks had some real competition, which forced them to become more competitive, such that they lowered the cost of borrowing by slicing one to two points from their traditional interest margin. Businesses themselves, however, had to borrow less, able to finance investment out of retained earnings as a result of their improved performance and profitability.

By the time they lost the elections to the neoliberal right, then, the Socialists had reversed their macroeconomic policies completely, going from Keynesian expansionism to liberal austerity, and from *dirigiste* policies focused on expanding the purchasing power and social benefits of workers to liberal ones concentrating on promoting the productive power and investment of business. A similar reversal also occurred for the nationalized enterprises, although it was not quite as dramatic, with informal privatization and a renewed respect for the traditional autonomy of public enterprises beginning in March 1983, about the same time as the great U-turn.

[61]*Rapport 1986 du Haut Conseil du Secteur Public* (Paris: Documentation Française, 1988); and Michel Durupty, *Les privatisations* (Paris: Documentation Française, 1988), p. 23.
[62]OECD, *France 1991–1992*, p. 160.

Changes in government policies toward business

That the Socialists nationalized when the rest of the world seemed swept up in a tidal wave of privatization and state disengagement from the economy, spurred on by the examples of Reagan and Thatcher, reflects not only French "exceptionalism" but also the long history of French acceptance of nationalization as a solution to economic problems. Although the Socialist nationalizations were the first in many years and provoked great controversy, they were nevertheless in keeping with past practice, following not only the example of the Fourth Republic by extending nationalization to the rest of the banks and to all essential or key industries but also that of de Gaulle in the Fifth by nationalizing industries in the new or growing sectors of the economy and by restructuring industries in the mature as well as the new sectors of the economy. The Socialist nationalizations really only consolidated the already extensive influence of the French state over the economy.

The nationalization of financial and industrial concerns

This is not to suggest, however, that nationalization was enthusiastically welcomed by all in the nation. Public opinion was more favorable than not, although this waned over time, as the nationalized industries lost money and the neoliberal right stepped up its attacks. In April 1980, 40% were in favor of nationalization versus 38% opposed; by October 1983, only 34% remained in favor versus 46% opposed. And by 1986, only 10% of the French claimed to be satisfied with the nationalization of the banks and industry.[63]

Business heads, by contrast, were initially for the most part opposed, and only with hindsight were willing to admit that nationalization turned out all right, primarily because it restructured, recapitalized, and streamlined operations, most importantly by allowing them to dismiss employees almost at will.[64] CEOs in general had been extremely apprehensive of the Socialist victory, given the prospects of nationalization, so much so that when the Socialists came into power, many companies panicked. Shell even asked one major consulting company to examine whether it should pull out of France altogether.[65] Even top managers on the left were not all convinced that nationalization was a good thing: one saw it as "a

---

[63]SOFRES, *L'état de l'opinion 1988*, p. 30.

[64]This was basically true for all but one of the CEOs interviewed for this study, whether on the left or the right.

[65]Comment by a top manager in a major consulting firm. Interview with author, May 1991.

little stupid," and was afraid that the result would have been like Renault. But he recognized subsequently that "without nationalization, French industry would not be where it is today."[66] Another, echoing the sentiments of CEOs generally, noted that the nationalizations did bring about important changes, although not what the Socialists had intended: "They did in fact fire people, and they recapitalized."[67] Yet another, Jean Gandois, who had himself resigned from Rhône-Poulenc because of the restructurings in his sector of industry, nevertheless admitted the need for restructuring – given that business in all countries, whether public or private, had to adapt to the new situation, and to modernize.[68] This view was shared by others such as Jean-Louis Beffa of Saint-Gobain, who also noted that not only was the state not too *gourmand,* or hungry, a shareholder in its demand for dividends (thus allowing it to reinvest its profits), it also enabled the company to take on a level of debt that was a bit excessive, that might have disquieted a private shareholder, and to set up certain deals that would otherwise have been impossible.[69] Even those such as Marc Vienot of the Société Générale, who found the logic of nationalization "peculiar," nevertheless thought that nationalization of his bank worked out fine.[70] And almost all agreed that, at the very least, some of the major industries were protected from foreign takeover and saved, in particular, Bull, Thomson, Péchiney, and Usinor-Sacilor. Only one banker, in fact, was reluctant to say that the nationalizations had turned out all right, insisting that the only way to gauge their performance adequately as public enteprises by contrast with how they might have done had they remained private would be to compare performance not with the past, as most do, but with the growth period in the eighties itself.[71]

Business and public views of nationalization, in any event, made little difference to the outcome. Nationalization was the product of an extremely restricted group of Socialist members of the government and close advisors. The group included the Prime Minister and a few top

[66]José Bidegain, number two in the Ministry of Industry as special assistant to Minister Fauroux and former director of personnel at Saint-Gobain. Interview with author, Paris, March 7, 1991.

[67]Descours, interview with author.

[68]Jean Gandois, CEO of Péchiney at the time of interview. Interview with author, Paris, July 2, 1991. See also the discussions in Chapter 9.

[69]Jean-Louis Beffa, CEO of Saint-Gobain. Interview with author, Paris, May 13, 1991.

[70]Testimony by Marc Vienot, CEO of Société Générale, *Rapport de la Commission d'Enquête sur les conditions dans lesquelles ont été effectuées les opérations de privatisation d'entreprises et de banques appartenant au secteur public depuis le 6 août 1986,* Assemblée Nationale no. 969, 3 vols., *Journal Officiel,* October 29, 1989, vol. 2, p. 823.

[71]Lévy-Lang, interview with author.

individuals in his office, including Jean Peyrelevade, in charge of arbitrations; the President and a few men in his cabinet, including Jacques Attali, Alain Boublil, and F. X. Stasse under Pierre Bérégovoy's coordination; the Ministry of Finance under Jacques Delors, which quickly took charge of the banking and finance nationalizations; and the Secretary of State, Le Garrec, who dealt mainly with the industrial nationalizations together with Minister of Industry Pierre Dreyfus and his cabinet director, Loïk Le Floch-Prigent. Outside of these individuals, there was little or no consultation other than with the leaders of the various groupings in the governmental majority: Jean-Pierre Chevènement, Charles Fiterman, Michel Jobert, and Michel Rocard, who, as ministers, were consulted in the official meetings. The political parties as such had no direct role in the formulation process and were not consulted as such.[72] And Parliament, although of course an integral part of the process, also had little real impact on the policy, which it passed with great speed despite a good deal of debate.[73]

The Socialists' nationalizations of industry left the state owning thirteen of the twenty largest firms in France and a controlling share in many other French companies. These nationalizations provided the government with at least a foothold if not a full share in most sectors of the economy: in mature sectors of industry such as heavy manufacturing, chemicals, textiles, aluminum, and steel; and in growing sectors such as arms, electronics, computers, and communications. More specifically, the government acquired 100% of the shares in the Compagnie Générale d'Électricité (CGE – a heavy manufacturing and engineering conglomerate), the Compagnie Générale de Constructions Téléphoniques (CGCT), Thomson-Brandt (the electronics and communications giant), Rhône-Poulenc (textiles and chemicals), Péchiney-Ugine-Kuhlman (PUK – in aluminum and chemicals), and Saint-Gobain–Pont à Mousson (in glass, paper, and metals). It converted state debt into majority ownership (95%) in the case of the two steel companies Sacilor and Usinor. In addition, it

[72]Barreau and Le Nay, "Du programme commun," p. 29.
[73]The nationalization bill, drafted over the summer, was first submitted to the Conseil d'État for its advice, which it gave September 17; it was adopted by the Council of Ministers on September 23, and discussed in the National Assembly beginning on October 13. The special commission charged with examining the first law on nationalization considered 1,400 amendments, and completed its work relatively quickly, in 63 hours, 20 minutes of debate. A full debate on the law was allowed, with twice the number of amendments considered, and took 118 hours, 45 minutes. The first reading of the bill took two weeks, during which time the opposition engaged in a long procedural battle and offered over 2,500 amendments. The final vote occurred on December 17, 1981, at which point the Constitutional Council, *saisi*, or appealed to, by the opposition, rendered its opinion, which recognized the constitutional character of the nationalizations but criticized the price paid, requiring the government to redraft the law, which was finally adopted by Parliament on February 11, 1982.

acquired 51% of the shares of the two arms and aeronautical manufacturers Dassault-Breguet and Matra, majority control over CII-Honeywell Bull (in computers – with Honeywell retaining a 19.99% share), and a minority share of Roussel-Uclaf (in pharmaceuticals – with Hoechst retaining a majority share).[74]

The nationalizations of thirty-six small banks and two investment banks (Suez and Paribas) and the takeover of the remaining minority of private shares in three nationally controlled banks (the Crédit Lyonnais, BNP, and Société Générale) went hand in hand with the nationalizations of industry. These nationalizations left the state in control of 96% of deposits. But even here, nationalization represented no real break with the past since the largest French banks had been under state control since the Fourth Republic and, through them, the government had in any case virtual control over the flow of funds.

With all this pre-existing government control, the Socialists' actions with regard to the banks might have seemed excessive and perhaps unwise, given the adverse publicity attached to certain bank nationalizations, most notably the Rothschilds' bank. But it must be understood that many of the bank nationalizations followed naturally from the nationalizations of a number of industries that had themselves absorbed and/or created their own banks; for example, Dassault held the Vernes Bank; PUK, the CFP-Crédit Chimique; and Thomson, Financière Électrique.[75] Moreover, the nationalizations reinforced the government's control and assured it the means for providing loans to those nationalized as well as private enterprises targeted for support in the effort to make French industry more competitive at home and abroad.

That the Socialists nationalized at 100% rather than at 51% might also seem extreme. This was in fact the only main area of dissension among the small group of major actors: on one side was a sizable minority of Socialists including Michel Rocard and Finance Minister Jacques Delors, in favor of nationalization at 51%, on the other were many others, including Jean Le Garrec, Secretary of State in charge of the nationalizations. When President Mitterrand decided in favor of nationalizing at 100%, he made the nationalizations a lot more expensive than they might have been. Had they nationalized at 51%, the Socialists could have saved 30 billion francs and avoided some of the severe financial problems they encountered in their first two years in office.[76] But in so doing, they might have jeopardized the nationalization program itself, not so much because they would have alienated their Communist coalition partners, the as-

[74]For a full discussion of the nationalizations, see: Delion and Durupty, *Nationalisations*. See also: Zinsou, *Fer de lance*, pp. 68–71.

[75]See: Bellon, *Pouvoir financier*, p. 19.

[76]*L'Express*, June 14, 1983, p. 40.

sumption by many at the time, but rather because nationalization at 51% would have been very lengthy and open to litigation.[77] According to Le Garrec, if the companies had not been nationalized at 100%, they would have had to be acquired through the stock market, adding to the time and the costs, since by the time all the shares could have been bought, the price of the companies would have increased astronomically while their subsidiaries might have been sold. In addition, there would always be the problem of a veto by shareholders holding large minority portions of the stock.[78]

The only part of the nationalization program that was halted in response to outside pressure was that involving foreign-owned banks and industries. This was because the French feared international repercussions. Thus, the Socialists left Honeywell with its close to 20% ownership of CII-Honeywell Bull and Roussel-Uclaf with its majority ownership by Hoechst. And they left all foreign-owned banks alone. Other than this, the only impact business had in the nationalization process had to do with the price paid. Here is where lobbying by business, in particular through the offices of the COB, the stock market oversight commission, and through personal contacts with top members of government, was highly successful.

The owners, in fact, although given no choice but to accept the expropriation, were more than amply compensated. Proof that the government was more than generous, as one Socialist deputy noted, is that there were no lawsuits. In fact, Minister of Finance Jacques Delors, worried about possible international court cases, established a generous evaluation system.[79] This, however, was not deemed generous enough by the Conseil Constitutionnel, which granted a higher level of repayment to the shareholders. The result was that, for example, each share of Rhône-Poulenc that had traded as low as 45 francs not too long before, was exchanged for a bond worth 126 francs paying 16% interest. The overall cost of the nationalizations, moreover, was increased by $8 million, for a 30% increase in their price.

Government industrial policy and its impact

The nationalizations were accompanied by an industrial policy, the *politique de filières,* which, unlike Giscard's policy of promoting industry lead-

---

[77]Zinsou, *Fer,* pp. 68–71.

[78]Jean Le Garrec, former Secretary of State responsible for the nationalizations – conversation with author in Paris, May 15, 1991.

[79]This was based on three criteria: (1) the average share price between January 1, 1978, and December 31, 1980; (2) the net value of the firm as of December 31, 1981; and (3) the average of the profit from 1978, 1979, and 1980 multiplied by a factor of 10.

ers, encouraged a sort of vertical integration of firms through parent companies, affiliates, and subsidiaries designed to strengthen the entire range of products in each sector so as to lose nothing to imports and, thereby, to "reconquer the internal market." The Socialists reasoned that "the ability of an economy to compete depends on the capacity of its industrial sector to satisfy the large bulk of domestic needs, on the existence of a tightly knit and diversified industrial fabric, and on an ample stock of large as well as small firms. It is time to realize that [in Pierre Dreyfus's words] 'there are no doomed industries, only outmoded technologies.'"[80] As a result, the government engaged in an ambitious policy that recapitalized the nationalized industries while mandating the restructuring of most of the newly nationalized industries and some of the old under its control, including the chemicals industry, electronics, computers, and steel. Moreover, it also sought to restructure in the private sector with plans focused on machine tools, textiles, furniture, leather goods, and toys.

The Socialists' industrial policies for declining sectors generally sought greater concentration, an increase in output, and a reduction in imports. For a declining nationalized industry such as steel, the merger of the two steel makers Sacilor and Usinor was to be accompanied by ambitious production targets: steel output was to rise from 18 million metric tons in 1982 to 26 million in 1986. The coal industry similarly was to go from 18 million tons in 1981 to 30 million in 1990. For the mainly privately owned machine tool industry, moreover, the industrial policy promised an increase in government financial support (4 billion francs in subsidies, 3 billion francs in loans, and more through public procurement) and was designed to encourage further concentration and to permit the industry to take a leadership role in numerically controlled equipment, to double the industry's output in three years, and to cut imports from 60% to 30%.

The policy for a growing sector such as the electronics industry, which consisted of all nationalized industries, was even more ambitious. The five-year action program pledged to provide some 140 billion francs in subsidies and loans, create 80,000 jobs, boost production to 9% from an annual growth rate of 3%, and transform a 19 billion franc balance of payments deficit into a 14 billion franc surplus. In addition, it proposed to restructure the operations of Bull, Thomson, CGE, Matra, and CGCT to ensure that each specialized only in one or two areas, and to make Saint-Gobain leave the sector entirely.[81]

[80]Ministère de la Recherche et de l'Industrie, *Une politique industrielle pour la France: Actes des journées de travail des 15 et 16 Novembre 1982* (Paris: Documentation Française, 1982), p. 387.
[81]Jocelyne Barreau and Abdelaziz Mouline, *L'industrie électronique française: 29 ans de relations état–groupes industriels 1958–1986* (Paris: Librairie Générale de Droit et de Jurisprudence, 1987), pp. 169–170; and Barreau et al., *L'état entrepreneur.*

Changes in government policies toward business

The government's overall industrial policy, thus, at least at first refused to distinguish between rising and declining sectors of the economy, assuming that France could compete successfully in all sectors of the international market. One drawback of this policy is that it reinforced rigidities in the French economic system and delayed the reallocation of resources from declining to growing sectors of the economy. And it remained a problem to the extent that the government did not have the wherewithal to finance as needed all sectors of the economy.[82] Moreover, although a number of the sectoral policies were successful, others were not.[83] Numerous are those who have been quick to point out the limits of French industrial policy, arguing that where a firm was weak or had a poor business strategy, no amount of industrial policy made a difference, as in the machine tool industry, textiles, and wood.[84]

What is more, in certain areas the Socialists' industrial policy delayed the radical restructuring that was necessary to turn some of the declining industries around. Thus, in the case of the steel industry, the government temporized in the beginning, unwilling to go back on Mitterrand's promise of 1979 to increase steel production, rather than to close plants, and it therefore made overly optimistic projections, much as in the past, to justify not engaging in the necessary restructuring. It took the government until 1984 to admit that "socialist *dirigisme* could mine more coal or roll more steel, but it could not create buyers for these products."[85]

In steel as in other declining sectors, shifting resources proved difficult, and the Socialists found themselves at first doing as the previous government had done, that is, supporting lame ducks rather than promoting the growth industries of the future, and thus reneging on their pledges of aid. The electronics industry, for example, received less than a third of the aid it was promised.[86] In some industries, moreover, the Socialists found it nearly impossible to streamline operations and, thereby, cut employment, so much so that subsidies to firms to keep workers were so high that it would have been cheaper to pay workers not to produce.[87]

By 1983, paralleling the Great U-turn in macroeconomic policy, how-

[82]For a full discussion of Socialist industrial policy, see: Hall, "Socialism in One Country," pp. 89–95; Vincent Wright, "Industrial Policy-Making under the Mitterrand Presidency," *Government and Opposition,* vol. 19, no. 3 (summer 1984), pp. 290–293; and Bela Belassa, "Politique industrielle Socialiste."
[83]On the failures and the reasons why, see: Pierre Dacier, Jean-Louis Levet, and Jean-Claude Tourret, *Les dossiers noirs de l'industrie française* (Paris: Fayard, 1985).
[84]For example, Lévy-Lang and Lebègue, interviews with author.
[85]Levy, "Tocqueville's Revenge," p. 64.
[86]Le Bolloc'h-Puges, *Politique industrielle* – cited in Levy, "Tocqueville's Revenge," p. 64.
[87]Levy, "Tocqueville's Revenge," p. 65; and Cohen, *État brancardier,* pp. 230–231.

ever, the Socialists did begin to support the necessary streamlining, eliminating jobs and, thereby, increasing unemployment. For the nationalized industries in particular, after a brief countercyclical increase in employment in 1982 (up by 3% over 1981, largely as a result of the restructurings), public sector employment in industry followed the downward trend of the private sector, such that between 1981 and 1985, public industrial employment decreased by 7.2% whereas industry as a whole lost 11.5% of its labor force.[88]

It was only in 1984, however, that the steel, coal, shipbuilding, and automobile industries felt the turnabout in policy. Steel, which had a $1.2 billion projected deficit for 1984 that was 60% higher than that of 1983, first felt the effects in January, when Usinor was refused a 6.2 billion francs request for funding, and instructed, along with Sacilor, to balance its budgets by 1988, which meant cutting jobs by close to 40,000 employees and production by 30%. By March 1984, moreover, the new industrial policy for the steel industry called for reducing capacity from 25 million tons a year to 18 million tons by 1987, with a projected loss of 30,000 jobs, or one in three steelmaking jobs. In 1984 alone, 20,000 job losses were to be accepted. In exchange, however, the Socialists promised to have invested a total of 17.5 billion francs between 1982 and 1986 in the attempt to modernize the industry. The coal industry, which had a projected deficit of $100 million, had a similar experience. It, too, was first instructed to cut jobs (by an estimated 25,000) and production (by 30%) by 1988. And things were not much better in the automotive industry, where manufacturers also had to streamline operations by cutting jobs.

In the end, for all its faults, the Socialists' industrial policy did have a positive impact. Most importantly, this policy, together with the nationalization of major banks and industries, served to preserve the industrial base of the nation in a time of world recession and low business confidence, thus priming the pump when no one else was going to.[89] Moreover, it ultimately helped transform that industrial base, by serving not only to recapitalize the nationalized industries but also to rationalize them, engineering their change from horizontally diversified firms to vertically integrated ones at the same time that it enabled them to cut jobs without the labor unrest they would have encountered as private concerns. Although in the previous decade the conservative government had in its own *dirigiste* way attempted to encourage such reorganization and restructuring, it had failed in a number of the areas most in need because

[88]Durupty, *Privatisations,* pp. 10–11. See also: *Rapport 1986 du Haut Conseil du Secteur Public.*
[89]Bob Kuttner, "France's Atari Socialism," *The New Republic,* March 17, 1983, p. 21.

it did not have the same kind of control over industry which only nation-alization allowed.[90]

Through nationalization, in brief, the Socialist government was able to do for the newly nationalized industries what those industries had been unable to do enough of for themselves as private enterprises during the previous decade, that is, restructure, eliminate jobs, close obsolete plants, and so forth. Instead, as private concerns, they had for the most part been continuing to finance with their profitable operations what Georges Besse, the late head of Renault (and former head of Péchiney), called the "cash-flow incinerators," or losing operations.[91] The reorganization and restructuring of the nationalized industries, by focusing each of their efforts on one main kind of product, made it possible to avoid destructive competition, duplication, and the dispersion of investments, sites, and research programs, as well as to establish companies of a size to make them internationally competitive. Moreover, because the state was much less demanding in terms of dividends, it enabled the firms to reinvest their profits and raise their level of savings.

More generally, it was only once the state became controlling stock-holder in Elf-Aquitaine, Péchiney, Rhône-Poulenc, and CDF-Chimie that it was able to reorganize the chemical industry effectively, despite numerous previous efforts. Péchiney gave up its losing operations in the area while the other three divided up the various parts of the industry among themselves, for example, with Rhône-Poulenc in pharmaceuti-cals and *chimie fine,* Elf-Aquitaine in halogens and petrochemicals, and CDF-Chimie in organic chemicals and plastics. With the exception of CDF-Chimie, which ended up with the losing operations of the oth-er companies, the redistribution of activities along with the new capital proved salutary.[92] Similarly, moreover, restructuring in electronics proved successful. Thomson and Matra took electronic components; Thomson also gained consumer electronics; Bull took over computers; CIT-Alcatel (CGE) and Bull got office electronics; and CGE took pub-lic telephones. The restructurings in this area saved Bull, and consoli-dated CIT-Alcatel, Thomson, and Matra. There was only one major failure, that of CGCT.[93]

Restructuring also proved helpful to the banking and financial con-cerns. UAP took back Worms; CCF got Rothschild-Européenne de Ban-que; Suez took over the industrial sector, mining, and real estate opera-tions of Rothschild as well as of the Vernes bank; and CIC took charge of

[90]For a discussion of the successes of the conservative government's restructuring efforts, see: Cohen, "Informed Bewilderment," pp. 21–48.
[91]Bruno Thomas, "Défense et illustration des nationalisations," *Le Monde,* Oct. 25, 1985.
[92]See Zinsou, *Fer de lance,* ch. 5.
[93]Ibid., ch. 6; and Bauer and Cohen, *Grandes manoeuvres.*

BUE.[94] In fact, even those who were vehemently opposed to the nationalizations, and worked hard for privatization, had good things to say about the performance of the banks. Thus, Jean-Maxime Levèque, nominated head of the Crédit Lyonnais in July 1986, a major opponent of nationalization who saw himself as the prime mover behind the idea of privatization between 1982 and 1986, nevertheless praised the performance of his bank under previous CEOs, finding that they had managed to put the bank back on its feet since the crisis of 1974 that had hit the Crédit Lyonnais much harder than its two large rivals, the BNP and Société Générale.[95] Similarly, the Société Générale did well under nationalization, with the period between 1983 and 1986 resulting in an average increase of 16% in gross income (*revenu brut d'exploitation*).

The financial implications of the nationalizations

Proof of the success of the nationalizations is evidenced by the fact that the nationalized industries went from tremendous losses to financial health in a relatively short period of time. In 1982, the newly nationalized industries lost 16 billion francs and the older public enterprises of EDF (electricity), GDF (gas), SNCF (railroad), RATP (Paris transport), Air France, and Charbonnages (coal) lost some 27 billion francs, compared with total losses of 19 billion francs in 1981 and 2.2 billion in 1980.[96] The steel industry alone lost $1.3 billion in 1983, 66% of the total losses of the nationalized industries.[97] For the public industrial enterprises in particular, losses in 1982 were at 12.3 billion francs; in 1984 they had sunk to 19.7 billion francs.[98]

By 1985, however, the picture had grown rosier. The public industrial enterprises' losses were down to 9.9 billion francs.[99] But more importantly, many companies had rounded the corner to renewed profitability. Five of the biggest industrial groups nationalized in 1982, for example, turned a combined profit of over 6 billion francs in 1985 – close to 2 billion better than in 1984 and clearly a whole lot better than the losses they racked up in 1982 of close to 5 billion francs.[100] By contrast, some of

[94]Hubert Bonin, "Les banques d'affaires et la sortie de la crise," *Le Débat,* May–September 1986, pp. 146, 155–156.

[95]Testimony of Jean-Maxime Leveque, *Rapport sur les opérations de privatisation,* vol. 2, pp. 685–686.

[96]Hall, "Socialism in One Country," p. 90.

[97]*Business Week,* April 23, 1984, p. 40.   [98]Durupty, *Privatisations,* p. 19.

[99]Ibid., p. 19.

[100]Net profits between 1981 to 1985 went from −286 million francs to 2.4 billion francs for Rhône-Poulenc, from 586 million francs to 1.185 billion francs for CGE, from −167 million francs to 583 million francs for Thomson, from 227 million francs

the other nationalized industries remained in trouble, such as CDF-Chimie, Renault, and the steel companies.[101] The nationalized industries, in short, were on their way to recovery, but some were closer than others.

The Socialists' restructuring and reorganization of industry could not have been successful without the vast infusion of public capital in the nationalized enterprises (see Table 4.1 above). This was something that went far beyond any previous such infusions, and was certainly one of the most important elements in promoting economic recovery. It was money, more than anything else, that gave the newly nationalized industries the chance to become competitive again. Even those heads of industry interviewed who insisted that nationalization had made little difference to the health of business and the economy had to admit, however grudgingly, that the infusion of capital at this high a level made a significant difference.[102] Ambroise Roux, for example, in noting that the state had recapitalized Péchiney and made up for the company's immense losses, admitted that he could not see how private investors could have righted the situation, given that Péchiney was losing 3 billion francs per year.[103] Only one respondent, the banker Lévy-Lang, suggested that the market could have performed the same function even without nationalization, given the opening of the markets.[104]

In the comparatively short period the Socialists were in office for the first time, government grants and loans for capital investment for modernization were an estimated $5 billion – according to one source this represented approximately twenty times more than had been invested privately over the previous twenty years.[105] Outside of loans, the subsidies and capital grants that public enterprises received between 1980 and 1986 went from 21.8 billion francs to 65.9 billion, for an increase of 202%.[106] The big five in particular, that is, CGE, Saint-Gobain, Péchiney,

to 1.524 billion francs for Saint-Gobain, and from −1.636 billion francs to 809 million francs for Péchiney.

[101]CDF-Chimie, which had absorbed the losing operations of Péchiney and Rhône-Poulenc, continued to post losses of −965 million francs in 1985, down from its high of −2.855 billion in 1983. Renault, recovering from its failed association with American Motors, had a deficit of −10.925 billion francs in 1985, down from its high of −12.555 billion francs in 1984. And the steel companies were still posting losses of −5.386 billion francs for Sacilor and −3.487 for Usinor in 1985, although this was down from their high in 1984 (when the government finally bit the bullet) of −8.141 billion for Sacilor and −7.399 for Usinor. Observatoire des Entreprises Nationales, *Le secteur public industriel en 1985* (Paris: Ministère de l'Industrie, des P. et T. et du Tourisme, 1986).

[102]See the discussion in Chapter 6.

[103]Testimony by Ambroise Roux, CEO of CGE before nationalization, *Rapport sur les opérations de privatisation*, vol. 2, pp. 787–788.

[104]Lévy-Lang, interview with author.   [105]*Boston Globe*, Dec. 8, 1985.

[106]Durupty, *Privatisations*, p. 20.

Thomson, and Rhône-Poulenc, did very well, especially by comparison with the ten years prior to nationalization, when these companies had only received on average 150 million francs per year from private share-holders (see Table 4.1).[107] Between 1982 and 1984 alone, these enterprises received ten times more in capital than private shareholders had provided in the eight years between 1974 and 1981. This in turn enabled those companies to have a capital investment growth rate of more than 8% a year and an increase of research spending of 23% in three years, with the percentage of research spending in the overall budget going from 3.45% in 1981 to 4.7% in 1984.[108]

Of the capital grants given to industry, however, it was often the older, declining industries that received the lion's share, convincing some that Mitterrand was continuing the lame duck policy of his predecessor by favoring declining over growing sectors of industry. Companies in difficulty such as steel, Renault, and CDF-Chimie received 47.3 billion francs in capital grants, or 68% of the total, while the electronics industry received only 11.7 billion francs, or 16.9% of the total. This led the High Council of the Public Sector to question whether, at the risk of compromising the construction of industries of the future, these grants were indeed ensuring the efficient recovery of those of the past.[109] The Council's fears were premature, however, because the capital infusions enabled the very companies that could have been written off as hopelessly in decline, such as steel, to turn themselves around.

Other problems remained, however, primarily the fact that the very enterprises that received the least in capital grants from the state provided the most in dividends to the state. France Télécom, most significantly, was used by Jean-Pierre Chevènement, whose ministry included post and telecommunications, to finance the restructuring project, turning the DGT, the Direction Générale des Télécom, into what critics saw as a "milking cow."[110] Not only was the DGT contributing to the general budget amounts totaling 2.1 billion francs in 1984 and 2 billion in 1983, it was also providing capital grants of 1.7 billion francs directly to Bull, Thomson, and CGCT. Moreover, Saint-Gobain, which between 1982 and 1986 turned over 557 million francs to the state, only received one capital grant for 200 million from the SFPI in 1982.[111] This resulted in an unsatisfactory situation on the purely financial level, according to the Senate Fi-

[107]Ibid., p. 20.   [108]Messine, "Nationalisations," p. 6.
[109]*Rapport 1986 du Haut Conseil du Secteur Public* – cited in Durupty, *Privatisations,* pp. 20–21.
[110]*L'Expansion,* September 21–October 4, 1984 – cited in Nikolaos Zahariadis, *The Political Economy of Privatization in Britain and France,* Ph.D. dissertation, University of Georgia, Athens, 1992, p. 324.
[111]Durupty, *Privatisations,* p. 21.

nance Commission, because it made profitable companies pay for the losses of unprofitable ones, and in effect penalized firms for being profitable.[112] Although this may have been true, it was also the case that the state was a less greedy shareholder than private shareholders had been in the past. In the case of Saint-Gobain, for instance, before nationalization shareholders took three-fourths of profits, with the banks demanding a big distribution in terms of dividends, leaving the firm without the ability to invest. Although top management had been worried about state ownership, it turns out that the state took much less than the shareholders, by a ratio of 5 to 1.[113]

Moreover, between the capital grants and the greater savings, investment by the nationalized enterprises grew enormously. During the three-year period between 1981 and 1985, investment in the newly nationalized industries grew by 87% and those of the old public sector industries by 52%, by contrast with the investments of private enterprises, which increased by only 38%.[114] Moreover, the growth rates of investment varied by company, with some of the newly nationalized industries such as steel at 128%, Matra at 303%, Bull at 224%, Thomson at 102%, and Rhône-Poulenc at 91%, outdistancing others, such as Péchiney at 14%. Many of the long-nationalized companies also did quite well, with SNIAS increasing its investments by a rate of 301%, EMC by 103%, and CDF-Chimie by 132%.[115]

Nationalization thus did a tremendous amount for industry. The state turned out to be more generous financially than the previous shareholders and more helpful in the modernization process than any private shareholder could possibly have been. In fact, only the infusion of capital at this high a level could have revived traditionally undercapitalized French industry. And politically, only nationalized industries could have received such an infusion of public capital. Had the newly nationalized industries remained in private hands while receiving such public capital, people would surely have cried foul, claiming that the government was using public revenues to line the pockets of private individuals. Nationalization thus proved an extremely effective way of recapitalizing French industry and of putting it back on the road to economic recovery.

The shift to market-oriented policies

Moreover, the fact that a Socialist government was in power enabled firms to dismiss employees without the kinds of difficulties that any right-wing

[112]Commission des Finances du Sénat, *Rapport d'information*, no. 8 (1986) – cited in Durupty, *Privatisations*, p. 21.
[113]Bidegain, interview with author. [114]Durupty, *Privatisations*, p. 14. [115]Ibid.

government would have had. Numbers of companies were able to shed one-third of their workforce without significant labor problems. Saint-Gobain, for example, laid off some 20,000 workers out of 60,000.[116] But although the Socialists managed this process successfully, that is, without the significant and sustained labor unrest a conservative government might have faced (albeit with numbers of demonstrations by steel workers and strikes by CGT members in Renault plants), they did this at significant political cost, since they necessarily alienated a goodly portion of their national constituency and lost their coalition partner, the Communist Party, in the process. But they really had no other choice, especially with the nationalized industries such as Renault, Sacilor, and Usinor, which had been overmanned for years while their profits, competitiveness, and productivity had kept dropping. Once they changed their macroeconomic policies from expansionist to restrictive, and there was no more money to fund these operations as there had been in the past, the microeconomic decisions were in some sense made for them, and not only in employment policy.

The change in direction at the macroeconomic level, from expansionist to restrictive policies, was accompanied at the microeconomic level by a gradual shift in views of the appropriate role of the state with regard to industry, from a highly interventionist one toward the progressive disengagement of the state. Between 1981 and 1983, government policies toward the nationalized industries in particular were, in the formulation at least, much more interventionist than they had been in the past, even precipitating an occasional resignation.[117] In fact, as we shall see later, the implementation of industrial policy under the Socialists, much as under previous regimes, involved as much accommodation and even co-optation as it did confrontation. Nonetheless, Ministry of Industry Chevènement's replacement by Laurent Fabius in May 1983 does mark a significant shift in the view of the appropriate formulation of government policy toward industry. The Ministry of Industry thereafter returned to its traditional respect for the autonomy of public enterprises, and to maintaining control over the nationalized enterprises in the same way previous regimes had.[118] This meant leaving most internal management decisions up to the firms themselves and relying on negotiated contracts between the state and the public enterprises on the firm's goals and objectives and the state's commitments.[119] Mitterrand himself underlined this change when

---

[116]Bidegain, interview with author.   [117]See the discussions in Chapters 7 and 9.

[118]A notable exception to this new policy occurred in the summer of 1984, when the chairman of the Crédit Commercial de France, Daniel Deguen, was fired because he refused to lend to Creusot-Loire which, as it turned out, went bankrupt a few months later.

[119]See Chapter 7.

he declared his new determination that "the nationalized industries should have total autonomy of decision and action."[120]

Under Fabius's direction, the Ministry of Industry began a different set of relationships with industry: it not only reaffirmed the traditional autonomy of public enterprises, it also began putting its faith in the market (with Fabius warning that "heads would roll" in companies that failed to return to profitability by 1985) and put profit back into fashion (with Fabius exhorting French firms to "get out of the red").[121] Moreover, planning took an even lesser role than before as Fabius explained that his view paralleled that of the German socialists of the past thirty years, that is: "The market as much as possible, the Plan as much as necessary."[122]

Finally, Fabius abandoned the policy of rescuing lame ducks that had begun under Giscard. This was symbolized by Fabius's refusal to rescue Creusot-Loire, the private steel and mechanical engineering conglomerate, one month before he became Prime Minister, which triggered the largest bankruptcy in French history. The refusal itself, however, was nothing Fabius had himself initially wanted; it was thrust upon him as the result of the failure of a complex set of negotiated attempts at rescue.[123] But it became a symbol of the turnabout in policy and of the disengagement of the state that Fabius was to pursue as Prime Minister.

The disengagement affected all aspects of government policies toward industry. In emphasizing firm profitability, Fabius had to accept the layoffs and increasing unemployment that were necessarily involved in streamlining operations. Moreover, in asserting public enterprise autonomy, he could no longer intervene when companies withdrew from government planning priority areas, for example, when Thomson sold its activities in telecommunications to its only domestic competitor.[124] And finally, in demanding firm competitiveness, he could no longer subsidize as before the oversized, underproductive sectors in decline such as the steel, coal, shipbuilding, and automotive industries.

The disengagement also affected that seemingly most sacred of policies: nationalization. Very early on, the Socialists had passed a variety of laws including the law on savings of 1983 designed to enable the nationalized enterprises themselves to dilute state ownership through the sale of nonvoting shares. And they contemplated others, including one as early as October 1982 that was to allow nationalized industries to "acquire or cede shares in enterprises as a function of their strategic objectives," that

---

[120]*Le Monde,* May 28, 1983.

[121]Bruno Thomas, "Laurent Fabius, PDG dénationalisateur," *Le Monde,* March 31, 1985.

[122]Laurent Fabius, "Qui a peur de l'économie mixte," *Le Monde,* Feb. 28, 1989.

[123]For the bankruptcy of Creusot-Loire, see: Cohen, *État brancardier.*

[124]See the discussion in Levy, "Tocqueville's Revenge."

is, to acquire or sell off subsidiaries; but this was never put on the agenda of the National Assembly for fear of the reaction of the Socialists' own majority.[125] Later, in 1985, the projected *loi de respiration,* which was to allow the subsidiaries of nationalized enterprises to go back to the private sector, was debated but never passed. But even before this, numerous nationalized industries, in need of capital that the government was no longer willing or able to provide at the desired level, had already started down the path to privatization, either legally, by using the law on savings of 1983 to issue *titres participatifs* and to float *certificats d'investissement,* or nonvoting shares, or illegally, with the tacit agreement of the government, by selling off subsidiaries.

The *titres participatifs* were first used in 1983 as a way to raise money by the nationalized enterprises. Saint-Gobain was the first to do this for 700 million francs, followed by Rhône-Poulenc for 600 million, as well as CGE and Renault for 1 billion each. All told, 25.358 billion francs were raised in this way.[126] By 1985 and even more so in early 1986, however, as the market developed, the less costly *certificats d'investissement* became more popular, with nationalized enterprises such as Péchiney, Thomson CSF, Alcatel, CII (Crédit Industriel et Commercial), and Saint-Gobain seeing this as a way of increasing their capital as well as of beginning the privatization process. The banks, too, issued nonvoting shares to raise capital, with Suez by the end of January 1986 already putting together a capital funding issue which would take it down the path to denationalization.[127]

Moreover, numbers of nationalized companies also sold off their subsidiaries, illegal though this was, with the full knowledge of the government. This was the case for approximately seventy affiliates of the nationalized enterprises, a majority of which were sold to foreign buyers.[128] In addition, the heads of such nationalized concerns as Rhône-Poulenc, Thomson, CGE, Paribas, and Suez had also been working on denationalization plans long before the right's return to power.[129] Already in 1984, moreover, André Rousselet, CEO of Havas (the communications giant that had been nationalized in 1945 because its owners had been collaborators), had approached the Prime Minister to propose his firm for

[125]Durupty, *Privatisations,* pp. 26–27. [126]Ibid., p. 25.
[127]*Financial Times,* January 25, 1986.
[128]These included five sales by CGE, the largest of which was to a French buyer for its activities in small electric motors, and a sixth by Thomson of the Compagnie des Lampes to Philips; three other sales by Thomson; five by Péchiney, including two of its aluminum operations to Spanish firms and its dye operations to the British ICI; one by Renault of its electronic subsidiary Rénix to the American Bendix; and so on. René Foch, "Fantasmes anciens et réalités modernes," *Le Monde,* Aug. 20, 1986; and Durupty, *Privatisations,* pp. 18, 28.
[129]*London Financial Times,* January 25, 1986.

privatization by the Socialists, as a way of enabling the left to demonstrate the difference between that which naturally was of the public domain and that which should be returned to the private sector.[130] This, however, was too much to ask.

In short, the need of the nationalized industries for more capital at a time when the government couldn't spare any led Fabius to allow privatization in through the back door, and thereby to back into an everyday policy that paved the way for the neoliberals' heroic policies with respect to privatization. Thus, there is every reason to believe that, had the neoliberal right not won the 1986 elections, the Socialists themselves would have continued the process of denationalization. The very fact that Mitterrand had initially been willing to go along with Chirac's intention to use the *loi d'habilitation* or enabling legislation to privatize by decree, rather than through the normal more lengthy parliamentary process, lends further support to this suggestion. Mitterrand's subsequent refusal to sign the first actual privatization decree in July 1986 indicates not so much a change of heart as a protest at the extent of the denationalization proposed. Moreover, even though there were certain denationalizations that the Socialists would never have countenanced, such as that of the television station, TF1, the Socialists themselves had begun the process of deregulation in this area by liberalizing the programming of radio and television, freeing up local radio stations completely as of November 1981 and local television stations as of December 1985

CONCLUSION

Ironically enough, the Socialists lost the parliamentary elections just as it was becoming clear that they had managed to put the French economy back on the road to recovery. Inflation was the lowest that it had been in years, having dropped close to ten points, from 14% in 1981 to 4.7% in 1985. Business confidence was up. Private entrepreneurs even credited the Socialists with "renewing the capitalist spirit in France" and improving business generally by producing a favorable labor climate, as evidenced by the relatively few strikes and the lower rise in wages.[131] The stock market was booming – so much so that the bull market that began with the economic austerity program of 1983 had meant a 150% rise in the general stock market index. The companies nationalized in 1982 were on the whole doing quite well. And even those nationalized enterprises that

---

[130]Testimony by André Rousselet, CEO of Havas before privatization, *Rapport sur les opérations de privatisation*, vol. 2, pp. 764.
[131]*Financial Times*, June 26, 1986.

had been in serious trouble for a very long time – Renault and the newly merged steel companies, Sacilor and Usinor – had started showing signs of improvement.

The overall value of the nationalized concerns, moreover, had increased threefold, with the nationalized banks and industrial groups having gone from being worth 45 billion francs at the time of their acquisition in 1982 to approximately 150 billion francs at the beginning of 1986. Public finances were also in reasonably good shape, as even the new right-wing neoliberal government had to admit when the report which it had itself ordered found that the Socialists had left neither a bad nor a disorganized situation.[132] Unemployment, however, had increased by 874,200 between May 1981 and October 1985, and the real rate of growth in the GDP for 1981 to 1985 was only 1.5%, by contrast with 2.4% for the OECD countries all together. But buying power after all adjustments to income, which had increased significantly in 1981 (up 2.8%) and 1982 (up 2.6%) only to decrease the following two years by 0.7%, had started to rise again, increasing by 1.1% in 1985. And the deficit in the foreign balance of payments had stabilized. The Socialists' economic success had been such, in fact, that even the conservative English weekly *The Economist* editorialized long before the elections of March 1986 that, based on economic performance alone, Mitterrand and the Socialists should be given a second chance.[133] They were not.

[132]*Le Monde*, April 30, 1985.   [133]*The Economist*, October 19, 1985.

5

Dirigiste *disengagement (1986 to 1988)*

When, four months before the elections of March 1986, Alain Madelin, who was to be Minister of Industry in Chirac's neoliberal government from 1986 to 1988, declared that "Today, everyone is a liberal," he was not far from the truth.[1] For if liberalism meant the easing of state *dirigisme* and the loosening of state regulation, then it was something that actually started with the Socialists, although the neoliberals would have been the last to admit this. During the first five years the Socialists were in power, neoliberal theorists attacked them for greatly increasing the traditional state interventionism in the economy and, often using arguments based on the experience of the United States or borrowed from Anglo-American proponents of laissez-faire capitalism, they contended that on-going authoritarian state *dirigisme* was responsible for the sorry shape of France's economy. During this same period, many politicians on the right who only a few years before when in power had themselves been the staunchest supporters of state *dirigisme* and a centralized industrial planning process became born-again neoliberals who began calling for liberty in all things economic, demanding the denationalization of banking and industry and the deregulation of price controls, exchange rates, and the financial markets as well as of the workplace.

These demands for "less state" and more "*liberté*" constituted the economic program for the right's winning electoral campaign of 1986. In large measure, Jacques Chirac's neoliberal right government of 1986–1988 kept to this program, taking state disengagement much further in the direction first charted by the Socialists by championing extensive privatization and deregulation. Moreover, it brought down inflation

---

[1]Alain Madelin stated on the "Club de la Presse" on Europe 1 on November 3, 1985, that the liberalism of a Giscard, a Chirac, or a Barre "all go in the same direction. Today, everyone is a liberal. We no longer even pose the problem of socialism. Laurent Fabius buried it once and for all in his debate with Chirac." *Le Monde,* November 5, 1985.

while promoting industrial competitiveness through even more supply-side measures, for example, through cutting taxes, eliminating restrictions on business, opening the markets further, and overhauling monetary policy.

For all this, however, a certain amount of *dirigisme* did remain. Not only did the government not go nearly as far as the campaign rhetoric suggested in instituting "less state," but the way in which Chirac's government implemented its policies was also no less *dirigiste* than that of previous governments. Privatization in particular was a centrally controlled, highly regulated affair in which the government picked the *noyau dur,* or small group of hard-core investors, to whom to sell a controlling interest in the privatized companies while limiting the amount of foreign investment, at the same time that it provided for no representation of small, individual shareholders on the board of directors. But it was also true in the deregulatory realm, where liberalizing policies on the one hand were balanced out by state control on the other. This was nevertheless the beginning of the change in the structure of ownership and control of French business that only accelerated under successive governments of the left and right.

THE NEOLIBERAL ECONOMIC PROJECT

Once the Socialists came to power in 1981, neoliberal thought flourished. Countless books were published by neoliberal theorists who traced the French roots of liberalism in the work of the Abbé Sieyès, Jean-Baptiste Say, Alexis de Tocqueville, and Benjamin Constant or who combined the work of French and Anglo-American philosophers as diverse as Montesquieu, Rousseau, Bela Farago, and Friedrich von Hayek in a modern version of liberalism.[2] There were also neoliberals who instead explicated and applied to France the Anglo-American version of economic liberalism as elaborated by members of the Chicago School of Economics and, again, Hayek.[3] And there were the neoliberals who focused on American "liberal" political practice either by describing the politics of Reagan and the neoconservatives or by contrasting the American "liberal" reliance on law to mediate conflicts

[2]See, for example, Guy Sorman, *L'état minimum* (Paris: Albin Michel, 1985), for the French roots of liberalism, and Jean-Marie Benoist, *Les outils de la liberté* (Paris: Laffont, 1985) for a modern version of liberalism. See also: Yves Cannac, *Le juste pouvoir* (Paris: Lattès, 1982); Jean-François Revel *Le rejet de l'état* (Paris: Grasset, 1984); Jacquillat, *Désétatiser.*

[3]See Henri Lepage, *Demain le capitalisme* (Paris: Librairie Générale Française, 1978); Florin Aftalion, E. Claasen, Pascal Salin, et al., *La liberté à refaire* (Paris: Hachette, 1984); and Guy Sorman, *La solution libérale* (Paris: Fayard, 1984).

with the French *dirigiste* reliance on the state.[4] Finally, there were the neoliberal politicians who focused almost exclusively on France and the program that was to unleash the productive forces in the society by liberalizing the economy.[5]

The neoliberals generally were committed to implementing policies related to (1) reducing the size of the state and the extent of its intervention in the economy; (2) allowing market mechanisms to operate as freely as possible; and (3) introducing as much flexibility as possible in the workplace. These three general policy commitments, moreover, were related to the two major principles underlying all neoliberal thought as noted above: more *liberté* and *moins d'État*.

But how much liberty and how little state they desired is what served to differentiate the specific policy recommendations of the three main groups of neoliberals. First, there were the "ultra" neoliberals, to borrow Raymond Barre's term, who urged radical change in the French polity through complete state disengagement from the economy and an end to most aspects of the welfare state. These were mostly academics who were for (1) total denationalization of banks and industry as well as an opening up of all monopolistic sectors of industry to private competition; (2) total deregulation in the financial and banking systems as well as in the workplace, meaning an end to the minimum wage (SMIC), an end to unemployment compensation, and a significant weakening of the power of the unions; (3) a dramatic reduction in public expenditures ensured by a constitutional requirement for a balanced budget; (4) a significant diminution in the *prélèvements obligatoires* and an end to the inheritance tax, to corporate taxes, and to corporate contributions to social security; and (5) a shrinking of the size of the welfare system by encouraging the growth of private charity and of competition from the private sector as well as by jettisoning all formulae for determining aid in favor of decisions arrived at on a case-by-case basis.[6] Only one politician was squarely in this camp, Alain Madelin, who in his regular columns for *Le Figaro* and in his numerous books popularized many of the ultra themes,[7] and

[4]See Guy Sorman, *La révolution conservatrice américaine* (Paris: Fayard, 1983); and Laurent Cohen-Tanugi, *Le droit sans l'état* (Paris: Presses Universitaires de France, 1985).

[5]See Raymond Barre, *Réflexions pour demain* (Paris: Hachette, 1984); and the work of Jacques Chirac's close collaborator Philippe Auberger, *L'allergie fiscale* (Paris: Calmann-Levy).

[6]Bruno Théret, "'Vices publics, bénéfices privés': Les propositions économiques électorales des néo-libéraux français," *Critiques de l'Économie Politique* no. 31 (April–June 1985), pp. 105–106.

[7]Among his many recommendations were a voucher system for the schools similar to that advocated by Milton Friedman. See: Alain Madelin, *Libérer l'école* (Paris: Laffont, 1985).

who, as Minister of Industry under Chirac, virtually dismantled the ministry. Other ultra politicians tended to support various aspects of ultra neoliberalism, but tended to shy away from the extremes, and certainly did not seek to undermine their own ministries.

The most powerful politicians were "moderate" neoliberals who encouraged a reform of the polity through limited state disengagement from the economy and a gradual retreat from the welfare state. They wanted to get rid of all so-called bureaucratic controls over industry; to lower the "excessive" taxes which discourage initiative and individual incentives to work hard; and to denationalize because the state is, by definition, a bad manager. Their focus tended to be more on business than on anything else and on the cult of *la liberté d'entreprendre*.[8] Thus, the common platform of the RPR-UDF in the election campaign deliberately used the theme of "restoring liberties," instead of liberalism, to dissociate themselves from the ideological position of the ultras, while the social program of the RPR of November 1985 declared itself for "liberalism but not anarchy" with a reasonably cautious program of liberalization and deregulation in such areas as the administrative authorization of layoffs, in the costs to industry of hiring the young, and so forth.

Among the politicians, few expected the future Prime Minister and leader of the RPR, Jacques Chirac, to be anything other than a moderate neoliberal, not only because of his own very recent Gaullist interventionist history but also because he was perceived as "a man without firm long-term convictions. His career is scattered with contradictory statements and broken political alliances."[9] Nevertheless, his commitment to some form of neoliberalism was not in question, as evidenced by the privatization program he had instituted as mayor of Paris, in which he reduced the overall size and cost of city government by contracting out for a number of municipal services.[10]

Members of the center right were equally cautious. For Valéry Giscard d'Estaing, privatization was a practical, not an ideological, issue based on the need of the nationalized industries and banks for more capital and on the ability of an enlarged competitive sector to promote growth and create productive jobs. In addition, he proposed deregulation in the new

[8]See Colette Ysmal, "Les programmes économiques des parties de droite," *Critique de l'Économie Politique* no. 31 (April–June 1985).
[9]*London Financial Times*, March 19, 1986.
[10]Note that at the time Chirac took over the city from the prefect of Paris in 1977, as the first elective mayor of Paris, he did not seem to mind the incredibly large and expensive bureaucratic machine (with more than 40,000 employees) he inherited. As a matter of fact, between 1977 and 1982, he increased the number of city employees by 6,400 (*Le Monde*, September 3, 1986). It was only in 1981 that Chirac began his neoliberal initiatives. For the privatization program itself, see: *Le Monde*, Oct. 29, 1985.

technological areas, in the rules requiring administrative authorization for layoffs, and in controls over prices and financial markets, but not in the minimum wage.[11]

Among top politicians, though, Raymond Barre was probably the ideal-typical moderate. At the same time that he argued that in the "liberal society . . . [one] doesn't sacrifice the individual to the state," he noted, nevertheless, that the state had played an essential role in French history, resisting those who blamed it for all societal ills;[12] and admitted that the inequality that goes along with liberty should be introduced gradually because the Frenchman has a "pronounced taste for security and equality."[13] As for actual proposals, he would introduce greater flexibility in the workplace[14] and free economic development from direct governmental intervention by providing indirect aid to industry in the form of fiscal incentives and research grants for the purpose of promoting the modernization of industry.[15]

The moderates, in short, unlike the ultras, were not interested in challenging the basic architecture of the French state. They were for a reduction in state intervention but were unwilling to reject the state completely, and understandably so. As major political figures in previous conservative governments who in those times had little problem with the reality of a strong interventionist state, they began talking about "less state" only when they lost control of it. All of a sudden, the ability to formulate programs and use the bureaucracy to implement them with total disregard for opposition views became anathema to the very parties that had heretofore lauded the efficiency of such a system.

While the moderates wanted to reform the state and the ultras to change it radically, the "modern" neoliberals wanted to modernize the state, using all of the latest in managerial and technological innovations to promote state disengagement from the economy but not from the welfare state except in certain strategic areas. Henri Lepage, for example, proposed a technological solution to the problem of state interventionism by substituting for central government decision-making a political exchange system relying on advanced communications technology to poll citizens' wishes.[16] Guy Sorman, by contrast, relied on modern managerial techniques to strike the right balance between state and market, coming up with proposals that in some instances were closer to those of the ultras, and in others smacked of socialism.[17] Thus, he was willing to countenance even lifetime employment and worker participation as long

---

[11]*Le Monde,* October 31, 1985.   [12]Barre, *Réflexions,* p. 435.   [13]Ibid., p. 39.
[14]Ibid., pp. 104–105, 302.   [15]Ibid., p. 56.   [16]Lepage, *Tomorrow,* pp. 208–211.
[17]Sorman, *L'état,* pp. 53, 60; and Sorman, *Solution,* p. 72.

as they promoted salary flexibility;[18] he favored keeping a modest form of progressive taxation instead of a flat rate for taxes;[19] and he recommended transferring public services to the private sector only where it could be advantageous.[20] At the same time, however, he went far beyond a moderate such as Barre when he suggested setting up a French equivalent to the Federal Reserve Bank to control the money supply.[21]

These modern neoliberals were influential more as a result of the numerous books they published popularizing neoliberal themes than for any strongly stated and logically reasoned economic ideology, like the ultras, or for any political clout and party ties, like the moderates. Of all the politicians, only Philippe Séguin, as Minister of Social Affairs, seems to have taken to heart some of the modernist recommendations with regard to labor legislation, by championing not only moderate neoliberal proposals, ultimately passed, to allow greater flexibility in the workplace, to end the administrative authorization for layoffs (itself Chirac's own initiative of 1975), and to facilitate youth employment (which reduced the costs to employers of hiring workers under twenty-five years of age), but also modernist and socialist proposals, which in most instances did not pass. Thus, he supported government funding of workers' retraining leaves (opposed by Balladur), measures promoting employment for the long-term unemployed and the handicapped (opposed by industry), and projects to encourage more part-time and temporary work or to recognize the underground economy, at the same time that he opposed the government-sponsored proposed regulation of public workers' right to strike.

Once the neoliberals came to power in the March 1986 legislative elections, the number of neoliberal books published slowed to a trickle. It was almost as if, once in power, the neoliberals, just as the Socialists before them, felt that they had neither the time nor the need to expand on their theories, only the imperative to put them into practice and, thereby, to reverse the effects of five years of socialism. Moreover, just like the Socialists, they began backing away from some of their more radical promises as soon as they came to office.

When, on March 13, 1986, Jean Lecanuet, president of the UDF, outlined the "project" of the new government – which included the liberalization of prices and interest rates, denationalization, starting with the banks, and lightening the *charges des entreprises,* notably in allowing businesses to hire the young at below minimum wage[22] – already excluded were a number of unpopular measures supported by the ultras

---

[18]Sorman, *Solution,* pp. 196–198.   [19]Sorman, *L'état,* pp. 80–83.   [20]Ibid., p. 41.
[21]Ibid., pp. 75, 147.   [22]*Le Monde,* March 15, 1986.

such as partially privatizing health insurance and taking apart the social security and social welfare systems.[23] From the very beginning, in
other words, the main question was to be how many concessions to
the ultras would the moderates make in legislating deregulation and
denationalization. And the answer was: Not too many. Neither Chirac
nor most of his cabinet appeared in many cases willing and in others
able to fulfill the promises of the neoliberal RPR-UDF electoral program – and this included the ultras themselves. By mid November
1986, members of the Parti Républicain were already beginning to
maintain that "Our ministers have become the hostages of this government. . . . [They] have not been able to become the liberal locomotive
of this government."[24]

In fact, once Chirac became Prime Minister and his good friend,
Edouard Balladur, Minister of Finance and the Economy, it was clear
to the ultra neoliberals that their own more radical policy recommendations were unlikely to see the light of day. Chirac, as already discussed, had at best a lukewarm commitment to liberalism, and he was
certainly unwilling to dismantle the state, as illustrated in a speech to a
group of lawyers in 1987, when he stated that "Privatization is not 'destatization' – the complete retreat of the state would not allow an equitable distribution of the fruits of growth – while a deregulation
which establishes a situation of competition, an end to public monopolies, and the development of private initiative must occur without risk
to the general interest of the country."[25] Balladur, moreover, as a man
of the state, having been a secretary-general at the Elysée under Pompidou before becoming head of two subsidiaries of the nationalized
CGE (which he successfully turned around), was no more a standard-
bearer for liberalism than Chirac. By mid November, the ultra neoliberals of the Parti Républicain had found that on budgetary matters
at least, Balladur had "shown himself to be more pompidolian and
conservative" than even they had anticipated.[26] Balladur himself remained cautious, claiming that his gradual reduction of the role of the
government in the economy was the only way, and that those who
urged more drastic measures were being "irresponsible."[27] Moreover,
the ambitious privatization program for which he was the principal architect, although true to neoliberalism in its scope, smacked of old-
style *dirigisme* in its control of the process and the final outcome. And
yet, despite the disappointment of the ultras, Chirac and his Finance

[23]Ysmal, "Les programmes," p. 70.   [24]*Le Monde,* Nov. 15, 1986.
[25]*Le Monde,* April 14, 1987.   [26]*Le Monde,* November 15, 1986.
[27]*International Herald Tribune,* Nov. 17, 1986.

Minister liberalized more than ever before, taking many of the policies the Socialists began much farther as well as instituting new ones.

LIBERAL *DIRIGISME* IN STATE MANAGEMENT OF THE ECONOMY

The Chirac government, like that of Fabius, focused first and foremost on the macroeconomic environment of business, using restrictive monetary policies and tight budgets to bring down inflation and the budget deficit, which it reduced (with the aid of the privatizations) by over 30 billion francs, from 153.3 billion francs in 1985 to 120 billion francs in 1987. It was also dedicated to diminishing the size of government by shrinking the government's share of GDP from 45% to 35%, a level which Chirac insisted was more appropriate for "a society of liberty and responsibility."[28] Moreover, Chirac pledged to decrease government spending by 1% of GDP every year, and to replace only one of every two retiring civil servants, thereby eliminating 20,000 posts in two years.[29] In addition, the government abolished a dozen or so central administrations, including the FIM, or Fonds Industriel de Modernisation (along with its 9 billion francs in subsidies for the technological innovation of small and medium-sized enterprises),[30] and drastically cut the budgets of others.[31] It also eliminated numbers of interministerial committees while stopping the funding for others, with the exception of the Committee on Industrial Restructuring (CRI). Finally, although the Plan was spared, it was left with little to do other than produce an advisory report on economic conditions and spending priorities.[32]

In addition to cutting government spending and the size and funding of government agencies, if not simply eliminating the agencies themselves, the government also reduced taxes on industry in an effort to promote their competitiveness. Thus, it cut payroll taxes, corporate taxes (by 37

[28]*Le Monde,* January 19–20, 1986.   [29]*Le Monde,* January 13, 1987, p. 9.

[30]Other agencies abolished were the ADI (Agence de Développement de l'Informatique), and the CESTA (Centre d'Étude des Systèmes et des Technologies Avancés). This was in response to the Bellin-Gisserot Report commissioned by Finance Minister Balladur, which called for the elimination of thirty central administrations (out of 250 studied). *Le Monde,* July 5, 1986, and July 8, 1986.

[31]These included the Ministry of Industry (by 50%, at the recommendation of the Minister himself), ANVAR (with a 40% reduction in budget in 1987), DATAR (which went from 1 billion francs in 1983 to under 600 million), and the FRT, or Fonds de la Recherche et de la Technologie (which lost 30% of its funds to help defray the costs of joint public and private research ventures, with 70% paid by private industry). *Le Monde,* May 19–20, 1991; *La Tribune de l'Economie,* Oct. 4–5, 1986; Levy, "Tocqueville's Revenge," p. 76.

[32]Hall, "State and Market," pp. 178–179.

billion francs over two years), and the business tax. Moreover, in order to increase consumers' buying power and indirectly, therefore, the revenue of business, it cut individual taxes (by 31 billion francs over two years) and abolished the inheritance tax (the only unpopular move of the government with regard to tax reduction). Overall, it reduced taxes by 69 billion francs for the budgets of 1987 and 1988.

The government also significantly diminished potential governmental control over the economy by instituting a vast array of deregulatory reforms which went far beyond what the Socialists had begun. Primarily among these were the freeing up of the securities, futures, and foreign exchange markets; the ending of most price controls; and the passage of the law on competition that replaced the two ordinances of June 30, 1945 (along with the approximately 30,000 rules which grew up around them) and created a Council on Competition to replace the Competition Commission.[33]

On top of policies that simply extended those of their Socialist predecessors, the neoliberals also introduced a number of entirely new policies. Most notably, they overhauled monetary policy as of January 1, 1987, by replacing the system of rationing bank credit, the *encadrement du crédit* (which they themselves had instituted in 1974 when they were known as conservatives, and which was the main way in which the French state influenced the growth of the money supply and the direction of investment), with a system in which the Banque de France would control the money supply by manipulating interest rates.[34] They also liberalized controls on corporations' stock issues and passed the law on savings that facilitated leveraged management buyouts (LMBO) and employee stock ownership plans (ESOP) as well as encouraged employees generally to buy shares in the firms for which they worked (especially in the newly privatized ones).

Finally, they created what Balladur dubbed the *petit bang* which broke the 180-year monopoly of the sixty official French stockbrokers, replacing the old system with one in which the administrative tasks related to the running of the stock market are separated from the regulatory and oversight functions carried out by an elected council.[35] This anticipated well in advance of 1993 the scheduled end to the stockbrokers' monopoly, when the twelve member countries of the EC would be able to trade on the Paris Bourse and the six regional stock exchanges. And it made pos-

[33]For a full discussion, see: Michel Bazex "L'actualité du droit économique: La déréglementation," *L'Actualité Juridique. Droit Administratif* no. 11 (Nov. 20, 1986).

[34]This, according to Michel Camdessus, governor of the Banque de France, would help lending competition among French banks, thereby encouraging lower interest rates. And it would escape the problems of the old system which discouraged competition for loans by setting annual loan limits. *New York Times,* November 29, 1986.

[35]Philip Cerny, "The 'Little Big Bang' in Paris: Financial Market Deregulation in a *Dirigiste* System," *European Journal of Political Research* no. 17 (1989), pp. 169–192.

sible the further expansion of a stock market that, on the eve of privatization, was capitalized at only 600 billion francs, a little higher than that of Amsterdam, lower than that of Zurich, barely a quarter of that of London, and with a volume which, at 166 billion francs, was a third that of Zurich, a fourth that of London, a fifth that of Frankfurt, one-seventeenth that of Tokyo, and a fifty-third that of New York.[36]

Most of these measures had salutary effects on the economy. In 1987, economic growth climbed to 2.3%, after 2.2% in 1986 and 1.6% in 1985. But deregulation and the elimination of the many restrictive regulations over business did not serve to create anywhere near the 350,000 jobs the neoliberals had predicted. Unemployment remained high even as it was dropping elsewhere in the European Community, although it did drop in 1988 to 10.3% from 10.7% the year before. Moreover, although the French economy got a boost from the lowering of oil prices in 1986 and the worldwide economic boom which ensured that in 1987, the volume of trade in manufactured products grew by 6.4%, exports of French manufactured products grew only by 1.8%, thus leaving France with a 4.6% loss of market share.[37] What is more, the franc was threatened within the EMS, forcing very high levels of interest rates which in turn made the cost of loans high and slowed economic growth. In addition, the balance of trade went from a surplus of 20.5 billion francs in 1986 to a deficit of 21.1 billion francs in 1988. In manufacturing alone, the trade deficit nearly quadrupled to over 50 billion francs from 13 billion.[38] And as if this were not enough, French commentators noted "holes in the industrial fabric."[39] In fact, liberalization, or the retreat of the state, which was to free the "entrepreneurial spirit," was not enough. Much more needed to be done in a positive way to strengthen start-up companies that were weak and isolated, without sufficient ties to local support networks of local authorities and employers associations, as in Germany, or access to the university research support or venture capital found in the United States.[40] This had been neglected by the neoliberals who, like Thatcher, had an implicit trust in the market when it came to entrepreneurial activity.

For all this liberalism, however, the neoliberals kept certain industrial policy instruments for themselves, and did not leave everything to the market. For example, in the 1986 ordinance on the control of mergers

---

[36]Michel Durupty, *Les privatisations* (Paris: Documentation Française, 1988), pp. 33–34; and Michel Pébereau, "Les Promesses de la privatisation," *Projet* (January–February, 1987).

[37]*Le Monde,* May 5, 1988.

[38]INSEE, *Rapport sur les comptes de la nation, 1990* (Paris: INSEE, 1991), p. 261; Levy, "Tocqueville's Revenge," p. 80.

[39]Levy, "Tocqueville's Revenge," p. 80.   [40]Ibid., pp. 80–81.

and acquisitions, Balladur kept for himself the sole power to refer questions about particular mergers and acquisitions to the new Competition Council, which was itself limited to giving advice, and not allowed to provide binding opinions, as is the case in England (where the minister cannot forbid a merger once a favorable opinion has been given by the Monopolies and Mergers Commission), or in Germany (once a merger has been authorized by the BundesKartellamt). This meant not only that the Minister of Finance could accept or reject the decisions of the new Council, but also that, because there is no automatic system of referral to the commission, when the Minister chooses not to question a merger or acquisition, the system does not go into effect. This necessarily leaves everyone in the dark until a takeover is complete, even if the takeover violates the rules. (This was used to great effect by Prime Minister Rocard a few years later in the case of the acquisition of Air Inter by Air France.)[41]

Moreover, although as of January 1987, prices were entirely decontrolled and left to the discretion of the heads of business, there were certain significant exceptions: The state refused to allow insurance companies to raise their rates as high as they wanted (in February 1987) or to let the banks charge for checks. In addition, they ordered EDF (the giant public electric utility) and GDF (the gas utility) to lower their rates, despite the facts that EDF had a level of debt close to 230 billion francs and that GDF was in bad shape. Moreover, although prices were technically free, in exceptional cases a decree by the Council of State could allow the government to take temporary measures where excessive increases in prices were found.

In addition, for all the governmental emphasis on the supply side, French industries still received large subsidies, and this despite the valiant efforts of Minister of Industry Alain Madelin, who insisted that "From now on . . . this ministry must adopt, and no longer orient, much less direct, the life of companies."[42] For example, when Madelin refused to grant Renault a 2 million franc subsidy or to reclassify certain automotive equipment as defense materials to get around European Community competition, Minister of Finance Balladur provided the money and agreed to reclassification. Moreover, Madelin's reduction of his own budget by 1.5 billion francs in the name of liberalism and his support for the elimination of the FIM simply left him without any real flexibility of action for the 1987 budgetary year (significantly, he reduced his next

[41]The threshold was 7 billion francs in sales and 25% market share. See: Hervé Dumez and Alain Jeunemaître, "L'état et le marché en Europe: Vers un état de droit économique?" *Revue Française de Science Politique* vol. 42, no. 2 (April 1992), pp. 260–270.
[42]*International Herald Tribune*, November 17, 1986.

budget by only 10%); and while Madelin was no longer in a position to help growing industries in the electronics sector, to encourage more research and development, or to support technological innovation in the SMEs, the traditional sectors of the economy were continuing to receive their traditional subsidies from the Ministry of Finance.[43] Commentators noted at the time that the problem with Madelin was that the less flexibility he gave himself, the more he left the field open to less liberal others, especially the Ministry of Finance, because "he is simply a little island of liberalism in an ocean of colbertism, and his projects therefore constantly backfire."[44]

In other ways, however, even Madelin was not quite the ultra he appeared. Although a sworn enemy of direct subsidies, he was not against indirect subsidies, whether in the form of employment zones to facilitate job creation or enterprise zones for business creation, in both of which the fiscal and regulatory environment of business was to be made "as favorable as in other European countries," with the reduction of payroll taxes and tax on profits (in the enterprise zones, ten years' freedom from all tax on profits). Moreover, although in industrial policy Madelin could still qualify as a neoliberal, this was less true in energy policy, where he put off the campaign promise to abrogate the law of 1928 that regulates oil imports and allows for the government to prohibit importation from certain countries on commercial or political grounds, making only minimal changes in favor of independent importers; and he maintained the obligation to import crude oil in ships under French flags. On social issues, moreover, such as Minister of the Interior Charles Pasqua's anti-pornography campaign and his remarks on shipping immigrants out of the country by train (at the height of the Klaus Barbie trial), Madelin's only comment was, "it's best to be quiet. In any event, a liberal Minister of the Interior would have fallen on his face."[45]

However ambivalent Madelin was in his commitment to liberalizing reform, other ultra neoliberal ministers were even more so. For example, Pierre Méhaignerie, Minister of the Infrastructure (*équipement*), Housing, the DATAR, and Transportation, and the centrist president of the CDS, not only proposed to make up for governmental cuts in aid to industry for job creation by taking over some of the costs of road maintenance and construction in interested regions,[46] he also proposed to return to the only recently abandoned *dirigisme* of the DATAR, to encourage the relocation to the provinces not only of industries but also of Paris ministries.[47] Moreover, in the transportation area, he did not seek to rees-

[43]*Le Monde,* September 19, 1986.   [44]Claire Blandin, *Le Monde,* April 13, 1987.
[45]*Le Nouvel Observateur,* August 8–14, 1986.   [46]*Le Monde,* October 31, 1986.
[47]*Le Monde,* September 20, 1986. With the new law on housing, though, he did give in to the neoliberal demand to abrogate the *loi Quilliot* (a Socialist law supporting

tablish competition between the railroads and other means of transportation: There was to be no privatization for the subsidiaries of the SNCF and no abrogation of the monopoly of the *artisans bateliers* in the transport of cereals. Equally little occurred in air transport, despite the fact that Méhaignerie's Deputy Minister, Jacques Douffiagues, was one of the most neoliberal members of Chirac's cabinet, an *énarque* who had had a civil service as well as a political career. As Douffiagues himself put it, "I want to go as far as possible, if it is possible,"[48] and the possible was determined by considerations of the international competitiveness of Air France, by negotiations within the EC, and by pressure within France for liberalization by the head of the travel agency Nouvelles Frontières and by UTA (Union de Transports Aerien). The result was an increase in competition only in those areas most subject to protectionism: Air Inter's monopoly on domestic flights and Air France's on international flights were breached when charter companies and UTA were allowed to compete on certain routes.[49] The charter companies considered Douffiagues to have provided de facto deregulation because although "officially, one still is not allowed to cheat . . . since Douffiagues is here, there isn't any more control."[50] Nevertheless, all was not completely unofficially deregulated; and we can surely believe Douffiagues when he claimed that "I am not an ayatollah of liberalism."[51]

In telecommunications and culture, the neoliberal agenda was also pushed only so far. François Léotard, the Minister of Culture (and Communications until the title was abolished), and head of the PR subgroup most in favor of neoliberal reform, was certainly faithful to the neoliberal project in his privatization of TF1, highly symbolic given its "governmental image" (even though it was itself a compromise on his original plan to privatize Antenne 2 with Chirac, who wanted to privatize only the less important third channel). He was equally faithful to neoliberalism with the deregulation of television, through the creation of the CNCL (the

tenants' rights) and he sought to favor housing investment and the sale of public housing; but he introduced only a moderate plan for the liberalization of rent control policies (by setting a schedule for decontrolling rents which would not be felt fully until 1991). *Le Monde*, July 25, 1986.

[48]*Financial Times*, June 15, 1986.

[49]See Eric Le Boucher, *Le Monde: Bilan économique et social 1986*, January 15, 1987.

[50]Comment by Jacques Maillot, head of Nouvelles Frontières, *Le Nouvel Observateur*, June 26–July 2, 1987.

[51]Douffiagues made this comment when talking about his remedies for the second half of his mandate: the small transportation concerns which, he insisted, he would neither put to death nor rescue through *"l'acharnement thérapeutique"* or extensive governmental aid, but rather would help through only an intermediary set of *"plans sociaux de reconversion"* or reconversion plans. *Le Nouvel Observateur*, August 8–14, 1986.

Commission Nationale de la Communication et des Libertés, or the National Commission for Communications and Liberty). This commission was to regulate public as well as private and newly privatized television stations, and to guard against concentration in the media.[52] It replaced the Haute Authorité and had ten times its budget and greater financial autonomy.[53]

Léotard was less faithful to neoliberalism in other areas under his jurisdiction. Although he claimed that the separation of communications from the state was like a modern-day version of the separation of church and state, he was not about to stop state interventionism in the movie industry by abolishing subsidies to French cinema because, as he explained, he wanted to keep French cinema first in Europe.[54] Moreover, even in the area of television deregulation, Léotard was unable to ensure complete freedom from state influence. The independence of the CNCL was jeopardized by the politicization of the appointments to the commission and the fact that in the telecommunications area, the Ministry of Post and Telecommunications retained almost total regulatory power, which it was unwilling to give up.

The Ministry of Post and Telecommunications, headed by Secretary of State Gérard Longuet – an *énarque* who had primarily followed a political career,[55] and who, although described as the most serious of the *bande à Léo,* was a "liberal-Colbertist" – did little to dilute the historic

---

[52]Because the August law was found in September 1986 by the Constitutional Council to guard insufficiently against concentration in the media, in October the majority had to pass a law limiting such concentration, to be implemented by the CNCL.

[53]The CNCL was in charge of regulation as well as of the privatization process, and elaborated rules related to its responsibilities which included ensuring the free and pluralistic expression of opinions on the air, guaranteeing public access, overseeing the competition between public and private sectors, ensuring the defense and illustration of the French language, and making certain that the owners of TF1 complied with the conditions of sale. These conditions required the TF1 owners to provide cultural and educational programs, programs originating in French, and programs promoting the contribution of French culture in foreign countries, in addition to promising a certain number of hours for new, original productions, a limitation on the number of commercials, etc. For a full account of the reform, see: Marie-Christine Henry-Meininger, "La réforme du statut de la communication audiovisuelle (lois du 30 septembre et du 27 novembre 1986)," *La Revue Française d'Administration Publique* no. 41 (January–March 1987), pp. 165–174. See also *Le Monde,* April 4, 1987.

[54]Similarly, despite the fact that the RPR-UDF platform proposed to abolish all state *tutelle* over the funding of local cultural activities, Léotard preferred a partnership between state and locality on the grounds that the localities are too often inadequately endowed in such areas. *L'Express,* April 25–May 1, 1986.

[55]In fact, he was graduated toward the bottom rather than the top of his class at the ENA and, faced with what would certainly be a rather mediocre civil service career compared to his *camarades de promotion* in top-ranking graduating positions, moved into politics at a relatively early age, and then on to a ministerial post equally early.

power of his ministry, especially by comparison to other major ministries. To begin with, Longuet indicated that he would not favor private industry over the nationalized ones, that he would continue public financing of telecommunications research, and that he was quite willing to recognize that development in the area was largely due to the efforts of the public sector.[56] Moreover, a number of promises contained in the RPR-UDF platform were not forthcoming, such as the transformation of the Direction Générale des Télécommunications from a government bureau (*administration*) to a nationalized enterprise, which meant that major decisions continued to be left up to the Minister.

In addition, the proposed deregulation of the sector did not go very far: Already in August 1986, Longuet had made it clear that he would proceed slowly, putting off the definition of the rules for competition until the end of 1987, at which time it was dropped because of fears of union opposition and a lack of support from Chirac, worried about the political repercussions of a PTT strike. Nonetheless, Longuet did decide in November 1986 that although the telephone services would not be opened to competition, the computer communications area would be (and this despite objections from industry);[57] and in spring 1987, Longuet did deregulate radio telephones.[58] The reorganization of telecommunications, however, would have to wait until the Socialists returned to power.

Even planning was not abandoned entirely, despite electoral promises and periodic threats to that effect. The initial arguments (in September 1986) of the Minister of the Civil Service and the Plan, Hervé de Charette, to eliminate the plan altogether (opposed, significantly enough, by Balladur, who sought only to reduce the numbers of civil servants in the planning area), changed in a matter of months (by November) to a discussion of how important it was in the planning effort to have the widest consultation possible. In this, de Charette was supported from all sides, whether from those who had been central to the planning process, such as Pierre Massé, General Commissioner of the Plan from 1959 to 1966, and Jacques Méraud, a member of the Economic and Social Council; or those who participated in the process on the side of labor, such as Pierre Héritier, national secretary of the CFDT; or on the side of business, such

---

[56]*Le Monde*, August 21, 1986; *Le Monde*, August 6, 1986.

[57]The state's monopoly was broken with the decree allowing the creation of Axone, a subsidiary of Paribas and the Crédit Agricole, associated with IBM. Jacques Stern, head of the French computer group Bull, saw this as anti-liberal, because it would in short order mean monopoly power for IBM, and thus lead to less rather than more competition. *Le Monde*, Nov. 5, 1986.

[58]Since the deregulation of radiotelephones, the Générale des Eaux, in association with CGE, became number two next to the state.

as Guy Brana, president of the economic commission of the CNPF.[59] In brief, the *"partenaires"* still saw something worthwhile in the planning exercise, even if everyone knew that the recommendations were not very important to the national economic policymaking process. We should not forget, moreover, that the regional planning process had become increasingly significant, and required a national plan to connect up with.

The government's commitment to neoliberalism, in brief, had its limits. The macroeconomic reforms clearly went farther than the microeconomic, as deregulation came face to face with industry resistance and ministerial footdragging. Privatization, however, went even farther faster than the neoliberals themselves anticipated.

DIRIGISTE DISENGAGEMENT IN STATE OWNERSHIP AND CONTROL

With privatization, the neoliberals remained true to their campaign promises, and in a very real sense broke with the Socialist policies of 1981 to March 1983, even if one might argue that they took later Socialist policies to their logical conclusion. Privatization, the linchpin of the right's common "program to govern together," was to end the state interventionism that limited firms' flexibility of operation and politicized the appointment process, to reduce the state's budgetary burdens while allowing the newly privatized enterprises new sources of funding, and to ensure greater recourse to the national and international financial markets of the privatized companies after their return to profitability.[60] In addition, privatization was to enable France to meet the challenge of European integration, by enabling firms to be as free as their European competitors for strategic purposes as well as by giving a boost to the newly opened French *bourse*. In all of this, the neoliberals were successful.

The privatization of financial and industrial concerns

The response to privatization follows a pattern similar to that of the nationalizations, where a positive initial response was followed by a more negative one. Even before the actual program, privatization enjoyed widespread support. This was evidenced by the increasing public confidence in the private sector, which in 1986 was at 62%, an increase of 11 points over 1982, at which time public trust for public enterprise, at 57%, had

---

[59]*Le Monde*, November 4, 1986.
[60]Durupty, *Privatisations*, pp. 33–34; and Pébereau, "Promesses de la privatisation."

outstripped that of private enterprise.[61] The response to the privatizations themselves was favorable: In May 1987, 41% of the French approved of privatization versus 27% who disapproved and 32% who either refused to take sides (20%) or respond (12%).[62] By 1990, however, the public was no longer as keen on privatization, as evidenced by a survey that found that only a third of the French (31%) thought that privatization would make public services work better, while 17% thought that it would make them work less well, and 38% felt that it would make no difference.[63]

Business heads, by contrast, initially greeted privatization with almost as much trepidation as they had nationalization. Some businesspeople feared the effects of privatization on the companies while others were concerned about the impact on the stock market and the economy more generally. Even the former heads of companies nationalized by the Socialists who had at the time they lost their jobs decried nationalization nevertheless expressed concern about privatization, fearing that the same loss of legitimacy and disruption which occurred with Socialist nationalization would be reproduced when the neoliberals privatized.[64] And others, even well before the March 1986 elections which brought the neoliberals to power, warned about the harmful effects of going too fast because it could entail the unbalancing of the stock market, the multinational acquisition of French companies, and the potential disruption of the economy if the left were to return quickly to power and renationalize.[65]

Only the heads of the nationalized enterprises – and by no means all – seemed unequivocally in favor of privatization. For most, however, privatization was simply a sensible next step for firms requiring a new infusing of capital rather than an ideological imperative, as it was for the neoliberals. Thus, Alain Gomez, CEO of Thomson, stated in June 1986 that

[61]Most interestingly, perhaps, these changes occurred in the least likely sectors, those of women (+13 points), workers (+13), and Socialists (+15). SOFRES, *L'état de l'opinion 1988*, p. 31.
[62]Ibid., p. 32. Contrast this with the British, 47% of whom thought the privatization of British Gas was a "bad thing" in November 1985, against 36% in favor.
[63]SOFRES, *L'état de l'opinion 1990* (Paris: Seuil, 1990), p. 184.
[64]Jacques de Foucher, former head of the Compagnie Bancaire and then the Banque de Paris et des Pays-Bas, for example, suggested that the only way to restore that legitimacy would involve having the presidents charged with privatization not only renew ties with the former owners by allotting them their former share in the company but also reinforce the loyalty of the company's personnel by allotting them a certain share in the company as well. And he argued that the only way to avoid the tremendous disruption and potential losses that rapid privatization would bring would be to proceed slowly and to provide protection to those firms until they became used to their new status. Jacques de Foucher, "Les avatars de la légitimité," *Le Monde*, July 8, 1986.
[65]*Le Monde*, November 9, 1985. See also the private study by Jean Loyrette, reported on by the *International Herald Tribune*, October 19–20, 1985; and the views of Pierre Moussa, *Le Monde*, February 5, 1986.

he was satisfied both with the nationalization of his conglomerate and with its future privatization (although this has yet to happen) because, while nationalization saved the company by bringing in financial resources at the time unobtainable from the private sector, privatization would enable it to be more flexible in its strategies now that Thomson had turned itself around.[66] Moreover, by flexibility, the heads of the nationalized concerns generally meant new ways of raising capital and greater ease in entering into strategic alliances rather than, as the neo-liberals would have insisted, an end to excessive Socialist *dirigisme*. Because Georges Pébereau, CEO of CGE, had difficulties with the negotiations for an agreement with ITT, the president of which had as a condition never to deal with a nationalized group, he felt that the privatization of CGE was "something to be desired" since it put it "in a situation of equality with respect to its global competitors and not completely in the hands of public powers."[67] For many industrial heads, such as the CEO of Elf, however, privatization "would not change things much for us. We are already an international company confronted by international competition, and we seek the state's help neither financially nor politically. It would only mean a greater involvement of private shareholders."[68] This was equally true for Saint-Gobain, which CEO Beffa welcomed primarily because it would reduce the company's level of debt. For Beffa, once the company had brought to a successful conclusion its restructuring and had modernized, "its status as nationalized industry did not have much justification" and "a private status seems natural."[69] Most nationalized industries, now financially solvent, modernized, and streamlined, were interested in going out to world conquest. This would be made easier by being private, although this would not stop the nationalized companies.

For the bankers, too, privatization meant increased flexibility, and was therefore welcomed, provably even more so than by the industrialists. Renaud de la Génière of Suez, for example, complained that being nationalized decreased Suez's flexibility because it did not have a hard core of investors to enable it to take advantage of a wide variety of opportunities, and instead had to depend upon the state for capital – or on floating nonvoting shares for up to 25% of its capital.[70] For some bankers, however, support for privatization also had other sources. CCF, for example,

[66]*Le Point,* no. 718, June 23, 1986.
[67]Testimony of Georges Pébereau, CEO of CGE before and during nationalization, *Rapport sur les opérations de privatisation,* vol. 2, pp. 720–721.
[68]*Petroleum Economist,* May 1986, p. 175 – cited by Zahariadis, *Political Economy of Privatization,* p. 332.
[69]Beffa, interview with author.
[70]Testimony of Renaud de La Génière, *Rapport sur les opérations de privatisation,* vol. 2, p. 659.

had had difficulty adjusting to nationalization because it went counter to the bank's corporate culture, which was founded on an image of it as the major French private deposit bank in a system where there was a preponderance of publicly owned banks (even its matchboxes reflected this).[71] Even CCF, however, benefited from nationalization, in that it helped with the creation of close relationships between CCF and two smaller nationalized banks, without which the smaller banks would have had difficulty surviving, given their loans to high-risk countries. But privatization was to help here as well, since it seemed the natural way to work out the banks' need for further working capital.[72]

In any event, within a short period, the government was able to allay most business leaders's fears as it laid out more detailed plans for privatization, which included establishing a core group of large investors for the privatized firms, and as it became clear that the to-be-privatized companies themselves were unlikely to change drastically their manner of operation after denationalization. The process of privatization itself, moreover, tended to reassure established businesses since it did not unleash the unbridled forces of competition the ultras had promised. Much the contrary, since privatization in many cases appeared to be an orderly divvying up of the market by the government in favor of larger investors.

Privatization was very much a "heroic" policy and, as such, was a strictly governmental affair which had its major outlines sketched out even before the government was elected. A committee formed toward the end of 1985 or the beginning of 1986 and led by Edouard Balladur, future Minister of Finance, had drafted the law even before the election, without input from the ministries or public enterprises on the list, or from other experts from outside the administration. Moreover, after the election, the only input for the preparation of the text of the law came from the cabinet and services of the Ministry of Finance, although later, needless to say, the

[71]It also had problems as a result of frequent changes in leadership, unavoidable in the cases of the death of its first CEO after nationalization and of the resignation of the third, Claude Jouven, in November 1985, but avoidable with the replacement of its second in 1984, Daniel Deguen, who had by all accounts managed to reestablish trust in the enterprise, and of the fourth, Gabriel Pallez, in 1987. Testimonies of Gabriel Pallez, CEO of CCF as of 1985, and of Michel Pébereau, CEO of CCF as of 1987, *Rapport sur les opérations de privatisation*, vol. 2, pp. 708–714, 733–734.

[72]In particular, the Européenne de Banque (the former Rothschild Bank) had had mediocre management and could not recover without financing either from the state or from another banking group and without vigorous reorganization efforts, the fruits of which appeared by 1987 and 1988. By contrast, the smaller Union de Banques à Paris (U.B.P.), which served small and mid-sized businesses, was quite solid at the time of nationalization, and therefore a natural complement to CCF. These, together with another smaller bank, became part of a CCF group of banks. Testimonies of Gabriel Pallez, CEO of CCF as of 1985, and of Michel Pébereau, CEO of CCF as of 1987, *Rapport sur les opérations de privatisation*, vol. 2, pp. 708–714, 736–739.

technicalities of the application of the law were worked out with advice from the ministries and discussion with the companies concerned.[73]

Parliament itself, moreover, was even less involved for the privatizations than it had been for the nationalizations. Much more important were President Mitterrand and the Constitutional Council. The legislative approval process went very quickly for the bill that authorized the government to draw up the list of enterprises to privatize, establish by ordinance the rules for privatization, end the mandates of the presidents of the firms to be privatized as well as their boards of directors, and decide the conditions under which the administrative authorities could authorize the transfer of public property to the private sector.[74] Even the Constitutional Council, which on June 26 declared the law constitutional, did not slow up the process much by stipulating that a commission of independent experts set the price for the companies to be privatized according to the rules of the market. This law of July 2, 1986, allowed the government to begin the privatization process, but not before it was forced to pass another law, rather than the ordinance establishing the rules governing privatization that it had anticipated, following Mitterrand's announcement July 14 that he would not sign the ordinance on the grounds that it did not sufficiently safeguard national independence. But this meant only a delay of approximately two weeks, given that the government simply went back to the Assembly for a judgment which came even more swiftly than the first set of deliberations.[75]

[73]Testimonies of Edouard Balladur, Minister of Finance in the Chirac government, and Jean-Marie Messier, technical councilor to Balladur and previously director of the cabinet of the deputy Minister for Privatization, Camille Cabana, *Rapport sur les opérations de privatisation*, vol. 1, pp. 6–7, 213–214. Members of the committee did include one civil servant, an *inspecteur de finances*, Jean-Marie Messier, who had participated in a study group on foreign privatization and published a short piece on privatization in Germany. The other members were: Jacques Friedmann, Edouard Balladur, Alain Juppé, Antoine Pouilleute, Paul Mentré, Renaud de la Génière, and François Heilbronner.

[74]By April 9, 1986, exactly fifteen days after the formation of the government, the *projet de loi*, or bill, was brought to the National Assembly. The Finance Commission of the Assembly considered the bill for all of fourteen hours, while on the floor of the Assembly it received a mere sixty-six hours of discussion (with only twenty minutes on the article that established the list of companies to be privatized) before the Prime Minister cut off debate using Article 49.3 of the Constitution, and turned instead to the rules to govern privatization. Moreover, the Senate did not provide any modifications to the law which was adopted on June 2 after only one reading in each of the assemblies.

[75]On the very day of its deposition in the National Assembly, the Finance Commission examined and adopted it. In the National Assembly, debate was cut off almost as soon as it started by the Prime Minister's use of Article 49.3; in the Senate, the discussion was tabled. Only the joint committee made any modifications to the project, and these were not significant. By July 31, the final version of the law on the rules governing privatization was adopted in each assembly. For an account of the various legal issues involved, see: Durupty, *Privatisation*, pp. 35–59.

In the privatizations, Balladur was in full control from the outset. Not only was he given full responsibility for privatization by the Prime Minister and, as the only minister of state, was clearly seen as above all over ministers on this question, but it was Balladur who appeared to lead, and Chirac to follow. Thus, as Balladur explained the deliberation process between the Prime Minister and himself: "I sent the information to the Prime Minister, and I decided after." As the Commission of Inquiry into the privatizations noted, the testimony of one of Balladur's technical councilors, Jean-Marie Messier, made clear that the Minister of Finance "had a special delegation in this matter and that the interventions from the Hotel Matignon (the Prime Minister's residence) were, as a result of this, exceptional."[76] The Prime Minister in fact intervened only in three cases: the sale of CGCT (which was in any case not part of the regular privatizations), the choice of television station to privatize, and the privatization of the Crédit Agricole.

Moreover, although there was a deputy minister for privatization, Camille Cabana, previously the architect of Chirac's privatization program for the city of Paris, he was placed under the authority of the Minister of Finance, Edouard Balladur, and therefore had little power because no direct access to the Prime Minister. (This contrasts with Le Garrec for the nationalizations who, although in a lesser position as a secretary general, had direct access to the Prime Minister, and therefore more power.) Cabana, who shepherded the bill through Parliament, was quickly sidelined by Balladur not only because his very presence complicated the formulation process, so much so that Treasury officials went to see Balladur's cabinet director Jean-Claude Trichet a number of times, as he recounts, "pulling their hair out," because "the deputy-minister asked for this, while a note of the Minister of State asked for that." It was also because Balladur had substantive disagreements with Cabana, in particular on the use of the golden share.[77]

Privatization, in short, was almost entirely the responsibility of the Minister of Finance; and it was he who decided, rather than the President or the Prime Minister, on the only matter that created dissension here, just as it had with nationalization: whether to privatize at 100% or at 51%. For Balladur and the majority of the government, the decision to privatize at 100%, rather than gradually for a large number of enterprises, at say 20%, had to do with a desire not to continue with the mixed economy, and a fear that if they proceeded gradually, *étatisme* would persist, and privatization would not be fully imple-

[76]*Rapport sur les opérations de privatisation,* Report volume, p. 25.
[77]Ibid., pp. 26–28.

mented.[78] Privatization at 100%, moreover, would have the opposite effect of the nationalizations at 100%. Instead of depleting state coffers, it would fill them, and allow the government to provide new capital infusions from the privatizations rather than out of the operational budget. Thus, they dismissed fears by Treasury officials about the potential weakening of certain nationalized enterprises, given the difficulties of reconstituting stable shareownership through the market,[79] and by some CEOs on the left such as Jean Peyrelevade, who feared that firms would be unable to find sufficient capital and stable enough shareholders to substitute for the state. Peyrelevade recommended instead that the state be left for a transitory period as the "ultimate shareholder" to thereby allow slowly privatizing firms to reinforce their savings rates, avoid instability in their shareownership, and guarantee their independence without recourse to questionable techniques such as the "golden share."[80] Needless to say, the government did not welcome these suggestions, and Peyrelevade found himself out of job almost immediately thereafter, his company privatized at 100% a short while later.

Denationalization actually went way beyond the neoliberals' electoral promises in terms of its extensiveness. The privatization law finally passed in July 1986 anticipated denationalizing sixty-five nationalized enterprises plus the television station TF1 (which has its own law) over the next five years, but with only a few companies scheduled for privatization before the next presidential elections. Saint-Gobain was to be the flagship of privatization, followed by Paribas, Assurances Générales de France (AGF), Havas, and TF1.[81] In addition, the law established conditions for the "respiration" of public sector enterprises, legitimizing the prior illegal sale of subsidiaries and determining how and when investment certificates would convert to voting shares, at the same time that it set up new rules of the game, e.g., the evaluation of sale prices by independent experts.[82]

---

[78]Testimony by Jacques Friedmann, *chargé de mission* in the cabinet of Balladur, *Rapport sur les opérations de privatisation*, vol. 1, p. 122, and in the Report volume, p. 99.

[79]Testimony by Daniel Legègue and Philippe Jaffré, *Rapport sur les opérations de privatisation*, vol. 1, pp. 268–269, 304.

[80]Testimony by Jean Peyrelevade, president of Suez before privatization, *Rapport sur les opérations de privatisation*, vol. 2, pp. 744–745.

[81]That Saint-Gobain should have been chosen as the flagship of neoliberal privatization is not at all surprising, given that it was one of the first nationalized enterprises to have one of its subsidiaries go public, as well as one of the many to float nonvoting shares. The floating of nonvoting shares alone was actually enough to suggest to some that Saint-Gobain was to be one of the first nationally owned industries to be privatized. *Financial Times*, May 31, 1986.

[82]The decision on pricing was the work of an independent Commission on Privatization, appointed by the government, advised by consultant banks (themselves picked by

Privatization, though, went faster than anticipated. First of all, even as the privatization law was being deliberated, informal privatization through the floating of nonvoting shares continued apace.[83] Formal privatization did not have to wait much longer: By July 1987, all from the original list of to-be-privatized companies except AGF had been sold off along with TFı (the oldest of the television stations), the Compagnie Générale d'Électricité (CGE), Suez, the Crédit Commercial de France (CCF), the Société Générale, and three small banks: the Banque du Bâtiment et des Travaux Publics (BTP), the Banque Industrielle et Mobilière Privée (BIMP), and Sogenal, as well as the first of the insurance companies: Mutuelle Générale Française-Accidents and Mutuelle Générale Française-Vie. All were sold on the stock market except the insurance companies which, because they are not publicly traded corporations, were privatized by decree through a change in the company charters. In addition, the government allowed for the sale of a number of subsidiaries of nationalized enterprises. As a result of all of this, the government managed to privatize close to 40% of the companies on the original list.[84] And if this pace had been kept up, the government could have accomplished in three years what it had anticipated completing in five.

This pace could not continue, however, primarily because of the stock market crash of October 1987. The only privatizations that occurred after the crash were those of Matra (January 20, 1988) and the Caisse Nationale de Crédit Agricole (January 18, 1988), which was in any case

another committee), who heard testimony from the companies (which had hired their own consultant banks) and the Treasury. Where there were differences in opinions about the value of companies, generally it was the Treasury that overvalued, given its interest in achieving the highest profits for the state as possible, and the companies that undervalued, given their interest in having as successful a public offering as possible and in being able to provide as high dividends as possible. Often, a compromise was reached. Thus, in the privatization of CGE, which involved also an increase in capital at the same time, primarily so that the company could pay off its acquisition of the European subsidiaries of ITT (which cost it between 4 and 5 billion francs), the company asked for 7 billion francs to finance its capital increase, the Treasury suggested 5 billion, and the Minister of Finances decided on 6.3 billion francs, judging that otherwise the company would have had to go too soon to the market for more capital. See the testimony by Pierre Chatenet, head of the commission on privatization, *Rapport sur les opérations de privatisation*, vol. 1, pp. 361–385; and by Daniel Lebègue, *Rapport sur les opérations de privatisation*, vol. 1, p. 285–286. On the evaluation process and on how prices were arrived at, see: Durupty, *Privatisations*, pp. 61–69.

[83]By May 1986, an industrial firm such as Saint-Gobain had sold 8 million nonvoting shares (with 40% reserved for small investors) to raise 2.4 billion francs, while bank after bank had already gone to the market for a total of over 11 billion francs ($1.5 billion), with Crédit Lyonnais having put out a 2.7 billion franc issue. Moreover, as early as autumn 1986, the government had sold part of its shares in Elf-Aquitaine (11% of the 66% owned by it).

[84]For a good overview of privatization, see: Durupty, *Privatisations*.

not sold on the market, but "mutualized." Even without the crash, however, privatization was unlikely to have continued at the previous breakneck speed because the market would not have been able to continue to absorb both denationalization and the capital needs of industries more generally. Moreover, even though people had been continuing to bring their money back into the country or out of savings to invest in the market while a number of private investment groups were still interested in acquiring large blocks of stock in the denationalized firms,[85] how long this would have lasted remains in question. Although the popularity of the privatizations was very high initially, due in part to the government's below-market value pricing of shares[86] and to the continuing bull market, the threat of a market downturn was always present, while government pricing of shares was already getting closer to real value (see Table 5.1). And the question was: Would people continue to buy if a sure profit were not guaranteed? The answer, as seen from the aftermath of the crash of 1987, was clearly in the negative.

In any event, privatization, as long as it lasted, generated great interest in large and small investors alike, with most stock issues heavily oversubscribed (see Table 5.1). And with all of this, needless to say, the government made a lot of money. The initial program to add 50 billion francs to the Treasury each year was accomplished in a mere six months. Most of the nationalized enterprises that were privatized brought in at least three times what had been paid for them, leading one Socialist to suggest, ironically, that the Socialists had turned out to have been extremely good corporate raiders, having recapitalized and returned to profitability the nationalized enterprises so that they could then be sold at a profit. Even CGE, which many complained was undervalued by as much as 1 billion francs, was valued at close to six times its purchase price. On CCF, though, the government did not even break even.[87] On the Crédit Agri-

[85]Among large investors, there were a number who had taken their money out of the country at the time of nationalization, e.g., the Franco-British financier Sir James Goldsmith who was reported to have £500 million ready to invest. Other French investors pooled their resources in anticipation of the deals to be made; among them were the heads of major companies in such areas as insurance – Claude Bébéar of Axa, Bernard Pagezy of the Compagnie du Midi; construction – Francis Bouygues, the major contractor in buildings and public works; and liquor – Alain Chevalier of Moët-Hennessy; to say nothing of investment banking – David de Rothschild of P.O. Banque. In addition, new investment firms were set up such as Frandev, created by Pierre Moussa, former CEO of Paribas; and Saint Honoré Matignon, created by David de Rothschild again along with Bernard Esambert, head of the financial company of Edmond de Rothschild. With denationalization, many of these became major stockholders in the newly privatized companies.
[86]See the criticism of the entire system of evaluation in the *Rapport sur les opérations de privatisation*. Report volume, pp. 159–199.
[87]Ibid., vol. 1, pp. 293–294. In 1982, the Socialists paid 17.7 billion francs – or 2.3

Table 5.1. *The privatizations: 1986–1988*

Company (date sold)	Share price[a] (in FF)	Trading[b] (in FF)	Share-holders (in mill)	Times oversub-scribed	% shares held by hardcore	% capital reserved for employees	% employees holding shares	Price of privat[a] (bill FF)	Net rec'd by state (bill FF)
Saint-Gobain (11/24/86)	310	402	1.5	14 x	17.06%[c]	18%	50%	13.6	8.4
Paribas (1/19/87)	405	513.7	3.8	40 x	18.2%	7.5%	50%	18.9	12.8
Sogenal (3/9/87)	125	170	0.85	46 x	51%	4.43%	78.5%	1.4	0.63
BTP (4/6/87)	130	146	1	65 x	51%	10%[d]	88%	0.416	0.4
BIMP (4/21/87)	140	181	0.52	29 x	51%	9.35%	81%	0.352	0.41
CCF (4/27/87)	107	137.6	1.65	11 x	30%	10%[d]	80%	4.4	2.2
CGE (5/11/87)	290	331.6	2.24	7x	31.7%[c]	7.9%	50%	20.6	8.6
Havas (5/25/87)	500	530.8	0.73	20 x	20%	4.24%	55%	6.3	2.8
Soc. Gén. (6/15/87)	407	428	2.3	5.4x	20%	7.8%	69%	22.5	17.2
Suez (5/10/87)	317	268	1.6		28.4%	10%[d]	59%	20	14.9
Matra (1/20/88)	110	123	0.3	5x	22%	6.2%	50%	4.1[e]	0.96
TF1 (6/29/87)	165	178[f]	0.4	4x	50%	2.4%	----	4.5[g]	4.4

a: As established by Minister of Finances.
b: Average trading price during first trimester.
c: Technically, not a hard core, since control gained through dissolution of SFPI.
d: a percentage of all shares offered rather than a percentage of the capital.
e: For the 51% share the state held in the company.
f: Share price on the first day of trading.
g: Public offering was 1.5 billion francs, with the additional 3 billion ceded in a block.

Source: Derived from Rapport de la Commission d'Enquête sur les conditions dans lesquelles ont été effectuées les opérations de privatisation d'entreprises et de banques appartenant au secteur public depuis le 6 août 1986 Assemblée Nationale no. 969, 3 vols., Journal Officiel, October 29, 1989.

cole, which was privatized by being sold to agricultural professional organizations, some felt the price was also too low.[88] On Matra, moreover, privatized in January 1988, the share price was lower than the cost of nationalization.[89] This contrasts greatly with Paribas, where the official valuation was over three times the 1982 purchase price, while the actual stock flotation brought in over double that.

Privatization, in short, was a great success both in terms of the money it brought to the state treasury (at 70.8 billion francs, it was close to the total corporate and income tax breaks granted during Chirac's time in office),[90] and in terms of its popularity. The number of shareholders jumped from 1.5 million to 8 million. The popularity itself, moreover, led Finance Minister Balladur to proclaim privatization a success in its creation of "people's capitalism."

Government policies with regard to privatization

The government had sought to promote "people's capitalism" in a variety of ways. To begin with, they sought to encourage share ownership by employees of the privatized firms as well as the general public. Thus, the government had reserved up to 10% of shares for employees (see Table 5.1). Moreover, they gave them deep discounts on shares purchased.[91] In some companies, the result was large-scale employee ownership: in the cases of Saint-Gobain, CGE, Paribas, and Matra, 50% of all the employees gained shares in the company; in all the other cases, it was higher (see Table 5.1). The government also promoted wide-scale individual ownership by limiting the number of shares individuals could buy in the initial offering to a maximum of ten, by providing free shares under certain circumstances (e.g., in the case of TF1, the general public received one free share for every five purchased), and by promoting the retention of

---

billion in 1987 francs, plus 2 billion francs in state funds to bring the company up to snuff, an amount which it did not seek to collect when it sold the company at an official valuation of 4.42 billion francs (thus taking in only 2.2 billion francs).

[88]See the discussion in: *Rapport sur les opérations de privatisation*, vol. 1, pp. 297–299.

[89]Ibid., p. 284.

[90]John Vickers and Vincent Wright, "The Politics of Industrial Privatisation in Western Europe: An Overview," *West European Politics* vol. 11, no. 4 (October 1988), p. 22.

[91]Up to 20% of share price if they kept them for two years in the case of Saint-Gobain; a 20% reduction in price plus one free share for every two bought in the case of TF1; a 5% discount to buy, with 20% if kept two years, in the case of Paribas. And CGE, which sought to encourage employee ownership (in part because there was to be no official "hard core"), gave employees a 30% discount if they kept the stock for five years.

shares with the general rule that individuals who keep their shares for eighteen months are given one free share for every ten they own.

The overall success of the attempt to encourage people's capitalism was nevertheless at least at first open to question. The incentive to retain stocks did not stop approximately 20% of the people from selling their stocks immediately in order to get a quick profit in the cases of Saint-Gobain and Paribas. By September 1987, 29% of the original purchasers had sold their stocks, and by February 1988, 45%. (This was nonetheless a lot lower than in Great Britain, where 50% had sold their stocks six months after most companies' privatizations.)[92] Moreover, although the limitation of shares purchased to ten per individual did indeed increase the number of shareholders appreciably (from 2 million before denationalization to upwards of 6 million by 1987), there is some suggestion that there was less a broadening of shareownership than a multiplication of the numbers of accounts in families which already owned stock.

More serious a challenge to the notion of people's capitalism than either of the above issues, however, was the fact that individual shareholders generally had no representation on the board of directors, and that many of the newly privatized companies were not interested in doing anything to encourage shareholder democracy.[93] Paribas specifically had been under attack by small shareholders, but resisted giving them representation on the board on the grounds that their interests were well enough represented by the larger shareholders.

But even if such "people's capitalism" was relatively successful by increasing the number of shareholders, its "liberalism" was offset by other limitations on shareownership determined by the government. To begin with, the government was highly *dirigiste* in the manner in which it apportioned shares. After all, even the attempt to promote neoliberalism in the population at large through a people's capitalism is interventionism of a certain kind. But this is nothing compared to the fact that the government decided what proportion of stock was to be given to a *noyau dur*, or hard core, of investors (generally between 15% and 30%) and how much was to be allowed foreign institutions (up to 20% in most privatized firms and 0% in defense-related firms like Thomson and Matra).

The government's decision to sell a controlling interest in the nationalized enterprises directly to a *noyau dur* of large investors who paid a premium over the public price in return for a block of shares and a say in the future of the company or bank resulted from its desire to provide the

---

[92]*Rapport sur les opérations de privatisation,* Report volume, p. 88.

[93]Actually, even if they did want to encourage shareholder democracy, they would have found it very hard because of the mechanics involved. Most companies keep no shareholders' roll and generally send little or no information out to stockholders. This makes it impossible to have proxy fights, etc.

privatized enterprises with stable leadership as well as to protect them from foreign acquisition and corporate raiders. The Treasury officials who came up with the idea thought that a *noyau stable* "was necessary to protect the privatized enterprises, to allow them to progressively reform their shareownership and to have a stable pole. . . . [It was] a good idea which came from the desire not to let the big French industrial and financial groups drift."[94] There was also fear that public offerings would lead to a fragmentation of capital that would increase the risk of French and foreign takeover attempts, and a sense that these enterprises needed a "tuteur, in the *arboricore* sense of the term, at least until the logic of the enterprise and its ties with its partners ended up by recreating an *affectio societatis* among those persons feeling most responsible for the fate and development of the enterprise."[95]

No one in a position of authority, moreover, thought that an open bid system as practiced by the "Anglo-Saxons" was a good idea. The Director of the Treasury agreed with the Minister of Finance that although such a system might maximize the state's revenue as well as choose shareholders according to an "incontestable" criterion, that of the best price offered, it was not right (*digne*) to put public enterprises to an auction "*à la bougie*," and to leave to the highest bidder the benefit of becoming a shareholder – even if this left the government open to accusations of arbitrariness.[96] By the same token, however, they were unwilling to allow for an *actionnaire de reference*, or one major shareholder, to take charge, despite the publicly expressed desire of certain firms to do so.[97] They were concerned not only for the government, because it would be open to countless accusations of political favoritism, regardless of the choice, but also for the interests of the company and the country if the choice were made only on financial grounds.[98] In addition, some felt that there would not be enough firms capable of acquiring 10 to 15% of the capital of these companies.[99] The nationalized enterprises, and in particular the

---

[94]Testimony by Daniel Lebègue, *Rapport sur les opérations de privatisation*, vol. 1, p. 280.

[95]Testimony by Philippe Jaffré, *Rapport sur les opérations de privatisation*, vol. 1, p. 304.

[96]Testimony by Daniel Lebègue, *Rapport sur les opérations de privatisation*, vol. 1, p. 279.

[97]The CEOs themselves, however, were not nearly as keen on this. In his testimony, the CEO of Suez, Renaud de la Génière, acknowledged that the formula which excluded any majority shareholder would be to the advantage of the sitting CEOs, noting that it was not even a fault, given that the CEO could always be replaced if he did not do his job well. *Rapport sur les opérations de privatisation*, Report volume, p. 127.

[98]Testimony by Philippe Jaffré, *Rapport sur les opérations de privatisation*, vol. 1, p. 304.

[99]Testimony by Jacques Friedmann, *Rapport sur les opérations de privatisation*, vol. 1, p. 123.

banks, agreed that a dispersed shareholdership by a hard core of investors was the most appropriate approach.[100]

But this meant that privatization was as a whole implemented in a rather *dirigiste* or at least not highly neoliberal manner. Unlike privatization in Thatcher's Great Britain, which was truly neoliberal in its sale of all shares of a company on the stock market, privatization in France was true to the *dirigiste* tradition.[101]

Moreover, the limitation on foreign ownership alone violated the laws of the European Community.[102] But because the limitation was ineffective, given that nothing could stop the privatized holding companies from selling off their subsidiaries to foreigners once privatization occurred,[103] it led the government to resort to using the *noyau dur* much more than originally intended. And this even though Balladur himself admitted that "such a method was not very liberal," and would therefore be resorted to only for the next five years.[104] Moreover, even where the hard core was not used, as in the case of Saint-Gobain, the government guarded against foreign takeover by allowing a sizable bloc of shares to remain with state-owned banks (which had held 12.5% of the shares directly or through the SFPI – Société Financière de Participants Industriels – a holding company created at the time of nationalization). And similarly, even though there was no official hard core in the case of CGE, there was a natural one

---

[100]*Rapport sur les opérations de privatisation,* vol. 1, p. 280.

[101]There were other differences as well between French and British privatization. The French did not in fact look to the British case when contemplating privatization (although the cabinet of Camille Cabana, in charge of privatization, did travel to England), because they saw tremendous differences between the two cases. Not only were most privatizations in Britain of long-standing monopolies in the noncompetitive sector, by contrast with the French, which were relatively recently nationalized, in the competitive sector, and therefore long-used to working according to the rules of the market, with strong financial management and an international strategy, but also the British administration and company management had to make major efforts to make the companies ready to bring to market, by contrast with the French companies that had already been turned around, with capable people running them. Testimony by Philippe Jaffré, *Rapport sur les opérations de privatisation,* vol. 1, p. 305.

[102]*London Times,* July 20, 1986. In this, however, the French were not alone; they were simply more inept. All European governments have found ways around Community rules that forbid discrimination in acquisitions of the companies of one European country by others that are also Community members. The Germans or the British, however, tended to camouflage their actions better through the use of antitrust criteria, e.g., Germany's Office of Cartels objected to Thomson's acquisition of Grundig on the grounds that Thomson would thereby gain a dominant position in the German market in consumer electronics.

[103]The parent companies often have very few employees by comparison with their subsidiaries. CGE, for example, has only 350 employees; and although it is covered under the "golden share" rule, its much larger subsidiary CIT-Alcatel is not. *Libération,* July 17, 1986.

[104]*Le Monde,* September 12, 1986.

with the shares of the SFPI going mainly to the BNP, Société Générale, and the Crédit Lyonnais.

In the case of the privatization of CGCT, which was sold April 30, 1987, for 500 million francs to a Franco-Swedish consortium, Matra-Ericsson, the government was even more blatant in its control of the process. Thus, Henry Ergas found that "Far from seeing a liberalization of the market, we're seeing a freezing of market share" as the search for an international buyer for the government-owned CGCT (Compagnie Générale des Constructions Téléphoniques) was influenced by the large companies which were to be its competitors.[105]

The neoliberal government's *dirigisme,* though, was most apparent in the simple fact that it chose the hard core of stockholders. As Alfred Grosser quite rightly noted, "When I see Mr. Chirac doling out the privatized television stations rather than publicly selling them, I don't see any liberalism."[106] And the doling-out process involved assuring the members of the hard core clear control over the denationalized companies. In a number of cases, majority ownership was the key to control. In the case of TF1, for example, Francis Bouygues, the construction magnate, along with a group of associates, was awarded 50% interest in the company. With the three small banks, the buyers were sold 51%, with BTP, for example, having five hard-core members but one clear controller, the Fédération Nationale du Bâtiment, at 20.5%. In the other cases, the amount was lower and ownership (and therefore control) somewhat more diffuse among the hard core. For example, Havas had a hard core owning 20% of the stocks split among five major institutions. Paribas had a *noyau dur* consisting of a group of seventeen investors holding 18.2% of the stock, but no single investor having more than 3%. And CCF had a group of nine investors – holding between 4.5% and 2.5% – for a total of 30% ownership.[107]

In choosing the hard core, the government not only decided who was to control the privatized enterprise (and thereby left itself open to accusations of political favoritism).[108] It also took much of the financial risk out of the acquisitions since it almost guaranteed the hard core windfall profits, given the undervaluation of shares and the increase in share prices immediately after the privatization (see Table 5.1). Bouygues and associates seem to have spent the most for the greatest risk when they paid 40% more than the public offering per share for their 50% interest in TF1 (even if they were guaranteed a ten-year license). The hard core of most

[105]*International Herald Tribune,* November 17, 1986. See also the discussion in Chapter 9.
[106]*International Herald Tribune,* February 9, 1987.
[107]For a full discussion of hard-core ownership and control, see Chapter 13.
[108]See the discussion in Chapter 10.

other privatized enterprises paid comparatively less for what were likely to be much higher immediate profits. The hard core paid 8% above the market price for a 20% interest in Havas; only 2.5% above for Paribas; 4% above the public price for CCF. The only problem these groups had in taking their profits was time. For the government generally set conditions for ownership, requiring the members of the hard core to keep their shares for a specified number of years, generally two. Thus, the hard core of CCF had to keep 90% of its shares for two years. And this meant that they could not cash in on what would have been guaranteed profits prior to the stock market crash of 1987, when most stocks returned to their original asking price after an initial drop.

With its use of a hard core, thus, the government was being rather antiliberal, given that it was in fact protecting the denationalized industries from market – or at least stock market – forces. In addition, the end result of privatization may be less free competition since many of the previously nationalized companies such as CGE have no French competitors in certain markets as a result of Socialist restructuring, and may in others even be in a position of monopolistic control.[109] And this situation surely contradicts the neoliberal presupposition that denationalization destroys monopoly and encourages competition.

Finally, as often as not, members of the hard core were nationalized banks and industries, thus raising questions about privatization itself as "destatization."[110] Although some might argue that it was natural that nationalized enterprises slated for privatization would be part of the hard core, the facts that relatively few companies were scheduled for privatization before the next election, and that there was no guarantee that the right would win that election, suggest rather that the government saw little contradiction between getting the state out of total ownership and control of the means of production and allowing them back in through partial ownership and control.

It is one thing to have a little state ownership, though, and another for nationalized concerns to have a central place in the system of hard-core investors. The government's overlong hesitation in withdrawing UAP from consideration for privatization after the crash of October 1987 had a lot to do with the fact that it saw UAP, which held shares in most of the privatized companies, as the key to the whole system of hard-core investors. And it was afraid that the system would be undone if it lost the

---

[109]CGE, the state's biggest supplier, is in a monopolistic situation with regard to nuclear power (with Framatome) and the railways (with Alsthom), and has close to a monopoly at 84% of the market with Alcatel. *Libération*, May 11, 1987.

[110]See Chapter 13 for a list of the nationalized enterprises that own shares in privatized enterprises.

elections or, worse, that UAP would be used as a Trojan horse by the state to seek to exercise control over the privatized companies.[111]

CONCLUSION

Despite the great success of privatization, then, it was not quite the liberal panacea originally intended, at least by the ultras; and this despite the fact that Chirac in his speech on privatization claimed that: "Statism and bureaucracy are in the past. The future belongs to a free and independent private enterprise."[112] For all the neoliberals' efforts to distinguish themselves from the Socialists by insisting that they alone were the champions of "less state," they were in many ways as *dirigiste,* if not more so, than the Socialists had been in their last few years in office. The heroic policies of the left had been followed by heroic policies of the right, in both cases with strong government initiatives that altered the French industrial and industrial policy landscape. Subsequent governments were to continue this process, but with much less heroism. François Léotard may very well have been more prophetic than he himself knew when, on the eve of the March 1986 elections, he declared that "the true modernization of political life . . . means the appearance of two major forces, one social-democratic and the other liberal" in which *l'alternance,* instead of producing a civil war with each change in government, would become *"banalisé."*[113] This normalization arrived with the 1988 elections, when everyday policymaking substituted itself for the heroism that had come before, and the pace of reforms in the direction set since 1983 only intensified even as the heroic rhetoric subsided.

Europe, moreover, was to become an increasingly important element in the mix. Although the impact of European integration had already been felt as of 1983 with regard to the macroeconomic sphere, the effects on the microeconomic sphere of the Single European Act, ratified in 1987, were yet to be felt. The public as a whole was generally unaware of the changes that were about to take place, and would remain so until the ratification of the Maastricht Treaty in 1991 brought a major public debate. French business, however, was already very much aware of the potential changes, and very much in support of them. In a survey of European managers taken in 1987, the French were far and away the most enthusiastic when it came to reinforcing the European Community, followed by the Germans, the Spaniards, and then the British (see Table 5.2). French business would remain a key promoter of European integra-

---

[111]*Le Point,* no. 791, November 16, 1987, p. 84.
[112]*Libération,* July 17, 1986.   [113]*Le Monde,* March 15, 1986.

Changes in government policies toward business

Table 5.2. *Managers' attitudes toward the reinforcement of the European Community in 1987, in percentages*

	Favorable	Somewhat Favorable	Opposed
France	88	10	2
Great Britain	65	24	11
W. Germany	77	12	11
Spain	69	25	6

Source: Le Monde Affaires, October 10, 1987.

tion, along with French politicians of the right and the left who, having staked their political careers on its success, would continue to support it wholeheartedly even in the face of popular fears of a loss of sovereignty and a recession brought on at least in part by France's unwavering adherence to the European Monetary System, despite other EC members' temporary departure.

6

Everyday disengagement (1988 to 1995)

For governments from 1988 forward, the direction of economic policy was set. Deregulation and privatization, either officially or unofficially, remained the order of the day, pushed by the imperatives of European integration as well as the capital needs of firms. These had become every-day matters, however, as the heroic policies formulated without significant consultation gave way to ones that seemed to follow business much more than to lead it, and as the *coup par coup* took the place of any coordinated industrial policy. In this period, there were to be no heroic economic projects, whether on the left or the right, and certainly no heroic industrial policies to make them reality.

In fact, heroic policymaking seemed a thing of the past, the heroism of those initial seven years during Mitterrand's first presidential mandate having exhausted the public and the politicians, as well as the font of ideas. The lesson, gleaned from seven years of *va-et-vient,* or back-and-forth, on economic policies and ideology, is that through nationalization and privatization, through state control of business and proclaimed state nonintervention, as well as through government-sponsored industrial co-operation and government promotion of seemingly unbridled competi-tion, business operates as business. Moreover, the lesson from the neo-liberals in particular, with their Thatcherite and Reaganite policies of laissez-faire capitalism, was that the free market, with all that that en-tailed in terms of unbridled competition and uncontrolled business, was not the panacea anticipated. When the public voted for the Socialists in 1988, they were voting for stability and an end to economic ideology, whether of the right or the left.

Heroism, if anything, was transferred to the supranational level, with governments focusing on the making of Europe, with the Maastricht Treaty, and on the making of European industrial policy. The results, however, were not always as anticipated. French leaders had expected that by giving up control over national monetary policy, they could manage to control European and French macroeconomic policy from the EC, and thereby better handle the external constraints that had made the economic environment so unpredictable in the seventies. Moreover, at the microeconomic level, they had assumed that by liberalizing and thereby giving up many of their industrial policy instruments at the national level, they could regain these and more at the European level, by creating an interventionist European industrial policy.

At first, at least, the French were not wrong. As long as the world economy was booming, everyone profited (except the unemployed) from an integrating economic system and the tight monetary policies that were required. However, as the world slid into recession, led by the United States, French economic growth began to slow, and French leaders more and more began questioning the politics of the strong franc to which governments remained faithful, even though this meant slowing economic growth and doing little to reduce unemployment. Similarly, moreover, the early hopes for European-level industrial policy, fueled by the EC history of programs such as Esprit, Brite, Euram, Race, Eureka, and Jessi, were disappointed, particularly in the high technology area.

Heroism, in short, no longer characterized industrial policymaking at either the European or the national level. And yet, important changes nevertheless occurred. As much if not more was done to alter the structure of French capitalism in this time of everyday policymaking than in the previous, more heroic period. By progressively diminishing state ownership and weakening state control over the course of Mitterrand's second *septennat,* governments of the left and right succeeded in creating a truly mixed economy in which public and private, nationalized and privatized financial and industrial concerns owned and controlled one another following the German model of banking–industry partnership.[1] Only instead of resulting from sweeping governmental policies formulated absent societal input, it came from a growing consensus between government and business about what should be done, and from government decisions that were much more responses to the needs of the moment than any publicly proclaimed heroic policies.

By the early nineties, in short, France's statist pattern of policymaking, distinctive for its heroism and at its apogee throughout the *trente glorieuses,* had lost not only much of the means to make heroic industrial policies but also the will, thus having become at least in comparison to the past an empty shell devoid of its traditional content. But much of this, at least, had been accomplished in heroic, statist fashion.

[1] For details on how French capitalism was restructured, see Chapter 13.

Everyday disengagement (1988–1995)

THE END OF HEROIC ECONOMIC PROJECTS AND THE NEW CONSENSUS

During the period between 1988 and 1994, as everyday policymaking substituted itself for the heroic, and as a united Europe became an increasing reality, a new view of the role of the state in the economy emerged. This was one in which liberal macroeconomic and microeconomic policies are accompanied by a certain amount of state interventionism, and where business works together with government to conceive of the strategies for the future. Jonah Levy calls this new view "Tocquevillean liberalism" because it mixes a broad distrust of state intervention with a recognition of the need for something more than the free play of market forces, and therefore accepts the importance of nonstate institutions and organized interests making policy with the state.[2] This is reflected in the more everyday policies of governments that, although serving as vehicles for change as significant as those precipitated by the earlier more heroic policies, were formulated much more in conjunction with societal interests than in spite of them. In the case of the reorganization of French capitalism, more specifically, it is as if succeeding governments, having exhausted their own capital of ideas, turned to the capitalists for proposals.

The groundwork for these changes was created by the previous period of backs and forths in industrial policy, in particular the nationalizations and privatizations. When Mitterrand declared a pause in the process with the policy of *ni-ni*, the public as well as the CEOs seemed relieved. The CEOs in particular welcomed an end to the seesaw, although many continued to push for some form of privatization. Their reasons, now as earlier, had nothing to do with ideology but rather with firm flexibility and need for capital. Their views of both nationalization and privatization, moreover, had undergone a major transformation. Whereas at the time of both the nationalizations of 1982 and the privatizations of 1986 to 1988, they had had great trepidations about their impact on the economy, now they insisted, with hindsight, that neither nationalization nor privatization had made much difference: ownership was less important than firm strategies and market conditions. As one high level Treasury official put it, neither nationalization nor privatization had anything to do with the success of the economy because "legal possession has nothing to do with performance."[3] And even Gandois, who had resigned in protest at governmental interference in the internal management of the firm, insisted that nationalization and privatization did not disturb, in a good

[2]Levy, "Tocqueville's Revenge."   [3]Interview with author, Paris, May 28, 1991.

167

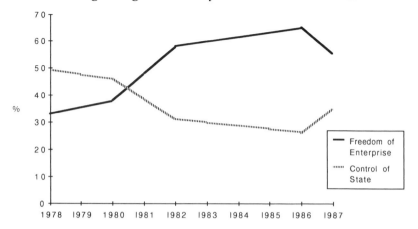

Figure 6.1. Evolution of public attitudes on freedom of enterprise and control of the state.
Source: SOFRES, *L'état de l'opinion 1988* (Paris: Seuil, 1988), p. 34.

or a bad sense, that which would have been done anyway.[4] By this time, the CEOs, like everyone else, had become convinced that, public or private, business operates as business. And the question then becomes how best to enable business to operate.

Public attitudes reflected this evolution in views. The public's initial enthusiasm for both nationalization and privatization had been almost immediately tempered by concerns in the first instance related to too much state control of and too little freedom for nationalized industry and in the second instance to too little state control of and too much freedom for privatized industry (see Figure 6.1). More specifically, whereas in September 1978 49% of the population agreed that to solve economic problems, the state should control business and regulate it more strictly, the proportion who believed this plunged to 31% in December 1982, right in the middle of the Socialist government's nationalization and restructuring program. It then dropped to a low of 26% by October 1986, during the initial phase of the neoliberal government's privatization and deregulation program, only to increase to 35% by May 1987, as if to say that the decrease in state control had gone far enough. By contrast, whereas in September 1978 33% of the public agreed that to solve economic problems, more faith should be put in business and it should be given greater freedom, the proportion who believed this jumped to 58% by December 1982, as if to show disapproval of the Socialists' interventionism, reaching a high of 65% in October 1986. It then dropped to 55% in May 1987, as if to say that privatization and deregulation had

[4]Gandois, interview with author.

168

gone far enough. In the end, however, the public remained much more in favor of greater freedom for business and of less state control than it had been at the outset.

The public's response to change, whether to nationalization or privatization, in short, was measured, demonstrating it to be less ideologically driven than its governments, concerned to liberalize but not to go too far. As former Prime Minister Rocard explained it, France had in ten years undergone a considerable modernization, and "The French have acquired an economic culture that they didn't have before and which makes them at the same time clearseeing and severe with regard to demagogues."[5] Within this context, Rocard's official declaration of an end to heroic industrial policymaking appeared perfectly appropriate, since it went along with the public's own evolving views of the role of the state in the economy. Moreover, the incremental change in the structure of state ownership and control of business that began under Rocard's leadership was very much a response to business needs and desires. But although such change ultimately ended up being as dramatic as that of previous regimes, it was not the result of any well-thought-out heroic state policy, and was not clearly articulated until it was already taking place.

It was only beginning in the early nineties that a consensus emerged on restructuring French capitalism in a manner akin to the German model, where the main banks have large interests in industrial firms and thereby provide stability and protection from hostile takeover, as well as a longer-term view and investment capital in the event of an economic downturn. It was at this time, too, that the grumblings about the lack of any clear industrial policy under Rocard were fully articulated, with a consensus also emerging on the need for a continued state role in industrial policymaking. And it was also at this time that Europe became a central preoccupation, with government and business leaders alike recognizing that effective industrial policy only had a future at the European level.

In 1991, a plethora of books and articles appeared lauding the Germans and castigating the Americans and the British for their approaches to industry. Of these, the most significant was Michel Albert's *Capitalisme contre capitalisme*,[6] in which he opposed the "neo-American" model characteristic of the United States and Great Britain, which values individual achievement, risk-taking, and short-term profitability, with what he described as the superior "Rhinish" model, most closely linked with Switzerland, Sweden, and Germany as well as Japan, which values collective success and long-term industrial development. Thus, he hoped that the history of France, which he saw as characterized in 1791 by

---

[5]*Le Monde,* May 10, 1991.
[6]Michel Albert, *Capitalisme contre capitalisme* (Paris: Seuil, 1991).

"capitalism against the state" and then in 1891 by "capitalism with the state," would be characterizable as of 1991 by "capitalism in place of the state."

French policymakers and business leaders more generally embraced this view, seeing the whole panoply of government–industry, banking–industry, and labor–management relations characteristic of German corporatism as the model to emulate.[7] Already in November 1990, Jean-Louis Beffa had called for more cooperation between financiers and industrialists along the lines of the German model. For him, "The real question is whether we can pass from the French model, which leaves a very special role to the state, to a German model, which seems to me can become the most important in Europe."[8] To emulate the German model, however, did not mean that they thought to abandon the state, not possible in any case given the different traditions and institutions; they sought only to change the way "the state does what it does," in the words of Beffa, and to recognize that for the state it is better "to have done (*faire faire*) than to do for itself," by leaving a more important role to the market and the actors themselves, including CEOs of public enterprises.[9]

To allow a more important role to the market, however, did not mean going overboard as they saw the Americans and British as having done, whether by allowing their industries to be acquired by the Japanese or by allowing their industries to go under because of the lack of any coherent industrial policies, whether guided by the state, as in France, by the banks, as in Germany, or by a business–government partnership, as in Japan.[10] Among French business and government officials, a consensus had emerged that suggested that the state still had a role to play, if only in strategic areas linked to the national interest, such as defense, energy, and high technology, and that continued state intervention to promote the growth industries of the future, in particular in high-technology areas, was appropriate. As part of this, many were concerned about an overemphasis on macroeconomic policy, to the detriment of the microeconomic, the result of the primacy of the French Ministry of Finance and its basically "Anglo-Saxon" vision. In fact, although most were perfectly satisfied with the strict monetary policies and budgetary austerity that sought to create a favorable macroeconomic environment for business, many were distressed about the declared rejection of any industrial policy by the Rocard government, especially once the economy began to slow down.

Only the bankers and Ministry of Finance officials were convinced that

[7]See: "L'état c'est l'Europe: A Survey of France," *The Economist* November 23–29, 1991, p. 14; *Wall Street Journal*, July 23, 1991.
  [8]*Le Figaro*, November 14, 1990.   [9]Beffa, interview with author.
  [10]See the discussion in Chapter 12.

macroeconomic policies, coupled with financial deregulation, were alone responsible for the economic recovery, and that industrial policy was therefore on the whole superfluous. For a banker such as André Lévy-Lang, president of Paribas, the changes in the opening of the markets beginning as early as 1982 were the only reasons for recovery.[11] Others, such as Jean-Paul Betbèze, chief economist at the Crédit Lyonnais, agreed with the overall point, although he saw the change coming a bit later, as of 1985–1986.[12] Daniel Lebègue, director-general of the BNP and former director of the Treasury, did not go quite as far. For him, industrial policy may have done something, but it was entirely secondary to the macroeconomic policies beginning with the Delors plan of 1983 (of which he was one of the architects), which created a favorable environment for business; to company strength and business strategy; and to worldwide market conditions. State intervention might help where the firm was well run and made good strategic decisions, as in the cases of Péchiney and the steel industry, but it could do little where a firm was weak or had poor business strategy, as in textiles and wood.[13] Another high-level Treasury official confirmed this view, arguing that the key to healthy industry is a low inflation rate, and that therefore the Treasury's emphasis on macroeconomic equilibrium over dynamism was perfectly justified. Even he admitted, however, that this was not enough, and that there is a role for the Ministry of Industry because you need *actions structurantes,* such as research and development, or providing Thomson and Bull with a needed infusion of extra capital.[14]

Most economists, business executives, and Ministry of Industry officials went a lot farther than this. Many economists were convinced that a strong industrial policy focused on investment in the manufacturing industry was the key to future economic growth, in contradistinction to the British emphasis on services, let alone its laissez-faire approach to state involvement in industry. Philippe Delmas, for example, maintained that the state alone was capable of ensuring industry's continued health because only it could manage time, that is, allow industries to take a more long-term view and invest.[15] Expanding on this theme, former Prime Minister Raymond Barre argued that the state, in giving business time for the management of the future, must place a priority on investment in industry as well as on training, following the example of Germany.[16] Jean-Louis Levet, moreover, insisted that the French should feel less apol-

[11]Levy-Lang, interview with author.   [12]Interview with author, Paris, April 30, 1991.
[13]Lebègue, interview with author.   [14]Interview with author, Paris, May 28, 1991.
[15]Philippe Delmas, interview in *Tribune de l'Expansion,* May 21, 1991. See also his
Le maître des horloges (Paris: Odile Jacob, 1991).
[16]Barre, *Le Monde,* May 24, 1991.

ogetic about their traditional protectionism and interventionism since other states do this too, they just show it less. And he pleaded for a real economic policy capable of overcoming the government's mistaken strategic decisions, remedying its poorly coordinated implementation of those decisions, and better defending French interests in the EC, including properly addressing the Japanese menace.[17]

Business executives on the right and the left also envisioned a continuing role for industrial policy. Gandois of Péchiney, for example, noted that the state has had and will always have a tendency to occupy itself in areas it thinks fundamental for the future and for defense, that is, electronics, computers, aerospace, and in areas which cause problems for the society at large, such as the declining industries.[18] Moreover, Michel Drancourt, director of the Business Institute, although ideologically in favor of less state, admitted that a strong industrial policy was necessary because the state must compensate for the fact that Europe didn't exist industrially as yet. Nonetheless, although Drancourt suggested that France had the best-directed economy in the world, he wondered if it was still possible in this day and age.[19]

In fact, most French government and business leaders agreed that industrial policy as they knew it was no longer possible at the nation-state level, but that it could and should be done at the European level. Most in particular pushed for a Europewide electronics policy, insisting, as did Prime Minister Cresson, that Europe dared not depend on other countries to supply products essential to its technological future or its defense;[20] and some even advocated the creation of a European electronics agency, as did Paul Quilès, Rocard's Minister of the PTT, feeling that the Community needed to do for electronics what it had done for space when it made Europe first in commercial satellite launching.[21] In addition, many supported Europewide infrastructural projects such as high-speed trains linking all of Europe; automotive industry policies, in particular to confront the Japanese challenge, as Jacques Calvet, CEO of Peugeot, put it; and high-technology policies more generally, with many more projects on the scale of those initiated on space.[22] In fact, even those who saw little role for a strong industrial policy in France, such as Rocard's Minister of Industry Roger Fauroux, wanted a real European industrial policy, based more on cooperation than competition among European partners, with

[17]Jean-Louis Levet, editorial in *Le Monde,* June 12, 1991. See also his *Une France sans complexes* (Paris: Economica, 1990).

[18]Gandois, interview with author.

[19]Michel Drancourt, director of the Institut de l'Entreprise. Conversation with author, Paris, May 15, 1991.

[20]*Le Monde,* May 24, 1991.   [21]*Le Monde,* April 26, 1991.

[22]Jean-Baptiste de Boissière and Bertrand Warusfeld, *La nouvelle frontière de la technologie européene* (Paris: Calmann-Lévy, 1991).

France playing the role of leader.[23] Thus, he would have liked to see the use of customs (high to protect young industries such as electronic components), standards, and public markets to protect the Community from unbridled competition as well as to reinforce research and cooperation among industrial groups, especially in the case of electronic components.[24] But the problem with Europe, as Fauroux among others insisted, was that it was "very liberal, too liberal."[25]

Although probably not all would have gone as far as the above-mentioned top Treasury official did, to call the Community "stupidly Englishly liberal," all would probably have agreed with him that the Community would have done better to take its lessons from the Germans and the Japanese rather than the British. Not many, however, were very hopeful about this possibility, with most complaining, as did Louis Gallois, at the time CEO of SNECMA and subsequently of Aerospatiale, that the EC mistook competition policy, or the control of mergers, for industrial policy, which created the conditions for development.[26] The problem with the EC, as Fauroux's successor as Minister of Industry, Dominique Strauss-Kahn, put it, was its ideological commitment to the free market, and the failure to recognize that, although Leon Brittan may have been right in theory, "real life is far from the theoretical world in which we would like to live. . . . In real life, market forces are imperfect: today's sophisticated industrial products tend to emerge more as a result of costly research and development, than in response to consumer demand." And technological development, therefore, cannot be left to market forces alone.[27]

The French concern with the liberalism of the European Union was not limited to unhappiness with the lack of coordinated, full-fledged industrial policies. It extended to what many saw as the EU's all-too-liberal approach to competition policy as well. Pierre Suard, CEO of Alcatel-Alsthom, for one, complained vociferously about "a certain state of mind that prevails in Brussels," insisting that "the single market should not be opened any larger than competing markets are; one shouldn't impose on European industries structural constraints that are not applied to their competitors." In particular, he cited the agreement signed with Fiat that still awaited approval from Brussels after six months, at a time when the Canadian Northern Telecom, itself protected from takeover by Canadian legislation, needed no approval for its rapid takeover

[23]Roger Fauroux, Minister of Industry in Rocard's government, former head of Saint-Gobain from before nationalization through 1986, and graduate of the ENA. Interview with author, Paris, April 4, 1991.
[24]*Le Monde,* April 4, 1991.   [25]Fauroux, interview with author.
[26]Louis Gallois, CEO of SNECMA. Interview with author, Paris, May 3, 1991.
[27]*Financial Times,* June 8, 1992.

of the British STC.[28] The French, in short, were upset not only by the fact that the EU did not do in the industrial policy area what they themselves could do no longer, but also that what it did do, it did not do well.

The French upset with the European Union had a lot to do with the fact that they recognized that France itself could no longer follow its traditional interventionist model of industrial policy, not only because of the role of Europe and the globalization of the economy, but also because of the weakening of the traditional policy instruments that had made interventionism possible in the past. This, however, did not entail the total abandonment of industrial policy in France, only the development of a more indirect kind. For Louis Schweitzer of Renault, for example, it meant developing infrastructural policies, aid for research and development, work on training and employment, and so forth, and with the Ministry of Industry providing recommendations in terms of industrial strategies, but only in the role of shareholder.[29] For Gallois, the answer lay in making industrial policy indirectly, by using the ministries of PTT, transports, defense, and agriculture as well as the public procurement policies of the major nationalized industries in the noncompetitive sector such as the SNCF and EDF to structure demand and to encourage research and development, as they had in the past.[30] For Paul Quilès, at the time Minister of the PTT in charge of France Télécom, such an approach, where "public powers play an orientation and incentive role," was essential to the health of the economy because "If we leave private enterprises to work solely in terms of their own strategy, we have no chance of resisting Japanese competition."[31] Nationalized enterprise in the noncompetitive sphere such as EDF and France Télécom, in fact, were to continue to play an important role. All remained convinced that some nationalization was always necessary, with most CEOs, whether on the right or the left, arguing that the state was in particular needed for the *grands projets*.

In short, a consensus had emerged over time that maintained that the state still had a role to play, but now in conjunction with business rather than in spite of it. By fall 1992, this consensus was consecrated by the Ministry of Industry in its "Made in France" study, modeled on MIT's "Made in America" study, which saw a role for the state in all the areas noted above, that is, in public procurement policy, in aid for research and development, in training and apprenticeships, in infrastructural projects and *grands projets*, in bringing industrial and financial concerns closer together through the creation of bank–industry "poles," or spheres of

[28]*Le Monde*, April 5, 1991.   [29]Schweitzer, interview with author.
[30]Gallois, interview with author.   [31]*Le Monde*, April 26, 1991.

influence, and through the furthering of the "mixed economy," by having private and foreign concerns participate in the capital of nationalized enterprises.[32] In an internal document of the Ministry of Industry in August 1992, moreover, the Ministry outlined an industrial policy that was to "create the conditions for a balanced and competitive industrial development" which would move from voluntarist policies focused on sectoral plans to strategic policies focused on the future, but which would also seek to reorient EC priorities toward industrial objectives with regard to funds for research and social and regional reconversion. Moreover, they sought to convince Brussels of the appropriateness of continued French state funding of its public enterprises, as a policy focused on defending the "hard core of the French industrial patrimony," and a goal they felt was simply achieved by different means in the United States through technology policies implemented by the Department of Defense, in Japan through its *keiretsus,* or in Germany through its banking–industry coupling.[33] Thus, although the French state was no doubt in retreat, it still saw a need for government planning and promotion of industry, but now more in partnership with business.

But how to make this work? According to Beffa, less state required politicians and industrialists together reaching a consensus on the model of development, with an industrial policy focused on firms with competence in their *métiers,* or core activities, the support of the state, and a vision of the long term. This consensus, he felt, could be built through macroeconomic, financial, and fiscal policies, through microeconomic policies involving targeted aid to industry, and through the careful choice of the composition of shareholders in the nationalized and privatized companies.[34] This is exactly what occurred, as the continuing liberalism in state management of the economy was joined by a certain measure of "voluntarism" in state industrial action, even as the restructuring of French capitalism proceeded apace.

THE TRIUMPH OF EVERYDAY LIBERALISM

When the Socialists returned to power in 1988, they continued with the liberalization begun in 1983 and accelerated as of 1986, maintaining tight monetary policies to keep inflation down while cutting taxes even further as well as freeing up business from even more restrictions – now as much in response to European Community directives as anything else. Moreover, the emphasis of successive Socialist governments on what Bé-

[32]Dominique Taddei and Benjamin Coriat, "Spécial: Made in France," *Industries* special edition (September 1992).

[33]Ministry of Industry, "Réflexions sur la politique industrielle," August 19, 1992.

[34]Beffa, interview with author.

régovoy, as Minister of Finance for Prime Ministers Rocard and Cresson, and then as Prime Minister himself, called "competitive disinflation," giving priority to budget reduction and focusing on supply-side micro-economic policies, only continued under the Balladur government. For all this conversion to liberalism, however, state intervention in areas deemed of strategic importance was not halted. Certain nationalized industries continued to receive large infusions of capital while others were encouraged to merge, regardless of their anti-competitive effects and despite the possibility of censure by the European Community. Nevertheless, heroic industrial policymaking appeared to be over.

Michel Rocard's government, by promising a return to stability and an end to ideologically inspired economic policies, was hailed as spelling the true end not only to *dirigisme,* but to industrial policy altogether. Although when Edith Cresson became Prime Minister in 1991 she proclaimed its revival with a new *"volontarisme,"* this was more rhetoric than anything else, and even this ended when Pierre Bérégovoy took over as Prime Minister barely a year later. Finally, yet another year later, Prime Minister Edouard Balladur on the right was no more heroic than the left. Even privatization had become an everyday affair.

Everyday policymaking under successive governments of the left and the right nevertheless succeeded in bringing about changes in the structure of French capitalism that rival in significance, although not heroism or speed, the nationalizations of the early 1980s and the privatizations of the mid 1980s. During the *ni-ni* period (1988–1991), when neither nationalization nor privatization was to have taken place, the Rocard government gradually diluted state ownership of nationalized enterprises by allowing exceptions to the policy to promote strategic alliances and decreased state control by arranging for the recapitalization of industry through the trading of shares among nationalized industrial and financial concerns. During the post-*ni-ni* period (1991–1993), when up to 49% of nationalized enterprises could be sold off, this process continued with the trading of shares among public and private, nationalized and privatized enterprises. And with the Balladur government beginning in 1993, the intermixing picked up speed as privatization began anew, with nationalized firms along with private ones buying into the privatized ones.

The result has been a restructuring of French capitalism, with an end to a model in which the state directly owns and controls the bulk of French industrial and financial concerns. Instead, the state now only indirectly controls its firms, with the bulk of major nationalized and privatized, public and private firms controlling one another through *noyaux durs* of investors that are to ensure stability and good management.

Everyday disengagement (1988–1995)

The Rocard government, 1988–1991

When Rocard took office in 1988, he benefited from the favorable economic environment that had started in 1986, which was linked to the reduction in oil prices that had fueled first an increase in consumption and then a rise in business investment. The French stock market was at its highest level ever, even if unemployment and foreign trade remained problematic. The year 1989 was even better, spelling the end of the crisis begun in 1974 that was characterized by underinvestment, stagnation of production and consumption, and the growth of unemployment.[35] The returning health of the nationalized enterprises, together with the general improvement in businesses' profit margins enabled French industry to expand worldwide through acquisitions and enabled French companies to remedy some of their problems related to inadequate size and internationalization.[36] By 1990, however, a number of firms began to experience sizable losses, and started laying off tens of thousands of workers. In 1991, the end of the Gulf War produced only a momentary recovery from the slowdown.

Throughout this period, the Rocard government had a lot more money available to it than all previous governments since 1983. Nonetheless, under the influence of Finance Minister Bérégovoy and in keeping with the policies of previous governments since 1983, the Rocard government also gave priority to budget reduction and focused on supply-side microeconomic policies. It reduced corporate taxes by 10 billion francs in its 1989 budget, cut taxes on individuals by 5 billion francs and increased public spending in line with inflation, that is, by 4.5%. Moreover, it reduced taxes on revenue from savings and on consumption (by reducing the VAT, or value-added tax, as mandated by the EC, despite Rocard's criticism of its "pauperizing" effect on the state).[37]

At the same time, however, the government spent a lot on a minimum job reentry revenue (RMI), on public employees' salaries (in particular the nurses, transport workers, postal employees, and tax collectors), on the national education system (which grew from 198 billion francs in 1988 to 250 billion francs in 1991), and on modernizing the public sector (expected to cost over the next seven years 42 billion in constant francs, of which the state was to pay 22 billion).[38] Thus, the worker was not forgotten. But this was still a long way from 1981. Not once was worker control mentioned; the best the Socialists did in the 1988 party platform was to

[35] Alain Gélédan, *Le bilan économique des années Mitterrand 1981–1993* (Paris: Le Monde Editions, 1993), pp. 125–30.
[36] See the discussion in Chapter 12.
[37] Gélédan, *Le bilan économique,* pp. 119–25.   [38] Ibid.

note that "to change life in the workplace is an ambitious project that takes time," and that "there is no citizenship project in the firm which is prefabricated and deliverable without delay."[39] There was also no mention of a reduction of hours in the workweek; no promises on salaries or on the minimum wage. Finally, instead of the traditional promise to maintain purchasing power, they noted that "In a competitive economy, the notion of a strict maintenance of purchasing power cannot be a mobilizing objective for the long term. Salaries must therefore benefit from the positive effects of austerity policy, that is, to share the fruits of refound competitiveness."[40] In short, all the emphasis was on maintaining a sound economy, with the assumption that all would benefit as a result. And instead of any talk of changing the workplace, all the focus was on promoting the health of business, small as well as big.

Moreover, this was not to be done with any heroic industrial policy or any more nationalization or privatization, Rocard having declared an end to industrial policy and Mitterrand an end to nationalization or privatization with the policy of the *ni-ni*. In fact, in the 1988 "propositions" of the Socialists, although they were clearly willing to allow some change in the structure of state ownership and control, they had no clear idea of what that would mean, especially given the *ni-ni*. Thus, the Socialists announced that the shape of the public sector could be "adjusted" according to "the strategic economic objectives of the nation" and according to the principle of "respiration" that would allow firms to exit as much as to enter the public sector. But although they anticipated circumstances under which nationalization would be beneficial – for example, to avoid foreign takeover, to provide financial aid, or to create new enterprises, in particular in high risk domains – they made no suggestions for renationalization other than that of TF1 (which never happened, of course).[41] Moreover, there was still no mention of a National Investment Bank, proposed in the 1972 and 1980 platforms.[42] (Only when Dominique Strauss-Kahn was Minister of Industry in the Cresson government did the subject resurface.)

The lack of any declared industrial policy or plans for nationalization or privatization, however, did not mean that no change occurred. Much the contrary. In the case of the nationalized enterprises in particular,

---

[39]*Le Monde*, January 8, 1988.   [40]Ibid.

[41]Defeated amendments by two Socialist groupings did, however, anticipate extensive renationalization. The amendment of the Socialisme et République faction proposed renationalizing CGE, Société Générale, Paribas, and Suez. That of the "Nouvelle Composante" faction of Jean Poperen stated that no denationalization was "irreversible" and that the renationalization of the entire banking and insurance industry was "indispensable."

[42]*Le Monde*, January 8, 1988. For why it was dropped, see Chapter 7.

although the official *ni-ni* policy called for no change, holes were progressively punched in the policy as the government decreased state ownership by allowing for foreign acquisitions or mergers and diminished state control as it arranged for the trading of shares among nationalized enterprises. Such changes came in a piecemeal fashion, the result not of heroic policies but rather of the everyday policies that emerged from the politics of accommodation between ministry and industry.[43] These "industrial actions," as they were termed in the Ministry of Industry to differentiate them clearly from industrial policies, were very much a response to requests by individual corporations, as part of a clear policy of the government to allow the CEOs to do what they wanted.[44] For Minister of Industry Roger Fauroux, this was as it should be, because "the violent shocks and countershocks of nationalization and privatization were things of the past, as was state interventionism, to be followed by a more peaceful period where appointments to head the nationalized industries are no longer politicized, and where the relationship of the state to industry is that of a shareholder."[45]

The first breach in the policy of *ni-ni* came in the spring of 1989, when Péchiney was allowed to create a wholly owned subsidiary, Péchiney International, and to sell 25% of its shares on the market to finance its acquisition of American Can. Other companies, however, still could only float nonvoting shares up to 25% of their equity capital, in keeping with the law of 1983. It was a year later that the policy of *ni-ni* came to an end unofficially, with the entry of Volvo in the capital of Renault (a 25% share) in April 1990 – and a change in law to allow it – and yet another year later when the *ni-ni* was for all intents and purposes reversed just before Rocard's resignation as Prime Minister. At that time, private companies were allowed to buy up to a 49% stake in nationalized companies, provided they entered into industrial, commercial, or financial agreements, and that they increased the company's capital without jeopardizing the state's majority holding.

The slow reversal of the *ni-ni* policy effectively provided nationalized companies with further capital, diluting state ownership without doing much to alter the state's control. But as a result of another set of little-noticed capital transactions involving the trading of shares in nationalized companies in an effort to generate new capital which the state could not provide directly, Rocard's government also ensured that the state no longer directly controlled most public enterprises in the competitive sector. Instead, these companies gained control of one another. The opposition actually criticized this not so much from the standpoint of the

---

[43]See the discussions in Chapter 9.   [44]Bidegain, interview with author.
[45]Fauroux, interview with author. See also the discussion in Chapter 7.

changes in control as from the financial, seeing it as the state acting as a "capitalist without capital."[46]

Here, too, the restructuring of French capitalism proceeded in a case-by-case manner. The process began when two nationalized companies, the insurer UAP and the bank BNP, were allowed to exchange 10% of their shares because this changed nothing in their status as nationalized enterprises and helped raise money for both enterprises. The process continued as the BNP took over the Bank of Brittany, and GAN acquired CIC. In 1990, the activity really picked up when the Crédit Lyonnais bought Thomson-CSF's subsidiary Altus and in return Thomson received 14% of the Crédit Lyonnais, leaving the latter partially controlled by private investors (6%) in consequence of Thomson's 60% ownership of Thomson-CSF. In addition, in July 1990, the state gave Rhône-Poulenc its 35% share of Rousself-Uclaf in exchange for new shares in Rhône-Poulenc, which it in turn gave AGF and Crédit Lyonnais in exchange for shares in them. A similar strategy was used for BNP and AGF to enter into the capital of Péchiney. In the meantime, Péchiney had transferred the whole real estate portfolio of the Crédit Chimique, its banking subsidiary, to the Banque Hervet in exchange for a 7.24% share. And a year later, in April 1991, France Télécom, through Cogecom, its subsidiary, acquired an 8.3% share of the Banque Hervet, bringing the bank 200 million francs in equity capital. France Télécom also participated in the recapitalization of Bull and Thomson, acquiring a 17% stake in Bull alone. In fact, there was so much trading of shares, with banks and insurers taking stakes in one another as well as with the nationalized industries, that the result was a "spider's web" which left the state not directly controlling any public enterprise in the competitive sector.[47]

Thus, although Rocard was roundly criticized for giving up on industrial policy by all and sundry once France began sliding into recession, his government nevertheless began a process that has enabled French business to gain greater independence from the state and greater interdependence between industrial and financial concerns, thus emulating a more German set-up. And this only accelerated under subsequent governments.

What is more, Rocard's government also sought to free public enterprises in the noncompetitive sphere from the burdens of excessive state intervention. Thus, EDF, in what Fauroux hailed as a revolution in ministry–industry relations, was freed from the worst of state interventionism when the ministry signed a contract in which the company agreed to try to increase productivity and the state engaged itself in a pricing policy that was *convenable,* meaning not arbitrary, calculated on costs, and so forth. The EDF was helped in its attempt to alter the situation not

[46]*Le Monde,* February 22, 1991.   [47]*Le Monde,* April 7–8, and 9, 1991.

only because financial pressures on the state had eased and the Ministry of Finance finally recognized how essential this was for EDF's health, but also because of pressure from Brussels to increase the freedom of all national utilities.[48] Moreover, the statute of France Telecom was modernized in response to mounting pressures to free it from excessive government financial regulations as well as to enable it to meet increasing European competition (spurred on in particular by Sir Leon Brittan's 1987 Green Paper calling for competition in the telecommunications market).[49] The change, which came from within and reflected the agency's engineers' desire to have "a large autonomy on its procurement, research, personnel, and finance policies,"[50] turned the *administration* into an *établissement autonome de droit public* on the model of EDF (its desire to become a *société nationale* was refused), giving it freedom to set rates and prices on products and services subject to competition (15% of its gross sales). But the Minister of Post and Telecommunications still fixed strategic economic and social objectives, and the Minister of Finance still fixed rates on monopoly services and kept the right of oversight over the company's industrial policy.[51] What is more, France Télécom still had to play a role in the government's industrial policy, as well as pay the state $2.5 billion to support research and development in other sectors until 1993. Finally, instead of Télécom regulating itself, as it had in the past, operations were separated from regulation, which went to the Direction de la Réglementation Générale (DRG), and an administrative council was established.[52]

The Rocard government promoted business in other ways as well. While the large industries were essentially let alone to do as they wished, the government sought to take a more active leadership role on a lower plane, by encouraging the development of small and mid-sized enterprises in conjunction with regional authorities, and on a higher one, by seeking to increase France's influence on European industrial policy.[53] Most important to the government, in fact, were small and mid-sized enterprises, which had become a priority area. It concluded that these firms were crucial to the health of the economy as a whole, especially given their close links as "just-in-time" suppliers to large industries. In 1988 alone, 15 billion francs in state-sponsored industrial bonds were diverted to

---

[48]Fauroux, interview with author.

[49]See the discussion in Elie Cohen, *Le colbertisme "high tech": Économies des Télécom et du Grand Projet* (Paris: Hachette, 1992); and Zahariadis, *Political Economy of Privatization*, pp. 355–360.

[50]*L'Expansion*, April 4–17, 1986, p. 93—cited in Zahariadis, *Political Economy of Privatization*, p. 342.

[51]*Le Figaro*, February 11, 1991.   [52]Zahariadis, *Political Economy of Privatization*, p. 359.

[53]Jean-Pierre Jouyet, cabinet director of the Minister of Industry, Roger Fauroux. Interview with author, Paris, May 14, 1991.

small and medium-sized businesses, while they were offered 600 million francs in subsidized loans.[54] In September 1990, moreover, using a mix of tax breaks, exoneration from social security charges for new hires, and low-interest loans, the Rocard government sought to "muscle" the SMEs. Thus, the government had shifted its attention to the SMEs, leaving the large industries essentially to do as they wished, even when this appeared to go against "liberal" tenets.

For the large industries, mergers and acquisitions were allowed even if they appeared anti-competitive. Rocard permitted Air France's acquisition of Air Inter and UTA, even choosing not to refer it to the Council on Competition, despite the fact that it went far beyond the threshold level anticipated by the ordinance of 1986.[55] This was the last time, however, that the French government would be able to do this without European Commission oversight. As of 1991, the European Commission gained jurisdiction over mergers and acquisitions of companies where overall sales were above 5 billion écus. For the French, this came home quite forcefully with the refusal by the Commission to allow the takeover of the Canadian firm Havilland by Aérospatiale and Aléna on October 2, 1991. It is important to note, though, that this was the only case among hundreds of takeovers looked into by the EC.

This is not to say, however, that large industries were totally left to their own devices when it came to subsidies. The Rocard government provided more direct aid to industry than the previous neoliberal government, although it certainly reached nowhere near the levels of Mauroy's government. For certain sectors in trouble deemed strategic, the government continued the provision of capital grants, as in the case of computers in 1991, promising Thomson 1.8 billion francs and Bull 2 billion francs, with another 2 billion for the following year, plus 2.68 billion for aid for research.[56] It might have done more had it not been for the European Community, which was scrutinizing more and more all the capital grants to industry for evidence of unfair competition.

As it turns out, the Commission investigations of aid to French nationalized enterprises mostly resulted in decisions favorable to France. For example, in 1991, just as the French were gearing up for what they were sure would be EC rejection of direct and indirect (through other public enterprises) capital infusions, the Commission approved the 6.68 billion francs in aid to Bull because although it saw the aid as a subsidy (since it would not have received a similar amount under similar conditions from an investor on the market), the Commission recognized it as part of a

[54]Hall, "State and Market," pp. 182–183.
[55]The threshold was 7 billion francs in sales and 25% market share. See: Dumez and Jeunemaître, "L'état et le marché," pp. 269–270.
[56]*Les Echos,* April 5, 1991.

radical restructuring plan. Only Renault, in any earlier capital infusion, had to give some money back.

Moreover, for all this talk of the absence of industrial policy, the government did not abandon voluntarism completely. It was in favor of certain *"grands programmes,"* big technological programs such as the clean car, high-definition television (HDTV), and the third generation of the high-speed trains (TGV). These went from 300 million francs in the 1989 budget to 450 million in that of 1990 and 625 million in that of 1991. Although the government had given up on seeking to intervene in all sectors of the economy, it continued to insist that it needed to play a role in strategic areas. As Rocard's Minister of Industry, Roger Fauroux explained it, "The change in action occurred in part because Europe stops the state from lots of actions – and this is not wrong. We understand that coal and steel are now no longer necessarily strategic, but HDTV is."[57] Moreover, the government recognized that even these projects could not be successful without European cooperation. Thus, the government focused its efforts on persuading the EC to institute Europewide industrial policies, most of which did not pan out.

While the Rocard government sought to encourage industrial policy at the EC level, albeit unsuccessfully, it saw no need for industrial policy at the national level. And for a time, no one else did either. As France progressively slid into recession and the Gulf War ended, however, more and more people began to discuss the need for a reinvigorated industrial policy and a renewed state. On the left, Louis Mermaz, Minister of Agriculture, argued in May 1991 that France needed a real economic strategy, because "To rely on the laws of the market and of profit, at a time of the globalization of industrial activity, is to forbid us to win back a mastery of our economy."[58] On the center right, Raymond Barre wrote an editorial in *Le Monde* calling specifically for a renewal, not a retreat, of the state.[59] In industry, numerous heads of nationalized enterprises publicly and privately criticized the lack of state initiative, including Francis Lorentz, CEO of Bull, who complained about the lack of unity of command, of vision, and of conviction in industrial policy by comparison with the early 1980s, even if it was a time of madness.[60] And there was even an appeal for a revival of the plan, now focused on ensuring the competitiveness of French industry worldwide.[61]

[57]Fauroux interview. [58]*Le Monde,* May 30, 1991.
[59]Raymond Barre, editorial in *Le Monde,* May 24, 1991.
[60]Lorentz, interview with author. In my interviews with CEOs, in February 1991 I was often told that industrial policy was a thing of the past. But by May I was hearing nostalgia for a time when the state led, with numerous business executives, primarily on the left, lamenting the lack of clear industrial policy direction.
[61]Gérard Lafay, editorial in *Le Monde,* June 12, 1991.

Changes in government policies toward business

The Cresson and Bérégovoy governments, 1991–1993

Prime Minister Edith Cresson's voluntarism was in great measure a response to this enlarging chorus of those interested in more state involvement, as well as to Mitterrand's judgment that to win the next election, an opening to the left, to the Communists, needed to replace the opening to the center that had worked under Rocard. Cresson's *dirigiste* language and flamboyant style brought back echoes of the Mauroy government. But it was more language and style than substance, mainly because the government no longer had the means to pay for the policies, given the continued tight monetary policies of Minister of Finance Pierre Bérégovoy, or the policy instruments to enforce them, given the heroic policies of previous Socialist and neoliberal governments that had deregulated and privatized business. Cresson had little room for maneuver in particular because there was little in the way of state funds for capital investment in nationalized companies, and the nationalized banks were unlikely to help with this because they, too, were in difficulty.

From the pronouncements alone, however, one would not have known of the limitations. Thus, Cresson proposed to "revive the industrial imperative" in order to combat unemployment; to modernize the productive apparatus, focusing on small and mid-sized as well as large enterprises; to provide more public financing to business through the Ministries of Industry and Foreign Trade; and to change the work environment through the automation of the workplace and worker training programs in order to promote greater worker autonomy and initiative.[62] Initially, some welcomed this voluntarist discourse, feeling that symbolically at least, it would make a difference.[63] Very quickly, however, this changed, as people were turned off by the Japan-bashing and the remarks about British men.[64]

Ultimately, Cresson, despite the rhetoric, did little to change the policies of her predecessors. She continued with the tight monetary policies that were to ensure a low inflation rate and a strong franc. She continued spending on the modernization of the public sector, even though she reduced it for the health sector and for the military. She too focused on the small and mid-sized enterprises, although her "global plan" for the SMEs, initiated in July 1991, faltered, since the package of concessions was offset by an increase in the inheritance tax.[65] In addition, Cresson's legislation that was to institute workplace codetermination, double the

[62] *Tribune de l'Expansion,* May 23, 1991.
[63] Elie Cohen, interview in *Tribune de l'Expansion,* May 21, 1991.
[64] Her remarks about the Japanese being "ants" or "yellow dwarfs" who "sit up all night thinking of ways to screw us" and that 25% of British men were homosexuals did not go over very well.
[65] *Liberation,* December 19, 1991.

number of engineers in France by 1993, and triple the number of apprentices within five years, from 200,000 to 600,000, met a similar fate, since French employers proved hostile to codetermination and indifferent to apprenticeship programs.[66]

Finally, Cresson's industrial policies also continued in the direction first charted by Rocard, despite the proclaimed renewal of "voluntarism." Ongoing deregulation and Europeanization ensured that however "heroic" Cresson may have intended to be, she had less potential control over business than her predecessors. And therefore, despite initial resistance, her government allowed for increased privatization (up to the 49% Mitterrand had declared permissible in 1991, just before the end of Rocard's mandate) and cross-border mergers and acquisitions, although it did not completely abandon *dirigisme,* in the form of large state subsidies to some nationalized enterprises.

Cresson's criticism of France's lack of industrial policy – the fact that "Today, we don't even know what we want to do in nuclear power or electronics. We also don't know what we expect of the public enterprises; we concern ourselves with them every three years at the time of the appointment of the CEO and nothing else. No control, no directives"[67] – was behind her promise to play a more active role in directing the nationalized industries. Her justification for this was that "This is not a question of practicing a *dirigisme tatillon* (nitpicking interventionism), but rather of assuming one's responsibilities as shareholder, just like any shareholder, [which means] not only to pay . . . but to get involved, to understand the strategy, to discuss this strategy and then to come up with conclusions."[68]

Cresson was not alone in her insistence on the need for greater governmental involvement in the strategies of the nationalized enterprises. One commentator complained that the emptiness resulting from the lack of state policy led to numerous incidents where the heads of the nationalized enterprises turned toward the state for guidance, and state officials turned toward the heads of industry.[69] Fauroux's successor as Minister of Industry, Dominique Strauss-Kahn, explained the Ministry's failure to provide any effective policy for the large enterprises as resulting from the fact that they had "had their hands slapped too many times," leading them to effect "an escape toward the higher level of Europe, with its mythical qualities, and toward the lower level of the small and mid-sized enterprise, something more manageable for them."[70]

[66]Levy, "Tocqueville's Revenge."   [67]*Le Monde,* May 17, 1991.
[68]*Le Monde,* June 4, 1991.
[69]Bertrand Warusfeld, co-author with Jean-Baptiste de Boissière of *La nouvelle frontière de la technologie européene* (Paris: Calmann-Lévy, 1991). Conversation with author, Paris, May 13, 1991.
[70]Strauss-Kahn, interview with author.

Cresson's "assuming of responsibility" had two major manifestations: first, she questioned a decision by the previous government to allow the Japanese firm NEC to gain a 4.7% share of Bull on the grounds that no Japanese should be able to gain a share in French nationalized industries, only to capitulate because of Bull's clear need for Japanese participation.[71] Second, the new 90 billion franc electronics-to-nuclear-energy superfirm, proposed with great fanfare in December 1991, which was to merge Thomson Consumer Electronics (TCE), the loss-making manufacturer of audiovisual equipment and household appliances, and SGS-Thomson, the producer of microchips, with CEA-Industrie, the nuclear fuel and reactor group, came to naught when CEA balked. (Once Bérégovoy became Prime Minister, CEA acquired only minority stakes in the two Thomson subsidiaries.)

Cresson's efforts to get the EC to do in industrial policy what the French could no longer do also failed. Despite her best efforts, she was unable to get Europe to adopt the standard D2-Mac on HDTV. Moreover, the proposed electronics policy continued to languish in Brussels.

Other, more modest changes which continued liberalizing the economy while restructuring French capitalism did succeed, however. Thus, in need of money to fund its programs, the Cresson government reduced the state's direct stake in Total in June 1993 from 31.7% to 5% (although public sector enterprises such as AGF and GAN were to buy in, thereby keeping public sector ownership close to 15%), but kept the right to appoint the chairman and to vet its international agreements. There were also partial sales of Elf (2.3%) in March 1993, and of Crédit Local de France (22.5%) earlier. In addition, there was more trading of shares among nationalized enterprises: the BNP invested 1 billion francs in Air France for a 10% share, and Crédit Lyonnais put 2.5 billion francs into the steel giant Usinor-Sacilor for a 10% share. This last set of actions, moreover, survived the scrutiny of the European Commission, with the injection by Crédit Lyonnais of money into Usinor-Sacilor in particular considered by EC Commissioner Leon Brittan to be in keeping with the principle of sound free market investment.

These more everyday initiatives were much more to the liking of Cresson's Minister of Industry, Dominique Strauss-Kahn, who remained when Bérégovoy became Prime Minister. Strauss-Kahn was not as "voluntarist" as his first Prime minister, but he was nevertheless very interested in encouraging the further restructuring of French capitalism along

---

[71]The story goes that in order to smooth Japanese feathers, ruffled by Cresson when she called them ants, Dominique Strauss-Kahn went to see the Japanese Prime Minister with the La Fontaine fable of "La Cigale and la Fourmie" (the grasshopper and the ant) in hand, to convince him that he ought not take offense because the French admire ants as hard workers.

the lines of the German model. The problem, according to Strauss-Kahn, is that "we have lived for the past thirty years in a situation in which the financial establishments have fed off of industry, and did so all the more easily in that they were not shareholders. Only when they become shareholders will they feed off it less, because a gain on the one side is a loss on the other."[72]

In other words, what had begun under Fauroux as a set of industrial actions in response to the requests of CEOs of nationalized enterprise became a full-fledged industrial policy under Strauss-Kahn, where nationalized and privatized, public and private financial and industrial concerns were encouraged to trade shares for strategic reasons. The state, therefore, continued to act like a shareholder, but it was a more active one. As Strauss-Kahn argued, "Why should the state be more passive than a private shareholder? It can manage well or badly, but it is not being interventionist in itself to try to manage one's assets as efficiently as possible."[73] He insisted that "If the 1980s were dominated by financial questions and financial regulations, the 1990s will be the time for states to intervene in industry in the same way as they do in finance, as regulators – but not just as regulators, as co-ordinators as well."[74]

In fact, although when Pierre Bérégovoy took over the reigns as Prime Minister, even the illusion of voluntarism was gone, his government nevertheless continued to facilitate the change in the structure of ownership and control in every way it could. Again, privatizations occurred primarily because of a need for money. With the partial privatization of Rhône-Poulenc, the government went beyond the principle of the "post-*ni-ni*" by selling enough shares to go below its majority stake, down to 43.4% from 57%. Bérégovoy himself even wanted to substitute for the *ni-ni* the *et-et*, that is, continued nationalization for public enterprises in monopolistic service sectors and total privatization for those in competitive sectors. In this, however, he did not get his way. He did in most else, however.

Bérégovoy's priority, like that of all previous governments since 1983, was to keep inflation down in order to maintain stable prices and to keep the franc strong and in the EMS. This he did in the face of an unemployment rate that continued spiraling upward, reaching close to 3 million by the time the Socialists lost the elections. In addition, he reduced fiscal pressures on business yet again, in particular in lowering the rate of taxation on profits (it went from 50% at the beginning of the eighties to 33% for 1993). Although he had made unemployment a priority, there was little he could do about it, since the slowing economy could not be helped by anything other than a drop in interest rates, something that depended upon the Bundesbank, and was not forthcoming. He too, how-

[72]Strauss-Kahn, interview with author.   [73]*Financial Times*, June 8, 1992.   [74]Ibid.

ever, provided help for the SMEs with a "support plan" passed in October 1992.

Outside pressures, however, were becoming increasingly important. A major preoccupation for Bérégovoy was European integration, given the deadline for the single market of January 1, 1992. The uphill battle in the referendum on the Maastricht Treaty, with its all-too-close victory for the partisans of European unity (51% in favor vs. 49% against), an indicator of public reluctance to take any great leaps forward with respect to European integration, did not stop the continuing liberalizing movement toward monetary and economic union. And the GATT was equally important in terms of liberalization, although the major battle here was fought by the Balladur government.

The Balladur government, 1993–1995

When the right returned, its policies were very much in continuity with those of the Socialists. The electoral campaign of 1993 had none of the ultra neoliberal rhetoric of 1986. Rather than major pronouncements on how to reform the economy, it had minor proposals on changing the retirement pensions and the family allowance system. Its "Twenty Reforms to Begin Changing France," much like the title itself, were modest proposals, without any suggestion of major tax cuts or new job initiatives. The linchpin of its program, though, as in 1986–1988, was to be privatization for firms in the competitive sector and greater autonomy for firms in the noncompetitive sector. On macroeconomic matters, Balladur followed along the lines of Bérégovoy as well as his own of 1986 to 1988, when he was Minister of Finance.

Balladur's major preoccupation was keeping the franc strong and inflation down, even if this meant keeping interest rates high and thereby slowing growth in an already recessionary economy. As more and more businesses went bankrupt, one began hearing comments such as, "The Bundesbank is making all of Europe pay for German unification." But despite strong pressures on the franc resulting from the run on the franc that, by the end of July 1993, had precipitated the monetary crisis that had already led Great Britain and Italy to take themselves out of the ERM altogether, Balladur made it a matter of pride not to devalue. The easing of the exchange rate mechanism, allowing much larger bands of fluctuation, relieved the problem, but not before the Bank of France had spent vast sums to shore up the franc. Thus, although Balladur managed to resist the challenge to the franc and remain in the ERM, this was at great cost to the country. And it continued to be so as French interest rates remained too high to help a flagging economy in which the unemployment rate had climbed to over 12% by 1994.

The Balladur government also continued the process of liberalization, and not only with privatization. In December 1993, it went so far as to present a bill that was to remove the Bank of France from central control, which included creating a monetary policy council made up of a governor and two deputies appointed for six-year terms and six members appointed for nine years, none of whom could be removed for any reason other than incapacity or grave error. The reform was passed, although certain key parts were struck down by the Constitutional Council. The government was also successful in cutting back the welfare state in many areas. In the first few months, it pushed through measures intended to control costs, such as reducing retirement payments, lowering reimbursements for medical expenses, and shortening the time period for unemployment benefits. It was not successful in lowering the SMIC, or minimum wage, for youth, though. Its winter 1994 proposal to allow employers to pay between 30% and 80% of the minimum wage to youth was greeted with so much student opposition, including demonstrations and other actions, that the government withdrew it, substituting in its place a much more expensive plan to reimburse employers who hire youths. Moreover, its education reforms were a failure: the January 1994 proposed revision of the Falloux law, which would have made it easier to finance private education, was withdrawn while Minister of Education François Bayrou's school reform project of a year later was suspended, both in response to much protest. And despite public pronouncements by the Prime Minister himself, there was no appreciable increase in apprenticeship programs (the number of apprenticeships grew only minimally, from 406,000 in March 1993 to 432,000 in September 1994).[75]

Again, the Balladur government, like all previous governments regardless of politics, continued to see no contradiction between its supply-side economics and providing large subsidies to industry. In fact, this government had the all-time record in amount of subsidies, at 21 billion francs in capital grants – to be funded in part with the money that was to come from the privatizations, paid for in advance by the floating of government bonds to the tune of 110 billion francs.[76] Public enterprises received 40% of the receipts of the privatizations of 1993 (out of 46 billion francs, they got 18.8 billion).[77] In addition, the government increased funding for research and development by 1.8 billion francs in the 1994 budget. Particular programs increased significantly: for example, a new 800 million

[75]*Le Monde,* January 19, 1995.
[76]The government had expected the loan to be for 40 billion francs at 6% interest, but its popularity meant that the government gained much more.
[77]Aérospatiale received 2 billion francs, Bull 4.5 billion, CEA 1.3 billion, CEPME 500 million, CGM 500 million, and Crédit Lyonnais 3.5 million. *Le Monde,* May 8–9, 1994.

franc fund to aid investment by small and medium-sized firms in rural zones; incentives for innovation in small and mid-sized industries, up by 16% over the previous years; research funds for the aeronautics sector, up by 25%; 21% more for the environment and energy, and so on.[78]

Moreover, particular companies received large capital infusions: The Compagnie Générale Maritime received 500 million francs, SNECMA 750 million francs. Bull was promised 11.7 billion francs over two years for restructuring, something that was investigated and accepted by the EU Commission on condition that the company be privatized before the end of 1995. Air France was promised a 20 billion franc capital injection for restructuring, despite the possibility of objections by the European Commission, given that the company had received injections totaling 5.84 billion francs in 1991 and 1992, and that the Commission was already investigating a 1993 aid package of 1.5 billion francs made through convertible bonds and other paper in response to British Air's attack on this as a subsidy rather than a restructuring aid.[79] Although the government won its gamble, since the Commission's final decision was to allow the capital infusion, this has been challenged by British Air and other airline companies. Finally, the government even came to the aid of the Crédit Lyonnais with three rescue plans, one in March 1994, a two-round attempt in September 1994, and again in March 1995. While the government's 1994 rescues followed the traditional pattern by providing the bank with 5 billion francs of fresh capital, in the more complicated 1995 rescue the government, concerned about possible protests from the bank's competitors and the EU Commission, took a more liberal approach. It guaranteed the company against 50 billion francs in potential losses in exchange for significant cost-cutting through the sale of assets and a heavy reduction in staff, with the understanding that privatization would be scheduled in five years' time.

The Balladur government also engaged in a policy of bailing out companies in distress that was reminiscent of the Giscard years as well as of the Socialists until Fabius's tenure as Prime Minister. Here, only the justifications for the large subsidies to paper companies such as La Rochette and Cellulose du Rhône et de l'Aquitaine (CDRA) and to the marine company Sud Marine remained within the liberal discourse, as Minister of Industry Gérard Longuet argued that his actions were meant to redress unfair competitive imbalances that had come about as a result of the currency devaluations of the northern European countries.[80]

The right-wing government, just as the left before it, in short, was unwilling to give up the interventionist role of the state entirely. And this

---

[78]*Le Figaro,* September 21, 1993; *Le Monde,* November 17, 1993.
[79]*Financial Times,* March 10, 1994.   [80]*Les Echos,* November 26, 1993.

was equally true when it came to state ownership and control of business, even though, here too, liberal disengagement proceeded apace.

Prime Minister Balladur put through Bérégovoy's unfulfilled recommendations on the "*et-et*," by proposing extensive privatization in the competitive sector but not in the monopolistic sectors, which instead were to have their statutes changed in order to give them greater flexibility. Of the twenty-one companies to be privatized in the competitive sector, twelve had been on the 1986 list, and nine were added.[81] These included major banks such as the BNP and minor ones such as the Hervet Bank, top insurers such as UAP and AGF, and industrial giants such as Rhône-Poulenc and Elf. The privatizations brought in 47.6 billion francs in 1993 and 60.4 billion francs in 1994, while those of 1995 were expected to reach 55 billion francs. Even before the official privatizations, moreover, in June 1993, the state had reduced its shares in the Crédit Local de France from 25.5% to 8%, and had the Caisse des Dépôts et Consignations reduce its own from 25% to 12%, with 7.16 million shares sold at 386 francs each.

The privatization of the BNP in October 1993 was a spectacular success: it was five times oversubscribed and brought in 2.8 million shareholders and 28 billion francs, with approximately 6% (8.29 million shares) held by 68% of employees (active and retired). The privatization of the state's 43.4% share of Rhône-Poulenc in November 1993 brought in 13 billion francs, with a majority of shares reserved for individuals, for a total of 2.9 million shareholders. The privatization of 37% of the capital of Elf-Aquitaine in February 1994 yielded 33 billion francs, with 10% reserved for a *noyau dur*, 4% for the employees, and 13% retained by the government through Erap. The privatization of UAP in April 1994 was to bring in 28 billion francs, with 1.9 million shareholders buying shares valued at 152 francs. AGF, scheduled toward the end of 1994, was expected to yield 15 billion francs. The Bull privatization was completed by the end of 1994, and involved primarily the sale of stakes to industrial partners, with only a small public offering. Moreover, one firm not on the original list, Renault, was successfully partially privatized, with 49% of its shares sold, and with over 65% of the employees buying shares in the firm.

Thus, the privatizations of firms in the competitive sector proceeded on schedule, ultimately engendering a 27% increase in individual share-

[81]The twelve on the 1986 lists were: AGF, GAN, UAP, Bull, Thomson, Banque Hervet, Crédit Lyonnais, Banque Nationale de Paris, Péchiney, Rhône-Poulenc, Elf, and Société Marseillaise de Crédit. The nine new companies were: Aérospatiale, Société Nationale Industrielle, Air France, Caisse Centrale de Réassurance, Caisse Nationale de Prévoyance-Assurances, Compagnie Générale Maritime, Renault, Seita, SNECMA, and Usinor-Sacilor.

holders over two years.[82] By contrast, the promised revision of the statutes of firms in the noncompetitive sector hit a number of snags. France Télécom's proposed change in statute, which was to have allowed it to become a *société anonyme* and thereby enable it to enter alliances and trade shares with foreign as well as domestic firms (it lost an opportunity to ally with MCI in the summer of 1993 because it could not trade shares with it), was withdrawn after a walkout by 75% of the Télécom workers. Moreover, Balladur's major reform of the Caisse des Dépôts et Consignations, promised in April 1993, was no longer anything very significant by January 1994, mainly because the government did not want to give up a cash flow that had served to recapitalize Crédit Lyonnais by 1.5 billion francs and to save Air France with 1.5 billion francs.[83]

State interventionism was not entirely a thing of the past, however. On the Volvo-Renault merger, the government tried to get Louis Schweitzer to renegotiate downward Volvo's participation before the Prime Minister agreed to the merger. This, together with the scant likelihood of an early privatization, may very well have increased the Swedish directors' concern about potential government interference, despite French government assurances to the contrary, sealing the fate of the merger.[84] In fact, once the deal fell through, once Volvo's shareholders rejected the merger, there was even less reason for the government to go ahead with the privatization plans, in particular because it feared further worker unrest given Renault's symbolic position. Thus, when in September 1994 the government announced that it would sell off some of the car manufacturer, it sought to circumvent worker unrest by retaining a 51% share in the firm.

More importantly, perhaps, the Balladur government in the fall of 1993, with shades of *déjà vu* from the late seventies, asked CEOs of public sector firms to slow the pace of worker firings. This was directed at such firms as Air France, Bull, Thomson-CSF, and SNECMA, which together had announced redundancy plans that would have laid off about 13,000 workers, as well as at the SNCF, which in particular had been asked to reconsider the closing of certain sites. However, the government also hoped that private firms would follow suit, using job cuts only as a last resort, and indicated that it would consider limiting state aid for job reduction packages where private firms had not first tried alternatives to firings.

[82]*Le Monde,* October 11, 1994.   [83]*Le Nouvel Economiste* no. 939, April 4, 1994.
[84]The government promised not to use its *"action spécifique"* to bring the voting rights of Volvo down to 20% in the eventuality that the agreement were to break down, given that it did not anticipate this happening for twenty-five years (the length of the contract tying the two companies) (although all other foreign concerns would still have to have government authorization to go above the 10% mark).

In the case of Air France, moreover, which suffered a strike in protest against a severe restructuring plan proposed by the CEO Bernard Pache (which the government itself had demanded), the government backed down and the CEO resigned.[85] Finally, even the "*Meccano industriel*" for which the right itself had criticized the left reappeared, this time with a proposal to merge Thomson-CSF and Thomson Consumer Electronics, the military and civil subsidiaries of Thomson SA, which was scheduled for privatization in 1994.[86]

Heroic industrial policy, in short, is not entirely dead. But its purview has been greatly restricted by the changes in the state's capability with regard to industrial policy.

CONCLUSION

Over the course of Mitterrand's presidency, then, after an initial expansion in size and activity through nationalization and restructuring, the state has retreated as a result of deregulation, privatization, and Europeanization. By the nineties, the traditional *dirigisme,* in which French governments set macroeconomic policy relatively independently of the international economic climate and engaged in "micromanagement" of the microeconomic sphere, had ended. France had given up its macroeconomic independence to remain part of the European Monetary System, and it had retreated from the more direct microeconomic interventionism of the past in order to comply for the most part with EC competition policy. The lesson of the first Socialist government, taken to heart by all subsequent governments, was that on the macroeconomic front, there was little room to maneuver: much depended upon fellow members of the EC and major trading partners. They all agreed, moreover, that microeconomic policies had to be more on the supply side than on the demand side, in part because of the new macroeconomic environment, but also because of the move toward greater emphasis on the market. The state leadership evident in the heroic industrial policies of the sixties and seventies and focused on producing national champions and *grands projets* culminated with the Socialist nationalizations, and has subsequently given way to a greater emphasis on profitability and private financing of public as well as private sector enterprises. Moreover, there

[85] Many were in fact surprised at this, seeing it as an unnecessary government capitulation since all including the unions knew that Air France was in terrible shape, at 6 billion francs in the red, and would have to be restructured. One expert noted that "this panic before a very traditional conflict is incomprehensible. We were in the middle of professional elections in the enterprise, which leads the unions to up the ante. Any knowledgeable negotiator would have allowed the elections to pass."

[86] For further details, see: *L'Expansion,* November 4–24, 1993.

has been a real shift in government focus, from large-scale industry to small and mid-sized industries.

Within the new limits, however, government leadership in industrial policy remains, albeit as a pale shadow of what it was. Business as well as government leaders are convinced that industry needs leadership that only the state can provide, given its ability to take a long-term view. French business, although increasingly independent of the state as a result of continuing deregulation as well as increasingly interdependent, given the *noyaux durs,* nevertheless continues to look to the state for leadership, albeit of a kinder and gentler variety than that of the past. Whether the state will be able to provide such leadership effectively, however, is another matter.

The problems of leadership go beyond the difficulties involved in finding appropriate market-oriented ways to manage the economy and to promote industrial development. From the late eighties on, there has been an ever-growing crisis of confidence in the political class resulting from the ever-widening number of corruption scandals that have taken down numerous ministers of both the left and the right. The first scandals involved top Socialists: the tainted blood affair where top ministers including Prime Minister Fabius were accused of unnecessarily allowing hemophiliacs in the mid eighties to be infected with the HIV virus because they delayed ensuring the safety of the blood supply so as to enable a French blood heating process to come to market; the corrupt election financing scandals that began in the mid eighties with a number of affairs concerning kickbacks from construction contracts awarded in Socialist-controlled regions and which, by March 1995, had led to the trial and conviction of the Socialist Party chairman, Henri Emmanuelli, and sixteen other defendants for illegal party financing practices between 1988 and 1991 (Emmanuelli received a two-year suspended sentence); and the game fixing involving the football team owned by Socialist politician and entrepreneur Bernard Tapie, which left him facing eighteen months in prison in 1995. The right, however, has also not been spared. Three ministers in Balladur's government had to resign in 1994, implicated in scandals involving illegal election financing – as in the case of Foreign Aid Minister Michel Roussin, who was accused of siphoning money for the party from the Paris region public housing authority; fraud and misuse of public funds – in the case of former mayor of Grenoble Alain Carignon, who went to jail; and abuse of public trust – in the case of Minister of Industry Gérard Longuet, who accepted favors from private building societies.

Even the new government of Prime Minister Alain Juppé under President Jacques Chirac in its first months in office had been tarnished in this climate of scandal, with questions raised in the media about Juppé's housing arrangements with the city of Paris, which generously provided him and members of his family with below-market rents. Leaving aside this problem, the new government appeared to be charting a middle course between the policies of its conservative and Socialist predecessors. It remained committed to the *franc fort* and to pursuing European integration. It was concerned about the budget deficit and its potential impact on European monetary union if it was not brought down to 3% of GDP, and therefore sought to reduce it from a forecast level of 5.7% to 5.1% for 1995 with the goal of reaching 3% by 1997. The Juppé government also proposed to wipe out the 60 billion franc social security deficit by 1998 through a reform of the pension system and changes to the country's health care services. Privatization was to continue apace (although the target for revenues was reduced to 40 billion francs, due to the interruption of the presidential campaign), with Usinor-Sacilor the first to be privatized (as of June 1995). But unemployment was also a target, with a 60 billion franc package that promised to create 700,000 new jobs by the end of 1996 through reductions in employers' social security contributions paired with special financial incentives, which were to cut the cost of employing low-paid workers by 10% and of hiring the long-term unemployed by approximately 40%; a series of programs related to training, apprenticeships, and youth in difficulty were also planned. This was to be paid for by some tax increases, including a temporary increase of 10% in the corporation tax, a temporary rise in the VAT from 18.6% to 20.6%, and a symbolic 10% jump in the wealth tax. It was also to come from public spending cuts of 22 billion francs in the last half of 1995, affecting all ministries except Justice and Culture, with over a third coming from the Ministry of Defense. Moreover, with a 4% increase in the minimum wage and a 0.5% increase in state pension payments, the government sought to demonstrate that it had the interests of both the worker and business at heart. Thus, it provided a small dose of neo-Keynesianism to accompany the austerity budget and, as Alain Juppé explained, sought to rescue the economy with a plan based "on the logic not of an accountant but of an entrepreneur."[87]

Compared to the 1981 Socialist initiatives, these measures to stimulate growth and reduce the 12.2% unemployment rate were quite modest. To the European markets, however, they represented an aggressive spending plan that would stimulate inflation and increase the budget deficit. The franc was put under pressure accordingly, sending a clear message to the new President and the Juppé government that interventionism, however modest, was to be avoided. This kind of sanction from the markets, together with the policy of the *franc fort,* the goal of European monetary

[87]*Financial Times,* June 23, 1995.

union, and the authority of the European Commission, ensure that the Juppé government is playing in a different world from that of 1981, with neither the macroeconomic autonomy nor the *dirigiste* policy instruments of the past to allow it to dominate the economy. And yet it is clear that at the same time that the Juppé government, like all governments since 1983, has thoroughly accepted a more market-oriented approach to economic policymaking, it, too, is unwilling to abandon interventionism entirely.

PART III

The process of policymaking

7

In the ministries

The vision of the French state is generally one of unity, where heroic governments backed by a strong bureaucracy make policy often without significant input from societal interests. And yet, behind the unity and the strong bureaucracy is a great deal of fragmentation. The centralization of the structure of government decision-making, in which all major issues flow up to the Prime Minister or President for a final decision, helps perpetuate this illusion of unity. But even the most heroic of policies, unveiled with such fanfare, heralded as the coherent response to the economic climate, the result of deep intellectual inquiry applied to practical matters, are in truth the results of bargains and compromises among a variety of interests. These are not, however, the results of pluralist bargaining as in the United States, where the pressures of outside interests make their indelible imprint on the resulting policy; nor are they the results of corporatist concertation, following the model of Germany or the smaller European countries, where the cooperation of privileged interests with government makes policy. Rather, these are the bargains within the context of the statist pattern of policymaking.

At the formulation stage, this means that they are the bargains within and between government ministries and parties, and in particular high-level bureaucrats and politicians. The government, after all, is most often made up of a coalition of parties within which are different *frondes,* subgroups with often conflicting agendas. Leaders of those different subgroups, moreover, are put at the head of ministries which themselves often have divergent agendas. And the French bureaucracy, despite the strength which is based in large measure on its elite recruitment pattern and its relative lack of permeability to outside interests, is nevertheless highly fragmented. Interministerial and intraministerial rivalries are as much factors in the shaping of policies as interparty and intraparty rivalries. And they are more significant factors than pressures brought to bear by Parliament, which talks a lot but changes little and initiates less.

At the implementation stage, the bargains are between ministries and industries. It is important to note that, however impermeable to outside interests France's statist pattern of policymaking may appear when compared to other countries' pluralist or corporatist patterns, certain groups nevertheless find a way in. However heroic a policy may be, and therefore however little societal interests, and in particular business interests, may influence the formulation of the policy, they are generally heard at the implementation stage. And here, the structure of decision-making follows the same overall pattern as at the formulation stage, with major issues arbitrated by the Prime Minister, except that in this context societal interests are the ones to raise the issues, and ministers, rather than making the rules, make exceptions to them to accommodate societal interests.

The key institutions for both formulation and implementation are the ministries, in which occur the internecine battles for power and influence that business interests have often been able to exploit for their own ends. In the postwar period, these battles were primarily between the Planning Commission and the Ministry of Finance, which tended to retain the upper hand, while in the Mitterrand years, the Ministry of Industry had replaced the Planning Commission as the Finance Ministry's less powerful rival. Although in the first years of the Socialists' tenure in office, the Ministry of Industry had new responsibilities and even, for a short time, new resources that enabled it to hold its own with regard to the Ministry of Finance, by 1986 the latter had managed to prevail, helped by Madelin's disastrous tenure as minister. Subsequently, the Ministry of Industry was a pale shadow of itself, acting more as a partner to business than a leader, and dominated by the Ministry of Finance. But whichever ministry was ascendant, business managed to profit, able to take advantage of interministerial rivalries by playing off one ministry against another with great effect. Moreover, this was as true for the nationalized enterprises as it was for private firms. Despite the formal powers ministry officials have over nationalized enterprise, public sector heads have benefited from a tradition of autonomy that has enabled them to manage their firms and set overall strategies with a minimum of interference from the state.

THE CIRCUITS OF POWER

The illusion of unity results from the centralization of the final decision-making process, and the fact that very few individuals actually contribute to that decision. For heroic policies in particular, this ordinarily includes the Prime Minister and/or the President and their chief economic advisors, a couple of ministers and their top cabinet (staff) aides, and perhaps a few top, upper-level civil servants. In the case of disagreement among the ministers, it is the Prime Minister or the President who has the final word as the "arbiter." Often, but not always, everyday policymaking is outside this heroic loop that includes arbitration by the Prime Minister or the President, and remains in the domain of the minister or ministers of the particular ministries in charge of the policy area. In the implementation process, moreover, although the politics of accommodation and co-optation also tend to remain in the ministries, where there is confrontation, the final decision is often also the Prime Minister's or President's.

Much more peripheral to the process are such bodies as the Council of State and the Constitutional Council, which may render opinions that delay the passage of a law (as in the cases of nationalization and privatization), but rarely deny it entirely. Parliament is essentially outside the loop, able to offer friendly amendments to government bills but not to obstruct unduly, given that whenever there is even the slightest hint of this, governments can reach into their bag of parliamentary mechanisms to ensure passage without further debate.[1] Least important to the formulation process are outside interests, which nevertheless do have a variety of ways in, either by exploiting interministerial rivalries[2] or through the personal relationships based on state school and career ties. But because they are the least influential, where they attempt to exert influence may tell us more about where power lies than more direct accounts.

Despite the centralization of governmental decision-making, which would make it appear impermeable to outside interests, and the fact that lobbying is regarded as illegitimate and influence peddling corrupt, there are ways in which outside interests, and business interests in particular, do gain a hearing. But the way to gain such a hearing is quite unlike in the United States, where lobbying efforts focus on Congress, and may involve buttonholing someone in the halls of the Capitol, testifying at Congressional hearings, or upping the pressure on members of Congress through grass-roots efforts. Not only is some of this simply unacceptable in France, it also makes little sense, since Parliament is not the main locus of power, and party discipline serves to insulate members from special-interest pressures. Although a certain amount of lobbying of the more powerful members of Parliament does go on – after all, these are likely to be future government ministers – it is minimal by comparison with the attention paid to the ministries. Most telling is the fact that relatively few groups are actually involved in concerted efforts to build sympathy for their cause in Parliament. In 1985, there were only thirty such groups.[3]

[1] See the earlier discussion in Chapter 1.

[2] Jean-Pierre Anastassopoulos, "Les entreprises publiques entre l'autonomie et la dépendance: Une analyse des divers instruments de régulation des entreprises publiques par l'état," *Politiques et Management Public*, June 1985, pp. 76–77, 85–87.

[3] Thierry Bréhier, "Les groupes de pression à l'Assemblée Nationale," *Pouvoirs* no. 34 (1985): 107–119.

The process of policymaking

The upper-level administration, where the main drafting of proposed legislation occurs, receives the bulk of attempts by outside interests to influence the formulation process. In times of the elaboration of laws, the Prime Minister is generally bombarded with notes (written on white paper so as not to give the appearance of lobbying) from the professional organizations and companies concerned, oftentimes on matters that are still under consideration by the services of the state.[4] Having influence involves not only having one's notes read, but more importantly having appointments and, better, lunches with ministers or, if that is not possible, with members of the minister's cabinet, the cabinet director if you're lucky. The main focus of all of this, of course, is Matignon, but failing access to the Prime Minister or his or her staff, the technical ministries are acceptable.

The practice of lobbying is a subtle game in France, much of which would now be seen as corrupt in the United States. It takes a variety of forms, the most obvious of which might involve providing fresh produce or meats to the Minister of Agriculture or his cabinet members, trips to an oil platform in Norway for the administrator in charge of energy, and so forth.[5] For the public enterprises, less obvious but equally helpful is hiring a *trésorien,* or former member of the Treasury, who is of necessity an *énarque,* to head the company's financial department. Here, because the *trésorien* will be dealing with former fellow-classmates, not to mention former fellow-administrators, the ties that bind run deep.

Most important in terms of influencing the policy process are the personal contacts between interest group leaders and top ministers and their staffs. In fact, personal relationships based on old school ties, *grand corps* membership, or common histories, whether through working in politics, in ministries, or in industries together, are the key to having an effect on policy, so much so that this more than anything else is seen as "lobbying" *à la française.*[6] Even where personal ties and *corporatisme* are not at issue, however, CEOs generally have special access, if only because of their position at the head of one of a relatively small number of firms. Being represented on the thousands of statutory bodies that allow for formal consultation between interest groups and civil servants and politicians, by contrast, does little in terms of policymaking, given that formulation tends to be prior to consultation.[7]

[4]Frèches, *Voyage au centre du pouvoir,* p. 132.   [5]Ibid., pp. 128–135.

[6]One book that only details these interpersonal relationships actually takes "lobbying" for its title: Thierry Lefébure, *Lobby or Not to Be* (Paris: Plume, 1991).

[7]See: Frank L. Wilson, "France: Group Politics in a Strong State." Paper prepared for delivery at the Annual Meeting of the American Political Science Association, Atlanta, August 31–September 3, 1989, pp. 18–19.

For French business, in short, personal contacts based on personal relationships or positions of power which are focused on swaying the Prime Minister or, failing that, the ministers of the more technical ministries, are the main means of influencing policy formulation. Also helpful would be the President as long as his party controls the government. When policies are the heroic initiatives of new governments, however, business influence is minimal, no matter with how many notes business leaders bombard the Prime Minister.

Of all the players in the policy formulation process, the President is without a doubt the most powerful as long as the governmental majority is of the same political color, acting as the final arbiter in disputes that cannot be resolved at lower levels. In times of *cohabitation,* or power sharing, with a Prime Minister of the opposition, the Prime Minister is the most powerful in economic policymaking, and the arbiter – even if the President is the ultimate authority. Especially in the years 1981 to 1986, the centralization of power around Mitterrand was extraordinary. This had actually started in the Socialist Party even before the Socialists gained power, but only increased once Mitterrand went to the Elysée.[8] Mitterrand often maintained a hierarchical decision-making process within the Socialist government, having the final word in the debates that frequently set one minister against another, occasionally making pronouncements about what was to become government policy without consulting any of his ministers. Thus, he was the arbiter on such questions as acquiring 100% of the shares of the nationalized industries rather than 51%, on reducing the work week to thirty-nine hours without a concomitant loss in pay, and on the Great U-turn in macroeconomic policymaking. And without consultation, he decided to exempt works of art from the wealth tax in 1982 and to reduce the tax burden by 1% in 1983.[9]

The Prime Minister was only slightly less important, and made the final decisions on all the important economic policy issues that did not elicit so much controversy as to force the matter to the presidential level – except, of course, in the case of right-wing governments, where the Prime Minister remained the ultimate arbiter in economic matters. It was often at the prime ministerial level that political considerations were introduced as counters to the more technical ones that came out of the ministries. For example, in the case of the privatization of CGCT, the preferences of the firm and of the technical ministries were ignored in the interests of greater

[8]William Shonfeld, "French Socialism in Power: Change and Continuity," *Tocqueville Review* vol. 6, no. 2 (fall 1984), pp. 343–359.

[9]Northcutt, *Mitterrand,* p. 95; and Howard Machin and Vincent Wright, eds., *Economic Policy Making Under the Mitterrand Presidency* (New York: St. Martin's, 1985), p. 16.

inter-European cooperation when Prime Minister Chirac awarded the company to a Swedish acquirer.[10]

It was at the prime ministerial level that most of the battles between ministries were fought out, with varying results for the ministries involved. Generally, before 1981, these battles pitted the Planning Commission against the Ministry of Finance, and after, the Ministry of Industry against the Ministry of Finance. Sometimes, policies were even formulated at this level, and imposed on the ministries in question. In the sixties and seventies, for example, electronics policy was formulated in the cabinet of the Prime Minister and the Ministry of Finance and imposed on the Ministry of Industry.[11]

It is also at the level of the Prime Minister that most major issues are resolved involving the strategic decisions of French firms in which the state has an interest, either because they are nationalized enterprises under the state's *tutelle* or a major firm, whether public or private, contemplating a large foreign or domestic sale, acquisition, or merger. The decision-making process here tends to be very personalistic, involving interaction between high-level government officials and top managers. On the more important *dossiers,* or issues, often the CEO, the Minister of Industry (or other relevant ministry), and the Minister of Finance are active in the negotiation process, with the Prime Minister or even the President asked to arbitrate whenever there is disagreement between ministers (which there generally is, in particular between the Ministry of Finance and the technical ministries). In fact, as former Director-General of Industry Louis Gallois noted, "to avoid that the *dossier* goes to sleep, arbitration is necessary," and is therefore generally part of the ministry's tactics to ensure that an issue gets resolved at the level of the Prime Minister, whether or not to its own satisfaction.[12]

The ministries are probably the most important level in the structure of decision-making for policy formulation. It is here that the fragmentation of the supposedly monolithic French state is at its greatest. Although the hierarchical nature of the system ensures that a very few individuals initiate the bulk of the major decisions, these individuals, as the heads of different ministries, often have very different interests to represent. As often as not, ministers become the champions of their own particular bailiwick, taking on the prejudices and preferences of their particular ministry. The fragmentation does not necessarily stop here, however, because rivalries between ministries are often compounded by rivalries within ministries between *directions,* or divisions, and within *directions,*

[10]See the discussion in Chapter 9.   [11]Zysman, *Political Strategies,* p. 64.
[12]Gallois, interview with author.

between *bureaux*.[13] Moreover, on top of the bureaucratic rivalries are the political differences that may separate the minister and his or her cabinet members, who are clearly politicized, from the civil servants in regular ministerial ranks, who are traditionally not (although this has been changing in recent years).[14]

Outside interests that have an in, meaning those with personal contacts in the ministries, have learned to exploit these differences. Depending upon circumstance, political affiliation, or simply personal preference, CEOs seeking to influence a decision may choose to deal with the regular civil servant in charge of their *dossier*, the director of a given service, the political appointee (often also a civil servant) in the ministerial cabinet, or the minister directly. (For example, Fauroux, when he was CEO of Saint-Gobain, would see the Director-General of Industry, while Georges Besse would go to the cabinet director, and others, the minister.)[15] But whomever they first went to see, if they were dissatisfied with the response, they would move higher up in the given ministry, on to another ministry, or up to the prime ministerial level for contact with the Prime Minister and/or the prime ministerial cabinet while, in every case, seeking to play off one set of actors against the other. And there is a lot off of which to play.

The relationship between the actors, in particular that between the political appointees, the ministers, and their staffs, on the one hand, and the regular civil servants, the directors of ministerial departments, and their staffs, on the other, is an intricate one. Ministers often dominate their ministries – their cabinets ensure that their political agendas are put into force, and help insulate them from the pressures of permanent civil servants more readily than in Great Britain, for example, where the civil servants' vaunted political neutrality does not mean that their own policy preferences do not hold sway. This means that forceful ministers in France can do a lot – but they still cannot ride roughshod over their ministries. For the bureaucrats themselves have a great deal of power, which is only enhanced by political instability and frequent changes in ministers. The weight of the bureaucracy is heavy, and reforms are therefore most successful when implemented in the "honeymoon" period of a minister's stay in office, preferably at the beginning of a new government's mandate. Nationalization and decentralization under the Socialists and privatization under the neoliberals were all effective because they were passed within the first six months or so of the government's arrival in power.

In fact, during the Mitterrand years, ministers and their political *cabi-

[13]Suleiman, *Politics, Power, and Bureaucracy*, pp. 137–154.
[14]On the politicization of the civil service, see Chapter 10.
[15]Gallois, interview with author.

nets tended to dominate their ministries much more than in the past, as changing political agendas dictated very different ministerial policies from one government to the next, and as regular civil servants tended to be relegated to the more technical aspects of policy formulation and to implementation.[16] This stands in striking contrast with the postwar period, where upper-level civil servants who prided themselves on their independence from government tended to be paramount, originating heroic policies for governments rather than merely providing technical support. During this period, individuals such as François Bloch Lainé were typical of the powerful, generally respected civil servant who influenced governments.[17] Moreover, much of the industrial planning and policy agenda was not only identified by a small group of the administrative elite, the *"milieu décisionnel central,"*[18] or central decision-making milieu, but also implemented by it with minimal public debate. This was especially true for bodies such as the Plan and the DATAR, and was most apparent in the cases of nuclear power, urban planning, and the reform of the health-care system.[19] The result of such a system was that the administrative elite preferred *"grands projets"* instituted by the state, such as the Plan Calcul in computers or the renovation of the telecommunications area,[20] over less interventionist policies that would have given precedence to market forces, which were regarded simply as one more inconvenience, one more factor to take into account.[21]

INTERMINISTERIAL RELATIONS AND RIVALRIES

To talk of a single administrative elite, then, suggests a unitary state that was more illusion than reality. The interministerial rivalries were such that any particular action was generally the result of a compromise among various views, of one ministry prevailing over the others, or of industry successfully resisting, as often as not by playing one ministry off against another. In the industrial policy area, the main rivalries have always been between the Ministry of Finance on the one hand and all the other ministries given responsibility in this area on the other, in particular the Planning Commission in the early postwar years, but increasingly the Ministry of Industry, as industrial policy slowly replaced planning as the government's main microeconomic tool.

[16]For the changing role of the civil servant, see Chapter 10.

[17]See: François Bloch Lainé, *Profession: fonctionnaire* (Paris: Seuil, 1976).

[18]Catherine Grémion, *Profession, décideur: Pouvoir des hauts fonctionnaires et réforme de l'état* (Paris: Gauthier-Villars, 1979).

[19]Pierre Muller, "Entre le local et l'Europe: La crise du modèle français de politiques publiques," *Revue Française de Science Politique* vol. 42, no. 2 (April 1992), p. 277.

[20]Cohen, *Colbertisme "high tech."*   [21]Muller, "Entre le local et l'Europe," p. 277.

Between the Ministry of Finance and other ministries

The Ministry of Finance, described by its own civil servants as a temple surrounded by "a halo of mystery and esotericism,"[22] has always been the most powerful ministry in France, primarily because it controls the purse strings: within it is the Bureau of the Treasury, the Direction du Trésor. Although the power of the Ministry of Finance devolves primarily from its financial resources, it also comes from its central role in economic policymaking at both macro- and microeconomic levels.

In the postwar period, the greatest challenge to the power of the Ministry of Finance was the Planning Commission, which had a totally different conception of how to ensure economic development and, at least at first, its own financial resources. Whereas the Planning Commission's mission was growth, first and foremost, the Finance Ministry's was to maintain fiscal stability, even if this undermined growth. Moreover, while the perspective of the former was long-term and focused on investment strategy for the future of the economy, the latter's was necessarily short-term and concentrated on the day-to-day health of the economy. Thus, while the Ministry of Finance sought to damp inflation wherever possible, the Planning Commission saw deflation as more of a danger than inflation, which it in fact encouraged in the early years in order to promote growth.

These philosophical differences led to increasing conflict between the Plan and the Ministry of Finance, which, in the early years at least, could be managed by senior officials.[23] But as the Commission's purview expanded into global resource planning, the two came into direct conflict with predictable results, given the unequal balance of power and resources. While the planners may have had political access, public exposure, and their own sources of funds from the Marshall Plan in the early years, this was nothing compared to the Finance Ministry's control over all direct public investment and the allocation of credit, along with all the Plan's own financial incentives. In consequence, the Ministry of Finance managed to impose deflation in a number of significant cases over the objections of the planners, in particular the interruption of the Third Plan in 1960, the stabilization policy of 1962, and Barre's 1976 program.[24]

But while the Planning Commission may have been outflanked by the

[22]Claude Alphandéry et al., *Pour nationaliser l'état* (Paris: Seuil, 1968), p. 52.

[23]Pierre Grémion, "La Concertation," in *Où va l'administration française,* ed. Michel Crozier (Paris: SEDEIS, 1974).

[24]Hall, *Governing the Economy,* p. 173. See also: Jacques Lautman and Jean-Claude Thoenig, *Planification et administrations centrales* (Paris: Centre de Recherches et des Sociologies d'Organisation, 1966), p. 40; Cohen, *Modern Capitalist Planning;* J. J. Bonnaud, "Les instruments d'exécution du plan utilisés par l'état à l'égard des entreprises," *Revue Economique* (July 1970).

Finance Ministry, it nonetheless was able to undermine the traditional ministry–industry relations for the more specialized ministries. Because the planners provided individual firms with more direct access to funding through the Ministry of Finance, the traditional ministries of *tutelle* which often dealt with the industry's trade associations found their power undercut. In consequence, in order to retain their influence over their appointed industries, these ministries in turn found themselves having increasingly to act as advocates rather than supervisors.[25] The phenomenon is similar to that of the department in charge of the *notaires* in the Ministry of Justice, which found itself scrambling to defend its "tutees" in order to keep its clientele from abandoning it in favor of allies in other ministries.[26]

The public enterprises in particular managed to exploit these rivalries among the ministries, and in particular that between the horizontal and vertical ministries. For example, the electric power company EDF in the seventies enlisted the support of the Minister of Industry against the Minister of Finance in support of its nuclear program, while it enlisted the latter against the former when it sought to institute a dynamic commercial strategy to increase sales.

The structure of many of the ministries facilitated this game. The Ministry of Industry, for example, retained the long-standing structure associated with the trade association pattern: It was divided into seven sectoral administrations, each charged with the oversight of a particular industry, but each becoming, in a very real way, a lobby for industry within the government "to show that it is capable of obtaining the aid of the state."[27] And the more responsibility shifted away from ministries charged with sectoral oversight to those with more general mandates, such as the Planning Commission and the Ministry of Finance, in particular as a result of the increasing role of financial incentives, the more the Ministry played this lobbying role. Only with the Socialists' arrival in power did this change – and only for a while – when the Ministry of Industry gained major new industrial policy responsibilities with the restructuring of the nationalized industries, and even, for a short time, new sources of funding.

When the Socialists took over the government, they brought in a set of strong ministers with major initiatives that ensured that the traditional

---

[25]Hall, *Governing the Economy,* pp. 173–174. See also: Bruno Jobert, "Le Ministère de l'Industrie et la cohérence de la politique industrielle," *Revue Française de Science Politique* vol. 23, no. 2 (April 1973); Pierre Grémion, "La théorie de l'apprentissage institutionnel et la régionalisation du Cinquième Plan," *Revue Française de Science Politique* vol. 23, no. 2 (April 1973).

[26]Suleiman, *Private Power and Centralization.*

[27]Conversation cited by Zysman, *Political Strategies,* p. 64.

balance of power among ministries would shift. The Planning Commission, already in decline, did not regain its previous powers. On the contrary, it became symbolically at least a political Siberia, with Michel Rocard its most prominent prisoner. Moreover, although the Commission was to have been responsible for the planning contracts negotiated between state and industry, the Prime Minister put the Ministry of Industry in charge, leaving the Commission a mere participant for the contracts signed in 1983, and out entirely for the 1984 renewals.[28] Finally, by the time such contracts were reintroduced as the objective-setting contracts in 1988, the Plan had nothing to do with them at all.

This is not to say that the Ministry of Industry therefore was the prime player in the state–industry planning contracts, or in any other area of industrial action for that matter. In the case of the planning contracts, although the Ministry of Industry was able to block other ministries (e.g., Plan and DATAR, Women's Rights, Environment, etc.) from imposing too many constraints on the twelve industrial groups over which it exercised tutelage, it still came up against the superior financial power of the Ministry of Finance. The heads of public enterprises, having initially assumed that the Ministry of Industry would be able to decide on the amounts of the capital grants, soon found that, as always, the Finance Ministry had the last word, and adjusted their appointment schedules accordingly. Only when the Ministry of Industry got its own resources, when a new circuit of financing was set up (through the FIM, or the modernization investment fund – funded by the CODEVI, which was to provide capital to industry) at the time Fabius became Minister of Industry did the Ministry of Industry gain a certain independence of action and increased attention from the CEOs.[29] But this did not last long.

With the FIM, the Ministry of Industry for the first and only time had a tool that permitted it to operate independently, without the oversight of the Ministry of Finance and even against its advice. This, needless to say, displeased the Treasury, which had always opposed the kind of voluntarist (not to say *dirigiste*) policies of which the Ministry of Industry was generally the architect.

There have always been fundamental philosophical differences between the two: The Treasury insists that only macroeconomic policy, which sets the environment for business, is appropriate, and favors a case-by-case solution to problems rather than the Ministry of Industry's "fresco that traces an industrial perspective."[30] It should come as no surprise, therefore, that Daniel Lebègue, the Director of the Treasury at the time but subsequently Director-General of one of the three largest banks, the BNP,

[28]Barreau, "Les relations état–groupes nationalisés," p. 63.   [29]Ibid., p. 64.
[30]Gallois, interview with author.

made a point of telling Louis Gallois, in his role as Director-General of Industry, that he had sent a note every week to the Minister of Finance asking for the FIM's elimination on the grounds that "we cannot allow a financial instrument to be at the disposition of a ministry without its being under the control of the Ministry of Finance."[31] The Treasury was not to succeed in its aim until Alain Madelin's tenure as Minister of Industry in Chirac's government, when the FIM was abolished, and heads of public enterprise again turned to the Ministry of Finance for all major financial support.

The Treasury was more successful in vetoing an earlier attempt to create an independent source of funding for the nationalized enterprises: the National Investment Bank, a kind of holding company for public investments, which had been supported by numerous Socialist bankers, industrialists, and ministry officials who saw it as a way of financing the newly nationalized industries.[32] Treasury opposition, together with government fears of appearing even more *dirigiste,* or more "gosplan" in mentality, than they were already perceived, as Dominique Strauss-Kahn put it, scuttled the project.[33] And it never did see the light of day, despite the later attempt by Minister of Industry Strauss-Kahn under Cresson and Bérégovoy to revive the idea. (It is interesting to note, in this respect, that Jacques Attali, who had also wanted a National Investment Bank in France, at least got one at the European level.)[34]

The Ministry of Finance, in short, kept as tight a control as it could on the financial resources of the country. Its capability in this, moreover, FIM or no FIM, was almost guaranteed after the imposition of economic austerity in 1983, since, as money got tight, the spending ministries, such as industry, telecommunications, and so forth, had less and less to give out. And it was always the Ministry of Finance that decided how much they would have.

What is more, this monopoly of the Ministry of Finance with regard to financing was only reinforced at the time of the privatizations, since the returns from the privatizations as of 1987 were paid into a special Treasury account out of which came capital grants for public enterprises. As a result, instead of being part of the classical budgetary procedure that goes through Parliament and that would of necessity involve the Ministry of Industry, the negotiation for capital grants became a direct one between the CEO and the cabinet of the Minister of Finance, leaving the Minister of Industry the role of defender of the dossier presented by the enterprise, if that.[35]

---

[31]Lebègue, interview with author.
[32]In particular, Deflassieux, interview with author.
[33]Strauss-Kahn, interview with author.   [34]Deflassieux, interview with author.
[35]Barreau, "Les relations état–groupes nationalisés," p. 94.

The Ministry itself has power not only because of its financial resources, but also because of its central role in economic policy formulation. The Delors plan in 1983 which brought about the Great U-turn in macroeconomic policy, for example, was the work of a very small group in the Ministry of Finance led by Delors's cabinet director, and the director of the Treasury, along with the head of the Bank of France, Jean Peyrelevade from the Prime Minister's cabinet, and Daniel Lebègue, financial councilor in Mauroy's cabinet.[36] Financial deregulation, moreover, was the brainchild of a small group of people in the Ministry of Finance, primarily Treasury technocrats, who did it with little or no input from the financial community, let alone the general public.[37]

The Ministry of Finance was probably at the pinnacle of its policymaking power in the neoliberal government of 1986 to 1988. Privatization was for all intents and purposes the product of the Minister's cabinet along with the Bureau of the Treasury. Other ministries that one might have assumed to have been involved, such as the Ministry of Industry, were carefully kept out of the process of privatization in the case of every industrial enterprise that was traditionally under its tutelage except for CGCT.[38] Even the Ministry of Culture and Communication, which by the decree of April 8, 1986, was to be "part of the preparation and implementation of the privatization program for the communications sector," was kept out of the privatization of Havas altogether. In the case of the privatization of TF1, moreover, although the Ministry of Culture was certainly the prime actor in the choice of television station to privatize, it became less and less central to the process as the Ministry of Finance progressively took over major decision-making responsibilities.[39] Of the outside ministries, only the Ministry of Agriculture seemed to have predominated over the Ministry of Finance, when the Minister of Agriculture François Guillaume overcame the resistance to the privatization of the Crédit Agricole not only by the banking concern itself, but also by the Treasury and the Ministry of Finance through a direct appeal to the Prime Minister, who arbitrated in his favor.[40]

Within the Finance Ministry, moreover, the Minister and his cabinet

---

[36]Lebègue, interview with author.

[37]See: Christian de Boissieu, "Recent Developments in the French Financial System: An Overview," in *Banking in France*, ed. Christian de Boissieu (London: Routledge, 1990), pp. 1–25.

[38]Roger Fauroux, Minister of Industry in Rocard's government, when asked by the Commission of Inquiry on Privatization for documents on the privatizations from his ministry, had to respond that, other than the special case of the CGCT, there were none, demonstrating that the Ministry was indeed not at all involved. *Rapport sur les opérations de privatisation*, Report volume, p. 30.

[39]*Rapport sur les opérations de privatisation*, Report volume, pp. 30–36.

[40]Ibid., pp. 36–37. See also the discussion in Chapter 9.

tend to predominate in matters considered political. Thus, in the privatizations, the Minister and his advisors were responsible for the list of privatizations, the ordinance putting into effect the application of the *loi d'habilitation,* and the decision over which companies were to participate in the *noyau stable.* They also chose the members of the various commissions of audit and evaluation as well as members of the boards of directors of the to-be-privatized companies.[41] The Bureau of the Treasury, by contrast, was very much involved in all technical decisions and the technical aspects of the political decisions. Thus, the Treasury provided technical advice on the text of the ordinance and on many of the privatizations once the choices were made as well as commented on the evaluations by outside banking consultants of the companies to be privatized.[42] Moreover, the Treasury had the idea for the *noyau stable.*[43] Thus, while the government minister and the prime ministerial cabinet made up of political appointees are clearly the most powerful when it comes to formulating policy, the regular civil servants in the Bureau of Treasury are nevertheless key players.

In the Ministry of Industry

Although the Ministry of Finance clearly towers over all the other ministries as a result of its financial resources and economic policymaking role, other ministries nevertheless do have some leverage. Money, after all, is not the only basis for power. And the power the Ministry of Industry had in the first few years of the Socialists' tenure in office was due to the personalities of its ministers as well as to its responsibilities. Because the Ministry of Industry was responsible for the newly nationalized industries, with a mandate to restructure them, it had a charge that went far beyond its more traditional one of oversight over nationalized industry and of granting subsidies to public and private industries, which it had to negotiate with the Ministry of Finance (with the exception of the FIM for a short period). Moreover, because its first ministers were all in different ways powerful personalities, the ministry had the kind of clout it had not had in the past, and was soon to lose, never to regain.

The power of Pierre Dreyfus, the first Minister of Industry in the Mauroy government, who presided over the actual program of nationali-

---

[41]Testimony by Daniel Lebègue, *Rapport sur les opérations de privatisation,* vol. 1, pp. 272–278. On how these commissions were set up, see: Durupty, *Privatisations,* pp. 61–66.

[42]See the testimonies of Daniel Lebègue, Philippe Jaffré, and Jean-François Théodore, *Rapport sur les opérations de privatisation,* vol. 1.

[43]Testimony by Daniel Lebègue, *Rapport sur les opérations de privatisation,* vol. 1, p. 280.

zation, came not only from his prestigious past (as CEO of Renault) but also from his personal relationships with the CEOs with whom he had to deal. This enabled him to manage a highly interventionist set of actions without appearing very *dirigiste*. According to one top manager, François de Wissocq, a senior executive vice president at Elf-Aquitaine and member of the Managing Board (and former CEO of Cogema), Dreyfus was reasonable during the process of nationalization, able to work matters out cooperatively in one- or two-day meetings with the companies involved, because he "is a man with a deep understanding of the way in which businesses should be managed, not fundamentally different from the managers' views themselves, and has a respect for the autonomy of public enterprises." If he had been a politician, in the view of de Wissocq, it might have led to battles, but he wasn't and it didn't.[44] Because he was a former CEO himself and one of the most respected business leaders in the country, Dreyfus was able to persuade and cajole where others, such as his successor as Minister of Industry, Jean-Pierre Chevènement, merely offended.

Chevènement, who was in charge of major restructurings, was certainly as powerful as Dreyfus, although his prickly personality and his insistence on reviewing the nationalized industries' strategic plans made for more strained relations with the CEOs, and ultimately made for his early departure from the job. Chevènement oversaw the restructuring of the computer and chemical industries and started discussions on the division of the telephone industry between Thomson and Alcatel. He reorganized the Ministry of Industry in order to facilitate this restructuring, making the Direction Générale de l'Industrie, with its new Services des Entreprises Nationales (SEN) containing ten to fifteen experts, the hierarchical superior of the sector divisions in charge of the coordination of the *tutelle,* of the capital grants, of information gathering on the performance of the nationalized industries, and of the planning contracts.

Chevènement was widely perceived as heavy-handed, intervening on a daily basis, and occasioning the most rancor. The oft-repeated story used in illustration of this involved the Ministry of Industry's request, sent to all nationalized industries, for a list of the number and kinds of typewriters used in all factories as a preliminary to creating a national factory to supply all public enterprises and administrations. In the opinion of more than one top government official, this represented a return to Marxism or the Gosplan. In fact, Chevènement himself was not to blame. According to Louis Gallois, the Director-General of Industry at the time (and also subsequently under Fabius, Cresson, and Madelin), an overzealous sub-

[44]François de Wissocq, a managing director in the Comité de Direction Générale of the oil company Société Nationale Elf-Aquitaine and former CEO of Cogema. Interview with author, Paris, April 24, 1991.

director responsible for internal management took it upon himself to expand a study of office equipment in the Ministry of Industry by sending the circular to all nationalized enterprises. And everyone then wrongly imputed this action to the Minister. In Gallois's view (somewhat partial, perhaps, given his long working history with Chevènement), Chevènement made decisions, and was not necessarily more *dirigiste* than Prime Ministers Mauroy or Chirac, who themselves occasionally demanded actions that went against the advice of the Minister of Industry. Moreover, Chevènement's decisions, even if seen as interventionist, were in Gallois's view necessary ones: "We felt that we did not nationalize for no reason. We did it to put in order French industry that was nearly bankrupt: Péchiney, Bull, CDF-Chimie, all were in catastrophic shape."[45]

But even if necessary, Chevènement's actions alienated many heads of the nationalized enterprises. In addition to many clashes, his actions even occasioned the resignation of the non-Socialist CEO of Rhône-Poulenc, Jean Gandois (only five months after having been reappointed to his position), who complained that the Socialists at the time were "like children who have a new toy," thinking that they could intervene in the management of the enterprise.[46] The resistance of Gandois and other heads of the nationalized industries to Chevènement's leadership ensured that his tenure was short.

Laurent Fabius, Minister of Industry from May 1983 to July 1984, was probably the most powerful Minister of Industry during the Mitterrand years. Because Fabius was clearly seen as a rising star, a *ministrable,* he had more clout, as evidenced by the fact that he had managed to have some *arbitrages* (arbitrations) by the Prime Minister of disputes between the Ministries of Finance and Industry go in his favor, and that he had gotten funds for the ministry alone to distribute, the FIM.[47] Thus, Fabius had the tools to be even more *dirigiste* than Chevènement, and was no less *dirigiste,* but he was not perceived as such. As their shared Director-General, Gallois, tells it, the main reason for this was that the two men had different objectives: for Chevènement, it was restructuring; for Fabius, it was a return to a balanced budget. Needless to say, a minister who tells CEOs that they must balance their books, something that they try to do anyway, is likely to be more welcome than one, such as Chevènement, who tells them that they must do more research and development, or who asks what their strategy is (since they don't like telling this to anyone). While the CEOs' relationships with Fabius were for the most part "*tout rond,*" all smooth, even if Fabius could be *rude,* or brutal, once he made a decision, with Chevènement they tended to be bumpy, albeit

---

[45]Gallois, interview with author.   [46]Gandois, interview with author.
[47]Barreau, "Les relations état–groupes nationalisés," p. 63.

always courteous, leading to "reticences rather than confrontations," because with the rather weighty restructurings "all was a question of power relations."[48] And when the power relations went in the direction of the interests of the CEOs, with greater liberalization, a renewal of a respect for the traditional autonomy of public enterprises, and a focus on the financial health of firms rather than their industrial strategies, the Minister of Industry was certain to be better appreciated.

When Fabius became Prime Minister, he took most of the powers of the Ministry of Industry and Telecommunications with him. It was Fabius, together with his cabinet and the councilors of the President, who were responsible for the major decisions in the industrial area. Nonetheless, with what powers that were left to her, Fabius's Minister of Industry, Edith Cresson, only furthered the process of liberalization begun by Fabius, taking more of a case-by-case approach than her predecessors. In addition, her relations with the CEOs were more variable than those of her predecessors: she did well with some, very poorly with others – who would then go to the Ministry of Finance for a solution to their problem. This only accelerated a process already under way: for as the Ministry of Industry liberalized, it was giving up the greater power it had had under previous Socialist ministers, at the same time that the Ministry of Finance was beginning to take back its prerogatives.[49] This process was to reach a climax under the neoliberal government of Jacques Chirac. If the Ministry of Industry could be said to have been in its heyday under Chevènement and at its zenith under Fabius, it certainly reached its nadir under its next head, Alain Madelin, the neoliberal ideologue.

Alain Madelin, who gave away most of his resources and practically dismantled the Ministry of Industry, had the least clout of all as a result of his own actions. Not only did Madelin, as we have already seen, cut his budgets in such a way as to destroy the Ministry's ability to conduct any industrial policy, leaving to the Ministry of Finance all of the industrial responsibilities that the Ministry had traditionally handled.[50] But Madelin also nearly reorganized the Ministry out of existence, replacing the SEN with a Mission aux Entreprises Publiques et aux Privatisations made up initially of three people, which was rapidly reduced to two (with one of them half-time), and reducing the size of the Ministry by getting rid of three out of five directors. This was "madness," according to José Bidegain, number two in the Ministry of Industry under Madelin's successor, Roger Fauroux, given that the best civil servants left because they had no room for advancement while the worst stayed.[51] And even Mad-

48Gallois, interview with author.
49Barreau, "Les relations état–groupes nationalisés," p. 93.
50See the discussion in Chapter 5.   51Bidegain, interview with author.

elin's second Director-General of Industry, Jacques Maisonrouge, a former head of IBM, admitted that Madelin's reorganization of the Ministry (for which Maisonrouge himself made a point of claiming no responsibility) was reasonably poorly carried out and was guaranteed to garner internal resistance since Madelin engaged in no consultation as he created horizontal services in place of the vertical fiefdoms serving the different sectors of industry.[52] Madelin's objective, according to Gallois, who was his Director-General of Industry for six months and left in order "not to bury the ministry he had served for four years," was to destroy the Ministry. And in that, in Gallois's view, Madelin succeeded.[53]

Even the CEOs were not very pleased with Madelin. Although they were happy to be let alone to do what they wanted, they did not wish to do this absent all financial support. Maisonrouge himself, although in agreement with Madelin's attempt to return a sense of competition to industry by providing management consulting help rather than subsidies, saw those policies as hard to put in effect because of the resistance of the industrialists themselves, who were used to the old system where they asked for subsidies and got them. This was not to change, moreover, as Maisonrouge noted that Rocard also complained that industrialists have a liberal discourse but are always asking for something.

While Madelin intended to destroy the Ministry of Industry, his successor, Roger Fauroux, sought to revitalize it, without, however, returning it to its traditional functions. Fauroux was also quite liberal, although nothing like Madelin, seeing his role as that of a "partner" to, rather than "leader" of, industry, and understandably so, since the Ministry no longer had either the capability or the means to lead.[54] As a former head of industry himself, he felt that industry was first and foremost a matter for the industrialists,[55] and he saw his own job as much like that of the chief executive of a diversified holding company.[56]

In consequence of this, Fauroux, like the Minister of Finance of the time, Pierre Bérégovoy, was seen as a liberal who didn't know exactly what industrial policy meant and was criticized for a "lack of voluntarism."[57] But Fauroux himself retorted that he wanted to "let businesses do their work. . . . To intervene on a daily basis would be a disaster. This kind of voluntarism makes no sense."[58] He argued that the role of the Ministry was no longer to direct: "We are becoming a modern state

[52]Jacques Maisonrouge, Director-General of Industry under Madelin and former president of IBM World Trade. Interview with author, Paris, April 9, 1991.
[53]Gallois, interview with author.
[54]Ibid.   [55]*Le Monde*, May 17, 1991.
[56]*Financial Times*, June 8, 1992.   [57]*Le Monde*, May 17, 1991.
[58]*Le Monde*, March 2, 1990.

where power is exercised in a gentler manner, by persuasion and the influence of competence."[59]

Because of his view of the role of the Ministry of Industry, Fauroux also planned to reorganize the Ministry by turning the Direction Générale de l'Industrie, or Bureau of Industry, into one of industrial strategy where, instead of dealing with procedural matters, ministry officials were to act as industrial analysts advising the Minister on policy and, along with outside consultants, were to help industries assess their strengths and weaknesses.[60] He lost his job before the reorganization took place, much to the relief of ministry civil servants who felt that this, too, would have been a disaster for the Ministry, given that the vertical bureaus are the ones with power and an ability to do something.[61]

Fauroux's successor, Dominique Strauss-Kahn, was more of a voluntarist.[62] For Strauss-Kahn, the best policy was one that would take a middle road between the extremes of previous interventionism – which determined from Paris "whether shoes with laces or without would be produced in the provinces" – or of recent noninterventionism under Rocard. More specifically, for Strauss-Kahn, "between the Gosplan *tatillon,* or nitpicking, on the one side, and simply saying that we will intervene only on the economic environment and the rest is the market, there is an action of the state in the structuration of business capital which does not involve setting business strategy, but instead creates a different context for business, a different relationship between the financial system and the industrial one."[63] Thus, he saw the role of the Minister of Industry as a more active one than Fauroux, but still basically as shareholder rather than leader.

He too could do little, however, caught as he was between a voluntarist Prime Minister, Edith Cresson, who wanted to do all herself, and a liberal Minister of Finance, Pierre Bérégovoy, who then became his Prime Minister, and who, by comparison at least, wanted no one to do anything much at all in the area. Moreover, because Strauss-Kahn was a deputy minister under the Minister of Finance in the Cresson government, being promoted to a full minister only once Bérégovoy became Prime Minister, his power was limited. (This was symbolically brought home by the fact that the Minister's offices moved to Bercy, the very home of the Ministry's traditional rival, although the Ministry as a whole managed to resist such a move.) This arrangement ensured that not only did Strauss-Kahn report to him, but Bérégovoy also got to see any information that Strauss-Kahn

[59]*Le Monde,* February 4, 1990.   [60]Fauroux, interview with author.

[61]Upper-level civil servant in the Ministry of Industry. Interview with author, Paris, December 1992.

[62]See also the discussion in Chapter 6.   [63]Strauss-Kahn, interview with author.

may have requested from the Treasury twenty-four hours before his deputy minister, thus giving the Finance Minister time to prepare a response and impose his will. This was only partially balanced out by the fact that Strauss-Kahn was to receive enough advance notice of Bérégovoy's decisions to have time to respond, and that he could always go to Matignon for arbitration, although this could cause him problems. But if he did not seek arbitrations, and relied on the Ministry of Industry alone, he would still have problems because, as one former Finance person put it, "the Ministry of Industry doesn't have either the rapidity or the technical competence to oppose the Finance Ministry" and, as a result, "All my buddies from X (Polytechnique) who went to the Ministry of Industry left running."[64]

The Ministry also did not have the funding, primarily because Strauss-Kahn was unable to include in his mandate the Ministry of Telecommunications and therefore France Télécom, which had substantial profits and power, with its 17% of the capital of Bull, its partnership in SGS-Thomson and in HDTV, as well as its proprietorship of the satellites. (His predecessor, Chevénement, and his successor, Longuet, were luckier in this regard.) Strauss-Kahn himself had hoped that Cresson would follow through on her idea to create a strong Ministry of the Economy (dealing with industry) to balance out the powers of the Ministry of Finance, as in Germany. However, he himself conceded that this was not likely to be, since Bérégovoy, the Minister of Finance and the Economy, was unlikely to relinquish any of his power, given that all of the services related to aid to industry and oversight would have to be detached from the Treasury in order to create such a new ministry.[65]

For all this, however, Strauss-Kahn did manage to do a lot, in particular with regard to the continued restructuring of French capitalism. Thus, although he saw the role of the Ministry also as a partner of industry, he sought to encourage firms to be entrepreneurial by insisting that instead of having the state fund them at 100%, they needed to go find banks and insurance companies to accompany their actions before he was willing to talk. The CEOs did not mind this at all, and saw the Ministry as an ally and a defender of their interests. This extended even to their battles to get funding from the Ministry of Finance, with the Ministry of Industry able to play the Ministry of Finance divisions off against one another.[66]

Balladur's Minister of Industry, Post, Telecommunications, Space, and Foreign Trade, Gérard Longuet (until October 1994), had more money, a larger mandate, and therefore greater independence than his predecessor,

---

[64]*Le Nouvel Observateur*, July 4–10, 1991.   [65]Strauss-Kahn, interview with author.
[66]Comments by upper-level civil servants in the Ministry of Industry. Interviews with author, December 1992.

with 25% of the GNP in some sense under his control.[67] (He symbol-ically moved his offices out of Bercy and into that of the Post at 20 Avenue Ségur.) Although he had a reputation as a neoliberal, he was a rather Colbertist one. He too saw his role as that of partner, but a partner who, judging from his actions, had more muscle than most of his predecessors since Fabius.

Longuet, however, was equally unlikely to be able to bring the Ministry back to its former glory, or to be any kind of serious rival to the Ministry of Finance. As Gallois remarked, with what Madelin did on the one hand and Bérégovoy's approach on the other, the balance of power between the two ministries maintained under Chevènement and Fabius was destroyed, so much so that "to make the Ministry rise again would take decades."[68] This view of the diminution in the power of the Ministry of Industry has been shared by business heads, a majority of whom (54%) in a 1990 survey did not think the Ministry of Industry useful to their enterprise (as opposed to 46% who did), even if 79% thought that the Ministry did serve some purpose (vs. 11% who did not).[69]

Privatization and deregulation also diminished the power of the Minis-try of Industry, as it did all the other ministries. Privatized enterprises, for obvious reasons, no longer had the state as a *tuteur,* nor did they have to go to the state for capital investments. Nonetheless, most such enterprises notified the relevant ministry as a matter of courtesy. André Lévy-Lang, head of Paribas, noted that for the acquisition of a firm, only as a courtesy does he inform the Ministry of Finance by telephone or in person of what actions he intends to take. Otherwise, since they became private, they have had no need to deal with the ministry of *tutelle* in any other way.[70]

Deregulation has affected the Treasury bureau probably more than other *directions* in the Ministry of Finance, and more than the Ministry of Industry. The Treasury is no longer able to limit credit through monetary policy, enforce price controls, or finance large projects through the FDES (the Fond du Développement Économique et Sociale, or Economic and Social Development Fund). Moreover, it is no longer the privileged inter-locutor of industry in the way in which it was in the early 1980s, when close to half of industry's loans were discounted.[71] Evidence of the changed status of Ministries of Industry or Finance is also reflected in the fact that there is no longer even the caricature of a relationship in which the young head of a department in the Ministry of Industry or in the Treasury calls up a CEO to chew him out.[72] Now, CEOs no longer have

---

[67]For an in-depth account, see: *L'Expansion,* September 23–October 6, 1993.
[68]Gallois, interview with author.   [69]*L'Usine Nouvelle,* no. 2253, February 1, 1990.
[70]Lévy-Lang, interview with author.   [71]Ibid.
[72]Strauss-Kahn, interview with author.

to go to the Ministry of Finance for permission to raise their prices or bankers to distribute loans. But the Treasury, nonetheless, retains tremendous power, especially by comparison with the Ministry of Industry.

In the nationalized enterprises

The diminution in the power of the Ministries of Finance and Industry as a result of deregulation has naturally also affected the nationalized enterprises. But even before this, despite the formal powers of the Ministries over the nationalized enterprises exercised through their *tutelle,* or oversight function, through their ability to nominate and revoke the CEO, and through the state–industry planning contracts,[73] CEOs of state-owned enterprises have nevertheless managed to maintain their independence. This results in large measure from the CEOs' own personal power, from their collective influence as members of the *grands corps,* and from their role as protectors of the national interest as much as from the inability of the ministries to exercise control through the planning contracts. In fact, the planning contracts that were to balance out public enterprises' autonomy by ensuring their accountability were for the most part little more than gentlemen's agreements, generally consecrating public enterprises' own decisions.

Political clout and corps membership are major sources of CEO power and independence. Thus, it was Pierre Dreyfus's personal power that enabled him to grant Renault workers a fourth week of vacation against strong Gaullist government opposition and Pierre Guillaumat's position as head of the Corps des Mines, or Mining Corps, that enabled him to

[73]The *tutelle* is exercised first of all through the nomination and revocation of the CEOs, and through the board of directors (*conseils d'administration*), of which one-third are state appointees (although this is generally only formal). Second, it is exercised economically and financially through the Ministry of Finance, and in particular the Bureau of the Treasury, which can allow or refuse operations on the financial markets; the Bureau of Competition, which controls prices (now only in the case of nationalized enterprises in the social service and noncompetitive sectors); and the Office of the Budget, which determines the size of subsidies. Third, there are the *controleurs de l'état* who are billeted to the companies, acting as go-betweens. Fourth, the technical ministries, e.g., the Transport Ministry for the SNCF and Air France, the Ministry of Industry for Renault and the EDF, the Ministry of Defense for the defense industries, and so forth, review the strategic decisions of the firm, although they generally leave managerial decisions to top management's discretion. There are also interministerial commissions that are asked to give their advice on certain plans of public enterprises. Finally, Parliament in principle has the ability to exercise tutelage through the voting of the budget, but in practice this never occurs, especially since governments have generally preferred to operate on the basis of decrees and ordinances when it comes to individual firms so as not to have Parliament interfere. For more on this relationship, see, for example, Anastassopoulos, "Entreprises publiques et pouvoir politique."

engineer the creation of a new petroleum company (Total) to be populated by members of the Corps.[74]

The independence of the heads of the nationalized industries is also
supported by the tradition of the nonpolitical, public manager, whose
position is assumed to be more long-term and stable by comparison with
the more transient, politically motivated ministers and whose responsibilities include protecting the nationalized enterprises from being buf-
feted about by the winds of faction.[75] Public managers have tended to
clothe themselves in this tradition and to suggest not only that they are
best qualified to intervene in economic policy matters but also that they
do it as guarantors of the general interest and guardians of the state
against the political vagaries of the moment.[76] As such, they are also able
to resist political pressures. Thus, for example, the CEO of one major
bank noted that he received calls to help an enterprise from different
ministries all the time. When he responded that he could not do this, and
the minister then said, but surely you can, he asked for the minister to put
the request in writing, at which point he was left in peace.

The result is that ministers in France have tended to exert comparatively little control over public enterprise, other than in the appointment
of the CEO.[77] Reflecting this is Georges Vedel's comment that "Nationalizations are a procedure for selecting directors."[78] In the sixties, A. G.
Delion underscored the importance of the power of appointment, noting
that "power over acts is meaningless if the directors are not competent,
superfluous if they fulfill their duties."[79] Even the power of appointment,
however, may escape the ministers of *tutelle*. Often, the more powerful
CEOs together with their boards of directors name their own
successors.[80]

Moreover, ministers actually tended to conspire with the CEOs to
ensure their independence from government interference. Thus, when the
Council of State effectively made the sale of the subsidiaries of nationalized companies illegal by deciding against the 1984 sale by the Com-
missariat à l'Energie Atomique of its subsidiary Cogema on the grounds

[74]Feigenbaum, *Politics of Public Enterprise*, p. 62.

[75]Raymond Vernon, "Linking Manager with Ministers: Dilemmas of the State-Owned
Enterprise," *Journal of Policy Analysis and Management* vol. 4, no. 1 (1984), pp. 42–45.

[76]Anne Stevens, "'L'alternance' and the Higher Civil Service," in *Socialism*, ed.
Cerny and Schain, p. 144. See also: Jacques Chevallier, "Un nouveau sens de l'état et
du service public," in *Administration et politique*, ed. F. de Baeque and J.-L. Quermonne (Paris: Presses de la Fondation Nationale des Sciences Politiques, 1981).

[77]The appointment procedures do vary, however, with the government sometimes
appointing the CEO directly, other times indirectly, on the basis of the board's nominations. See: Daniel Derivry, "Managers of Public Enterprises," pp. 212–213.

[78]Quoted in: Derivry, "Managers of Public Enterprises," p. 213.   [79]Ibid.

[80]See Chapter 10.

that Parliament had to give authorization for such sales because they belonged to the state, thereby putting all the nationalized companies in a precarious or "delicate" position, the ministers nevertheless permitted the sales without, however, any official OK. The solution, as Georges Pébereau described it, was that he and the other heads of the nationalized enterprises "would send a letter to the tutelage Minister saying that they envisaged this or that operation. I did not receive a reply but I had informed and then I assumed the responsibility for what had been done. Had I not done that, CGE would not be what it is today."[81]

Ministerial protection of the independence of the CEOs extended to everyday operations as well. For example, Ministry of Industry officials charged with the *tutelle* often see their job as that of protecting the firm, and in particular the CEO, from the encroachments of politics, meaning the pressure of ministerial cabinets and ministers. In an interview, one explained that he acted as a screen to keep the company from daily interference, feeling that the state appoints the CEO for three years, and should therefore place its trust in the CEO.[82] Nationalized enterprise autonomy is ensured also by the fact that the government presence in nationalized industries is, and has always been, minimal. In defense firms, for example, whereas in the United States people from the Defense Department are everywhere – at GE, maybe 150 or 200 people – in a French firm such as SNECMA they only had three or four people from the Ministry of Defense.[83]

There are two sides to this relationship between ministry and nationalized industry, however. When the civil servant charged with the *tutelle* of a given firm disagrees with the proposed strategy, then the CEO has little choice in the matter if the civil servant has put together a case that convinces the Director-General of Industry and the Minister of Industry. Arbitration through the Prime Minister, moreover, provides no recourse, even if the Minister of Finance agrees to the CEO's strategy, because if the Minister of Industry refuses, the Prime Minister will not order it, and two signatures are necessary for the proposal to go through. In 1992–1993, this happened to Alain Gomez, CEO of Thomson CSA, who was kept from selling Thomson ElectroMénager.[84] Generally, however, the CEOs got their way, with ministerial control increasingly ineffective over time.

CEOs have also generally gotten their way because of the tradition of respect for the autonomy of public enterprise which has only increased over the years. In fact, in the "new society" government of Jacques

---

[81]Pébereau testimony, *Rapport sur les opérations de privatisation*, vol. 2, pp. 725–726.

[82]Upper-level civil servant in the Ministry of Industry. Interview with author, December 1992.

[83]Gallois interview.   [84]Ibid.

Chaban-Delmas of 1969–1972, the nationalized enterprises gained so much new autonomy that Pierre Dubois wrote about the "death of the *Etat patron*."[85] The Nora report, which recommended treating the nationalized enterprises "like the others," even led Albin Chalandon to declare that "I no longer consider that Elf has a public service mission" (although he was rebuked by the Minister of Industry for this).[86]

The increasing autonomy of public enterprise, however, raised the question: How does one establish governmental control of public enterprise, thus ensuring ministerial accountability, without at the same time destroying an autonomy of action that has been largely responsible for public enterprise success?[87] The problem, as Harold Seidman has argued, is that all the tradition of public autonomy really does for everyday affairs is to leave ministers free to intervene without fear of being held responsible for their actions. And this lack of ministerial accountability is not only dangerous in principle but may also prove highly detrimental in practice because the ministerial control exercised may be misguided: the ministers and their staffs often don't speak the same language as the managers of public enterprises and don't understand the differences between commercial undertakings and traditional government activities.[88]

Beginning in the seventies and extending through Mitterrand's presidency, the state's answer to this problem of accountability was to be found in the contractualization of its relationship with industry.[89] Plan-

[85]Pierre Dubois, *Mort de l'état-patron* (Paris: Editions ouvrières, 1974); and René Mouriaux, "Trade Unions, Unemployment, and Regulation: 1962–1986," in *Searching for the New France*, ed. James F. Hollifield and George Ross (New York: Routledge, 1991), pp. 178–179.

[86]*The Economist*, December 23, 1974 – cited in Feigenbaum, *Politics of Public Enterprise*, p. 74.

[87]It has also raised another, more philosophical question: If public enterprises are truly autonomous, then how does one ensure that they will indeed act in the public interest? And if, as Bernard Chenot has remarked, they are given no guidance by the central government, then they will, as had increasingly been true in the 1970s, interpret their guardianship as one involved solely with the goal of making a profit. If that is the case, if all they strive to do is to act like private enterprises, then what is the point of their being public enterprises in the first place? Bernard Chenot, "Philosophie des nationalisations françaises," *Revue Française d'Administration Publique* no. 15 (July–September 1980); pp. 494, 497.

[88]Harold Seidman, "Public Enterprise Autonomy: Need for a New Theory," *International Review of Administrative Sciences* vol. 49, no. 1 (1983), pp. 68–70.

[89]The state–industry contracts started with the "program contracts" recommended by the Nora report of 1969–1970 and continued with the "enterprise contracts" of 1978–1980. Under the Socialists, they encompassed the "planning contracts" foreseen by the nationalization law of February 11, 1982, and the planning reform law of July 28, 1982, with eleven such contracts having been signed and put into effect by the end of 1983. André Delion, "Le contrôle des entreprises publiques," *Cahiers français* no. 214 (January–February 1984); p. 43. See also: Vernon, "Linking Managers," p. 41. For a discussion of the experiences of industry under these contracts, see: J.-P. An-

ning contracts were to allow ministers to set goals for public enterprises to achieve, thus leaving the nationalized enterprises autonomous but not without state direction.[90] In fact, they primarily left the nationalized firm autonomous. The state–industry planning contracts, originally conceived of as a way of ensuring managerial and ministerial accountability, had no more of a coercive function than those with private sector firms. Because these planning contracts, like the industrial plans of the past, involved negotiating with industry rather than commanding, because they often legitimized actions already taken by industry, and because they generally contained promises to promote national economic priorities such as economic decentralization, they tended to play what Durand has called a "pedagogical" rather than a "directive" role.[91] Put another way, in the words of Philippe Messine, the negotiation of planning contracts was "mainly the occasion for a useful and courteous exchange of information between the enterprise and the government" and was in "the domain of the gentleman's agreement more than in that of the directive."[92]

The Socialists in no way sought to change this arrangement, or to challenge the autonomy of public enterprise. Even in the Common Program of the left in 1972, with its rhetoric of a break with capitalism and an end to exploitation, the management of the nationalized enterprises was to retain its traditional autonomy, with the control by the state an *a posteriori* one of review.[93] In their campaign, the Socialists pledged to guarantee the traditional autonomy of the public enterprises, with only the planning contracts between state and enterprise to serve as guides, and with state oversight to be *a posteriori*.[94] With some exceptions during the short-lived Chevènement period, the Socialists kept their promise.

Generally, the negotiations between top management and ministry officials were amicable and cooperative.[95] This tended to be ensured by the

astassopoulos and J. P. Nioche, eds., *Entreprises publiques: Expériences comparées* (Paris: FNEGE, 1980).

[90]There were differences between the contracts of the past and the Socialists' state–public enterprise planning contracts. The program contracts tended to provide more autonomy to public enterprises in the service sector, providing for a certain liberty in setting tariffs and prices, a multiyear investment program, and obligations in modernization and internal management. The planning contracts apply to public enterprises in the competitive sector and require them to adhere to the national plan and to meet the objectives set out for the national interest, at the same time allowing managerial autonomy in day-to-day operations.

[91]Durand et al., "Dirigisme," p. 254.   [92]Messine, "Nationalisations," p. 5.

[93]*Programme Commun.*   [94]Barreau and Le Nay, "Du Programme Commun," p. 24.

[95]The planning contracts also required large-scale consultation with the personnel in arriving at the firm's strategies and objectives. But although this was often confirmed in the planning contracts themselves (e.g., those of CGE, Bull and Thomson), little actual consultation took place, as the High Council of the Public Sector made clear in its report. However, even had it occurred, it would have had little impact, given that the major decisions were generally made outside the context of the planning

ministers themselves. For example, in his instructions for the first Socialist planning contracts, the Minister of Industry, Pierre Dreyfus, was careful to make sure that the planning contracts would be understood as noncoercive documents, insisting that "It would be better to speak of *convention* (agreement) rather than planning contract, so that the enterprises do not understand it as a protocol as constraining as the contract in commercial law."[96] Dreyfus's successor as Minister of Industry, and the person who was to see the first planning contracts to their conclusion, Jean-Pierre Chevènement, was less concerned about the enterprises' fears of *dirigisme*. He put managerial autonomy at the very end of a list of objectives for the planning contracts that included ensuring that the group's medium-term strategies cohered with the industrial policy of the state, that the group was associated with "the objectives of the national interest, national solidarity, the Government's policies of employment, research and development, foreign trade balance and the relations with small and mid-sized enterprises and industries," and that the group mobilize the personnel around these objectives.[97]

Whatever his intentions, however, the first planning contracts signed by the nationalized industries during Chevènement's tenure as Minister served largely as a way of accommodating industries' views. What is more, even as pedagogical documents, they were not very worthwhile. The planning contracts signed by the nationalized industries tended to include vague generalizations that were merely simplified versions of the companies' own strategic plans;[98] they contained formulations such as "to pursue foreign expansion," "to prepare the long-term future of the branch," "to maintain profits," "to reestablish an international position," "to develop its capacity," "to consolidate its dominant position in the world market," to ensure a strong growth," and so forth. Actual figures were almost nonexistent (three in Bull's first contract, one in those

contracts and involved a very small group of people, generally the top three managers and ministry officials. Thomson's decision to reinforce its semiconductor activities in 1983, for example, was decided together with the state by three top managers of the group. Barreau, "Les relations état-groupes nationalisés," p. 64.

[96] Charzat Report, p. 267 – cited in Barreau and Le Nay, "Du Programme Commun," p. 47.

[97] Barreau and Le Nay, "Du Programme Commun," pp. 47–48. In many ways, Chevènement's more *dirigiste* approach conformed to the earlier discussions of the CERES, where the CEOs were to be not just accountable for their results, "*comptables que de leurs résultats*," as declared Pierre Mauroy and Michel Charzat (speaking for the CERES) in the parliamentary debates of winter 1981–1982, but also "accountable for the national interest." Ibid., p. 49.

[98] This was actually deliberate: Dreyfus's first set of instructions that became the ground rules for the process established that the basis for negotiation would be a simplified version of the internal strategic plans of the parent companies of the nationalized groups.

of CGE and Thomson). The 1984 contracts were no more precise, although the sections on training were more extended, in response to instructions from Fabius.[99]

Moreover, even had they been precise documents that did lay out overall company strategy – not likely since the company heads were unwilling to allow their rivals to know their plans – they would have been largely superseded by events. For the largest nationalized companies, major decisions are the result of ongoing discussions with other corporations on joint ventures, licensing agreements, distribution agreements, mergers, or acquisitions, which are unlikely to fit the time-bound requirements of planning documents of the kind required by the state, or to work smoothly in a process that requires consultation with a large number of actors. If anything, the planning contracts ended up simply confirming the decisions of the companies' CEOs, in consultation with top ministers. The planning contract for Saint-Gobain, for example, essentially took the company's own internal strategic plan.[100]

Fabius's approach to the planning contracts essentially took account of these realities. Because he recognized that the planning contracts were not terribly useful, rather "heavy documents" designating the whole of the enterprise's strategy, Fabius found it simpler to establish more informal relations with the enterprises, as shareholder, except of course in the case of major restructuring.[101] As part of this, moreover, Fabius sought "to define rules that would ensure the managerial autonomy of the heads of the public enterprises and could guarantee them against the nit-picking intervention of the bureaucracy," in particular in the planning contracts.[102]

After something of a hiatus under the Chirac government, the planning contracts continued, although in a less formal manner, under the Rocard government, returning as the *contrats d'objectifs,* or objective-setting contracts. Here, the process, which again began with the submission of a strategic plan by the enterprise, involved a number of meetings between top management and Ministries of Industry and Finance officials. These were held in order to reach a consensus between the management of the group and the state, now understood more as shareholder than "*tuteur,*" on the group's overall strategies and finances. The state's role was, if anything, less coercive than with the planning contracts. Since there was

[99]Barreau, "Les relations état–groupes nationalisés," p. 62.

[100]According to its president, Roger Faroux, "Une experience de réussite industrielle," *Cadres CFDT* (July 1986), p. 9 – cited in Fridenson, "Atouts et limites," p. 188.

[101]Louis Schweitzer, CEO of Renault (director general at the time of the interview), interview with author, Paris, May 10, 1991.

[102]Laurent Fabius, "Qui a peur de l'économie mixte," *Le Monde,* February 28, 1989.

no industrial policy to which the Ministry could refer in order to reject any given corporate strategy, it could only raise questions with regard to company finances, and reject proposals for external expansion if these negatively affected the company's balance sheet.[103] In fact, by the late eighties and early nineties, the only criterion used to assess nationalized enterprises' performance was their profitability. And increasingly, the ambitious sectoral plans and policies were replaced by the *coup-par-coup*, or the day-to-day relations between ministry and individual firms. Even before this, however, the more important actions affecting the nationalized enterprises in particular were essentially those between the state and the individual firms, and were personalized in terms of minister–CEO relations.

CONCLUSION

Thus, although the nationalized enterprises were less free *a priori* to do what they wished by comparison with private enterprise, they nevertheless had a great deal of freedom. And this only increased over time as companies generally became more independent of the state as a result of government deregulation and business internationalization and more interdependent in consequence of the trading of shares in public and private firms. European integration, moreover, has only added to this independence, at the same time that it has served to unbalance the entire structure of decision-making, as we shall see in the next chapter.

This is not to suggest, however, that French ministries have lost all their power. Much the contrary, since they remain the locus of decision-making in France, with the Ministry of Finance predominant and the Ministry of Industry a distant second. But they have lost their independent authority, as the European Commission and Court may review, and reject, their actions in an ever-growing number of areas.

[103]Barreau, "Les relations état–groupes nationalisés," pp. 66–68.

8

Between the ministries and the European Union

Complicating relations in the ministries as well as between ministries and industry in recent years has been European integration. The growth of the EC/EU as a locus of decision-making has in a very real way altered the traditional structure of French decision-making, where governments have typically formulated policy unilaterally but allowed societal interests in at the implementation stage with the politics of accommodation, co-optation, or confrontation. The primacy of Brussels in policy formulation has decreased the independence of government, which no longer has the authority to make policy unilaterally, while it has further increased the independence of business, which now looks as much to Europe as to the nation-state for policymaking. Moreover, the introduction of the EU regulatory model has reduced the flexibility of government at the implementation stage, given that it demands an arm's-length relationship between business and government and the even-handed application of the rules. This has served to weaken France's traditional pattern of policymaking even further, since it calls into question the administrative nature of the French state, where making exceptions is the rule. The result is that in the application of EU rules or of those of the new French regulatory agencies, all societal interests, and not only business, will find less accommodation and therefore may engage in more confrontation, albeit with less success. Only where the traditional relationship between ministry and industry remains will business find more co-optation with regard to state oversight.

Thus, while business has become less dependent on national governments and more interdependent and international, the French state has become more dependent on the European Union. The result is that the French state has been losing many of its traditional powers and some of its national sovereignty, which has been jeopardized by the government's loss of the freedom to determine independently its macroeconomic policy and its domestic policy agenda in the economic, social, and environmental spheres. (This is more than symbolic: a constitutional argument supporting the transfer of sovereignty has been developed that sees sovereignty limited "by a sovereign consented act.")[1] The power of the central government, moreover, has diminished not only as a result of the liberalization of the economy and the abandonment of its traditional interventionist policy instruments, but also in consequence of the decentralization reforms which gave increased powers over local economic development to the regions, which themselves have a direct relationship with the EU unmediated by the central government.[2]

And yet, in exchange for all this, the French government has gained other benefits: Most importantly, it has greater influence at the supranational level. France, after all, is a member of the Council of Ministers which acts as the legislative body; French bureaucrats, as members of the European Commission, help shape the directives that are then imposed on France; and French businesses lobby Brussels to ensure that they will remain in a competitive position by comparison with those of other European countries. France also has gained greater control over its macroeconomic environment and a larger arena for its ambitious industrial policies. However, as both of these have begun to prove elusive, some may increasingly question whether all of this has been worthwhile, especially given the problems for French democracy resulting from the impact of the EU on policy implementation.

THE IMPACT OF EUROPEAN INTEGRATION ON POLICY FORMULATION

European integration has meant that the government has lost much of its ability to formulate policies independently, thereby significantly weakening one of the most distinctive features of the statist pattern of policymaking. In the first place, French national interests, like those of other member states, are no longer defined independently, but rather "are defined and redefined in an international and institutional context that includes the EC."[3] Moreover, the sphere in which French policymakers can act independently, without attention to the EU, has gotten narrower and narrower. French bureaucrats are more and more in the business of

[1]*Le Monde* May 6, 1992; and Robert Ladrech, "Europeanization of Domestic Politics and Institutions: The Case of France," *Journal of Common Market Studies* vol. 32, no. 1 (March 1994).

[2]See: Schmidt, *Democratizing France*.

[3]Wayne Sandholtz, "Choosing Union: Monetary Politics and Maastricht," *International Organization* vol. 47 (winter 1993). For a discussion of how French ministries have reconciled French national interests with European ones, see Christian Lequesne, *Paris–Bruxelles: Comment se fait la politique européenne de la France* (Paris: Presses de la Fondation Politique Nationale des Sciences Politiques, 1993).

implementing policies formulated in Brussels rather than in Paris.[4] They themselves admit that they can no longer impose, and that instead they "have been obliged to accept the idea that they were becoming instruments of execution as much as of decision in Community matters."[5] In addition, because EU member governments no longer have veto power over decisions, given the shift to qualified majority voting with the Single European Act that went into effect in 1987, the French administration could even be implementing policies that the French government opposed. Because of this, effective interaction with Brussels at all levels has become crucial.[6]

French influence with the EU bureaucracy, however, is not nearly as great as the French would wish, even if it is quite clearly a lot greater than that of smaller member states with less power or influence. Although the French have been key players at the level of grand strategy, having been instrumental in accelerating European integration through the European Monetary System, the Single Market, and the Maastricht Treaty, as well as in promoting grand industrial policy initiatives such as Esprit, Eureka, and Race, they have been less effective in imposing their views in the day-to-day affairs of the Commission.

French business and government officials complain in particular of what they see as the distinctly "Anglo-Saxon" bias, or the liberal economic ideology, that they insist has pervaded DG4, the Directorate charged with competition policy, especially under Leon Brittan. Epitomizing this was the de Havilland case, where the French criticized EC civil servants for basing their decision not to allow acquisition by Aérospatiale and Aléna on purely "liberal" grounds, that is, on the effect of the takeover on world competition, rather than, say, on what position this would leave Aérospatiale in by comparison with its major competitors.[7] (It is important to note, however, that in three years of EU merger regulation, from 1991 to 1994, it was the only case of a deal being outlawed. The next such attempt by the Competition Directorate – to block a three-way merger between French, German, and Italian steel-tube manufacturers in January 1994 – was rejected by the European Commission. Moreover,

[4]See: Charles Debbasch, "L'influence des transferts de compétences vers les instances communautaires sur les compétences des administrations," *Administration* vol. 149 (October 15, 1990).

[5]Yves Mény, "Formation et transformation des policy communities: L'exemple français," in *Idéologies, partis politiques et groupes sociaux* (Paris: Presses de la Fondation Nationale des Sciences Politiques, 1989), p. 363.

[6]See: Jean-Louis Quermonne, *L'appareil administratif de l'état* (Paris: Seuil, 1991); and Muller, "Entre le local et l'Europe," p. 287.

[7]See the discussion in Hervé Dumez and Alain Jeunemaître, "La France, l'Europe et la Concurrence: Enseignements de l'Affaire A.T.R./De Havilland," *Commentaire* no. 57 (spring 1992).

most French subsidies to state-owned enterprises have been approved by the Competition Directorate, despite protests from competitors.)[8] For the French at the time, the de Havilland case symbolized the end of France's ability to control its own destiny, burying not only French industrial policy but also any hope for a European industrial policy.[9] Even French CEOs, despite their general support for accelerating European integration (in a September 1992 poll, 58% of respondents wanted more Europe as opposed to 21% wanting less, 17% neutral, and 4% with no opinion), were nevertheless quite hostile to competition policy (with 47% negative responses vs. 33% finding such policy positive and sufficient, and 14% positive and insufficient), selecting it out for their most negative assessment of the whole panoply of EC policies, including social and labor policy.[10] The source of the CEOs' fears, as one director of Peugeot remarked, "is very simple; we have never seen so much power concentrated in one single institution since the Holy Roman Empire and the Hanseatic league."[11]

Although the main target of French criticism is the liberal content of economic policy decisions, the complaint is also directed at the entire regulatory structure of the institutions. The difficulty the French have with the structure comes from two sources: The first stems from the minimal French civil service and business presence in Brussels until comparatively recently; the second from the French lack of understanding of EU administrative culture.

The French presence in Brussels

The first source of difficulty results in large part from French ministries' long-standing underestimation of the importance of the EC administration. Because French bureaucrats were slow to recognize the significance of the EC as an administrative, as distinct from a political, policymaking body, they were even slower at encouraging the "best and the brightest" of the younger civil servants, that is, graduates of the ENA or Polytechnique, to forsake national for EC service. This in turn has ensured that comparatively few find themselves in the upper levels of an administration where civil servants start low and stay long in the Directorates, acceding only late in their careers to major positions (by contrast with the French system in which young graduates of the ENA start high, go higher, and then move out to head a private or public enterprise).[12] The fact that European civil servants of French nationality tend to be law graduates or

---

[8]See Chapter 6.   [9]*La Tribune*, October 3, 1991.
[10]*L'Expansion*, September 3–10, 1992, p. 57.   [11]Ibid.
[12]For the career path, see Chapters 10, 14, and 15.

products of the Institut d'Études Politiques rather than *camarades de promotion*, or fellow classmates, of top French ministry officials closes off one way of easing relations between the Commission and a French administration which has had a tendency to remain somewhat distant and suspicious of its supranational counterpart.[13] And this has only been reinforced by the more general French perception that the most senior ranks of the civil service are dominated by the British, in particular Leon Brittan when Competition Commissioner, and the Germans, in particular Martin Bangemann when Industry Commissioner, who tend to be less charitable toward public ownership and state intervention than the French,[14] and less supportive of the kinds of industrial policy initiatives spearheaded by predecessors such as the Belgian Industry Commissioner Viscount Etienne Davignon and his French chef de cabinet Pierre Defraigne or director-general of DG XIII Michel Carpentier. With Edith Cresson in charge of the research and technology portfolio as of 1995, it will be interesting to see whether the French complain less and dominate more in the industrial policy sphere.

Equally important, the ministries themselves were late in feeling the need for their civil servants to know European policy and law,[15] or to have a continuous presence in Brussels. The French Conseil d'État, or Council of State, even made a point of chastising the French administration on the first issue in 1990, deploring the fact that the ministerial services were poorly prepared to deal with the increasing numbers of directives because of their insufficient knowledge of community law, insufficient resources, and too frequent dissociation between the tasks of negotiation on the one hand and the too-often neglected tasks of follow-up on the other.[16] As for the second issue, Jacques Maisonrouge, the Director-General of Industry under Minister of Industry Alain Madelin, expressed his shock that when he was appointed in 1987 there was not much of a relationship between the Ministry of Industry and Brussels.[17] France, however, was not the only country that was slow to appreciate the importance of Brussels. Even Great Britain, although often seen by others as one of the most effective countries in its lobbying efforts, was caught short in the financial services sector, when British business interests and Treasury officials, preoccupied with the Big Bang in London, were slow to

[13]Jean de la Guérivière, *Voyage à l'intérieure de l'Eurocratie* (Paris: Le Monde Editions, 1992).

[14]*L'Expansion*, September 3–6, 1992, p. 50.

[15]Lequesne, *Paris-Bruxelles*, pp. 55–57; Dominique Le Vert, "Ouverture et adaptation," *Administration* vol. 149 (October 15, 1990), pp. 62–63; and "La formation des fonctionnaires en droit communautaire," *Revue Française d'Administration Publique* vol. 48 (October–December 1988).

[16]De la Guérivière, *Voyage à l'intérieure.* [17]Maisonrouge, interview with author.

realize the implications of the single market and the need for close ties with DG XV.[18] What is more, Maisonrouge's shock is itself not surprising, given his previous experience as former head of IBM World Trade, in which role he had had extensive involvement with the Commission in the early eighties because of the EC's antitrust suit against the firm.[19]

In fact, the heads of most French multinationals probably had a much greater appreciation of the importance of Brussels than the ministries at the time, given not only their obvious interest in EC regulation where it affected their products and operations but also their early support for accelerating European integration. French members of the European Roundtable such as Roger Fauroux, CEO of Saint-Gobain at the time and future Minister of Industry (1988–1991), Olivier Lecerf of Lafarge Coppée, and Antoine Riboud of BSN, were highly influential not only at the EC level, through their close and continuous contacts with top EC officials such as Viscount Etienne Davignon and Jacques Delors, but also at the national level, through their easy access to the French president and their influence over the top French business group, the CNPF, which they were instrumental in moving toward a more European agenda.[20]

But although the largest, most internationalized French firms were early on very much aware of the importance of Brussels, the majority of French businesses were not. This is due to a variety of factors, but in particular to the comparatively low level of internationalization of French firms until relatively recently. Moreover, awareness is one thing, effective action another. Although French business had organized itself to lobby in Brussels as charter members of European business associations such as UNICE and of the various European groupings of national umbrella organizations; as members of national associations such as the CNPF, the main general business association; and as individual firms, government studies found French business in all sectors other than agriculture less active, more tardy, and less efficient than those of other countries.[21]

---

[18]Robert Hull, "Lobbying Brussels: A View from Within," in *Lobbying in the European Community*, ed. Mazey and Richardson, p. 89.

[19]The antitrust suit against IBM lasted from 1980 to 1984, when the case was suspended in exchange for an agreement from IBM to make available more information on its computers so that rival companies could design equipment for IBM's System/370. IBM was also accepted as a participant in ESPRIT at that time. See: Daniel van den Bulcke, "Multinational Companies and the European Community," in *The European Community in the 1990s*, ed. Brian Nelson, David Roberts, and Walter Veit (New York: Berg, 1992), p. 113.

[20]Maria Green, "The Politics of Big Business." Paper prepared for presentation at the European Community Studies Third Biennial Conference (May 27, 1993, Washington, DC); Henri Weber, *Le parti des patrons: Le CNPF, 1946–1990* (Paris: Seuil, 1986).

[21]Jacqueline Nonon and Michel Clamen, *L'Europe et ses couloirs: Lobbying et lobbyistes* (Paris: Dunod, 1991).

French business has been less present in Brussels than many other countries: At one point, it had been said that Toyota's delegation in Brussels was comparable in number to all of French industry's representatives combined.[22] Much of this had changed for the better by the early 1990s, however. In just the two years between 1988 and 1990, the number of people employed in the Brussels office of the CNPF quadrupled from seven to thirty-one.[23] In 1990, the French had fifty permanent presences: fourteen from local governments, twenty-five for individual businesses or sectoral groups, and fifteen for general associations such as the CNPF and the French Chamber of Commerce.[24] By 1993, the Planning Commission could report that French groups had finally been establishing permanent presences not only individually or as members of sectoral associations, but also as specialized lobbies such as the French Association for the Environment (made up of fourteen big French businesses including Rhône-Poulenc, EDF, Usinor-Sacilor, and Lyonnaise des Eaux) and the French Association of Private Enterprises charged with defending private corporations' interest in fiscal and juridical matters. Nonetheless, the Planning Commission concluded that French initiatives were still fewer than those of their European competitors, let alone the Japanese. Moreover, there was still little representation for small and medium-sized enterprises and comparatively few French represented among lobbyists operating in Brussels: Of the 4,000 lobbyists the Planning Commission estimated to be in Brussels, fewer than 100 were French.[25] The fact that a majority of Brussels-based professional lobbyists, consultants, and legal experts represent British (and U.S.) firms adds to the impression of non-U.K. groups that the Anglo-Saxons have the advantage in lobbying efforts.[26]

What is more, unlike the British, French industry had limited access to the French mission in Brussels (although it of course had indirect access through the French national ministry under whose jurisdiction it fell) because of a lack of manpower and little sense of the need. It was only in the early 1990s that the DREE (Direction des Relations Economiques Extérieures) put a branch in place under the authority of the French permanent representative to the EC.[27] Although Edith Cresson as Minister of European Affairs beginning in May 1988 did provide for greater access through advisory boards made up of civil servants, local elected

[22]Ibid., pp. 215–216.   [23]*Fortune*, June 1990, p. 78.

[24]Nonon and Clamen, *L'Europe et ses couloirs*, p. 230.

[25]Commission Général du Plan, *La France et l'Europe d'ici 2010*, ed. Jean-Baptiste de Foucauld (Paris: Documentation Française, 1993), p. 92.

[26]Sonia Mazey and Jeremy Richardson, "Introduction," in *Lobbying in the European Community*, eds. Mazey and Richardson, p. 9.

[27]Nonon and Clamen, *L'Europe et ses couloirs*, p. 223.

officials, and representatives of business and social groups (the GEM, or Groupes d'Études et de Mobilisation), their influence was short-lived (under Cresson's successor, Elisabeth Guigou, they were for the most part ignored) and their contribution to policy minimal, with the exception of the social GEM (headed by Martine Aubry, future Minister of Labor), which contributed to the European Social Charter, and the environmental GEM, which recommended the creation of a European Environmental Agency.[28]

By the early nineties, of course, French awareness of the importance of Brussels had increased dramatically. At this time, the Minister of Industry was spending between one-fourth and one-third of his time on Europe (including the four two-to-three-day meetings per year with member-country ministers of industries), having seen that one-third of all decisions were already being made in Brussels.[29] Moreover, ministerial officials were increasingly becoming part of European policy networks at the same time that the ministries had been reorganizing themselves internally in order better to respond to the growing importance of Europe.[30] In addition, French government officials who typically frowned on lobbying when it involved the national government even encouraged it when it involved the EU.[31] One need only make note of the countless exhortations in the late eighties and early nineties by French officials to French business to, as Edith Cresson put it when Minister of European Affairs, "Agir pour ne pas subir," or act so as not to be acted upon,[32] or the CNPF conference put on with the support of the Ministry of Industry in late 1988 to familiarize French businesses with the potential impact of the single market. This was nothing, however, by comparison with the British government, which inundated businesses with pamphlets, films, and the like in 1993 at the same time that the French government put out only a series of four elementary informational brochures.[33]

Finally, although French awareness of the need for French participation in standard setting had increased over time, actual participation remained comparatively low. Despite the fact that Maisonrouge had as early as 1987 criticized the French standard-setting association, the Association des Normes, as having only a negative influence, rejecting proposed standards rather than working to develop them,[34] and despite the fact that Cresson beginning in 1988 had expressed the need for greater participation of French experts in standard-setting committees, France remained

---

[28]Lequesne, *Paris–Bruxelles*, pp. 72–76.   [29]Bidegain, interview with author.
[30]Lequesne, *Paris–Bruxelles*, pp. 38–53.
[31]Jean François-Poncet and Bernard Barbier, *1992: Les conséquences pour l'économie française du marché intérieur européen* (Paris: Economica, 1989).
[32]*Bruxelles mode d'emploi* – cited in Lefébure, *Lobby*, p. 113.
[33]Lefébure, *Lobby*, p. 117.   [34]Maisonrouge, interview with author.

far behind countries such as Germany and Great Britain in the number of secretariats of technical committees it controlled. In the mid 1990s, Germany tended to dominate, with 39% of secretariats, followed by Great Britain at 20%, France at 14%, and Italy at 8%.[35]

French influence in the policymaking process

France's lesser influence in the EU bureaucracy, at least in the more everyday matters, together with the late recognition by French business and civil service of the importance of the EU, was only compounded by the fact that neither government nor business officials were culturally attuned to the European policymaking process. French civil servants do not always do a very good job of representing French national interests within the EU administration (although they may very well at the level of the Council or the Commission) because of the culture clash between EC and French administrative practices. As Pascal Lamy, director of the cabinet of Jacques Delors, has remarked, French civil servants have been finding the culture of consensus of the EU bureaucracy difficult to deal with, since they are used to much more conflictual relations in interministerial committees, with the Prime Minister or President called upon to mediate the conflict and to make the decision.[36] Business, too, assumes that the solution is to go to the top; as one CEO observed, "The French think that a phone call to Jacques Delors can solve everything. They're wrong."[37]

The cultural problems for the French, while significant in the drafting of regulations or directives, where civil servants negotiate and France is officially represented in the *tour de table,* are even more so in the case of decisions, which are more internal to EC administration.[38] In France, as we have already seen, lobbying is regarded as illegitimate, ultimate decision-making in the ministries is political, and the most important level of decision-making is at the top, so that any decision on a *dossier,* however technically competent, may be reversed higher up, by the Minister or even, in the case of particularly sensitive cases, by the Prime Minister or President.

By contrast, in the EU general directorates, lobbying is regarded as a

---

[35]Michelle Egan, "The Politics of European Regulation: Bringing the Firm Back In." Paper prepared for the Conference of Europeanists, Council for European Studies (Chicago, March 31–April 2, 1994).

[36]Remarks by Pascal Lamy in an interview by Denis Olivennes, "Choses vues . . . d'Europe," *Esprit* (October 10, 1991), p. 70.

[37]*L'Expansion,* September 3–10, 1992, p. 56.

[38]On the differences between regulations, directives, and decisions, see: B. Guy Peters, "Bureaucratic Politics and the Institutions of the European Community," in *Euro-Politics,* ed. Alberta M. Sbragia (Washington, DC: Brookings, 1992), pp. 102–103.

legitimate activity in policy formulation and even encouraged by the European Commission; decision-making is by comparison only minimally political for the vast majority of decisions, although on the larger issues politics of course play a role; and the most important level is at the bottom, where the first-level senior civil servant charged with a given dossier has the most weight.[39] Needless to say, personal and in particular *"corporatiste"* contacts are rare at this bottommost level, even if they may occur at higher levels on the more strategic or political cases. The actual process of lobbying in the EU, moreover, unlike in France, involves providing detailed technical information to the civil servant in charge of the *dossier,* not simply an excellent lunch for the Commissioner.[40] Because universal suffrage is not here to legitimate their actions, these first-level civil servants make every effort to hear all sides and to base their decisions on purely technical and economic arguments. They are therefore more open to persuasion by technical rather than political arguments. What is more, once they make a recommendation, it is quite difficult to reverse. At the level of the Commission, changes on the basis of anything other than technical arguments are hard to bring about (although political decisions are, of course, made, and then couched in technical arguments); but changes that come through the Parliament, which increased its powers as a result of the Single European Act, tend to be minor, technical changes. One estimate (albeit hotly contested) suggests that on average, the final proposal adopted by the Council contains 80% of the proposal generated by the civil servant responsible for the initial preparation process (involving first draft, consultations with the Commission, consultations with interested parties, subsequent drafts, and navigation through the Commission).[41]

In short, exerting influence in the policymaking process of the EC cannot be more different from what it is in France, and French government and business officials have understandably, as a result, often had difficulty adapting themselves to this very different administrative culture. The French themselves make repeated reference to this problem, with remarks in how-to books on lobbying the EU such as: "The Dutch and British are virtuosos, the Irish excellent, the Germans (as always) efficient, and the French (as often) lightweight and late, in particular because they tend to wait until the last minute to act, and because they are too abstract, especially by contrast with the British who tend to bring with them ready-

---

[39]For the complexities of the decision-making structure, see: Martin Donnelly, "The Structure of the European Commission and the Policy Formation Process," in *Lobbying in the European Community,* eds. Sonia Mazey and Jeremy Richardson (Oxford: Oxford University Press, 1993).

[40]On lobbying in France, see: Frèches, *Voyage au centre du pouvoir,* p. 132.

[41]Hull, "Lobbying Brussels."

to-use amendments."[42] The fact that lobbying is comparatively under-developed in France and business interest groups not always very cohesive makes French business less effective at the EU level than the business groups of those countries with better-developed lobbies and more cohesive peak associations such as Germany. Because they are used to very close, symbiotic relationships that allow them great leeway at the implementation stage but little impact at the formulation stage, French businesses find it hard to adjust to the greater openness, or porousness, of the EU formulation process. Moreover, in regulatory decisions, because they expect to interact with a bureaucracy that tends to operate without much technical input from business at the formulation end but is accommodating at the implementation end, it has had difficulty organizing itself to get information quickly enough to the civil servants in charge of the *dossier* that affects them. Finally, because they are used to an interaction where they were generally the privileged interlocutors, they find it hard to adapt to a situation in which they have to deal with a whole range of interests from a variety of countries – and where French bureaucrats have themselves in some sense become lobbyists. The result is that despite the fact that French business was in the vanguard with respect to pushing for European integration as well as in promoting European industrial initiatives, it has been less successful at getting its way on the day-to-day matters of standard setting.

The cultural misunderstandings were amply demonstrated in the de Havilland case, where most French incorrectly assumed that the process was political, not technical. In fact, business and national civil servants were simply not up to the lobbying task, having failed to provide early the kind of technical information that might have swayed the Commission.[43] That the people from Aérospatiale felt that the Eurocrats had already made their decision before hearing them out was probably not wrong; just as the Nestlé people felt "in front of a wall" when they were trying to buy Perrier (in which they succeeded, in their view, only because the Danes had just said no to Maastricht and Commissioner Brittan was worried about the upcoming French referendum). But it may have been because they had not gotten there early enough to have their arguments heard.[44] Some French firms such as Elf had certainly recognized that "the only way to do things is to anticipate difficulties by maintaining permanent contact with the Commission."[45] France, however, is not the only country where ministry and industry did not fully understand the importance of early and constant discussion with the Commission. In the sale of

[42]André Fourcans, *L'entreprise et l'Europe* (Paris: Interedition, 1993), pp. 21, 32.
[43]See the discussion in Dumez and Jeunemaître, "La France, l'Europe."
[44]*L'Expansion*, September 3–10, 1992, p. 50.   [45]Ibid., p. 56.

Rover to British Aerospace, for example, BAe did not have any discussions with the European Commission on the instructions of the DTI (the Department of Trade and Industry), which took upon itself the negotiations. Although the deal was ultimately approved, unlike the de Havilland case, this was not before much back-and-forth, including a call to the President of the Commission by Prime Minister Thatcher, the substantial revision of the deal, and eleventh-hour financial "sweeteners" by the government, which were then also challenged by the Commission.[46]

Such a miscalculation, however, is more of an exception for the British, who have generally been quick and successful in organizing EC-level lobbying, given producer interests' century-long history of involvement in national policymaking processes.[47] By contrast, Japanese business community members in Brussels are less effective in presenting their positions than other outsiders such as the Americans, for cultural reasons similar to those of the French with regard to other insiders. The Japanese themselves explain their problem in much the same way as the French, referring to their cultural disadvantage, given business reliance on government and informal relationships to influence decision-making in Japan rather than on active political participation.[48] Even the Germans, however, have difficulty in organizing and being effective at the European level in the more heavily regulated sectors such as energy, which are populated by small and medium-sized enterprises and characterized by dense political networks.[49]

Such cultural generalizations based on institutional arrangements, however, cannot explain the whole story. There are also great differences according to sector of business that depend upon degree and length of time of internationalization as well as level of effectiveness of individual firms or business associations. Many French multinationals, especially those that have long been in the international arena, have been extremely successful at playing the lobbying game individually or as part of business associations. This has been particularly true of certain individual firms, such as the pharmaceuticals giant Rhône-Poulenc, which has managed to have influence not only on its own but also as part of the pharmaceuticals industry association, which has been well organized and effective for a

---

[46]Andrew McLaughlin and Grant Jordan, "The Rationality of Lobbying in Europe: Why Are Euro-Groups So Numerous and So Weak? Some Evidence from the Car Industry," in *Lobbying in the EC,* eds. Mazey and Richardson, pp. 141–142.

[47]Mazey and Richardson, "Introduction," in *Lobbying in the EC,* eds. Mazey and Richardson, p. 9.

[48]Andrew McLaughlin, "Outsiders Inside? Japanese Lobbying in the European Union." Paper prepared for presentation for the Conference of Europeanists (Chicago, March 31–April 2, 1994).

[49]Beata Kohler-Koch, "Changing Patterns of Interest Intermediation in the European Union," *Government and Opposition* vol. 29, no. 2 (spring 1994), p. 178.

very long time, having succeeded in becoming the equivalent of a private interest government.[50] By contrast, the automobile industry's Euro-group has been notoriously weak and French car firm Peugeot a veritable disaster when it came to lobbying. The most notable instance of Peugeot's problems was when it lobbied individually against new higher standards introduced in 1989 for 1992, which forced the company to adopt a catalytic converter instead of pursuing its large research investment in a lower-polluting engine. The French generally blamed the German ecologists and German automakers for having bested the French automotive company and Peugeot CEO Jacques Calvet, who had not lobbied, giving the advantage to the Germans, who had been behind in pollution control.[51]

In other cases, where an industry has been in the forefront of Europe, it has generally managed to dominate EU policymaking. In the energy sector, for example, the Community took much of the French view on the free circulation of energy service and conservation. French firms have also had successes in sectors such as cosmetics, construction, and machine tools (in particular with the adoption of the machine tool directive of the early 1990s). But they were less effective in distribution, the environment, and the chemical industry.[52] One of the greatest successes, however, which also flies in the face of the cultural stereotype, was by the French construction materials industry producers of *granulats* who as early as 1987 proposed the creation of a European industrywide association (the Union Européenne des Producteurs du Granulat, or UEPG) that pushed for standardization and a system of certification to ensure the quality of materials, and that led to the creation of a technical committee with a French-controlled secretariat.[53] This is more the exception than the rule, however, because French business effectiveness in lobbying is generally compromised by the differences in administrative culture.

The French not only have difficulty playing the regulatory game in Brussels because of differences in administrative culture; they often have difficulty accepting the results of the regulatory process. This is mainly because they are used to an entirely different model of policymaking, in particular with regard to the role of the courts, which have traditionally had much less power next to France's administrative state (although this has been changing in recent years), and the role of the Commission, where regular civil servants generally have more independence of action than in

---

[50]Justin Greenwood and Kersten Ronit, "Interest Groups in the European Community: Newly Emerging Dynamics and Forms," *West European Politics* vol. 17, no. 1 (January 1994), pp. 37–38.
[51]Thibaud Dornier, *En finir avec les bureaucrates européennes* (Paris: Première Ligne, 1994), pp. 45–48; McLaughlin and Jordan, "The Rationality of Lobbying."
[52]Nonon and Clamen, *L'Europe et ses couloirs*, pp. 215–216.   [53]Ibid., p. 227.

France, especially given the rising importance of ministerial cabinets in recent years.

For the French, therefore, the decisions of EU regulatory bodies or the courts are much harder to take than EU directives or regulations. Because both regulations and directives come out of a lengthy process of negotiation at the European level, with directives in particular leaving governments great leeway in determining how to implement them, French governments feel that they have a significant amount of control over them.[54] In the environmental protection area, for example, the directives are the compromises resulting from hard bargaining by member countries, with all giving up something and getting something in return.[55] More generally, there has been little outcry at the loss of the government's traditional economic policy instruments because this was voluntary, a result of the French decision in 1983 to stick with the EMS they had joined in 1979, to pursue the goal of a common market more rapidly with the Single European Act, and to attempt monetary union with the Maastricht Treaty. In fact, in contrast with the early eighties, when top civil servants were "reticent to accept control coming from an outside body such as the European Community,"[56] by the mid eighties on, after the publication of the white paper on the single market in 1985, most saw the European Community as a way to ensure the modernization of France. Community rules became the means to "rationalize" outdated internal legislation and even to push through reforms of civil and commercial law that would have been impossible otherwise.[57]

By contrast, where the policies do not result from a process of negotiation or legislation, as in the binding decisions of regulatory bodies or the European Court,[58] the French tend to be much readier to question their legitimacy. It is telling that whereas the French state was ahead of many member states in translating European directives into national law, it was far behind in heeding warning letters from the Commission or orders of the Court of Justice.[59] This is because French

[54]On the leeway of national governments in the implementation of EC directives, see: Heinrich Seidentopf and Jacques Ziller, eds., *Making European Policies Work: The Implementation of Community Legislation in the Member States* (London: Sage, 1988).

[55]See David Vogel, "Environmental Protection and the Creation of a Single European Market." Paper prepared for delivery at the 1992 Annual Meeting of the American Political Science Association (Chicago, September 3–6, 1992).

[56]See Vlad Constantinesco, "Synthèse nationale sur la France," in *L'application du droit communautaire par les états membres,* ed. Giuseppe Ciavarini Azzi (Paris: IEAP, 1985), p. 56.

[57]Lequesne, *Paris–Bruxelles,* p. 54.

[58]See Alexandre Carnelutti, "L'Administration française face à la règle communautaire," *Revue Française d'Administration Publique* vol. 48 (October–December 1988).

[59]Report to the Ministry of the Civil Service and European Affairs by Jocelyne de Clausade – discussed in Le Vert, "Ouverture," p. 62.

officials are generally uncomfortable with what they see as the European Court of Justice's judiciary activism,[60] or what they assume to be the lack of responsiveness of regulatory bodies, as in the de Havilland case. Pierre Rosanvallon summed this up quite well when he complained that Europe was conceived of "essentially as a legal space" and that "the Community is in the process of becoming a kind of closed regulatory area isolated from political forces," and recommended urgently therefore that "the Community rebalance the judicial with the political."[61] This may have been an added reason for the French push for the Single European Act and the Maastricht Treaty, since they constituted limitations on judicial power (even as they consecrated judicial decisions, as in the standard of mutual recognition) in favor of political power.

This preference for the political over the judicial is even apparent in the arguments that the French national courts used to get the Conseil d'État to accept the supremacy of the European Court of Justice. In the Niccolò case of 1990, the Commissaire du Gouvernement cajoled the Conseil d'État with arguments based on transnational reciprocity that suggested that France would have been alone among member states in denying its citizens the ability to rely on a regulation the principle of which had been accepted not only by Germany eighteen years before but even by Italy in 1984.[62]

In any event, whatever the source of the policy, and whether it be regulation, directive, or decision, there is a general acknowledgement that the French government has lost its independence, and that instead of directly preparing the rules it administers, the bureaucracy now implements rules forged in Brussels, where it can act in the creation of such rules only as a "lobbyist" representing one state out of twelve,[63] or now one out of fifteen. For business in particular, the fact that the EC can impose has affected its traditional relationship with the French government.

---

[60]On judicial activism, in particular as it relates to the Cassis de Dijon case and the standard of mutual recognition, see: Karen J. Alter and Sophie Meunier-Aitshahalia, "Judicial Politics or Politics as Usual? The Pathbreaking *Cassis de Dijon* Decision," paper prepared for the European Community Studies Association conference, May 7–29, 1993; and Kalypso Nicolaïdis, "Legal Precedent and Political Innovation in the European Community: Explaining the Emergence of Managed Mutual Recognition," paper prepared for discussion at the Center for European Studies, Harvard University, March 16, 1993.

[61]Pierre Rosanvallon, "Bruxelles, Tu nous étouffes," *Le Nouvel Observateur,* February 6–12, 1992, pp. 26–27.

[62]Joseph H. H. Weiler, "A Quiet Revolution: The European Court of Justice and Its Interlocutors," *Comparative Political Studies* vol. 26, no. 4 (January 1994).

[63]Bocquet and Delleur, *Génération Europe.*

The changes in the relationship of business and government

Business, despite its privileged relationship with French ministries, now recognizes that this relationship neither is nor can be enough. Brussels is becoming as important as Paris, especially since Paris no longer has veto power over decisions taken in Brussels (with the qualified majority rule). As of September 1992, a majority (52%) of French CEOs had become convinced that although the EC was less important than France, it would become more important than France by the year 2000 (by contrast with 24% thinking that the EC was and would stay less important, and 17% thinking the EC was already more important).[64] Moreover, business is expected by Brussels to make its views heard directly, and not only through the intermediary of the French mission. Unlike in the traditional French policy process, where business interests had their main input at the policy implementation stage, in the European process business interests have their main input at the formulation stage.

Thus, lobbying activities that are still regarded as illegitimate at the national level and are therefore still not very highly developed have become quite sophisticated at the supranational level. And however much French business might complain that it is at a disadvantage in the lobbying process, it nevertheless plays a role – whether as part of European business associations, as part of national associations, or as individual firms – not only in influencing policy but also, in some instances, initiating it, since European business often participates with the European Commission in seeking to impose a policy on reluctant governments.

With business as the primary interest being heard at the EU level, though, neither corporatism, which demands a relatively equal balance among industry, labor, and government,[65] nor pluralism adequately describes the relationship. For although the system may be "transnational pluralism" in form,[66] it is not so in content, at least ideally, given the one-sided nature of interest-group politics, where industry dominates and opposing interests representing consumer groups, labor, and so forth are much less present. In fact, while French business was quick to recognize the need to organize at the European level as well as to prepare for the new, competitive European environment, many of the major unions were slow to organize, too busy trying to defend themselves against that very

---

[64]*L'Expansion*, September 3–10, 1992, p. 57.
[65]Wolfgang Streeck and Philippe Schmitter, "From National Corporatism to Transnational Pluralism: Organized Interests in the Single European Market," *Politics and Society* vol. 19, no. 2 (June 1991).
[66]Ibid.

environment, fearing a loss of jobs and privileges.[67] But even had the French unions paid more attention to the EC, they would have had little impact because there is no cohesive, pan-European labor movement to make their case at the European level at the same time that they have been losing ground at the national level.[68] It is only recently that there has been some indication that labor has been organizing more effectively.

Whatever the problems for French businesses of lobbying the European Commission, the very fact of their access to the decision-making process at this level has increased their independence from the national government, since they are now as much partners with national ministries in efforts to influence the EU as they are supplicants of national ministries to influence the EU for them. As actors in the EU lobbying effort, moreover, the government tends to see business more as a defender of the interests of the French nation than as a lobby that might have its own interests at heart, and not those of France in particular or Europe at large. It is as if the old notion attached to public enterprise, in which it was seen to act as a catalyst for social reforms and industrial innovation, leading the nation forward, has been generalized to all big French businesses, despite the fact that increasing numbers are private or on the road toward privatization, and that their goals whether public or private, is profitability above all.

This sense that however independent business is, it still serves the national interest, not only pervades interaction related to European policy formulation, but also continues to characterize the entire French business–government relationship. The only problem, however, is that it has becoming increasingly one-sided, as government gives and business takes. As Elie Cohen explains it, the "attributes of sovereignty" that French business gained in the past from its relationship with government remain, leaving unchallenged the idea that French business operates in the national interest through the creation of French jobs and plants and through the trade balance, and that in exchange the state owes it attention, assistance, and protection. That this is not challenged, according to Elie Cohen, has to do with the fact that the state has not yet figured out how to operate in its new, more modest role, and reflects the continued crisis of national sovereignty.[69]

That crisis, in fact, has ensured that as the French state has lost its authority for this and other reasons (including scandals related to corrupt election financing and the distribution of HIV-infected blood), business

---

[67]Michael Jehan Rose, "Les syndicats français, le jacobinisme économique et 1992," *Sociologie du Travail* vol. 31, no. 1 (1989).

[68]George Ross, "French Labor and the 1992 Process," *French Politics and Society* vol. 8, no. 3 (summer 1990).

[69]Elie Cohen, "Dirigisme, politique industrielle et rhétorique industrialiste," *Revue Française de Science Politique* vol. 42, no. 2 (April 1992), pp. 217–218.

has gained in stature (although this has been undermined of late by the scandals involving top businessmen).[70] This has only been enhanced by the fact that at the head of the major business firms, as often as not, are individuals whose education and career paths have been state-centered.[71] This means that in many cases the very civil servants who helped shape the policies formulated by French governments are now the CEOs helping shape the policies formulated by French governments in conjunction with their European partners (e.g., the current head of Renault was in Delors's cabinet; the number two at the BNP was formerly Director of the Treasury; the current head of Aérospatiale was director-general of industry, etc.).

THE IMPACT OF EUROPEAN INTEGRATION ON POLICY IMPLEMENTATION

Business's new stature, together with the changes in its size and organization,[72] has meant that it has gained increasing independence from government. In fact, although the politics of accommodation, co-optation, and confrontation remain to some extent, their rate of incidence has changed. Businesses with greater access to policy formulation at the EU level are much less likely to need the politics of accommodation in the implementation process. Where they do need it, however, they are unlikely to get it, given the new regulatory model increasingly prevalent at the implementation stage as a result not only of the EU but also of the independent regulatory agencies created in conjunction with deregulation and privatization.

With the new regulatory nature of policy implementation, the incidence of confrontation has also increased, although less so for business than for other societal groups with less access to the policy formulation process at the EU level. Because societal interests had come to expect that even if they had little input into policy formulation, they would at least be heard during the implementation process, tensions in what has always been a more conflictual model than the cooperative one of other EU countries are likely only to get worse. In the past, where societal interests did not approve of a policy, they were generally more successful at blocking its application than in working with the administration to make it acceptable to all concerned.[73] Now and until societal interests generally

---

[70]See the discussion on the changes in attitudes toward business in the eighties in Chapter 4.

[71]See Chapter 10.   [72]See Chapters 13, 14, and 15.

[73]For a comparative study, see: Heinrich Seidentopf and Christoph Hauschild, "L'application des directives communautaires par les administrations nationales (étude comparative)," *Revue Française d'Administration Publique* vol. 48 (October–December 1988), p. 553.

organize themselves to influence policy formulation at the EU level, they are likely to be confronted with decisions which they cannot block. In certain sectors, especially where the EU has imposed a policy decision not to the liking of societal interests, confrontation is more likely to occur because the government has no option other than to implement the decision. The administrative model where making exceptions was the rule by which French civil servants managed to control interests and to promote accommodation has had to make way for the regulatory model, where exceptions are illegitimate. This has been most apparent in the agricultural sector in the context of the GATT talks. Vegetables on the highways and pigs in the street, however, have not been as effective as they have in the past at gaining much more than verbal concessions from the French government, because the government is no longer as free to bend, or not, to the pressures of confrontation.

Not that the government hasn't tried to continue in its old ways. In fact, the ministries have sometimes been remiss in implementing EU directives in the manner that the EU regulatory model demands. As one set of commentators put it already in 1988, the French administration, following Tocqueville's maxim, "has not dedicated itself to the consistent implementation of policies."[74] The French government has been chastised by the European court for making countless exceptions to rules that, in the view of the EU, allow none.

The regulatory model, moreover, has complicated life generally for the bureaucracy, since it results in two different systems of law: the old administrative one and the new regulatory one. The French constitutional scholar Guy Braibant has remarked on the inequities that result, given the two different processes, with different avenues for recourse[75] – a bit like the differences in the United States between cases taken up by the Federal Trade Commission, which go through an administrative law process before any appeal can be made to the courts, and those taken up by the Justice Department, which go directly to the judiciary.

The EU has not been the only spur for change in the traditional administrative model of policy implementation. Deregulation and privatization both, to the extent that they set up independent regulatory agencies, have also been responsible for altering the relationships of the past, where ministries and industries were often free to work things out amongst themselves, and where, in the words of one Ministry of Industry official charged with overseeing the energy sector, "on s'arrange."[76] Deregula-

[74]Ibid., pp. 536–537.
[75]Guy Braibant, Speech at the Conference: "La décentralisation en France et L'Europe," sponsored by the Institut de la Décentralisation and *Le Monde* in Strasbourg, November 17–18, 1992.
[76]Interview, November 1985.

tion, in fact, has not meant an end to government regulation, only a different kind of regulation,[77] while privatization has often simply substituted increased government regulation for government ownership. And together, they have complicated the traditional circuits of power and influence, leaving many of the traditional actors frustrated.

Parliament, for one, has been frustrated by its inability to move regulatory bodies in the way it had been able to move governments, when a particular issue concerned it. For example, in the face of public and business pressure over Francis Bouygues's decision to permit home shopping and the absence of any action taken by the regulatory body, the CNCL, certain members of the majority proposed a law outlawing this, while the Prime Minister solved the problem by proposing a law directing the CNCL to deal with the matter.[78]

French businesses, similarly, have been having a hard time getting used to dealing with the new regulatory bodies. The more arm's-length relationship demanded by these bodies often leaves businesspeople even more upset than they had been in the past by the traditional, near-symbiotic relationship with the ministries, since at least there they were likely to be able to arrive at some kind of accommodation, if they could not get their way altogether. For example, the CEO of the privatized television station, TF1, found that the regulatory body set up to monitor television and radio simply substituted increased government regulation for government ownership, and complained that "the regulations have become more and more constraining to the point that they appear promulgated to make it impossible for us to function."[79] Where the regulations involve standards that originate at the EU level, however, the upset is likely to be lesser because businesses have been able to participate in the standard-setting process.

Deregulation itself, moreover, has not necessarily led to "less state," only a different kind. The laws on competition are likely to lead to a larger bureaucracy than the one which was used to control prices; and the Council on Competition gained larger powers than the Commission on Competition which it replaced.[80] The burdens to industry, moreover, have not always been reduced. The legislation easing the administrative authorization for layoffs is a case in point, since it may have substituted a

[77]For the many different aspects of deregulation, see: Bernard Chenot, ed., *Les déréglementations* (Paris: Economica, 1988).

[78]Frèches, *Voyage à l'intérieur*, pp. 133–135.

[79]Testimony of Patrick Le Lay, *Rapport sur les opérations de privatisation*, vol. 2, p. 681. He in particular complained that the lawyers of the CSA (Conseil Supérieur de l'Audiovisuelle), much like those of the previous council, the CNCL, which it replaced in 1988, were especially difficult on the subject of original French content of TV shows.

[80]For a discussion of the particulars of the law, see: *Le Monde*, November 5, 1986.

more cumbersome process which may also have encouraged more confrontations between workers and managers.

The new regulatory model, in short, has upset the traditional model of policy implementation, and in many cases further weakened the traditional business–government relationship. This, together with the primacy of the EU in policy formulation and the new access of business at this level, has ensured that business is more independent from government than it has ever been.

CONCLUSION

European integration, in sum, has served to unbalance the traditional statist pattern of policymaking at both formulation and implementation stages. While most societal groups have lost access and influence, French business has gained it. It has become increasingly independent of the nation-state, with its formerly close relationships with the French bureaucracy loosening as it develops closer ties to the EU bureaucracy and its European business counterparts. This independence is only enhanced by the authority with which it was endowed by the past role of public sector enterprise, which allows it, despite liberalization and the loosening of the ties that bind business and government, to retain its aura of operating in the national interest.

This is not to suggest, however, that French ministries have lost all their power. Much the contrary, since they remain the locus of decision-making in France, with the Ministry of Finance predominant and the Ministry of Industry a distant second. But they have lost their independent authority, as the European Commission and Court may review, and reject, their actions. Relations between ministries and industries have changed accordingly.

9

Between ministry and industry

The term "*dirigisme,*" or state intervention in the economy, has always indicated a set of both interventionist policies and directive policymaking processes. In the postwar period, the policies were epitomized by the indicative plans and industrial policies, the processes by the ways in which planners and industrial policymakers used their tremendous resources to gain acquiescence from business. During the Mitterrand years, the nationalization and restructuring of major industries represent the culmination of this *dirigiste* policy tradition, with deregulation and privatization ensuring the move away from a state-directed to a more market-oriented economy. And yet, even as *dirigiste* policies were superseded by liberal policies as early as 1983, *dirigiste* policymaking processes continued, as the policies with regard to privatization attest. It was really only as of 1988 that *dirigisme* as a set of policymaking processes also waned, as governments began to follow business more than to lead it, despite occasional rhetorical flourishes or grand initiatives, but where significant changes in state ownership and control nevertheless occurred along with further deregulation.

However, even at the height of *dirigiste* policymaking, state interventionism was not all it was assumed to be. *Dirigisme* as a set of policymaking processes is synonymous with only the first part of the "statist" pattern of policymaking, where governments formulate heroic policies absent business input. Generally left out of the equation is that part of the statist pattern that has always attenuated the *dirigisme*. As we have already seen, however strong the state may appear, it suffers from many weaknesses, with ministries that are subject to fragmentation and policies that are often more everyday than heroic. Most importantly, however, governments' ability to be *dirigiste,* that is, to take unilateral action at the policy formulation stage without prior consultation with those most interested in the policy, is tempered by their need to respond to societal interests at the implementation stage, where policymaking is characterized by the politics of accommodation, co-optation, or confrontation.

Although French governments in the postwar period have on the whole been seen as highly *dirigiste*, or interventionist, in industrial policy and planning, they have in fact been much more accommodating to business than normally supposed, if they have not been downright co-opted. In the 1960s, Andrew Shonfield found that planning in France "has reinforced the systematic influence exerted by large-scale business on economic policy."[1] In the 1970s, Charles Lindblom remarked that French planning is "in some part even an explicit exchange of favors: industry offers performance – expansion, relocation, technological innovation and the like – in exchange for governmental favors like tax rebates, subsidies, or credit advantages."[2] By the 1980s, Jack Hayward argued that industrial policy, which had replaced planning as the preferred governmental tool, was "usually a symbolic, unitary fiction to cover a multitude of piecemeal, improvisatory and portentous claims by governments to be pursuing a comprehensive and consistent medium and long-term industrial strategy," and he concluded, therefore, that "it should not be surprising that it frequently amounts to an industrialists' policy."[3]

Industry, in other words, often got its way. How this happened, however, changed somewhat over time, as planning began to lose importance while industrial policy was on the rise. When national planning was in its heyday, with policies formulated in formal consultation with business, implementation was more bound up with the formulation process, as business agreed in planning sessions to the goals, plans, and policies essentially initiated by civil servants. As industrial policy progressively took over from national planning, however, there was an increasing separation of policy formulation, which often occurred without even any formal consultation with business, and policy implementation, which took form more and more through sectoral planning and policymaking as well as individual state–firm negotiations. The lack of input at the formulation stage was generally offset at the implementation stage by the politics of accommodation, where business and government officials cooperated in the setting of strategies, and of co-optation, where business imposed its strategy on government. Confrontation, by contrast, where government sought to impose over the objections of business, was relatively rare. Moreover, when it occurred, it as often as not led to capitulation on the part of government.

With the changes in the eighties, if anything, this pattern was rein-

[1]Shonfield, *Modern Capitalism*, p. 139.
[2]Charles Lindblom, *Politics and Markets* (New York: Basic, 1977), p. 183.
[3]Hayward, *State and the Market Economy*, p. 230.

forced. Although nationalization and privatization were truly heroic policies, with little consultation in the formulation, their implementation certainly allowed for accommodation and even co-optation. Restructuring, publicly decried as the most *dirigiste* of policies, nevertheless accommodated industry in most instances. Moreover, as everyday policies began to take precedence over the heroic from 1988 on, as the state lost many of its interventionist policy instruments and a growing consensus developed on the model to build, business increasingly gained the initiative. This is not to say, however, that heroic gestures did not occasionally appear, in particular under Cresson, but these were largely emptied of substance, and still more consultative than those of the past.

By the nineties, in short, ministry–industry relations had changed. Governments no longer had the means to persuade, let alone impose, as they had in the past, given the heroic policies of privatization, deregulation, and Europeanization that had diminished state independence in macroeconomic policymaking and state control over industry in microeconomic policymaking. The system of rationing credit and the selective granting of exemptions from exchange and price controls that ministries had used to gain compliance from industry were gone, as was the leverage afforded ministries through such means as the administrative approval of layoffs or public procurement policies. Moreover, planning was no longer significant, and the kinds of sectoral industrial policies such as the *grands projets* that involved tremendous investment in high technology or infrastructure such as the high-speed trains had become things of the past.[4] Governments lacked not only the money, but also the will, given the greater market orientation and the emphasis on nongovernmental, meaning business, initiatives, whether coming from the public or private sectors. Everyday policymaking had become the norm, blurring the lines between formulation and implementation stages, as business increasingly took the lead and government followed.

MINISTRY–INDUSTRY RELATIONS PRIOR TO 1981

National industrial planning began in the late forties and early fifties by accommodating business and ended in the seventies by being co-opted by it in certain areas as national planning became less and less heroic, supplanted by industrial policy and undermined by sectoral plans and individual state–firm agreements. As government and business became increasingly distant from each other at the formulation stage, with governments making heroic pronouncements absent business input, ministries got closer and closer to industry at the implementation stage, with predictable results.

[4]See the excellent summary in Levy, *Tocqueville's Revenge.*

The process of policymaking

National planning

At its height in the fifties with the Monnet plan, Shonfield saw a "conspiracy to plan" involving "an act of voluntary collusion between senior civil servants and the senior managers of big business," bypassing the politicians and the representatives of organized labor, which worked because "both sides found it convenient."[5] Although the relationship was cooperative, it was not corporatist: the state retained the upper hand not only because it controlled the content of the plan – in the early sixties, civil servants and independent members (including professional planners) occupied leading positions on the *commissions,* accounting for nearly 50% of total membership and serving as chair or vice-chair and *rapporteur* who not only guided the work but was also responsible for interpreting it[6] – but also because its power "either to persuade the recalcitrant or to reward the obedient" could exert irresistible pressure on business to do as the plan indicated.[7]

The planners, moreover, did not deal with just any businesses; they chose their interlocutors, that is, those who were to be their legitimate partners. Thus, instead of the business associations representative of small and medium-sized businesses that had originated as cartels to fight recession during the Third Republic, they preferred to deal with larger businesses, the "national champions" that were to receive the lion's share of subsidies and low-interest loans. While the latter were open to cooperation with government planners and relatively easy to deal with, given the small number of large firms and clear authority lines, the former tended to be suspicious of government, taking a more adversarial view toward the planners, and could not, in any case, speak authoritatively for their members. Therefore, while the planners saw large businesses as the vehicle for modernization and innovation, they saw the smaller businesses as backward and opposed to modernization.[8] The result is that the major business associations grouping small and medium-sized businesses were marginalized in favor of one-on-one contacts with the larger firms. This was to last a long time, to the detriment of the smaller firms that were essentially left out of the modernization process – by contrast with countries such as Germany, where the associational relationships were stronger, and Japan, where larger firms took responsibility for the smaller firms in the planning relationship with MITI.

As the government's attention shifted to industrial policies designed to create national champions and to the *grands projets,* in the planning area government led less and the initiative often shifted to industry. Actual

[5]Shonfield, *Modern Capitalism,* p. 128.   [6]Ibid., pp. 158–159.   [7]Ibid., p. 145.
[8]On business associations, see Ehrmann, *Organized Business.*

decision-making became more and more a matter of individual negotiations between government officials and individual firms, and took place outside the official institutions of the planning process, even as the number of participants in the official process grew exponentially.[9] The response of organized labor, which was conspicuously left out of the informal loop, was to withdraw from participation – the CGT and FO as early as the Second Plan, the CFDT by the Sixth Plan.[10] The planning process, as a result, began to resemble a cartel arrangement, which was made all the more effective by the fact that civil servants and top managers shared not only a common educational background but also similar ways of conceiving of the issues, such that heads of banks, nationalized industries, and private enterprises "think and want what those in charge of the policy decisions think and want."[11]

As this continued, moreover, the process of accommodation between government and industry began to look increasingly like co-optation. This culminated in the Sixth Plan (1970–1975), when the CNPF, the national confederation of France's major businesses, which had previously kept its distance, decided to take the initiative in the preparation of the plan, recommending changes in the organization of the process and in the policies, in particular to direct resources to industrial investment rather than social consumption.[12] Because the government followed these recommendations, it left the government with the appearance of having been captured by industry, and with *l'impératif industriel* having become *l'impératif des industriels.*[13]

With more and more of the real decisions being made behind closed doors and less and less oversight being exercised or realistic planning being performed, the planning commissions remained useful primarily as forums in which industrial policymakers gathered information and gained the acquiescence of industrialists. For the key industrial actors, it served as an instrument of adult education[14] or as "an apprenticeship in social change" which provided them with new, more forward-looking attitudes favoring growth, innovation, and international competitive-

[9]Hall, *Governing the Economy,* pp. 157–158; McArthur and Scott, *Industrial Planning,* p. 26; Edgar Friedberg, "Administrations et entreprises," in *Où va l'administration française,* ed. Crozier.

[10]Hall, *Governing the Economy,* p. 158.

[11]Pierre Bourdieu and Luc Boltanski, "La production des idées dominantes," *Actes de la Recherche en Sciences Sociales* (June 1976), p. 54.

[12]See the discussion in Hall, *Governing the Economy,* pp. 169–171. See also, Bonnaud, "Les instruments d'exécution du plan."

[13]Atreize, *La planification française en pratique* (Paris: Editions Ouvrières, 1971) – cited in Hall, *Governing the Economy,* p. 171.

[14]Cohen, *Modern Capitalist Planning.*

ness.[15] By the seventies, moreover, probably as much industrial action was going on outside the planning process as inside. Here, too, the line between accommodation and co-optation increasingly blurred.

With Giscard's unofficial policy of rescuing lame ducks, for example, the refusal to contemplate nationalization of ailing industries led to a situation in which the government spent vast sums of money – and had the private sector lend even more – with little control and few guarantees. Between 1974 and 1981, the CIASI, or Comité Interministériel pour l'Aménagement des Structures Industrielles, granted loans from the FDES (Fonds de Développement Economique et Social) worth 1.5 billion francs, 474 million francs in loans tied to profits, and 815 million francs in subsidies from the *crédits de politique industrielle,* with every franc awarded permitting the company to raise 8 francs more from other sources.[16] The CIASI, composed of the head of the DATAR as chairman, the planning commissioner, the Director of the Treasury, the director of construction and public works (the DDE), the director-general of the Ministry of Labor, the director-general of credit of the Bank of Finance, and a representative of the Prime Minister, dealt primarily on a case-by-case basis with collapsing firms (although in a few cases, e.g., printing, shoes, and mechanical industries, it dealt with an entire sector). It would intervene only in response to reorganization plans by industrialists and bankers which would keep the firm private; and it helped obtain primarily private funds, with only 15 to 20% public funds from the FDES. Thus, it did not own, manage, or exercise any control over the firms it helped.[17] The results speak for themselves. Of the 700 cases awarded funds from a total of 1,100 reviewed, fully one-third resulted in failure within five years.[18]

The CIRI which replaced it under the Socialists actually did no better at first, with the government's policies seemingly dictated more by politics than by competitiveness, and designed more to rescue lame ducks than to promote growing businesses. The 1984 rescue of Chapelle-Darblay, the paper maker, which was in Prime Minister Fabius's electoral district, is a case in point, with the state granting 3 billion francs to a single individual, John Kila, a man of questionable professionalism.

Moreover, the involvement of the CIASI or CIRI generally devolved to the benefit of large industry, principally by favoring the takeover of small failing firms by the large industrial groups. But the benefits also went beyond this. Elie Cohen describes in wonderful detail how a large compa-

[15]Michel Crozier, "Pour une analyse sociologique de la planification française," *Revue Française de Sociologie* vol. 6, no. 2 (June 1965).
[16]Aujac, "Introduction to French Industrial Policy," pp. 23–24.
[17]Berger, "Lame Ducks and National Champions," pp. 172–174.
[18]Aujac, "Introduction to French Industrial Policy," p. 24.

ny such as Michelin, concerned about its relatively large investment in a smaller, failing firm, managed to get the CIRI to take charge of the firm, to get the banks to cover the losses, to arrange the company's merger with another failing company, and finally to engineer its sale at tremendous loss to government and banks to another large industrial group at 30 cents on the dollar.[19]

The proliferation of industrial policy instruments also undermined the coherence of the planning exercise, and this too devolved to the benefit of large industry. For example, in addition to the CIASI, which was to help enterprises in difficulty, there was the Comité Interministériel d'Orientation pour le Développement des Industries Stratégiques (CODIS), created in 1979 to promote strategic industries, primarily large ones; Fonds Spécial d'Adaptation Industrielle (FSAI), created in 1978; and the Comité Interministériel pour le Développement des Investissements et le Soutien de l'Emploi (CODISE), to promote employment and investment. There was also the ANVAR, the agency focused on the encouragement of high technology and applied research, which in 1979 gained increased funding to promote innovation; and the ADI, created in 1977, which was charged to encourage the diffusion of information technology. Although many of these programs ostensibly were directed at small and medium-sized enterprise, the traditional relationship between ministry and industry ensured that most of these programs favored big business to the detriment of the small, and that large industrial groups would receive the bulk of financial aid. The Hannoun report underlines that in 1976, six major industrial groups representing only 25% of employment and of added value received 50% of public aid to industry. The result is that while small and medium-sized enterprises continued to feel the crushing weight of the increasing tax burden, this was offset for big business by government capital grants and loans.[20]

All of these new industrial policy instruments only muddied even further the already murky waters of national industrial planning. In addition, whatever the announced national plans and industrial policies, they were increasingly being superseded by sectoral plans and state–firm agreements.

Sectoral planning and policymaking

However apparent accommodation and co-optation were in planning and industrial policy, writ large, they were even more clear with the state's sectoral plans and policies. The more routine the relationships, and the

[19]Cohen, *L'État brancardier,* pp. 172–175.
[20]Dacier, Levet, and Tourret, *Les dossiers noirs,* pp. 60–65.

closer particular ministries got to particular industries, the easier it was for accommodation to become co-optation, and for confrontation to lead often, but certainly not always, to government capitulation to the demands of industry. It was here, moreover, that the industries' technical expertise enabled them to prevail over ministries.

The slide into a relationship of co-optation was probably most pronounced with sectoral-level planning for declining industries, where the relationship was of necessity a close one given the needs of industry. This was especially the case for the privately owned but increasingly publicly indebted steel industry, where the confrontations of the late forties and early fifties gave way to the co-optation of the mid sixties and on. In the early postwar period, confrontations occurred mainly over the resistance of steel companies to the state-recommended reorganization of the industry into a small number of large companies (from fourteen to four), with a truce finally declared when the state provided a generous financial inducement which included a large reduction in interest rates on the companies' long-term and medium-term loans.[21] By the mid sixties, moreover, because the conservative governments (which had eschewed nationalization for political reasons) could impose their views only through a difficult process of negotiation, they relied increasingly on the industry's trade association, the Chambre Syndicale de la Sidérurgie Française (CSSF), and in particular on its head, Jacques Ferry, to mediate in the negotiations between rival companies and, until the crisis of 1977–1978, even to monitor company compliance with state–industry planning contracts, thereby abandoning even the pretense of traditional state controls on funding.[22] In the planning process itself, although all was allegedly being worked out in the planning commissions, the commission's business was actually prearranged by prior unofficial contact between government and business officials, and meetings among government officials in interministerial meetings on the one side, and business officials in CSSF meetings on the other, thereby cutting out organized labor completely. The relationship thus effectively involved a "corporatist-style collusion," orchestrated by the industrial trade association rather than government, in which "there was an abandonment of autonomous decision making by

[21]Philippe Mioche, "Le financement public de la sidérurgie: Réalité ou illusion d'un contrôle par l'état?" in *Le capitalisme français 19–20e siècle,* ed. Fridenson and Straus, pp. 83–96.

[22]Hayward, *State and the Market,* p. 93. See also: J. E. S. Hayward, "Steel," in *Big Business and the State: Changing Relations in Western Europe,* ed. Raymond Vernon (Cambridge, MA: Harvard University Press, 1974), pp. 255–271; Jean G. Padioleau, *Quand la France s'enferre: La politique sidérurgique de la France depuis 1945* (Paris: Presses Universitaires de France, 1981).

the steel firms and a rejection of arm's length remoteness from detailed policy intervention by the various government agencies and political leadership."[23]

Government leadership was still in evidence, but primarily only in two areas: first, in the overall industrial policy that encouraged the merger of firms into one or two "national champions," which in this case promoted the merger of the steel firms into a duopoly; and second, in its control over prices. The steel industry accepted the latter in particular as the cost of receiving government funds, a necessity given its inability to attract long-term investment from the market – even if this did not stop its constant complaints that the reduction in profits was financially crippling it. The quid pro quo was also evident in other areas: The industry was equally accommodating when the Chirac government before the elections of 1977 pressed for restraint in layoffs, fearful of the political repercussions.[24] In exchange, the industry received generous loans without being forced to take the appropriate steps to stem its own decline.

In the case of the oil industry, too, co-optation became the rule, but here the results were not at all disastrous. The oil industry prospered even though state elites became the "ideological captives of the private sector,"[25] as the oil companies in some sense dictated state policies as a result of their greater expertise.[26] The protectionism involved with the regulation of oil prices benefited the oil companies rather than the consuming public, and did not improve the security of supply.[27] Moreover, despite government pressures to take into account the needs of the consuming public and the imperatives of the national interest, the firms on the whole made their decisions almost solely on the basis of commercial considerations.[28] Finally, the oil companies were time and again able to use technical arguments to deflect government demands, as in the case of Total's successful resistance to searching for oil in French North Africa, despite strong government pressure.[29]

The relationship between ministry and oil industry was not entirely one of co-optation, however. There were also instances of accommodation. Although the state's representative on the corporate board exercised veto power only once in the memory of the top officials interviewed in the late seventies, informal bargaining did take place: for example, when Elf sought to invest in a U.S. petrochemical firm, the Treasury made it known that this would be acceptable only if that company opened a branch in France.[30] Confrontations also occasionally occurred, for example, the

[23]Hayward, *State and the Market,* pp. 87–88.   [24]Ibid., pp. 93–94.
[25]Feigenbaum, *Politics of Public Enterprise,* p. 14.   [26]Ibid., p. 94.   [27]Ibid., p. 53.
[28]Ibid., pp. 71–86.   [29]Ibid., pp. 59–60.   [30]Ibid., p. 95.

repeated clashes from 1978 to 1981 between the CEO of Elf-Aquitaine Albin Chalandon and the Minister of Industry André Giraud. But the government generally capitulated in the end.[31]

The nuclear energy sector was also a great success story (or at least was until recently when some began raising questions about its advisability and safety), with industry essentially left alone to make the technical decisions.[32] The result was that a comprehensive sectoral plan for the development of nuclear reactors was executed more swiftly, thoroughly, and economically than in any other Western industrialized country, meeting the extremely ambitious development targets to become the world leader in per capita nuclear power and second in total capacity.[33]

In other sectors, co-optation was not nearly so pronounced – but industry still got its way. In the cases of such industrial groups as Thomson and CGE, the various planning contracts and concomitant government support through both direct financial aid (e.g., research and development aid, financing of exports, and tax breaks) as well as indirect aid (e.g., government contracts, diplomatic support, and public research) ensured that while the state took the technical and industrial risks, the enterprises carried out the industrial projects and disposed liberally of the resulting profits. In these cases, as with many others, the factors that tipped the scale in industry's favor had to do with the unity and centralized power of the industrial group by comparison with the fragmentation of government ministries, and the continuity of industrial leadership by contrast with the ever-changing ministers and ever-rotating civil servants. In brief, industrial policy outcomes resulted not so much from government directives as from the uncoordinated decisions of the directors of the large industrial groups.[34]

For the automobile industry, too, sectoral policies essentially followed the desires of the companies. As long as companies did not need state funds, they could basically do what they wanted, and CEOs fought hard to maintain this. Thus, as early as 1954, Lefaucheux, head of Renault, declared, "The state created us. It does not nourish us at all and we do not seek to live in its shadow. We consider state control to be the worst evil which could befall Renault."[35] Dreyfus, his successor, followed this up by noting that

The Minister of Industry chose a man in whom he has confidence, a man who, he thought, would effectively manage this national patrimony which has a very

[31]For the special relationships that are involved between ministers and CEOs of nationalized firms, see the discussion in Chapter 10.
[32]Wilsford, "Tactical Advantages," p. 158.   [33]Ibid.
[34]Bauer and Cohen, "La politique, l'administratif," pp. 324–327.
[35]*Le Monde*, March 10, 1954 – cited in Derivry, "Managers of Public Enterprises," p. 217.

important role in the economy. But once having made his choice, the Minister must let this man be free. Lefaucheux understood things in that way, and he always succeeded in preserving his independence. I hope I will be able to do as much. . . . Renault is an enterprise belonging to the nation, but it is a free enterprise. I think that . . . Renault has oriented the policy of the public authorities rather than the opposite.[36]

Co-optation, in other words, was key to the relationship. This was certainly borne out through the history of the ministry–industry relationship, where only very exceptionally did government intervene at all.[37] In the seventies, in fact, when Renault and Peugeot were both cash-rich, they could resist the government interference that was a natural corollary to government financing. For example, Renault purchased much of the American Motors Corporation without direct state assistance. The marriage of Peugeot and Citroën, by contrast, was engineered by the government, concerned to keep Citroën, which had been in search of an international partner, in the family, and was sweetened by a 1 billion franc government loan (drawn on the FDES).[38] Where government takes the lead, in other words, business accommodation is bought by government capital grants and/or low-interest loans.

In the transportation sector, too, firms generally got their way, although this was sometimes harder given the fact that these were generally nationalized industries in monopolistic areas. Air France, for example, managed to use technical arguments successfully in its refusal between 1974 and 1978 to capitulate to government insistence on replacing the aging Caravelles with what Air France deemed the inappropriate but French-built Dassault airplanes, leasing thirteen American-built Boeings instead. (The confrontation did lead to a crisis for the company, though, which was resolved only when a new CEO was appointed in 1976, who then prevailed over the government by buying Boeing 737s.) By contrast, Air France was not able to resist the move to the new Charles de Gaulle airport on grounds that it would prove too costly.[39] After all, ministers

---

[36]Pierre Dreyfus, *La grande entreprise et l'économie moderne* (Paris: Les Echos), quoted by J. L. Bodiguel, *La réduction du temps de travail, enjeu de la lutte sociale* (Editions Ouvrières, 1969) – cited in Derivry, "Managers of Public Enterprises," p. 218.

[37]See: Fridenson, "Atouts et limites de la modernisation," p. 183.

[38]Stephen S. Cohen, James Galbraith, and John Zysman, "Rehabbing the Labyrinth: The Financial System and Industrial Policy in France," in *France in Troubled World,* ed. Cohen and Gourevitch, p. 67.

[39]Jean-Pierre C. Anastassopoulos, "The French Experience: Conflicts with Government," in *State-Owned Enterprises in Western Economies,* ed. Raymond Vernon and Yair Aharoni (London: Croom Helm, 1981), pp. 100–103. See also: Taïeb Hafsi and Howard Thomas, "Managing in Ambiguous and Uncertain Conditions: The Case of State-Controlled Firms in France." in *Strategic Issues in State-Controlled Enterprises,* Taïeb Hafsi (Greenwich, CT: JAI Press, 1989), pp. 121–123.

can and sometimes do impose. And this was very much the case with regard to the government's response to the TGV project of the SNCF, about which it temporized at first, despite the positive recommendation of the government's own commission that had worked from 1969 to 1972, and then continued to delay approval until 1976, under pressure from the SNCF's competitors and concerned about the size of the investment necessary.[40]

The politics of accommodation and co-optation were not the rule for all industries, however, especially in times of economic downturn for firms in less concentrated sectors of industry. The case of the textile industry is one where the kind of relationship characteristic of heavy manufacturing developed late, only when the shakeout resulting from international competition had already created the conditions for closer ministry–industry relations. It was only in the mid to late seventies that a kind of *concertation* developed between the state and the larger textile firms that allowed for some industrial planning. At the same time that this process marginalized labor and the smaller producers, it tended to benefit primarily the larger firms, which were the recipients of the bulk of the loans from the CIASI between 1974 and 1978. The focus, moreover, was on rescuing lame ducks through industrial takeovers. It was only beginning in the latter half of 1978 that attention was shifted to modernization of equipment and rationalization of production.[41] This shift was dramatized when the government pulled the plug on the textile mills of Boussac, by refusing to continue to cover its deficits, thereby forcing it into bankruptcy. But this is not to suggest that the government therefore left everything to the market – much the contrary, since the government managed the process very carefully, forcing the company to transfer its holdings to private companies which agreed to "temper the pace and the location of mill closures according to the state's calculations of financial urgency, humaneness, and political expediency."[42]

In cases where an industrial sector is in a weakened position and fragmented, in short, ministries tend to assert themselves over the industry much more than in cases where the industries in a sector are already strong and concentrated. Moreover, in these cases ministry interference generally leads to delays and added costs. For example, when Rhône-Poulenc sought in 1976 to streamline its operations in the textile sector

[40]Hafsi, *Entreprise publique et politique industrielle*, p. 64.
[41]Lynne Krieger Mytelka, "In Search of a Partner: The State and the Textile Industry in France," in *France in Troubled World*, ed. Cohen and Gourevitch, pp. 140–142.
[42]Cohen, "Informed Bewilderment," pp. 24–25. For the postwar history of the relationship of the textile industry with government, see: Robert Jim Berrier, "The Politics of Industrial Survival: The French Textile Industry." Ph.D. dissertation, Massachusetts Institute of Technology, 1978.

by reducing by half its 4,000 workers, it was government, not labor, that set up the roadblocks, delaying the textile plan until after 1978 and thereby costing the company between 6 and 10 billion francs. Moreover, when Rhône-Poulenc decided to sell its heavy chemical operations to BP, the government refused to allow it, forcing it to delay until it managed to make a deal with Elf in 1980.[43]

The experience with the textile industry was mirrored by that of the machine tool industry, where the results proved no better.[44] It was also the case for computers. The Plan Calcul, which involved the expenditure of vast amounts of money in an effort to create a national champion in computers to match those in other sectors, proved a disaster. Moreover, government intervention tended to be erratic and costly. When the government blocked the sale of Machines Bull to General Electric in 1964 only to capitulate the following year because Bull continued to lose money, the resulting deal was far less advantageous for the company.[45] Only with the national champions that were already well established did industrial success go hand in hand with relative industry independence from government interference.

In fact, even with the downturn in the economy in the seventies government policymakers had difficulty exerting control over the national champions. First of all, they had to continue to subsidize them as generously as they had in the past if they expected them to participate in the *grands projets*. Second, because they were generally the only one in a given sector, they had a virtual monopoly over it, making it impossible for French officials to exert pressure by going to a rival, as often happens in Japan, where there are ordinarily five or six large competitors. And third, by virtue of their size and therefore the numbers of jobs they controlled, government officials had little leverage.[46]

The state's sectoral plans and policies, in short, increasingly followed, rather than led, big business. Cohen and Bauer, in summarizing the relationship between state and industry, differentiate among three kinds of relationship, none of which suggests that government is very strong. In the face of powerful industrial groups such as Thomson, the firm, even if nationalized, imposes its own strategy on the government. However, even where the firm is in a weakened position through bankruptcy, the government does not manage to take a successful leadership role: its attempts to create powerful industries through mergers among weak firms, as in the

[43]Cohen and Bauer, *Grandes manoeuvres industrielles*, pp. 96–97.
[44]Ibid., pp. 117–131.
[45]John Zysman, "The French State in the International Economy," in *Between Power and Plenty*, ed. Peter Katzenstein (Madison: University of Wisconsin Press, 1978), pp. 285–287.
[46]Levy, "Tocqueville's Revenge," pp. 51–52.

machine tools industry, invariably fail. Finally, although the government may have great successes in sectors where no powerful industrial firms existed, such as its initiatives in oil, nuclear, aerospace, and armaments, these successes only lead to a reversion to the first instance, where the newly powerful firm can exert its influence over the government.[47] If an industry is viable, in other words, it controls itself; if it is not, nothing government does will alter that. This was as true after 1981 with the nationalization of the bulk of major industries as it was before.

The only exceptions were public firms in the noncompetitive sector. Unlike private firms or public firms in the competitive sector, that is, the "state's private enterprises" (in the terms of the Nora report), which had the freedom to fix salaries, wages, and prices without state interference, these "public interest enterprises" had to follow the principle of profitability for themselves and the nation, meaning that public authorities could utilize them to fight inflation, for example, by fixing prices below normal, or use them as an instrument for national economic policy.[48] Thus, although they had managerial autonomy and were able to devise their own strategies, they were subject to price or wage controls which in turn affected those strategies. The state's policies regarding prices and wages in the noncompetitive sector, in the view of many top managers at companies such as at EDF, Gaz de France, and the SNCF, represented evidence of the state's heavy weight and its *tatillon,* or nitpicking, control.[49] But for those in the ministries, this kind of control was perfectly justified for firms in monopolistic sectors. In Strauss-Kahn's view, these "states within states" wanted all the advantages, that is, to be without competitors and without state control. But they cannot have it both ways.[50] This view was echoed by a top Treasury official, who insisted that in the monopolistic sector, it was totally natural that the Ministry watched carefully and controlled, even if the weight of the Treasury was indeed heavy, through its fixing of prices, approving of loans, setting employee levels, and so forth. However natural, though, the state's heavy hand often had a negative effect on the company's balance sheets, especially in the early eighties as governments sought to keep inflation down and consumers happy.

MINISTRY–INDUSTRY RELATIONS THROUGH NATIONALIZATION AND RESTRUCTURING

With the extensive nationalization of industry under the Socialists, heroic policymaking returned full force. There was no consultation with the

[47]Cohen and Bauer, *Grandes manoeuvres industrielles,* p. 139.
[48]Derivry, "Managers of Public Enterprises," pp. 216–217.
[49]High-level professional at EDF. Interview with author, March 1991.
[50]Strauss-Kahn, interview with author.

banks or industry on the formulation of nationalization policy. Restructuring of the nationalized industries was the domain of the Ministry of Industry and the product of a very small group within the Ministry, primarily the Minister and his cabinet, with technical advice from regular civil servants, and some outside consultation with the CEOs. Several CEOs at the time of Chevènement's tenure as Minister of Industry actually had to read of the restructuring plans in the newspapers (e.g., the heads of Bull and Thomson).[51]

In the implementation of the restructuring policies, though, the politics of accommodation and co-optation were primarily at play. Although there was some confrontation between 1981 and 1983 under the Ministers of Industry Dreyfus and Chevènement, under Fabius and Cresson industry prevailed in every instance but one. Because Fabius, whether as Minister of Industry or Prime Minister, was more interested in the return to financial health of the nationalized enterprises than in ensuring a French presence in all strategic sectors, the firms were allowed whatever strategies they deemed best. As Louis Schweitzer, CEO of Renault, explains it, because Fabius had told the nationalized enterprises that their first responsibility was to make money, that firms in the competitive sector that didn't make money were bad enterprises, and that all CEOs would lose their jobs if they had losses in 1985, "it enabled the *patrons* to say no, because you told us to make money."[52] Increasingly over time, then, industry got exactly what it wanted. But even when it did not, however *dirigiste* the state might have appeared, it not only always sought some sort of accommodation by negotiating in good faith with the firm, it also generally sweetened the deal by providing financing.

Even at the height of its *dirigisme*, during the restructuring process, the state exercised varying degrees of control over industry, depending upon the kind of industry involved, its relative health and market position, its strategic position for the nation, and the government's policies involving the promotion of modernization, industrialization, and employment.[53] Moreover, while sometimes the state appeared to impose, other times it acted as an arbiter, and on yet other occasions it simply responded to the desires of industry.[54] Finally, however *dirigiste* the state was in terms of overall structural or strategic questions, it was not at all *dirigiste* in terms of the internal operations of nationalized enterprises, leaving them free to restructure on their own, to develop industrial strategies, and so forth. According to sociologists Claude Durand and his co-authors, this diverse

---

[51]Boublil, *Soulèvement*, p. 78.   [52]Schweitzer, interview with author.
[53]Claude Durand, Michelle Durand, and Monique VerVaeke, "Dirigisme et libéralisme: l'état dans l'industrie," *Sociologie du Travail* 27 (March 1985), p. 271.
[54]Ibid., p. 257.

range of motives led to so many different degrees of intervention in the various sectors of industry, from very high to very low, that it becomes pointless even to try to distinguish between Socialist *dirigisme* and neo-liberal *libéralisme*.[55]

The differing degrees of ministerial intervention, moreover, were no predictors in terms of industry response and the overall ministry–industry relationship. As much depended upon the financial health of the company and its importance to governmental policy as it did on the personality of the CEO, the history of ministry–industry relations, and the politics of the moment. It is therefore difficult to ascribe any general pattern to the interactions, or to predict when accommodation and co-optation was more likely to occur than confrontation. If there was any pattern or predictability, it had more to do with the history of business–government relations as well as the health of the firm itself than anything else.[56]

For example, the Socialist government was highly *dirigiste* indeed in the case of a declining industry such as steel, which was both financially weak and in a key governmental policy area, mandating industry restructuring, approving layoffs and plant closings, and so forth, because of concerns involving defense, modernization, and unemployment.[57] The fact that this was delayed until 1984, however, suggests that the industry (helped by political pressures and Mitterrand's own 1979 promise of increases in production) had managed quite effectively to co-opt government until then. And this was despite the fact that the government had the capability to exercise control, mainly because in place of the semicorporatist relationship of the past was government ownership, with state representatives in the majority on the boards of both companies able to enforce their views over the objections of labor if necessary, while the state-appointed head would have to negotiate with government officials. When the government chose to exercise that control, it did so from the highest levels rather than through the Ministry of Industry: Once Mitterrand announced the major restructuring program in spring 1984, it was clear

[55]Ibid., p. 271.

[56]Taïeb Hafsi and Christian Koenig, in describing the life cycle of state-controlled enterprises, find three stages in state-nationalized enterprise relations in any given industry: cooperation (equivalent to accommodation in our terms), confrontation, and then autonomy (equivalent to co-optation), the last stage being reached when the original objectives are achieved, the firm develops its own character, and the political circumstances are right, but which may then return to cooperation when the state begins to seek to intervene again. Taïeb Hafsi and Christian Koenig, "The State-SOE Relationship: Some Patterns," in *Strategic Issues in State-Controlled Enterprises* (Greenwich, CT, and London: JAI, 1989). Hafsi, *Entreprise publique et politique industrielle*, pp. 43–50, 63–68.

[57]On the policies themselves, see Chapter 4.

that the Prime Minister, if not the President himself, would have the ultimate power of decision.[58] By now, there was also a new CEO willing to do the government's bidding, ensuring that accommodation, not confrontation, would characterize the ministry–industry relationship.

While the interventionism in the steel industry was not only forceful, once it occurred, but also successful, in the machine tool industry it was an unmitigated disaster. Here, the goal was to create a national champion from the fragmented and weak set of companies in the industry, of which all but one of the top seven were either subsidiaries of major firms such as Renault, Schneider, CGE, and SNECMA, or controlled by financial concerns such as Suez and IDI.[59] Again, the formulation of policy was heroic for a sector deemed of strategic importance to the nation: in this case, because the Ministry lacked expertise in the area, it turned not to the professional organizations of the industry but to an American consulting firm, the Boston Consulting Group (BCG), for its ambitious plan that was to create one major interlocutor with the Ministry, and to offer financial incentives such as capital grants, loans, and public orders to convince the industries concerned to create "poles" of activity in three subsectors of the industry. But the large companies involved, in particular CGE, Schneider, Suez, and Renault, after brief initial cooperation, withdrew one after the other, unwilling to be involved in what were continuing to be money-losing operations, propped up only by government funds.[60] Here, then, there was no confrontation. And it was big business that decided the extent of accommodation.

Probably the most publicly confrontational of the restructurings was the case of Saint-Gobain, when top management protested the government's decision to force the company to abandon its diversification into computers (on the grounds that it was too risky) and to stay in the stagnant markets of its traditional heavy-industry core activities.[61] Top management had to give up its shares in Bull in 1982; its participation in Eurotechnique, a subsidiary with National Semiconductor (in which it was helped by the government electronic components plan of 1978), which it ceded to Thomson in January 1983; and its shares in Olivetti, sold in November 1983.[62] The state's constant intervention in Saint-Gobain's strategic decisions was very costly, most notably with its divestment of the company's 33% share in Olivetti, which made it lose a

---

[58]Hayward, *State and the Market*, p. 103.   [59]See Chapter 4.
[60]Cohen and Bauer, *Grandes manoeuvres industrielles*, pp. 111–117.
[61]Durand, Durand, and VerVaeke, "Dirigisme et libéralisme," p. 257.
[62]Saint-Gobain was also forced to reduce its holdings acquired in 1983 in the Compagnie Générale des Eaux (from 35% to 20%) because the Ministry thought it was too big an operation, that it would cause political problems, and was incompatible with the company's status as a nationalized industry.

potential 0.5 billion francs in profits in 1984. Thus, CEO Fauroux complained, "We tried to take advantage of the right moments, financially and industrially, to go beyond our traditional industrial *métier,* or core activity, and each time we were brutally forced to retreat. . . . We incontestably lost . . . a part of our freedom. . . . The moment we left our hole, we were shot down."[63] And yet Fauroux himself later suggested that intervention under public ownership was no greater than under private.[64] Moreover, despite his public objections, there are those who argued that CEO Fauroux could not have been nearly as upset as he proclaimed and the action not nearly as disastrous for the company as he insisted, since he did not do all he could to stop it – for example, by going to the Minister of Industry, Pierre Dreyfus, who would likely have accommodated him.[65] In other instances, in fact, the company showed itself quite capable of resisting government pressure, as in its refusal to help Chapelle-Darblay, a company situated in Fabius's electoral district.

But even if the state interfered with Saint-Gobain's strategic autonomy, it did not interfere with its managerial autonomy. It is important to note that other than the interventionism in the restructuring, Saint-Gobain was let alone, that is, in its implementation of the restructuring, its modernization, and so forth. As Jean-Louis Beffa, CEO of Saint-Gobain subsequent to Fauroux, noted, "It was management, as with any other shareholder, that proposed the strategy. . . . To be perfectly frank, the state let us do what we wanted at the point at which we did not ask for money." In fact, nationalization as a whole, he insisted, didn't change much of anything: "It was a parenthesis. It allowed Saint-Gobain to continue with its *politique* that has gone on for over 300 years."[66]

The chemicals industry experienced a similar set of interactions. Although even more dramatic confrontations occurred with the restructuring policy, with Gandois of Rhône-Poulenc resigning in protest against Chevènement's planned reorganization of the chemical industry and with Albin Chalandon not being renewed by Fabius in response to his recalcitrance with regard to certain financial conditions of the final agreement (in particular his unwillingness to compensate Total for certain acquisitions, despite Minister of Industry Fabius's explicit order to that effect),

[63]Roger Fauroux, "L'industriel et le fonctionnaire," *Le Débat* (May–September 1986), pp. 172–175 – cited in Fridenson, "Atouts et limites," p. 187; see also, Cohen and Bauer, *Grandes manoeuvres industrielles.*
[64]*Le Monde,* January 14, 1986.
[65]Commentators cite in particular the fact that Eurotechnique had yet to show a profit and that the head of Olivetti, Carlo de Benedetti, did not relish maintaining an alliance with a nationalized company. Barreau, "Les relations état–groupes nationalisés," p. 73; Boublil, *Soulèvement.*
[66]Beffa, interview with author.

accommodation otherwise characterized the ministry–industry relationship. The negotiations among the various industrial groups involved –
primarily Péchiney, Elf, Total, and Rhône-Poulenc – dragged on and on,
as ministerial officials charged with the restructurings held meeting after
meeting with the CEOs, until Chevènement preempted everything when
he announced his "devolution policy." This was the heroic policy that
was to resolve the matter (and led to Gandois's resignation), but which in
turn led to a renewed round of discussions, which then again dragged on
until Fabius became Minister of Industry – with the final resolution
occurring in June 1983, after Chalandon of Elf had been ousted. The final
outcome was to the satisfaction of most of the industrialists involved,
with all firms other than CDF-Chimie in a position to turn themselves
around, and with all expected to except CDF-Chimie.[67]

Thus, even in one of the most apparently interventionist of restructurings, the desires of most firms were accommodated. In all other ways,
moreover, co-optation was the rule. Thus, in the case of Rhône-Poulenc,
because the company was in relatively good financial shape, making its
money in the international market, the government had an essentially
hands-off policy, leaving it with basic control over its own planning,
restructuring, and social policies both before nationalization and after.[68]
It is telling that several top government and business officials interviewed
for this study ascribed the success of the company over time to Gandois's
strategic plans, which they said continued unchanged under successor
CEOs after his precipitate departure.

For similar reasons, Péchiney was also basically let alone. In fact, in the
view of Ambroise Roux, former CEO of CGE and member of the board of
directors of Péchiney before nationalization, Péchiney was able to turn
itself around during nationalization because it was no longer subject to
the bad industrial policy decisions of the previous government, which had
systematically blocked Péchiney's sale of its specialized steel and chemical
operations, "restructurings which were indispensable to allowing the
group to live." Instead, as of 1981, it benefited from the fact that "the
domain of industrial policy was left to the sitting CEOs, much as to those
who succeeded them after nationalization, thereby leaving them a greater
freedom of action than what had existed before."[69]

Elf-Aquitaine, too, continued to benefit from a great deal of freedom,
despite the fact that the CEO, Albin Chalandon, was a clearly identified
economic liberal and Giscard appointee. For example, the CEO was able
to convince Minister of Industry Pierre Dreyfus to allow Elf to purchase

---

[67]Cohen and Bauer, *Grandes manoeuvres industrielles*, pp. 99–108.   [68]Ibid., pp. 258–268.
[69]Testimony by Ambroise Roux, CEO of CGE before nationalization, *Rapport sur
les opérations de privatisation*, vol. 2, p. 787.

Texasgulf in 1981 by claiming that it could become a "little French Exxon."[70] Confrontation, however, began to build, first, when Chalandon failed to persuade the government to abandon political considerations in oil policy for purely commercial ones by allowing him to buy from commercially available sources instead of the Saudis and, secondly, with the financial arrangements surrounding restructuring. Upon his resulting ouster from Elf, he criticized the Minister on the grounds that he "wanted to make public enterprises simple extensions of administration."[71] Other than on this issue, however, Elf generally was let alone in decision-making by the state. It already had outside shareholders at the time of nationalization, and kept them, thus giving it an added reason for demanding, and obtaining, its independence from government intervention.[72]

The aerospace industry also experienced little state intervention, since government limited itself to the planning function and left operational aspects to the nationalized industries themselves.[73] Here, co-optation was the key even in the restructuring process: the government had a tendency simply to respond to the desires of industry, for example, when CIT-Alcatel, a subsidiary of CGE, was interested in taking over the aerospace operations of Thomson.[74]

Co-optation was equally the rule in telecommunications, especially once Fabius became Minister of Industry. In the agreement between CGE and Thomson which recapitalized Thomson-Telecommunications and placed it under the management of CGE, in fact, the two CEOs negotiated with each other without the most concerned ministries involved: the DGT (Télécom) and the PTT, which heard about the deal only very late and yet had to provide the financing for it.[75] Moreover, in the protocol of intent between CGE and ATT in July 1985, it was at the level of the Prime Minister and President that the decision was taken to leave to the next government a matter that they felt would harm France's economic independence.[76] (And they did this knowing full well that the next neoliberal government would approve it.) In the case of CGE more generally, in fact, Georges Pébereau noted that during the period of nationalization, "the state fulfilled all of its obligations as a shareholder and I never was subjected to the least constraint, in any domain, which was not the normal one of any shareholder."[77] Moreover, he was totally free to decide to

[70]*Le Monde,* June 17, 1983, p. 34.
[71]*Le Monde,* June 16, 1983, p. 38. See the discussion in: Zahariadis, *The Political Economy of Privatization,* pp. 324–327.
[72]De Wissocq, interview with author.
[73]Durand et al., "Dirigisme et libéralisme," pp. 258–268.   [74]Ibid., p. 257.
[75]Barreau, "Les relations état–groupes nationalisés," pp. 77–78.   [76]Ibid., p. 80.
[77]Testimony of Georges Pébereau, CEO of CGE until a few months before privatization, *Rapport sur les opérations de privatisation,* vol. 2, pp. 717–718.

whom to sell companies or which to buy and at what price, insisting that he would "not have stayed one lone minute if it had been otherwise."[78] As he explained, the state in its role as major shareholder could put him in a minority on the board of directors but, as he made clear to the different Ministers of Industry, "If at any given moment I was in disagreement with my shareholder, I asked to be received by the Minister himself and, on leaving, either we were in agreement or I was revoked."[79]

The electronics industry was similarly subject to relatively little unwelcome interventionism, with the government mainly creating incentives for development to interest private as well as public enterprises to invest in certain areas, for example, integrated circuits.[80] Thomson itself benefited the most from restructurings that led to confrontation for firms in other industries. For example, when Saint-Gobain was forced to give up one of its operational areas to Thomson, the electronics company saw the state not as highly *dirigiste* but, rather, as an arbiter in the restructuring process.[81]

Moreover, even when government decisions went against Thomson, it involved accommodation, or ultimately government capitulation. For example, when Chevènement vetoed the agreement between Thomson's subsidiary CGR and the American Technicare in January 1983 to cede its operations in magnetic resonancing and nuclear medicine, Thomson willingly acceded in exchange for government promises of financial support. In addition, Chevènement's veto of Thomson's proposed abandoning of its losing microlithographic operations by its subsidiary CAMÉCA in December 1982 on the grounds that France should have a presence in all areas of high technology, held for only a short time. By June 1983, Thomson was allowed to abandon these operations. What is more, as ministry concerns shifted from strategies to profits, Thomson found less and less interference. In December 1985, Thomson was authorized to sell another subsidiary, SOCAPLEX, to the American Amphenol Products, despite objections from the military firms it supplied that it was abandoning a strategic area, by arguing that this was essential to its profitability for 1986.[82] Finally, for every decision that Thomson did not like – for example, the Ministry of Industry's refusal to allow it to set up an agreement between its subsidiary SEMS and SEL, a subsidiary of the American firm Gould in January 1982, it found one it liked even more, as in the case of the sale of its troubled subsidiary SEMS in December 1982 to CII-HB, Bull's subsidiary.

Bull, by contrast, was not too happy with this; and even less so with the

[78]Ibid., vol. 2, p. 725.   [79]Ibid.
[80]Durand et al., "Dirigisme et libéralisme," pp. 258–268.   [81]Ibid., p. 257.
[82]Barreau, "Les relations état–groupes nationalisés," pp. 71–72.

ceding of CGE's subsidiary, TRANSAC, which management judged disastrous for the company.[83] In fact, Francis Lorentz, head of Bull, in response to the argument that industry mostly got its own way, suggested that maybe Georges Pébereau at CGE was happy to get rid of all its losing operations, but Bull certainly wasn't happy to acquire them.[84] This helps explain Lorentz's insistence that the first two years of the Socialists' tenure in office were "madness" because Bull lost big.[85] In fact, Bull got the raw end of the deal in most instances. Thus, although the government froze negotiations between Matra and the Norwegian firm Norsk on a joint venture in minicomputers in September 1984 on the grounds that any such agreement would jeopardize Bull's competitive position as well as its status as a national champion, the agreement was authorized in November 1984, and the venture even received a public purchase order from CNES. Nonetheless, Bull, too, over time got its way, in particular once concerns had shifted to profit from strategic presence. In 1984, Bull, even though the sole manufacturer of magnetic disks, was allowed to abandon its production of these without comment from public authorities.

Most firms, in short, but certainly not all, mostly got their way in the implementation of industrial policies even in the most interventionist of periods, at the time of the restructuring of industry. This should help explain why CEOs of major nationalized firms, although eager for denationalization as a way of increasing their flexibility and their access to capital investment, did not attack state control unduly.[86] Moreover, in the individual permissions to sell nonvoting shares and the government's turning a blind eye to the illegal sale of subsidiaries, firms not only essentially got their way, they effectively undermined the government's policy of nationalization, thus paving the way for the privatizations of the neoliberal government that were to follow.

Only firms in the noncompetitive sector did not for the most part get their way, either under the Socialists or the neoliberals who followed them. The pharmaceutical companies, for example, suffered from the fragmentation of state action: prices were kept artificially low because the Ministry of Social Affairs, which was more interested in the physical health of citizens, had tended to win the fight with the Ministry of Industry, which was interested in the economic health of companies, primarily because the Ministry of Finance, most interested in the macroeconomic health of the country, had tended to support the former over the latter.[87]

[83]Ibid., pp. 73–74.
[84]Francis Lorentz, CEO of Bull. Interview with author, Paris, May 28, 1991.
[85]Ibid.   [86]See the discussion in Chapter 6.
[87]David Wilsford, "Theories, Frameworks and Concepts: Disaggregating the French

For similar reasons, moreover, the Ministry of Finance subjected the electric utility, EDF, to a *contrôle tatillon* which kept its price rises well below the amount agreed upon in the planning contract and that was necessary for it to engage in the adequate industrial investment. Thus, although the EDF was in control of technical choices – for example, in the decision to go with nuclear power – it was not in financial choices, where the services of the Ministry set prices in such a way that it made it impossible for the EDF to make a profit, leaving EDF with a deficit three years running and unable either to lower its indebtedness or to invest.[88] This was in violation of the state–firm planning contract that, had it been honored, would have enabled EDF to save 35 billion francs.[89]

MINISTRY–INDUSTRY RELATIONS THROUGH PRIVATIZATION AND DEREGULATION

Privatization under the neoliberal government of 1986 to 1988 was as heroic an affair as nationalization and restructuring. There was no consultation on the choice of companies to privatize, although often the general inclinations of industry were followed. Moreover, only in a few instances was top management consulted for the choice of the hard core of investors. Otherwise, business was left to make its own strategic decisions, to which the government often, but not always, acceded.

Heroism in particular characterized the formulation of privatization policy. For example, the list of the companies to be privatized was essentially the decision of the Minister of Finance, with no outsiders involved, including the CEOs of the soon-to-be privatized firms – even if often, but not always, management's interest in privatization played a role. Thus, Saint-Gobain was sold first in part because the government decided that it was a good candidate for privatization, given its stable management and healthy profile, in part because management was favorable. AGF, by

State and Its Role in Industrial Policy." Paper prepared for presentation to the Annual Meeting of the American Political Science Association (Washington, DC, August 30– September 2, 1991), pp. 20–23.

[88]Bernard Couroux, *De la faculté d'adaptation d'un établissement public à son milieu: L'exemple d'EDF*, Ph.D. dissertation (Faculty of Law, Economic Sciences, and Management, University of Nice, January 11, 1991), p. 326.

[89]*Le Point*, February 5, 1990. The planning contract of 1984–1988 stipulated that the EDF was to be able to raise its rates to a level equivalent to inflation minus 1%. Instead, it was forced to lower them. Moreover, although the plan allows the state and public enterprise to determine together (*en concertation*) the level of investment for the renewal of intermediate and high-tension power lines, the FDES yearly establishes the amount of investment EDF is allowed, thus controlling an important part of its activity. See: Couroux, *Faculté d'adaptation*, p. 203.

contrast, was not privatized, first because there were certain technical problems involving the ownership of the company's insurance reserves that delayed its being put on the market as planned, and secondly because the company, although at first enthusiastic about privatization, later became more reticent. UAP was slated for privatization instead because it seemed to be more favorably inclined (although it was not ultimately privatized).[90]

In some cases, however, the government went against company desires, refusing to capitulate to pressures. The Crédit Agricole, for example, was very much against privatization and its director-general, Jean-Paul Huchon, quite vocal in his opposition (for which he was fired). In this, the firm was joined by the Minister of Finances and the Director of the Treasury, Daniel Lebègue, who protested the privatization not only on the grounds that it was sold too cheaply, but also that it was corporatist and "would put in the hands of a profession one of the ten largest banks worldwide under conditions that do not respect the equality of competition among banks. To privatize an enterprise with its state monopolies shocks me."[91] But the protest was to no avail, despite numerous difficult meetings between the Director of the Treasury and the top management as well as the Federation of the Crédit Agricole, given that the issue was arbitrated by the government and pushed by the Minister of Agriculture, François Guillaume, himself the former head of the main agricultural association, the FNSEA, which had been in favor of mutualization since the mid sixties.[92]

By contrast, Dassault was very much interested in its own privatization, but neither the Ministry of Finance nor of Defense was favorable.[93] Similarly, for the Crédit Lyonnais, even though the CEO, Jean-Maxime Levèque, thought privatization would have been easy and brilliant, he explained that "Unfortunately, I did not completely convince the Minister of Finance [of this], and you know what his importance is in this domain."[94] Moreover, when Matra as early as April 1986 pushed for privatization of the company through employee ownership under conditions that would have allowed the family group and management, under Lagardère's leadership, to regain control with a minimal investment, neither the

[90]Testimony by Philippe Jaffré, at the time of the privatizations chef de service, banks and financial institutions, *Rapport sur les opérations de privatisation*, vol. 1, p. 306.

[91]Testimony by Daniel Lebègue, *Rapport sur les opérations de privatisation*, vol. 1, p. 297.

[92]For testimony on this issue, see: *Rapport sur les opérations de privatisation*, vol. 1, pp. 71–91, 297–299, 314–316.

[93]Testimony by Daniel Lebègue, *Rapport sur les opérations de privatisation*, vol. 1, pp. 276–278.

[94]Testimony by Jean-Maxime Levèque, nominated CEO in July 1986, *Rapport sur les opérations de privatisation*, vol. 2, p. 686.

Director of the Treasury nor the Minister of Finance was in agreement, preferring instead that the company first increase its savings, and that management increase its stake before privatization. This did happen, with the Minister of Finance agreeing to the privatization in January 1988, although the Treasury remained uncomfortable about the privatization. The Director of the Treasury felt the valuation of the company in January 1988 was insufficient, while the former Director noted that the low valuation might have appropriately corresponded to the level of risk of the operation, given the market at that point.[95] Numerous members of the opposition, by contrast, saw politics as the real explanation.

Ministries and public enterprises were not the only ones involved in exerting pressure in the privatizations. In the case of the privatization of Sogenal, local elected officials of the Lorraine ensured that the bank would be sold on the Nancy regional stock market, despite concerns by Sogenal, the Société Générale, and the Treasury that the stock market's liquidity and level of capitalization were not high enough to ensure a good price.[96]

In short, once the government had decided on the firms to privatize, or not, it was often subject to great pressure – to which it only occasionally capitulated. The CEOs, however, were ordinarily out of the loop. And if they sought to exert undue pressure, their reward was as likely as not being shown the door.

Generally, it was only at the point that the CEOs were informed that their firms were candidates for privatization that they had any real contact with the Ministry of Finance, at which juncture the CEO generally met a number of times with the Minister of Finance while their "collaborators," or underlings, met with the bureau of the Treasury.[97] With membership in the *noyaux stables,* though, the CEOs had a bit more say, since they were allowed to make suggestions for candidates, despite the fact that the decision on membership remained the prerogative of Balladur. Ordinarily, the CEOs were asked by the Ministry if they had special preferences, related to international, industrial, or financial plans that tied them to specific companies, that would have been helpful if they were to be part of the structure of their capital. The CEOs rarely put

[95] *Rapport sur les opérations de privatisation,* vol. 1, pp. 230–235, 282–283, 334–339.

[96] Testimony by Daniel Lebègue, *Rapport sur les opérations de privatisation,* vol. 1, p. 289.

[97] For example, Renaud de la Génière, head of Suez as of 1986, noted that he had had no official contacts with the cabinet of the Minister of Finance nor with the Treasury until he was informed in the spring of 1987 that his bank was a candidate for privatization, at which point he had five or six meetings with the Minister of Finance while his collaborators met with the Treasury. Testimony of Renaud de la Génière, *Rapport sur les opérations de privatisation,* vol. 2, p. 654.

together a complete list. Rather, the list was put together by the Minister's cabinet on the basis of requests by companies interested in participating in the *noyau stable*,[98] and after, simply as a matter of politeness, the CEOs informed the heads of financial and industrial services or the Director of the Treasury of their ideas on the subject.[99]

In most cases, the Minister eliminated very few of the names recommended by the CEOs, and those he did were at the behest of the companies concerned. At most, he proposed enlarging the membership by including a significant international component.[100] In the case of the Société Générale, the Minister of Finance put an announcement in the *Journal Officiel* inviting those who wished to aquire stock in the Société Générale to present themselves to office B 25 in the North Wing in the Bureau of the Treasury, then put together the list of members, and subsequently went over the list with the CEO at the time, Marc Vienot. They got rid of no one, despite Vienot's objections to the Banco de Santander, and only reduced the size of the hard core from around 25% to 21%.[101] Vienot himself was reproached by Balladur for not being activist enough in seeking potential members of the *noyau stable*, but by his own account, he was not at the time convinced of its utility, although he subsequently changed his mind.[102]

Similarly, at Suez, the CEO Renaud de la Génière provided the government with a full list of suggestions of potential members of the *noyau dur*. But in this case, the government modified the list by asking the state's consultant bank for another list of suggestions, and constituted a hard core much more diversified than that for the industrial companies privatized.[103] At CCF, too, top management was consulted by the cabinet of Balladur and the Bureau of the Treasury on the type of hard core they wanted, and asked for particular suggestions, at which point they requested Lafarge Coppée, which had been a major shareholder before nationalization, and the Galeries Lafayette, with which they had had close relations since the beginning of the century. Moreover, the Ministry

[98]Testimony of Jacques Friedmann, *Rapport sur les opérations de privatisation,* vol. 1, p. 126.

[99]Testimony by Philippe Jaffré, *Rapport sur les opérations de privatisation,* vol. 1, p. 307.

[100]Testimony of Messier, *Rapport sur les opérations de privatisation,* vol. 1, p. 217. The only two candidates for membership who were eliminated were Decaux and Scopresse in the case of Havas.

[101]Testimony of Minister of Finance Balladur, *Rapport sur les opérations de privatisation,* vol. 1, p. 54, and of Marc Vienot, vol. 2, p. 825.

[102]Testimony of Marc Vienot, *Rapport sur les opérations de privatisation,* vol. 2, p. 825.

[103]Testimony of Renaud de la Génière, *Rapport sur les opérations de privatisation,* vol. 2, p. 654.

authorized them to make contact with certain potential candidates, which they did. None of their suggestions was rejected by the Minister, although they themselves rejected a potential candidate, the Lazard Bank, because it was one of their major competitors.[104]

In a few cases, however, the CEO of the public enterprise constituted the list of investors, making the initial contacts and keeping the Minister informed. This was the case with CGE, where Pierre Suard began contacting potential shareholders in the first months of 1987, and completed the list by the end of May.[105] A similar process occurred in the case of Paribas, where the bank put together the list of potential investors and contacted them.[106]

In the case of the privatizations by public offering on the stock market and private offering to a *noyau dur,* then, the process was primarily in the hands of the Ministry of Finance, with CEOs for the most part having a minor say on membership in the *noyau dur,* but that is all. When they had serious objections to any one member, however, this was taken into account, given that the Ministry of Finance had the best interests of the firm at heart.

Only in the case of the privatization of CGCT, the telephone switching manufacturer, were the best interests of the firm sacrificed in the name of a higher industrial policy, that is, greater inter-European cooperation. When Prime Minister Chirac awarded the firm to the Swedish firm Matra-Ericsson rather than to Siemens, he ignored the preference of CGCT itself for AT&T, which was technologically and financially superior, also the preference of CGE (which felt less threatened by it than by Siemens) and the director-general of France Télécom, who assumed that if it became one of its main suppliers (with CGE the other), it would be able to exert pressure in the service area on AT&T.[107] And even Madelin favored AT&T. The final decision, in fact, satisfied no one, and turned out to be disastrous for CGCT.

For the most part, then, privatization was a heroic affair which, although it involved minimal consultation on the choice of firms to be privatized and only somewhat more on the hard-core memberships, generally satisfied the participants with a few exceptions, and was not seen as highly *dirigiste* as a result. Policies with regard to mergers and acquisitions, by contrast, were occasionally much more interventionist.

---

[104]Testimony of Gabriel Pallez, CEO of CCF as of 1985, *Rapport sur les opérations de privatisation,* vol. 2, p. 717–718.

[105]Testimony by Pierre Suard, CEO of CGE during privatization, *Rapport sur les opérations de privatisation,* vol. 2, pp. 796–797.

[106]Testimony of Michel François-Poncet, PDG of Paribas at the time of privatization, *Rapport sur les opérations de privatisation,* vol. 2, pp. 610–611.

[107]*International Herald Tribune,* Nov. 17, 1986.

In competition policy, although the government was generally liberal, it nevertheless did not hesitate to intervene where it deemed necessary. Thus, although Chirac did nothing with certain big operations in 1987 – for example, the *épousaille,* or marriage, between BSN and Fiat, the merger of Moët-Hennessy and Louis Vuitton, the failed takeover attempt by Chargeurs on Textiles Prouvost, and the development of the consulting giant Cap Gemini Sogeti through various takeovers – he actively encouraged the takeover of Générale Occidentale by the privatized CGE. Similarly, moreover, although Minister of Industry Madelin agreed to Thomson's acquisition of RCA and the merger of its electronics operations with the Italian public enterprise SGS, he actively tried to exclude John Kila, placed as shareholder and CEO of the paper company Chapelle Darblay by Fabius, and to replace him with the French group Pinault. Finally, at the same time that in the interests of competition Minister of Transportation Douffiagues allowed UTA to compete with Air France on certain routes, he forbade UTA to land in New York under pressure from the CEO of Air France, Jacques Friedmann (a good friend of Chirac).[108]

MINISTRY–INDUSTRY RELATIONS THROUGH THE PERIODS OF NEITHER NATIONALIZATION NOR PRIVATIZATION, PARTIAL PRIVATIZATION, AND RENEWED PRIVATIZATION

As of 1988, with the shift from heroic policymaking to the everyday, ministry–industry relations became almost entirely ones of accommodation and co-optation. Succeeding governments for the most part lacked either the will or the means to impose decisions on business, which looked less to the government for guidance as it became increasingly subject to the imperatives of world competition, the constraints of the market, and the demands of technological advancement, and less to the government for support as alternative sources of financing grew. Most government actions came from the proposals of business, whether they involved the growing intermixing of the economy through the trading of shares in nationalized enterprises under Rocard, through the trading of shares between nationalized and private firms under Cresson and Bérégovoy, or through the outright privatization of nationalized enterprises under Balladur. There were, nevertheless, a certain number of instances where governments imposed, often over objections from business.

With the return of the Socialists to power, the industries' only problems with the ministries involved seeking to sell subsidiaries in strategic areas.

[108]See Eric Le Boucher, *Le Monde, Bilan economique et social 1986,* January 15, 1987.

Otherwise, the state was exceedingly accommodating, in particular in its allowing for the trading of shares in nationalized companies. This is where formulation and implementation blur, as the politics of accommodation became the everyday policies of governments without many heroic initiatives. But although business for the most part initiated, it did not always entirely get its way. Accommodation, rather than co-optation, was often the operative concept.

The Volvo-Renault alliance is a case in point. As the CEO, Louis Schweitzer, recounted it, the initiative came from the company, which kept all four authorities – the Ministry of Industry, the Ministry of Finance, the Prime Minister, and the President – informed of the project, but which formally submitted it to these parties at a meeting at Matignon (the Prime Minister's office) only when it thought that it had an agreement. Its project to turn Renault into a holding company, with the operational units as subsidiaries jointly controlled by Volvo, was vetoed by the President, who nevertheless accepted Volvo's entering the capital of Renault. On this basis, the company then negotiated with Volvo, with the approval of authorities. Thus, all the action was initiated by the enterprise, submitted to authorities when the project was set, and changed to make it acceptable. Although informal contacts had come before, at the moment of decision, the response came in a matter of days.[109]

Under Rocard, in fact, the relationship between ministry and industry was highly cooperative, leading to much accommodation and few confrontations. Even in the case of the restructuring of the chemical and nuclear industries, although the initiative came from the government, concerned that there was too much competition (it charged Le Floch-Prigent, former head of Péchiney, to consider the issues and to try to work something out with the CEOs involved), the process was characterized by lengthy consultation – which only half succeeded.[110] While the activities of CDF-Chimie, renamed Orkem, were divided between Elf and Total (which returned with this to the sector, having left it with the earlier restructurings), and the state's blocking vote in Roussel-Uclaf was transferred to Rhône-Poulenc, with the blessing of its German owner, Hoechst, the decision on EMC was put off in response to opposition to Elf's outright acquisition of the company.[111] By contrast, the restructuring failed entirely in the nuclear industry in the case of Framatome, where the dossier was ultimately shifted from the Minister of Industry to the Minister of Finance.

Under Cresson, the government was in certain instances more interventionist, but industry also for the most part got its way. In two major cases

[109]Schweitzer, interview with author.　　[110]De Wissocq, interview with author.
[111]*Les Echos*, April 8, 1991.

where company-proposed alliances had received the go ahead from the Rocard government, Cresson threatened to undo them, but ultimately capitulated in exchange for industry concessions. Thus, in the case of confrontation over Cresson's demand for the reexamination of the Japanese NEC taking a 4.7% share in Bull, after a few weeks and many discussions, an accommodation was reached in which the NEC–Bull accord was authorized with Bull agreeing in exchange to take total control of its American subsidiary Honeywell-Bull. Confrontation occurred also on the matter of Bull's American alliance with IBM, with Cresson and advisor Abel Farnoux having wanted it to reach an agreement with Hewlett-Packard instead, fearful that IBM would dominate Bull. In this case, however, the CEO Lorentz wanted, and got, an alliance with IBM (which was willing to inject more money and to sell its personal computers) with the support of Minister of Finance Bérégovoy and the "arbitrage" of President Mitterrand.

The Renault–Volvo accord also ran into problems with Cresson, who, the minute she became Prime Minister, wanted to know if Volvo's accord with Mitsubishi, which allowed the Japanese to manufacture cars in the Netherlands, was not a threat to Renault and to European automobile manufacturers. Her councilor Farnoux wanted the Swedes to renege on the agreement, but Raymond Lévy, CEO of Renault, along with his Swedish ally, managed to allay the fears of the government.[112] Mitterrand again saved the day: having been the one to agree to the link under Rocard, he sent word down that he was unwilling to allow a reexamination of the whole dossier. (Rumor had it that the main reason Cresson had cast doubt on the accord had to do with her dislike of Louis Schweitzer – number two at Renault and the architect of the accord, as well as a former cabinet director of Fabius – for political reasons as well as the fact that he was "too independent."[113] Political allegiances may also help explain why, after Cresson secretly refused the total merger between Volvo and Renault a few weeks before she was replaced, her successor Bérégovoy okayed it, given his close relationship with Laurent Fabius, and his ties to Schweitzer.)[114]

Which companies were subject to more government pressure, as in the past, depended upon the strategic importance of the industry as well as on questions of personality and history. Thus, numbers of industries had no problem in making alliances with foreign concerns, such as Elf with Sterling drug, the pharmaceutical subsidiary of Kodak, or Roussel-Uclaf with the Japanese Ajinomoto, and others such as Péchiney, Rhône-Poulenc, and Atochem were basically given a relative liberty of manage-

---

[112]*Le Figaro*, April 3, 1992.   [113]*L'Usine Nouvelle*, no. 2348, January 23, 1992.
[114]*L'Usine Nouvelle*, no. 2359, April 9, 1992.

ment and alliance as long as public funds were not requested. Others, however, in nuclear energy, computers, and electronics, were subject to a significant amount of interventionism. For example, when Framatome and KWU, the nuclear subsidiary of Siemens, agreed to export and construct a 1,000-megawatt reactor, the Cresson government started worrying about the lack of balance in the agreement.[115]

The Cresson government, in short, precipitated many more confrontations than the previous government, although ultimately its impact was little different. Moreover, such confrontations occurred not only in the case of alliances with foreign firms, but also in the trading of shares among nationalized enterprises. What under Rocard had been primarily a sometimes reluctant response to company initiatives was now actively encouraged by the government, and occasionally imposed. For example, although the BNP and Crédit Lyonnais insisted publicly that their acquisition of 10% stakes in Air France and Usinor-Sacilor respectively were done under their own initiative, privately the BNP acknowledged that it had only agreed to the Air France deal in return for government help with raising the bank's capital the previous year – and it did refuse to exercise its option to acquire shares in Usinor-Sacilor.[116] Moreover, although Paul Quilès, at the time Minister of Post, Telecommunications, and Space, insisted that France Télécom's participation in the capital of the Banque Hervet represented an opportunity for the company rather than an instance of state *dirigisme,* he made certain subsequently to institute state–industry planning contracts that protected France Télécom from such "opportunities" in the future.[117] In fact, the planning contract signed in November 1991, in which France Télécom agreed to cut its debt, modernize its network, and expand abroad, proved timely, since it helped protect it from the Cresson government's pressure soon thereafter to increase its share in Bull from the 17% stake it had already acquired.

Perhaps the most newsworthy of such cases was the proposed merger of Thomson and CEA into a superfirm, which was the brain child of Farnoux under the instigation of Thomson CEO Alain Gomez, who was looking for funding from somewhere. Here, CEA tended to resist, since while Thomson stood to gain a lot in terms of financial help, CEA stood to lose financial reserves that it had set aside to cover the costs of dismantling nuclear installations. Ultimately, Alain Gomez, CEO of the Thomson group, and Jean Syrota, head of Cogema, who was in charge of reporting on the legal and financial modalities of the operation, fell out so badly over how to value the shares in the new venture that the head of the Treasury, Jean-Claude Trichet, was asked to find a solution. The result

[115]*L'Usine Nouvelle,* no. 2348, January 23, 1992.   [116]*Wall Street Journal,* July 25, 1991.
[117]*Le Monde,* April 9, 1991.

was a tentative agreement for CEA to take a 20 to 25% share in the two Thomson subsidiaries. Once the Bérégovoy government came to power, however, this was reversed. CEA-Industrie took only a minority interest in the company, which meant that Thomson had to go elsewhere to find more capital.

This was not to be the end of the "*Meccano industriel,*" as the French call this kind of operation. Although the Bérégovoy government essentially encouraged continued trading of shares without such dramatic flights of "voluntarism," the Balladur government came up with a new suggestion for reinvigorating Thomson involving firm mergers. In other ways, too, moreover, the Balladur government took a more interventionist role.

Minister of Industry Longuet, for example, had a more interventionist, or at least directive, style than previous ministers. In the case of Bull, he warned that it could no longer expect to come to the state every year for millions of francs, and that it needed to recognize that "it could no longer do all, all alone, and everywhere."[118] It was he who decided that CEO Bernard Pache had to go because, in the words of one of his councilors, "When we saw Pache for the first time, we understood that we would get nowhere with him."[119] His naming of Jean-Marie Descarpentrie as head, along with a pledge for a capital grant of 7 billion francs, was evidence that the government was back to playing a stronger role, at least with companies in trouble.

This was equally true in the case of Air France. When Bernard Attali, CEO of Air France, submitted his restructuring plan to the Minister of Transportation Bernard Bosson in spring 1993, Bosson requested a much stronger program, and Attali complied with a new proposal submitted in September that anticipated cutting 4,000 jobs for 1994–1995 (in addition to the 3,000 already planned for 1992–1993), for 5 billion francs saved. But while Bosson publicly supported the CEO, in the Ministry his councilors complained about Attali's bad faith, so much so that union officials saw a weak spot to exploit. When the strike occurred, Attali was marginalized while Bosson managed the conflict. When the government decided to withdraw the restructuring plan, the CEO resigned. The new plan, put together by the new CEO Christian Blanc, had no compulsory firings. Moreover, Air France, too, was to receive a large capital injection (20 billion francs) to soften the impact of the restructuring.

Other than in these two cases, however, the Balladur government seemed to be following the same pattern as its immediate predecessors with regard to respecting the traditional autonomy of public enterprise. Once a new CEO was appointed who had the confidence of the govern-

118 *L'Expansion,* September 23–October 6, 1993.
119 *L'Expansion,* November 2–24, 1993.

ment, the hands-off policy returned. Privatization, moreover, would only serve to consecrate that autonomy.

The actual process of privatization in the Balladur government reflected the change in ministry–industry relations. It was more of an everyday affair than privatization in the Chirac government, and the work of more individuals. There was a consensus, in the first place, about the appropriateness of privatization and the process. Secondly, there was a great deal more consultation with the CEOs about which firms were ready, and about which shareholders should be part of the *noyau dur*. In the privatization of the BNP, for example, the president Michel Pébereau was responsible for recruiting the hard core of investors. And yet, here too, Balladur was at the center of the process, having decided on the list and the order of privatization for the twenty-one groups and appointed the members of the privatization commission. But Minister of the Economy Edmond Alphandéry, author of the 1993 law on privatization, decided on the price and the *noyau dur,* after advice by the commission.

The companies to be privatized were picked entirely on a pragmatic basis. Thomson was eliminated as a potential source of friction between the Ministry of Defense, concerned about its subsidiary Thomson CSF, and the Ministry of Industry. The Caisse Nationale de Prévoyance was passed over because only six months before it had undergone a change in status. The three insurance companies were also let alone not only because their real estate ventures were likely to prove less than profitable but also because GAN was waiting for a decision on the fate of its banking subsidiary CIC, while AGF and UAP were still trying to sort out their German ventures, AGF in terms of its takeover of the German insurer AMB, UAP trying to conclude its armistice with Suez over Victoire-Colonia. Moreover, the government was not about to privatize Renault because "To privatize Renault in the current state of affairs would result in giving the control of the Swedish manufacturer."[120] SEITA, on which the Bolloré group had designs, was also not soon to go on the block because including it in the privatization law would have immediately made it lose its monopoly on tobacco import, manufacture, and sale. (It was sold only in February 1995.) Three of the four companies to be privatized, by contrast, had made a profit: Elf, 6 billion francs; BNP, 2.1 billion francs; Rhône-Poulenc, 1.5 billion francs. The Hervet bank, by contrast, had lost 186 million francs in 1992; but CCF, which already owned 34% of the firm, remained an ardent suitor.[121]

Privatization, in brief, was also much more of an everyday matter than it had been in the past. And intervention in company management, although perhaps more pronounced than under Bérégovoy or Rocard, and

[120]*Le Monde,* July 23, 1993.   [121]Ibid.

probably matching that of Cresson, remained much less than it had been under the previous neoliberal or Socialist governments of 1981 to 1988.

CONCLUSION

Ministry–industry relations have always been ones in which industry has generally prevailed over ministry, with the plans and policies initiated by governments modified or even scrapped when business found them too burdensome. In the eighties, however, as business became more interdependent and independent of government while governments gave up their industrial policy instruments, business had been able to resist more and governments to persuade less. The days of encouraging the creation of national champions are over. It is business that decides if and how it wishes to concentrate, and government that acquiesces.

This is not to say, however, that government cannot and will not seek to impose on occasion. It is only that, given international economic constraints and European regulations, it will do so much more cautiously, with a recognition of the risks for business health and of EU sanctions.

PART IV

The players in the policymaking process

10

Elites in the ministries and industries

Through the heroic policies of "more state" and "less state" between 1981 and 1988, which first brought nationalization and then deregulation and privatization, and the more everyday policies thereafter, which continued with deregulation and brought increasing Europeanization, only one aspect of the state changed not at all: the elite recruitment patterns. The new heads of public enterprise shared with their predecessors, their counterparts in private enterprise, and their interlocutors in government the same elite background in terms of class, education, and membership in the prestigious civil service corps. The only difference in patterns of recruitment to the ministries or industries has been in terms of political coloration. In the ministries, civil servants appointed to major positions were increasingly identified with one or another political party. In the industries, where the Socialists often but not always appointed CEOs with left-wing sympathies whose careers spanned government and business, the neoliberals appointed ones with right-wing sympathies. But this was the extent of it. Neither sought to alter the traditional profile of top ministry or industry officials. What is more, in the case of nationalized enterprise in particular, neither expected the new heads to infuse the firm with the government's stated political values, whether Socialist or neoliberal. While the Socialists appointed no union activists who could embody socialist egalitarianism, the neoliberals named no self-made entrepreneurs who would promote neoliberal laissez-faire.

In the industries, moreover, the newly appointed heads, even when civil servants politically aligned with the left or right, were themselves intent on not allowing ideology into the firm, conceiving of management as value-neutral and seeking to protect the firm from the incursions of politics. In the ministries, by contrast, the vaunted neutrality of the civil service was challenged by the increasing politicization of administration, with civil servants increasingly seen as in the service of governments as opposed to some higher public interest. This politicization, the result of changing governments, has been accompanied by a transformation in civil servants' perceived roles and responsibilities, themselves the result of changing government policies in favor of the retreat of the state. While this has led to a modernized civil service that is more responsive and responsible, it has also brought greater instability, less productive work, fewer chances for advancement, and lower pay. All of this, in turn, has encouraged top civil servants to move out of the ministries and into industry, leading to even more blurring of the distinctions between administrative and managerial elite.

IN THE MINISTRIES: RENEWING THE ADMINISTRATIVE ELITE

During the Mitterrand years, there was little change in the profile of those recruited to the highest ranks of the ministries other than that involving political allegiance. This was as true for the regular civil service ranks, the directors in the central ministries, as it was for the ministerial cabinets, the ministers' staffs charged with carrying out the minister's policies and the government's agenda. Moreover, although politics played no greater a role in the appointment process than it had in the immediate past, the politicization of the upper levels of the administration in general was much more significant, as governments of the right and left succeeded one another in rapid succession, expecting civil servants to carry out their policies faithfully. By the same token, however, the "bureaucratization" of politics was equally pronounced, as civil servants moved out of the ministries into political positions as well as industries. All of this, together with the retreat of the state engineered by top civil servants themselves, has had a profound impact on the civil service. Civil servants, affected by diminishing budgets and responsibilities, politicized and less well-paid, have been moving in increasing numbers into the private sector, leaving the civil service, despite its recent modernization and the redefinition of civil servants' roles, in crisis.

The large majority of appointments to top civil service positions by governments of the left and the right were either graduates of the ENA, the École Nationale d'Administration (National School of Administration), among whom many had first received diplomas from the Institut d'Études Politiques (Institute of Political Studies), or of X, the École Polytechnique, most of whom followed with a degree from one of the professional engineering schools, in particular the École de Mines (School of Mines) or the École des Ponts et Chaussées (School of Bridges and Roadways). They then became members of one of the *grands corps de l'état*, or elite civil service corps, the most prestigious of which are the Inspection des Finances, the corps ordinarily made up of the top graduates of the

ENA who go to work for the Ministry of Finance immediately upon graduation; and the two engineering corps: the Corps des Mines, made up of the top graduates of X and the École des Mines, and the Corps des Ponts et Chaussées, for which the École des Ponts et Chaussées and X are the feeders. (Only ten per year enter the Corps des Mines or the Inspection des Finances, and twenty enter the Corps des Ponts, such that, altogether, each of the smaller corps contains approximately 350 to 500 members, including retirees – 1,000 for the larger corps.)[1]

When the Socialists came to power, if anything they increased the dominance of graduates of the *grandes écoles* and members of the *grands corps* in the upper levels of the administration. After 1981, much as before, only 20% of the directors in the central ministries had attended only universities. By contrast, four out of five had attended a *grande école*. Moreover, for the graduates of the ENA alone, the number of directors increased slightly, from 42.5% before 1981 to 43.7% after.[2] What is more, their profile changed little: a large majority were children of the upper-middle classes, 66% of directors in May 1981, 71% in December 1983.[3] Women did increase by 700%, however, although in absolute numbers it was not very high, since women remained only 5% of all directors in the central administration (understandable, perhaps, since they were not admitted to the *corps* of the Inspection des Finances until 1975, even though they could attend the ENA since 1945 – and they could not even attend Polytechnique until about the same time).[4]

Traditionally, the ministerial cabinets generally have had a wider range of appointees, given their political function, than the directorates of central ministries, although even in the cabinets most were typically civil servants. While in the Third Republic, 60% were civil servants, by the seventies, over 90% were civil servants.[5] And in the eighties, the preponderance of upper-level civil servants in ministerial cabinets only increased, with elite *corps* members having a predominant role. Whereas in the 1981 Mauroy government 65% of members of ministerial cabinets were upper-level civil servants, in 1986 under Chirac, 66% were, and in 1988 under Rocard, 70% (see Table 10.1). *Énarques* alone made up, in September 1990, 21% of the cabinet of the President of the Republic, 37% of that of the Prime Minister, 38% of the Minister of National Education, and 58% of the Ministers of Finance, Industry, and the Interior. More-

[1]*Le Monde*, June 19, 1991.
[2]Danièle Lochak, "La haute administration à l'épreuve de l'alternance," in *Les élites Socialistes au Pouvoir: Les dirigeants Socialistes face à l'état 1981–1985*, ed. Pierre Birnbaum (Paris: Presses Universitaires de France, 1985), pp. 176–77.
[3]Ibid., p. 172.   [4]Ibid., p. 177.
[5]Jeanne Siwek-Poudesseau, "French Ministerial Staffs," in *The Mandarins of Western Europe*, ed. Mattei Dogan (New York: John Wiley, 1975), p. 200.

Table 10.1. *The number of civil servants in ministerial cabinets, in percentages*

	Mauroy (1981)	Chirac (1986)	Rocard (1988)
Upper-level civil servants	65	66	70
Teachers	10	4	7
Party militants	15	14	9
Private sector	8	14	7

Source: Monique Dagnaud and Dominique Mehl, "L'élite rose confirmée," Pouvoirs vol. 50 (1989), p. 142.

over, they were generally in the position of director or deputy director, preferring that to more technical positions.[6] In 1995, this pattern continued, with *énarques* making up 70% of ministerial cabinet directors in the Juppé government.[7]

This increasing pattern of elite recruitment has not only been a function of the growing hold of the *grands corps* over government. It also has had a lot to do with money: because the finances accorded to the ministerial cabinets have been limited (and increasingly so after 1983), ministers have found it cheapest to employ members of the *grands corps* who are *mis à disposition,* or freely attached to the cabinet, without any money having to be spent, other than the *primes* (or bonuses) that make serving in a cabinet position so attractive.

The growing hold of members of the *grands corps* over ministerial cabinet positions probably had less to do with a desire for money or even power, however, than it did with the fact that service in a ministerial cabinet was a sine qua non for those interested in a major position in government or business. Politics, in other words, was a way of increasing a *grand corps* member's chances of getting to the top faster. For those already on the fast track, this meant moving into a position of a ministerial cabinet once their party came to power. And out into a secure position, *"se faire caser,"* when the opposition returned to power or, more simply, when they deemed it opportune to move on. Consider, for example, all the Socialist cabinet members and directors who moved into top positions in public enterprise in 1986 and 1987, some before they were told to leave by the right, others once they received their marching orders. There is nothing new about this, however. Generally, the reward for ministerial cabinet service is a sinecure such as that of Balladur who, after four years in Prime Minister Pompidou's cabinet, became president of the French company for the construction of the Mont Blanc tunnel, or

[6]Irène Bellier, "Vocation ou goût du pouvoir?" in *Faire la politique: Le chantier français, Autrement* no. 122 (May 1991), p. 178.
[7]*Le Monde,* July 1, 1995.

who, after five years in the secretariat-general of President Pompidou, became head of two subsidiaries of CGE, thanks to his good friend Ambroise Roux.[8] For others, not on the fast track in the *grands corps,* getting to the top even meant leaving the public sector for political office, and then coming back triumphant as minister. Gérard Longuet, Minister of Industry under Chirac and Balladur, is a case in point: he left early on to distinguish himself in politics, having done poorly at the ENA and having therefore started as a subprefect.

In fact, whatever the complaints about the politicization of the civil service, one must also talk about the "bureaucratization" of politics, given the large number of civil servants who have been members of governments during the Fifth Republic – at an average of 54% between 1958 and 1986. Of these, upper-level civil servants were the large majority between 1958 and 1981, at between 66% and 88%, and again in 1986, at 81% (with seventeen upper-level civil servants out of a total of twenty-one members). By contrast, under the Socialist government of 1981 to 1986, teachers were the main category, at from 56% to 76%, by contrast with upper-level civil servants who were at 40% in the short-lived first Mauroy government (with nine out of twenty-three), 23% in the second Mauroy government (with five out of twenty-two) and 24% in the Fabius government (with five out of twenty-one).[9] Of the main players, however, an increasing number were former top-level civil servants. Thus, among Prime Ministers, although Pierre Mauroy, Edith Cresson, and Pierre Bérégovoy were not elite civil servants, with Mauroy and Bérégovoy in particular having come up the hard way, the others were all *énarques* with careers in the civil service as well as government: Laurent Fabius, Jacques Chirac, Michel Rocard, and Edouard Balladur.

Although politics was quite clearly a main criterion for appointment to ministerial cabinets, it played less of a role in the appointments to central ministry directorates than one might ordinarily have expected. There were certainly a number of political appointments, but these were fewer than the nonpolitical ones. Generally, under the Socialists, the appointments reflected an attempt to name left-leaning civil servants if possible, but expertise was the key criterion.[10] Only certain ministers, moreover, moved quickly to replace the directors. Thus, in the Ministry of Industry, whereas Pierre Dreyfus left previous directors for the most part in place,

---

[8]Thierry Pfister, *La république des fonctionnaires* (Paris: Albin Michel, 1988), p. 51.

[9]Francis de Baecque, "Les fonctionnaires à l'assaut du pouvoir," *Pouvoirs* vol. 40 (1987), p. 65–66.

[10]Lochak, "La haute administration," pp. 189–193. On the differences in style among directors with clear left-wing affiliation and those without, see: Jean-Luc Bodiguel and Marie Christine Kessler, "Les directeurs d'administration centrale," in *Élites Socialistes,* ed. Birnbaum, pp. 195–218.

the minute Jean-Pierre Chevènement arrived, he replaced five very quickly between September 1982 and January 1983.[11] The turnover rate during this time period was, nevertheless, greater than the average over the long term. But this was less a peculiarity of the Socialists than a phenomenon of civil service politicization that had started under Giscard d'Estaing's presidency in 1974. Turnover of department heads, which had been about 14% between 1958 and 1974, increased to 25% between 1974 and 1976, and climbed to 31.4% between 1981 and 1984, to reach 40.5% between March 1986 and March 1987.[12] In 1988, the pace of change of directors slowed. But again, certain ministries were quicker to replace directors than others. In the first six months of 1988, while the Ministry of the Interior replaced seven, Education three, and Foreign Affairs three, the more technical ministries such as Transport, Infrastructure, and Industry replaced none. In the Ministry of Finance, a year later none had yet been replaced, despite the fact that the directors of the Treasury and the Budget had been former ministerial cabinet members in Chirac's government.[13]

One might actually have expected to see more change for political reasons. After all, the left had been out of power for twenty-three years, and had been quite suspicious of the upper levels of the civil service when they took over. Paul Quilès, national secretary of the Socialist Party (PS) and a deputy from Paris, at the time of the first Socialist Congress in Valence in October 1981 noted that the government would have to deal with the resistance of the opposition and its allies, including "certain spheres of the higher administration," and although he was not suggesting a witchhunt, he thought that it would be "naïve to leave in place people who are determined to sabotage the policy desired by the French (rectors, prefects, heads of nationalized enterprises, upper-level civil servants)." Moreover, when Anicet LePors, former Communist senator, took over as Minister of the Civil Service, he stated that changes would first have to take place with the 200 to 300 upper-level civil servants whose appointments were set by decree from the Council of Ministers. This was not new, however. In 1976, the Barre government did the same to all those suspected of being "chiraquiens."[14]

---

[11]Lochak, "La haute administration," p. 170.

[12]Ibid.; and Dominique Chagnollaud, "La nominations des hauts fonctionnaires ou les arcanes de la politisation," paper presented to the French Political Science Association (Bordeaux, October 1988) – cited in Jean-Luc Bodiguel and Luc Rouban, *Le fonctionnaire détrôné?* (Paris: Presses de la Fondation Nationale des Sciences Politiques, 1991), p. 41.

[13]Bodiguel and Rouban, *Fonctionnaire détrôné?* pp. 48–49.

[14]André Passeron, "Comment ils ont placé leurs amis," *Pouvoirs* vol. 40 (1987), pp. 26–27.

Even if the appointment process to the uppermost ranks of the civil service has not been entirely politicized, the upper-level civil service as a whole has become increasingly politicized, in large measure in response to the back-and-forths in government majority. In 1967, 90% of directors of central administrations claimed to have no party affiliation and only 15% admitted to any political leanings, while most ministerial cabinet members similarly belonged to no political party and only 44% admitted to any political leanings.[15] This has, needless to say, changed with the fact that political affiliation may now help, rather than hinder, a career (depending, of course, upon who is in power). In 1981, 69% of ministerial cabinet members admitted belonging to majority parties.[16] Moreover, a good 42% of members of ministerial cabinets between 1981 and 1986 had participated in study commissions of the PS.[17] This politicization only accelerated subsequently, with ministerial cabinets increasingly making day-to-day decisions that had previously been the purview of regular civil servants, so much so that middle managers began complaining about their interference.[18]

Most upper-level civil servants themselves acknowledge the politicization of the civil service generally, with 47.5% finding the civil service more politicized than a few years earlier (versus 44.9% who saw no change and 5.6% who saw less politicization). The large majority explain this positively as a result of the basic evolution of French democracy, whether because of the politicization of all public choices (37.1%), the new demands from elected leaders for more political responsibility (27.3%), or renewed interest in policy follow-up (22.4%), than negatively as a consequence of recent political change, "boss system" practices, or elected leaders' dismissal of state values (13.6%).[19]

In fact, there have been two sorts of polemics about the politicization. Many, beginning with the Socialists in opposition to Giscard's state but increasing with the right in opposition to the Socialists in government, have seen it as a negative factor, as the end of the moral independence of the highest levels of French institutions.[20] Most recently, critics have seen a loss of credibility for the upper-level administration, first, because pub-

[15] Jean-François Kesler, *L'ENA, la société, l'état* (Paris: Berger-Levault, 1985); and Luc Rouban, "France in Search of a New Administrative Order," *International Journal of Political Science* vol. 14, no. 4 (1988), p. 416.
[16] Monique Dagnaud and Dominique Mehl, *L'élite rose–Qui gouverne?* (Paris: Ramsay, 1982).
[17] Ibid.   [18] Rouban, "France in Search," p. 416.
[19] Luc Rouban, *Les cadres supérieurs de la fonction publique et la politique de modernisation administrative* (Paris: Presses de la Fondation Nationale des Sciences Politiques, 1992); and Rouban, "France in Search," p. 416.
[20] Bodiguel and Rouban, *Fonctionnaire détrôné?* pp. 38–41.

lic opinion sees the politicization as a kind of spoils system (the American term having entered the French vocabulary is itself indicative of a change), and secondly, because the politicization involves not "administration in the service of politics," but "administration against politics," meaning that the politicization has affected the details of administration, not the substance, leading to more politicking than real politics.[21]

For the most part, however, the politicization of the upper-level civil service has been depicted in a positive light. No longer a neutral force above governments and politics, commentators see *"l'administration"* as an instrument of elected governments and in the service of their politics.[22] The beginning of a true alternation of elected governments makes this transition understandable. When the right was in power for twenty-three years, civil service neutrality became a way of ensuring a place for nonmajority civil servants in the upper echelons of the bureaucracy, and of retaining an image of the civil servant as above the fray, implementing programs in the public interest without regard to the politics of the moment. Such a vision is no longer necessary when governments change on a regular basis, and are seen as responsible for their policies alone. Within this context, civil servants have gone from a neutral power to an increasingly politicized one, from impartial formulators and implementers of state policy to the implementers of changing governments' political agendas.

The changes in government policies promoting increasing liberalization, moreover, have had as much if not more of an impact on the civil service than the changes in governments that have brought politicization. After all, although the recruitment pattern changed little, other than sometimes in terms of political affiliation, the job changed greatly. As the state retreated, with the public sector progressively leaving place to the private sector, civil servants' actions have become an accompaniment, rather than an initiator. And civil servants have begun to conceive of their roles differently. Many members of the civil service have become more open to the outside, more willing to accept interest group activity as legitimate, and to allow the confrontation of experts in policymaking, much as in the American pluralist model of policy formulation. The upper-level civil service has also become more responsive, with some civil servants having begun to see themselves as the interlocutors of socio-professional groups or local governments rather than the vessels of an authority "as enigmatic as it is implacable."[23]

---

[21]Nicolas Tenzer and Rodolphe Delacroix, *Les élites et la fin de la démocratie française* (Paris: Presses Universitaires de France, 1992), p. 68.

[22]Bodiguel and Rouban, *Fonctionnaire détrôné?* pp. 38–41.

[23]Jacques Fournier, *Le travail gouvernemental* (Paris: Presses de la Fondation Na-

Some of this change in role also resulted from the fact that between 1988 and 1993, the Socialists lacked a clear majority, which meant that many policies that might heretofore have been heroic ones formulated by governments and passed by Parliament could not be. Instead, they became the everyday policies in which off-the-record arrangements, compromises with center and right politicians, and agreements with outside groups occurred in the ministries, far from public view. With this scenario, interestingly enough, policy evaluation, which had been resisted by "many upper level civil servants, especially those dedicated to controls and checks," now came to the fore as a "legitimation tool for political compromise."[24]

Much of this change in civil servants' conceptions of their role has also come about as a result of specific governmental policies favoring administrative modernization, begun in 1986 and extended by Rocard in 1989.[25] The modernization policy emphasized human resource management (in particular training sessions, professional and geographical mobility, career path renewal), personal accountability (through describing targets and resources in each ministry), policy evaluation (through new advisory and analytical institutions), and users' services (through better communications and more businesslike relations with the public).[26] Its success was ensured because it neither engendered union opposition nor raised ideological or legal questions about the status of the civil service. It led to the adoption of over 400 strategic plans in most ministries, hundreds of task forces on "quality improvement" (over 200 in the Ministry of Finance alone), and 85 quasi-contractual agreements between the Ministry of Finance, the Civil Service Ministry, and particular agencies that sought to promote financial and staff autonomy.[27]

Government policies, in short, have had the positive effect of encour-

tionale des Sciences Politiques, 1987), p. 124; Jacques Chevallier, "La gauche et la haute administration sous la Cinquième République," in *La haute administration et la politique,* ed. Jacques Chevallier (Paris: PUF, CURAPP, 1985); and Bodiguel and Rouban, *Fonctionnaire détrôné?* p. 50.

[24]Rouban, "France in Search," p. 415; and Jean-Pierre Nioche, *Institutionalizing Policy Evaluation in France: Skating on Thin Ice* (Jouy-en-Josas: Cahiers de Recherche HEC, 1991).

[25]Some of this was already in the works earlier, as attested to by the annual report of Jean Le Garrec, Minister of the Civil Service in the Mauroy government, who noted the effort at the "promotion of the *mieux d'état,*" or better state, by adapting the administration to the exigencies and evolution of modern society. See: Jean Le Garrec, *La fonction publique de l'état,* Annual Report (Paris: 1985).

[26]Rouban, "France in Search," p. 409. See also: Luc Rouban, "The Civil Service and the Policy of Administrative Modernization in France," *International Review of Administrative Sciences* vol. 55, no. 3 (1989), pp. 533–555.

[27]Ibid., p. 410.

aging the modernization of the civil service, making it more responsive to the public as well as to changing governments. They have also, however, had some negative effects, especially once combined with the politicization.

Most importantly, perhaps, the administration's long-admired ability to bring long-term projects to fruition has been seriously undermined. In France, political instability had for the most part had little impact on day-to-day operations in ministries concerned with the industrial sector, even as planning was becoming increasingly politicized. A comparison with Great Britain in the high technology area is illustrative. Whereas French instability had little impact on "entrenched forces with secure mandates," British instability resulted in "broad transfers of responsibility" that prevented the launching of certain projects altogether. Thus, for example, the French successfully completed the Charles de Gaulle airport, while the British abandoned the building of a third London airport.[28] The problem in Great Britain was that changes in ministers brought institutional reorganization and, therefore, "inadequate continuity in political instruction and oversight," with "mandates and criteria for decision-making . . . in constant flux, with new teams of civil servants assigned to a problem, or old teams given new instructions and new interlocutors." By contrast, in France, continuity remained despite political turmoil, so much so that ministerial change might actually enhance the power of the civil servants, while "units remain intact and the mandate remains immutable."[29]

During the Mitterrand years in the industrial policy arena, however, this changed as the increasing politicization of the civil servants themselves, together with increasing turnover, meant that units no longer remained intact or mandates immutable. Moreover, the constantly changing ministers with equally constantly changing agendas, all of which were focused on institutional reorganization, meant that in France, too, there were changing mandates and criteria for decision-making. Although the situation was probably most serious in the early to mid eighties, with the wide swings in policies and ideologies, other problems in the late eighties emerged that were equally threatening to the success of long-term endeavors, and to the survival of a respectable civil service itself.

Primary among these problems was the fact that the traditional attractions of the civil service, job security and upward mobility, were undermined by government austerity measures that from 1983 reduced the size of the civil service through attrition and through the elimination of budgetary lines: 2,200 in 1984, 7,500 in 1985, 11,300 in 1986, 19,100 in

---

[28]Elliot J. Feldman, *Concorde and Dissent: Explaining High Technology Project Failures in Britain and France* (New York: Cambridge University Press, 1985), p. 141.
[29]Ibid., p. 156.

1987, and 12,800 in 1988. As of 1986, for the first time since 1950, the overall number of employees diminished, going under 2.7 million.[30] The problems with this policy were dramatized by the 1986 and 1987 public service strikes that focused less on better salaries than on better careers, and demanded social recognition as professionals. Civil servants at the middle and lower grade in particular found themselves increasingly over-qualified, supervised by less qualified senior civil servants, and with few opportunities for advancement, given the constriction of the size of the civil service, and the radical separation between the lower-level and upper-level civil service.[31] Even upper-level civil servants faced problems, given that the *grands corps* system that guarantees top graduates of the ENA a stellar career also guarantees that the other graduates who find themselves in the much larger corps of *administrateurs civils* have little hope of moving up into top positions.[32]

Equally problematic has been the fact that government austerity policies have hit civil servants hardest in their pocketbooks (upper-level civil servants lost up to 20% of their average purchasing power between 1980 and 1988) at the same time that their counterparts in the private sector have been earning a lot more (in scientific and technical fields, the differential can be as much as 100%).[33] Moreover, the disengagement of the state from the economy has opened up opportunities in the private sector while closing many in the public sector, leaving upper-level national civil servants with fewer interesting things to do, a lot less power, and a much more complicated task requiring greater responsiveness to a public that has become more demanding. Both factors, money and a changed environment, have contributed to an exodus from government employment toward the private sector of younger managers (59.1% of managers between ages twenty-five and forty plan to leave the public sector for at least a while, by contrast with only 28.5% of upper-level civil servants, taken all together).[34] As one X-Télécom man, now at Alcatel, put it, he gave up the security of his civil service status at France Télécom for a salary that is two to three times what he could make in the public sector, and a job that is more challenging.[35]

The result is that civil servants have not only lost their central role in the economy as a result of the retreat of the state, they are paid less, have fewer chances for advancement, and have no more job security than in the

[30]*La fonction publique de l'état en 1988* (Paris: Documentation Française, 1989), ch. 1.
[31]Rouban, "France in Search," p. 405.   [32]Tenzer and Delacroix, *Les élites,* pp. 77–78.
[33]Ibid., p. 406.
[34]Rouban, "France in Search," p. 406. See also: Luc Rouban, *Les cadres supérieurs.*
[35]Conversation with author, November 16, 1993.

private sector. In sum, their special role as public servants is no longer special; they have become salaried employees like everyone else.[36] Moreover, at the upper ranks of the civil service, the politicization has led to a constant turnover that has led to an equally constant search for jobs. This in turn has created a chronic instability, a loss of morale, and increased concerns about job security even for the high flyers. Finally, it has led to a much more individualistic, by contrast with corps, spirit for the high-level functionaries, at the same time that it has increased the distance between the politicized upper levels of the civil service and the more neutral lower levels as well as the more technical services.[37]

In short, the rapid turnover in governments during the Mitterrand year, all of which from 1983 sought to diminish the size and purview of the state, led to a renewal of the top ranks of the civil service, which is now more modern, more political, and more elite in profile. But it is also less likely to bring long-term projects to fruition, given the alternation of parties. And it risks weakening over time, as underpaid top civil servants start moving out into industry at younger and younger ages, thus contributing to the renewal of the managerial elite as well as to a crisis for the civil service elite.

IN THE INDUSTRIES: RENEWING THE MANAGERIAL ELITE

In the industries, much as in the ministries, the appointments to top positions were based on elite educational credentials and *grand corps* membership. Despite a certain amount of politicization, especially in the first few years of the first Socialist and neoliberal governments, the appointments to the nationalized enterprises were based more on the candidate's administrative expertise and/or business experience than on political affiliation.

The shift in ownership from private to public, and subsequently from public enterprise to private, did little to engender change in type of personnel. Just as Pierre Mauroy found in 1982 that "We have nationalized the banks but not the bankers," so Jacques Chirac may have discovered that he denationalized the banks but, again, not the bankers.[38] The Socialist and neoliberal governments both appointed as heads of the nationalized enterprises managers who tended to have the same state educational backgrounds and career histories as their predecessors. Generally, the CEOs were graduates of the *grandes écoles* and members of a *grand*

---

[36]For an excellent discussion of the changes, see: Bodiguel and Rouban, *Fonctionnaire détrôné?*
[37]Ibid., pp. 50–53.   [38]*The Economist*, May 24, 1986.

corps, primarily ENA and the Inspection des Finances or X and the Corps des Mines or Corps des Ponts. In addition, a few CEOs were members of the corps of the Cour des Comptes, the accounting and auditing corps, made up of graduates of the ENA; and the Conseil d'État, the extremely prestigious judiciary corps which, however, rarely produces a head of industry or banking. As members of one of the elite corps, the future CEOs will all have spent a few years working in a ministry. And then, whereas some will have gone directly into industry, others will have first gained a high civil service position while yet others will have entered politics to gain a ministerial post before being "parachuted" into a vice-presidency or even a presidency of a major industrial group.

Both the Socialists and neoliberals, by doing little or nothing to change this pattern, at least as regards their appointments to head the nation-alized industries and banks, did little to challenge the dominance of the traditional interpenetrating political-financial-industrial elite held to-gether by family ties, old school ties, and *pantouflage,* or the shuttling (literally "slippering") of members from the higher levels of the civil service or politics into the highest reaches of private (or now public) enterprise.[39] After ten years of Socialist rule, of the thirty top managers in industry and banking, one-third came from X, one-third from the corps of the Inspection des Finances (and thus ENA), and close to one-half had also passed through a ministerial cabinet. Almost all of them had the same upper-middle-class social background, meaning the parents were from the liberal professions (i.e., doctors, lawyers, etc.), engineers, bank-ers, CEOs, and professors. There were only two farmers' sons and no workers.[40]

The main difference between the former heads and the new heads was that the latter were mostly younger and politically more on the left, "pink baby boomers" as they were sometimes called. There were few real mem-bers of the Mitterrand generation among them, except for André Rousse-let of Canal Plus; Jean-Pierre Aubert of CIC-Paris; and René Thomas of the BNP, a graduate of the ENA and member of the corps of Inspection des Finances, and thus much like his predecessor, Jacques Calvet, also an ENA-Finances, who moved to the private car-maker Peugeot.

Most of the younger members had the same elite credentials as the older: a large percentage were not only graduates of the elite schools, in particular the ENA and X, but also members of the elite civil service

[39]For a discussion of this elite, see: Pierre Birnbaum, Charles Barucq, Michel Bel-laiche, Alain Marie, *La classe dirigeante* (Paris: Presses Universitaires Française, 1978); and Pierre Birnbaum, *The Heights of Power* (Chicago: University of Chicago Press, 1982).
[40]*L'Express,* May 2, 1991.

Table 10.2. *CEOs of major nationalized (1982) and privatized (1986–1988, 1993) industries, from 1980 to 1993*

Firm	1980	1981	1982	1983	1984	1985	1986	1987	1988	1989	1990	1991	1992	1993
Nationalized '82, Privatized '86														
Saint-Gobain	Martin (X-Mines)	Fauroux (ENA-Fin)					Beffa (X-Mines)							
CGE (Alcatel-Alsthom)	Roux (X-Ponts/cab)		G. Pébereau (X-Ponts/cab)					Suard (X-Ponts/cab)						
Matra	Lagardère (Centrale/bus)													
Nationalized '82, Privatized '93														
Rhône-Poulenc	Gandois (X-Ponts)			Le Floch-Prigent (cab)				Fourtou (X/bus)						
Nationalized '82														
Thomson	Walhain (bus)	Bouyssonnie (X-Maritime)	Gomez (ENA-Fin)											
Péchiney	Thomas (ENA-Fin/cab)		Besse (X-Mines)		Pache (X-Mines/cab)			Gandois (X-Ponts)						
Dassault	Vallières & (Aéro/bus)	M. Dassault (family)						S. Dassault (X-Aéro/family)						
Sacilor	Mayoux (ENA-Fin/cab)		Dollé (HEC/cab)				Mer (X-Mines/cab)							
Usinor	Etchegaray (X-Harvard MBA/bus)		Lévy (X-Mines)		Loubert (X-Mines)		Mer (X-Mines/cab)							
Bull	Brulé (X/bus)		Stern (X-Aéro)						Lorentz (HEC-ENA/bus)				Pache (X-Mines)	Descarpentrie (X-bus)

Table 10.3. CEOs of major banks and insurers, from 1980 to 1993

Nationalized '82 Privatized '86

Firm	1980	1981	1982	1983	1984	1985	1986	1987	1988	1989	1990	1991	1992	1993
Société Générale	Lauré (X-Fin)		Mayoux (ENA-Fin/cab)					Vienot (ENA-Fin/cab)						
Paribas	Moussa (NmSup-Fin/cab)		Haberer (ENA-Fin/cab)				François-Poncet (IEP/bus)				Lévy-Lang (X-Stanford DBA/bus)			
Suez	Caplain (ENA-Fin)	Malet (X-Mines/cab)	Plescoff (ENA-Fin/cab)	Peyrelevade (X-IEP/cab)			de la Genière (ENA-Fin/cab)				Worms (X-Mines/cab)			
Crédit Agricole[a]	Lallement (Fin/cab)	Bonnot (law-pol/bus)				Huchon (ENA-Fin/cab)	Auberger (ENA-Fin/cab)		Barsalou (bus)					

Privatized '93

Firm	1980	1981	1982	1983	1984	1985	1986	1987	1988	1989	1990	1991	1992	1993
BNP	Calvet (ENA-Fin/cab)		Thomas (ENA-Fin)											M. Pébereau (X-ENA-Fin/cab)

Nationalized '82

Firm	1980	1981	1982	1983	1984	1985	1986	1987	1988	1989	1990	1991	1992	1993
Crédit Lyonnais	Pierre-Brossolette (ENA-Fin/cab)		Deflassieux (HEC/bus/cab)				Levêque (ENA-Fin/pol)		Haberer (ENA-Fin/cab)					Peyrelevade (X-IEP/cab)
UAP	Esteva (ENA-Fin/cab)		Chassagne (ENA-Comptes)				Dromer (ENA-Fin/cab)		Peyrelevade (X-IEP/cab)					
AGF	Plescoff (ENA-Fin)		Albert (ENA-Fin)											
GAN	Verdeil (ENA-Fin/cab)			Attali (ENA-Comptes)			Heilbronner (ENA-Fin/cab)							

[a] Crédit Agricole was "mutualized" but not privatized, such that its control was given over to the regional Caisses.

Table 10.4. *CEOs of major public industries, from 1980 to 1993*

Firm	1980	1981	1982	1983	1984	1985	1986	1987	1988	1989	1990	1991	1992	1993
EDF	Boiteux (IEP-NmSup/bus)						Delaporte (X-Ponts/cab)							
Renault	Vernier-Palliez (HEC-IEP-law/bus)		Hanon (HEC-Columbia PhD/bus)		Besse (X-Mines)			Lévy (X-Mines)					Schweitzer (ENA-Fin/cab)	
ELF	Chalandon (ENA-Fin/minister)		Pecqueur (X-Mines)							Le Floch-Prigent (cab)				Jaffré (ENA-Fin/cab)
CFP (Total)	Granier de Lilliac (X-Mines)					Ortoli (ENA-Fin/minister)					Tchuruk (X-Armement/bus)			
GDF	Alby (X-Mines/cab)								Fournier (ENA-Conseil/gov)					
SNCF	Pélissier (Agro/prefect/cab)	Chadeau (IEP-law/prefect/cab)			Essig (X-Ponts)									

corps.[41] Of the Socialist appointees to the major nationalized industries in the early eighties, all but one had been graduated from a *grande école,* all but two were also members of a *grand corps,* and these last two, along with three others, had been in a ministerial cabinet (see Table 10.2). Their predecessors, along with those whom the Socialists reconfirmed, were no less elite, albeit somewhat less state-centered in their credentials, with half having spent their entire careers in business. In banking and insurance, similarly, only one out of twelve Socialist appointees had not attended a *grande école* and three were not members of a *grand corps,* whereas all of their predecessors were elite graduate members of a *grand corps* (see Table 10.3).

For all their focus on elite credentials, however, the Socialists did not therefore totally ignore business experience in their appointments. In the first place, over 40% of Socialist appointees in major public industries, long-standing as well as newly nationalized, consisted of heads in place before the Socialist victory. They did not touch the heads of such groups as Saint-Gobain, Rhône-Poulenc, EDF, GDF, CFP (Total), Dassault, and Matra (see Tables 10.2 and 10.4). Moreover, many of the new Socialist appointees had extensive industry experience, either in the same firm or in a related industry. For example, Raymond Lévy, a graduate of X and the School of Mines, and thus a member of the mining corps (X-Mines), had managed the oil company Elf-Aquitaine before being named in April 1981 to head the Usinor special steel subsidiary, and then the following year to head all of Usinor. Alain Gomez, although an ENA-Finances, had spent only five years in the Ministry of Finance before going to work for Saint-Gobain, where he passed his entire career before being appointed head of the electronics company Thomson. Similarly, although Jean-Louis Beffa was an X-Mines with seven years in the Ministry of Industry, he had had eleven years of experience in the firm, and four in the number two spot as Director-General, before his elevation to CEO at Saint-Gobain.

Beffa's appointment, however, was also testimony to the Socialists' willingness to take the recommendation of the previous head, Roger Fauroux (an ENA-Finances). This was equally true in a number of other appointments: At CGE, Georges Pébereau, a graduate of X and the École des Ponts et Chaussées, and therefore a member of the bridge-building corps (an X-Ponts) with ministerial cabinet experience, but also with years of experience in the firm, was the anointed successor to Ambroise Roux (also an X-Ponts, with ministerial cabinet experience). And at Re-

---

[41]See: Elie Cohen, "L'état Socialiste en industries: Volontarisme politique et changement socio-économique," in *Les élites Socialistes au pouvoir (1981–1985)* (Paris: Presses Universitaires de France, 1985).

nault, Bernard Hanon, a graduate of the business *grande école,* HEC (the École des Hautes Études en Commerce), with an M.B.A. and Ph.D. from Columbia, whose career had been entirely in business, was the choice of Pierre Dreyfus, the CEO up to 1975 and the first Socialist Minister of Industry. (The previous two heads appointed between the early fifties and eighties were the choice of the board of directors.)

Political affiliation, moreover, did not play a major role in the appointments to industry. Of those heads newly appointed, most had no clear political affiliation, such as Bernard Pache, president of Péchiney and an X-Mines with cabinet experience. Some, however, had clear right-wing affiliations, such as Jean-Yves Habérer, an ENA-Finances, named head of Paribas, who was a classmate and friend of Jacques Chirac at the ENA, was cabinet director of a number of right-wing ministers, and served as director of the Treasury from 1978 to 1982, under Barre as well as under the Socialist Mauroy; and Edouard Balladur (ENA-Finances), reappointed as head of two subsidiaries of CGE even though he had been secretary general at the Elysée under Pompidou and was subsequently to become Chirac's Minister of Finance and the Economy in the neoliberal government of 1986–1988. Even where political affiliation was clear, as in the case of Claude Dollé, a graduate of HEC and a Socialist former member of Pierre Dreyfus's cabinet who was named to head Sacilor, industry experience probably weighed more heavily: he had been a commercial director of a medium-sized firm marketing steel products, linked with the Belgian Cockerill group.

Politics did play a larger role in the appointments to the nationalized banks and insurance companies, where the Socialists had decided to replace all former heads for politically symbolic reasons (see Table 10.3). But even here, experience played a large part. For the bank nationalizations, cases in point are Jacques Bonnot at the Crédit Agricole, who had a law degree and an entire career in banking, and Jean Deflassieux at the Crédit Lyonnais, a graduate of HEC who started at the bank he was later to head, although he had also had ministerial cabinet experience (1956–1957). This was equally true for the insurance companies, although here, the appointees also had impeccable elite credentials along with distinguished civil service careers: Yvette Chassagne, named president of the Union des Assurances de Paris (UAP), was a graduate of the ENA and member of the accounting corps (ENA-Comptes), and Bernard Attali, president of the Groupe des Assurances Nationales (GAN), was also an ENA-Comptes (he later became head of Air France).

In both industry and finance, however, there were a few individuals who did not fit the traditional profile and had not had major responsibilities in business prior to their appointments. The fact that, in interviews, almost all top ministry and industry officials, whether on the left or the right, were quick to point this out demonstrates how painfully aware they all were of the exceptions to the rule.[42] But even the exceptions had some claim to elite status; and they were certainly not the union leaders or grass-roots activists the right might have expected. Thus, although Loïk le Floch-Prigent had not held positions of great importance in industry prior to his appointment as chairman of Rhône-Poulenc in July 1982, and did not have an elite education, having attended the polytechnic of Grenoble and the University of Missouri, he was not a total outsider, having been Pierre Dreyfus's cabinet director in the Ministry of Industry (1981–1982). Moreover, appointments such as this one, or that of Jean Peyrelevade (a graduate of X and the Institut d'Études Politiques, nevertheless), made head of Suez in 1984, occurred only because Prime Minister Pierre Mauroy insisted on appointing people outside the usual circuits, as did Jacques Delors, himself not a product of the elite education system (even if his daughter, Martine Aubry, Minister of Labor in the Cresson and Bérégovoy governments, was).

With these exceptions, throughout their first mandate, the Socialists appointed to the nationalized firms individuals who, if anything, had greater elite status than those who had headed them before. Moreover, according to a study carried out in 1985, there was little variation in this across the five years of their government,[43] and this despite the fact that in 1983, the Socialist government itself seemed to suggest that there was a difference when it made a point of stating that, from then on, its appointments were to be based on professional qualifications above all.[44]

Further substantiation for the fact that the Socialists' main criteria for appointment were based on traditional elite credentials is the commentary of one of the major proponents of denationalization, Pierre Moussa (ENA-Finances), former president of Paribas (1978–1981). Even before the right's return to power, Moussa not only admitted that the worst had been avoided with nationalization because capable presidents were appointed, he also recommended retaining those self-same presidents in place for a time in order to ensure against any problems with denationalization related to rapid management turnover.[45] And the new government seemed to have heeded his advice, changing only twelve out of twenty-five heads of the nationalized industries in July 1986, and only fourteen out of twenty-nine bankers in September 1986 (although more changes came later).

The neoliberal government's appointments, moreover, seemed to have had more to do with political coloration than they did either with a

[42]In over forty interviews with the author between February and July 1991, all noted these exceptions to the rule.
[43]Bauer and Mourot, *Les 200*, p. 187.   [44]*Le Monde*, May 11, 1991.
[45]*Le Monde*, February 5, 1986.

commitment to neoliberalism or with some new kind of free-marketeering credential. Other than for political affiliation, the profile of the new heads was quite similar to that of the heads under the Socialist government as well as under previous régimes. There were no self-made individuals here. All new appointments were of men with elite credentials, while the reappointments primarily depended upon track record, even if there were certainly a number of politically inspired appointments and dismissals.

The neoliberals, although replacing many socialist appointees for political reasons, also reappointed a certain number (see Tables 10.2, 10.3, and 10.4). Holdovers included such clearly left-aligned heads as Chassagne of UAP and Gomez of Thomson, as well as Beffa of Saint-Gobain and Michel Albert (ENA-Finances) of AGF. The fired encompassed such heads clearly identified with the Socialists and, for the most part, without elite credentials as Peyrelevade of Suez, replaced by Renaud de La Génière, an ENA-Finances with ministerial cabinet experience, whose credentials were similar to those of Peyrelevade's predecessors; Claude Dollé of Sacilor, a graduate of HEC with experience in a ministerial cabinet, replaced by Francis Mer, an X-Mines with cabinet experience who, as simultaneous head of Usinor, replaced another X-Mines with cabinet experience, René Loubert; Deflassieux of Crédit Lyonnais, succeeded by Jean-Maxime Levèque, an ENA-Finances; Le Floch-Prigent of Rhône-Poulenc, displaced by René Fourtou, a graduate of X who had spent most of his career in business; and Jean-Pierre Huchon of the Crédit Agricole, an ENA-Finances with experience in a ministerial cabinet, who was followed by another ENA-Finances with cabinet experience, Bernard Auberger.

Some nonaligned heads also rolled, such as Pébereau of CGE, replaced by Pierre Suard, also an X-Mines with cabinet experience; and Pache of Péchiney, succeeded by Jean Gandois, an X-Ponts thereby pushing out an X-Mines. Even some heads clearly identified with the right whom the Socialists had kept on were fired, such as Habérer of Paribas, presumably because he had served his new masters too well, replaced by Michel François-Poncet, an IEP who had spent most of his career in business and was a good friend of Chirac. There were also the requisite number of rewards for services rendered, as when Jacques Friedmann, who helped draft the privatization legislation before the right gained power and subsequently became Balladur's right-hand man as *chargé de mission* in the cabinet of the Ministry of Finance, was made head of Air France in May 1987 (having refused the top position in any privatized firms on the grounds that it would not have looked right).[46]

---

[46]See the testimony of Edouard Balladur, Minister of Finance in Chirac's government, *Rapport sur les opérations de privatisation,* vol. 1, p. 7.

The next time around, moreover, after the Socialists' return in 1988, the recruitment pattern continued unchanged, with political criteria now being even less significant a factor. This time, however, they could appoint Socialist CEOs with a significant business track record, in particular many who had been turned out by the neoliberals, such as Peyrelevade, formerly of Suez, whom they named to UAP; Le Floch-Prigent, formerly of Rhône-Poulenc, to Elf-Aquitaine; and Attali, formerly of GAN, to Air France. Moreover, they also appointed non-Socialists who had also been fired by the neoliberals because they had served the Socialists, such as Habérer, formerly of Paribas, to Crédit Lyonnais.

The Socialists, however, also left in place a number of neoliberal appointees such as Raymond Lévy, an X-Mines, at Renault; Serge Dassault, the founder's heir but an X-Aéro nevertheless, at Dassault; Mer at Sacilor and Usinor; and even some who were clearly politically aligned with the right, such as François Heilbronner at GAN, an ENA-Finances, and Fourtou at Rhône-Poulenc. And it almost goes without saying that the Socialists also reconfirmed their own first-round appointees left in place by the neoliberals, such as Gomez of Thomson, Albert of AGF, and Thomas of the BNP.

Of the Socialists' new appointments, moreover, some were the anointed successors of the head, such as Francis Lorentz at Bull, a graduate of HEC and the ENA, and the longtime lieutenant of Jacques Stern, an X-Aéro. A handful also harkened back to the Socialists' earlier period of naming individuals with more ministry than industry experience. Louis Gallois, put in charge of SNECMA in 1989, the jet-engine manufacturer, had been Director-General of Industry under four Ministers (1982–1986), as well as earlier in Chevènement's cabinet in the Ministry of Industry and later in Defense (1988–1989). Others, however, had spent a few years in the company as second in command before being promoted, such as Louis Schweitzer, an ENA-Finances with cabinet experience, who was the number two at Renault for several years before being appointed head in 1992. And this seemed to be the new trend, with Daniel Lebègue, an ENA-Finances and former director of the Treasury, made the Director-General of the BNP, and clearly the heir apparent until the March 1993 elections. With the change in government, however, President René Thomas preferred to leave his place to Michel Pébereau, a former councilor to Giscard who was close to Balladur and an expert on privatization (having taken CCF private in 1987), because Thomas thought this might guarantee that the BNP would be high on the privatization list.[47]

The Balladur government actually proved to be no more politicized in its appointments than the more recent Socialist governments. Although

[47]*Le Nouvel Observateur,* September 30–October 6, 1993.

the requisite number of appointments of right-wing stalwarts were made (it is after all not only the privatization experience that made Thomas choose Pébereau over Lebègue), competence was as much a factor, as in the case of the appointment to head Elf of Philippe Jaffré, an *énarque* and inspector of finance who helped engineer the Socialists' "Great U-turn" in 1983, was number two in the Treasury in 1986 and a key player in the privatizations of the time, then went to the Stern Bank before landing as director-general of the Crédit Agricole in 1988, where he was responsible for the bank's "mutualization." In other cases, moreover, the replacement would in any case have been necessary given dissatisfaction with performance, as in the cases of Lorentz, who was blamed for many of Bull's problems, and was replaced by the budget-cutting Jean-Marie Descarpentrie, an X with private sector experience, having gone from Saint-Gobain to president of Carnaud Metall-Box; Habérer, whose overly ambitious acquisitions were seen as responsible for Crédit Lyonnais's red ink, who was replaced by Peyrelevade, a darling of the left who had been fired by the right in 1986; and Attali, who resigned when his restructuring plan was withdrawn by the government in response to a strike, to be replaced by Christian Blanc, previously head of the RATP.

The privatized companies did not change their heads either (see Tables 10.2 and 10.3). Of the privatized banks, de la Génière remained at Suez; Marc Vienot, an ENA-Finances, at the Société Générale; and François-Poncet at Paribas until 1991, when he was replaced by André Lévy-Lang, an X with a Stanford D.B.A. who had spent much of his career in business. Of the privatized industries, Beffa continued to head Saint-Gobain; Suard, CGE (now Alcatel-Alsthom); and Jean-Luc Lagardère, Matra, of which he was in charge before, during, and after nationalization. Thus, despite the fact that Balladur had promised that privatization was to rid industry of the suffocating effects of the "state bourgeoisie,"[48] this very bourgeoisie remained as the companies it controlled were transferred from public to private sector.

Moreover, the way in which Balladur had set up the privatizations (by often getting the CEOs themselves to pick the major shareholders in the *noyau dur,* many of whom were to have seats on the board) ensured that his appointees to head the nationalized companies slated for privatization would remain at their head once privatized.[49] What is more, he ensured that the right, and in particular individuals close to the RPR, would predominate in these firms, not only in the persons of the CEOs who would be kept on, but in that of the members of the hard core. In fact, many of the dominant members of the *noyau dur* were CEOs with close

[48]Edouard Balladur, *Je crois en l'homme plus que l'état* (Paris: Flammarion, 1987).
[49]See the *Rapport sur les opérations de privatisation.*

Table 10.5. *CEOs of major private industries, from 1980 to 1993*

Firm	1980	1981	1982	1983	1984	1985	1986	1987	1988	1989	1990	1991	1992	1993
PSA (Peugeot)	Parayre (X-Ponts/cab)		Calvet (ENA-Comptes/cab)											
Carrefour	Defforey (founder)										Bon (IEP-ENA-Fin/bus)			
Michelin	Michelin (inheritor)													
Bouygues	Bouygues (Centrale/founder)													
IBM France	Lemonnier (Centrale/bus)							Barazer (X/bus)						
Générale des Eaux	Dejouany (X-Ponts)													
Lyonnaise des Eaux	Monod (ENA-Comptes/cab)													
BSN	Riboud (founder/inheritor)													
Shell France	Carous (bus)					Pradier (X/bus)								

ties to the RPR, such as Jérôme Monod, president of the Lyonnaise des Eaux and on the board of Havas, who had been general secretary of the RPR; Michel François-Poncet, president of Paribas and also member of the *noyau dur* of Havas, who was a friend of Jacques Chirac; and Heilbronner, president of GAN, member of the hard core of Paribas and Société Générale, and also a friend of the Prime Minister.

Throughout the decade, in brief, the major nationalized and privatized firms were led for the most part by CEOs with elite educational credentials and *grand corps* membership. The pattern was quite different from the major private industries that had not been touched by either nationalization or privatization (see Table 10.5). Here, the large majority were business people who sometimes had elite schooling, but rarely elite schooling and *grand corps* membership. Among the banks, by contrast, even in the few that had not been nationalized or privatized, *corps* members predominated, and the *passerelle* between public and private remained open. Thus, Jean-Marie Messier, an *inspecteur de finances*, graduate of X and the ENA, director of the cabinet of the delegated Minister for privatization Camille Cabana, and technical councilor in the cabinet of Minister of Finance Balladur, in 1988 moved to the Lazard Bank as managing partner (having turned down numerous offers from privatized firms such as Saint-Gobain, as well as banking concerns such as Marceau-Investissements, on the grounds that it would not have looked right).[50]

Government takeover, in short, sanctified elite domination of the upper managerial ranks of business, despite ideological commitments which might have suggested a rejection of elite domination in favor of either socialist equality or neoliberal entrepreneurialism. Why was this the case?

THE VALUES OF THE NEW MANAGERIAL ELITE AND THE ISSUE OF DEMOCRATIC CONTROL OF THE FIRM

The members of the new managerial elite were quite different from the old in terms of their more dynamic approach to management, their greater openness to new management techniques such as participative management, and their age.[51] They were members of a younger generation, most of whom would probably in the end have acceded to the top position in the firm, but certainly not all. They resembled the older generation of business heads in one major way other than sharing elite background: they, too, believed that political ideology had little to do with manage-

---

[50]Testimony of Jean-Marie Messier, *Rapport sur les opérations de privatisation*, vol. 1, pp. 206–207.
[51]See Chapter 14.

ment. And they therefore did not try to imbue the firm with socialist or neoliberal values.

When asked why Socialist CEOs did not seek to imbue the firm with socialist values (whatever that might mean), almost all the business executives queried responded with the same refrain: "There is no such thing as management of the left or the right, there is only good management or bad management." This was as much the view of top managers on the left such as Lebègue of the BNP[52] as those on the right such as Gandois of Péchiney,[53] as it was for those who claimed no political allegiance whatsoever, such as Jean Grenier, head of Eutelsat and former top manager for France Télécom (as head of international operations), who noted that although the political may have intruded in the firing of people at the very top at France Télécom, none of this affected management lower down: "Underneath, the rest remained the same, and there was no political pressure to change anything in management."[54]

Only a handful of Socialist top managers, moreover, went on to suggest that socialist values could nevertheless be involved in some way in management. Thus, one Socialist banker insisted that socialist values served to differentiate what came afterwards, once the money was earned, in determining how to spend it, because while "capitalists take profits, socialists think of consumers, the community, and basically, all the social responsibility issues."[55] In most cases, however, it is as if the Socialists felt that ownership by the state of the means of production was sufficient, that, in the words of the head of Renault, Louis Schweitzer, socialism was in the very fact of nationalization, as proof that an enterprise could function well with the state as shareholder, that the state could ameliorate its efficiency (*efficacité*), and that it could do so within a market economy without seeking to protect nationalized enterprises from competition.[56] Schweitzer, like others, also noted that this went together with greater worker democracy through the Auroux laws on worker participation and those specifically for public enterprises. But such democracy did not extend to participation in top-management decision-making, or to *autogestion,* the rallying cry of the more grass-roots left in the seventies.

In the seventies, discussions of democratic control of the firm were focused at all three main components of economic enterprise: capital, management, and labor. Nationalization, and the participation of employees on the boards of directors, was to ensure democratic control at the top, in the capital of the firm; worker participation would ensure it at

---

[52]Lebègue, interview with author.   [53]Gandois, interview with author.
[54]Jean Grenier, Director-General of Eutelsat, formerly a top manager of France Télécom. Interview with author, Paris, April 17, 1991.
[55]Deflassieux, interview with author.   [56]Schweitzer, interview with author.

the bottom, for labor in its relationship with management; and *autogestion* was to ensure it in the middle, at the level of management.

With their accession to power, the Socialist government proceeded to fulfill expectations for democratic control in only two of the three areas: in terms of capital and labor, but not management. Nationalization, by establishing state ownership of the means of production and state appointment of the CEO, brought indirect forms of democratic control of capital by the government as representatives of the people. The law on public enterprises produced a more direct democratic control by labor of capital by establishing a tripartite system of representation on the board of directors of the nationalized enterprises: one-third salaried employees (i.e., six representatives from the labor force), one-third state representatives (i.e., six state appointees), one-third *"personalités qualifiées"* (i.e., six outside experts). The *lois Auroux* brought greater democratic control by labor of their working conditions, by setting up a requirement for regular direct worker–management consultation.

Whether these forms of democratic control actually led to real democratic control remains open to question: Although workers were given a voice on the boards of directors, they were not given a majority voice or control over the enterprise. Moreover, we have already seen that the boards of directors tended in any case to be rubber stamps of the CEOs' decisions, and lacked veto power over top management's decisions. Finally the Auroux laws, although ensuring greater communication between management and labor, reducing friction while enhancing performance and productivity, effectively weakened unions and the labor cohesiveness that is important for collective bargaining success.[57]

Whatever their effect, however, at least these forms of democratic control were passed. This was not the case with *autogestion,* or worker control over managerial decisions, which was never even contemplated because, unlike the first two forms that had a large constituency pushing for them, between traditional socialists and labor, the *autogestionnaires* were neither mainstream socialists nor mainstream labor sorts. They therefore had much less clout. Even though prior to their arrival in power, the Socialists had adopted the *autogestionnaires'* language and recommendations, they were never really serious about putting their proposals into practice. (The language, however, did convince the bulk of heads of businesses that they were serious. In a SOFRES-Expansion poll of 1976, a full 70% of those interviewed thought that if the left came to power in 1977, *autogestion* initiatives would be undertaken in a number of enter-

[57]See the discussion in Chapter 14.

prises.)[58] Just as the decentralization reforms never incorporated laws focused on encouraging local democracy through citizen participation and referenda, so the nationalization reforms never included laws providing democratic control of management of the kind recommended by the *autogestionnaires*. Moreover, whereas there was no clear constituency pushing for reform, there was one resisting such reform: top managers.

What little discussion there was of socialist management before nationalization suggested that there would be few "socialist" changes to the firm once the Socialists took power. Among managers, not only was there no support for the democratization of managerial power or *autogestion,* there was not even any theorizing about what such management might look like. At best, there was talk of Japanese management, quality circles, and management participation. But these were quite obviously not seen as socialist ways of managing; they were simply different or more modern ways of managing, with often better results. And in any case they were more focused on democratically managing labor, than on democratically controlling management.

Already three years before the Socialists' accession to power, one of the leading "pink" managers, Alain Gomez, at the time senior vice-president at Saint-Gobain but soon to become head of the newly nationalized Thomson, and who was also together with Chevènement one of the founders of the CERES, tellingly argued that within the context of a government of the right, "there was no difference between a *patron,* or boss, of the right and of the left: he is required to work within the rules of the game established by the environment and the society."[59] Those rules did not change with nationalization and a government of the left.

Moreover, while Gomez saw no possibility for socialist internal management practices because of the external environment, his wife at the time, Francine Gomez (who had a reputation for being more on the right in any case), then CEO of Waterman, was equally negative about the possibility of democratizing recruitment and promotion practices because of internal managerial necessities. She contended, specifically, that "you can't always be liked; you can't have the CEO elected, or you would end up like politicians. And then the best will not necessarily be in charge."[60]

[58]Jean Boissonnat, ed., *Les Socialistes face aux patrons* (Paris: L'Expansion/Flammarion, 1977), p. 212.

[59]Interview with Alain Gomez in "Patrons '78–91," a documentary film by Gérard Mordillat and Nicolas Philibert, produced first in 1978 but censored at the time because François Dalle, CEO of L'Oréal, among others, objected. This was at a time when the PDG had not been used to seeing themselves on TV, in interviews. They objected to the editing job.

[60]Interview with Francine Gomez in "Patrons."

Similarly, François Dalle, then CEO of L'Oréal and a close friend of President Mitterrand, contended that "One has to avoid ideology. Men can't manage themselves; they need to find a leader."[61] Recently, moreover, Beffa of Saint-Gobain explained that "When we did experiments with *autogestion*, or self-management, we found that parliamentary democracy is not necessarily adapted to the management of enterprises."[62]

At a time when the *autogestion* movement was in its heyday, then, top managers with ties to the Socialists seemed to intimate that the more democratic forms of management demanded by activists were not to be. Why, then, should we wonder that Socialist managers, once placed at the head of industries and banks nationalized by their comrades, did not seek to infuse the firm with socialist values?

In fact, infusing the firm with socialist values was one of the farthest things from the minds of most of the new Socialist heads of the nationalized firms. Rather, they sought to defend their firms against any encroachments by the Socialist government, and to ensure that the government continued to respect the traditional autonomy of French public enterprise. In other words, the CEOs resisted even democratic control of capital by way of the government. This was as true of those without elite corps membership, such as Peyrelevade, as it was of those who were nurtured by it.

Thus, the CEOs of the nationalized enterprises effectively sought to manage their companies with the same kind of independence, and lack of interference, as private sector firms. And they succeeded quite well at this. This is why, even at the height of the Socialist nationalizations, it was possible for a top Ministry of Industry official to respond, when asked to distinguish the operation of the newly nationalized companies from private ones, "I can't tell you, I don't see any differences."[63]

But are there any differences, then, between managers of the left and those of the right? A top manager clearly aligned at least in the early eighties with the Socialists and subsequently considered the pivot of the new establishment, Peyrelevade, agreed that "We are, it is true, very 'business-minded.'" But he still saw a difference because he found that CEOs of the left have a longer-term view and probably different relations with labor from such owner-capitalists as Bernard Arnault (Louis Vuitton Moët-Hennessy – LVMH), Jacky Letertre (Duménil Bank), or Vincent Bolloré (Bolloré Technologies).[64] But this is the extent of it.

Certainly none on the left felt any obligation to the Socialist Party, including the left-leaning CEOs appointed by the Socialists. For

[61]Interview with François Dalle in "Patrons."   [62]Beffa, interview with author.
[63]Quoted in Smith, "Nationalizations for What?" p. 90.   [64]*Le Monde,* May 11, 1991.

Peyrelevade, it was "The interest of the enterprise first."[65] And this may
in part explain how it was that Peyrelevade at UAP refused to go along
with the raid on the Société Générale in the fall of 1988 by Georges
Pébereau. Pébereau launched the raid at the behest of Pierre Bérégovoy,
who perceived the board of directors of the privatized bank as too favorable to the RPR. This is how Peyrelevade gained the name of "godfather
of the mixed economy," coined by the *Wall Street Journal*.[66]

CONCLUSION

The new administrative and managerial elites, in short, are no more
politically socialist in their actions than the old, nor are they any less elite.
They are, if anything, more elite in their educational background and
membership in the *grands corps*. After the wide swings in ideology, from
socialist to neoliberal, and in policy, from nationalization to privatization
to the *ni-ni* and beyond, it is safe to conclude that the leadership of
ministry and industry has been renewed; we cannot say that it has been
remade.

[65] *Le Monde*, May 11, 1991.   [66] *L'Express*, May 2, 1991.

11

Explaining elite dominance

The elite pattern of recruitment, as we have seen and contrary to what one might have expected from ideologically driven governments intent on changing the state, was actually reinforced during this period through the extension of elite domination in ministries and industries alike. Why did this occur? Following traditional elite theorists, we could simply argue that this was inevitable, a product of the iron law of oligarchy, of the circulation of elites, and of the bureaucratic conservation of any party in power. Certainly much of this can be supported by evidence of an elite training system which, although meritocratic in its policy of admissions through competitive examination, nevertheless is predominantly upper-middle-class in recruitment, and creates an elite that perpetuates itself through the *grand corps* system that monopolizes major government and business positions. Neo-Marxists, beyond this, would have us see the lack of change in this system as the result of the constraints under which all governing parties in capitalist society operate, and which ensure that the state serves the long-term interests of the bourgeoisie. Certainly this explains in large measure why no governing party of the left or the right, regardless of its promises, significantly challenged the elite recruitment or promotion system. The Socialists themselves, needless to say, would bridle at any suggestion that their purpose was to serve the interests of the bourgeoisie, arguing instead that their economic policies served the interests of all, and that their recruitment policies in particular conformed to the principle of economic efficiency, which dictated that the best-qualified, regardless of origins, be put at the head of ministries and industries. But French critics also see it as a phenomenon of caste, with the Socialist appointments in the early eighties a case of generational change in elites, with elites of the left replacing those of the right and ultimately, by the nineties, intermingling to form a single elite more united by its *corporatisme* than it is divided by politics.

Although all of these explanations provide insight, they do not do

314

enough to explain why there was so little consciousness on the part of the leaders of the way in which adherence to the traditional pattern of elite recruitment might undermine their overall goals, and little conscious attempt to alter the pattern. To account for this, another kind of explanation is necessary, one that considers culture and institutions. In France, it is the culture of the state, embodied in its institutions and embedded in the minds, words, and actions of its citizens, that so pervades the society at large that it would have been foolish to assume that any government, left or right, would have sought to refuse its representatives, that is, those trained for state service, their rightful place at its head. The hold that the state continues to have over French leaders, both as concept and as concrete representation, ensures that they could not have imagined change coming against the state, only through it. Thus, the Socialists nationalized in order to have greater control over the economy through the state – and assumed without question that those trained for state service would be the ones to ensure that control. Moreover, although the neoliberals may have inveighed against the state, they never sought to dismantle it or deny its privileges to those trained for it, only to diminish its purview. Even the latest changes in the relationship between ministry and industry under the governments of 1988 and beyond have not denied the French state continued influence over French business. For at a time when direct government control of business, regardless of ownership, is no longer feasible, given the deregulation and internationalization of the economy along with the Europeanization of industrial policy, the state maintains its hold not only through more indirect policy tools but also through the colonization of French business by state-trained former civil servants.

THE RATIONALE FOR THE ELITE PROFILE IN MINISTRY AND INDUSTRY

Why did the Socialists, who came to power vowing to alter the capitalist system, do little or nothing to change the system that put the control of the ministries and industries in the hands of a small elite consisting of the upper-middle-class products of elite schools who were members of the prestigious civil service corps? And why did the neoliberals who came to power promising to engineer the retreat of the state in an effort to promote laissez-faire capitalism do equally little to change this?

The importance of history, education, and corps membership

It is, in fact, not so difficult to understand why the neoliberals did not seek to go back on this elite pattern of recruitment. The neoliberals, after all, had only recently been reborn as laissez-faire capitalists, having been statist and credentialist in the twenty-three years they had been in power before the Socialist victory of 1981. This pattern of appointment to the nationalized industries had been their own prior to the Socialists' stay in power. Many of their own, moreover, had become accustomed to the comfort of knowing that they could move into a high-level private sector position after years in the public sector. Moreover, as we have already seen, the commitment to neoliberalism of those in positions of the greatest power in the appointment process to ministries and industries (i.e., Chirac and Balladur) was moderate at best. What is more, they and their staffs, as noted above, were themselves products of that self-same elite educational system and members of the most prestigious of the *grands corps*.

In short, whatever the rhetoric of entrepreneurialism and laissez-faire capitalism, the reality was otherwise. The neoliberals did not seek to appoint as heads of the nationalized firms entrepreneurs or self-made individuals who had a demonstrable commitment to laissez-faire capitalism or ability in free-marketeering methods. Moreover, it was said that the firms that were chosen to constitute the *noyau dur* or hard core of shareholders were often picked more on the basis of their friendships with the Prime Minister than on their neoliberal or entrepreneurial flair. Only the acquisition of TF1 by Francis Bouygues, the construction magnate (although himself a graduate of Centrale) could be said to fit the neoliberal logic. What is more, that the privatized industries and banks did not see fit to turn out the CEOs who had been placed there by neoliberals and Socialists alike is probably as much testimony to their good business sense – after all, these were good managers, and too much turnover is never good for a company – and their loyalty to the men who had in many cases chosen them to be members of their hard core of investors, as to their own comfort with their elite credentials.

But why, one must ask, did the Socialists, who had vowed to make radical social changes, respect the traditional elite recruitment patterns when they appointed new heads of the nationalized industries or directors in the ministries rather than try to engineer some kind of social revolution? The Socialists themselves would tell us that the answer to this question lies in their commitment to social justice and economic efficiency, two concepts which have their origins in the Socialist program of 1944.[1] In 1944, the Socialists were considering wide-scale nationalization and how "to manage these enterprises democratically, inspire them with socialist principles, allow them autonomy, and yet operate them efficiently." Social justice, or the desire for democracy, was served by the

[1]Kuisel, *Capitalism*, p. 175.

worker democracy laws (the *lois Auroux* and the 1983 law on public enterprises) and state ownership of the means of production. Economic efficiency, however, could only be appropriately ensured by recruiting those with top-managerial qualifications, that is, those with elite educational and career histories, and by allowing them autonomy in running the firm. As for the postwar pledge that the nationalized enterprises were to be inspired by socialist principles, this seems to have disappeared altogether. Certainly neither the new managers nor the government thought to infuse the firm with socialist principles in any way other than through the worker democracy laws and, in the nationalized enterprises, through employee membership on the board of directors (*conseil d'administration*).[2]

Thus, while Pierre Mauroy declared that the main objective of his government was "to become a major governmental party and to make major social reforms compatible with the management of the economy imposed by the international context," for Laurent Fabius, it was "the demonstration of the ability of the left to manage the economy while promoting social justice."[3] The Socialists were much more interested in the successful implementation of their programs than in questioning the pedigree of those charged with implementing them, especially given the fact that many government leaders had that very same pedigree (e.g., Fabius, Rocard), and that most assumed, in any event, that these were the best-qualified individuals for the job.

After all, these were the individuals recognized by the society at large as truly meriting their positions, having succeeded in the rigorous educational system which privileges those who are capable of passing more and more arduous written and oral tests – in particular in the areas of math, physics, and economics. This begins with entrance exams for the *lycées*, already a weeding-out process, because only some prepare for the *bacs* which are in turn necessary for entry into the more prestigious schools of higher education (in particular the *bac C*, physics and math, and the *bac B*, economics). It continues through the *bac* and the entrance exams to the *grandes écoles*, for which students often take up to three years of preparatory classes. It ends with the exit exams of the *grandes écoles*, in which the rank ordering of the graduates determines which *grands corps*, if any, they may enter.[4]

In theory at least, given the open examination process, the system is blind as to social origin; in practice, the children of the upper middle

[2]See Chapter 4.   [3]*Le Monde*, May 10, 1991.

[4]See: Marie-Christine Kessler, *Les grands corps de l'état* (Paris: Presses de la Fondation Nationale des Sciences Politiques, 1986). For an anthropological look at the educational experience of the ENA, see: Irène Bellier, *L'Ena comme si vous y étiez* (Paris: Seuil, 1993).

classes, or "the inheritors" who have all the advantages, benefit the most. But although this has led many over the years to clamor for a more democratic recruitment process, there have been comparatively few successful challenges to the basic premises of the recruitment system, which allows access to the uppermost reaches of the civil service only through the educational system, such that moving up the ranks from lower levels is not possible (except through the internal competition process for the ENA). The main reason for this is the hold the products of that educational system have over the entire system through the *grands corps*.

The persistence of the elite recruitment pattern has to do not only with the competitive educational system which, through the process of elimination, funneled the best and the brightest toward state service, but also with the "*corporatisme*," or stick-togetherness of the *grands corps,* which seek to promote the careers of their members and to maintain their members, and theirs alone, at the head of major ministries and industries.[5] The technical corps (Mines, Ponts, Télécom, Aéro) take care of their own through an efficient system. Generally, those in charge of the corps, in conjunction with the personnel directors of the concerned ministries (Industry, Infrastructure, PTT), decide on the position a young recruit is to take – the recruit has little choice in this, and may refuse a position only once or twice. The Corps des Mines tends to be the most *dirigiste,* even authoritarian, with regard to the placement of its members in jobs in state ministries, with the *chef de service,* or director, of the general council of the Mines in charge of careers, aided by a council of elders (*anciens,* or alumni). But corps members tend not to mind, given the jobs they do get, and often at a very young age – for example, Anne Lauvergeon (X-Mines), who at thirty replaced Jacques Attali as economic advisor to François Mitterrand. The Corps des Mines also looks after its own for those who go into industry, given the *grands patrons* who are corps members (e.g., Raymond Lévy, when president of Renault, was also vice-president of the Corps des Mines.)[6]

The *grands corps* watch over their members throughout their careers, and not only in the beginning. When they lose their jobs, they are helped to find other employment such that, as Jean Drômer (ENA-Finances, former head of UAP, now with Bernard Arnault at LVMH) suggests, "The objective is to keep the *compère* from being 'out of the picture.'"[7] This care to help one's own is most pronounced from the Corps des Mines, which is highly organized and hates losing a bastion, so much so

---

[5]For a full discussion of *corporatisme,* see: Bruno Jobert and Pierre Muller, *L'état en action: Politiques publiques et corporations* (Paris: Presses Universitaries de France, 1987).

[6]See *Le Monde,* June 19, 1991.   [7]*L'Express,* May 2, 1991.

that the graduates of the Mines even wrote an internal memo to express their concern over the appointment of non-X-Mines CEOs at Elf and CFP (Total), where the CEOs had traditionally been members of the corps.[8] In another case, one CEO recounts receiving an irate phone call from the head of the Corps de Mines when he fired a member of the corps.

The Inspection des Finances is reputedly not as aggressive. The members themselves tend to downplay the influence of their corps, which they claim offers them much less help than that received by members of the engineering corps.[9] By the same token, however, at the beginning of Prime Minister Cresson's tenure in office, with the proposed move to Bercy, the home of the ENA-Finances, of the Ministry of Industry, the main ministerial link of the Corps des Mines, many perceived the *Inspecteurs de Finances* as having gotten the upper hand in their competition with the *Mineurs,* who were now to be placed under the authority of their hereditary enemies. The fact that when all was said and done, only the Minister of Industry and his cabinet completed the move, allegedly because of space problems, suggests that the resistance of the corps to governmental whim won out. Moreover, the "delocalization" of the ENA as a school to Strasbourg, part of the decentralization policies of the Cresson government that was not reversed by the Balladur government, despite tremendous pressure from alumni, suggests that the *énarques* have themselves less control of the destiny of their members than they would like.

In any event, whatever their relative strength, the pressures from members of the *grands corps* who see most ministries and industries as their personal domain are notoriously hard to resist. This is why, despite the fact that there have been challenges to the *grand corps* system, none have managed to alter the *grands corps* or take away their privileges. The most notable challenge was the "revolt" against the ENA by sixty-eight students of the *promotion Charles de Gaulle* (class of 1972), who protested in 1971 the differential treatment of graduates on the basis of which ministry they entered and whether they became *administrateurs civils* rather than members of the *grands corps*. These students promised to refuse to join the *grands corps* upon graduation if changes were not forthcoming (four out of the six eligible carried through on the promise, joining the prefectoral corps rather than the Inspection des Finances).[10] But this too came to naught. The *grands corps* remain as Lüthy described them in the fifties, as constituting "a supreme and sovereign self-recruiting body, immune from political intervention, a rock against which all political storms beat ineffectively and in vain."[11]

[8]Bénédictine Bertin-Mourot, quoted in *Le Monde,* June 19, 1991.
[9]*Le Monde,* June 19, 1991.
[10]Suleiman, *Politics, Power, and Bureaucracy,* pp. 89–94 109–111.
[11]Herbert Luethy, *France Against Herself* (New York: Meridian Books, 1954), p. 17.

Upon its accession to power, moreover, the left did little to try to change this system. And this was despite early proclamations by Socialist Prime Minister Pierre Mauroy and the Communist Minister in charge of the civil service Anicet Le Pors that they would call into question the privileges of certain *grands corps* and the recruitment and training offered by the ENA,[12] proclamations that were already not nearly as radical as the proposed reforms in the Common Program of 1972, or the Communists' pronouncements of 1977 that had called for civil service recruitment from the universities by examination system. In tacit acceptance of the system as it was, the government only sought to democratize recruitment by opening a "third way" (the *troisième voie*) into the ENA to allow a select group of non-civil service recruits, including union leaders, grassroots activists, and the like, to enter the school. This, all agreed, proved not very successful, and was promptly abolished by the neoliberals in 1986. The Socialists subsequently set up a new, "third contest" (the *troisième concours*) in 1990 in which individuals under forty years of age who had eight years of professional activity or held an elective post were allowed to compete for ten or so reserved places in ENA in a process in which a select group of candidates for admission (in the first recruitment process, 40 or so out of 500 applicants) were offered special preparatory classes before taking the entrance exam to the ENA. In so doing, the Socialists hoped to democratize and diversify further the higher civil service without diluting its quality, as they were accused of with their first attempt at reform.

The neoliberals between 1986 and 1988 took another tack in the reform of the system by diminishing the size of the entrance class to the ENA. The stated goal of the neoliberal Deputy Minister of the Civil Service and the Plan, Hervé de Charette, however, was not focused so much on the elite system per se as it was on slimming down the administration to make it more efficient and thus "doing better with fewer" as well as on shaking up the civil service generally, by introducing a certain instability into the civil service which would "be enough to create a psychological change in their heads."[13] The means by which he chose to accomplish this, by cutting admission to the ENA in half in order to force ministers to look elsewhere for members of their cabinets, whether from the corps of "*attachés administratifs*" or even the private sector, linked fewer graduates of the ENA to a reduction in the size of the state, or "*moins d'ENA, moins d'État.*" Fewer *énarques,* however, really only entails greater elite status for those remaining. And the neoliberals, as we

[12]*Le Monde*, October 6, 1981 – cited in Pierre Birnbaum, "Que faire de l'état?" in *Les élites Socialistes au pouvoir: Les dirigeants Socialistes face à l'état 1981–1985*, ed. Pierre Birnbaum (Paris: Presses Universitaires de France, 1985), pp. 155–156.
[13]*Le Nouvel Observateur*, August 8–14, 1986.

have already seen, did nothing to question that elite status when it came to the appointments to the nationalized industries or to ministerial cabinets. But neither did the Socialists.

The role of political values, class, and caste

After all, the Socialists had little reason to distrust the graduates of the ENA and X. Elite education did not preclude left-wing values. In 1977, the executive bureau of the PS contained 19% *énarques*. In 1981, there were fourteen *énarques* in the Socialist group.[14] Moreover, among the generation of graduates of the ENA who were born between 1948 and 1966, a majority were solidly on the left, with 16.5% voting for the right, 1.1% for the extreme right, 3.5% for the Greens, and 53.5% for the left.[15] (This has been less true lately, however, with the classes of 1990 and 1991 coming from families in which 60% support the right as opposed to 40% for the left.)[16]

The new CEOs appointed in 1981, like the members of ministers' cabinets and heads of ministerial bureaus, were very much of this generation, in particular its earliest part. In the sixties, as students at the elite schools, they were part of a large majority who were solidly on the left (see Table 11.1). Among graduates of the École Nationale d'Administration who took the regular route (mainly students), those on the left made up 58.5% as opposed to 31.2% for the right. For those who took the ENA's alternate route, members of the civil service who are often older (up to the age of thirty), the differences were even more striking, with the left at 80.6% and the right at 11.1%. This division even went beyond the École Normale Supérieure, the humanities and sciences faculties, with 66.3% on the left and 17.1% on the right. The more technical professions were somewhat less on the left, although the graduates of the École des Mines, many of whom were themselves products of the École Polytechnique, or X (for which data is not available), remained decidedly on the left, at 54% versus 42.8% on the right. This was not the case for the less prestigious engineering school, Centrale, students' second choice behind the Polytechnique, where the right, at 46.9%, exceeded the left, at 44.2%; or the most prestigious business school, the École des Hautes Études Commerciales (HEC), where the right, at 48%, exceeded the left, at 45.2%.

Given this division, it is perhaps understandable that the Socialists, upon coming to power, turned for recruits to this generation of graduates of the ENA and of X-Mines, the most prestigious schools which prepare

[14]Pfister, *République des fonctionnaires*, p. 23; Kesler, *L'ENA*.
[15]Bellier, "Vocation," pp. 180–181.   [16]Ibid., p. 180.

exclusively for state service, and tended to ignore graduates of HEC, let alone Centrale, for top management positions. In so doing, they killed a number of birds with one stone: They renewed top managers and civil servants with a younger generation of appointees who were not only of the appropriate political color, but had legitimacy, given their elite educational background.

There was in consequence little need to worry that top managers and civil servants would sabotage the Socialists' efforts, as a result of either political conviction or incompetence. Thus, there was no thought of recourse to a dual system of management for the nationalized enterprises, such as that prescribed by Lenin in *State and Revolution,* where, because the bourgeois had to be kept on as managers of the industrial plants at least until such a time as the proletariat would be capable of taking over, party members were to oversee managers' decisions.[17] In fact, there was little or no attention to the class origins of the Socialists' appointments, the Socialists having little use for the sometime Marxian assumption that class background dictates beliefs and attitudes. Research indicates that they were justified in this view: there is little evidence to suggest that top managers' and civil servants' class status has any connection to their values.[18]

But regardless of values, bourgeois these managers and civil servants were. A quick look at the social class status of the parents of this cohort of future managers through an examination of the occupations of the fathers of graduates of the *grandes écoles* between 1966 and 1969 shows a clear bias toward upper-middle-class professions (see Table 11.2). Among graduates of the ENA's main route, of the groups that make up the Socialists' natural constituency, there are no children of workers and only 11.1% are children of middle managers, by contrast with 69.7% from the upper middle classes. The figures for the parents of the engineering school graduates are somewhat different: at Polytechnique, children of workers and middle managers together come to 15.1%, by contrast with 69.3% for the children of upper-middle-class professionals; and at the School of

---

[17]The relevant passage is: "We organize large-scale production from what capitalism has already created; we workers OURSELVES . . . shall reduce the role of the state officials to that of simply carrying out our instructions as responsible, moderately paid 'managers' (of course, with technical knowledge of all sorts, types and degrees)." V. I. Lenin, *State and Revolution* (New York: International Publishers, 1932), p. 42. In "Can the Bolsheviks Retain State Power?" (*Selected Works,* vol. 6, New York: International Publishers, 1940, pp. 269–270), Lenin expanded on this theme when he stated that the former capitalists who are to be employed in the service of the state will "have a higher rate of pay during the transition period. But we shall put them under comprehensive workers' control. . . . As for the organizational form of work, we shall not invent it, but shall take ready-made from capitalism the banks, syndicates, the best factories, experimental stations, academies, etc."

[18]See Suleiman, *Politics, Power, and Bureaucracy,* pp. 100–112.

Table 11.1. *Political allegiance of graduates of grandes écoles, in percentages (1966–1969)*

	ENA1[a]	ENA2[b]	Mines[c]	Polytech[d]	HEC[e]	Centrale[f]	NmSup[g]
Far Left	5.0	2.8	10.5	--	5.5	7.5	14.0
Left	28.3	36.1	33.8	--	28.6	30.6	45.6
Center Left	25.2	41.7	10.5	--	11.1	6.1	6.7
Center	4.0	5.5	18.0	--	20.0	27.6	10.9
Center Right	22.2	2.8	3.0	--	6.4	4.1	2.1
Right	5.0	2.8	9.8	--	21.6	15.2	4.1
Other	3.0	--	1.5	--	--	1.4	2.1
No response	7.1	8.3	12.8	--	6.8	7.5	14.5

Note: The studies were carried out over a three-year period, with the technical schools surveyed toward the end of that period.

[a] The first route into the ENA, taken by students.

[b] The second route into the ENA, taken by civil servants.

[c] École Nationale Supérieure des Mines, engineering students made up principally of graduates of Polytechnique and students from preparatory schools who passed the entrance exam.

[d] Data unavailable for the École Polytechnique.

[e] The second-ranked engineering school, after Polytechnique.

[f] École des Hautes Études de Commerce, the premier business school.

[g] École Normale Supérieure, the top academic faculty in humanities and sciences.

Source: Pierre Bourdieu, La noblesse de l'état: Grandes écoles et esprit de corps (Paris: Editions de Minuit, 1989), p. 354.

Mines, children of workers and middle managers come to 18.1% whereas those of upper-middle-class professionals are at 62.4%. Only the ENA's alternative route, open to civil servants, has a different recruitment pattern: it is the only place where the children of workers (13.9%) and farmers (13.9%), along with middle managers (16.6%), seem to have

Table 11.2. *Profession of fathers of graduates of grandes écoles, in percentages (1966–1969)*

	ENA1	ENA2	Mines	Polytech	HEC	Centrale	NmSup
Agriculture	3.0	13.9	5.2	2.3	1.8	4.8	2.6
Worker	0.0	13.9	5.3	3.9	.7	5.2	5.7
Employee artisan/	4.0	8.3	2.3	3.8	2.8	5.0	4.1
shopkeeper	5.0	5.6	3.0	3.1	5.5	7.5	4.7
middle mgr	11.1	16.6	12.8	10.2	8.5	12.9	13.5
Teacher	1.0	0.0	6.0	5.2	1.6	4.8	3.6
upper mgr/ lib. prof	69.7	44.5	62.4	69.3	77.8	58.7	65.8
No answer	1.0	0.0	3.0	0.2	9.6	0.7	0.0

Source: Pierre Bourdieu, La noblesse de L'état: Grandes écoles et esprit de corps (Paris: Editions de Minuit, 1989), pp. 192-193.

much chance of entry, even if, here too, the children of upper-middle-class professionals (44.5%) are the largest single group. But these ENA graduates are in any event less likely to be on a career path to top civil service or managerial positions, having entered later and not having attended the prestigious Institut d'Études Politiques (IEP) first. For the most part, they end up as *administrateurs civils* rather than members of the *grands corps*. The entry figures between 1953 and 1968 are revealing: Whereas students taking the main *concours* of the ENA (referred to here as ENA$_1$) made up 92% of entrants into the *grands corps* and 53.6% of *administrateurs civils,* civil servants following the alternative route (ENA$_2$) came to only 8% of the former, and 46.4% of the latter (see Table 11.3). On average, then, whereas the children of the Socialists' natural constituency of workers and middle managers make up 14.8% of graduates of the elite schools which produce the most CEOs (ENA$_1$, X, and Mines), the children of upper-middle-class professionals come to 67.1% of these graduates.

Even if one were to argue that upward mobility takes two generations, though, we cannot find entirely in the Socialists' favor. At first blush, however, the figures do suggest that the Socialists may have been promoting the lower classes, twice removed, because the grandfathers of our future CEOs are less privileged by one-third than their fathers. There is a differential of approximately 34 points on average in upper-middle-class professional status between the fathers (at around 64%) and grandfathers (at around 30%) of graduates of the elite *grandes écoles,* taken together (see Table 11.4), suggesting a significant degree of upward mobility. Moreover, when considering the grandfathers of the bulk of our future CEOs, the graduates of ENA$_1$, Mines, and Polytechnique, we find that although the largest single group among the grandfathers remains that of the upper-middle-class professionals (at 33%), it constitutes only one-third of all grandfathers as opposed to two-thirds of the fathers.

But lest one conclude too hastily, therefore, that the Socialists were promoting their own natural constituency at two generations removed, it is important to consider where the less privileged grandfathers came from. It was only minimally from the Socialists' natural constituency: Among graduates of the ENA's main route, only 8% are the grandchildren of workers and middle managers, while among graduates of Polytechnique, the numbers are only 11.2%, and at Mines, 13.5%. By contrast, the right's natural constituency of farmers, artisans, and shopkeepers is much more heavily represented, with close to two and a half times the number of their grandchildren at the ENA, at 21.3%, over two and a half times the number at Polytechnique, at 29.1%, and over two times the number at Mines, at 28.5%.

Explaining elite dominance

Table 11.3. *Entry into the grands corps and Corps of Administrateurs Civils by method of entry into ENA, 1953–1968*

Method of Entry into ENA	Grands corps		Administrateurs Civils	
	no.	%	no.	%
1st route (students)	246	92.0	391	53.6
2d route (civil servants)	21	8.0	338	46.4
Total	267	100.0	729	100.0

Source: Ezra Suleiman, Politics, Power, and Bureaucracy in France: The Administrative Elite (Princeton: Princeton University Press, 1974), p. 88.

Thus, although two-thirds of the grandfathers of our future CEOs and one-third of their fathers are not from the upper middle classes, only a relatively small percentage of these are from the Socialists' natural constituency, from those to whom the Socialists made appeal in their electoral campaigns.

This pattern of elite recruitment has not changed. In the early eighties (1981–1985), 65% of ENA students were still from the upper classes, by

Table 11.4. *Profession of paternal grandfathers of graduates of grandes écoles (1966–1969)*

	ENA1	ENA2	Mines	Polytech	HEC	Centrale	NmSup
None	5.0	--	0.7	1.0	3.2	3.6	1.0
Agriculture	13.1	19.4	16.5	13.5	6.8	12.0	12.9
Worker	3.0	13.9	7.5	8.1	3.6	8.4	10.3
Employee	5.0	6.3	7.5	9.6	5.2	6.8	6.2
artisan/							
shopkeeper	8.2	13.9	12.0	15.6	17.1	17.9	17.6
middle mgr	5.0	5.5	6.0	3.1	9.8	6.6	4.7
Teacher	3.0	5.5	--	3.1	1.2	2.9	5.7
upper mgr/							
lib. prof	40.4	19.4	28.6	31.0	42.5	24.0	30.0
Other	--	2.8	--	0.2	0.8	--	--
No answer	17.2	11.1	21.0	14.8	9.6	17.7	11.4

Note: The figures on maternal grandfathers are comparable, with at most a 2 point variation in a few categories.

Source: Pierre Bourdieu, La noblesse de l'état: Grandes écoles et esprit de corps (Paris: Éditions de Minuit, 1989), pp. 352-353.

325

Table 11.5. *Profile of students of the ENA, in percentages (1988, 1989)*

Competition	Internal		External	
	1988 (n=42)	1989 (n=48)	1988 (n=42)	1989 (n=48)
Sex:				
male	85.7	79.1	73.8	68.7
female	14.2	20.9	26.1	31.5
Birthplace:				
Ile de France	54.7	52.1	33.3	31.2
Provinces	38.1	37.5	40.4	56.2
Foreign	7.1	10.4	26.1	12.5
Diplomas:				
Bac, IRA, mother of 3	0	0	4.7	2.0
DEUG, DUT, BTS	0	0	4.7	0
Licence, Masters	2.3	2.0	16.6	47.9
DEA, DES, Doctorat	0	0	4.7	2.0
Agrégation	9.5	0	16.6	2.0
Science Po	78.5	85.4	26.1	31.3
Grandes Écoles, TPE	9.5	12.5	26.1	14.6
Father's profession:				
farmer	0	0	2.3	4.1
businessman	9.5	2.1	4.8	6.2
artisan	0	0	7.1	0
worker	2.3	0	21.4	8.3
upper level manager	21.4	39.6	7.1	25
middle level manager	2.3	4.8	9.5	8.3
employee	0	0	2.3	4.2
technician	0	2.1	0	0
liberal professions	23.8	12.5	7.1	12.5
grands corps, ENA, X	10.4	6.2	2.3	0
top civil service (A cat.)	9.5	8.3	7.1	4.1
lower civil service (B & C)	0	0	2.3	8.3
professor	7.1	12.5	14.3	6.2
schoolteacher	4.8	8.3	4.8	4.1
military officer (upper)	2.3	2.1	2.3	4.1
military officer (lower)	2.3	0	2.3	4.1
magistrate	2.3	2.1	2.3	0

Source: Irène Bellier, "Le changement passe-t-il par l'École Nationale d'Administration? Revue Politiques et Management Public vol. 8, no. 3 (Sept. l990).

contrast with 38.7% between 1955–1962.[19] In the late eighties (1989), the upper middle classes were still overrepresented among those who had competed in the external competition, with the children of the upper middle classes together making up over 85% of the class in both 1988 and 1989 (see Table 11.5). Equally interesting, perhaps, a majority were born in or around Paris, in the Île de France (with only slightly over a third from the provinces), and an average of around 80% had attended

[19]Rouban, "France in Search," p. 406. See also: Rouban, *Cadres supérieurs.*

the Institut d'Études Politiques, or Sciences Po, before the ENA in those two years. In the internal competition, by contrast, only a third were from Paris, while over half were from the provinces in 1989 (fewer in 1988, the difference being accounted for by foreign admissions); only 31.3% had attended Sciences Po, with close to half in 1989 having bachelor's (licence) and master's degrees; finally, a simple majority were the children of the lower middle classes in 1988, although they were only slightly over two-fifths in 1989.[20]

The most successful graduates of the ENA, moreover, were generally from the most advantaged milieus and had gained admission through the external competition. Thus, in 1990, of the fifteen top graduates out of a total of eighty-six, only two were from the internal contest (out of forty-one), and five were women (out of seventeen). Moreover, all of their parents were from the upper middle classes, with four retired military officers working as top managers, four liberal professionals, a director of a nationalized bank, a real estate promoter, a councilor of the Cour des Comptes, an agronomist, an engineer graduate of Centrale, and a professor of history and geography.[21] Finally, a recent study of top managers found that 71.9% of those who competed in the ENA's external competition were from the upper classes (families of public or private upper-level managers, engineers, or businessmen), 20.3% from the middle classes, and 7.8% from a lower class.[22] Thus, although the Socialists' natural electorate may have benefited from Socialists' policies, it did not implement them.

But elections, the Socialists might retort, are one thing; implementing social policies or running nationalized enterprises another. To do either efficiently, they felt they had to appoint those who could do the job, regardless of social origins; else they would also lose the support of even their natural constituency.

This was certainly the perception among CEOs on the right, who felt that the Socialists appointed to the nationalized enterprises individuals with elite credentials in order to retain credibility. According to Jean Gandois, head of Péchiney, former head of Rhône-Poulenc, and no Socialist, the Socialists wanted to change the system but didn't dare because they needed to find credibility after nearly a quarter-century of exclusion from power. Thus, they appointed non-Socialists such as himself because there were so few Socialists with the experience of leading the major firms, and they felt they had to find a balance between loyalty and managerial competence.[23]

[20]Irène Bellier, "Le changement passe-t-il par l'École Nationale d'Administration?" *Revue Politique et Management Public* vol. 8, no. 3 (September 1990), p. 44.
[21]Ibid., p. 48.   [22]Rouban, "France in Search," p. 412.
[23]Grandois, interview with author.

Although there is certainly much truth to this, the more cynical view, and the most widely cited, especially on the right, holds that the change in top managers was a phenomenon of caste. For Michel Drancourt, director of the Business Institute, it was simply a matter of the next generation of young Turks taking over a bit earlier, a question of clans taking power, as had happened before with the social democrats in the Fourth Republic, succeeded by the Gaullists, then the Giscardians, then the Socialists, who would stay on until the next renewal of the clan. And he saw little difference between them, remarking that Fabius would have been a good Giscardian.[24] In this same vein, Jean-Louis Descours, CEO of the Groupe André, the shoe and clothing retailer, went even farther, suggesting that the nationalizations and the privatizations were done by the same men, who had opted for one or the other camp not from deep belief but from their calculation of probability that they would get to the top that way.[25]

Critics on the left did not see this in quite the same negative light. Rather, nationalization was a way of wresting control of the economy away from the conservative elite, with the Socialist governing elite appointing their own to head the nationalized enterprises.[26] For some, moreover, especially those still steeped in the pre-election Marxist rhetoric such as Pierre Joxe, "Socialist nationalization is a class act," meaning, of course, an act of the working classes.[27]

In any event, whatever the reason, in the name of economic efficiency and despite their egalitarian ideology, the Socialists did little to challenge the dominance of the traditional interpenetrating administrative-financial-industrial elite. On the contrary, one could even argue that they increased it. François de Closets, in the planning commission report for the Tenth Plan, noted that this very small caste from the *grands corps* of the ENA and X had been exercising a growing hold on the positions of power not only in the administration but also in large industry, in finance, in insurance, and in politics.[28] Moreover, this caste's hold has only been reinforced as a result of the structural changes attendant upon the periods of privatization and of *ni-ni* in which business heads are now part of networks of interlocking directorships.

The interlocking directorships give these heads a tremendous amount of power that is only enhanced by relationships based on previous working experience and old school ties that cut across public and private sectors. These linkages can be seen among CEOs originally appointed by the Socialists, for example, between the heads of UAP, BNP, Suez, and

[24]Drancourt, conversation with author.   [25]Descours, interview with author.
[26]Jacques Julliard, "Mitterrand: Between Socialism and the Republic," *Telos* no. 55 (spring 1983).
[27]*Le Monde*, February 3, 1982 – cited in Birnbaum, "Que faire de l'état?" p. 157.
[28]François de Closets, *Le pari de la responsabilité* (Paris: Payot, 1989).

Saint-Gobain not only because they sit on one another's boards of directors, but also because of special relationships: Peyrelevade at Suez and Lebègue at the BNP are part of the Mitterrand generation; Worms was hired at Suez by Peyrelevade, who is a friend of Beffa at Saint-Gobain, who is in turn part of the Saint-Gobain "mafia" of former managers, which includes Gomez (Thomson), Mer (Usinor), Alain Minc (notable for his neoliberal books as well as his short-lived employment with Carlo DeBenedetti), Fauroux (former CEO of Saint-Gobain and Minister of Industry, 1988–1991), and José Bidegain (number two in the Ministry of Industry, 1988–1991).[29] The linkages are similarly close among CEOs of the privatized companies originally appointed by the right.

In fact, the networks of influence that prior to the Socialists' arrival in power dominated big business were not destroyed, only enlarged by the new CEOs, not only through interlocking directorships and personal relationships, but also through membership in certain exclusive clubs. These are the places where the CEOs have a variety of informal means of getting together, whether through monthly dinners of the 500-member Siècle, begun at the time of Liberation by Georges Bérard-Quélin, and now hosted by Jérôme Monod and Jean-Louis Beffa (with the rest of the members secret); through membership in Entreprise et Cité, Claude Bébéar's group that brings together entrepreneurs and heads of nationalized and privatized enterprises such as Jean-René Fourtou of Rhône-Poulenc, Didier Pineau-Valencienne of Schneider, Vincent Bolloré, Bernard Arnault, André Lévy-Lang, David de Rothschild, Michel Pébereau, Jean-Louis Beffa, Jean-Marie Descarpentrie, and so on; through the progressive Saint-Simon Foundation, created on the initiative of Roger Fauroux, in which not only is all the Saint-Gobain mafia included, but also Gérard Worms, Antoine Riboud, Marc Vienot, Jean Peyrelevade, Michel Albert, Serge Kampf, and so forth; or through the conservative AFEP (Association Française des Entreprises Privées), formed at the time the Socialists took power.[30]

These relationships increasingly cross political lines, such that members of the new Socialist establishment are more and more being accepted by members of the old, conservative establishment.[31] Not only have some of these Socialist-appointed CEOs been kept on by the neoliberal government and by companies once they were privatized, a number of them have also become part of the conservative establishment as part of the CNPF, the Confédération Nationale du Patronat Français (the association repre-

---

[29] *L'Express*, May 2, 1991.

[30] For a discussion of the clubs, see: Lefébure, *Lobby or not to be*, pp. 97–99.

[31] For a full account of how many Socialists find themselves on the boards of directors of private as well as public enterprises and the kinds of perks they gained as a result, see: Alexandre Wickham and Sophie Coignard, *La nomenklatura française* (Paris: Belfond, 1988).

senting large businesses): Lebègue of the BNP is a member of the economic commission; Frédéric Saint Geours, ex-director of the cabinet of the Minister of the Budget, Henri Emmanuelli, and now Director-General of Peugeot, is on the fiscal commission; and Claude Vincent, ex-CEO of CGCT, is head of the working group on Telecommunications.[32] There is nothing very surprising in this increasing acceptance of CEOs on the left by those of the right, according to Strauss-Kahn. He argues that the caste system created by the *grandes écoles,* in particular ENA and X, which very early on determines people's advantages for the rest of their lives, sets corps members apart, such that two *énarques* (graduates of ENA), one on the left and the other on the right, will have more in common than two individuals on the left, where one is an *énarque* and the other is not.[33]

Graduation from the ENA or X, however, is only one of a set of prerequisites, albeit a major one, that determines membership in this managerial elite. The social prestige that comes with having had a stellar career, possible in a majority of cases only with the initial educational credential, is also a must, and this brings with it membership in the exclusive clubs, seats on the boards of the top public and private enterprises, and the friendships that are a sine qua non of elite status and influence. In the financial inner circle in particular, social friendship networks that divide roughly into Socialist and conservative social circles with enough overlap to ensure overall cohesiveness or "enforceable trust," in the words of Charles Kadushin, are made up of individuals who share a background that includes having been graduated from the ENA and having worked in the Treasury, and who in addition share social prestige and club membership. Board memberships are often a consequence of rather than an indicator of membership in the financial elite.[34]

The new Socialist CEOs, in brief, had a lot in common with the conservative CEOs they replaced in terms of social background, education, and membership in the *grands corps.* They did nevertheless differ in a variety of ways from their predecessors. But they were not necessarily more socialist in their management practices. This, however, can be explained less in terms of the new heads' elite status than their view of management itself.

REINTERPRETING ELITE DOMINANCE

Traditional elite theorists would certainly not be in the least surprised at the persistence of the elite pattern of recruitment. Robert Michels's "iron law of oligarchy," which holds that an elite, by virtue of its organizational abilities, will always control the leadership positions in democracies, appears doubly validated, as the French administrative elite, in control of the state apparatus, extended its dominion through nationalization to a major part of business as well.[35] Vilfredo Pareto's view of the circulation of elites, where elites displace one another as a group, moreover, seems to fit admirably what French critics have described as the replacement of the conservative governing caste with the Socialist.[36] But Michels's insight, in a critique of Pareto, that "in most cases there is not a simple replacement of one group of *élites* by another, but a continuous process of intermixture," with the competition between successive cliques of the dominant classes ultimately ending in reconciliation,[37] even better explains the specific case of the CEOs, and the intermingling of Socialist CEOs with conservatives of the same pedigree in interlocking directorships and business associations.

But how, then, to evaluate this elite domination? It is first necessary to differentiate what we might call the Socialist governing elite, the members of which gained their status through democratic election and may lose it in this way as well, from our state elite, the members of which attained their positions through the educational system and a civil service recruitment process that ensures that, once gained, their elite status is rarely lost. With this latter elite, the main question to ask would be: Is there open access to this elite, and is it based on merit? In France, as we have seen, the answer is a qualified yes. Although the system is meritocratic, in that it rewards only those capable of meeting its exacting standards, the cards are nevertheless stacked against all but the upper middle classes. Thus, even though France could be said to meet Gaetano Mosca's ideal requirement that merit be the basis for access to the ruling class,[38] it also risks the danger Max Weber described: that by using educational credentials as a substitute for heredity, plutocratic privileges simply give way to professional ones, and we end up with the substitution of one caste system for another.[39]

But why did the Socialists, newly arrived in power in 1981, help perpetuate this state elite system? And to what end? Elite theorists would tell us that it was quite simply a question of the Socialists' desire to remain in power. Michels's prediction that party leaders act more in the interests of

[35]Robert Michels, *Political Parties: A Sociological Study of the Oligarchical Tendencies of Modern Democracy* (New York: Free Press, 1962).

[36]Vilfredo Pareto, *Sociological Writings* (New York: Praeger, 1966).

[37]Michels, *Political Parties*, p. 343.

[38]James H. Meisel, *The Myth of the Ruling Class: Gaetano Mosca and the Elite* (Ann Arbor: University of Michigan Press, 1962), pp. 60–61.

[39]Max Weber, *Economy and Society: An Outline of Interpretive Sociology*, vol. 3 (New York: Bedminster Press, 1968), p. 1000. See also the discussion of Suleiman, *Power, Politics, and Bureaucracy.*

bureaucratic conservatism, seeking to conserve their own power at the head of the state, than in adherence to ideology or in defense of their members' interest,[40] rings true not only in terms of their elite recruitment policies but also with regard to the great ideological U-turn in macro-economic policy and their policies toward the workers and *cadres moyens,* or middle-level managers, who represent their targeted constituency. Although the Socialists did institute "social justice" through worker participation laws and other social welfare policies, after the imposition of economic austerity they also kept wages down and social unrest at a minimum while accepting a high rate of unemployment.

Neo-Marxists also lend insight, adding that the Socialists could not have done much differently, short of revolution, given the internal and external constraints impinging on any government in capitalist society, where the safeguarding of private property and the preservation of capital markets are paramount. Not only did the entrenched power of the senior civil servants ensure that the Socialists could not have jettisoned the elite recruitment system (had it even occurred to them) without fear of civil service revolt, but the need to preserve the capitalist economy, the demands of organized labor, electoral politics, protest by marginalized groups, and international pressures such as those of the IMF, let alone those of the European Community, all ensured that the Socialists would be unable to fulfill their ideological commitments.[41] Once the Socialists decided in 1983 to attempt to resolve the national economic crisis from within the European Community as opposed to charting their own course, they had little option but to do everything they could to follow traditional prescriptions for economic stability through restrictive macro-economic and labor policies, even if this did mean seeming to turn on their own electorate in the short term.

But why did they not choose to chart their own course? According to Henri Weber, former member of Fabius's cabinet, it was because the Socialists were fundamentally administrators and elected officials rather than syndicalists or ideologists, and therefore their convictions tended to join their interests, ensuring their decision to abandon socialism in favor of pragmatism.[42] We could go on to suggest, following Pareto and Mosca,[43] that the Socialists' bureaucratic conservatism, evident in their willingness to set aside ideology and their members' immediate interest in

[40]See the discussion by Seymour Martin Lipset, "Introduction," in Michels, *Political Parties,* p. 19.

[41]On the internal and external constraints of capitalism in democratic states, see: Ralph Miliband, *Capitalist Democracy in Britain.* (Oxford: Oxford University Press, 1984), p. 104; Ralph Miliband, *Marxism and Politics* (Oxford: Oxford University Press, 1977), p. 72.

[42]Weber, interview with author.

[43]See Meisel, *Myth of the Ruling Class*; Pareto, *Sociological Writings.*

order to retain state power, served the interests of the bourgeoisie. Building on the neo-Marxists, moreover, we could argue that nationalization also served these interests, since it constituted government acquisition at a moment when the nation's capitalists were too weak to retain the means of production for themselves. Government nationalization, in other words, acted as a kind of trusteeship which, once these companies were put back on their feet, could be diminished, if not eliminated, through privatization, but which in the interim would leave state appointees to control the nationalized enterprises in the interests of capitalist profits and balance sheets. Undoubtedly, any number of disillusioned Socialists would see things in exactly this light. Others might even contend that government ownership served as a vehicle for bourgeois control, given the CEOs' elite status and value-neutral (meaning nonsocialist) approach to management.

But there is a danger in conflating the interests of the bourgeoisie and the state bureaucracy. Neo-Marxists such as Nicos Poulantzas caution against assuming that the functioning of the bureaucracy is determined directly by its class membership, even if its members are from the upper middle classes.[44] Ralph Miliband adds that state employees' interests are not necessarily identical with their class counterparts in capitalist enterprises: whereas capitalists are concerned mainly with economics and constrained by the imperatives of the capital they control and manage, ministers and civil servants have different concerns, primarily those of managing class conflict and maintaining the stability of the social system, even if this is not appreciated by some or all of the capitalist class.[45]

The performance of the heads of the nationalized enterprises who were formerly top ministry officials seems to bear out this distinction between state service and capitalist management: once they made the transition from state administrators to state capitalists, they became more concerned with the imperatives of capital than they were with larger concerns about the system as a whole, and even sought to protect the firm from the encroachments of the state. As state capitalists, however, their ideology was less capitalist in the traditional sense than it was managerial, or technocratic in the French sense – and this remained the case whether they became heads of privatized firms or stayed at the head of public ones. Thus, we could argue that they resemble Burnham's new managers, as part of a small, cohesive group, united by their managerial ideology, and replacing the traditional capitalist at the head of business.[46] (It is interesting to note in this context that Léon Blum wrote the preface to the 1947

[44]Nicos Poulantzas, *Pouvoir politique et classes sociales* (Paris: Maspero, 1971), pp. 166–168.

[45]Miliband, *Capitalist Democracy*, p. 7.

[46]James Burnham, *The Managerial Revolution* (London: Putnam and Co., 1943).

French edition of Burnham's book, convinced that all that was necessary to install socialism was the creation of a democratic, meritocratic recruitment system for a technocratic elite.)[47]

But this said, the French case does not therefore constitute a replay of the first managerial revolution, which separated ownership from control, already long true for much of French business. Rather, we might call it the second French managerial revolution. But here, unlike in the United States, where the expression is used solely to dramatize business displeasure with government regulation, by suggesting that government has substituted itself for management through stringent regulation of every aspect of business, the term is intended to denote the actual takeover and reorganization of business by government. In France, the second managerial revolution began with the nationalization of major banks and industries by government and the replacement of their top managers by top civil servants. This has not, however, as we have already noted, necessarily meant more government control and less capitalism – only different kinds. While government control remains no greater than that of the past, given its continued respect for the managerial autonomy of the enlarged public enterprise sector, capitalism in the aftermath of nationalization, understood as following the imperatives of the market, has become, if anything, more dynamic with the replacement of traditional private sector managers in wholly private *noyaux durs* by state managers in public and later privatized enterprises controlled increasingly by public/private *noyaux durs*. The second French managerial revolution, in short, has reinvigorated capitalism through the imposition of a new group of state-trained, business-oriented managers at the head of major public and private enterprises.

To say that the new managers constitute a group apart from the administrators of the state, however, is not to suggest that they have severed all ties with their fellow graduates of X and the ENA. Much the contrary, since their ability to protect their state firms from the state administration depends in large measure on their close ties with it. In other words, however much these managers may differ in their concerns and their sense of role once they leave state administration for state (or private and privatized) enterprise, they nevertheless remain part of the same interpenetrating state elite of top government and business officials. As such, they might appear akin to Milovan Djilas's "new class" in their seeming monopoly of positions of power in government and business.[48] But there is at least one significant difference between the French elite and Djilas's new class: they are not *the* ruling class. The state elite, however extensive

[47]Pfister, *République*, p. 24.
[48]Milovan Djilas, *The New Class* (London: Thames & Hudson, 1957).

its influence as a result of its members having colonized business and the governing party, does not therefore control government. It cannot impose its own particular policy agenda, as might an independent power elite such as that described by C. Wright Mills because, following the argument of T. B. Bottomore, its "policy-making powers are subject to the control of a political authority, which stems from party control, the ethical code of the bureaucracy, in particular ethical neutrality, and so forth."[49] In other words, despite André Siegfried's insistence already years ago that bureaucratic managers and government officials together were developing into a ruling elite,[50] and that this has since only been enhanced by old school and *grand corps* ties, this elite does not have a monopoly over political power: it may be a ruling elite, but it is not *the* ruling elite.

There are other loci of power, for example, in the Socialist governing elite and in opposition parties to which members of our interpenetrating state elite may belong but which they do not control; in the trade unions that remain independent from the parties, even if they have strong linkages with some of them; in the rivalries among ministries and the weight of the nonelite members who often look outside the pyramid rather than up for guidance;[51] in the powerful local elected officials who consistently resist encroachment by the centralized state, having set up their own circuits of power;[52] in private firms left outside the elite circuit; and so on. The elite in France, as elsewhere, in other words, is divided, as Raymond Aron put it years ago,[53] and in any event does not always get its way, given the ability of nonelites in the society to resist.

Our smaller interpenetrating state elite, although more cohesive as a result of its strong educational and professional ties, is therefore only one of a plurality of elites. Its power comes from the fact that it is at the center of this plurality of elites – as a loose association of like-minded because like-trained individuals who tend to be forward-looking, supportive of economic modernization, technocratic in approach to solving problems, and certain of their own superiority, and who bring coherence because they are pervasively, but not exclusively, at the center of power. As such, this elite may restrict the power of the rulers of the society at any given time, as Bottomore rightly noted, but it cannot rule the society itself.[54]

[49]T. B. Bottomore, *Elites in Society* (Baltimore: Penguin, 1966), pp. 86–87.

[50]André Siegfried, *De la IIIème République à la Quatrième* (Paris: Grasset, 1957), p. 246.

[51]See Jean-Claude Thoenig, *L'administration en miettes* (Paris: Fayard, 1985).

[52]See: Schmidt, *Democratizing France.*

[53]Raymond Aron, "Social Structure and the Ruling Class," *British Journal of Sociology* vol. 1, no. 1 (March 1950), pp. 1–16; and vol. 1, no. 2 (June 1950), pp. 126–143.

[54]Bottomore, *Elites,* p. 90.

The question to answer then becomes: How does this elite restrict the government, other than, as already mentioned, in its constraint on civil service appointments? And to what end? Although Bottomore insisted that instead of influencing policy as a result of its interests as a ruling class such as elite would do it more on the basis of class interests, we have already seen that class membership alone tells us little about the interests of our elite.[55] Political interests, moreover, are also unlikely to unite this elite in opposition to the governing elite, whether on the right or the left, given that its members come from all shades of the political spectrum, and that, if anything, the increasing politicization of the civil service at the uppermost levels suggests collusion between different portions of governing elite and state elite.

What is more, substantive policy interests are even more certain not to serve as a rallying point, given the tendency of the members of this state elite to defend the preferences and programs of the ministries in which they find themselves (e.g., the divisions between the Ministries of Finance and Industry), or the firms they lead. For example, the divergences of opinion on the role of the state in economic development between Daniel Lebègue, former director of the Treasury and then number two at the BNP, and Louis Gallois, former Director-General of Industry and then head of two defense manufacturers (SNECMA and then Aérospatiale), are marked, despite that fact that they are graduates of the same class and friends, having succeeded one another in a variety of positions throughout their careers, were together in the Treasury department, and are "part of the same mafia."[56] Illustrative of their differences is the exchange between them in which Lebègue insists that there is no industrial policy, only macroeconomic policy, arguing that money invested in tourism brought in more money in terms of the balance of payments and of foreign trade than money invested in industry, and Gallois responds that without industrial policy, France would be populated with theme parks and tourists, and that Lebègue "would create a superDisneyland covering all of France with Asterix in Auvergne, Bretagne, etc., and exalt the virtues of the climate on the Côte d'Azur."[57] Clearly, members of this state elite are not necessarily united over substantive policy issues.

At most, following from the earlier analysis, we could say that this elite acts in the long-term interests of the bourgeoisie. But this tells us little, other than serving as a general statement about the nature of the constraints under which any elite operates in a capitalist society. As such, it has no greater explanatory power than the account that members of the elite themselves might give: that, as servants of the state, they act in the

---

[55]Ibid., pp. 87–88.   [56]Gallois, interview with author.
[57]Lebègue and Gallois, interviews with author.

general interest. What is more, no alternative analysis, such as a pluralist one that would argue that the conflict among the many different interests in society, elite and nonelite, leads to the public interest, does any better. The problem is that none of these explanations tell us much about the impact of this elite on the polity, or exactly how it restricts the governing party and to what end. For that, another kind of analysis is required, one tied to an understanding of the place of the state in France.

ESPRIT D'ÉTAT COMME ÉTAT D'ESPRIT: THE IDEA OF THE STATE AS STATE OF MIND

The state in France is everywhere and nowhere. It is an idea and an ideal, a concrete reality and a state of mind. Georges Burdeau described this very well in his short classic on the state, when he remarked that the state is an idea which, unlike a concept that systematizes a number of facts about reality, is itself "all the reality that it expresses because this reality resides entirely in the spirit of the men who conceive it."[58] In Wittgensteinian terms, then, this is not a word used by experts to explain the meaning of other words in everyday use, it is a word that is itself in everyday use and for which its many meanings are therefore in the use.[59] As such, as Burdeau eloquently puts it, the state is the public power which men obey in order not to obey other men, at the same time that it is subject to capture by officials elected to power, and thus colonized by its own servants. The state, however, is not therefore simply a cover for the power of political factions, it is also the regulator of the battle for power of which it is the object.[60]

The state, in short, is an idea that takes on almost mystical qualities for the French. It explains everything and nothing. It comforts because it serves as an all-encompassing concept that summarizes all aspects of power, taking care of one's welfare. It frustrates, since it is the single entity to blame for any governmental problems – for example, when one is unhappy at the bank, in the post office, in the social security administration, about the arcane regulations that do not allow one to perform what should be a simple operation, *"c'est l'état."* More simply, it is. And as such, its top servants, the graduates of special schools that train them in the ways of the state and teach them to think of the national interest above all, are as irreproachable as the state itself, having acquired some of its mystical aura. More importantly, they are the protectors of the state against the political vagaries of the moment because, as Simon Nora, a

[58]Georges Burdeau, *L'état* (Paris: Seuil, 1970), p. 14.
[59]See Ludwig Wittgenstein, *Philosophical Investigations* (Oxford: Oxford University Press, 1968).
[60]Burdeau, *L'état*, pp. 14–19.

former director of the ENA, once put it, "The civil service, thanks to its accumulated memories, its extended prospective, its competence in the preparation and execution of decisions, is the legitimate manager of the 'long term' of the Nation."[61]

None of the left- or right-wing governments in the Mitterrand years ever really questioned the state or its servants. In the years 1981 to 1986, the Socialist leaders and their Communist coalition partners had no desire to dismantle the state – much the contrary, since they sought to use it for their own ends.[62] In fact, because they conceived of the state and its servants as in their service, if not always neutral,[63] the Socialists saw it as carrying out their own political agenda, not that of any one class. Interestingly enough, even their coalition partners, the Communists, not only agreed with this analysis, but went further never even to question the neutrality of the state[64] (although both before and after their stints in power, they went back to more class-based analyses). Thus, the Communist minister in charge of the civil service, Anicet Le Pors, in responding to a question about this view of the nature of the state, remarked, "Is it the state of Marx and Engels, the board of directors of the dominant class of the bourgeoisie? Is it the state of the monopolies? Obviously, we can no longer say this. In fact, it is a hybrid situation where the bourgeoisie has strong positions in the economy, while the political power affirms the values of liberty, responsibility, in brief, of republican citizenship."[65] For the Communists in government as much as the Socialists, the state was in the service of the political power, and therefore served the interests of the nation, not of the bourgeoisie. For both, in short, there was no alternative to utilizing the state and its bureaucracy in the way they did, and no need for an alternative.

It has been relatively rare, in fact, for any government in power to question the state. Only when the Socialist and Communist parties were in opposition did they in any way attack the state. But even then, it was not the state as such that they opposed but, rather, its being put in the service of the capitalists, of the "wall of money," the *mur d'argent*, a view articulated in 1936 by the Socialists and over and over again thereafter, the last time in 1981 by Mitterrand.[66] In their pre-1981 pamphlets, the

[61]Quoted in Pfister, *République*, p. 36.   [62]See: Birnbaum, "Que faire de l'état?"
[63]Pierre Birnbaum notes a certain confusion among the Socialists, who sometimes talk as if they are the state, other times as if the state is subject to bourgeois influence if not domination, and thus has to be dominated in turn. "Que faire de l'état?" p. 156–159.
[64]Ibid., p. 158.
[65]Interview in *Libération*, December 13, 1983 – quoted in Birnbaum, "Que faire de l'état?" p. 147.
[66]Birnbaum, "Que faire de l'état?" pp. 153–155.

Socialists described the state as an "instrument of the business class [*bourgeoisie d'affaires*], and a factor in inequalities," which "enslaves [*asservit*] the French"; and they insisted that "Never had the opposition between the general interest and the maintaining of privileges of all types been as great." They therefore argued that the state should be put in the service of the interests of the collectivity and no more in that of minority private interests.[67] And this meant changing the government, not the state. Thus, the Common Program of the Left did not anticipate any major change in the state or question the central role of the upper-level administration.[68]

This did not preclude, however, criticizing certain aspects of the state, including its role. Throughout the eighties, numerous books were written about the inequities resulting from state privileges and rules, and the capture of the state by special interests that masqueraded as the interests of the state.[69] Moreover, we have already seen how the neoliberals spoke and wrote extensively on the need for the retreat of the state. The Socialists, too, once they began outlining a new, less interventionist role for the state, complained about the dominance of the state. Thus, Mitterrand, in response to an accusation that statism was a problem of the left, responded, "Statism, the French suckle on it as they are born. This government is the first since the Revolution of 1789 to attack the root of the evil."[70] Even the Communists, once they had left the government in 1984, criticized the state, claiming that "The state is everywhere with us. Even in the head."[71]

But while government policies of decentralization and liberalization diminished the size and purview of the central state, no government ever did call into question the organization of the state or the elite recruitment of its servants. The reforms themselves, moreover, were not done against the state, to weaken it, but rather for the state, to strengthen it by ridding it of excess and onerous responsibilities, slimming the state down in order to enable it to regain its traditional *envergure* and effectiveness. And it was the servants of the state who willingly implemented the reforms, to the benefit of the country as well as themselves.

[67]See: Barreau and Le Nay, "Du Programme Commun," p. 21.
[68]Birnbaum, "Que faire de l'état?" pp. 153–154; and Hughes Portelli, *Le socialisme français tel qu'il est* (Paris: Presses Universitaires de France, 1980).
[69]François de Closets, *Toujours plus!* (Paris: Grasset, 1982), pp. 86–108; François de Closets, *Tous ensemble: Pour en finir avec la syndicratie* (Paris: Seuil, 1985); Jean-Pierre Gaudard, *Les danseuses de la république: Que fait l'état de votre argent?* (Paris: Pierre Belfond, 1984).
[70]*Libération*, May 10, 1984 – cited in Birnbaum, "Que faire de l'état?" p. 155.
[71]*L'Humanité*, November 21, 1984 – cited in Birnbaum, "Que faire de l'état?" p. 150.

As the state has retreated, these servants of the state, the members of the small interpenetrating state elite, have moved out into nonstate positions of power, populating the top positions in industry now that there are fewer interesting positions in the ministries. This has served both public purposes and private ones.

On the public side, it has performed a symbolic and legitimizing function, as well as a stabilizing one. Just as state elites served to legitimize business in the seventies by moving into it,[72] so in the nineties the much larger movement of state-trained civil servants into the private sector symbolizes as it legitimizes the shift to a greater emphasis on the market and the retreat of the state. At the same time, moreover, this has also limited any potential instability that could have followed from a total opening to a market economy. For although the state has given up direct control over business, it remains indirectly in control not only through the policy instruments remaining to it but also through its servants at the head of public and private enterprise. The result is that ministry–industry relations can remain informally close even as ministry and industry take their formal distance from one another, and that industry may retain a sense of the national interest at a time when capital is becoming more and more international.

Depending upon one's point of view, this continued indirect state control can be positive or negative. Most businesspeople, although in many instances condemning the state elite recruitment system as inappropriate for business,[73] have nevertheless seen as positive the resulting closer ministry–industry relations. For example, although Gallois, head of Aérospatiale, admitted that it was not so healthy to have a "monoculture" in which decisions may be made on the basis of relationships rather than on professional grounds, he nevertheless pointed to the fact that the system may also facilitate ministry–industry relations, given that on both sides many are not just members of the same corps, but *camarades de promotion,* or fellow classmates, and thus speak to one another with the informal "*tu.*"[74] This view was echoed by others, such as Bruno Boudrouille, a director of the Caisse des Dépôts et Consignations, who found that because the bank has so many dealings with governmental units, the multipositioned graduates of ENA and X who can go from one group to another are favored.[75] Even Maisonrouge of IBM World Trade, who had a whole raft of other criticisms, recognized the advantages to this aspect of the system, and the usefulness for companies to employ

[72]See the discussion in Ezra Suleiman, *Elites in French Society* (Princeton: Princeton University Press, 1978).

[73]See Chapter 15.   [74]Gallois interview.

[75]Bruno Boudrouille, Director of Strategy, Caisse des Dépôts et Consignations. Interview with author, July 3, 1991.

graduates of the *grandes écoles* because of their relationship with the ministries, their friends, and their graduation class, given the power of the state.[76]

Others, moreover, saw as useful the fact that these enterprises are led by members of the state elite who have been imbued with a sense of the general interest and taught a scrupulous honesty which they share with their former classmates in the ministries. Thus, Gallois notes that whatever the other problems with the elite recruitment system may be, the *esprit de corps* ensures against corruption.[77] In a similar vein, François de Wissocq of Elf remarked that the elite's training ensures that its members retain a sense of the general interest, even in industry, at the same time that, because they know the state so well, they can reinforce the autonomy of the enterprise.[78]

Whatever its other faults, in short, the *"corporatisme"* helps promote incorruptibility and devotion to the state, whether one works for ministry or industry. But this is because the state and the corps are almost seen as one. *"L'État c'est moi"* is no longer the purview of kings but of members of the *grands corps*. And corruption, therefore, may not take the form of dishonesty but, rather, of promoting one's own in government and in business, to the exclusion of others, or even hiding one another's mistakes – if, that is, they are recognized as such. For de Closets, there is an implicit corruption in the *pantouflage,* or back-and-forth between administration and industry.[79] For others, starting with Tocqueville and Michelet and ending with Blandine Barret-Kriegel, the corruption starts long before they even had a chance to move from ministry to industry, in their claims to represent the general interest, because there is much question as to whether they have ever risen above their factionalist interests to even get to the general interest.[80]

Whatever the public purposes, in other words, private purposes have also been well served by the changes in the ministries and industries. But rather than seeing these private purposes as representing yet another instance of the French state serving the interests of the bourgeoisie, as neo-Marxists might insist, we could conclude that it looks much more like a case of the state serving the interests of its own elite, through the colonization of French business by state-trained upper-level civil servants.

CONCLUSION

What is the effect of all this? The state remains as concept and concrete representation, but it is no longer what it was. It has renewed itself along

---

[76]Maisonrouge, interview with author.   [77]Gallois, interview with author.
[78]De Wissocq, interview with author.   [79]De Closets, *Le Pari*.
[80]Blandine Barret-Kriegel, *Les chemins de l'état* (Paris: Calmann-Levy, 1986).

with the administrative and managerial elite, becoming accompaniment to business action instead of initiator. Meanwhile, some of its aura has rubbed off onto business, which has gained in stature and in public trust as a result. Whether business, with the state-trained elite at its head, can maintain that trust, however, is open to question. This will depend not only upon its ability to lead the economy out of recession but also upon its ability to keep its distance from the corruption scandals wracking the political class. Whereas business seems to have been relatively successful in the former, it has been less so in the latter. Recent scandals affecting CEOs have included bad business decisions, as in the case of Jean-Yves Habérer's overly ambitious merger and acquisition program for the Crédit Lyonnais, which led to large losses and his dismissal, and under-handed business deals, as in the case of the acquisition of two Belgian companies by the CEO of Schneider, Didier Pineau Valencienne, which led to his brief detention in 1994 in a Belgian jail. Such scandals have also involved misuse of company funds, fraud, and illegal political financing, as in the cases of Guy Dejouany, CEO of the Compagnie Générale des Eaux, personally indicted in May 1995 for company-paid kickbacks while the company more generally was under investigation for illegal funding of local political parties, and Pierre Suard of Alcatel-Alsthom, replaced as CEO in April 1995 in consequence of such charges as billing home remodeling work to the company, involvement in a scheme to overcharge France Télécom by more than 100 million francs, and the illegal channeling of upwards of 20 million francs to political parties. All together, these scandals suggested that public trust for business may be waning.

The crisis of leadership, thus, is one that increasingly involves those at the top of business as well as government. Moreover, it represents not simply an indictment of individuals but also of the elite system as a whole, as the corruption scandals involving the few have generated a more general questioning of the cozy relationship at the top levels of government and business populated by graduates of ENA and X that enabled such corruption to fester. Even the presidential candidates in the April–May 1995 campaign joined this debate. Their response, interestingly enough, however, was not to denounce the elite system per se, but rather to insist that a revival of the political was necessary to reestablish balance. Thus, Socialist candidate Lionel Jospin noted that "Our society suffers from a democratic deficit. . . . The French have the feeling that too many decisions are taken without them, that power is too distant. . . . To restore the role and place of politics is indispensable because if the citizenry has broken down, if technocrats have taken power, it is because politicians have given up their responsibilities." In a similar vein, conservative candidate Jacques Chirac denounced "the gulf between the French and those who govern them" and the creation of a "technically competent caste" which is "politically irresponsible and sociologically distanced from the people."[81] For Chirac too, the solution was not to get rid of the technocratic elite, but rather to submit it to political authority.

For the presidential candidates of 1995, then, just as for those of 1981 and 1988, change was not to come against the state or its representatives, whether now in business or still in government. Rather, it was to come only through the state, with its elected representatives ensuring that the state be more clearly in the service of the people.

[81]*Le Monde,* May 5, 1995.

PART V

The changes in business

12

Revitalizing the economy

In economic matters as in many others, the French have often been their own harshest critics. By the early 1990s, their view of the state of the French economy appeared almost as pessimistic as at the beginning of the 1980s. They saw the country as far behind their main European rival, Germany, and in need of protection against what they termed the predatory Japanese. They despaired of solving such intractable problems as the high unemployment rate at the same time that they complained about slowing economic growth and insufficient levels of investment, the budgetary deficit and the negative balance of trade, the high level of public expenditures and the low rate of savings, the decrease in the size of the workforce and the inadequacies of the educational and training systems, the insufficient competitiveness of France's products internationally and its smaller market share worldwide, and the list goes on.

Such criticism, although accurate, obscures the great strides the French economy has made in the past decade, as it has rationalized and internationalized its industry, deregulated its markets, and prepared for the single European market. By the end of the decade of the eighties, it was clear that the economic decline that had begun in the seventies and continued into the early eighties had been reversed.[1] Most economic indicators had steadily improved since 1983, when the Socialists put an economic austerity program into place: inflation had been more than tamed; the rate of growth in the GDP remained ahead of most other countries until the early nineties even if per capita GDP had declined; the level of savings and investment compared favorably with other countries; industrial productivity had risen at an unprecedented rate; and the negative balance of trade had righted itself by 1992. French firms themselves were reaping the

---

[1]For discussions of the deindustrialization, see: Jean-Louis Levet, *Une France sans usines?* 2d ed. (Paris: Economica, 1989); Cohen, *L'état brancardier*; Dacier, Levet, Tourret, *Dossiers noirs*.

benefits of this improved economic profile with increased investment in research and development, greater industrial productivity, and large enough profits toward the end of the decade to finance ambitious international merger and acquisition programs.

Although specific industries continued to have problems, in particular computers and electronics, others had managed to pull themselves out of what had seemed at the beginning of the decade to be an irreversible decline. This was especially the case with steel, even if the unfavorable economic climate from 1992 on caused renewed crisis in this as in other industries. There were some industries, of course, that were never able to recover, such as the textile and machine tool industries.

Thus, despite the fact that there is much to criticize in French economic performance during the Mitterrand presidency, there is also much to praise. Many mistakes were no doubt made, in particular in the early period of the nationalizations, which delayed French recovery. But even the nationalizations proved salutary, not only saving French industry from foreign acquisition but also providing a climate for change, an excuse to clean house internally, and an opportunity to rationalize operations. Privatization, whole as well as partial, only continued in these same directions. The result is that by the end of the decade, French business had modernized and internationalized, while most economic indicators had improved significantly. The subsequent recession, although taking its toll, could not negate this. Nonetheless, the French complained, frustrated by the fact that, however well their country had done, some countries, such as Japan and Germany, had done better; and ignoring the fact that other countries, such as Great Britain, had done worse.

THE CRITICISMS OF ECONOMIC PERFORMANCE

Admittedly, as the French are the quickest to remind one, even after over a decade of economic renewal, certain "structural weaknesses" remain. Primary among these is unemployment, which increased from 1.6 million in 1981 to 2.6 million in 1991, for a jobless rate of 9.5%, and which rose to 11.7% in 1993 and to 12.5% for 1994.[2] France's 9.3% average for the decade of 1981–1991, however, was still slightly lower than that of the European Community as a whole (9.6%), and those of France's next-closest European rivals, the United Kingdom (9.6%) and Italy (9.5%), even if it was 3.4 points higher than Germany's average rate. In the case of Germany, though, the rate would have been higher if it had listed as

[2]Figures on the number of unemployed as a percentage of the civilian labor force are based on European Community data.

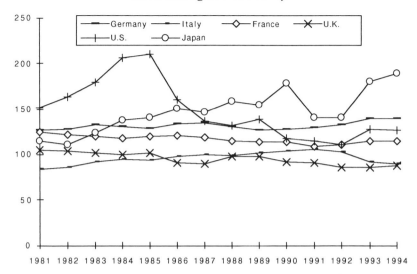

Figure 12.1. GDP per capita at current market prices (in écus, the European Community equals 100). Source: EC.

unemployed all those participating in the apprenticeship system or in retraining programs. Thus, even though Germany's 1994 unemployment rate was below that of France as well as most other EU countries (6.6% in West Germany and 8.4% in the East, compared to the U.K.'s 9.5%, Italy's 11.4%, and Spain's whopping 24.1%), the real figures, especially since German unification, were probably much higher. Unemployment, in other words, is something of an intractable problem for Europe as a whole.

France has also had a comparatively slow rate of increase in industrial production, growing by 11.7% from 1981 to 1991, close to Italy's 13.7% but about two-thirds as fast as the United Kingdom's 17.1% or the European Community's average 17.8% growth, a little under half as fast as Germany's 21.1% and a third as fast as the United States' 31%, and only slightly over one-fourth as fast as Japan's impressive 41.8%. Between 1991 and 1995, moreover, through the recession, it grew by only 0.7%, far behind the United States' 14% growth, the United Kingdom's 6.4%, and even the European Community's average of 2.4%, but ahead of Italy's 0.5% growth, Germany's decline of −0.7%, and Japan's of −7.8%.[3]

[3]Figures on industrial production (excluding construction) based on Commission of the European Community, *European Economy* no. 59 (1995), Table 12.

Changes in business

France was in fact much slower at recovering from the recession in the
1980s, in part because of its inflationary policies in the first two years,
and thus remained behind these other countries in terms of its industrial
production, which in turn affected its ability to respond to the recession
of the early 1990s.

In addition, France in the mid to late eighties suffered from a negative balance of trade, which went from +35.1 billion francs in 1980
and a high of +97.1 billion francs in 1984 to −70.3 billion francs in
1990, although this subsequently righted itself, with a trade surplus of
30.9 billion francs in 1992, of 80 billion francs in 1993, and 86 billion
francs in 1994. France's budget deficit, moreover, at approximately
130 billion francs for 1991 and around 2 billion francs in 1992, rose
to 315.7 billion francs in 1993, or 4.4% of GDP, and was close to 6%
of GDP in 1994. In addition, between 1981 and 1994 France's GDP
per capita declined by 9.2 points, in marked contrast with Japan's 74.3
point gain, Germany's 11.8 point gain, and even Italy's 6.6 point gain
(even if Italy's GDP per capita was close to 25 points lower than that
of France), although this decline was nothing compared to the 83.2
point drop of the United States from its high in 1985, or even the 17.1
point drop of the United Kingdom (see Figure 12.1). Finally, France's
market share worldwide receded from 8.5% at the beginning of the
eighties to 6.5% in 1991.[4]

Public expenditures in terms of local authorities' spending and social
welfare costs also remained high – too high according to the OECD,
which estimated France's ratio of public borrowings to deficits at 5.75%
of GNP in 1994, above the government's target of 5.1% for the year, and
a problem especially if France was to meet the Maastricht goal of bringing
the ratio to 3% or less by 1997. Public debt had also been mounting. In
1988, it represented less than 10% of budgetary expenditures; by 1992, it
had risen to over 14%, the same level as the United States.[5]

French industry in particular also is a source of concern. Most critics
see France as having too small an industrial base, industry having lost 1.3
million of its 6 million jobs between 1974 and 1991.[6] Industrial employment as a percentage of total employment declined by 18 points, most of
it in large industry, which lost 20% of its employees, while industry's
share of the GDP declined from 25.1% to 21.7% between 1980 and
1990.[7] Moreover, between 1991 and 1994, employment in manufacturing industries declined by another 11.1%, although this was less significant than Italy's 13.4% decline, on a par with Germany's 11.8%, but
worse than Great Britain's 7.8%.

[4]*Le Nouvel Economiste* no. 786, August 3, 1991.   [5]*Le Monde,* September 8, 1992.
[6]*Le Monde,* June 12, 1991.   [7]*Rapport Raynaud* (Paris: Documentation française, 1993).

Critics in addition complain about France's lack of industrial specialization: its focus on big contracts and on the South (meaning Third World
countries), with insufficient clients in OECD countries and in sectors with
a high return on investment. And they note that French products are too
bottom-of-the-line as a result of the lack of research and development
over the long term, and not competitive enough in pricing because of the
strong franc.[8]

Critics also find that the educational system does not produce enough
skilled employees at any level, and in particular engineers.[9] In the training
of managers, the problem is the elite system which rewards the few who
attend the *grandes écoles* and leaves the many, educated in the universities, with inadequate technical background and poor career chances.[10]
In the training of workers, the refrain, repeated over and over again in the
press, from the government, and from CEOs, is that they suffer from a
lack of *"formation"* that must be remedied through the creation of an
apprenticeship system similar to that of the Germans, which ensures the
Germans a more highly skilled workforce than the French. But this is an
old refrain: Elie Cohen notes that since the 1890s the French have every
year sent a technical study mission to Germany to learn from their apprenticeship program, with no results.[11] Many blame the failure of the
French training system not only on the government but also on industry,
which, when the government imposed a 1% tax for training, in many
cases simply assumed that it had done its bit, and left it at that.[12]

Moreover, critics find insufficient investment in industry, inadequate
reconversion policies, and insufficient research, with what there is focused on the military, thus putting France behind Germany and Japan in
consumer product innovation. They remark on the lack of specific, internationally competitive products, by contrast with Italy. And they deplore
the inordinate emphasis on large industry, to the detriment of the small
and mid-sized enterprises which are undercapitalized (only 1.5 billion
francs out of 25 billion francs in state aid to industry goes to the SMEs),
undersized, and without the necessary training.[13] They have been particularly concerned that French small and mid-sized industries are half
the size of those of Germany; almost half as numerous (in 1990, France

---

[8]*Le Monde,* June 12, 1991.   [9]*Le Nouvel Economiste,* March 3, 1991.

[10]All of those interviewed for this study, whether top managers in business or top
officials in government, made this point.

[11]*Le Nouvel Economiste,* March 3, 1991.   [12]Descours, interview with author.

[13]Remarks of contributors to a Conference of the Jean Jaurès Foundation entitled,
"What Industrial Policy for France?" in Paris, March 27, 1991. The speakers included
Henri Guillaume, head of ANVAR, the agency for the promotion of high technology;
Jacques Mazier, economics professor at the University of Paris XIII; Gérard Lafay,
deputy director of CEPII; Jean-Pierre Jouyet, director of the cabinet of the Minister of
Industry, Roger Faurou; and Jean-Louis Levet, Director of Strategy of SFPI.

had only 9,000 larger SMEs with between 50 and 1,000 employees next to Germany's 16,000); and lacking in the kind of close linkages with large industry found in Germany as well as Japan.[14] Moreover, the Raynaud Report, commissioned by the Balladur government in 1993, found that France's small and mid-sized industries, which in 1991 accounted for 55% of industrial employment and 42% of revenue for industry before taxes, suffered not only from problems of size, in particular intermediate enterprises with between 100 and 2,000 employees, but also of financing, with particularly high financial costs that translated into a greater call to indebtedness at higher rates than large industries.[15]

Innovation with regard to computer techniques has also been a problem. A 1991 study found that the small and medium-sized industries were behind in this regard, with 50% of those it interviewed having failed to reorganize their *ateliers* after the introduction of computerized machinery, or to reduce their production channel.[16] High-tech innovations, however, have not always been a success even with the larger firms. The problem, as a manager from Renault insisted, is that "Robots that are too sophisticated, handled by a poorly directed personnel, only automate disorder." Only companies such as Lafarge, Saint-Gobain, and Air Liquide got high marks in this area, having been generally seen as in advance of all others.[17]

Finally, critics point to the fact that even though over the past ten years the government has deregulated business, people still believe that savings are better invested in property than in industry, so business still suffers a lack of easy access to financing. "It is now reasonably easy to create a business; [it remains] Kafkaesque to finance it."[18] Risk capital is still hard to come by, despite tremendous improvements in recent years. Interest rates remain too high, thereby keeping borrowing down and slowing growth. But this is not something the French authorities have much power over, given the European Monetary System where, because the French franc is pegged to the Deutschemark, the Bundesbank has virtual control over interest rates, which it has kept high to keep inflation under control in Germany. And the litany goes on.[19]

THE CHANGES IN ECONOMIC PROFILE

Even the critics, however, admit that France has certain trump cards, in particular its infrastructure, including nuclear energy, electricity, trans-

[14]*Les Echos*, April 8, 1991.   [15]*Rapport Raynaud.*
[16]*Le Nouvel Economiste*, March 3, 1991.   [17]Ibid.
[18]Eric LeBoucher, *Le Monde*, June 12, 1991.
[19]There has been a spate of books on the problems of the French economy in the last few years. See, for example, Levet, *France sans usines?*; Cohen, *L'état brancardier.*

portation, communications, and in aeronautics, oil, and engineering. Moreover, it is interesting to note that however harsh the French were when assessing the competitiveness of their own industries, they were even more so with respect to the United States, let alone Great Britain, in marked contrast to their views of Germany and Japan.[20] In interviews with top business and government officials in 1991, whereas Germany was time and again touted as the country to emulate and Japan the country to fear, the United States was invariably dismissed as "deindustrialized." U.S. industry was seen as scarred by a decade of irresponsible "financial capitalism," hampered by its short-term view because you "cannot run industry looking at quarterly reports,"[21] and sold off to foreigners, including, naturally, to the French (which seems for the French to be proof positive of its decline – bringing to mind that old Groucho Marx line that any club that would have one as a member is no club to which one wants to belong). Great Britain never came up at all. But when asked, the response was always that it no longer counted, and that its industry was totally foreign-controlled.

Such assessments of the relative competitiveness of countries are of course notoriously unreliable, given that they tend to change at a moment's notice with new macroeconomic figures or changes in perceived performance, and often have little to do with reality. In 1988, at a time when the French economy was ascending, a study of elite attitudes found that a majority (58%) of the elite was convinced of France's decline (as opposed to 38% who did not see any or felt the contrary).[22] At this same time, moreover, in direct contrast to the 1991 view of top managers, 82% of the elite saw the United States as the greatest economic power in the world, 15% named Japan, and only 1% West Germany.[23] By 1993, moreover, this earlier more positive attitude toward the United States seemed to be returning to popularity, with U.S. corporations regaining respect as competitors and envied for their lower labor costs in manufacturing (the 1992 hourly labor costs in manufacturing were $16 in the United States and Japan, a dollar higher in France, Italy, and Canada, and

---

[20]In a SOFRES poll of French and German top managers' views of one another, there was on average at least a 20- to 30-point spread between French views of German performance and management practice and German views of French performance and management practice, whether in terms of the quality of products and services (96% to 71%), the conception of marketable products (88% to 68%), respect for engagements (89% to 59%), commercial dynamism (88% to 56%), quality of management (82% to 55%), long-term vision (79% to 42%), technological advancement (91% to 42%), productivity (91% to 43%), profitability (86% to 36%), work organization (91% to 35%), or labor–management relations (81% to 29%). SOFRES, "Perceptions croisées de la France et de l'Allemagne," *Les Rendez-Vous d'Évian*, October 4, 1992.

[21]Gallois, interview with author.

[22]SOFRES, *L'état de l'opinion 1989* (Paris: Seuil, 1989), p. 37.   [23]Ibid., pp. 36–37.

almost $10 higher in Germany) and higher productivity (in 1992, U.S. productivity rose 2.7%, while in 1991, U.S. workers were counted as the world's most efficient workers, with Japan and most Europeans in the 70–80% range).[24]

Ironically, foreign top managers have tended to be more charitable toward France and its economy than the French themselves. In a 1991 SOFRES survey of CEOs in Europe, Japan, and the United States, the French saw their country as less internationalized than did foreign CEOs (at 2.29 out of 4 for French CEOs as opposed to 2.69 for foreign ones), less prepared for European integration (at 2.28 vs. 2.97), and having a workforce less well trained (at 2.18 vs. 2.66). The only place where French CEOs were more optimistic than foreigners was on France as offering attractive investment opportunities (at 2.62 vs. 2.40), which could very well be another instance of misperception on the part of the French. Moreover, although they were more positive about the technological innovativeness and the quality/price ratio of their products than foreign CEOs (for a differential of +.45 and +.44 respectively), the French were less so about the internationalization and marketing capabilities of their firms (for differentials of −.31 and −.25 respectively). Finally, as regards the evaluation of individual sectors, the French were by far the more optimistic, whether it involved the agro-alimentary industry (a differential of +.53), pharmaceuticals (+.76), automotive (+.49), insurance (+.53), or banking-finance (+.41).[25] This suggests that while the French may have undervalued themselves when it came to more general categories related to international competitiveness, they overvalued, or they might insist appropriately valued, themselves when it involved specific industries.

Although France remains behind in comparison to some of its neighbors in the EC, it has nonetheless shown dramatic improvements in its economic outlook over the past dozen years or so, reversing the downward spiral of the mid 1970s to the early eighties. To begin with, inflation has been so successfully brought under control that France, which had one of the highest rates in Europe at the beginning of the decade, had one of the lowest by the end, remaining below that of Germany since June 1991, at 2.4% in 1992 by comparison with the EU average of 4.6%, and below 2% from mid 1993 on. Moreover, even though France's GDP per capita declined its overall GDP continued to grow at an acceptable rate, behind Italy from 1981 through 1994 and the United Kingdom from 1987 on, but remaining ahead of the United States, Germany, and Japan

[24]*Wall Street Journal,* July 16, 1993.
[25]SOFRES, "L'image internationale de la France et de l'enterprise française auprès des dirigeants d'entreprise en Europe, aux Etats Unis, et au Japon" (December 1991).

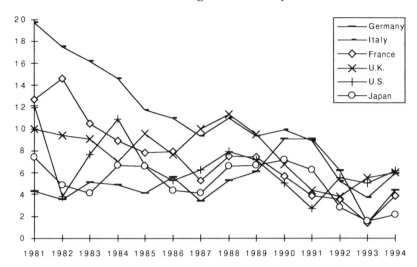

Figure 12.2. Growth in GDP (annual percentage change at current market prices, in national currency). Source: EC.

through the 1980s, although it slipped below them in the early 1990s (see Figure 12.2). In addition, despite the fact that France's budgetary deficit reached record highs in the early nineties because of the worldwide recession, the problem of the deficit steadily improved from 1984, when it was close to −150 billion francs, to 1990, when it was reduced to −93.15 billion francs – further testimony at the time to the recovery of the French economy, and a significant contrast with the United States, which had been unable to make much of a dent in its own deficit. Moreover, France remained in better shape than Germany: the budget deficit was only 2.1% of the GDP in 1991, by contrast with Germany's 2.9% (although this was largely a result of unification with East Germany).[26]

Other economic indicators also suggest that France, although not a top performer, has done reasonably well. France's economic growth between 1980 and 1992, at an average of 2.2% a year, was comparable to the average of the members of the European Community, and higher than that of Great Britain (+1.9%), Germany (+2.1%), and the United States (+2%), even if lower than that of Japan (+4.1%).[27] Moreover, despite the fact that France had a savings rate that declined slightly between 1981 and 1994 (from 21.1% to 18.6%) and in 1994 remained lower than that of Germany (21.1%) or Japan (32.6%), it was above that of Italy (18.4%) and well above those of the United States (15.5%) and the United King-

[26]*Financial Times*, September 24, 1992.   [27]*Rapport Raynaud.*

Changes in business

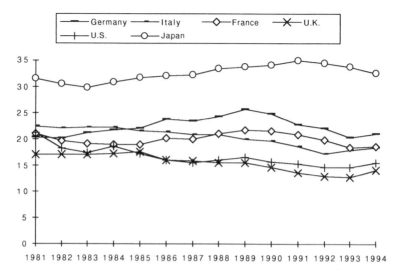

Figure 12.3. Gross national saving as a percentage of GDP at market prices. Source: EC.

dom (14.2%) (see Figure 12.3). In addition, French investment, although still insufficient in the view of many critics, having declined from 22.1% in 1981 to 18.7% in 1994, nevertheless remained in 1994 ahead of the United States' 15.5% and the United Kingdom's 15%, on a par with

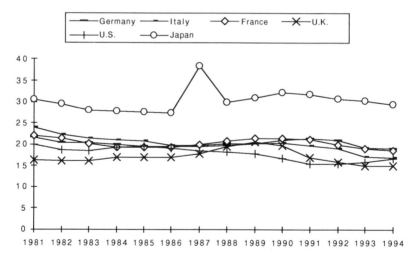

Figure 12.4. Investment (gross fixed capital formation at current prices, as a percentage of GDP at market prices). Source: EC.

Germany's 19.1% and Italy's 16.9%, and, like all other advanced indus-trialized countries, far behind Japan's 29.4% (see Figure 12.4).

France has also become extremely competitive in terms of salaries and wages. The Socialists' years in power, contrary to what one might have expected of a "workers' party," managed to hold wages down. The rise in hourly wage costs over the decade were kept in check, so much so that they ended up 16% below those of Germany as of September 1992.[28] By 1993, France had one of the lowest wage rates in the EU: at $17.79, it was higher than Britain's $14.61 and Spain's $14.70, but well below Ger-many's $26.90, Sweden's $24.64, the Netherlands' $21.64, and Italy's $19. Moreover, although this was still higher than the United States' $15.89, it was lower than Japan's $19.23. Paid vacation days as specified in union contracts were also toward the low end: France's 35 days were on a par with those of Britain and lower than Spain's 36 days, Sweden's 38, Italy and the former West Germany's 40, and the Netherlands' 41, even if they were still a lot higher than the United States' 23 vacation days and Japan's 25.[29]

Nonetheless, French managers still complained, not so much about the salary rate as the lack of flexibility in hiring and firing, and the expensive social *charges* or payroll taxes attached to the wages. Although France's wages are much lower than those of the former West Germany, its ratio of wages to benefits and taxes is close to Germany's 46%. For employers paying the minimum wage of 4,830 francs a month ($810), payroll taxes for social security programs take it up to 8,500 francs ($1,420), or anoth-er 43%. Contrast this with the 28% in payroll taxes over wages in the United States.[30] Or contrast French with American workplace flexibility. Whereas in America, as François Périgot, head of the CNPF, maintained, companies are able to change work conditions with relative freedom, even radically revising work rules and production methods for productiv-ity gains, this is not so in France, where "rigidities" in labor rules and "in our minds" inhibit change. But this is no less a problem in Germany, where the chief economist of the Bayerische Vereinsbank of Munich com-plained that unions block weekend work, among other efforts to improve productivity.[31] In fact, much of Europe has come of late to envy American flexibility, which has contributed to a lower unemployment rate, even if this has meant lower-paying jobs for many of the recently reemployed.

However, even if payroll taxes remain comparatively high, taxes on profits have regularly diminished since 1985, when they were approx-imately 50% (the rate since 1958), to a low of 33.3% in 1993 (see Figure 12.5). This compares favorably with Germany, where the maximum tax

[28]*Financial Times,* September 24, 1992.   [29]*New York Times,* August 9, 1993.
[30]Ibid.   [31]*Wall Street Journal,* July 16, 1993.

Changes in business

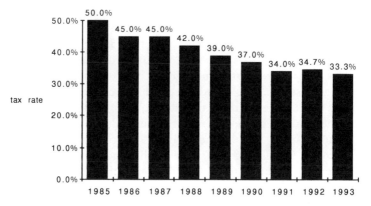

Figure 12.5. Change in tax rate on business profits, 1985–1993. Source: Francis Lefebvre, reproduced in "Raisons d'investir en France," Ministère de l'Economie, 1994.

on profits is as high as 60%, and Japan and Italy, where it is over 50%; and it is only slightly ahead of Great Britain. In July 1995, however, the Juppé government temporarily raised the corporation tax by 10%.

THE CHANGES IN BUSINESS

French business has become increasingly dynamic: Although industrial production grew slowly, industrial productivity rose at an unprecedented average rate of over 5.5% per year between 1981 and 1989.[32] Investment in research and development, not a strong point for French industry after de Gaulle (when the average annual increase was +7%), having experienced negative growth of −4% per year from 1968 to 1974 and zero growth from 1974 to 1981, increased under the Socialists at a respectable annual average rate of +4.2% between 1981 and 1986, regressed under the neoliberals between 1986 and 1988, and then jumped by +8% in 1988, bringing it back to the level lost in 1986.[33] And capital investment in French firms rose considerably, growing by 40% from 1988 to 1990 (+15% in 1988; +13% in 1989; +12% in 1990), even if the rate of increase in cash flow slowed during the same period (+20% in 1988; +3% in 1989; −10% in 1990; +5% in 1991).[34]

What is more, the ten top nationalized companies, which were losing more than 13 billion francs in 1981, made over 26 billion francs in profits

[32] Albert Merlin, "Réponse aux Cassandres industriels," *Politique Industriel* no. 18 (winter 1990).
[33] Levet, "Réindustrialiser la France," pp. 24–25.
[34] BNP newsletter on the state of the economy, March 1991 – quoted in *Le Monde*, May 17, 1991.

Table 12.1. *The sales and net income of public and private firms:*
1981, 1990

	Sales (in billions of francs)		Net Income (in billions of francs)	
	1981	1990	1981	1990
Public Enterprises[a]				
Elf-Aquitaine	104.4	175.5	3.7	10.6
Renault	87.7	163.6	-0.6	1.2
EDF	74.7	156.5	-4.6	0.1
France Télécom	50	103	1.9	5.4
Usinor-Sacilor	42.2	95	-7.1	3.7
Rhone-Poulenc	35.9	78.8	-0.3	1.9
Péchiney	40.9	76.9	-2.5	4.9
Thomson	43.7	75.2	-0.1	-2.4
Postal Service	40.8	69.1	-3.4	1.3
Air France	19.1	56.8	-0.3	-0.7
Total Public	539.4	1,050.4	-13.4	26.1
Private Enterprises				
Peugeot S. A.	72.4	160	-2	9.3
Alcatel-Alsthom	56.7	144.1	0.4	5.1
Total CFP	123.1	128.4	1	3.9
Générale des Eaux	20.3	117	0.3	2.2
Lyonnaise-Dumez	18.2	72	0.4	1.4
Saint-Gobain	43.5	69.1	0.5	3.4
Michelin	31.3	62.7	0.8	-4.8
Bouygues	9.3	56.7	0.2	0.6
BSN	19.3	52.9	0.4	3.1
Schneider	37	51.4	-0.3	0.9
Total Private	431.1	914.3	1.6	25.1

a More than 50% control by state

Source: Le Nouvel Economiste no. 795 (May 10, 1991).

by the end of 1990, about the same as private enterprises, which themselves had been barely breaking even in 1981 (see Table 12.1). Overall,
businesses' profit margins jumped from 25.8% in 1981 to 32.7% in
1990. And although these decreased with the recessionary trend begun in
1991, they enabled French industry as of 1987 to use its profits to expand
worldwide through acquisitions, most notably in the United States. In
1990, direct foreign investments came to 147.6 billion francs (or close to
$30 billion at the exchange rate of the time), a big shift from earlier in the
decade, when the government had embarked on a campaign to reconquer
the domestic market and frowned on foreign acquisitions, which until
1985 did not exceed 20 billion francs on average, and fell to 14 billion
francs in 1983.[35] Of the 1990 amount, over $12 billion went to finance
corporate acquisitions in the United States alone, putting it ahead of
British companies (at $11.3 billion) and Japanese (at $8.2 billion), as well
as far ahead of its own acquisitions in previous years (see Figure 12.6).[36]

[35]*Le Monde* July 6, 1991.   [36]*Wall Street Journal*, April 24, 1991.

Changes in business

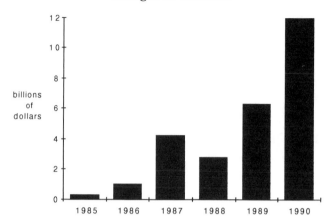

Figure 12.6. French acquisitions of U.S. companies, in billions of dollars. Source: *Wall Street Journal*, April 24, 1991.

This ambitious merger and acquisition program enabled French companies to remedy some of their problems related to inadequate size and internationalization, even if French industry's globalization remains behind other countries, with its 276 billion francs invested in OECD countries as of 1991 still one-sixth of the U.S. figure, one-third the British, and one-half the German.[37]

A major impetus for this shopping spree was European integration, and the recognition not only by French CEOs but by European managers more generally that the only way to compete was to penetrate other markets in Europe and elsewhere, primarily through joint ventures, mergers, or acquisitions. These decisions, in other words, were not mergers and acquisitions solely for financial profit, as were many in the United States in the eighties, but rather for strategic reasons.[38] In 1989, there were close to 1,300 cross-border mergers in Europe valued at more than $45 billion. In 1990, in France alone there were 1,759 mergers and acquisitions for a total of 311.8 billion francs. Moreover, although these figures dropped off dramatically in succeeding years because of the recession, with 1,605 mergers and acquisitions for 250.9 billion francs in 1991, 1,191 for 238.6 billion francs in 1992, and 979 for 178.3 billion francs in 1993, the beginnings of recovery in 1994 brought the franc amount back up to almost the 1990 level, with 991 mergers and acquisitions valued at 299.1 billion francs.[39]

[37]*Le Nouvel Economiste*, no. 778, November 11, 1991.
[38]"Stratégie du capital et de l'actionnariat," working document, Institut de l'Entreprise (January 1991).
[39]*L'Express*, March 16, 1995.

The French mergers and acquisitions were in all areas between 1987 and 1991, when the merger and acquisition fever died down. Most of these mergers and acquisitions proved expensive, causing most companies to go into debt. But they were also highly successful in increasing company size, sales, and often, if not always, profits. Michelin's acquisition of Uniroyal-Goodyear in 1989 made it the number one manufacturer of tires worldwide, although the high debt it took on contributed to its subsequent serious financial problems. Thomson's acquisition of RCA/GE in 1987 for 33 billion francs made Thomson Consumer Electronics number four worldwide, but also gave it debts of 10 billion francs and 1.4 billion francs in interest payments (figures from 1991), thereby contributing to its later difficulties. Other companies, although also taking on high debt, benefited from the increase in size without experiencing such financial difficulty. Péchiney's takeover of American National Can in 1988 put it in fourth place by 1991, just behind Usinor-Sacilor, and first for packaging. BSN's acquisition of Nabisco's European operations put it in the third place for Europe in the agro-alimentary sector. Schneider's acquisition of the electricity distribution firm Square D for 13 billion francs made it number one worldwide in its sector. Rhône-Poulenc's aggressive acquisitions plan, involving Union Carbide's pesticides division and Stauffer Chemical's inorganic chemicals division in 1988 and the American pharmaceuticals firm Rorer in 1990 (for $2 billion), meant that the group went from the twelfth rank worldwide in 1985 to the seventh in 1993, increasing its sales by 50% (at 81.7 billion francs).[40]

Other acquisitions in the United States included Accor's purchase of Motel 6 (for 7 billion francs); Saint-Gobain's of the abrasives manufacturer Norton; Bull's of Zenith (the computer division); Axa's of the insurance company Equitable Life (for $1 billion), and the tandem Altus-Maaf's of Executive Life. Purchases in Germany included Groupe Tapie's acquisition of Adidas, and Moulinex's of Krups; in the United Kingdom, Cap Gemini Sogeti's of Hoskyns. In addition, Elf went to Spain, gaining a fourth of the gasoline market with its acquisition of Ertoil, and Lafarge to East Germany.

Major alliances were also created. In Europe, the computer services firm Cap Gemini Sogeti joined with Daimler-Benz (through the acquisition of a 34% share in it); Renault with Volvo, through the exchange of shares; and Saint-Louis with Wiggins Teape (through the creation of a subsidiary which was to become the number three in European paper). In the United States, pharmaceutical companies such as the French Sanofi (a subsidiary of Elf) merged with Sterling Drug (a subsidiary of Eastman Kodak). In Europe, retailers such as Chaussures André started a joint venture with the English company Sears PLC to enter the markets in Holland and Germany.[41] Finally, under the impetus of the European Union's proposed European Nervous System (ENS), a web of computer systems that would track people, goods, and services across borders in the unified market, Olivetti, Bull, and Siemens-Nixdorf formed a consortium that put together a joint venture to develop applications for data exchange among EC governments, the Trans-European Information Systems (TEIS).[42]

Although the jury is still out on these joint ventures, mergers, and acquisitions, they already suggest that the initial pessimism of commentators who were convinced that much of the rush to concentration was ill-advised, tending on the whole to produce less profitable companies except in cases involving restructuring, divestment, and a return to core businesses, was premature. Collaborative ventures in the EC over the previous twenty-five years were few, due in part to legal and antitrust barriers and in part to cultural differences related to management practices and styles;[43] they were often unprofitable, such as Agfa-Gaevert and Dunlop-Pirelli, and sometimes failed because of cultural clashes, such as Unidata, a partnership between the West German Siemens, the Dutch Philips, and the French CII, dissolved in 1975.[44] The realities now, however, are different. Top managers are more aware of the need to adapt culturally. And they are taking steps to ensure that partners in collaborative ventures want the relationship to succeed. Thus, they seek to avoid the kinds of problems Renault experienced in the United States: not only the general one of buying too high a company in bad shape and then leaving it to local managers, as in the case of AMC, but also the more specific one of engaging in a limited joint venture with a partner (in this case Chrysler) that found it easier to make money by modifying the distribution of costs and profits, rather than trying to earn it. Renault itself learned its lesson: its relationship with Volvo has been one of cross-sharing holdings with a clear sense of one another's obligations.[45] French firms, in other words, are going in with their eyes open, well aware of the potential problems. But they are also clear as to their necessity.

Moreover, despite the fact that this merger and acquisition frenzy may

[41]Descours, interview with author.

[42]Jonathan Levine, "A Helping Hand for Europe's High-tech Heavies," *Business Week*, July 13, 1992, pp. 43–44.

[43]P. Lemaitre and C. Goybet, *Multinationals in the EEC* (Chichester: IRM Multinational Report, no. 1, 1984).

[44]J. Dunning and P. Robson, "Multinational Corporate Integration and Regional Economic Integration," *Journal of Common Market Studies* vol. 26, no. 2 (December 1987), p. 120.

[45]Schweitzer, interview with author.

have helped push France into recession and some French companies into the red as a result of heavy debt loads, it means that French industry is in a better position to weather regional economic ups and downs in the future, and to compete internationally. And even though their foreign acquisitions have made them more vulnerable to currency fluctuations of the dollar and the yen, they ensure that French industry is now not only inextricably linked to a European web of firms, but to a global web as well. Testimony to the good sense of French corporate strategy is the fact that as France pulled out of recession in 1994, the twenty-five largest French companies had on average doubled their profits over the previous year while lowering their debt loads.

The increasing internationalization of French business beginning in the late eighties, in short, has contributed to the improving economic profile of the country. Other problems have remained, however, that only in some instances began to be remedied at this same time.

Certain French industries were particularly threatened by European integration. The French agro-alimentary sector, for example, was still too dispersed in too many small firms (only one group, BSN-Gervais-Danone ranked among the twenty largest European firms) and not innovative enough (in investment in research and development, Nestlé by itself having outspent the entire industry).[46] Moreover, it was penalized by the distribution system of the large supermarkets.

The automobile industry, although appropriate in size given that the two major manufacturers, Renault and Peugeot, each had 4% of the world market, and in better shape than in the early eighties, was not necessarily ready to meet the challenge of international competition in a more open Europe (given previous tariff barriers that had kept the Japanese down to 3%).[47] It was also fragile because it could not rely on strong supplies.[48] Although Peugeot made 3.1 billion francs in profits in 1994 after a loss of 1.4 billion francs in 1993, it still had a long way to go to become internationally competitive. Moreover, although Renault had turned itself around by the early 1990s, with profits at 5.6 billion francs in 1992, up by 84% from 1991, it was the only world automotive company that was handicapped by its indebtedness. As of early 1994, it was still not doing well enough for the Balladur government to be willing to risk an early privatization – which sealed the fate of the Renault-Volvo merger – even though by the fall of 1994 it was willing to go ahead with a partial privatization. By the end of the year, Renault had 3.63 billion francs in profits and, most importantly, had wiped out its debts.

Other industries were already weakened by international competition

---

[46]Bocquet and Delleur, *Génération Europe.*   [47]Ibid.
[48]*Le Monde*, June 12, 1991.

that European integration could only intensify. The textile industry, slow to modernize with computer-aided production techniques, was under siege from lower-wage Asian countries. Only certain segments of the market, such as quality fibers, haute couture, and luxury ready-to-wear, remained highly competitive and out of danger.[49] For the regular ready-to-wear, problems of clothing manufacturers included ones of size next to their larger Italian and German rivals. For cloth manufacturers, the problems were ones of cost, given a still relatively labor-intensive industry which therefore favors low-wage countries.[50]

The paper industry also did not fare very well. Once the French government renounced its effort to find a French firm to dominate what it had for a long time considered a strategic sector, French paper production by and large fell under foreign control, going in three years from 15% to 36% as a result of acquisitions by American and European firms.[51]

By contrast, by the late eighties, although the chemicals industry still suffered from problems of size (the largest companies, e.g., Atochem – subsidiary of Elf-Aquitaine, Orkem, and Rhône-Poulenc – were still under half the size of their German competitors) and were not world leaders in any given product, they were nevertheless doing very well. Rhône-Poulenc, Elf, Total, and Air Liquide were in the top five slots for vaccines, pesticides, synthetic fibers, CFCs and their substitutes, inks, and industrial gas. After 1989, however, profits in the sector declined by between 20 and 50%.[52] In 1992, although Elf had 6 billion francs in profits, with its operations in pharmacy, cosmetics, and even haute couture (having bought Yves Saint Laurent in early 1993), it was still down by 37.6% over 1991. In fact, as of 1992, only the pharmaceuticals end of the industry continued to do well. Rhône-Poulenc had profits of 1.5 billion francs, for an increase of 23.6% over 1991. In 1993, moreover, it reported 0.962 billion francs in profits, and in 1994, 1.9 billion francs, by contrast with Elf, which posted a 5.4 billion franc loss in 1994 (at least partially due to a change in accounting method), and only a 1.1 billion franc gain in 1993.

But although the pharmaceuticals industry was in decent shape, it suffered from the price controls imposed in order to control health costs, which put reimbursed drugs at 40% of the price of German ones, and left French firms less likely to innovate (France had fallen to eighth place in the creation of new drugs by 1989 from second in the sixties).[53] The modest measures to encourage research had not offset the fact that low drug prices, intended to contain health care costs, had limited the size of

[49]Bocquet and Delleur, *Génération Europe.*   [50]*Les Echos*, April 8, 1991.
[51]Ibid.   [52]*Les Echos*, April 8, 1991.
[53]Bocquet and Delleur, *Génération Europe.*

profits and concomitantly the amount of money put into research. This resulted in French pharmaceutical companies being in a less competitive position than their neighbors. And because they had been spending more on consolidating their positions in the domestic market rather than on expanding in competitor markets, they were likely to be less competitive as time went on.[54]

In heavy industry, some of the larger manufacturers did well, while others did poorly. For example, in 1992, Péchiney, although not in the red, since it had earned profits of 0.203 billion francs, was down by 75.2% on profits of the previous year. In 1993, it showed a 0.98 billion franc loss, and in 1994, a 3.7 billion franc loss. Saint-Gobain was also down in 1992, although not as severely, with 2.13 billion francs in profits, for a reduction of 16% in profits over 1991. In 1994, however, its profits rose to 4.7 billion francs, up from 1.2 billion francs in 1993. By contrast, Alcatel-Alsthom remained strong throughout this period up until 1994, with 7 billion francs in profits in 1993 and in 1992, for an increase of 14.1% over 1991. It was only in 1994 that Alcatel began having problems, with company profits down 40% as a result of problems in Germany, Turkey, and Brazil (although the company still showed a profit of 3.6 billion francs), and with the stock price having lost half its value in response to this as well as to the problems of CEO Suard.

The steel industry was the greatest success story, having already attained the right size as the largest European steel producer in 1986, having introduced modern production techniques for *tôles* which allowed it to remain competitive with low-wage steel producers, and having as early as 1988 reached agreements with other European steel producers to enable them together to rationalize steel production.[55] However, the turnaround of the late eighties was followed by another period of decline, with 1992 leaving Usinor-Sacilor with a negative balance sheet of 2.4 billion francs, and with 1993 worse, with a loss of 5.7 billion francs as a result of the bankruptcy of its German subsidiary Saarstahl. The problems were the result of a slowing of demand in Europe generally, in particular by a decline in automobile sales, which had left all European firms with the exception of British Steel in tough shape, facing problems of overcapacity.[56] The company was not in dire straits, however, as evidenced by the fact that it was the first company slated for privatization by the new government of Alain Juppé under President Chirac, and was successfully privatized in June 1995.

The new technologies are another story, however. In the late eighties,

[54]David Wilsford, "Facing European Economic Integration: The French Pharmaceutical Industry," *French Politics and Society* vol. 8, no. 3 (summer 1990).
[55]Bocquet and Delleur, *Génération Europe*.   [56]*Le Monde*, November 17, 1993.

France was only in the fifth place worldwide in terms of exports of high-technology products (at 6%), after not only Japan (at 22%), the United States (18%), and Germany (12%), but even the United Kingdom (8%).[57] But here, international competition has put all European companies on the defensive, since they are all of insufficient size and lack mastery of the domestic market. They are dispersed by country and by *métier*, or core activity, with Bull and Olivetti only in computers, Thomson and Philips having abandoned the computer and telecommunications sector. Outside the Siemens, none are vertically integrated like the Japanese, from semiconductors to finished products, which allows them to finance one sector by another, or to lower prices in one area to recuperate them in another.[58] Some change has occurred in the nineties, as Bull reached an alliance with NEC. But Thomson and Bull have both been hurting enough to go to the government for large subsidies, which the EC Commission on Competition only grudgingly allowed.

Bull in particular has had the worst problems. It went from being one of the few nationalized firms operating in the black in 1981 to a deficit of 18 billion francs in 1989, at a time when most other firms were making large profits, and on to a record loss of $1.2 billion in 1990, which was followed by another $600 million loss in 1991, $825 million in 1992, and $883.2 million in 1993. Its attempts to staunch its losses by closing plants (six out of thirteen as of 1991), firing employees (one-fifth of a total of 445,000 as of 1990, with an additional 12,157 between 1990 and 1992, and another 3,000 in 1993), and rationalizing product lines did not turn the company around. Moreover, government subsidies did little to staunch the losses, whether the 4.6 billion francs subsidy of 1991, or the 2.45 billion francs ($438.3 million) injection in 1992 by the French state along with state-owned France Télécom. All in all, with the 1994 infusion, Bull will have received a total of 20 billion francs in just five years.

Although Bull itself claims that its problems result from difficult economic times and a general acceleration in the decline of prices,[59] in particular in minicomputers, most observers attributed Bull's losses to bad management under Francis Lorentz – which included remaining focused on the mainframe market for their long-term institutional customers while failing to take into account the demand for personal computers, work stations, and minis – and to a government more focused on national pride and preserving jobs than the bottom line.[60] This changed with the Balladur government, when Minister of Industry Longuet first demanded that the recently named CEO Bernard Pache bring the compa-

[57]Bocquet and Delleur, *Génération Europe.* [58]*Les Echos,* April 5, 1991.
[59]*Wall Street Journal,* July 30, 1993.
[60]Paul Klebnikov, "Bull? or Albatross?" *Forbes,* March 30, 1992, pp. 118–120.

ny to profitability as fast as possible, and then replaced him with Jean-Marie Descarpentrie, a man noted for slashing budgets and jobs. Descarpentrie attributed the problems of Bull to "bad organization, bad reporting. Maybe when you're backed by a government you do not have enough pressure [to perform]." He was depending upon the 11.7 billion franc government injection to complete his planned turnaround of the company, where instead of laying off workers he intended to slash operational costs (as much as three billion francs) in areas such as purchasing, subcontracting, and moving facilities to cheaper locations.[61] This has helped: the company lost only 1.94 billion francs in 1994.

The banking and insurance industries have also undergone tremendous change, especially as of the mid eighties with the financial deregulation that has brought increasing competition and exposure to risks. From protected, conservative enterprises, they have expanded and internationalized, becoming increasingly dynamic while modernizing their operations, with deposit banks creating new kinds of financial products and the business banks transforming their full range of services.[62] The financial concerns' new role as "accompaniers" of industry has meant that instead of passive lenders to industry, they are investors in industry, and as such have been major players in the restructuring of French capital. Although they have not quite taken on the role that the German banks have had with regard to industry, providing leadership or long-term stability, they have become at the very least junior partners, participating in the risks and gaining a vested interest in the success of the firm.

There have been differences in strategic approaches among financial concerns, however. Whereas the BNP and the Société Générale followed a bank-based model, playing a relatively cautious game in investing, the Crédit Lyonnais preferred a market-based approach modelled on the German industrial banks, and was extremely aggressive in its foreign financing policies, quadrupling its industrial holdings to 25 billion francs in just two years. This occasioned some criticism from fellow bankers and caused a number of particularly splashy problems, for example, the MGM-Pathé deal that soured, leading to recriminations from all sides; and the losses of 6.9 billion francs in 1993 and 12 billion francs in 1994. Ultimately, these problems brought an end to the bank's ambitions to become a major bank along the lines of the German ones. Once the 5 billion francs in new capital pledged by the government in 1994 failed to stabilize the bank, downsizing became inevitable, and was consummated in the March 1995 rescue plan, which involved the sale of assets (primari-

[61]*Wall Street Journal,* March 18, 1994.
[62]Hubert Bonin, "Les banques d'affaires et la sortie de la crise," *Le Débat* (May–September 1986), pp. 146, 155–156.

ly retail banking holdings outside of Europe) worth up to 135 billion francs and pledges to sell off more than 80% of its assets within five years and all its industrial stakes within three.

Finally, the air transportation industry, or more precisely, Air France, has done quite poorly. Having absorbed a number of smaller companies, including Air Inter, Air France has been unable so far to rationalize its operations or reduce its personnel sufficiently to make it competitive, especially by comparison with privatized British Airways, and this despite the 20 billion franc capital injection from the government on top of earlier subsidies. Moreover, Air France remains in the red, having lost 8.5 billion francs in 1993 and 2.35 billion francs in 1994, although the CEO Christian Blanc anticipated being in the black by spring 1996.

CONCLUSION

The early nineties found French business in much better shape than in the early eighties. And yet, problems remained for all industries as a result of the recession that seemed to have hit France harder and longer, and for certain sectors as a result of traditional weaknesses. Nonetheless, underneath it all, French industry had become relatively healthy in consequence of the changes in business and the economic environment in the past decade. As if to confirm this, the OECD in 1991 gave France a clean bill of health, noting that although it had a problem with high unemployment, inflation was under control, wage increases were appropriately moderate, the currency was strong, and the rate of growth in the foreign trade deficit moderated. And this led it to conclude that "a prudent macro-economic policy linked to audacious micro-economic reforms" will allow France to overcome progressively the problems left to resolve.[63] By 1993, moreover, further confirmation of France's underlying economic health came from a group of six Nobel prizewinners who urged the French government to withdraw from the EMS in order to avoid the slide into a pointless recession, given France's low inflation rate and otherwise competitive economy.[64] By 1995, France had started pulling out of recession, having stayed with the EMS; the national economy was in a strong position, despite continuing problems, including relatively slow economic growth.

[63]*Le Monde,* June 8, 1991. It is important to note that, despite the primarily favorable report, the headlines read: OECD criticizes the SMIC (the minimum wage) for contributing to the high unemployment figures by keeping the young, least skilled workers from getting jobs. The French government, clearly, did not take this criticism to heart, since in June 1991, it raised the SMIC by 2.3%.
[64]*London Times,* July 29, 1993.

13

Restructuring French capitalism

The revitalization of the French economy owes much to the changes in the structure of French capital, which were dramatic over the course of the Mitterrand years. French business went first from the "protected capitalism" of the pre-1981 period, in which hard cores of private enterprise investors controlled one another through cross-shareholdings, to the nationalization of major industrial and financial concerns, which instituted total state ownership and control. It then proceeded to the privatization of some nationalized enterprises to the benefit of hard cores of investors, which began the intermixing of French capital not only by including banks and insurers for the first time in industrial investment but also by having nationalized concerns acquire shares in the privatized companies. It led next to the partial privatizations in the *ni-ni* period and the post *ni-ni* period, then on to the renewed privatizations in which hard cores of public and private enterprise investors controlled one another again through cross-shareholdings. The end result is the "dynamic capitalism" of the mixed economy in which cross-shareholdings and interlocking directorships ensure that French business now looks much like the German in terms of banking–industry partnerships and like the Japanese in terms of affinity groups of industries, banks, insurers, other service providers, and suppliers. It also means that private and public firms formally control one another, with state control where state ownership remains having become increasingly indirect.

Within this new capital structure, the CEO remains all-powerful. The traditional powerlessness of boards of directors has only been increased by the cross-shareholdings that ensure that control, whether by the public or private sector investors that make up the hard core, is barely exercised. Whereas oversight over top management is insufficient in the case of the outside directors, it is eliminated entirely in the case of inside directors. The cross-shareholdings, in brief, have only reinforced the CEO's hand, even as they immobilize capital that could be otherwise used for investment purposes.

FROM NATIONALIZATION TO PRIVATIZATION

At the time of the nationalizations in 1981, French business was characterized by a "protected capitalism" in which a majority of publicly quoted French firms were controlled by a small group of investors with enough shares in the company to capture all seats on the board. In the financial sector, the investors tended to be other financial concerns; in the industrial sector, other industries. There was little cross-ownership between banking and industry, with the exception of the *banques d'affaires,* or business investment banks, Paribas and Suez, which had close relations with industry, forming rival spheres of influence.[1]

Nationalization changed all this by taking over not only major industries but also major financial concerns, including Paribas and Suez. As of January 1, 1986, the state held a controlling interest in over 50% of the 50 largest industrial firms in France, family-owned firms accounted for approximately 25%, and foreign concerns about 20%. Once we expand the list to the 150 largest companies, the three main kinds of controlling interests converged at around 25% each. The banks controlled next to nothing (under 5%).[2] Moreover, there were a negligible number of companies where there was no controlling interest. Of the 200 largest companies, only six met this description as of January 1, 1986: Air Liquide, Lafarge Coppée, BSN, Club Méditerranée, Compagnie de Navigation Mixte, and Valeo (soon to be acquired by Benedetti), up by only one from 1971 (when, in place of the last four, the list included Marine-Firminy, CGE, and Péchiney – the latter two nationalized in 1981).[3] And yet, even if these firms had no shareholders with a controlling interest, they nevertheless often had some kind of stable, major shareholders.[4]

Privatization began the process of change in this scenario, reducing state control as it essentially re-created something akin to the traditional

---

[1] For the pre-1981 situation, see in particular: François Morin, *La structure financière du capitalisme français* (Paris: Calmann-Levy, 1974).

[2] Bauer and Mourot, *Les deux cents,* pp. 106–107.

[3] Bauer and Mourot, *Les deux cents,* p. 107, fn. 7; and Morin, *Structure financière.*

[4] For example, in the case of Lafarge Coppée, the second largest cement manufacturer in the world, although 40% of the shares are held by small shareholders (the only other French firm like this is Air Liquide) and no one holds more than 5% of the shares, 35% of the shares are held by institutions which look at the medium-short term and 25% are held by ten French industrial and financial investors with long-term commitments. Thus, as the president of the group, Bertrand Collomb, notes, although there is no *noyau dur,* the firm is still protected from any surprises. *Le Monde,* February 22, 1991.

Table 13.1. Board membership and holdings by major players (two or more) in the hard core of privatized enterprises, in percentages (holdings at privatization – 1986–1987/holdings in 1989)

	Paribas	Suez	Soc Gen	CGE	St Gobain	CCF	TF1	Matra	Havas
Paribas[a]									bd 4/4.5
Suez					bd 3.8/4.5		bd[b] 1.2/3.3		
Société Générale				bd 5.8/8.8			bd 2/2.6		bd 4/4.5
BNP				0/0.6	bd 3.9/4			bd /2	bd /.9
Crédit Lyonnais							1.1/1.7	bd /2	
UAP	bd 3.5/5	bd 1/4.6	1/1	bd 2.6/3.5	bd 1.7/2.2				bd /3.8
AGF	bd 2/2.2	1/0.67	bd 2/3.5						bd /4.3
GAN		1/0.83	bd 2/4.5					2	
Axa	bd 2/4		bd			/3			
Rhône-Poulenc			bd 2/2.5			bd /3			
CGE			bd 2/4			/4.5			
Générale des Eaux	0.6/0.6		bd 0.5/0.5	bd 2.6/2.9	3.4 / 8.2				
Caisse des Dépôts			1/2.4						bd 2.5/2
Société Gen. Belg.		bd 1.5/5.9		1.8/4					

a Paribas is listed because, although it participates in only one noyau dur, it is an important player in the new set of relationships and alliances.
b Suez shares held through its subsidiary, Indosuez.

"protected capitalism" of the pre-nationalization period. There were three significant differences, however.

First, financial institutions, primarily the banks and insurance companies, acquired a significant share of industrial capital for the first time. Before this, the banks had held a negligible interest in industry, lending money but for the most part not holding shares in the companies or seats on the boards. In consequence of this move, an industrial giant such as Saint-Gobain had a hard core and board membership that included financial giants such as BNP, Suez, and UAP in addition to the water resources giant Compagnie Générale des Eaux (see Table 13.1 and Figure 13.1); CGE similarly had UAP and the Société Générale (as well as the BNP as of June 1989), along with the Compagnie Générale des Eaux and the Belgian bank Société Générale de Belgique; and Matra had the BNP, Crédit Lyonnais, and GAN. By the same token, industrial concerns gained a share in major banks and insurance companies to a much greater degree than ever before. Thus, a financial giant such as Société Générale had a hard core that included industrial giants such as CGE and Rhône-Poulenc (for which they were the major banker), the CEOs of which sat on the board along with the CEO of Peugeot and the number two at Renault (whose firms did not hold shares), in addition to assorted insurance companies which held shares and seats on the board such as AGF (with which the bank has had long relations) or only seats such as Axa, and again the Compagnie Générale des Eaux. CCF was similarly controlled by CGE, Lafarge-Coppée, Rhône-Poulenc, and Thomson CSF, although it was also held by insurance companies such as Mutuelle du Mans and the retailer Galeries Lafayette. Paribas, by contrast, although itself not well represented in shareholdings, was controlled mainly by insurers such as UAP, GAN, and Axa, investment firms such as Bruxelles-Lambert, and firms in control of natural resources such as Total and, again, the Compagnie Générale des Eaux, in addition to the industrial firm Péchiney, with a seat on the board (but no shares). Suez was controlled by industrial firms such as Saint-Gobain, other financial concerns such as UAP, Cerus, GAN, AGF, Marceau Investissements, and the oil company Elf, along with the foreign Société Générale de Belgique and another water resources company, Lyonnaise des Eaux (on the board with no shares). Finally, the communications giant Havas was controlled primarily by banks and insurers such as Paribas, Société Générale, Crédit Agricole, AGF, and UAP, along with Société Générale de Belgique and Lyonnaise des Eaux. The major players (i.e., two or more major holdings) in the *noyaux durs* of the privatized enterprises, in short, were first and foremost other privatized enterprises such as CGE, Société Générale, and Suez; two private enterprises, Compagnie Générale des Eaux and Axa; one foreign banking concern, Société Générale de Belgique; and certain

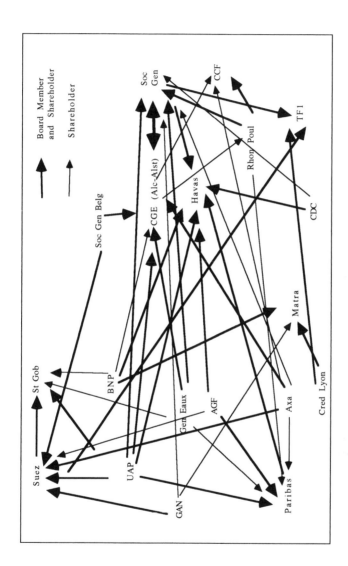

Figure 13.1. Board memberships and holdings of major players in privatized companies (as of 1989).

nationalized enterprises such as UAP, BNP, AGF, GAN (see Table 13.1 and Figure 13.1).

This last category of shareholder in the privatized enterprises, in fact, brings us to the second major difference from the past: the nationalized banks and industries also held shares in the privatized enterprises, making the distinction between nationalized and privatized firms in terms of ownership and control a bit confusing. Among the nationalized enterprises acquiring major shareholdings in privatized firms, UAP was probably the most ubiquitous, becoming a major shareholder and member of the board in most of the privatized firms, including Saint-Gobain, Paribas, CGE, Havas, and Suez, and only a shareholder in the Société Générale (see Table 13.1 and Figure 13.1). The BNP was also in the hard core and on the board of Saint-Gobain, Matra, and Havas. The Caisse des Dépôts et Consignations had a seat on the board and shares in Havas, and only shares in the Société Générale; while AGF had shares and a seat in Havas and in the Société Générale, and only shares in Suez. GAN held shares but no seat on the board of Paribas, Société Générale, Suez, and Matra. Crédit Lyonnais had a seat and shares in Matra, Total in Paribas, and Elf in Suez. Rhône-Poulenc was on the board and in the hard core of CCF and Société Générale, while Thomson CSF was on the board and in the hard core of CCF. Moreover, the number two at Renault, Louis Schweitzer, was on the board of the Société Générale even though Renault was not part of the hard core of shareholders. The result is that most privatized firms came to be controlled by a mix of public and private, nationalized and privatized enterprises.

Third, and again in contradistinction to the past, the privatizations created patterns of reciprocal shareownership, where companies held shares in one another, and interlocking directorships, where CEOs sat on one another's boards (whether they held shares or not in one another's companies).[5] Thus, just as Suez acquired major shareholdings in Saint-Gobain at the time of its privatization, so Saint-Gobain did Suez (even before Suez was privatized). A similar pattern obtained with CGE and the Société Générale.

There were other ways in which the changes reproduced patterns of the past that only reinforced the web of influence among the small group of major financial and industrial firms. First, in a pattern reminiscent of the pre-1981 situation, many firms subsequent to privatization had subsidiaries acquire major shareownership in a parent company in order to reinforce the power of the CEO on the board.[6] This inside control, pres-

[5]Testimony by François Morin, Professor at the University of Toulouse I, *Rapport sur les opérations de privatisation*, vol. 2, p. 856.
[6]Ibid.

ent before 1981 in such enterprises as Paribas, Suez, and CGE (at 14% of
its capital), returned after 1987 or 1988: CGE increased the holdings of
its subsidiaries (the Compagnie Immobilière Méridionale and the Société
Financière et Immobilière de Contrôle et de Gestion) in the parent company to around 7% from nothing at the time of privatization; Saint-
Gobain increased its own to 4.67%; the Société Générale, to a whopping
10% (the top amount allowed by law); and Paribas, to 9% through its
subsidiaries (Compagnie Bancaire and Copeba, its Belgian subsidiary),
with an additional measure of quasi-inside control coming from the 3.6%
held by Bruxelles-Lambert, run by the former CEO of Paribas, Gérard
Ashkenazi. Not included in this list, moreover, are the shares held by
pension funds (e.g., for CGE, which constituted an additional 5%); by
employee shareholders, who were also reserved places on the board; and
by employee representatives who might or might not vote with top management (two at Saint-Gobain and two at Suez, while at CCF, it was eight
out of nineteen board members excluding the CEO – two were top management, one was a former CEO, and five were employees).

Second, the hard cores essentially re-created the strategic alliances of
the past, such as those between CGE (Alcatel-Alsthom), Société Générale
(CGE's traditional banker), and CCF; Suez and Saint-Gobain; and Paribas, Générale des Eaux, and Schneider. These were the alliances that
symbolized to the highest degree the French capitalism of the sixties. It
was almost as if, according to François Morin, these companies wished to
make it clear that nationalization was merely a parenthesis. But it was a
parenthesis with a difference, because with financial powers as part of
these renewed alliances, they became very different in terms of their potential for financing their ventures. The network around Paribas in 1989
had a capacity of 1,250 billion francs in terms of ability to mobilize
financial resources; Suez had 921 billion; CGE-Société Générale 988
billion; and the Crédit Agricole 1,144 billion.[7] Moreover, the potential
for full networks to be created around the three major poles was significant. Paribas and Suez, through their shareownerships in rival companies,
had already divvied up major portions of industry. For example, while
Paribas had Générale des Eaux, Suez had Lyonnaise des Eaux; while
Paribas had Generali (investment), Suez had Cerus; while Paribas had
Bruxelles-Lambert, Suez had Société Générale de Belgique; and while
Paribas had CFP (Total), Suez had Elf. In addition to these parallel shareownerships, there were strong alliances on the one side between Paribas
and the insurer Axa Midi (as of September 1989, Paribas gained a 10%

[7]François Morin, *Le Monde*, September 17, 1987; *Rapport sur les opérations de privatisation*, Report volume, p. 128; and Morin testimony, *Rapport sur les opérations de privatisation,* vol. 2, pp. 859–860.

interest in Drouot, one of the main firms in the Axa Midi group), on the other Suez and Victoire.[8] (This was not to last long, however, since by 1993 Paribas had sold most of its holdings to go back to its core business banking activities.)

With privatization, then, the right-wing government created a situation in which there were connections among hard cores, and where closed networks of capital were created, with a majority of the members of the hard core, and in particular those on the boards of directors, part of either reciprocal shareownership or inside control. Paribas's board, for example, had eight out of fifteen board members who were linked to the network through either inside control (five) or reciprocal ownership (three); Suez had seven out of twelve, including four with inside control and three with reciprocal ownership (including Beffa of Saint-Gobain, de Benedetti of Cerus, and Lamy of the Société Générale de Belgique). CGE is similarly controlled.[9]

The main advantage of this set-up is that it created a "community of interests" or one of collective control that represented a line of defense against foreign takeover attempts, given that between inside control, re-ciprocal shareownership, and the other members of the hard core, in almost all cases approximately 50% of the capital was held in fifteen or twenty friendly hands.[10] As of 1989, for example, CCF's *noyau dur* controlled close to 50% of its capital, between its hard core at 30%, its employees at 6%, its clients with 8%, and CCF itself with over 5% of the capital.[11] The only vulnerability for privatized firms with such control would come from dissension within that small group of shareholders.[12]

This power of the hard core to resist takeover came about essentially subsequent to privatization, generally as a result of a few of the major shareholders increasing their holdings on top of the rise in inside control (see Table 13.1). For example, Paribas went from a hard core of 18.2% in January 1987 to 25.1% in July 1989, with only three firms showing major increases: UAP (which went from 3% to 5%); Axa (from 2% to 4%); and Bruxelles-Lambert (0.6% to 3.6%). Saint-Gobain's major shareholders, although not an official hard core (since they came from the dissolution of SFPI), nevertheless went from 17.06% in June 1987 to 24.49% in June 1989, with the major increase being that of the Compagnie Générale des Eaux (at 8.15% – up from 3.39%). For CCF, the only major change in its hard core (at 30%) was the increase in the holdings of the Groupe des Mutuelles du Mans (from 3.8% to over 9%). At CGE,

[8]*Rapport sur les opérations de privatisation,* Report volume, p. 128; and Morin testimony, *Rapport sur les opérations de privatisation,* vol. 2, pp. 866–867.
[9]Morin testimony, *Rapport sur les opérations de privatisation,* vol. 2, pp. 854–855.
[10]Ibid., pp. 858, 863.   [11]Ibid., p. 742.   [12]Ibid., pp. 858, 863.

where the hard core increased from 31.7% in December 1987 to 45.4% in June 1989, one major player, the Société Générale, increased its stake significantly (to 8.8% from 5.8%). At Havas, as of December 31, 1988, there were many changes in the hard core from the beginning of the year, but only one major increase: Lyonnaise des Eaux (to 7% from 4%), and two new players, the Caisse des Dépôts et Consignations (at 5.8%) and Canal + Finance (at 5.6%). At the Société Générale, the only major increase was the jump by Marceau Investissements from a negligible amount (0.5%) at privatization to over twice the control of any other shareholder (at 10%) by July 1989.

The solidity of the alliance created by the hard core, moreover, was reinforced by various pacts among the shareholders. The most significant such agreement was among the major shareholders of CGE (Alcatel-Alsthom), which ensured that in the case of a desire to divest themselves of shares in the company, they had to sell to one another, and that no shareholder could have voting rights in excess of 8%, regardless of the percentage of capital owned.[13] The hard cores, in short, had been made harder through increases in capital and agreements of major share-holders, and thereby less vulnerable not only to foreign takeover but also to internal takeover attempts, as Bérégovoy later found when he tried to engineer the takeover of the Société Générale.

FROM PRIVATIZATION TO THE MIXED ECONOMY

By the time the Socialists returned to power in March 1988, the land-scape had changed. Many of the firms they had nationalized in 1982 were now privatized, and many of the still-nationalized companies were share-holders in the privatized enterprises, leaving a situation in which the mixed economy had become even more intermixed, with the ownership and control of privatized firms one that included privatized and nation-alized, public and private enterprises. The Socialists after 1988 were only to complicate this even further, as the *ni-ni* period saw the intermixing of share ownership in the nationalized enterprises, and the post-*ni-ni* period saw the further intermixing of share ownership with the acquisition of shares in the nationalized enterprises by privatized firms. Moreover, the nationalized enterprises also continued to acquire shares in private and privatized companies.

The banks in particular, whether nationalized or privatized, gained shares in industry. In 1990 alone, Crédit Lyonnais acquired shares in Novalliance, Zanier, Sicli, Bidermann, Seribo, Guillin Emballane, Bouy-gues, Pinault, Arnault and Associates, DMC, Essilor, and Lyonnaise des

[13]*Rapport sur les opérations de privatisation*, Report volume, pp. 130–131.

Eaux, for a total investment of 18 billion francs (as of July 1990), quite a change from the 1.30 billion francs in shares in industry that it held in 1987. BNP, by comparison, had a total investment of 13 billion francs with holdings acquired in 1990, up from 2 billion francs in 1987, including Novalliance, Bidermann USA, Cap Gemini Sogeti, Valeo, Strafor, Saint-Louis, Saint-Gobain, Générale des Eaux, Matra, Facom, Péchiney, and Boiron. Société Générale also increased its holdings in industry, going from 2.5 billion francs in 1987 to 18 billion in 1990, with 5% of SAE, 10% of SPEP (which holds 58% of Schneider), 7.8% of CGE, and shares in Perrier, Pernod-Ricard, Michelin, Peugeot, Péchiney, Rhône-Poulenc, Air Liquide, Générale des Eaux, Devanlay, and Salomon. Even Paribas, which traditionally invests in companies, saw a major increase in its industrial shareholdings, from 12.75 billion francs in 1987 to 30.5 billion francs in 1990, having taken control of Buyomac'h and gained shares in Valeo, SPEP, Beghin-Say, Rochette, Fougerolle, Poliet, Sommer-Allibert, Rhône-Poulenc, and Total. Suez, however, was by far and away the biggest player, with 104 billion francs in industrial shareholdings, up from 9 billion francs in 1987, which included the takeover of the Compagnie La Hénin, the reinforcement of Lille Bonnières Colombes, the creation of Eurosuez, and control of the Société Générale de Belgique (51%), as well as shares in Lyonnaise des Eaux, Saint-Gobain, Eurotunnel, and Pernod-Ricard.[14]

This was not a one-sided relationship, however. Industry held shares in banks and insurance companies as much as the latter did the former as well as in one another (see Table 13.2 and Figure 13.2). By 1991, UAP and BNP each owned 10% of each other; Thomson owned 14% of the Crédit Lyonnais; Crédit Lyonnais and AGF held shares in Rhône-Poulenc; and BNP and AGF held shares in Péchiney. By this same time, Crédit Lyonnais controlled 9.4% of the chemical group Rhône-Poulenc, 14% of the military electronics manufacturer Thomson CSF, and 20% of the steelmaker Usinor. AGF held 6.8% of Rhône-Poulenc and 10% of Péchiney. Moreover, France Télécom held 8.3% of the Hervet Bank, 17% of Bull, and, by 1992, 14% of Thomson.

The structure of ownership of the public companies was often quite complicated given these cross-shareholdings as well as the fact that subsidiaries were also generally not held exclusively by the parent company, especially where they involved joint ventures. The case of Thomson is illustrative. While the parent company Thomson SA was held by the state at 82%, France Télécom at 14%, and the banks at 4%, Thomson SA itself held 100% of Thomson CE, 100% of Thomson Electro Ménager, and only 60% of Thomson CSF. This last in turn held only 45% of SGS

[14]*L'Usine Nouvelle* no. 2277 (July 19, 1990).

Table 13.2. Hard-core investors in major public and private enterprises, in percentages (holdings in April 1994)

Firms	BNP	*UAP	Soc Gén	*Cr Lyon	*AGF	Pari-bas	Suez	Axa	CDC	Alc Alst	Saint-Gob	Gen Eaux	Lyon Eaux	*Pch-iney	Rhôn Poul	*Elf	Total	Hav-as
BNP		19			3.7						3.7	1.6		7.5	2.4	1.4		
*UAP	15						5				4.4	4	6			3		2.7
Soc Gén					1.8					4.5					4.3		2	8
*Cr Lyon					2.8										7.4		3.4	
*AGF				6.4		8.3								8.7	6.6		3.4	
Pari-bas								4								1		5
Suez		5									6.9		12.4		1.4#	1		
Axa			5			6.9	3			4.5					1.25	1		
CDC		0.7	5.6		2.5										0.5	5		6
Alc Alst			6									2.5						
Saint-Gob	1.8	1.2	1.5				6					10.5						
Gén Eaux	0.5	2.2								2	9.5							
Lyon Eaux										1								
*Pch-iney	1																	1
Rhôn Poul	1.1		2.5															
*Elf	2.1						3.8					2.5						
Total Hav-as																		

Note: Reading across gives amount of firm's investments in other enterprises. Reading down gives amount of firm's equity held by investors.

* Majority owned by the state (UAP 52.3%; AGF 65.5%; Crédit Lyonnais 55.3%; Péchiney 55.8%).
# Held through its subsidiary Société Générale de Belgique.

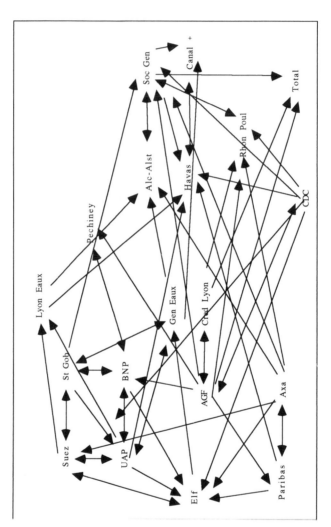

Figure 13.2. Holdings by hard-core investors (as of April 1994). Source: Adapted from *L'Expansion* November 4–24, 1993, and other information.

Thomson, another 45% of which was held by Italian IRI and another 10% of which was held by the British Thorn EMI.[15]

In the meantime, the privatized companies also saw changes, and even more complicated arrangements with respect to ownership and control. Matra-Hachette, for example, was held at 37.6% (with 50.3% voting rights) by the holding company Lagardère Group,[16] which in turn was controlled by the CEO Jean-Luc Lagardère, who held 12.6% of the holding company (with 18.8% voting rights) through Lagardère Capital and Management, along with a hard core of investors that included the financial concerns GAN at 3.9% (with 3.7% voting rights), BNP at 8.1% (with 12.1% voting rights), Crédit Lyonnais at 8.3% (with 11.2% voting rights), and Paribas at 5.6% (with 4.3% voting rights); the industrial firms GEC at 7.3% (with 5.5% voting rights), Daimler-Benz at 8.6% (with 6.5% voting rights), and Northern Telecom at 7.5% (with 5.7% voting rights); the Floirat group at 11.7% (with 12.8% voting rights); and public shareholders and others at 20.1% (with 19.1% voting rights). While the industrial firms' holdings represented for the most part alliances, the financial concerns represented capital investment, and they were therefore in close contact with the CEO. It might seem surprising, therefore, that Lagardère remained at the head, given the problems that Matra-Hachette had had with the failures of the TV channel, La Cinq, the football team, and the automatic metro of Orly, which cost the company 4 billion francs. Clearly relationships mattered. This was amply demonstrated when Pierre Dauzier, the head of Havas, who had started buying shares in Hachette in an effort to force an audit of the group, was dissuaded from pursuing this by Chirac as head of the RPR; Jérôme Monod, CEO of Lyonnaise des Eaux and member of the board of Havas; and Jean-Marc Vernes, also a member of the board as well as CEO of the Vernes Bank.[17]

With renewed privatization as of 1993, moreover, the changes in equity stakes and intermixing increased. By now, most of the players had become convinced that the best way to overcome the weakness of French capitalism – which had neither the strong banking interests invested in industry since World War II, as in Germany, nor the large pension funds that control 20% of a vastly larger stock market, as in the United States – was by interlocking ownerships seen as business partnerships. Certain close relationships, something like *keiretsus* – although the Japanese example is rarely mentioned by this time – had established themselves.

However, as business partnerships, the relationships had to make business sense. Thus, although the insurance companies had initially been

[15]*L'Expansion*, May 21–June 3, 1992.
[16]Another 24.4% (with 27.3% voting rights) was held by the Arjil Bank.
[17]*L'Expansion*, November 4–24, 1993.

playing a godfather role, this ended with the downturn in the economy. Claude Bébéar of Axa made clear that "My role is clearly not to carry French industry. It is not my money but that of my insured."[18]

Some of the banks, too, were no longer interested in playing a very active role. The Caisse des Dépôts et Consignations had taken a back seat ever since the failed raid on the Société Générale of 1989. Although it still held a sizable number of shares in major companies (see Table 13.2 and Figure 13.2), it saw itself as playing the role of a stabilizer rather than that of a restructurer or active member of the hard core of investors.[19] According to top management, it was more a question of placing its funds than of exercising control. In many cases, it put its money in particular companies because it was asked to do so by the state. It could have refused, but it didn't.[20] Paribas and Suez, traumatized by their losses in real estate and in the markets, were also less willing to be active players, with Paribas in particular, according to its head Lévy-Lang, having given up its traditional alliances and focused on its core activities instead, on medium-sized firms with growth potential in need of capital and advice.[21]

The privatizations beginning in 1993 reinforced the patterns of mutual influence that had already been established. The core of stable investors in the privatization of BNP, each of which held between 0.5% and 2% of the capital, included Saint-Gobain at 1.8%, which simply returned the favor that the BNP had provided when it participated in its privatization at 3.7%. Peugeot-Citroën, despite its financial problems, with a 1 billion franc loss for the first semester of 1993, bought into its banker for 1.03%. Péchiney, similarly, took a 1% stake in the bank which held 7.5% of it. In addition, UAP held a 15% equity from previous share swapping. Rhône-Poulenc's privatization, which reserved 6% for new hard-core investors, led to a situation in which the hard core controlled 24%, made up of those that had already had equity in the firm, primarily financial concerns, with Crédit Lyonnais at 7.4%, AGF at 6.62%, BNP at 2.4%, and the Société Générale, the company's traditional banker, at 4.33%. Rhône-Poulenc's new entrants included two more financial concerns: Axa, which holds the company's life insurance business worth 4 billion francs, with 1.25%, and Crédit Suisse with 1%; along with one industrial firm, Fiat-France, with 1%, which has an industrial alliance with the company in the fibers market through SNIA and will also have a seat on the board. Elf's privatization in February 1994 reserved 10% of the capital for the *noyau dur,* with UAP at 3%, BNP at 1.4%, Sofexi (a

[18]Ibid.

[19]Comments of the new Director-General, Philippe Lagayette, *L'Expansion*, November 4–24, 1993.

[20]Conversation with a top manager, November 1993.

[21]*L'Expansion*, November 4–24, 1993.

subsidiary of Renault) at 1%, Paribas at 1%, Axa at 1%, Crédit Agricole at 0.5%, Union des Banques Suisses at 0.5%, the Belgian group Albert Frère at 0.5%, and the Société Général de Belgique, a subsidiary of Suez, at 1.4%. Finally, UAP's privatization in April 1994 reserved 10.8% to hard-core investors consisting of the Compagnie Générale des Eaux at 2.2%, Soparinvest (Albert Frères, Belgium) at 2.2%, Westdeutsche Landesbank (Germany) at 2.2%, Saint-Gobain at 1.2%, Meiji Mutual Life (Japan) at 1%, Grande Armée Participations (Peugeot) at 0.8%, Caisse des Dépôts et Consignations at 0.7%, and Crédit Local de France at 0.5%. These investors joined long-standing shareholders BNP (at 19%) and Suez (at 5%).

These new privatizations only reinforced the new spheres of influence that by 1993 had established themselves, building on previous traditional alliances (see Table 13.2 and Figure 13.2). A large sphere of influence was created through the reinforcement of the traditional alliance of Suez and Saint-Gobain with the new coupling of UAP and BNP (instigated by the Socialists in 1989), by BNP holding shares in UAP and Saint-Gobain; UAP in Suez and Saint-Gobain; and Saint-Gobain in Suez and BNP. These were not exclusive relationships, however, since UAP and Saint-Gobain both held shares in Générale des Eaux, while Suez held shares in Générale des Eaux's rival Lyonnaise des Eaux Dumez. Moreover, both water resources companies were also tied to the second sphere of influence, made up of the traditional allies Alcatel-Alsthom (formerly CGE) and Société Générale, along with CCF, and two new partners, Havas and Canal Plus (the first holding 8.4% in the second, which held 23.5% of the first), both of which had shares held by Société Générale (8% of Havas, 5% of Canal Plus). These, too, were not exclusive relationships, however, since all but Havas were tied to the first sphere of influence through shares held in and by Générale des Eaux, while Havas had shares held by UAP. In addition, a third sphere of influence around AGF and Crédit Lyonnais seemed to have developed, albeit tied to the second through shares held by AGF in Société Générale and shares held by both AGF and Société Générale in Rhône-Poulenc. Axa was also tied to this sphere of influence through its ownership of shares in Société Générale, Rhône-Poulenc, and Alcatel-Alsthom, and it brought Paribas into this sphere through its interlocking shareownership (although Paribas was also a part of it through its shares in Havas). The oil companies belonged to different spheres, with Elf tied to the first through its shares in Suez and Générale des Eaux and UAP's shares in it, and with Total tied to the third through shares held by AGF and Crédit Lyonnais as well as the second through shares held by Société Générale.[22] In addition, the

[22]Ibid.

Table 13.3. *Cross shareholdings of selected hard-core investors, in percentages (holdings in June 1995)*

Firms	BNP	*UAP	Soc Gen	*Cr Lyon	*AGF	Pari bas	Suez	Alc Alst	St Gob	Gen Eaux	*Elf
BNP		19					5		3.7		1.4
*UAP	14.4						6.8		4.1		2.9
Soc Gén					1.6			9.1			
*Cr Lyon					1.3						
*AGF			2.5	2.3		6.6					
Pari bas					1.5						
Suez	5								6.5		1.4
Alc Alst			3.4							2.5	
St Gob		1.2						5.7		10.5	
Gén Eaux								1.9	7.7		
*Elf	4	2.9					3.8				

Note: Reading across gives amount of firm's investments in other enterprises. Reading down gives amount of firm's equity held by investors.

* State Ownership (UAP 3.4%; AGF 57.1%; Crédit Lyonnais 55.3%; BNP 2.4%; Elf 13.4%)

Source: Adapted from The Economist, July 1, 1995.

Caisse des Dépôts et Consignations held shares in a number of these firms, although these were solely as investments rather than also as strategic alliances, as it was for the other firms.

By June 1995, moreover, the spheres of influence had reshuffled, the results of shifts in business alliances, changes in state ownership, and financial problems of some of the major firms. Générale des Eaux, AGF, and Paribas were now clearly part of a close-knit, *keiretsu*-like network including the Société Générale and Alcatel-Alsthom, while Suez, Elf, BNP, UAP, and Saint-Gobain were all part of another. Crédit Lyonnais had bowed out, given its financial troubles (see Table 13.3 and Figure 13.3).

These spheres of influence have only been enhanced by a more European set of cooperations. The internationalization of French capital is found not only in the acquisitions and joint ventures, but also in participation in the capital of foreign firms. The CEO of Alcatel-Alsthom, for example, is on the board of directors (*conseil d'administration*) of Fiat to represent the company's 2% share, alongside Mediobanca (3.19%), Gen-

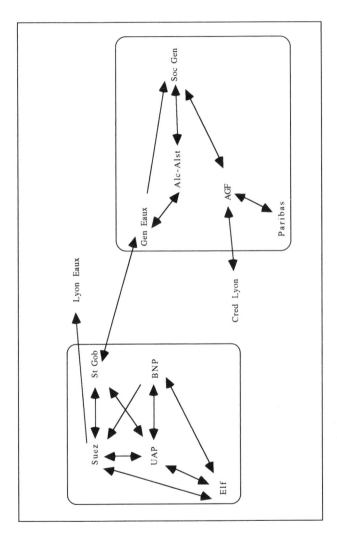

Figure 13.3. Networks of cross shareholdings of selected hard-core investors (as of June 1995). Source: Adapted from *Economist*, July 1, 1995.

erali (2.42%), and the Deutsche Bank (2.39%), two members of the Agnelli family (Giovanni as president and his nephew Giovanni Alberto Agnelli), two representatives of the company, two representatives of the Lazard Bank, and one from the Swiss business bank Ab Golding.[23] Moreover, most firms, nationalized as well as privatized, had a foreign member of the hard core. Shares in UAP, for example, were held by Wintherthur (2.9%), in addition to BNP's 20%, France Télécom's 0.6%, and the state's 53%. This pattern began with the privatizations of 1986–1988. Société Générale had two foreign concerns, Commercial Union and Nippon Life, as members of its hard core.

Thus, French firms are now tied into a set of international as well as national alliances that not only provide stability, funds for investment, and partners for future ventures, but also protect them from takeover. There are, nevertheless, a number of problems.

PROBLEMS WITH THE NEW STRUCTURE OF CAPITAL

One of the major problems with the new structure of French capital is that with the trading of shares between companies or the holding of shares by the company, much capital that could otherwise be used to invest is immobilized, and corporate finances may suffer as a result. Moreover, inside control through subsidiaries' shareownership in the parent company has tied up a lot of capital in a nonconstructive way, given that the money is not available for investment. For example, at the time of the first set of privatizations, the Société Générale's inside control represented the immobilization of 3 billion francs, and this was similarly true for Suez, Paribas, and CGE, all of which had 2, 3, 4, or 5 billion tied up in this manner.[24] These problems have only worsened since the first set of privatizations. By 1993, even more capital was immobilized, with Saint-Gobain at 7 billion francs, Alcatel-Alsthom at 6 billion, and Paribas at between 15 and 18 billion. Moreover, this amount of immobilized money brings in only 2.5% from dividends, while the cost of borrowing is at 7%. Recognizing this, a number of companies such as Air Liquide, Lafarge-Coppée, and CCF simply floated stock issues without interlocking shareholdings, banking on protecting themselves through technical means such as limiting voting rights or setting a very high threshold for control.[25]

Another possible negative effect is that competition will suffer either because a company holds equity in competing firms or because the relationships among firms become too cozy, much like the pre-1981 situation. On the first issue, which CEOs admit can cause uneasiness, the

[23]*Le Monde*, Nov. 17, 1993.
[24]Morin testimony, *Rapport sur les opérations de privatisation*, vol. 2, pp. 859.
[25]*L'Expansion*, November 4–24, 1993.

answer is to keep the rival firms separate. For example, in the case of UAP, the insurer, which holds shares in Suez and Paribas, and in Lyonnaise des Eaux-Dumez and the Générale des Eaux, CEO Jean Peyrelevade insists that the company puts up the equivalent of the great wall of China to avoid transmitting confidential information and to ensure that it is represented by different people on the boards of the companies.[26] On the second score, there are those who insist that there is little to worry about, given the character of contemporary French CEOs, who are much less likely to maintain a peaceful and cooperative fraternity than in the traditional "protected capitalism" of the past. As Jacques de Fouchier, president emeritus of Paribas and, along with Ambroise Roux, a leader of the pre-1981 fraternity, remarked, "After nationalization, privatization, and despite the *ni-ni,* our top managers seek new brands at the risk of fratricidal battles."[27] This is because French CEOs are individualists, and many strategies involve alliances with different groups to ensure that rivals don't get the upper hand.

A more significant problem with the new structure of French capital than the immobilization of capital or the potential impact on competition involves the overall control of the company, which, given the new structure of ownership, is one that devolves primarily to the benefit of top management. This is because although a hard core could in principle exert control, the percentage of shares held by any one member is generally so small — often at 0.5 to 1%, and even for the major shareholders infrequently over 3% and rarely much more than 5% (see Tables 13.1 and 13.2) — and the number of such shareownerships is so relatively large (anywhere from twelve to twenty) that control is diffuse. Moreover, top management's independence was not only reinforced by the increase immediately after privatization of inside control, through subsidiaries' shareholdings and inside directors who, as the heads of subsidiaries, were unlikely to go against their own hierarchical superior. It was also helped by the fact that the outside directors, themselves CEOs, would be unlikely to impose on the CEO, given that there was every possibility that they faced that selfsame CEO on their own board of directors. François Morin called this the principle of "I got you, you got me."[28]

What is more, the fact that with the privatizations the CEOs were in many cases responsible for picking the hard core ensured that they had the gratitude if not the loyalty of the new board. This probably also explains the fact that all the CEOs of the privatized enterprises kept their

[26]Testimony by Jean Peyrelevade, president of Suez before privatization, *Rapport sur les opérations de privatisation,* vol. 2, pp. 746.

[27]*L'Express,* May 2, 1991.

[28]Morin testimony, *Rapport sur les opérations de privatisation,* vol. 2, pp. 856–858, 862.

jobs once the general shareholders' meetings occurred immediately after privatization.[29]

The result has been an absence of sanctions on CEOs. Responsibility has been diluted and personal relations have had great weight.[30] Not only do they sit on one another's boards, but they also belong to the same club, the Entreprises et Cité, organized by Claude Bébéar. Thus, the *noyau dur* of investors that characterizes French public and private enterprise ensures stability, but not necessarily good management.

There is little difference in this lack of oversight from the past. And it was as true for the nationalized enterprises as it was for the private ones. At Renault, for example, from the early fifties to the eighties, the board of directors and the CEO never had a conflict. As one top Ministry of Industry official with experience on boards of directors explained, "The boards of directors meetings are essentially rubber stamps. . . . If there are any questions, they come before and after, even though during the presentations, questions are asked, of course, but these never cause conflict. The boards of directors are more places for networking."[31] (In this regard, it is significant that in none of the interviews for this study did the CEOs ever bring up the boards of directors.) In fact, even the employee members of the board raise no significant issues. Thus, as this same civil servant noted, "Although the employees often have a Marxist or class-based discourse, that is mainly for appearance. They always go along with the CEO." Moreover, the general assembly meetings of the shareholders are even less significant, since they are generally over in five minutes. Any important meetings occur beforehand, with any issues solved in private.

There are a variety of reasons for the singular authority of the CEO. In private firms in the past as much as at present, the combination of interlocking directorships, diffuseness of ownership, and personal relations that characterized membership in the *noyaux durs* ensured the absence of any real oversight. In public firms, where the state owns and controls, the dynamic has been somewhat different, but the results have been the same. The tradition of public sector autonomy has certainly played a large role in protecting the nationalized firm from state interference with the decisions of the CEO;[32] but there is more to it than this. At least since the fifties, state administrators on the boards of directors of nationalized

---

[29]There were actually two instances of CEOs fired by the board after privatization. This was the case of the heads of the BIMP and the BTP, both of whom were opposed to control of the firm by a *noyau dur*. See the discussion in *Rapport sur les opérations de privatisation*, Report volume, p. 127.

[30]Comment by Philippe de Lagayette, Director General of the Caisse des Dépôts et Consignations *L'Expansion*, November 4–24, 1993.

[31]Interview with author, Paris, December 1992.   [32]See Chapter 7.

enterprises have generally had close ties with those they were charged to supervise as a result of sharing the same schools, the same *grand corps* membership, and the same state career track.[33] In 1957, of the 134 state administrators of public enterprises in energy, transportation, and mechanical industries, 23 were *inspecteurs de finances* and 35 were technical corps engineers (17 of which were mining engineers).[34] The percentage is probably as great today. The result of this shared corps membership between engineers of the technical ministries and those in public enterprises is, in the words of Alain Griotteray in a report written in the early seventies, that the former "are hardly equipped for looking at the latter's suggestions with a critical eye. Not really capable of exercising their duties, they are gradually brought down with anemia."[35] Another motivating factor is that top civil servants also see their careers as ultimately leading to top positions in the firms which they are charged with overseeing, given the phenomenon of *pantouflage*. There is little, therefore, that encourages them to do anything other than to adopt a cooperative attitude.

Within the nationalized enterprises, moreover, the fact of the CEOs' appointment by the Prime Minister and President only enhances their power and incontrovertibility. As one top manager explained it, "Although in public enterprises, the president of the administrative council is de jure elected by council members, he/she is de facto appointed by the two *responsables* of the state, the Prime Minister and the President. Naturally, it is of superior essence."[36] The result is a system in which CEOs are treated as monarchs, making them very difficult to dissuade once they have decided on a particular course of action. The Crédit Lyonnais disaster is a good illustration of the problems. The reason Jean-Yves Habérer could not be stopped by the state, the members of the administrative council, or top management of the bank was that, as Jean Peyrelevade explained, "By definition, in a monarchical system, no one, with the exception of the monarch, understands the full situation."[37] In the nationalized sector, then, as much as in the private sector, despite state ownership, CEOs remain essentially free to do as they choose for better or for worse.

Finally, the recent interlocking directorships among nationalized enterprises make for even less exercise of control by state administrators, since

[33]Pierre Bauchet, *Propriété publique et planification* (Paris: Cujas, 1962), p. 262; see also Derivry, "Managers of Public Enterprises," p. 213.

[34]André Delion, *L'état et les entreprises publiques* (Paris: Sirey, 1959).

[35]A. Griotteray, "Rapport sur les entreprises nationales" (Document no. 2010), first ordinary session of the National Assembly, 1971–1972, p. 13 – quoted in Derivry, "Managers of Public Enterprises," p. 215.

[36]*Le Nouvel Economiste*, no. 956, July 29, 1994.   [37]Ibid.

the major investors of the *noyau dur* are seen as the principal actors, even if they do not sit on the board. Thus, although the state formally still directly controls nationalized firms, given the law governing the composition of the boards of directors (one-third employees, one-third state representatives, and one-third "*personalités qualifiées*") and the fact that nothing guarantees a seat on the board to firms that have bought into a given nationalized company, such control has become for all intents and purposes indirect, as informal control resides with members of the *noyau dur*. But core investors, whether in public or privatized firms, have rarely exercised control except where they have been concerned about serious mismanagement or scandal, and even this has only been since the spring of 1995, in the cases of Suez, once UAP successfully blocked an increase in capital, of the Compagnie de Navigation Mixte, which had its entire board replaced at the instigation of Paribas, and of the Alcatel-Alsthom board's reluctant removal of CEO Suard. Unless the *noyaux durs* or the boards of directors of public as much as private companies begin to exercise control on a more day-to-day basis, whether officially or unofficially, recent changes in the structure of oversight will represent little more than a guarantee of continued top management autonomy.

The main sanction possible today is the stock market, which nearly doubled in size from 1986, when it was capitalized at 1,150 billion francs, to 1993, when it came to 2,200 billion francs. But it is a sanction that can be exercised by investors primarily only through the trading of shares, since there is little to support stockholder activism. The "people's capitalism" promoted by the right in the first wave of privatizations, as we have already seen, did little to give the small individual stockholder access to and influence over corporate decisions.[38] In fact, there were noticeably fewer individual holders of publicly traded shares (*action cotée*) at the end of 1992 (34%) than there were in 1977 (although the number is about the same, around 20%, when privately held and publicly traded shares are taken together). Moreover, the percentage of individual shareholders in the stock market in 1992 made them of little consequence compared to the larger investors, whether the financial concerns (23%), industrial concerns (21%), foreign concerns (20%), or public authorities (2%). Among nontraded stock, business held far and away the largest share (65% by contrast with 16% for individual shareholders).[39]

Finally, although there is more talk today of American-style corporate governance to ensure better oversight, it remains for the most part just talk. Even Michel Albert, the main pundit on the appropriate structure of French capitalism and now member of the monetary policy council of the

[38]See Chapter 5.   [39]*Le Monde*, October, 11, 1994.

Bank of France,[40] although full of praise for American innovations such as audit committees and outside members for the boards of directors, insists that any such changes should be left up to the companies themselves, and not imposed by law.[41] This means that wide-scale change in corporate governance will be slow in coming, although there are some indications that it is coming. Elf, for example, changed its accounting procedures for the 1994 exercise to conform to the standards set by the American FASB (Financial Accounting Standards Board). Casino and Générale des Eaux created board committees with new powers, while Paribas added a director to represent minority stockholders (the head of the Association of Minority Stockholders). Finally, Lyonnaise des Eaux, in seeking to improve its image after a variety of recent scandals, in April 1995 brought in two outside directors and established audit, salary, and ethics committees for its boards of directors, and at the end of June published full details of top executives' compensation.

The market nonetheless is likely to become increasingly important. Although it may not attain the importance of the New York or London stock exchanges, it is already much larger than the German. Thus, for all the talk of restructured French capital resembling the German model, there remain significant, and necessary, differences. By restructuring French capital by way of hard cores of investors and all the while opening the markets, the French sought a compromise between the German model of banking–industry relations, which even the greatest proponents of the model such as Beffa admitted lacks flexibility, and the American dependence upon the stock market, which, as Beffa insisted, has too short-term a focus for French industries in need of a stable source of financing because they are not giants as in the United States.[42] For Lévy-Lang, this middle road between the two models was to be recommended, contingent upon the further expansion of the financial markets. For although he agreed that the developing networks of participation may provide managers with sufficient stability to allow them to develop medium and long-term strategies, they will still have to go to the market because French companies have an insufficient level of savings.[43]

Thus, although the restructuring has certain elements in common with the protected capitalism of before 1981 – in the *noyau dur* control of both public and private industries attendant upon the privatization and the *ni-ni* periods – and with the German model – where the participation of the banks and insurance companies in the capital of industry ensures greater stability and sources of financing as well as protection from take-

---

[40]See the discussion in Chapter 6.   [41]*Le Monde,* October 11, 1994.
[42]*Le Figaro,* November 14, 1990.
[43]André Lévy-Lang, head of Paribas, quoted in *Le Figaro,* November 14, 1990.

over – there are also significant differences, the reliance on the market being the major one. Certain weaknesses associated with the pre-1981 model remain, however, including the lack of meaningful control of the CEO by investors, not only the small but also the large, whether as members of the hard core or as directors on the board. As long as the CEOs are competent and far-seeing, this is not necessarily a problem. But the question is: Is there any way to know this before disaster strikes, given the lack of oversight?

CONCLUSION

For the decade of the eighties, at least, the new CEOs seem to have performed well, modernizing operations, expanding and internationalizing, and improving labor–management relations. The problems of the nineties, however, which include overreaching in terms of mergers and acquisitions (e.g., the Crédit Lyonnais), failing to anticipate changes in market trends (e.g., Bull), and failing to deal sufficiently with problems of overstaffing (e.g., Air France), suggest that some greater oversight by boards of directors might have been in order. Nonetheless, these CEOs were responsible in large measure for the modernization of French enterprise.

14

Reforming managerial practice

During the Mitterrand years, French management practice changed dramatically in a variety of spheres. Much of this must be understood against the background of changes in French societal attitudes toward business. As we have already seen, in the case of the nationalizations, the public along with the Socialists who had disapproved of business and mistrusted its business heads, seeing them as exploiters of labor, came to see business as the creator of riches and business heads as heroes and friends of the worker. And privatization, rather than generating a wide-scale conversion to laissez-faire capitalism, elicited a popular rejection of all economic ideology with the realization that business operates as business, whether it is nationalized or privatized.[1] This sea change in French attitudes toward business was evident not only in the rehabilitation of business generally but also in an amelioration in labor–management relations, both on the labor side, where studies showed a softening of labor militancy and a more positive approach to the firm by workers, and on the management side, where business heads shifted their attention from problems with personnel to questions of profitability, and where modernization became the watchword.

The greatest changes in French managerial practice in the Mitterrand years have been in personnel and labor relations and in the introduction of modern management techniques; the smallest have been in the CEOs' management style and in top management recruitment and promotion. Although decentralization of managerial decision-making has occurred at the lower levels of the hierarchy, major decisions still remain centralized in the hands of the CEO, who, given the increasing size and internationalization of French industry along with the restructuring of ownership and control, has now a great deal more power than in the past.

Of all areas of internal management practice affected by the policies of

---

[1]See Chapters 4 and 6.

the past decade, management recruitment and promotion have been least changed. By doing little to alter the elite profile of the CEOs they appointed to the nationalized enterprises, the Socialists and the neoliberals ensured that there would be no direct challenge to the long-standing patterns of recruitment and promotion to top management positions. The typical profile of the French top manager, private as much as public, as we have already seen, remains that of elite education at one of the *grandes écoles,* elite civil service corps membership, extensive state service, and comparatively brief business career. The French recruitment system remains more exclusive in terms of education than those of all other advanced industrialized nations except Japan, while promotion continues to be more state-centered and thereby less based on business experience than in any other advanced industrialized nation.

MANAGERIAL DECISION-MAKING

Most CEOs agreed that significant changes occurred in French managerial practice during the Socialists' tenure. They credited the Socialists with promoting an entrepreneurial spirit and unblocking labor–management relations. They also noted the beginnings of change in the CEOs' management style, which has traditionally been highly centralized. Moreover, although not all CEOs interviewed agreed that modernization started with the Socialists – for some it started in the seventies with the introduction of modern management techniques, for others it came after 1968 with greater attention to human resources management, and for yet others it represented a gradual process going as far back as the fifties – they were all convinced that it accelerated under them, beginning with the new appointments to head the nationalized enterprises. Most saw these new CEOs as younger, better trained, more professional, more technically sophisticated, better able to manage human resources, better at devising management strategy, and more open to the world than their predecessors, whom they often described as more paternalistic and less competent, having abandoned industry to focus on the consumer instead of the enterprise. The sociologist Elie Cohen has described these new CEOs as "true capitalists" who, even if they had gone to the same schools as their predecessors, "are, compared to their elders, carriers of a modern capitalism, of movement, conquerors and European."[2]

As "carriers of modern capitalism," these CEOs were at the forefront of promoting the adoption across French industry of modern management techniques. Over the past decade, French managers have come to recognize that the client needs to penetrate the enterprise, and that the

[2]Elie Cohen, quoted in *Le Monde,* May 11, 1991; and conversation with author, Paris, February 20, 1991.

strategy of marketing that starts from the needs of the client works. Japanese management techniques have been all the rage. On the production line, JIT, or Just-In-Time, for inventory control has become *de rigueur*. In many cases, moreover, major French firms have decentralized their operations, democratized their management, and modernized their personnel evaluation systems.[3] As early as 1984, the management consulting firm Cofremca found these changes in evidence, with a greater concern for productivity and efficiency on the parts of workers and management; new market strategies, innovation, and diversification; and greater managerial cohesion resulting from the process of decentralization, the increase in autonomy and responsibility, and the social transformation of the enterprise.[4] By 1988, however, the same consulting firm found that greater acceleration in the changes in French enterprise was needed for it not to be left behind, outdistanced by more flexible and inventive competitors more open to today's realities.[5]

Although there has been a transformation of French management techniques in production, marketing, and corporate organization, changes in management decision-making style have come more slowly. The more modest changes are perhaps understandable, given that the new heads of the nationalized and privatized firms, although from a younger and more open generation, are little different in training from their predecessors, for whom hierarchy and centralization were the stock in trade.[6] And as if this were not enough, those who might be inclined to alter their leadership style come face to face with the expectations of their subordinates, who are used to leaders who manage in an autocratic and paternalistic style.

The modest changes in top management centralization
of decision-making

Confronting the new CEOs of the early eighties was a rigidly centralized and hierarchical structure which ensured that only the highest levels of management had decision-making power and that the president alone bore responsibility for the company's activities.[7] Compared to Great Brit-

[3]See, for example: Renaud Sainsaulieu, ed., *L'entreprise, une affaire de société* (Paris: Presses de la Fondation Nationale des Sciences Politiques, 1990); G. Archier and H. Sérieyx, *L'entreprise du 3e type* (Paris: Seuil, 1984); and Antoine Riboud, *Modernisation, mode d'emploi* (Paris: Union Générale d'Editions, 1987).
[4]"Meilleur pilotage dans les entreprises," *L'Observatoire de la Cofremca*, no. 12 (1984).
[5]"L'accélération du changement des entreprises," *L'Observatoire de la Cofremca*, no. 27 (1989).
[6]See, for example: Pierre Dupont Gabriel, *L'état patron c'est moi* (Paris: Flammarion, 1985).
[7]For empirical pieces on French management before the eighties, see: Roger Pri-

ain and Germany, France has had the strongest degree of centralization of authority, with the CEO monopolizing decision-making power on most major issues and having an exalted status unparalleled in either other country.[8] Moreover, unlike German managers who reward individual creativity and see the organization as a coordinated network of rational individuals, or the British who focus on interpersonal communication and negotiation skills and view the organization as a network of relationships among individuals who seek to influence one another, the French have traditionally emphasized the ability to manage power relationships and to work the system, primarily because they looked at the organization as "an authority network where the power to organize and control the actors stems from their positioning in the hierarchy."[9]

The hierarchical structure of the firm, along with the focus on power relations, ensures that all attention in French firms is focused on the top. This is only enhanced by the fact that French firms traditionally have boards of directors or workers' councils that play minor roles, unlike in the United States or Germany. The lack of control by boards of directors or workers' councils in both public and private firms has been such that it led one CEO of a major industrial group to insist that "We are the only Western country where one man alone conceives of the strategy of the enterprise, applies it, and controls it without the board of directors exercising any counterpower."[10] Given all of this, it becomes all the more understandable why, as one CEO put it, the entire system "leads to a solitary power at the top," and although decentralization is necessary to combat all of this, it requires "fighting a natural tendency."[11]

Such a situation, where centralization of decision-making, autocratic rule, and paternalism hold sway, is very difficult to overcome. But despite the fact that "the French CEO is seen more as a monarch who makes decisions all alone, perhaps with some princes," many CEOs did seek to diminish the authoritarianism, decentralize operations, and introduce into the enterprise information-sharing and decision-making with the

ouret, *La France et le management* (Paris: Denoël, 1977); André Harris and Alain de Sédouy, *Les patrons* (Paris: Seuil, 1977); Dominique Xardel, *Les managers* (Paris: Grasset, 1978); Philippe Vasseur, *Patrons de gauche* (Paris: Lattès, 1979).

[8]Christel Lane, *Management and Labour in Europe: The Industrial Enterprise in Germany, Britain and France* (London: Edward Elgar, 1989), p. 105; J. Horovitz, *Top Management Control in Europe* (New York: St. Martin's, 1980), p. 67; G. P. Dyas and H. Thanheiser, *The Emerging European Enterprise: Strategy and Structure in French and German Industry* (London: Macmillan, 1976), p. 246.

[9]André Laurent, "The Cross-Cultural Puzzle of International Human Resource Management," *Human Resource Management* vol. 25, no. 1 (spring 1986), p. 96. For the implications of this for internal management in France, by comparison with the United States and the Netherlands, see: Philippe d'Iribarne, *La logique de l'honneur: Gestion des entreprises et traditions nationales* (Paris: Seuil, 1989).

[10]*L'Expansion*, January 9–22, 1992.   [11]Gallois, interview with author.

managers and wage earners.[12] But this depended very much on questions of personality as much as on firm history, sector, structure, and degree of internationalization.

To begin with, long-internationalized firms such as Péchiney, Rhône-Poulenc, Saint-Gobain, and Elf were in the view of many CEOs less likely to be centralized than more recently internationalized firms. At Elf, for example, the relatively small head office set the overall direction of business policy and controlled the finances, but otherwise operations were decentralized, with the heads of subsidiaries used to autonomy, to managing on their own, and to having their own business strategies.[13] At Saint-Gobain, the operations of which have been highly decentralized and internationalized for a very long time (they have been in Germany since 1865, in Italy since 1892, in Spain since 1903, and in the United States since 1968), CEO Beffa explained that only certain responsibilities were centralized, such as strategic policies, which were nevertheless proposed by subordinates; finances, because "you can only spend what you earn"; and human resources, "in order to give people promotional opportunities on an international basis."[14] Roger Martin, former CEO of Saint-Gobain, confirmed this view when, in explaining his own lack of interest in financial questions related to the privatizations, he commented that "One cannot run a bazaar like Saint-Gobain without a great deal of decentralization; and to have decentralization, people given responsibilities should not feel that the boss is always looking over their shoulder, and that he has, *a priori,* always a view of what will happen."[15]

But whereas Gandois of Péchiney insisted that the centralization of decision-making was mostly a legend[16] and Beffa of Saint-Gobain maintained that the question itself "was not *sérieuse*" (having already spent one and a quarter hours in the interview itself without interruptions), others took the question seriously indeed. Peyrelevade of UAP (now Crédit Lyonnais) insisted that centralization was still a major problem across industries, including his own insurance industry, and even for the new generation of CEOs, including Beffa, although he felt that the CEO was not alone to blame, given that subordinates sent decisions up the hierarchy.[17] Similarly, Gallois of the jet engine manufacturer SNECMA found the entire culture of the enterprise centralized, and complained that he himself had to make all the strategic decisions, with people com-

[12]Lebègue, interview with author.   [13]De Wissocq, interview with author.
[14]Beffa, interview with author.
[15]Testimony of Roger Martin, *Rapport sur les opérations de privatisation,* vol. 1, p. 390.
[16]Gandois, interview with author.
[17]Jean Peyrelevade, CEO of Crédit Lyonnais, at the time of interview head of UAP (and before that head of Suez), interview with author, Paris, May 1994.

ing to him all day long. But he considered SNECMA's partner GE no less centralized.[18] Louis Schweitzer of Renault similarly admitted that his company was totally centralized in its decision-making, but that this was likely a function of the automotive industry worldwide, with its single big profit center – GM, he felt, was equally centralized.[19]

Sector of industry is only one variable that might explain centralization of decision-making. Personality also plays a role. Jacques Calvet of Peugeot, for example, has a reputation as an autocrat who insists on seeing all dossiers ahead of time and then quizzing his directors on a particular problem.[20] Moreover, while Bernard Attali, head of Air France until 1993, was reputed to have centralized all decisions in his office, so much so that it created something of a bottleneck, his predecessor, Jacques Friedmann, was seen as someone who consulted the personnel.[21] In fact, personality plays a much larger role than even political sympathies, since decentralization has been implemented by CEOs on the right as much as the left, most notably by Beffa at Saint-Gobain, Peyrelevade at UAP, Riboud at BSN, and Descarpentrie at Carnaud Metal Box.[22]

The democratization at the middle management level

Although some firms have successfully democratized decision-making at the uppermost levels, the most progress has been made at the lower managerial levels. Companies such as Péchiney reorganized in 1990–1991 to give more autonomy, creativity, and responsibility to factory worker and director alike.[23] Saint-Gobain flattened its hierarchical levels and virtually got rid of the separation of supervisory and maintenance personnel in order to enhance the diversity of tasks and to increase span of control. In addition, it reorganized and subsidiarized its operations to give younger cadres the opportunity to work in lighter structures, where they knew one another, could make their own decisions, could deal on their own with their labor problems, and more generally could feel more responsible for their decisions and avoid feeling that they worked in bureaucratic, hierarchical structures.[24] Aging monoliths such as the Caisse des Dépôts et Consignations also underwent significant changes, having been decentralized and reorganized through the creation of subsidiaries with precise ends in terms of core activities, and having replaced the old egalitarian system of seniority where the boss was far removed with a manager much closer to the team and a merit system to reward perfor-

[18]Gallois, interview with author.   [19]Schweitzer, interview with author.
[20]Conversation with a management consultant, Paris, April 1991.
[21]Conversation with a manager at Air France, November 1993.
[22]Lebègue, interview with author.   [23]*Le Nouvel Economiste*, March 3, 1991.
[24]Beffa, interview with author.

mance.[25] Even the most seemingly hidebound of public bureaucracies, Post and Télécom, was reformed by way of massive participation of the employees, proving that "in a country where corporations are strong and unions weak . . . a modern negotiation is possible." They created two autonomous entities, set up a new salary scale, modernized job classifications, and renewed all regulations for telecommunications.[26]

These changes in managerial practice have been generally successful in democratizing management practice at the lower levels in the hierarchy. In a 1989 study of three major firms, Michel Crozier found that managers were very open to participative management, were unanimously in support of quality circles, and greeted the reduction in hierarchical levels with not nearly the opposition that might have been expected, because it speeded up the decision-making process. Nonetheless, he found that many problems resulted from the fact that, despite the more modern form of decision-making at lower levels, major decisions still mounted the hierarchy.[27] For Crozier, in brief, centralization remained, even as decentralization increased.

A number of CEOs interviewed confirm this view. Francis Lorentz of Bull, for example, complained, "We still function within a hierarchy, and wait for the hierarchy to tell us what to do. Otherwise, nothing is done."[28] What is more, once the orders are given, Lorentz noted that they are not followed, because of a "mix of centralization and anarchy" in which subordinates

rethink the decisions, seek all the reasons for why another decision than the one that was taken should have been, such that you find that eight days later, what is done is 180° different from the decision taken. . . . Anarchy results not from the refusal of order, but this sort of individualism, when each one protects himself individually or assumes that he alone is best or knows bests what needs to be done. Rather than working with those at their own level, they prefer to go up the hierarchy for an arbiter. It's the *peur du face à face,* or fear of face-to-face relations.[29]

This description suggests that the relationship first outlined in Crozier's "bureaucratic phenomenon" continues.[30] Others, however, have another perspective on the same set of phenomena, seeing them less as a sign of ongoing French unmanageability than as simply a cultural fact which may have positive or negative consequences for the firm.

Philippe d'Iribarne, for one, sees this individualism as an ingrained cultural trait to be worked with, rather than opposed, in order to get the

---

[25]Boudrouille, interview with author.

[26]*Le Monde,* April 26, 1991. For the full story on the transformation of the Télécom side in particular, see: Cohen, *Colbertisme hi-tech.*

[27]Michel Crozier, *L'entreprise à l'écoute* (Paris: Interéditions, 1989).

[28]Lorentz, interview with author.　[29]Ibid.　[30]Michel Crozier, *Bureaucratic Phenomenon.*

most from employees. He characterizes such individualism as involving the "logic of honor," based on long-standing French traditions governing interpersonal relations, in which each individual thinks of himself as a kind of sovereign power who has, at most, to account for his actions only to his own conscience and to his own sense of honor, at the same time that he still has a sense of the good of the whole organization, so that challenges only go so far.[31] This contrasts with the "logic of virtue" as found in the United States, where people respect laws that apply to all, and are very much wedded to formal rules, to contracts, and to job descriptions. The French are much less bound to contracts and rules, creating their own informal rules within the organization, and maintaining a strong sense of independence, even deciding whether to go to a regular meeting with a superior on the basis of whether it is more important than something else they need to do.[32] Moreover, even where centralization is the stock in trade of a company (and d'Iribarne actually found little uniformity in the pattern of hierarchical relations, with centralization characterizing some firms and decentralization others, and with some managers having much power, others little),[33] there is often open conflict and disagreement, even shouting matches, all of which is acceptable as long as it doesn't go too far – in fact, the shouting is often necessary in order to be heard. This makes for informal adjustments to the rules which may go so far as to violate those very rules, with the informal rules often dominant in creating a sense of what one can legitimately do.[34] Centralization, where it exists, therefore, may not be nearly as serious a problem in the French organization, given the informal ways around it, than it would be in an American one, where rules are sacrosanct and informal arrangements are seen as illegitimate.

Successful management, therefore, is for d'Iribarne a question of working within the French culture of individualism, knowing how to motivate and to encourage responsibility within the bounds of the "logic of honor." It involves recognizing that French employees organize themselves in informal ways that render unnecessary the heavy overlay of rules and regulations that define the American workplace. And it helps explain why American management practices imported to France, such as MBO, or Management by Objectives, are likely to be short-lived fads. The French management culture, d'Iribarne insists, is not better or worse than the American emphasis on contractual relations and teamwork, it is simply different. In this view, moreover, he is backed up by a recent study conducted by the Lyon Business School and the European Round Table which suggests that despite the fact that, unlike American and Japanese

[31]D'Iribarne, *Logique de l'honneur,* pp. 28, 34.   [32]Ibid., pp. 23–26.   [33]Ibid., pp. 35–37.
[34]Ibid., pp. 29–35.

corporations, European corporations are based on the individual because "Europeans do not work well in teams," European corporations nevertheless do well because, as the head of the Japanese NTT remarked, "these qualities actually require a more dynamic and productive individual."[35]

Through the eighties, top managers were largely successful at democratizing firms at the lower management levels in a manner that worked with, rather than against, French cultural traits, even if decisions continued to mount the hierarchy in many companies. Progress was even more dramatic, however, at the level of the workers, where a near-revolution in labor relations occurred as a by-product of the rehabilitation of business and the end of economic ideology.

The near-revolution in labor–management relations

Traditionally, France has had poor labor relations, with management attitudes toward workers characterized by mistrust and coldness, and with management style a mixture of autocracy and paternalism. This translated itself into management by fiat or decree, a rejection of all worker participation or meaningful involvement of subordinates in decision-making,[36] and limited worker discretion accompanied by close supervision.[37] Rewards for good performance were accorded in an individualistic way, so that rewards were seen as part of management's discretion.[38] For example, in large enterprises, management rewarded "seniority in the family" and good behavior, and punished bad behavior such as participation in strikes by denying merit bonuses or promotions. In smaller ones, the more paternalistic approach was followed.[39]

The observation by Daniel Halévy in the early thirties that labor and capital "faced each other like two hostile nations, each having its great men, its slogans, its newspapers, it books, and soon its own syntax and its own language," remained largely true until the beginning of the eighties.[40] For many CEOs, the Socialist victory in 1981 only spelled trouble for them in labor relations and legislation. Business executives were concerned that the state would, among other things, limit their ability to fire,

[35]*Euromanagement: A New Style for the Global Market*, École Supérieure de Commerce and the Table Ronde Européenne (forthcoming).
[36]Lane, *Management and Labour*, pp. 105–106; D. Gallie, *Social Inequality and Class Radicalism in France and Britain* (Cambridge: Cambridge University Press, 1978).
[37]M. Maurice, F. Sellier, and J.-J. Silvestre, *Production de la hierarchie dans l'entreprise: Recherche d'un effet sociétal* (Aix-en-Provence: LEST, 1980).
[38]Gallie, *Social Inequality*, p. 182 fn.   [39]Lane, *Labour and Management*, p. 105.
[40]Daniel Halévy, *Décadence de la liberté* (Paris: 1931), p. 89 – quoted in Ehrmann, *Organized Business*, p. 273.

so much so that many claimed that they had frozen hiring, preferring not to hire at all or to subcontract outside of the country, rather than be forced to decrease further their flexibility. In addition, the CEOs worried that the Socialists would deny them greater freedom to set wages, at the very least to go above established minimums to reward initiative and effort.[41]

Much of this changed in the eighties. Although the worker democracy laws (the Auroux laws of 1982 and the law of July 1983 applicable only to public enterprises) may not have been terribly effective in increasing worker democracy, their unintended consequences helped to transform labor–management relations.[42] As Schweitzer of Renault noted, "even if it did not change the world, it is a success."[43] This success was measured, however. As Strauss-Kahn made clear, even though the Auroux laws were lived as revolution – by those who wanted them and those who feared them – they only brought France up to the level of the countries that surround it.[44]

After an initial period of resistance, the worker democracy laws won the support of top managers in private and public sector enterprises who discovered that these laws tended to facilitate internal communication, ameliorate working conditions and the quality of working life, and even increase productivity.[45] As an added bonus, some managers found that the worker democracy laws further weakened the traditionally weak trade unions by providing for direct management–worker interaction. Not only did these laws undermine unions with the creation of work councils which mandated direct communication between workers and management, they also encouraged the replacement of industry-level bargaining agreements with firm-level agreements, and increased labor flexibility.[46] In the view of the CEO of Péchiney, the resulting improvement in labor relations had been such that there was "a century of difference" between 1978 and the present, with labor now taking an approach more focused on individuals and more concerned with issues involving the

[41]"L'état et les chefs d'entreprises," *L'Observatoire de la Cofremca* no. 5 (1981).

[42]For the Auroux laws specifically, see: Michèle Millot and Jean-Pol Roulleau, *L'entreprise face aux lois Auroux* (Paris: Les Editions d'Organisation, 1984); Holton, "Industrial Politics," pp. 77–78; Gallie, "Les lois Auroux"; W. Rand Smith, "Towards *Autogestion* in Socialist France: The Impact of Industrial Relations Reform," *West European Politics* vol. 10, no. 1 (January 1987); Frank L. Wilson, "Democracy in the Workplace: The French Experience," *Politics and Society* vol. 19, no. 4 (December 1991); Chris Howell, *Regulating Labor: The State and Industrial Relations Reform in Postwar France* (Princeton: Princeton University Press, 1992), ch. 7.

[43]Schweitzer, interview with author.   [44]Strauss-Kahn, interview with author.

[45]*Les Echos*, June 27, 1985.

[46]Chris Howell, "The Dilemmas of Post-Fordism: Socialists, Flexibility, and Labor Market Deregulation in France," *Politics and Society*, vol. 20, no. 1 (March 1992), pp. 85–89; and Howell, *Regulating Labor*.

health of the company itself and not simply the size of their salaries.[47] In the view of a top manager at Saint-Gobain, they helped facilitate better communication between management and workers, diminished the importance of unions, provided workers with better understanding of the requirements of the firm, and gave management a better grasp of issues important to the workers. What is more, board meetings that had lasted three-quarters of an hour before nationalization, with directors obliged to call CEO Roger Martin to tell him what they wanted to say ahead of time, because he didn't like much discussion, changed entirely. With nationalization, the board, now made up of six elected employees out of eighteen, had meetings that at first lasted from 9:00 a.m. to 3:00 p.m., and only later went from 9:00 a.m. to 1:00 p.m., then broke for lunch.[48] Testimony to the success is that even after privatization, Saint-Gobain kept three employees on the board.

A variety of polls confirm these perceived changes in management–labor relations. A 1984 Cofremca study found management, on the one side, closer to the personnel, notably in the factories, and more cooperative as well as communicative, having abandoned its anti-union stance. On the other side, they found workers less interested in ideology, preferring negotiated solutions to battles over grand principles, and the personnel in general expressing a greater trust in the enterprise and less interested in recourse to the state, which it had come to regard as temporary and dangerous.[49]

A 1986 SOFRES poll went further to uncover a transformation in labor's attitudes toward the firm, which was no longer the place of alienation, and work, which was no longer exploitation. Instead, personnel at all ranks came to characterize their relations with the firm primarily in terms of trust (55%), solidarity (43%), and *sympathie* (33%), as opposed to antipathy (2%), contempt (2%), hostility (3%), discord (12%), or mistrust (19%). Even if workers were less enthusiastic about the firm than upper-level managers, having less trust (53% vs. 67%), feeling less solidarity (39% vs. 56%), and finding it less *sympathique* (27% vs. 33%), this was still a significant change from the past, where words like trust, solidarity, and *sympathie* were hardly part of their vocabulary at all.[50] The personnel had even more positive views of top management. By 1986, over two-thirds of the personnel had come to see top management as *sympathique* (69% vs. 14% who did not), while around three-quarters found them competent (78% vs. 10%) and worthy of trust (73% vs. 18%). As for their views of their direct management supervisors, around

[47]Gandois, interview with author.   [48]Bidegain, interview with author.
[49]"Meilleur Pilotage," *Cofremca*.
[50]SOFRES, *L'état de l'opinion 1987* (Paris: Seuil, 1987), pp. 141, 143.

three-quarters saw them as *sympathique* (75% vs. 12%), competent (73% vs. 15%), and worthy of trust (70% vs. 18%). Ironically enough, the personnel's improvement in attitude toward managers was balanced by a deterioration in their views of union representatives, who, although similarly *sympathique* (75% vs. 12%), were seen as less although still competent (51% vs. 28%) and less although still worthy of trust (54% vs. 27%).[51]

Labor militancy also diminished. Anecdotal evidence suggests that even the CGT had to moderate its approach in order to retain worker support. For example, in a conference with union members from all of Saint-Gobain's operations in Europe, everyone laughed at the class conflict discourse of the CGT, and no one from the other countries wanted to sit with them. The CGT itself changed as a result.[52]

This is not, of course, to suggest that all problems have been resolved: the high rate of unemployment alone ensures a high level of alienation among the many workers who remain out of a job, while the recession of the nineties is certain to have increased tensions even within the firm as employers try to keep wages down and to cut where they can. CEOs are no longer the "golden boys" that they were through the eighties, and no longer so trusted by personnel, who fear for their jobs, or by the public, who worry about the excesses apparent in insider trading and influence peddling scandals. Moreover, privatization, greeted with general enthusiasm in the mid eighties, no longer generated the same support in the mid nineties. Employees at Rhône-Poulenc saw the company's privatization as a "threat," bringing "insecurity" not only in terms of employment but also in terms of the future of the company, which they feared would be broken up with the sale of the less profitable operations and would lose its long-standing culture (Lyonnais in origin, infused with democratic socialist values or inspired by the Catholic grande bourgeoisie, but which they all saw as guaranteed by the state).[53] Similar fears were expressed at Elf, while walkouts greeted planned restructurings that were to prepare the way for privatization at France Télécom and Air France. However, even with the increase in labor unrest under the Balladur government and worker dissatisfaction related to privatization, the overall point about the transformation of labor–management relations remains true, not only because of the changed attitudes of labor but also because of the weakening of organized labor more generally.

Labor was not the only group to undergo a transformation in attitudes, though. Management, too, changed its tune. Before the Socialists took over, management focused on labor/management issues almost exclu-

[51]Ibid., p. 148.   [52]Bidegain, interview with author.
[53]*Le Monde*, November 17, 1993.

sively; after a decade of Socialists in power, the watchwords had become profit, productivity, investment, and modernization. In a 1978 documentary (not released at the time), the CEOs were obsessed by labor–management questions, talking primarily of labor conditions, labor disputes, and the dangers of acquiescing to worker demands for *autogestion,* or self-management. There was no real discussion of the company, as Michel Bon, at the time head of Carrefour, the supermarket chain, noted in commenting on the 1978 documentary. By 1991, in contrast, the entire discussion had shifted to one centered on profits and performance, and on the client.[54] This continues to be the focus, as the globalization of business and the internationalization of the economy have created an increasingly competitive situation in which managers must get the most out of all their resources, human as well as capital and technological.

MANAGERIAL RECRUITMENT AND PROMOTION

The overall success of the decade of the eighties had much to do with the leadership put at the head of the nationalized industries. Respect for autonomy of public enterprises was only reinforced by the fact that the Socialists and neoliberals alike followed traditional recruitment patterns. This ensured that the new leadership retained a certain kind of legitimacy which helped minimize the disruption that any abrupt change in ownership and management might have caused, ensuring the smoothness of the transition from private to public and, in some cases, back to private sector enterprise. The price of the legitimacy, however, was the reinforcement of the elite system of control of business and government which, although helpful as a source of stability in the eighties, may serve as a source of blockage in the nineties.

The career path of top managers

One of the most striking features of French management is the pervasive credentialism. In the interviews for this study, every time top managers were asked about their confrères, they without exception offered up a full accounting of educational histories and corps memberships before any discussion of career histories or accomplishments, leaving the impression that the former are more important than the latter. This is in marked

[54]*Patrons '78–91,* a documentary film by Gérard Mordillat and Nicholas Philibert, produced first in 1978 but censored at the time because François Dalle, CEO of L'Oréal, among others, objected. This was at a time when the PDG had not been used to seeing themselves interviewed on TV. They objected to the cutting. It was only aired in the early 1990s, with an update and commentary by a few of the "new generation" of CEOs.

contrast to both the United States and Germany, where schooling may be important at first, but loses importance very quickly, supplanted by achievements and positions attained. The French themselves note the greater openness of both systems, seeing hiring in the United States solely on the basis of one's schooling as more the exception than the rule, given the greater competition among schools,[55] or finding that competence progressively replaces academic degree as a basis of judgment in Germany, where a foreign, nongraduate of a *grande école* can become president of Volkswagen (as the Frenchman Daniel Goeudevert did), unlike in France, where it is inconceivable that the president of Crédit Lyonnais or AGF would not be a graduate of a *grande école* and member of a *grand corps.*[56]

French management recruitment and promotion remains quite distinct from most other advanced industrialized countries. In Germany, top managers tend to be regular university graduates, with little distinction made among universities. In Great Britain, the home of the "amateur tradition," they are often public school products who went directly into business rather than to the university, although many are also university graduates. In the United States, no easy pattern can be discerned: at the same time that the heads of major firms may be self-made individuals, the large majority are college graduates in the liberal arts from elite schools as well as from the top business schools. The Japanese model, where the heads of industry tend to be the graduates of Tokyo University, probably comes closest to the French, although it does not place the same emphasis on technical schooling.[57]

France probably has the most exclusive recruitment system for top managers among advanced industrialized nations. In France, the heads of business are the products of an elite education that emphasizes advanced technical training at one of the top schools, the *grandes écoles*. Of the CEOs of the top 200 firms in January 1986, half were graduates of one of six first-class *grandes écoles* (see Table 14.1). What is more, over one-third of the CEOs were graduates of two of these schools: Polytechnique (X), for the training of engineers, and the National School of Administration (ENA). In all, graduates of X made up slightly over a quarter of the total, at 25.5%, followed by the École des Hautes Études de Commerce (HEC), the premier business school, at 8.5%; the ENA, at 6.5%; the Institut d'Études Politiques (IEP), at 5%; the École Nationale Supérieure des Mines (Mines), at 3%; and Centrale, the second-ranked engineering

---

[55]Comments by Ludo Van der Heyden, Dean of Insead. *Le Monde*, June 19, 1991.
[56]Comments by Maurice Dommensath, a former director of CEGOS and a graduate of X. *Le Monde*, June 19, 1991.
[57]For the comparisons, see: David Granick, *The European Executive*, reprint ed. (New York: Arno Press, 1979).

Table 14.1. *The educational credentials of the CEOs of the top 200 firms in France*

	Industry		Services and Commerce		Total	
Grande école, 1st cl.	77	(52.4%)	24	(48.9%)	101	(51.5%)
Grande école, 2nd cl.	35	(23.8%)	8	(16.3%)	43	(21.9%)
University	8	(5.4%)	5	(10.2%)	13	(6.6%)
Foreign	11	(7.4%)	1	(2.0%)	12	(6.1%)
Self-made men	16	(10.8%)	11	(22.4%)	27	(13.7%)
Total	147	(100 %)	49	(100 %)	196	(100 %)

Note: Data as of January 1986.

Source: Michel Bauer and Bénédicte Mourot, <u>Les 200: Comment Devient-on un Grand Patron?</u> (Paris: Seuil, 1987), p. 181.

school after Polytechnique, at 2.5%. The universities, by comparison, were in dismal shape, turning out a mere 6.6% of CEOs of the top firms, far behind even those who had no formal higher education at all (at 13.7%).[58] As of 1992, moreover, little had changed. Of the CEOs of the top 200 firms, over one-quarter (27%) were still graduates of X, many more than before (19%) were graduates of the ENA, and slightly fewer (7%) were from HEC.[59] What is more, of the CEOs of the top ten firms in 1991, seven were graduates of X, and two of the ENA (only Loïk Le Floch-Prigent, head of Elf, was not an elite graduate). HEC was far behind, its highest-placed graduate in 16th place out of the top 100 firms (Didier Pineau-Valenciennes of Schneider), and with only 9 in the top 100, by contrast with 26 from X and 7 from ENA. The elite recruitment was up overall from 1981, however, when there were 24 from X, 3 from ENA, and 4 from HEC (2 of which had both HEC and ENA credentials). The Centraliens, by contrast, had decreased from 7 in 1981 to 4 in 1991.[60] In 1995, finally, the percentages remain virtually unchanged.[61]

In many ways, this is probably a somewhat more open recruitment pattern than in Japan, where most CEOs are the graduates of Tokyo University. The comparison, however, ends upon graduation. Whereas most Japanese destined to lead their firms enter business immediately after graduation, few French do. In France, the best and the brightest have traditionally gone to work for the state, and only later if not at the end of their careers do they enter business. Thus, it is perhaps understandable that in France, of the top 200 heads of business in 1991, 44.53% rose to

[58]Bauer and Mourot, *Les 200*, pp. 180–181.   [59]*L'Expansion*, January 9–22, 1992.
[60]*L'Expansion*, November 1–December 1991.
[61]Michel Bauer, Bénédicte Bertin-Mourot, and Pascal Thobois, *Les no. 1 des 200 plus grandes entreprises en France et en Grande Bretagne* (Paris: Boyden, 1995).

the top through state-centered careers, by comparison with 21.88% through business-centered careers (with the rest through having founded or inherited a business). The contrast with Germany is striking, where only 7.96% had state-centered careers while 65.49% had business-centered careers.[62]

The French pattern can be explained in part by the fact that the most prestigious of the *grandes écoles,* the ENA (created after World War II) and X (a military engineering school set up by Napoleon which did not even admit women until relatively recently), both prepare students for state service and demand a certain number of years of subsequent state employment as reimbursement of tuition costs (generally ten years, which is forgiven only in exceptional circumstances, or if the graduate is bought out by a private firm). As discussed earlier, after the ENA, the best go on to work in the Ministry of Finance and become members of the corps of the Inspection des Finances. After X, the best go on to the Écoles des Mines and the École des Ponts et Chaussées, although they may go on to one of the other technical engineering schools, such as Télécom for telecommunications training or Aéro for aeronautics training. They then become members of the engineering civil service corps made up of alumni of their school, the Corps des Mines being the most prestigious, followed by the Corps des Ponts.

Equally if not more important than degrees for the future top manager, therefore, is belonging to a *grand corps*. Elite corps membership may be the most significant distinguishing characteristic for top managers. Graduation from X or ENA may very well be secondary, although these are the obligatory paths to membership in a corps.[63] Of the CEOs of the top 200 firms in France in 1986, fully one-quarter were members of a *grand corps,* with 38 of the 50 graduates of X members of a corps and 10 out of the 13 graduates of the ENA members.[64] Of the CEOs of the top 200 firms in France in 1992, 45%, or 90, were upper-level civil servants, two-thirds of whom, or 60, were members of a *grand corps*.[65] Moreover, because elite corps membership always means state service while elite education alone most often suggests some state service, the preponderance of CEOs with one or both of these credentials ensures that more CEOs of top French firms have had more experience working for the state than for business. This pattern has not changed in the postwar period.[66]

A major reason for the pattern is that working for the state has traditionally been seen as more prestigious than working for business at any-

[62]Michel Bauer and Bénédicte Bertin-Mourot, "*Les 200 en France et en Allemagne,*" CNRS and Heidrick & Struggles International (Paris, 1994), pp. 40–41.
[63]Bauer and Mourot, *Les 200,* p. 268. [64]Ibid., p. 183.
[65]*L'Expansion,* January 9–22, 1992. [66]See Suleiman, *Elites in French Society,* p. 115.

thing other than the highest levels, after a distinguished career in state service, and as its reward. Before the Socialists' tenure, business was looked down upon, and industry was depicted in a prejorative light, if it was considered at all. As one commentator noted in 1980, the system was one in which it was more "noble" to be an *inspecteur de finances* or a civil service engineer than to be the financial or technical director of a private company.[67] Typical was the experience that Jean Gandois, head of Péchiney and former head of Rhône-Poulenc, a graduate of X and Ponts, confronted thirty years ago, when he left state employ to work in business. As he recounts it, all and sundry insisted that "To work for business was unthinkable, it was simply not done." And he himself worried that business "was not as noble as working for the state."[68] If anything, this attitude only intensified in the sixties and seventies. In the late seventies, Jean-Marie Messier recounts that upon graduation from X, after a long hesitation between going to the ENA or going to a top business school like INSEAD in order then to go into the private sector, he went to the ENA, having decided that "given French realities, a good knowledge of the public sector was indispensable," even though he remained ready from one moment to the next to choose the private sector.[69] His career path reflects this: after a number of years in the Ministry of Finance in the cabinets of various ministers, he became in 1989, at the age of thirty-two, a managing partner of the Lazard Bank.

This path by which future CEOs go to elite state schools and then into state service helps to explain why the French are by far the oldest when they start careers in business. The figures are quite dramatic when compared with Japan and the United States (see Figure 14.1). By age twenty-six, 84% of America's top managers and 81.2% of Japan's had begun their careers in business, by contrast with only 49% of the French. By thirty-five, moreover, whereas virtually all of America's future CEOs (99%) and Japan's (97.8%) had started their business careers, a sizable number of France's soon-to-be top managers (20.2%) had yet to begin theirs.

The figures are equally striking when considering the age at which CEOs had entered the firm which they were ultimately to lead (see Figure 14.2). Here, the French remain far behind the Americans, and even farther behind the Japanese. By age twenty-nine, only 29.8% of future French CEOs had begun their in-house careers, 20.2 points behind the Americans (at 50%) and 47.6 points behind the Japanese (at 77.4%).

[67]M. Vulliez, former head of HEC and head of the Paris Chamber of Commerce education department – cited in NEDO, *Making of Managers,* p. 73.

[68]Gandois, interview with author.

[69]Testimony of Jean-Marie Messier, *Rapport sur les opérations de privatisation,* vol. I, p. 206.

Changes in business

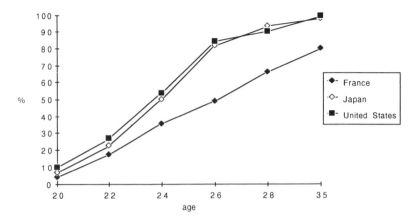

Figure 14.1. Age at which CEOs first entered business, in percentages. Source: Michel Bauer and Bénédicte Mourot, *Les 200: Comment Devient-on un Grand Patron?* (Paris: Seuil, 1987), p. 252.

Moreover, after forty-years of age, at a time when they would presumably enter only in the top management ranks, if not as CEO, 25% of the French began their in-house careers, a proportion close to double that of the Americans (at 13.5%), and close to quadruple that of the Japanese (at 6.5%).

Among the top 200 firms in France, only the CEOs of subsidiaries of foreign multinationals come close to matching the Japanese pattern of

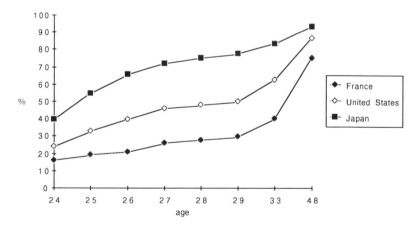

Figure 14.2. Age at which CEOs first entered the firm they direct, in percentages. Source: Michel Bauer and Bénédicte Mourot, *Les 200: Comment Devient-on un Grand Patron?* (Paris: Seuil, 1987), p. 252.

long in-house business careers and elite educational credentials. Of the sixteen French heads among the twenty largest foreign subsidiaries in 1986, eight attended *grandes écoles* (but only three went to the most prestigious, X), only one had any state experience, and all but one (94%) entered business and the firm in which they were later to become CEO in their twenties (as opposed to the French firm percentage of 66.3% for entry into business and 29.8% for entry in the firm they were later to lead), at an average age of twenty-six.[70] This profile has not changed much. As of 1992, of the thirty-six heads of foreign subsidiaries, thirty-three had business careers and only three had state experience -- and none were from the ENA.[71] Thus, CEOs of foreign-owned subsidiaries differ greatly from the typical French management profile: they may share elite credentials, but they have long in-house business careers and no corps membership.

The family-owned firms constitute the greatest exceptions to the typical French management profile of elite education, civil service corps membership, and brief business career, since they are not only long on in-house business careers, they are also short on elite educational credentials. In all, of the forty-two heads of family-owned firms run by the founder, there were three times as many *autodidactes,* or self-made men (eighteen or over 85%) as there were graduates of the *grandes écoles* (three, or less than 15%).[72] Of the remaining twenty-one run by the inheritor, only six out of twenty-one, or 28%, attended elite schools.[73]

By comparison with the rest of France's top firms, then, the CEOs of family-owned firms are quite lacking in the typical credentials, having spent their entire careers in business, and with only a few having elite educations and even fewer having corps memberships. But they are still well ahead of Great Britain's top 100 owner-managed firms, where only 5% of CEOs have a degree and 91% have the O-level (not quite equivalent to the *bac*) or below.[74]

If we were to exclude family-owned firms as well as foreign-owned subsidiaries from consideration, we would find relatively few top managers with a regular career in business, and in particular in the firm which they lead. Of the sixty-four French, nonfamily or foreign-owned firms among the top 200 in January 1986, slightly over half (thirty-four) were led by those whose careers were primarily based on state service. Of the remaining thirty firms, led by those whose careers were exclusively based

[70]Bauer and Mourot, *Les 200,* p. 244.   [71]*L'Expansion,* January 9–22, 1992.
[72]Bauer and Mourot, *Les 200,* pp. 117–119.
[73]On the differences between firms run by founders and inheritors, see: Dean Savage, *Founders, Heirs, and Managers* (Beverly Hills, CA: Sage, 1979).
[74]*The British Entrepreneur 1988,* quoted in *The Independent,* December 29, 1988 – cited in Lane, *Management and Labour,* p. 91.

on and in business, only twelve had had full careers in the firm which they then led.[75]

For all firms other than the family-owned firms or the subsidiaries of foreign multinationals, then, managers' career paths are more likely to depend upon their education and membership in a corps than on their accomplishments, in particular if they lack the elite educational credentials and corps membership. This is only partially due to the highly competitive educational system which, through the process of elimination, funnels the best, or at least those most capable of succeeding in the French examination system, to the ENA and X. It also has to do with the *corporatisme* or stick-togetherness of the *grands corps,* which ensures that where there are X graduates or *énarques* at the head of a company, they surround themselves with their fellows.

French-style corporatism

The *corporatisme* of many French CEOs is legend; and it affects the private sector as much as the public. Quite typical is the story told of Claude Bébéar, head of Axa, the insurance group, when he took over another, larger insurer. In his first meeting with the top few hundred managers, Bébéar, a product of Polytechnique, singled out the seven or so other X graduates by greeting them with the familiar "*tu*" (a peculiarity of graduates of X that distinguishes them from all others) rather than the formal "*vous,*" the usual greeting. From this simple gesture, everyone in the firm immediately understood that a new management team, made up exclusively of polytechnicians, was being formed.

Members of the two main corps are in top management positions throughout major French firms (see Tables 10.2, 10.3, 10.4). As we have already seen, the number one position in banking and insurance companies tends to be the domain of the ENA-Finances. The top position in industrial companies tends to be held by X graduates who are also members of the engineering corps, in particular the Corps des Mines.[76] The level of domination of top managerial ranks by X or ENA graduates, however, does differ among companies. This is often related to the firm's history and level of internationalization.

X-Mines and X-Ponts tend to dominate companies in the energy sector and in infrastructure. CGE (Alcatel-Alsthom), in energy and services, was headed before, during, and after nationalization by X-Ponts. In 1972, out of the twelve members of the board of directors, nine were graduates of X and one of HEC, of which two were X-Mines and

---

[75]Ibid., pp. 247–248.   [76]See Chapter 10.

three X-Ponts.[77] A decade later, just before nationalization, of the eleven members of the executive committee, eight were graduates of X and one of ENA, all of whom were members of *grands corps,* with one ENA-Finances, four X-Ponts, three X-Génie Maritime, and one X-Télécom.[78] According to Jean-Claude Thoenig, the Corps des Ponts' control of CGE was part of a deliberate strategy to control certain industries – electrical construction, road and bridge building, transportation, and the like – which began in 1969 with Georges Pébereau's arrival with many of his comrades from the corps, fresh from having completed a reform of the DDE, or Department of Infrastructure.[79] This control ended, however, with the appointment in June 1995 of Serge Tchuruk, former head of Total and an X-Armement.

At the SNCF, the state-owned railroad company, there were thirty-three members of the Corps des Ponts as of January 1986, including the CEO, one deputy director-general, the director of transport, and the director of capital investment. At this same time, the EDF-GDF had twenty-two X-Ponts, including the directors-general of both EDF and GDF.[80] By later in 1986, moreover, its CEO was also an X-Ponts. At GDF, by contrast, the CEO until 1986 was an X-Mines, at which point an ENA-Conseil d'État took over. But there were still three X-Mines left.[81]

The X-Mines are most prevalent in such companies as CEA, where in 1986 there were twenty-three, including the CEO; CFP (Total), where there were seven including the top position until Ortoli, an ENA-Finances, claimed the job in 1985 and Tchuruk, X-Armement, took over in 1989; Péchiney, where there were nine X-Mines, including the CEO, until Gandois, an X-Ponts, took over in 1986; Cogema, where there were four X-Mines including the head; and Elf, where there were nineteen, including the head as of 1986.[82]

At Elf, the dominance of the X-Mines has been such that some suggest that "not to be a *'mineur'* is a tragedy."[83] This changed, though, with the appointment of a new head with a nonelite profile, Le Floch-Prigent, in 1989. Although outside the firm it may have been a cause of protest from X-Mines, inside it was greeted as *"une grande beauté"* by François de Wissocq, a top director at Elf-Aquitaine, former CEO of Cogema, and, naturally, an X-Mines, who noted that this appointment was the first

[77]Pierre Bourdieu, *La noblesse de L'état: Grandes écoles et esprit de corps* (Paris: Editions de Minuit, 1989), p. 518.
[78]Bauer and Mourot, *Les 200,* p. 132.
[79]Jean-Claude Thoenig, *L'ère des technocrates* (Paris: Editions d'Organisations, 1973), p. 233.
[80]Bauer and Mourot, *Les 200,* p. 127.   [81]Ibid., p. 127.   [82]Ibid.
[83]Comment by Claude La Santé, cited in *Le Monde,* June 19, 1991.

time that a CEO of Elf was not a *fonctionnaire,* but, rather, an engineer with a modern profile.[84] The appointment of his successor in 1993, an ENA-Finances, also departed from tradition.

France Télécom is, understandably perhaps, made up primarily of graduates of X and the School of Télécom. In 1991, the president, the director-general, and one of the two deputy directors-general had this profile (the other deputy is a product of X and ENA). Moreover, eight out of thirteen in the governing board (*comité de direction*) were X-Télécom, two of the remaining were X and another *grande école* (Mines or ENST), while there was only one university product, a doctor in economics. Aérospatiale's top management team was mainly from the *grandes écoles* or ministers' cabinets,[85] with the CEO appointed in 1992, Louis Gallois, no exception (although he is not a member of a *grand corps,* having refused to join one upon graduation from the ENA in 1972).[86]

In banking and insurance, graduates of the ENA tend to hold sway, although not to the exclusion of graduates of X. At the Caisse des Dépôts et Consignations, the very top level of management consists of graduates of the ENA or X-Ponts, and this, according to Bruno Boudrouille, director of strategy and himself an X-Ponts, was not likely to change, even if change had been going on at lower levels.[87]

Not all companies, however, have this extreme kind of *corporatisme.* Bull, for example, has had a varied profile, perhaps due to its particular history as a GE subsidiary and to the fact that computing has no *grande école* attached. Its CEO from the late eighties until 1992, however, Francis Lorentz, a graduate of HEC and the ENA, had the traditional elite profile, as did his replacement, Bernard Pache, an X-Mines, and his replacement in turn as of November 1993, Jean-Marie Descarpentrie, an X.

Some companies, moreover, have been diminishing the hold of a single *grand corps.* At SNECMA, the jet engine concern, the CEO (1989–1992), Louis Gallois, admits to being the first *énarque,* the only one of two CEOs who was not an X-Mines (the other was his immediate predecessor, an Air Force general). At SNECMA, Gallois claims there is no mafia. There are only three X graduates out of twelve or thirteen members of top management: the directors of finance, human resources, civilian trade. The others are graduates of Centrale, Arts et Métiers, HEC, even the university in public law, and one *énarque,* whom he himself brought in.[88] At Saint-Gobain, similarly, of the nine divisional directors, three were *énarques* or *polytechniciens* (two with civil service experience) who entered the industry as directors; the other six were engineers, in-

[84]De Wissocq, interview with author.   [85]*Le Monde,* June 19, 1991.
[86]See the discussion in Chapter 10.   [87]Boudrouille, interview with author.
[88]Gallois, interview with author.

cluding an engineer with an evening degree who entered the enterprise as a technician.[89] The CEO, Jean-Louis Beffa, however, is an X-Mines, as was the CEO up until 1980, with an ENA-Finances in between. In many firms, in other words, although the CEO remains an elite graduate with administrative career history, the other directors have become increasingly diversified.

But while in some companies, the *grands corps* have been loosening their hold, in others they have been increasing it. At Renault, for example, a management team heavily dominated by graduates of *grandes écoles* was parachuted in at the top in the eighties. Before this time, and despite the fact that it was nationalized, all previous heads had managed to maintain their independence, and the company had been able to decide on its own who was to be the new head. Pierre Dreyfus, head from 1955 to 1975, had been the choice of the directors of the nationalized company. And he had managed to impose his own choice for successor, who in turn chose his own, Bernard Hanon, whose career was entirely in-house. Hanon, however, in turn appointed outsiders to top positions. And in 1983, another outsider was appointed to replace him. Georges Besse, an X-Mines, was parachuted in, in response not to politics but to the internal troubles at Renault and the directors' loss of confidence in the CEO. Besse was then replaced by Raymond Lévy, another X-Mines, and the *grands corps* had gained another bastion, but only for a time.[90] With the promotion of Louis Schweitzer from the number two position in 1992, the Corps des Finances replaced Mines in the top slot.

Generally speaking, however, the more global the company and the greater the diversity of its activities, the less serious the problem of domination by one *grande école* and/or *grand corps*. Thus, Rhône-Poulenc is less dominated by one corps because of the range of its activities and therefore of recruitment. Out of 6,000 managers, only 4% come from the School of Chemistry of Lyon, despite the company's Lyon base (in the 1970s, the percentage was much larger). And today, the six members of the executive committee come from different schools.[91]

Moreover, multinational companies that are truly international, as in the case of Airbus,[92] or are foreign-owned, such as IBM, Sony-France, and so forth, tend to be places for those outside the networks tied to the state.[93] But this does not necessarily mean that the recruitment of French top managers in these companies is not based on elite educational credentials. IBM's recruitment, for example, is still based on elite education; its

[89]Beffa, interview with author.   [90]Bauer and Mourot, *Les 200*, pp. 218–240.
[91]*Le Monde*, June 19, 1991.   [92]Ibid.
[93]Octave Célinié, president emeritus of CEGOS and graduate of the Mines, quoted in *Le Monde*, June 19, 1991.

presidents are all graduates of the *grandes écoles,* but it recruits from a wider range of *grandes écoles* directly at graduation. Jacques Maison-rouge, former head of IBM World Trade, for instance, is a *centralien.*

The top ranks of a majority of the top 200 firms in France, in brief, are dominated by products of the elite schools. Only the heads of the family-owned firms are an exception to this rule. In addition, they, together with heads of the subsidiaries of foreign-owned multinationals, are the only ones with long in-house careers. The typical profile of the French manager is long on elite education and corps membership, short on business career.

CONCLUSION

Management practice, in short, underwent significant changes during the Mitterrand years. The structure of corporate decision-making, however, became only somewhat less centralized, with hierarchy remaining the defining pattern for many firms even as lower management levels were democratized and labor–management relations were transformed. And the CEO, having become the head of a much larger, global firm with a complex network of relationships to other French as well as foreign industries, banks, and insurers, has only gained in power and responsibility without any concomitant increase in accountability. Given this, the appointment process for the CEO becomes all-important. But it is here that the least change has occurred. And the question to ask is, therefore, is this good for management?

15

Evaluating the elite management recruitment system

Top managers of major French firms tend to be divided over whether the elite educational system, with the attendant *corporatisme* and state service, is good or bad for business management. Although some, most often themselves the beneficiaries of the system, see the products of the elite system as the best and the brightest, many more, including numbers of the beneficiaries, see the system as the source of many of the ills of French management. The detractors cite, in particular, the attention paid to elite credentials over achievements, which leaves most managers with little hope of getting to the top, thus hurting morale while failing to make the most of the human resource potential of the firm. And they question the value of an educational system that favors theoretical knowledge over practical, whether managerial or technical.

Much of this is in the process of changing, however. To begin with, the traditional management profile is beginning to diversify, with more women and university graduates gaining positions of responsibility. In addition, elite recruits are entering the firm earlier, and spending more years learning the business before being catapulted to the top. Moreover, although the pressures of internationalization have brought little change as yet at the top, they have ensured that younger managers have been gaining experience abroad. In short, even if the French still have a long way to go to approximate the American or German models of advancement, where university education and business achievement tend to be the main criteria for advancement, they are at least beginning to resemble more the Japanese, by supplementing elite education with longer business careers. But whether this represents enough change for French top managers to meet the challenges of the twenty-first century remains to be seen.

Changes in business

THE EFFECTS OF THE ELITE EDUCATIONAL SYSTEM

Top managers disagree over the appropriateness and adequacy of the elite educational system. Whereas many, especially the products of the system, see it is as an excellent way to identify and train future business leaders who are not only gifted but honest, others criticize the kind and quality of the education, in particular its engineering focus, and the narrowness of the recruitment pool, which breeds homogeneity in management teams and excludes many with talent.

Arguments in favor of this narrow system of recruitment tend to emphasize the fact that the elite corps members, graduates of ENA and X, are the best and the brightest, having succeeded in an extremely rigorous educational system, and who therefore not only deserve the best, but also serve the country best. Needless to say, the upholders of this faith are generally members of the corps themselves. André Giraud, a former minister and former director of the Corps des Mines, exemplified this view when he insisted that "it is to be expected that the Republic (which has spent a lot on their education) employs these young people to the best of their ability, in their interest, of course, but above all in the interests of the nation. I don't see anything scandalous in this."[1] Although Jean-Louis Beffa, CEO of Saint-Gobain and an X-Mines, agreed with this logic, he nevertheless saw a problem if recruitment was based solely on these criteria, remarking, "It is normal that the good students go to difficult schools. . . . It is not abnormal that they would accede to the good jobs. What would be shocking is if there were elements of exclusivity."[2] Roger Fauroux, Beffa's predecessor at Saint-Gobain, a director of the ENA, and Minister of Industry under Rocard, similarly saw the elite system as a source of strength, and was even a little sorry that the system was starting to crumble. The advantage of the system, he noted, is that its members are "good soldiers, of whom you can ask almost anything," such as Francis Mer, an X-Mines, who was willing to take on the thankless task of running Usinor-Sacilor, and that "it is helpful to have 300 young who are devoted, intelligent, ready to serve, and who have a certain kind of spirit. . . . The *inspecteurs de finances* and *ingénieurs des mines* always work hard. The United States also has something like this, Japan too. Every state has a certain elite, it just shouldn't be the nobility of the *ancien régime*."[3] Although Fauroux admitted that this system, laudable for its meritocratic basis, may nevertheless be a bit "*corporatiste*," he did not see this as such a problem.[4] Much the contrary, since he worried that the diminution of the system would make it much more difficult to know

---

[1]*Le Monde*, June 19, 1991.   [2]Beffa, interview with author.
[3]Fauroux, interview with author.   [4]Ibid.

who is good and who isn't, and more mistakes would be made: "When I hire a graduate of the Mines, eight out of ten times, I know I have a good one. If I put an ad in *Le Figaro,* or go to a personnel agency (*consultant*) the chance is five out of ten."[5]

Not all top officials in business or government, needless to say, were convinced by these arguments. Many, in particular those who had not had the advantages of the elite education and/or corps membership, were quick to raise questions about whether the education prepared students adequately for management leadership, and in particular whether future managers were best served by an engineering education which is highly theoretical.

One of the main criticisms traditionally made of the French elite educational system is that its engineers are trained too theoretically, and know too little about practical application. One commentator found that upper-level managers from the elite engineering schools, whose education emphasizes quantitative techniques, rapid problem-solving, and abstract analytical reasoning, "may well be capable of deploying their abstract expertise with brilliance to those problems reserved for their attention. But these generals of the industrial army would never be able to base any claim to lead 'the charge with the spanner' upon their experience of tightening nuts."[6] Former Prime Minister Edith Cresson herself remarked in an interview, "although the *grandes écoles* have high quality instruction, they inculcate an elitist culture . . . there needs to be another mode of training next to the *grandes écoles* which produces technicians and engineers more aware of the realities."[7]

There is an oft-repeated story illustrative of the problems with the elite educational system for managers and engineers. You have three engineers, one a graduate of Polytechnique, one from Centrale, and one from Arts et Métiers (the three schools of engineering with a clear pecking order, where if you don't get into Polytechnique, you go to Centrale; and if you don't get into Centrale, you go to Arts et Métiers). They each build a bridge. For the first, the bridge collapses, and he knows why; for the second, the bridge collapses, and he doesn't know why; and for the third, the bridge stays up and he doesn't know why. There is another version of the story where the *polytechnicien* doesn't know why and the *centralien* does. But what is important is that only the clearly nonelite graduate of Arts et Métiers can do the job.

On this score, however, the French engineering elite graduates are not

[5]Ibid.
[6]M. Rose, "Universalism, Culturalism, and the AIX Group," *European Sociological Review* vol. 1, no. 1 (1985), p. 72 – quoted in Lane, *Management and Labour,* p. 90.
[7]*Libération,* January 31, 1991.

much worse off than their German counterparts, about whom employers also complain of the lack of practical training and insufficient attention to the technological changes in industry.[8] But whereas practical competence on the whole is generally highly valued in Germany, where engineers from the second-string schools are more popular with employers and those who have some vocational qualification or have served an apprenticeship are more appreciated, it is undervalued in France.[9] Thus, while the ultimate results tend to be more equilibrated in Germany, in France, the theoretical tends to win out, leading to brilliant invention and conceptually excellent design, regardless of costs, as in the case of the Concorde; to disdain for the more mundane and practical tasks of the production engineer; and often to poor implementation of strategy.[10]

The French and German models of education, nevertheless, are quite similar, with the French *grandes écoles* and German university engineering faculties seconded by the less prestigious *écoles d'ingénieur* and German polytechnics. This can be explained by the fact that the Germans copied the French model of engineering education, developed by Napoleon, in the early nineteenth century; even if, already by the beginning of the twentieth century, the Germans had far outstripped the French in output of professional engineers and in the reputation of its engineers and engineering schools.[11] And it remains that way today: as of 1991, Germany had well over twice as many certified engineers (31,000) as France (14,000).[12]

Both models, whatever the differences, are far and away better than in Great Britain, where engineers do not have the same prestige – the term itself applies to anyone from grease monkey and computer repairman to university-trained engineer in a desk job. Until recently relatively few British engineers were trained in universities, and British technical training is on the whole weaker than in either France or Germany.[13] The result is that managers in Great Britain tend to have nontechnical and often non-university training, by contrast with the engineering bias of France,

[8]Institute of Manpower Studies, *Competence and Competition – Training and Education in the FRG,* Report for the NEDO and the MSC (London: IMS, 1984) – cited in Lane, *Management and Labour,* p. 80.

[9]Lane, *Management and Labour,* p. 93.   [10]*The Economist,* October 15, 1988.

[11]Lane, *Management and Labour,* pp. 79–80. See also G. Ahlström, *Engineers and Industrial Growth* (London: Croom Helm, 1982).

[12]*Le Nouvel Economiste,* March 3, 1991.

[13]Lane, *Management and Labour,* pp. 79–81. For an in-depth discussion of the view of engineers in Great Britain, see: J. C. Gerstl and S. P. Hutton, *Engineers: The Anatomy of a Profession* (London: Tavistock Publications, 1966). An opinion poll of the early 1970s illustrates the differences in view: when oil workers were asked to define the outer limits of their class, 30% of the British classed engineers as working-class, whereas 14% of the French in the South did and only 8% of the French in the North. Gallie, *Social Inequality and Class Radicalism,* p. 36.

where in the mid eighties, engineers made up 74.3% of younger managers (25–34 years of age), and nearly two-thirds of these engineers were graduates of a *grande école*.[14] This makes for a striking contrast with Great Britain's "amateur tradition" – where future civil servants read the classics at Oxford or Cambridge to prepare themselves for state service while future managers read nothing practical, if they read much at all beyond their public school training, given that until recently most did not even go on to university. A study in the seventies and early eighties found that only 24% of British managers were university-educated, by contrast with 65% of the French, 62% of the Germans, and 85% of Americans and Japanese.[15] Even in 1995, although the numbers had changed dramatically, the percentage of British CEOs of the top 200 firms without higher education, at 37%, far exceeded the French, at 17% (although many more British had had further training at work, usually in accounting).[16]

But although the French, like the Germans, have more technical training than the British, they also share some of the preference for the amateur tradition. The emphasis on *polyvalence,* or on being a generalist more than a technician, has been highly prized for a long time in France.[17] Testimony of the graduates themselves seems to confirm their pride in their technical ignorance; witness the remark of one member of a *grand corps:* "The education I had gave me no ideas, and hence no preconceived ideas about the science of management. If I have a few today, they can only be the fruits of a pure autodidacticism."[18]

But is an elite higher education system focused on training engineers with little hands-on technical know-how appropriate for future managers? Many French criticize this system, insisting that while there is nothing to guarantee that it will identify those with the best managerial potential, it at the same time shuts people out very early on, disqualifying those who for whatever reason do not test as well, or who have skills other than those for which the *concours* test. Many point to the fact that among the most successful heads of enterprises, two-thirds are *autodidactes,* or self-made men, suggesting that elite schooling is not necessarily the best way to gain entrepreneurial skills.[19] And some, such as Dominique Strauss-Kahn, Minister of Industry under Prime Ministers Cresson and Bérégovoy, go one step farther to question whether success based on educational performance has anything to do with the qualities needed for the management of either state or industry, given that some of

---

[14]NEDO., *Making of Managers,* p. 7, Table 2.   [15]Ibid., p. 2.

[16]Bauer, Bertin-Mourot, and Thobois, *Les No. 1 des 200.*

[17]See: Suleiman, *Elites in French Society.*

[18]Quoted in Ezra N. Suleiman, "The Myth of Technical Expertise: Selection, Organization and Leadership," *Comparative Politics* vol. 10 (October 1977), p. 146.

[19]Bauer and Mourot, *Les 200,* pp. 182–183.

the most successful managers such as Vincent Bolloré, Bernard Arnault, and Bernard Tapie clearly did not excel in their studies.[20]

Critics also question whether an elite educational system focused on training people for state service as engineers (X) or as administrators (ENA) can produce managers capable of running a business enterprise. There are those who fault the education of the *polytechniciens* in particular by arguing that although they are all good at solving technical problems, while some may be decent managers, others are not because they lack training in management and don't know anything of human relations because they haven't learned about the world.[21] And there are those who have similar things to say about the *énarques* because "they haven't really even managed a team, or sensed where people are, what people are, and the like. They don't know team spirit, are individualists, careerists. Some went into enterprise very early, and succeeded. But only if they agreed to learn. Parachuting is a very bad idea."[22] Thus, many feel that although the *énarques* may make good administrative staff members, given that at the crux of the ENA education is "the transmission of methods, even recipes, to treat as rapidly as possible the multiple problems of a modern administration,"[23] they are not necessarily good business managers.

Even those thoroughly approving of the elite education system, however, acknowledge that problems arise from an educational system that is too theoretical and lacks a focus on the interpersonal. One such supporter of the system noted, "French cadres are trained very rationally and find it difficult in front of people older than themselves and with considerable work experience to accept that things are never perfect or completely solveable."[24] A direct attack also came from the growing literature insisting that managers required greater "professionalism," meaning that their competence was to be defined on the basis of their understanding of the company and their experience of real problems and interpersonal relations, and not only on academically acquired knowledge.[25] The result of the demand for increasing professionalism, however, has led to an emphasis on more training in interpersonal skills in the firm, rather than an abandonment of the elite recruitment system.[26]

Beffa of Saint-Gobain, himself a product of this system, might agree with part of this analysis of the problems, since he acknowledged that

[20]Strauss-Kahn, interview with author.
[21]Bertrand Warusfeld, conversation with author, Paris, May 13, 1991.
[22]Descours, interview with author.   [23]Bellier, *L'Ena.*
[24]M. Le Gorrec, assistant personnel director of EDF-GDF, and president of the French Association of Training Managers, cited in NEDO, *Making of Managers*, p. 67.
[25]Ibid., pp. 73–74.   [26]Ibid., p. 74.

even if the elite recruits were the best and the brightest, nothing guaranteed that they had good sense or the ability to deal with others, and so forth. But those with these added qualities, he insisted, can't be all bad.[27] The question, however, is whether those without the added qualities will be weeded out. The problem with the *corporatisme* that accompanies the elite educational system is that, in taking care of its own, the corps ensures that even the bad ones get a *"placard doré,"* a golden closet, or sinecure, since "one doesn't abandon one's young."[28]

But even if the less competent are weeded out, the *corporatisme* in and of itself breeds other problems related to issues of access and outlook. An example of this is the comment of a top manager at a major bank who approved of the elite recruitment system on the grounds that "it was easier to work with a homogeneous group than with people with disparate backgrounds and expectations." The response of Strauss-Kahn (who did HEC and a Ph.D. in economics, and when asked why he did not do the ENA, responded, "I thought I could do better"), noted that it may very well be easier and less tiring to work with people who think the same things and say the same things, but it is less profitable."[29] This view was confirmed by the management consulting firm Cofremca in 1987, which argued that for French business to respond appropriately to the increasingly diverse and complex environment, it needed a more heterogeneous management team, noting that "in a period of change, a management team that is too homogeneous, in which its members resemble one another too much, could be a major handicap for an enterprise, leading it to share the fate of the dinosaur, if its competitors have a more polymorphous management top." Where top managers come from the same one or two schools and even the same corps, and are about the same age, the result is too much internal competition and not enough diversity in terms of innovation. Moreover, they all look alike and think alike, and have been selected on the basis of an intellectual competition based on high intellectual agility and precocity.[30]

Many complained that the elite educational system, together with the *corporatisme,* breeds uniformity of thought and arrogance of character, in addition to cronyism. Thus, Octave Célinié, president emeritus of CEGOS and a graduate of the School of Mines, decried "the arrogance of the corps, an impermeable and homogeneous network which monopolizes thought in a caricatural manner, to the great stupefaction of foreign-

[27]Beffa, interview with author.
[28]Comment by Bénédicte Bertin-Mourot, cited in *Le Monde,* June 19, 1991.
[29]Strauss-Kahn, interview with author.
[30]"Homogénéité des états-majors: Danger de mort," *L'Observatoire de la Cofremca,* no. 30 (1987).

ers."[31] In a similar vein, François de Closets, in the report on the Tenth Plan, remarked that even though they may be the brightest, their power system results in homogeneity; and because they see themselves as the best, they lose that rare quality, doubt, without which all other qualities are spoiled. One is better off, he suggested, with mixture and heterogeneity, in particular because "the best managers reveal themselves in the field in contact with men and concrete situations." And he therefore recommended the diversification of recruitment, something which he recognizes cannot be done without getting rid of the privileges of the ENA or X.[32]

But is this likely to occur? Criticisms of the elite recruitment and training system have been made for a long time. By the sixties, already, the French were concerned about the training of their managers. But they sought to remedy this management gap not through changing the recruitment system but through improving the education of their elite recruits: instead of increasing the M.B.A.s recruited, they gave those already selected for top positions the opportunity to do M.B.A.s.[33] Not much has changed since. The training may have improved, but the elite recruitment system remains basically untouched.

Thus, the *corpsards,* because of their similar training and their assured future together, tend to form a small club of like-minded, arrogant, but competent individuals. When they join the firm at the top managerial ranks after years in state service, they will perform splendidly. But their very presence in the firms signals to all those who come up through the ranks that firm loyalty and business success are not rewarded nearly as much as elite educational credentials and a career in state service.

THE EFFECTS OF THE STATE-CENTERED CAREER TRACK

Most arguments against the elite recruitment and promotion system tend to focus less on the future CEOs' education than on their career track. The problems start with the fact that those with elite educational backgrounds first go to work for the state – and therefore know the ways of administration better than those of business – and end with the fact that, because they are parachuted into the top ranks of business, they block access to everyone else, thus lowering morale and undervaluing business achievement.

This pattern has not gone uncriticized over time. In the early seventies,

[31]*Le Monde,* June 19, 1991.   [32]De Closets, *Pari de la responsabilité,* pp. 59–63.
[33]Jane Marceau, " 'Plus ça change, plus c'est la même chose': Access to Elite Careers in French Business," in *Elites in France: Origins, Reproduction, Power,* ed. Jolyon Howorth and Philip G. Cerny (London: Pinter, 1981), pp. 121–122.

Evaluating the elite management system

Alain Griotteray complained that this system of recruitment to the public enterprises denied access to top positions to all but the few who followed an elite educational and civil service career track which in no way provided them with the experience best suited for public sector jobs. He regretted that recruitment was not open to political figures in cases where large corporations with tens of thousands of employees that could benefit from leadership by "persons who have the habit of treating business from a perspective larger than a strictly technical viewpoint" or to specialists from the private sector, for example, in the case of the reorganization of an enterprise or group of enterprises.[34]

More recently, many on both the right and the left have bemoaned above all the fact that the most gifted go into state service rather than directly into business. On the left, Strauss-Kahn criticized the fact that a large percentage of the best and the brightest are pulled toward state service, and therefore not toward industry, with predictable effects. On the right, Michel Drancourt of the Business Institute claimed it a pity for business that the best, the smartest, were *énarques* and X-Ponts, X-Mines, and so forth,[35] while Maisonrouge of IBM World Trade found it a waste, since even though the size of the entering class of the ENA was reduced by half, 50% of the graduates still went to work for the state.[36] Others went even further to criticize a system in which the graduates of the most prestigious of the *grandes écoles* ended up working for the administration and/or in a political cabinet for ten or fifteen years before being parachuted into a top managerial position in business.

Those who have extensive business careers tended to be the harshest critics of this system, whether on the left or the right. For example, the Socialist banker Jean Deflassieux, who attended HEC and the London School of Economics, saw this caste system as killing France, with the elite poorly educated for leadership in business, and of middling quality. There are, as he put it, "gratteurs de rapports," or scratchers of reports, but what is needed are "rapporteurs de grats," or people who bring in the scratch. France, he insisted, "has good public administrators, but they should stay in public administration. They are made to administer, not to command. They need to remain number two, not be number one." Thus, Deflassieux maintained that if they are to enter business at all, "civil servants need to leave public service before they are forty years old, to agree to obey in the firm, and to learn for ten years."[37]

---

[34]A. Griotteray, "Rapport sur les entreprises nationales" (Document no. 2010), first ordinary session of the National Assembly, 1971–1972, pp. 14–15 – quoted in Derivry, "Managers of Public Enterprises," p. 220.
   [35]Drancourt, conversation with author.   [36]Maisonrouge, interview with author.
   [37]Deflassieux, interview with author.

425

On the other side of the political spectrum, moreover, a number of CEOs added to this by complaining that the state experience of elite school graduates left them "too marked by the civil service and the ENA or X." For Descours, this meant that they ended up not being real leaders of their enterprise.[38] For others, it may very well have meant the bureaucratic ethos and the preoccupation with hierarchy and discipline which undervalues profit-making, a criticism of long standing.[39] For Maisonrouge of IBM World Trade, a *centralien* who had an in-house business career, those who work in public administration and then "leave ten years later to go into industry, are a bit deformed by the administration; because in administration, it is too bureaucratic, and one doesn't learn how to make decisions."[40] Others such as André Lévy-Lang of Paribas, himself a graduate of X (who it is said would have been valedictorian had he not been foreign-born and thus part of a separate competition), but who also attended Stanford University and went early on into business, also thought it better to take *polytechniciens* and *énarques* at thirty rather than forty-five because "they need to know something about business,"[41] although he appeared less convinced that state experience bred indecision.

Top business managers with extensive state experience, needless to say, disagreed with the notion that such experience is a serious problem. De Wissocq of Elf, having himself had long experience in administration (always in the energy sphere) before becoming head of Cogema, wouldn't go as far as Maisonrouge to say that people who have had ten years of experience in the administration couldn't make decisions, although he agreed that it was a risk, but not a serious one, if one looked at the examples such as that of Roger Martin, an X-Mines, at Saint-Gobain.[42] Gallois, with the bulk of his career in administration, retorted that Maisonrouge's opposition to the elite system could be explained in part because he is a *centralien* (meaning that he did not attend a state school such as ENA or X, and so he cannot understand the importance of the system). Although Gallois agreed that "it may not be so good that so many French business *patrons* are obliged to take the administration route; it may not be such a good education for heads of industry; and the *grand corps* may not be a good system"; he himself, after all, as he explained, did learn to make decisions in the administration, as cabinet

[38]Descours, interview with author.

[39]M. Levy-Leboyer, "The Large Corporation in Modern France," in *Managerial Hierarchies,* ed. A. Chandler and H. Daems (Cambridge, MA: Harvard University Press, 1980), p. 133.

[40]Maisonrouge, interview with author.   [41]Lévy-Lang, interview with author.

[42]De Wissocq, interview with author.

director in the Ministry of Industry.[43] But Gallois, too, disapproved of the state-focused system of education: "The French don't love their industries enough; the best don't go into industry, the education and training at all levels is not targeted enough on industry; the solidarity of the *tissu indus-triel* is insufficient, especially compared to Japan and Germany."[44]

Not all who defended state service as an acceptable pre-business career track, however, approved of all aspects of it. Giraud, former director of the Corps des Mines, criticized its political aspects, in particular the now almost requisite experience in ministerial cabinets. He was most concerned about "the ministerial cabinets which destroy the stable administration for which our country was envied. Engineers of the Mines are frequently named to these, and this is not the best use of their services. They were educated to be scientific or industrial leaders rather than political ones."[45] Descours of the Groupe André tended to agree with this, arguing that the *énarques* in particular, because they have systematically sought political careers, have ended up confounding politics and administration. And this is only made worse, he suggests, when the *camarades de promotion* of the young minister sees his *camarades* in administration.[46] These criticisms may be becoming moot, however, given that of late the numbers of graduates of ENA and X in ministerial cabinets are diminishing, supplanted in government by the *agrégés,* or university graduates who have passed the *agrégation,* or special test which assures them of a teaching position.

But whether they faulted the political aspects of state experience alone or the simple fact of state experience, most critics condemned business recruitment from the outside for the top-level positions. They found that it created a glass ceiling, and signaled to all in the firm that one's loyalty and dedication, let alone one's achievements, were clearly not rewarded anywhere nearly as handsomely as elite educational credentials and a career in state service. Thus, although almost all critics of the elite system of recruitment and promotion had no complaints about the people put at the head of the nationalized enterprises, they nevertheless condemned it for its deleterious impact on the personnel.

For example, Bertrand Warusfeld, a management consultant and university lecturer, contended that French industry suffered a double loss in that it lost good engineers when *polytechniciens* became managers – and as managers, they blocked advancement for everyone else. For in firms where X graduates are top managers, all others know that they can't go any higher.[47] Maisonrouge of IBM similarly insisted that although the

[43]Gallois, interview with author.   [44]Ibid.   [45]*Le Monde,* June 19, 1991.
[46]Descours, interview with author.   [47]Warusfeld, conversation with author.

parachuting worked because the Socialist government made good choices, it was bad for the mass of employees and bad for morale.[48] Jean-Claude Porée, a top administrator of ANVAR, the government agency for applied research, also felt that the system was a disaster for France because there was so little chance for someone to come up from nothing, so much so that there weren't even any stories or fables about this, as in the United States with its Horatio Alger myth. After all, he noted, even Bouygues, whose career provides the media with its most popular rags-to-riches-story, is a *centralien*.[49]

A 1986 SOFRES study confirms these concerns about the impact of the elite recruitment system. At this time, and despite the improvement in worker–management relations and in attitudes toward management, three-quarters of all employees complained that they were not rewarded for their merits, with one-quarter (24%) of them finding their merits unrecognized and unrewarded, while close to half (48%) saw their merits recognized but unrewarded. The responses according to size of the firm only further highlight the problem: the personnel of firms with fewer than ten employees felt the most recognized and rewarded (at 36%); those in firms with more than 200 employees felt least so (at 21%); and those in firms between the two extremes were intermediate in their feelings (at 25%).[50]

Low morale and a sense of going nowhere, of being *plafonné*, are clear indications of the effects of the elite recruitment system. The contrast with Germany is most striking, where the pattern of in-house career and inside promotion is said to encourage employee loyalty to the firm and its objectives, leading to the development of a long-term view.[51] Because promotion to top management positions in Germany is the reward for high performance over the long haul, it also gives Germans a sense that they have something to work toward, by contrast with France, where no amount of achievement will help. Drancourt illustrated this by comparing Germany, where the greater importance of middle management is such that there are more captains and fewer generals, to France, where the generals come from elsewhere, and the captains aspire only to be colonels. And for the captains, this results in a profound resentment, because people can't advance far enough.[52]

The figures speak for themselves. France is the country with the highest

[48]Maisonrouge, interview with author.

[49]Jean-Claude Porée, top administrator at ANVAR. Conversation with author, Paris, April 8, 1991.

[50]SOFRES, *L'état de l'opinion 1987*, p. 145.

[51]J. M. Bessant and M. Grunt, *Management and Manufacturing Innovation in the United Kingdom and West Germany* (Aldershot: Gower, 1985).

[52]Drancourt, conversation with author.

Evaluating the elite management system

Table 15.1. *Method by which managers are chosen in Europe, in percentages*

	Germany	Great Britain	Nether-lands	Belgium	France	Italy	Spain	Total
Outside recruitment	57%	66%	74%	71%	76%	57%	60%	65%
Internal promotion	43%	34%	26%	29%	24%	43%	40%	35%
No. of positions (in thousands)	109.5	233	38	21	156	101	68.5	727

Source: APEC, Panel Europe 90; and Dominique Taddei and Benjamin Coriat, "Spécial: Made in France," Industries Special Edition (September 1992).

percentage of outside recruitment of managers, at 76%, or 156,000 in absolute numbers, with only 24% internal promotion, by contrast in particular with Germany and Italy, which tie for the lowest outside recruitment, at 57%, and the highest internal promotion, at 43% (see Table 15.1). It also has the highest percentage of managers compared to employees overall – 14% in France versus only 9.3% in Germany, as compared to the European average of 12.5%. This makes the sense of going nowhere even more profound.[53]

The system, moreover, results in a serious lack of "capacity catching," or of taking advantage of all the human potential at one's disposal, in particular that of university graduates, who are left almost entirely out of the loop. What is more, in addition to limiting the careers of the noncaste members, according to Strauss-Kahn, it also leads to bitterness for those who don't fulfill their expectations: not everyone can be head of Thomson, after all.[54]

Even those who had themselves benefited from being placed at the top after a career in administration admitted that there were problems. Daniel Lebègue, himself parachuted into the number two position at the BNP, granted that it was not normal to put people who come from outside an enterprise at the top. But he noted that the real question was not whether the state was wrong to put *énarques* or *polytechniciens* at the head of major enterprises, but rather why the French system of education did not produce similarly well-qualified people from the universities.[55]

The CEOs were in fact unanimous in their condemnation of the university system. Lévy-Lang of Paribas contended that the problem was not with the *grandes écoles* but with the dual system of higher education that

[53]Dominique Taddei and Benjamin Coriat, "Spécial: Made in France," *Industries*, special edition (September 1992), p. 9.
[54]Strauss-Kahn, interview with author.   [55]Lebègue, interview with author.

claimed to provide equality but didn't.[56] Jean Gandois, CEO of Péchiney and himself an X-Ponts argued,

the bias of the recruitment system in favor of graduates of X and ENA is understandable, given that the universities do not produce enough students at a high enough level of competence in technical and economic subjects: The only places where recruitment is possible is from the *grandes écoles,* and it is natural that the best go to X. This bias in favor of the *grandes écoles* may have another source: the fears of the French that they have an elitist system that can only train people who serve the state. It is part of the nonmodernity of France.[57]

To understand why the elite recruitment persists, in other words, requires an explanation of why the university system is so bad. And this takes us back to the elite educational system and the bias in favor of state service.

INITIATING CHANGE IN HUMAN RESOURCES

Just about all top government and business officials interviewed, regardless of their view of the traditional elite education and recruitment system, agreed that it was changing, primarily through the diversification of management recruitment, with an increasing number of graduates of less elite *grandes écoles* and from the universities, as well as women, being given positions of responsibility. By contrast, the pressures of recent internationalization have brought little change at the top, although they have ensured that younger managers have been gaining experience abroad.

What change has occurred as regards recruitment and promotion to top managerial positions for women and university graduates has come about as a result of efforts by CEOs with elite credentials to diversify their teams. For women, although lower-level management positions have been increasingly opened up, higher level positions remain male-dominated. Although women represent between 40% and 50% of students in business schools and 16% at engineering schools, only 4% of senior managers are women, and 90% of female managers are in the service sector.[58] There is little difference here, however, from most other advanced industrial societies, other than Japan, where the women in top management positions in major firms are nonexistent. In Germany, the number of women in top management positions in 1982 was estimated at between 2 and 3%;[59] in Great Britain in 1984, women constituted only 2.51% of the British Institute of Management.[60] In Japan, according to the Prime Minister's Office, in 1980 women in all management positions, senior and junior, came to 6.7%, by contrast with 23.5% in the United States and 39.8% in West Germany.[61]

[56]Lévy-Lang, interview with author. [57]Gandois, interview with author.
[58]NEDO, *Making of Managers,* p. 75. [59]Ibid., pp. 52–53. [60]Ibid., p. 89.
[61]Ibid., p. 96.

The pay statistics are also significant. In 1987, the incomes of men with full-time employment were 25% higher than those of women, explained in large measure by the differentials among senior managers and professionals.[62] Admission to the École Polytechnique, the Cours des Comptes, and the Inspection des Finances began only in the 1970s. The coeducational École Nationale d'Administration, however, was not much better: it was 90% male in the 1970s, and by the mid eighties had reduced that only to 75%.[63]

Nonetheless, there are examples of CEOs making a concerted effort to alter the pattern. For example, Gandois of Péchiney, noting that heavy industry tended to be rather macho, although not as much as steel, hired a woman, Martine Aubry (subsequently Minister of Labor under Rocard) as one of his main deputies, one of four executive vice-presidents. He found that it had a positive impact on internal management practice by breaking through the traditional "court phenomenon" of yes-men that is often apparent in power circles and by serving as an example to lower management levels, encouraging them to promote women as well.[64] At SNECMA, Gallois started the process of change a bit lower down. In seeking to diversify recruitment to create a more "exotic profile," he explained that they were recruiting women *and* university graduates. "No, better," he corrected himself, tongue in cheek, "You see, we are recruiting blacks, Arabs, women, *and* university graduates."[65] From his somewhat ironic comments, he was making it quite clear that women with elite educational backgrounds were still more likely to succeed than men or women with university credentials.

University graduates have nevertheless made inroads. In terms of recruitment to career positions in large firms, only 40% now come from the *grandes écoles*, a big change from 1980.[66] Moreover, significant changes have been occurring at the lower managerial levels over the past ten or twenty years. For example, although the top ranks remain ENA and X at the Caisse des Dépôts et Consignations, the lower ranks up to the top level minus one have changed significantly from twenty years ago, when management as a whole was 90% ENA. Now, a diminishing number are from the ENA and state service, with the majority from the private sector (80%) who may even run one of the 400 subsidiaries with 200 employees.[67]

Part of the explanation for these changes has to do with reforms of the

[62]*Données sociales 1987* (Paris: Insee, 1987), pp. 159–161.
[63]Joni Lovenduski, *Women and European Politics: Contemporary Feminism and Public Policy* (Amherst: University of Massachusetts Press, 1986), p. 222.
[64]Gandois, interview with author.   [65]Gallois, interview with author.
[66]*Le Monde,* May 14, 1991.   [67]Boudrouille, interview with author.

universities, with new degrees such as the B.T.P. and new professional education units such as the IUT. But real overhaul of the system is difficult if not impossible. The general perception is that the government has been able to do little about this, given the strength of the national education union on the one hand, and opposition from students to any reform, whether from the left (the *loi Savary*), the neoliberal right, or the left again.

There seems to be a general sense among all business executives interviewed that the major firms are opening up recruitment to those who have not gone to the *grandes écoles*. Moreover, they also see less significance to the administration route, finding that most of those wishing to succeed in business, whether or not they have elite educational credentials, have to go into the enterprise earlier than traditionally, and at a lower level, in the middle rather than at the top.

For those who start at the bottom, however, as opposed to those who start at the middle or the top, and who lack university education of any kind, there is little hope of reaching top management levels. It is perhaps significant that although three-fourths of the personnel complained in 1986 that they felt unrewarded, whether their merits were recognized or not, upper-level managers, for all their fears of being *plafonnés,* were the least upset about this (at 51%) and workers the most (at 81%), with foremen and employees (at 71%) still concerned, but less so.[68] Workers, in effect, have little hope of climbing the ladder.

This is in marked contrast with Great Britain where, for all its other faults, a large proportion of managers (38% according to a recent survey) started their careers in a manual occupation.[69] Access to management positions is probably more open in Britain than elsewhere because there have traditionally been fewer credentialist barriers to surmount, such as university degrees, since people who went into business were not thought to need a higher-level degree. (Barriers do exist, however, and come even earlier than with the French: a third of British CEOs of the top 200 firms came from twenty of the top public schools, with a tenth from Eton alone.)[70] In France, on the contrary, in 1985, of all cadres, or managers, staff and line, in firms of all sizes, from the largest to the smallest, a full 68.7% have the *baccalauréat,* or *bac,* and of these, 36.6% have *bac* + 4/5, equivalent to four or five years of higher education, suggesting that even managers in the small and mid-sized firms are reasonably well edu-

---

[68]SOFRES, *L'état de l'opinion 1987,* p. 147.
[69]P. K. Edwards, *Managing the Factory* (Oxford: Basil Blackwell, 1987), p. 41 – cited in Lane, *Management and Labour,* p. 89.
[70]Bauer, Bertin-Mourot, and Thobois, *Les No. 1 des 200.*

cated.[71] In the early eighties, nearly half of the CEOs of the SMEs in all sectors had had a higher education qualification.[72]

At the same time that more women and more university graduates are making their way into responsible positions in firms and up the hierarchy, however slowly, given that the glass ceiling remains a reality, there is also a new pattern of larger numbers of graduates of the *grandes écoles* moving directly into business, without passing through the state first. As Strauss-Kahn explains it, things are in the process of changing because the decrease in state influence on the economy is weakening the hold of this "'closed shop': elite graduates know that state service won't necessarily net them the leadership of a major state bank such as the Crédit Lyonnais, whereas a career in business may."[73]

Of course, not all companies have been diversifying their recruitment patterns. Although some firms are trying to "exit from the ghetto" by a strategy of *"mixage de compétences,"* often those that need it the most may succeed the least at this "grafting of new blood."[74] Certainly, the prejudice in favor of elite graduates remains even where the recruitment has been diversified. Illustrative of this is a recent story of the first meeting of Serge Dassault (an X-Aéro), CEO of Dassault, with the two hundred or so managerial recruits of the year 1992. Turning to his assistant, in front of all of the recruits, he asked: "How many are *polytechniciens*?" "Twelve." At that, he responded: "Ah, isn't that a bit low?"

The internationalization of French business has also helped loosen the hold of the graduates of elite schools, with the M.B.A. increasingly becoming the degree of choice among the up-and-coming. Moreover, because the internationalization of firms has also ensured that there is the need for more than one network, elite membership is no longer a guarantee against dismissal. This is why, according to Every de Rochechouart of Korn and Ferry, the personnel agency, "Ten years ago, one never fired an X. Now, yes."[75]

Foreign experience has become an increasingly important part of a manager's career profile. More and more managers on their way up of late have been spending years heading foreign operations. And some CEOs have even had foreign experience: The head of Lafarge Coppée had ten years' experience in the United States; the head of Air Liquide, eight years in Canada and the United States. This is more the exception than

[71]NEDO, *Making of Managers*, p. 64.
[72]L. Vickery, "France," in *Small Business in Europe* (London: Macmillan, 1986), p. 24; and Lane, *Management and Labour*, p. 90.
[73]Strauss-Kahn, interview with author.
[74]Claude La Santé, quoted in *Le Monde*, June 19, 1991.
[75]*Le Monde*, June 19, 1991.

the rule for CEOs, however. In 1986, of the 144 CEOs of the top French multinationals, only 16 had foreign managerial experience, and only 8 of these, or 5.5%, worked for the company they were later to lead. Of the rest, 112, or 78%, had no foreign experience.[76] Part of the problem here, as Maisonrouge explains it, is that French firms don't have an internal management system that enables them to handle their expatriates well. It is something akin to the "'Glenn,' or reentry, problem: They go away and, when they come back, management doesn't know what to do with them, so most have little desire to go abroad."[77]

The French have similar problems bringing foreign nationals in to the topmost positions in the firm. Although the French are on the whole not quite as bad as the Germans on this score (although the Germans at least had a French president of Volkswagen), they are a lot worse than U.S. and British firms, let alone the most internationalized of multinationals, those of the smaller countries, such as Holland (Royal Dutch Shell) and Switzerland (Nestlé).[78] The executive committees tend not to be very internationalized even if the operations are. At Péchiney, although the executive committee has not been successfully internationalized (it was attempted briefly with an American from its subsidiary American National Can), the next level below is.[79] At Elf, only French are in the executive committee, in part because of the history, in part because of the language problem; but this is likely to change in the next ten to fifteen years.[80] Saint-Gobain has an Italian head of packaging, as well as a Spanish and even a Brazilian top manager.[81] And Thomson has at the very least been conscious of the need for a "multicultural" approach.[82]

The more French firms internationalize, and the less important the internal market becomes to the company, the more likely it will be that foreign heads of subsidiaries take the top positions in the firm.[83] And the more this is the case, the less the graduates of the elite schools will hold sway; unless, that is, they are the ones who have the greatest international experience, and the best language skills, and who have managed to prove themselves in the firm before they are considered for high-level positions. The problem, in fact, is that often those with the greatest advantages in the educational system will continue to dominate. The recession, moreover, has slowed down the pace of change, as companies, less willing to take chances in an unfavorable economic climate, have been turning away

---

[76]Bauer and Mourot, *Les 200*, p. 255.   [77]Maisonrouge, interview with author.
[78]*Business Week*, May 14, 1990.   [79]Gandois, interview with author.
[80]De Wissocq, interview with author.   [81]Bidegain, interview with author.
[82]Janice McCormick and Nan Stone, "From National Champion to Global Competitor: An Interview with Thomson's Alain Gomez," *Harvard Business Review* (May–June 1990): 127–135.
[83]Maisonrouge, interview with author.

from their more open recruitment of university graduates to the surer bets, the graduates of the *grandes écoles*.

CONCLUSION

For the moment, then, the typical top management team remains remarkably like that of the past: very French, very male, and very elite. As such, it continues to raise questions not only of fairness, given the upper-middle-class bias of the elite educational system, as discussed earlier, but also ones of capacity catching. After all, if only those children of the upper middle classes who test well at an early age are marked for success, then what of all those who are equally gifted but mature later, or are talented in other ways? They are forever left out of the loop which takes the privileged few from the topmost ranks of the civil service, perhaps with a detour to a ministerial cabinet, into those of business. The result is a system in which these privileged few monopolize top positions, limiting upward mobility in the corporation, and blocking access to the topmost ranks for those making their way internally up the corporate ladder. By rewarding credentialism at the expense of achievement, this recruitment and promotion system lowers morale and fails to take full advantage of the human resources at its disposal in the corporation. Moreover, the elite promotion system, combined with the continued centralization of power in the hands of the CEO in many French firms, risks leaving the personnel feeling disenfranchised in the firm, and more likely than ever to seek individual arrangements outside of the formal rules in order to retain their "honor."

Management practice has been changing, however. Most large firms have successfully democratized at the middle management level while labor relations have improved immeasurably. And even the system of management recruitment and promotion has been changing, however slowly. But whether such change will come fast enough, and produce a sufficiently diverse cohort of future top managers with the training and range of experience essential to dealing effectively with the rough-and-tumble of the new competitive environment generated by European economic integration and the internationalization of trade, remains to be seen.

Conclusion

During Mitterrand's presidency, France underwent a major transformation in business and its relationship to government. The *dirigiste* state, so carefully built up during the postwar period, was effectively dismantled. In pursuit of European economic integration and international competitiveness for French business, governments of the left and right deregulated and privatized, stripping the state of its long-standing interventionist powers in the economy and loosening the ties that have traditionally bound business to government. The results speak for themselves: Not only is the economy as a whole much freer and more market-oriented, but the very structure of French capitalism has changed. Business has not just modernized and internationalized, it has become more interdependent and independent of the state as successive governments almost immediately following upon the 1981 nationalizations found ways to dilute state ownership and/or diminish state control of public enterprise, leaving a situation in which public and private, nationalized and privatized firms control one another through cross-shareholdings, in a manner akin to the German model. Although French business slid into recession in the early nineties, most major elements for recovery are there, including sound investment strategies, better labor–management relations, and democratization at the lower management levels – even if problems remain, including high unemployment, undersized and underfinanced small and medium-sized businesses, and the continued centralization of decision-making in many firms.

Underlying this transformation has been a major shift in the French view of their country's place in the world economy. French leaders, with few exceptions, fully accepted that France could no longer go its own way in an integrating Europe and an internationalizing economy. They recognized that to prosper they would have to give up their close control over the domestic economy in favor of a more indirect and "liberal" approach to industrial policymaking in France and of a larger role for Europe.

Conclusion

The conflict between competing strands of economic management policy — the postwar *dirigisme* that saw the role of government as promoter of industry on the one hand, and the EC-inspired liberalism that pushed France ineluctably away from a state-directed economy toward a more market-based one on the other — was resolved in the early eighties in favor of liberalism. This was probably inevitable, as France struggled to emerge from the crisis of the seventies brought on by a great number of external constraints and by internal failures. The external constraints included the end to the fixed exchange rate system, the oil shocks, and the increasing competition resulting from European integration. Internal failures responsible for the 1970s crisis included a business–government partnership that could not effectively spur economic modernization because it excluded small and medium-sized enterprises as well as labor from the policymaking process; the national champions that had turned into lame ducks because they had failed to address their structural problems; and the government industrial policies that increasingly focused on rescuing lame ducks or creating industry leaders in certain sectors rather than on promoting overall competitiveness. But the triumph of liberalism was nothing that the Socialists who came to power in 1981 had themselves anticipated — far from it.

At the time the Socialists entered office, they had pledged to turn the economy around through an increase in state *dirigisme,* in particular with reinvigorated planning and industrial policy, worker democracy, and a break with old-style French capitalism and the "wall of money." It was only after an initial, highly interventionist period characterized by expansive macroeconomic policies and expensive microeconomic policies, which included the nationalization and recapitalization of major French financial and industrial concerns, a fifth week of vacation, a thirty-nine-hour work week, and so on, that the Socialists changed direction. A general belt-tightening in the microeconomic sphere accompanied the restrictive monetary policies in the macroeconomic sphere, while deregulation and informal privatization became the order of the day. Worker democracy was all but forgotten, as was the central role of planning. Moreover, while labor lost jobs as well as wages, business, which went in the popular rhetoric from "exploiter" to "creator of riches," gained greater access to government financing, new nongovernmental sources of funds, lower taxes, lower interest rates, and greater flexibility in the workplace. Ultimately, the Socialists broke not with capitalism but with the failures of capitalism, and with the Socialist economic project both as ideology and as policy.

For the neo-liberal right who followed them, Socialist liberalism was not liberal enough. Wide-scale privatization and stepped-up deregulation, with supply-side measures focused on decreasing government spending, cutting the size and funding of government agencies, lowering taxes, eliminating restrictions on business, and further opening the financial markets, were the neoliberals' responses to what they saw as the excessive *dirigisme* of the Socialists. However, they did not themselves completely abandon *dirigisme,* which was apparent in their policy style if not in the policies themselves. Privatization was as heroic an affair for the neoliberals as nationalization was for the Socialists: It was centrally controlled and highly regulated, with government picking the hard core of investors, limiting the amount of foreign investment, and marginalizing small shareholders. Deregulation, moreover, did not go nearly as far as the right's campaign promises or its "ultra" neoliberal members' expectations, with certain controls over business retained, while subsidies to business continued as before. The neoliberals' calls for "more liberty" and "less state," in brief, did institute less state, but not as little as promised.

Heroic policies of the left and the right, then, were instrumental in transforming the economy in Mitterrand's first *septennat,* or seven-year term, with "more state" followed in short order by "less state," and *dirigiste* economic management policies very quickly replaced by more liberal ones. In Mitterrand's second seven-year term, heroism was no longer desired, nor possible, and everyday policies substituted themselves for the heroic.

The lesson gleaned from the back-and-forth on economic policies and ideology, in particular from nationalization and privatization, was that, public or private, business is business, and that neither total control by the state nor total retreat of the state was a panacea. Under successive prime ministers of the left and then the right, privatization and deregulation continued, but these had become everyday policies for governments that seemed to follow business more than to lead it, despite occasional rhetorical flourishes or grand initiatives. Although the *dirigiste* reflex was not gone, reemerging when the economy appeared in trouble, it no longer had the force of the traditional *dirigiste* state behind it. Heroism, if anything, had moved to the European level, with the making of the Maastricht Treaty, even if French hopes for more interventionist European industrial policies in strategic areas had been disappointed. And yet, at the national level, significant change nevertheless occurred, with the restructuring of French capital the result of a growing consensus on the need for French business to emulate the German model of banking–industry partnership.

By the end of Mitterrand's second seven-year term, as France suffered from prolonged economic recession while European integration appeared stalled, the demise of heroic policymaking no longer occasioned the same sense of relief as in 1988, when the economy was flourishing. Although the French would not necessarily have desired a return to the ideologically inspired heroism of the recent past, they nevertheless felt a sense of loss for what that heroism had represented in terms of forceful leaders with clear plans of action and political certainties about what was to be done to resolve French economic problems. This was expressed in a SOFRES survey just preceding the April 1995 elections, in which 64% of respondents wished for "a real leader who will bring back order and command" (by contrast with the 1981 survey results which emphasized promoting political and social change or those of 1988 which preferred maintaining established rights and consensus). What is more, 67% recommended that the state intervene more in the economic life of the country (with respondents on the left, for obvious reasons, more interested in state intervention, at 74%, than those on the right, at 61%). European integration and trade liberalization, interestingly enough, were not connected to this sense of loss: 63% of respondents actually called for an acceleration of integration (vs. 25% against), while 69% insisted on the continued acceptance of free trade (vs. 21% against).[1]

This sense of loss manifested itself in the disaffection of the electorate, in the rising extremism on the right, and in the general malaise that came from the increasing banality of political discourse and the lack of new ideas that followed the disintegration of left-wing and right-wing ideological divisions. It was also apparent in the increasing disillusionment with government officials who appeared unresponsive to citizen desires; incapable of solving the problems that they cared about the most, such as high unemployment; and increasingly corrupt, given the scandals related to illegal election financing, insider trading, misuse of public funds, and the distribution of HIV-infected blood.[2]

The restiveness of the French public suggests a crisis of political leadership. In the 1990s, a majority of the population has had a negative view of how well democracy functions in France, although the numbers for 1994 are slightly better than those for 1992. In 1994, 49% thought that French democracy functioned not very well (35%) or poorly (14%), which was three points higher than 1992, while 47% thought that it worked very well (4%) or all right (*assez bien*) (43%), which was two points higher than 1992.[3] Interestingly enough, this does not reflect any more deep-seated dissatisfaction with French institutions per se, at least not yet. In a major poll by SOFRES in late 1992, a majority of French thought that even though democracy was doing poorly, the structures of government

[1]*Le Monde,* April 11, 1995.
[2]See Yves Mény, *La corruption de la République* (Paris: Fayard, 1992).
[3]Jean-Philippe Roy, "1994–1995: Recomposition ou pérennité du spectre politique," *Revue Politique et Parlementaire* no. 969 (January–February 1994).

were functioning well. Although they saw major problems with unemployment, poverty, and the tainted blood scandal, they remained happy with their institutions, with 61% convinced that they worked well, as opposed to 32% convinced that they did not work well (and 7% with no opinion). This compares favorably with the views expressed in 1983, when 57% were pro and 25% con (and 18% had no opinion); and in 1978, when 56% were pro and 27% con (and 17% had no opinion).[4] What the general public has not yet recognized is that although the structures of government with which they are happy remain unchanged, the processes by which those structures function have been modified as a result of the policies of the recent past. The crisis of leadership has a lot to do with the changes in these processes, because the leaders no longer have the means to do what they did before.

The statist pattern of policymaking, where governments may formulate heroic policies largely independently of societal interests only to accommodate them in the implementation, is no longer what it was. At its apogee during Mitterrand's first presidential mandate, when heroic economic and industrial policies made a radical break with the past, it had become a pale shadow of its former self by the end of Mitterrand's second presidential mandate, when the very policies that had been so heroically formulated had undermined the very processes that made such heroism possible. Those policies, in other words, emptied the statist pattern of policymaking of much of its substance.

The heroic policies of the past had for the most part given way to more everyday ones as governments, absent their traditional interventionist policy instruments, could no longer command, and therefore consulted a great deal more. Although relations between business and government were still close, the ties that had bound them inextricably to one another throughout the postwar period, first through planning and then through industrial policies, had been loosened. Ministries had become partners rather than leaders of industry, while industries that used to look almost exclusively to the state for guidance and resources now turned more to one another for strategic advice and equity investment, and to the enlarged stock market for funds. Even the nationalized enterprises had become mostly autonomous, as the state–industry planning contracts became vaguer and less binding, and as the trading of shares among

---

[4]*Le Monde,* November 19, 1992. In fact, the only constitutional dispositions a majority of the French were against were the governmental power to adopt a law without parliamentary vote other than a vote of censure (54% opposed this, 28% favored it, and 18% had no opinion) and the president's seven-year mandate (which 75% preferred to see reduced to a five-year term, renewable one time, while 12% favored a nonrenewable seven-year term and 11% favored the current renewable seven-year term).

nationalized enterprises substituted an indirect system of state oversight for the more direct state *tutelle*. Finally, the European Union had reduced the independence of government at the formulation stage and its flexibility at the implementation stage.

This is not to suggest, however, that France has abandoned its statist model for a more pluralist or corporatist one. The state, both as concept and concrete representation, remains embedded in French culture and embodied in its institutions, with change able to come only through the state, not against it. The executive is still comparatively strong next to the weak legislature and bureaucratic politics are more significant than interest group politics. Governments have not stopped seeking to guide business, albeit in more indirect ways, more in keeping with the new international economic environment and the dictates of the European Union; and they as always play a primary role in deciding the direction of economic growth and the shape and organization of economic activity, even as they engineer the retreat of the state. Ministries continue to be the main locus of decision-making, with major issues flowing up to the Prime Minister or President for arbitration, even if the European Union has taken away much of their autonomy. The Ministry of Finance, after a brief challenge by the Ministry of Industry, persists as the major force in economic matters, even if deregulation has diminished its power and the EMS has usurped its authority. Finally, business interests still get their way, not only as in the past by exploiting intra- and interministerial rivalries or trading on personal relationships, with the politics of accommodation and co-optation the norm, but now also through lobbying at the EU level.

Europe, however, looms increasingly large in all of this as a challenge not simply to the statist model of policymaking but to the very foundations of French democracy. National democracy has been threatened by the fact that the French government together with Parliament have become increasingly something of a rubber stamp for directives issued from Brussels by a Council of Ministers that relies more on the European Commission and its bureaucracy for all recommendations than on the European Parliament, which performs only a consultative role.[5] Although the role of the legislature has been enhanced with the revision of the constitution attendant upon the Maastricht Treaty ratification in April 1992 which enables deputies and senators "to vote resolutions and not just express opinions,"[6] this has done little so far to increase French

[5]See, for example, Bernard Bosson, "Les transferts de compétences nationales vers les organes de la Communauté s'analysent-ils ou non comme un déficit démocratique?" *Administration* vol. 149 (October 15, 1990).

[6]*Le Monde*, June 25, 1992; and Ladrech, "Europeanization of Domestic Politics and Institutions."

parliamentary influence on EU decisions. Moreover, although the "return of law" may be a factor in promoting "a democratic ideal" based on fundamental principles and "a system of judicial recourse largely open to citizens against national states,"[7] it is also a factor in increasing the rigidity of the state, and in undermining the state's ability to accommodate societal interests in the implementation of laws drafted without their input.

In fact, the "democratic deficit" that has characterized policymaking at the European level,[8] added to the weakening of France's traditional statist model of policymaking, has contributed to a crisis that the French have yet to address fully (although a beginning was made with the Maastricht Treaty debates), let alone resolve. The crisis for French democracy has two sources in the changes in the policymaking process. First, elected governments that were traditionally solely responsible for policy formulation have less and less control over it because policy decisions occur increasingly at the EU level in conjunction with other member states, with only certain interests, primarily business, pressuring, and with national government bureaucrats, not elected officials, negotiating. Second, societal interests that were traditionally kept out at the policy formulation stage but allowed in at the implementation stage may progressively be excluded even here, given the gradual replacement of the administrative model, where making exceptions is the rule, by the regulatory one, where exceptions are illegitimate. Citizens, denied the traditional politics of accommodation and co-optation, may therefore increasingly find confrontation their only recourse. Moreover, policymaking will be left to only a few top elected officials – speaking through their civil service representatives; to large business interests – speaking through their lobbies; and to bureaucrats, whether those at the EU level responsible for formulating policy or those at the national level responsible for implementing them. The result is a crisis of democracy for France's traditional statist pattern of policymaking. Until the French find ways to adapt their policymaking processes to the new realities, or possibly even to reform their institutions, the crisis will only deepen.

Thus, this book runs counter to those who argue without qualification that European integration has strengthened the nation-state.[9] Although it

---

[7]Interview in *Le Monde,* May 5, 1992 – cited in Ladrech, "Europeanization of Domestic Politics and Institutions."

[8]Shirley Williams, "Sovereignty and Accountability in the European Community," in *The New European Community: Decision-Making and Institutional Change,* ed. Robert O. Keohane and Stanley Hoffmann (Boulder, CO: Westview, 1991), pp. 155–176.

[9]A. S. Milward, *The European Rescue of the Nation-State* (Berkeley: University of California Press, 1992); Andrew Moravscik, "Preferences and Power in the European

generally agrees that the power of national governments has increased at the European level, as the bilateral negotiations of the past have given way to the common European policies of the present, and that this has in turn collectively "rescued" the economies of European Union members, it disagrees at least in the case of France with those who maintain that national governments have also increased their power at the domestic level, by enhancing their autonomy with regard to societal interests. Part of the problem with this last argument is that the international relations literature of which it is a part tends to assume a pluralist model in which societal interests constrain government, by which it means executive, action in policy formulation. In the pluralist or even the corporatist context, the EU surely does "enhance the autonomy and initiative of national political leaders," strengthening the hand of the executive in terms of its "domestic agenda-setting power."[10] But in France's statist model of policymaking, as we have already seen, the hand of the executive has always been very strong and autonomous at the formulation stage, since it is primarily at the implementation stage that societal constraints operate. European integration has diminished that autonomy at the formulation stage, while it has undermined the executive's flexibility at the implementation stage. At the formulation stage in particular, the government's loss of its traditional *dirigiste* policy instruments makes it appear weaker to a populace that continues to feel a sense of loss for the heroism of the past – and a sense of frustration with leaders who lack clear plans and grand projects to resolve the major concerns of the day. Moreover, although one could argue that instead of seeing a loss of flexibility at the implementation stage one could see strengthening, since the executive is no longer constrained to accommodate itself to societal interests, such strengthening comes at great risk: the loss of government legitimacy and increased confrontation.

There is another problem with the arguments favoring the strengthening of the nation-state, however. Even more importantly, they imply a limited definition of the nation-state, since they equate the nation-state with national governments, and national governments with the executive power, thereby ignoring the role of legislatures and societal interests as partners in ensuring a strong, meaning healthy and stable, nation-state. For France, as for many other countries, European integration has unsettled the traditional state–society relationship. And until France, as much as the other countries, finds ways to readjust that relationship to respond

Community: A Liberal Intergovernmentalist Approach," *Journal of Common Market Studies* vol. 31, no. 4 (December 1993).
[10]Moravscik, "Preferences and Power," p. 507.

to the new realities, the strength of the nation-state, as understood in terms of its overall health and stability, will not have been enhanced.

The problems for democracy posed by European integration are only compounded by the fact that decision-making in France, despite a range of reforms designed to provide greater access in business and government, remains centralized in structure and concentrated in relatively few hands. Although the decentralization of local government and the democratization of management practice have made a difference, power continues to be the purview of a small elite.

Even as the policies have undergone radical shifts and the policymaking processes have been readjusted, the players have remained largely the same. Whether in the ministries or in industry, the same state-trained elites as before run the show. Although they may be younger and more dynamic, they remain overwhelmingly upper-middle-class graduates of the *grandes écoles,* in particular the ENA and X, and members of the *grand corps,* in particular the Inspection des Finances and the Corps des Mines. In addition, they have had extensive state administrative experience, including in a ministerial cabinet, before they move on into industry in a top management position, if not in the top position.

Moreover, as the state has retreated, increasing numbers of its servants have moved into business, thus ensuring that the state maintains its hold through the colonization of French business by state-trained former civil servants. Although this has conferred legitimacy on business in a country that until recently had regarded it as less "noble" than working for the state, it has only increased the problems of morale for the majority of business employees who lack elite credentials, by blocking their access to the topmost positions. What is more, it puts a special burden on members of this elite to be competent and worthy of the trust that has been placed in them. The main challenge for France's top managers – trained in the hothouse atmosphere of the French state and therefore, in the view of critics at least, best equipped to interact only with their fellow *camarades de promotion,* who all think, talk, and act very much alike – is whether they can adapt to the larger, less structured world around them.

Until now, admittedly, French top managers have done remarkably well in responding to that challenge. Adherence to traditional French elite management recruitment and promotion practices can certainly largely be credited with the successes of the nationalized industries during the eighties, ensuring that highly qualified individuals were responsible for shepherding their firms through turbulent times. Moreover, top managers in the eighties and into the nineties have not only been behind the modernization of business and the democratization of management practice, they have also been instrumental in promoting the restructuring of French capitalism.

But the question remains whether French business will continue to prosper if the restricted system of access to top management positions persists. The internationalization of French business alone demands a greater acceptance of diversity based on personal characteristics, training, and career track than in the past, as well as a greater willingness than many French CEOs have to date shown to decentralize decision-making. Moreover, the increasingly unpredictable and unprotected international market in which French businesses operate only reinforces the need for those who have practical experience in it on top of a theoretical under-standing of it. An education and career track centered primarily in the French state, whatever its benefits, cannot prepare adequately for leading business in an increasingly interdependent and competitive world econ-omy. Thus, although French business in the past may have benefited from the state-centered elite system of recruitment and promotion, it is less likely to do so in the future. And the future of French business, therefore, depends upon the continued opening up of its recruitment and promotion system, and a shift from an emphasis on educational credentials and substantial state career track to one focused more on business achieve-ment, as is the case in most other advanced industrialized nations.

But what then of the state and its relationship to business? Who leads, and to what end, remains open to question. While business has gained legitimacy, not only through the presence of state-trained upper-level civil servants at its head, but also as a partner in the EU lobbying efforts and as the "creator of riches" for France as a whole, the state has lost it. Not only has the politicization of its administrators undermined its credibility, but the various scandals related to corrupt election financing and the transfusion of tainted blood have cast doubt even on the incorruptibility of the state in the persons of its elite civil servants and its political leaders. It is telling that in an April 1995 SOFRES survey, 62% of respondents agreed that most political leaders were corrupt (vs. 31% who dis-agreed).[11] Lately, such doubts have also extended to business heads, with scandals raising questions about their probity and leadership capability, so much so that the legitimacy of business has also been undermined, thus adding to the overall crisis of leadership.

Moreover, as government has become less autonomous in its decision-making as a result of the increasing power of the EU at the supranational level and regional governments at the local, business, headed by the for-mer servants of the state, has become more autonomous, benefiting from nongovernmental sources of funds, less government intervention, and its

[11]*Le Monde,* April 11, 1995.

Conclusion

role as a partner in national efforts to influence the EU. Finally, whereas business has a clear set of goals, profitability, government has lost much of its traditional sense of purpose other than that of serving business and its goals. The question, then, really is: Has the state colonized business through the presence of its representatives at the head of major firms? Or has business colonized the state through the redirection of government policy and economic principles from state- to market-oriented ones? Regardless of the answer, the servants of the state will have benefited. Let us hope that the country as a whole will have as well.

Bibliography

GENERAL METHODOLOGICAL AND EPISTEMOLOGICAL WORKS

Almond, Gabriel, *A Discipline Divided* Newbury Park, CA: Sage, 1990.

Causey, Robert T., "Structural Explanations in Social Science," in *Scientific Discovery, Logic, and Rationality,* ed. Thomas Nickles. Dordrecht: Reidel, 1980.

Dray, William, *Philosophy of History* Englewood Cliffs, NJ: Prentice-Hall, 1965.

Dryzek, John S., "The Progress of Political Science," *Journal of Politics* vol. 48 (1986).

Dryzek, John S., and Leonard, Stephen T., "History and Discipline in Political Science," *American Political Science Review* vol. 82, no. 4 (December 1988).

Emmet, Dorothy, *Function, Purpose and Powers* Philadelphia: Temple University Press, 1972.

Kuhn, Thomas, *The Structure of Scientific Revolutions,* 2d ed. Chicago: University of Chicago Press, 1970.

March, James G., and Olsen, Johan P., *Rediscovering Institutions: The Organizational Basis of Politics* New York: Free Press, 1989.

Martin, Raymond, "Beyond Positivism: A Research Program for Philosophy of History," *Philosophy of Science* vol. 48, no. 1 (March 1981).

Moe, Terry M., "Political Institutions: The Neglected Side of the Story," *Journal of Law, Economics, and Organization* vol. 6 (1990).

Ostrom, Elinor, "An Agenda for the Study of Institutions," *Public Choice* vol. 48 (1986).

Putnam, Robert, *Making Democracy Work: Civic Traditions in Modern Italy* Princeton: Princeton University Press, 1993.

Schmidt, Vivien A., "Evaluating the State–Society Debates: Lessons from the Philosophy of Science." Paper prepared for presentation at the XVIth World Congress of the International Political Science Association, Berlin, August 21–25, 1994.

Schmidt, Vivien A., "Four Models of Explanation," *Methodology and Science* vol. 21, no. 3 (1988).

Schmidt, Vivien A., "The Historical Approach to Philosophy of Science: Toulmin in Perspective," *Metaphilosophy* vol. 19, no. 3 (July–October 1988).

Schmidt, Vivien A., "Four Approaches to Science and Their Implications for Organizational Theory and Research," *Knowledge* vol. 9, no. 1 (September 1987).

Schutz, Alfred, *The Phenomenology of the Social World* Chicago: Northwestern University Press, 1967.

Bibliography

Shepsle, Kenneth, "Studying Institutions: Some Lessons from the Rational Choice Approach," *Journal of Theoretical Politics* vol. 1 (1989).

Toulmin, Stephen, *Human Understanding* Princeton: Princeton University Press, 1972.

Walsh, W. H., "Colligatory Concepts in History" in *The Philosophy of History*, ed. Patrick Gardiner. London: Oxford University Press, 1974.

Winch, Peter, *The Idea of a Social Science* London: Routledge and Kegan Paul, 1970.

Wittgenstein, Ludwig, *Philosophical Investigations* Oxford: Oxford University Press, 1968.

POLITICAL INSTITUTIONS, PROCESSES, AND POLICIES: GENERAL WORKS

Allison, Graham, *Essence of Decision: Explaining the Cuban Missile Crisis* Boston: Little Brown, 1971.

Armstrong, John, *The European Administrative Elite* Princeton: Princeton University Press, 1973.

Aron, Raymond, "Social Structure and the Ruling Class," *British Journal of Sociology* vol. 1, no. 1 (March 1950).

Beer, Samuel, *British Politics in the Collectivist Age,* rev. ed. New York: Random House, 1969.

Bottomore, T. B., *Elites in Society* Baltimore: Penguin, 1966.

Bulcke, David van den, "Multinational Companies and the European Community," in *The European Community in the 1990s*, ed. Brian Nelson, David Roberts, and Walter Veit. New York: Berg, 1992.

Burnham, James, *The Managerial Revolution* London: Putnam and Co., 1943.

Cawson, Alan, *Corporatism and Political Theory* Oxford: Basil Blackwell, 1986.

Dahl, Robert, *Who Governs* New Haven: Yale University Press, 1961.

Diamant, Alfred, "Bureaucracy and Public Policy in Neocorporatist Settings," *Comparative Politics* vol. 14, no. 1 (October 1981).

Djilas, Milovan, *The New Class* London: Thames & Hudson, 1957.

Dogan, Mattei, ed., *The Mandarins of Western Europe* New York: John Wiley, 1975.

Donnelly, Martin, "The Structure of the European Commission and the Policy Formation Process," in *Lobbying in the European Community*, ed. Sonia Mazey and Jeremy Richardson. Oxford: Oxford University Press, 1993.

Dore, Ronald, *Flexible Rigidities* Stanford: Stanford University Press, 1987.

Dyson, Kenneth J. F., "West Germany: The Search for a Rationalist Consensus," in *Policy Styles in Western Europe,* ed. Jeremy Richardson. London: 1982.

Dyson, Kenneth J. F., *The State Tradition in Western Europe* New York: Oxford University Press, 1980.

Dyson, Kenneth J. F., *Party, State, and Bureaucracy in West Germany* Beverly Hills, CA: Sage Publications, 1977.

Easton, David, "The Political System Besieged by the State," *Political Theory* vol. 9 (1981).

Elder, N., *Modern Sweden* Oxford: Pergamon Press, 1970.

Freeman, Gary P., "National Styles and Policy Sectors: Explaining Structural Variation," *Journal of Public Policy* vol. 5 (October 1985).

Gallie, D., *Social Inequality and Class Radicalism in France and Britain* Cambridge: Cambridge University Press, 1978.

Bibliography

Gamson, William, *The Strategy of Protest* Homewood, IL: Dorsey, 1975.

Gerlich, Peter, Grande, Edgar, and Müller, Wolfgang, "Corporatism in Crisis: Stability and Change of Social Partnership in Austria," *Political Studies* vol. 36, no. 2 (1988).

Greenwood, Justin, and Ronit, Kersten, "Interest Groups in the European Community: Newly Emerging Dynamics and Forms," *West European Politics* vol. 17, no. 1 (January 1994).

Guérivière, Jean de la, *Voyage à l'intérieure de l'Eurocratie* Paris: Le Monde Editions, 1992.

Heclo, Hugh, "Issue Networks and the Executive Establishment," in *The New American Political System*, ed. Anthony King. Washington, DC: American Enterprise Institute, 1978.

Heclo, Hugh, *Modern Social Politics in Britain and Sweden* New Haven: Yale University Press, 1974.

Heclo, Hugh, and Wildavsky, Aaron, *The Private Government of Public Money* Berkeley and Los Angeles: University of California Press, 1974.

Hogwood, Brian W., *From Crisis to Complacency? Shaping Public Policy in Britain* New York: Oxford University Press, 1987.

Hull, Robert, "Lobbying Brussels: A View from Within," in *Lobbying in the European Community* ed. Mazey and Richardson.

Jordan, A. Grant, "Iron Triangles, Woolly Corporatism and Elastic Images of the Policy Process," *Journal of Public Policy* vol. 1, no. 1 (February 1981).

Katzenstein, Peter, "International Relations and Domestic Structures," *International Organization* vol. 30 (Winter 1976).

Kingdon, John W., *Agendas, Alternatives, and Public Policies* New York: Harper-Collins, 1984.

Koh, B. C., *Japan's Administrative Elite* Berkeley: University of California Press, 1989.

Kohler-Koch, Beata, "Changing Patterns of Interest Intermediation in the European Union," *Government and Opposition* vol. 29, no. 2 (Spring 1994).

Lehmbruch, Gerhard, "Introduction: Neo-Corporatism in Comparative Perspective," in *Patterns of Corporatist Policy-Making,* ed. Gerhard Lehmbruch and Philippe Schmitter. Beverly Hills, CA: Sage Publications, 1982.

Lenin, V. I., *State and Revolution* New York: International Publications, 1932.

Lijphart, Arend, *The Politics of Accommodation: Pluralism and Democracy in the Netherlands,* 2d ed. Berkeley: University of California Press, 1975.

Lindblom, Charles, *Politics and Markets* New York: Basic, 1977.

Lovenduski, Joni, *Women and European Politics: Contemporary Feminism and Public Policy* Amherst: University of Massachusetts Press, 1986.

Lowi, Theodore, *The End of Liberalism: Ideology, Policy, and the Crisis of Public Authority* New York: W. W. Norton, 1969.

Marin, B., "Organizing Interests by Interest Associations: Organizational Prerequisites of Cooperation in Austria," *International Political Science Review* vol. 4 (1983).

Mazey, Sonia, and Richardson, Jeremy, "Introduction," in *Lobbying in the European Community,* ed. Mazey and Richardson.

McConnell, Grant, *Private Power and American Democracy* New York: Vintage, 1970.

McLaughlin, Andrew, and Jordan, Grant, "The Rationality of Lobbying in Europe: Why Are Euro-Groups So Numerous and So Weak? Some Evidence from the Car Industry," in *Lobbying in the European Community,* ed. Mazey and Richardson.

Bibliography

Meisel, James H., *The Myth of the Ruling Class: Gaetano Mosca and the Elite* Ann Arbor: University of Michigan Press, 1962.

Michels, Robert, *Political Parties: A Sociological Study of the Oligarchical Tendencies of Modern Democracy* New York: Free Press, 1962.

Middlemas, R. K., *Politics in Industrial Society: The Experience of the British System since 1911* London: André Deutsch, 1979.

Miliband, Ralph, *Capitalist Democracy in Britain* Oxford: Oxford University Press, 1984.

Miliband, Ralph, *Marxism and Politics* Oxford: Oxford University Press, 1977.

Milward, H. B., and Francisco, R. A., "Subsystem Politics and Corporatism in the United States," *Policy and Politics* vol. 11 (1983).

Mitchell, Timothy, "The Limits of the State: Beyond Statist Approaches and Their Critics," *American Political Science Review* vol. 85, no. 1 (March 1991).

Moore, Barrington, *Social Origins of Dictatorship and Democracy* Boston: Beacon Press, 1966.

Nettl, J. P., "The State as a Conceptual Variable," *World Politics* vol. 20 (1968).

Nonon, Jacqueline, and Clamen, Michel, *L'Europe et ses couloirs: Lobbying et lobbyistes* Paris: Dunod, 1991.

Nordlinger, Eric, *On the Autonomy of the Democratic State* Cambridge: Harvard University Press, 1981.

Offe, Claus, "The Attribution of Public Status to Interest Groups: Observations on the West German Case," in *Organizing Interests in Western Europe,* ed. Suzanne Berger. Cambridge: Cambridge University Press, 1981.

Pareto, Vilfredo, *Sociological Writings* New York: Praeger, 1966.

Peters, B. Guy, "Bureaucratic Politics and the Institutions of the European Community," in *Euro-Politics,* ed. Alberta M. Sbragia. Washington, DC: Brookings, 1992.

Poulantzas, Nicos, *Pouvoir politique et classes sociales* Paris: Maspero, 1971.

Richardson, Jeremy J., and Jordan, A. Grant, *Governing Under Pressure: The Policy Process in a Post-Parliamentary Democracy* Oxford: Robertson, 1979.

Salisbury, Robert H., "Why No Corporatism in America?" in *Trends Toward Capitalist Intermediation,* ed. Philippe C. Schmitter and Gerhard Lehmbruch. Beverly Hills, CA: Sage Publications, 1979.

Schmidt, Vivien A., "The New World Order, Incorporated: The Rise of Business and the Decline of the Nation-State," *Daedalus* vol. 124, no. 2 (spring 1995).

Schmidt, Vivien A., "La dérégulation aux États Unis." *Revue Française d'Administration Publique* no. 41 (January–March 1987).

Schmitter, Philippe C., "Corporatism Is Dead! Long Live Corporatism," *Government and Opposition* vol. 24, no. 1 (winter 1989).

Schmitter, Philippe C., "Neo-Corporatism and the State," in *The Political Economy of Corporatism,* ed. Wyn Grant. New York: St. Martin's, 1985.

Schmitter, Philippe C., "Reflections on Where the Theory of Neo-Corporatism Has Gone and Where the Praxis of Neo-Corporatism May Be Going," in *Patterns of Corporatist Policy-Making,* ed. Gerhard Lehmbruch and Philippe C. Schmitter. Beverly Hills, CA: Sage Publications, 1982.

Schurmann, Franz, *The Logic of World Order* New York: Pantheon, 1974.

Scott, James, *Weapons of the Weak: Everyday Forms of Peasant Resistance* New Haven: Yale University Press, 1985.

Seidentopf, Heinrich, and Ziller, Jacques, eds. *Making European Policies Work: The Implementation of Community Legislation in the Member States* London: Sage, 1988.

Bibliography

Skocpol, Theda, "Bringing the State Back In," in *Bringing the State Back In,* ed. Peter Evans, Dietrich Rueschemeyer, and Theda Skocpol. Cambridge: Cambridge University Press, 1985.

Skocpol, Theda, "Political Response to Capitalist Crisis: Neo Marxist Theories of the State and the Case of the New Deal," *Politics and Society* vol. 10 (1981).

Skocpol, Theda, *States and Social Revolutions: A Comparative Analysis of France, Russia, and China* Cambridge: Cambridge University Press, 1979.

Skowronek, Stephen, *The Building of a New American State* New York: Cambridge University Press, 1982.

Steiner, J., *Amicable Agreement vs. Majority Rule* Chapel Hill, NC: University of North Carolina Press, 1974.

Steiner, K., *Politics in Austria* Boston: Little, Brown, 1972.

Stepan, Alfred, *State and Society: Peru in Comparative Perspective* Princeton: Princeton University Press, 1978.

Streeck, Wolfgang, and Schmitter, Philippe, "From National Corporatism to Transnational Pluralism: Organized Interests in the Single European Market," *Politics and Society* vol. 19, no. 2 (June 1991).

Tarrow, Sidney, *Democracy and Disorder: Protest and Politics in Italy, 1965–1975* Oxford: Oxford University Press, 1988.

Truman, David, *The Governmental Process* New York: Knopf, 1951.

Turner, Lowell, *Democratic Corporatism and Policy Linkages* Berkeley: Institute of International Studies, University of California, Berkeley, 1987.

Weber, Max, *Economy and Society: An Outline of Interpretive Sociology,* vol. 3. New York: Bedminster Press, 1968.

Weiler, Joseph H. H., "A Quiet Revolution: The European Court of Justice and Its Interlocutors," *Comparative Political Studies* vol. 26, no. 4 (January 1994).

Wilson, Graham, "Why Is There No Corporatism in the United States?" in *Patterns of Corporatist Policy-Making,* ed. Gerhard Lehmbruch and Philippe C. Schmitter. Beverly Hills, CA: Sage Publications, 1982.

Wilson, James Q., ed. *The Politics of Regulation* Chicago: Chicago University Press, 1980.

Winkler, J. T., "Corporatism," *European Journal of Sociology* vol. 17, no. 1 (1976).

Wright, Maurice, "Policy Community, Policy Networks and Comparative Industrial Policy," *Political Studies* vol. 36, no. 4 (December 1988).

POLITICAL INSTITUTIONS, PROCESSES, AND POLICIES: FRANCE

Adam, Gérard, *Le pouvoir syndical* Paris: Dunod, 1983.

Aftalion, Florin, Claasen, E., Salin, Pascal, et al., *La liberté à refaire* Paris: Hachette, 1984.

Alphandéry, Claude, et al., *Pour nationaliser l'état* Paris: Seuil, 1968.

Ambler, John S., "Educational Pluralism in the French Fifth Republic," in *Searching for the New France,* ed. James F. Hollifield and George Ross. New York: Routledge, 1991.

Ambler, John S., "Constraints on Policy Innovation in Education: Thatcher's Britain and Mitterrand's France," *Comparative Politics* vol. 20, no. 1 (October 1987).

Ambler, John S., "Neocorporatism and the Politics of French Education," *Politics* vol. 8, no. 3 (July 1, 1985).

Auberger, Philippe, *L'allérgie fiscale* Paris: Calmann-Levy.

Bibliography

Balladur, Edouard, *Je crois en l'homme plus que l'état* Paris: Flammarion, 1987.

Barre, Raymond, *Réflexions pour demain* Paris: Hachette, 1984.

Barret-Kriegel, Blandine, *Les chemins de l'état* Paris: Calmann-Levy, 1986.

Bellier, Irène, *L'Ena comme si vous y étiez* Paris: Seuil, 1993.

Bellier, Irène, "Vocation ou goût du pouvoir?" in *Faire la politique: Le chantier français, Autrement* no. 122 (May 1991).

Bellier, Irène, "Le changement passe-t-il par l'École Nationale d'Administration?" *Revue Politique et Management Public* vol. 8, no. 3 (Sept. 1990).

Benoist, Jean-Marie, *Les outils de la libérté* Paris: Laffont, 1985.

Berger, Suzanne, *Peasants Against Politics: Rural Organizations in Brittany, 1911–1967* Cambridge, MA: Harvard University Press, 1972.

Birnbaum, Pierre, "Que faire de l'état?" in *Les élites Socialistes au pouvoir: Les dirigeants Socialistes face à l'état 1981–1985*, ed. Pierre Birnbaum. Paris: Presses Universitaires de France, 1985.

Birnbaum, Pierre, *The Heights of Power* Chicago: University of Chicago Press, 1982.

Birnbaum, Pierre, Barucq, Charles, Bellaiche, Michel, and Marie, Alain, *La classe dirigeante* Paris: Presses Universitaires Françaises, 1978.

Bodiguel, Jean-Luc, and Kessler, Marie Christine, "Les directeurs d'administration centrale," in *Les élites Socialistes au pouvoir: Les dirigeants Socialistes face à l'état 1981–1985*, ed. Pierre Birnbaum. Paris: Presses Universitaires de France, 1985.

Bodiguel, Jean-Luc, and Rouban, Luc, *Le fonctionnaire détrôné?* Paris: Presses de la Fondation Nationale des Sciences Politiques, 1991.

Boissonnat, Jean, ed., *Les Socialistes face aux patrons* Paris: L'Expansion/Flammarion, 1977.

Bonnaud, J. J., "Les instruments d'exécution du plan utilisés par l'état à l'égard des entreprises," *Revue Economique* (July 1970).

Boublil, Alain, *Le soulèvement du sérail* Paris: Albin Michel, 1990.

Bourdieu, Pierre, and Boltanski, Luc, "La production des idées dominantes," *Actes de la Recherche en Sciences Sociales* (June 1976).

Bréhier, Thierry, "Les groupes de pression à l'Assemblée Nationale," *Pouvoirs* no. 34 (1985).

Burdeau, Georges, *L'état* Paris: Seuil, 1970.

Cannac, Yves, *Le juste pouvoir* Paris: Lattès, 1982.

Carnelutti, Alexandre, "L'administration française face à la règle communautaire," *Revue Française d'Administration Publique* vol. 48 (October–December 1988).

Chenot, Bernard, ed. *Les déréglementations* Paris: Economica, 1988.

Chevallier, Jacques, "La gauche et la haute administration sous la Cinquième République," in *La haute administration et la politique*, ed. Jacques Chevallier. Paris: PUF, CURAPP, 1985.

Cohen-Tanugi, Laurent, *Le droit sans l'état* Paris: Presses Universitaires de France, 1985.

Cox, A., and Hayward, Jack, "The Inapplicability of the Corporatist Model in Britain and France: The Case of Labor," *International Political Science Review* vol. 77 (1983).

Crozier, Michel, *État modeste, état moderne* Paris: Fayard, 1987.

Dagnaud, Monique, and Mehl, Dominique, *L'élite rose – Qui gouverne?* Paris: Ramsay, 1982.

Daniel, Pierre, *Question de liberté* Paris: Desclée de Brouwer, 1986.

Bibliography

de Baecque, Francis, "Les fonctionnaires à l'assaut du pouvoir," *Pouvoirs* vol. 40 (1987).

de Closets, François, *Le pari de la responsabilité* Paris: Payot, 1989.

de Closets, François, *Tous ensemble: Pour en finir avec la syndicratie* Paris: Seuil, 1985.

de Closets, François, *Toujours plus!* Paris: Grasset, 1982.

Debbasch, Charles, "L'influence des transferts de compétences vers les instances communautaires sur les compétences des administrations," *Administration* vol. 149 (October 15, 1990).

Duverger, Maurice, *La monarchie républicaine* Paris: Robert Laffont, 1974.

Ehrmann, Henry, "Bureaucracy and Interest Groups in Fifth Republic France," in *Faktoren der politischen Entscheidung,* ed. Ernst Fraenkel. Berlin: Gruyter, 1963.

Ehrmann, Henry, "French Bureaucracy and Organized Interests," *Administrative Science Quarterly* vol. 5 (1961).

Ehrmann, Henry, *Organized Business in France* Princeton: Princeton University Press, 1957.

Ehrmann, Henry, and Schain, Martin, *Politics in France,* 5th ed. New York: HarperCollins, 1992.

Elbow, Matthew, *French Corporative Theory, 1789–1948* New York: Octagon Books, 1966.

Favier, Pierre, and Martin-Roland, Michel, *La décennie Mitterrand,* vol. 1 Paris: Seuil, 1990.

Feldman, Elliot J., *Concorde and Dissent: Explaining High Technology Project Failures in Britain and France* New York: Cambridge University Press, 1985.

Fournier, Jacques, *Le Travail Gouvernemental* Paris: Presses de la Fondation Nationale des Sciences Politiques, 1987.

François-Poncet, Jean, and Barbier, Bernard, *1992: Les conséquences pour l'économie française* Paris: Economica, 1989.

Frèches, José, *Voyage au centre du pouvoir* Paris: Odile Jacob, 1989.

Friedberg, Edgar, "Administrations et Entreprises," in *Où va l'administration française,* ed. Michel Crozier. Paris: SEDEIS, 1974.

Gallie, Duncan, "Les lois Auroux: The Reform of French Industrial Relations?" in *Economic Policy-Making under the Mitterrand Presidency 1981–1984,* ed. Howard Machin and Vincent Wright. London: Frances Pinter, 1985.

Gaudard, Jean-Pierre, *Les danseuses de la république: Que fait l'état de votre argent?* Paris: Pierre Belfond, 1984.

Gerbet, Pierre, *La naissance du Marché Commun* Brussels: Complexe, 1987.

Grémion, Catherine, *Profession, décideur: Pouvoir des hauts fonctionnaires et réforme de l'état* Paris: Gauthier-Villars, 1979.

Grémion, Pierre, *Le pouvoir périphérique* Paris: Seuil, 1976.

Grémion, Pierre, "La Concertation," in *Où va l'administration française,* ed. Michel Crozier. Paris: SEDEIS, 1974.

Grémion, Pierre, "La théorie de l'apprentissage institutionnel et la régionalisation du Cinquième Plan," *Revue Française de Science Politique* vol. 23, no. 2 (April 1973).

Halévy, Daniel, *Décadence de la liberté* Paris: 1931.

Hayward, Jack, "Mobilising Private Interests in the Service of Public Ambitions: The Salient Element in the Dual French Policy Style?" in *Policy Styles in Western Europe,* ed. J. Richardson. London: Allen and Unwin, 1982.

Hayward, Jack, *The One and Indivisible French Republic* New York: Norton, 1973.

Hoffmann, Stanley, *Decline or Renewal? France since the 1930's* New York: Viking Press, 1974.

Hoffmann, Stanley, "The French Constitution of 1958: The Final Text and Its Prospects," *American Political Science Review* (June 1959).

Jacquillat, Betrand, *Désétatiser* Paris: R. Laffont, 1985.

Jobert, Bruno, "Le Ministère de l'Industrie et la cohérence de la politique industrielle," *Revue Française de Science Politique* vol. 23, no. 2 (April 1973).

Jobert, Bruno, and Muller, Pierre, *L'état en action: Politiques publiques et corporations* Paris: Presses Universitaires de France, 1987.

Julliard, Jacques, "Mitterrand: Between Socialism and the Republic," *Telos* no. 55 (spring 1983).

Keeler, John T. S., "Patterns of Policymaking in the French Fifth Republic: Strong Governments, Cycles of Reform and Political Malaise," in *Ideas and Ideals: Essays on Politics in Honor of Stanley Hoffmann*, ed. Linda Miller and Michael Smith. Boulder: Westview Press, 1994.

Keeler, John T. S., "Opening the Window for Reform: Mandates, Crises and Extraordinary Policymaking," *Comparative Political Studies* (1992).

Keeler, John T. S., *The Politics of Neocorporatism in France: Farmers, the State, and Agricultural Policy-Making in the Fifth Republic* New York: Oxford University Press, 1987.

Keeler, John T. S., "Situating France on the Pluralism–Corporatism Continuum: A Critique of and Alternative to the Wilson Perspective," *Comparative Politics* vol. 18, no. 2 (January 1985).

Kesler, Jean-François, *L'ENA, la société, l'état* Paris: Berger-Levault, 1985.

Kessler, Marie-Christine, *Les grands corps de l'état* Paris: Presses de la Fondation Nationale des Sciences Politiques, 1986.

Ladrech, Robert, "Europeanization of Domestic Politics and Institutions: The Case of France," *Journal of Common Market Studies* vol. 32, no. 1 (March 1994).

La fonction publique de l'état en 1988 Paris: Documentation Française, 1989.

Lainé, François Bloch, *Profession: fonctionnaire* Paris: Seuil, 1976.

Lautman, Jacques, and Thoenig, Jean-Claude, *Planification et administrations centrales* Paris: Centre de Recherches et des Sociologies d'Organisation, 1966.

Leclerc, Gérard, *La bataille de l'école* Paris: Denöel, 1985.

Lefébure, Thierry, *Lobby or Not To Be* Paris: Plume, 1991.

Le Garrec, Jean, *La fonction publique de l'état* Annual Report, Paris: 1985.

Lenoir, René, and Lesourne, Jacques, *Où va l'état?* Paris: Le Monde Editions, 1992.

Lepage, Henri, *Demain le capitalisme* Paris: Librairie Générale Française, 1978.

Lequesne, Christian, *Paris–Bruxelles: Comment se fait la politique européenne de la France* Paris: Presses de la Fondation Nationale des Sciences Politiques, 1993.

Le Vert, Dominique, "Ouverture et adaptation," *Administration* vol. 149 (October 15, 1990).

Le Vert, Dominique, "La formation des fonctionnaires en droit communautaire," *Revue Française d'Administration Publique* vol. 48 (October–December 1988).

Levy-Leboyer, M., "The Large Corporation in Modern France," in *Managerial Hierarchies*, ed. A. Chandler and H. Daems. Cambridge, MA: Harvard University Press, 1980.

Lochak, Danièle, "La haute administration à l'épreuve de l'alternance," in *Les élites Socialistes au pouvoir: Les dirigeants Socialistes face à l'état 1981–1985,* ed. Pierre Birnbaum. Paris: Presses Universitaires de France, 1985.

Luethy, Herbert, *France Against Herself* New York: Meridian Books, 1954.

Madelin, Alain, *Libérer l'école* Paris: Laffont, 1985.

Marceau, Jane, " 'Plus ça change, plus c'est la même chose': Access to Elite Careers in French Business," in *Elites in France: Origins, Reproduction, Power,* ed. Jolyon Howorth and Philip G. Cerny London: Pinter, 1981.

Mény, Yves, "Formation et transformation des policy communities: L'exemple français," in *Idéologies, partis politiques et groupes sociaux* Paris: Presses de la Fondation Nationale des Sciences Politiques, 1989.

Meynaud, Jean, *Nouvelles études sur les groupes de pression en France* Paris: Armand Colin, 1962.

Meynaud, Jean, *Les groupes de pression en France* Paris: Armand Colin, 1958.

Muller, Pierre, "Entre le local et l'Europe: La crise du modèle français de politiques publiques," *Revue Française de Science Politique* vol. 42, no. 2 (April 1992).

Nioche, Jean-Pierre, *Institutionalizing Policy Evaluation in France: Skating on Thin Ice* Jouy-en-Josas: Cahiers de Recherche HEC, 1991.

Northcutt, Wayne, *Mitterrand: A Political Biography* New York: Holmes and Meier, 1992.

Olivennes, Denis, "Choses vues . . . d'Europe," *Esprit* (October 10, 1991).

Olivennes, Denis, and Baverez, Nicolas, *L'impuissance publique* Paris: Calmann-Lévy, 1989.

Passeron, André, "Comment ils ont placé leurs amis," *Pouvoirs* vol. 40 (1987).

Peyrefitte, Alain, *The Trouble with France* New York: Knopf, 1981.

Pfister, Thierry, *La république des fonctionnaires* Paris: Albin Michel, 1988.

Portelli, Hughes, *Le socialisme français tel qu'il est* Paris: Presses Universitaires de France, 1980.

Programme Commun de gouvernement du Parti Communiste et du Parti Socialiste Paris: Editions Sociales, 1972.

Quel avenir pour l'état? Paris: La Documentation Française, 1993.

Quermonne, Jean Louis, *L'appareil administratif de l'état* Paris: Seuil, 1991.

Revel, Jean-François, *Le rejet de l'état* Paris: Grasset, 1984.

Ross, George, "Labor and the Left in Power: Commissions, Omissions, and Unintended Consequences," in *The French Socialists in Power, 1981–1986,* ed. Patrick McCarthy. New York: Greenwood Press, 1987.

Ross, George, and Jenson, Jane, "Pluralism and the Decline of Left Hegemony: The French Left in Power," *Politics and Society* vol. 14, no. 2 (1985).

Rouban, Luc, *Les cadres supérieurs de la fonction publique et la politique de modernisation administrative* Paris: Presses de la Fondation Nationale des Sciences Politiques, 1992.

Rouban, Luc, "The Civil Service and the Policy of Administrative Modernisation in France," *International Review of Administrative Sciences* vol. 55, no. 3 (1989).

Rouban, Luc, "France in Search of a New Administrative Order," *International Journal of Political Science* vol. 14, no. 4 (1988).

Safran, William, *The French Polity* New York: Longman, 1991.

Savary, Alain, *En toute liberté* Paris: Hachette, 1985.

Schain, Martin, "Corporatism and Industrial Relations in France," in *French Politics and Public Policy,* ed. Philip Cerny and Martin Schain. New York: St. Martin's, 1980.

Schmidt, Vivien A., *Democratizing France: The Political and Administrative History of Decentralization* New York: Cambridge University Press, 1990.

Schmidt, Vivien A., "Unblocking Society by Decree: The Impact of Governmental Decentralization in France," *Comparative Politics* vol. 22, no. 4 (July 1990): 459–481.

Schmidt, Vivien A., "Decentralization: A Revolutionary Reform," in *The French Socialists in Power, 1981–1986,* ed. Patrick McCarthy. Westport, CT: Greenwood Press, 1987.

Seidentopf, Heinrich, and Hauschild, Christoph, "L'application des directives communautaires par les administrations nationales (étude comparative)," *Revue Française d'Administration Publique* vol. 48 (October–December 1988).

Shonfeld, William, "French Socialism in Power: Change and Continuity," *Tocqueville Review* vol. 6, no. 2 (fall 1984).

Siegfried, André, *De la IIIème République à la Quatrième* Paris: Grasset, 1957.

Siwek-Pouydesseau, Jeanne, "French Ministerial Staffs," in *The Mandarins of Western Europe,* ed. Mattei Dogan. New York: John Wiley, 1975.

Smith, W. Rand, *Crisis in the French Labor Movement: A Grassroots Perspective* New York: St. Martin's Press, 1988.

SOFRES, *L'état de l'opinion 1990* Paris: Seuil, 1990.

SOFRES, *L'état de l'opinion 1989* Paris: Seuil, 1989.

SOFRES, *L'état de l'opinion 1988* Paris: Seuil, 1988.

SOFRES, *L'état de l'opinion 1987* Paris: Seuil, 1987.

Sorman, Guy, *L'état minimum* Paris: Albin Michel, 1985.

Sorman, Guy, *La solution libérale* Paris: Fayard, 1984.

Sorman, Guy, *La révolution conservatrice américaine* Paris: Fayard, 1983.

Stone, Alec, *The Birth of Judicial Politics in France* New York: Oxford, 1992.

Suleiman, Ezra N., *Private Power and Centralization in France: The Notaires and the State* Princeton: Princeton University Press, 1987.

Suleiman, Ezra N., *Elites in French Society* Princeton: Princeton University Press, 1978.

Suleiman, Ezra N., "The Myth of Technical Expertise: Selection, Organization and Leadership," *Comparative Politics* vol. 10, no. 1 (October 1977).

Suleiman, Ezra N., *Politics, Power, and Bureaucracy in France: The Administrative Elite* Princeton: Princeton University Press, 1974.

Tenzer, Nicolas, and Delacroix, Rodolphe, *Les élites et la fin de la démocratie française* Paris: Presses Universitaires de France, 1992.

Thérèt, Bruno, " 'Vices publics, bénéfices privés': Les propositions économiques électorales des néo-libéraux français," *Critiques de l'Économie Politique* no. 31 (April–June 1985).

Thoenig, Jean-Claude, *L'administration en miettes* Paris: Fayard, 1985.

Tilly, Charles, *From Mobilization to Revolution* Englewood Cliffs, NJ: Prentice-Hall, 1978.

Tocqueville, Alexis de, *Democracy in America* New York: Doubleday, 1969.

Weber, Henri, *Le parti des patrons: Le CNPF 1946–1986* Paris: Seuil, 1986.

Wickham, Alexandre, and Coignard, Sophie, *La nomenklatura française* Paris: Belfond, 1988.

Williams, Philip, *Crisis and Compromise: Politics in the Fourth Republic* New York: Doubleday, 1966.

Wilsford, David, *Doctors and the State* Durham: Duke University Press, 1991.

Wilsford, David, "Tactical Advantages versus Administrative Heterogeneity: The

Bibliography

Strengths and the Limits of the French State," *Comparative Political Studies* vol. 21, no. 1 (April 1988).

Wilson, Frank L., "Groups Politics in a Strong State." Paper prepared for delivery at the Annual Meeting of the American Political Science Association (Atlanta, August 31–September 3, 1989).

Wilson, Frank L., *Interest Group Politics in France* New York: Cambridge University Press, 1987.

Wilson, Frank L., "French Interest Group Politics: Pluralist or Neocorporatist?" *American Political Science Review* vol. 77 (December 1983).

Wright, Vincent, *The Government and Politics of France,* 3d ed. New York: Holmes and Meier, 1989.

Ysmal, Colette, "Les programmes économiques des partis de droite," *Critique de l'Économie Politique* no. 31 (April–June 1985).

POLITICAL ECONOMY, BUSINESS, AND ECONOMICS:
GENERAL WORKS

Ahlström, G., *Engineers and Industrial Growth* London: Croom Helm, 1982.

Bessant, J. M., and Grunt, M., *Management and Manufacturing Innovation in the United Kingdom and West Germany* Aldershot: Gower, 1985.

Blank, Stephen, "Britain: The Politics of Foreign Economic Policy, the Domestic Economy, and the Problem of Pluralistic Stagnation," in *Between Power and Plenty: Foreign Policies of Advanced Industrial States,* ed. Peter J. Katzenstein. Madison: University of Wisconsin Press, 1978.

Boyd, Richard, "Government–Industry Relations in Japan: Access, Communication, and Competitive Collaboration," in *Comparative Government–Industry Relations: Western Europe, the United States, and Japan,* ed. Stephen Wilks and Maurice Wright. Oxford: Clarendon Press, 1987.

Chevallier, Jacques, "Un nouveau sens de l'état et du service public," in *Administration et politique,* ed. F. de Baeque and J.-L. Quermonne. Paris: Presses de la Fondation Nationale des Sciences Politiques, 1981.

Dertouzos, Michael L., Lester, Richard K., Solow, Robert M., et al., *Made in America: Regaining the Productive Edge* Cambridge, MA: MIT Press, 1989.

Dunning, J., and Robson, P., "Multinational Corporate Integration and Regional Economic Integration," *Journal of Common Market Studies* vol. 26, no. 2 (December 1987).

Dyas, G. P., and Thanheiser, H., *The Emerging European Enterprise: Strategy and Structure in French and German Industry* London: Macmillan, 1976.

Edwards, P. K., *Managing the Factory* Oxford: Basil Blackwell, 1987.

Freeman, John R., *Democracy and Markets: The Politics of Mixed Economies* Ithaca, NY: Cornell, 1989.

Gerstl, J. C., and Hutton, S. P., *Engineers: The Anatomy of a Profession* London: Tavistock Publications, 1966.

Goodman, John, *Monetary Sovereignty: The Politics of Central Banking in Western Europe* Ithaca, NY: Cornell University Press, 1992.

Granick, David, *The European Executive,* reprint ed. New York: Arno Press, 1979.

Hayward, Jack, "The Policy Community Approach to Industrial Policy," in *Comparative Political Dynamics,* ed. Dankwart A. Rustow and Kenneth Paul Erickson. New York: HarperCollins, 1991.

Bibliography

Hayward, J. E. S., "Steel," in *Big Business and the State: Changing Relations in Western Europe*, ed. Raymond Vernon. Cambridge, MA: Harvard University Press, 1974.

Holland, Stuart, "Europe's New Public Enterprises," in *Big Business and the State*, ed. R. Vernon. Cambridge, MA: Harvard University Press, 1974.

Horovitz, J., *Top Management Control in Europe* New York: St. Martin's, 1980.

Ikenberry, John G., *Reasons of State* New York: Cambridge University Press, 1989.

Johnson, Chalmers, *MITI and the Japanese Miracle* Stanford, CA: Stanford University Press, 1982.

Katzenstein, Peter J., *Small States in World Markets* Ithaca, NY: Cornell University Press, 1985.

Katzenstein, Peter J., "Introduction," *Between Power and Plenty: Foreign Policies of Advanced Industrial States,* ed. Peter J. Katzenstein. Madison: University of Wisconsin Press, 1978.

Krasner, Stephen D., *Defending the National Interest: Raw Materials Investment and U.S. Foreign Policy* Princeton: Princeton University Press, 1978.

Lane, Christel, *Management and Labour in Europe: The Industrial Enterprise in Germany, Britain and France* London: Edward Elgar, 1989.

Laurent, André, "The Cross-Cultural Puzzle of International Human Resource Management," *Human Resource Management* vol. 25, no. 1 (spring 1986).

Lemaitre, P., and Goybet, C., *Multinationals in the EEC* Chichester: IRM Multinational Report, no. 1 (1984).

Milner, Helen V., *Resisting Protectionism: Global Industries and the Politics of International Trade* Princeton: Princeton University Press, 1988.

NEDO, *The Making of Managers,* Report on behalf of the MSC, NEDC, and BIM. London: NEDO, 1987.

Okimoto, Daniel, *Between Miti and the Market: Japanese Industrial Policy for High Technology* Stanford, CA: Stanford University Press, 1989.

Pempel, T. J., "Japanese Foreign Economic Policies: The Domestic Bases for International Behavior," in *Between Power and Plenty: Foreign Policies of Advanced Industrial States,* ed. Peter J. Katzenstein. Madison: University of Wisconsin Press, 1978.

Pempel, T. J., and Tsunekawa, K., "Corporatism without Labor? The Japanese Anomaly," in *Trends Toward Capitalist Intermediation,* ed. Philippe C. Schmitter and Gerhard Lehmbruch. Beverly Hills, CA: Sage Publications, 1979.

Piore, Michael, and Sabel, Charles, *The Second Industrial Divide: Possibilities for Prosperity* New York: Basic Books, 1984.

Rose, M., "Universalism, Culturalism, and the AIX Group," *European Sociological Review* vol. 1, no. 1 (1985).

Samuels, Richard, *The Business of the Japanese State: Energy Markets in Comparative and Historical Perspective* Ithaca, NY: Cornell University Press, 1987.

Sandholtz, Wayne, "Choosing Union: Monetary Politics and Maastricht," *International Organization* vol. 47 (winter 1993).

Seidman, Harold, "Public Enterprise Autonomy: Need for a New Theory," *International Review of Administrative Sciences* vol. 49, no. 1 (1983).

Shonfield, Andrew, *Modern Capitalism: The Changing Balance of Public and Private Power* Oxford: Oxford University Press, 1965.

Streeck, Wolfgang, "Neo-Corporatist Industrial Relations and the Economic Crisis in West Germany, 1973–1982," in *Order and Conflict in Contemporary*

Bibliography

Capitalism: Studies in the Political Economy of Western European Nations, ed. J. Goldthorpe. Oxford: Oxford University Press, 1984.

Vernon, Raymond, "Linking Managers with Ministers: Dilemmas of the State-Owned Enterprise," *Journal of Policy Analysis and Management* vol. 4, no. 1 (1984).

Vogel, David, "Why Businessmen Distrust Their State: The Political Consciousness of American Corporate Executives," *British Journal of Political Science* vol. 8 (1978).

Zysman, John, *Governments, Markets, Growth: Financial Systems and the Politics of Industrial Change* Ithaca, NY: Cornell University Press, 1983.

POLITICAL ECONOMY, BUSINESS, AND ECONOMICS: FRANCE

Albert, Michel, *Capitalisme contre capitalisme* Paris: Seuil, 1991.

Alexandre, Philippe, and Priouret, Roger, *Marianne et le pôt de lait* Paris: Grasset, 1983.

Anastassopoulos, Jean-Pierre, "Les entreprises publiques entre l'autonomie et la dépendance: Une analyse des divers instruments de régulation des entreprises publiques par l'état," *Politiques et Management Public* (June 1985).

Anastassopoulos, Jean-Pierre, "The French Experience: Conflicts with Government," in *State-Owned Enterprises in Western Economies,* ed. Raymond Vernon and Yair Aharoni. London: Croom Helm, 1981.

Anastassopoulos, Jean-Pierre, *La stratégie des entreprises publiques* Paris: Dalloz, 1980.

Anastassopoulos, Jean-Pierre, and Nioche, J. P., eds., *Entreprises publiques: Expériences comparées* Paris: FNEGE, 1980.

Andersen, Sven, and Eliassen, Kjell, "European Community Lobbying," *European Journal of Political Research* vol. 20 (1991).

Andrieu, Claire, Le Van, Lucette, and Prost, Antoine, eds., *Les nationalisations de la libération* Paris: Presses de la Fondation Nationale des Sciences Politiques, 1987.

Archier, G., and Sérieyx, H., *L'entreprise du 3ᵉ type,* Paris: Seuil, 1984.

Atreize, *La planification française en pratique* Paris: Les Editions Ouvrière, 1971.

Aujac, Henri, "An Introduction to French Industrial Policy," in *French Industrial Policy,* ed. William James Adams and Christian Stoffaës. Washington, DC: Brookings, 1986.

Barreau, Jocelyne, and Le Nay, Jean, "Du Programme Commun (1972) au programme électoral du PS (1981)," in *L'état entrepreneur: Nationalisation, gestions du secteur public concurrentiel, construction européenne (1982–1993),* ed. Jocelyne Barreau et al. Paris: L'Harmattan, 1990.

Barreau, Jocelyne, and Mouline, Abdelaziz, *L'industrie électronique française: 29 ans de relations état–groupes industriels 1958–1986* Paris: Librairie Générale de Droit et de Jurisprudence, 1987.

Bauchard, Philippe, *La guerre des deux roses: Du rêve à la réalité, 1981–1985* Paris: Grasset, 1986.

Bauchet, Pierre, *Propriété publique et planification* Paris: Cujas, 1962.

Bauer, Michel, Bertin-Mourot, Bénédicte, and Thobois, Pascal, *Les no. 1 des 200 plus grandes entreprises en France et en Grande Bretagne* Paris: Boyden, 1995.

Bauer, Michel, and Cohen, Elie, "La politique, l'administratif, et l'exercise du pouvoir industriel," *Sociologie du Travail* no. 27 (March 1985).

Bibliography

Bauer, Michel, and Mourot, Bénédicte, *Les 200: Comment devient-on un grand patron?* Paris: Seuil, 1987.

Bazex, Michel, "L'actualité du droit économique: La déréglementation," *L'Actualité Juridique, Droit Administratif* no. 11 (Nov. 20, 1986).

Belassa, Bela, "La politique industrielle Socialiste," *Commentaire* no. 30 (summer 1985).

Bellon, Bertrand, *Le pouvoir financier et l'industrie en France* Paris: Seuil, 1980.

Berger, Suzanne, "Lame Ducks and National Champions: Industrial Policy in the Fifth Republic," in *The Impact of the Fifth Republic on France,* ed. William G. Andrews and Stanley Hoffman. Albany: SUNY Press, 1981.

Berrier, Robert Jim, "The Politics of Industrial Survival: The French Textile Industry." Ph.D. dissertation (Massachusetts Institute of Technology, 1978).

Bocquet, Dominique, and Delleur, Philippe, *Génération Europe* Paris: Editions François Bourin, 1989.

Bonin, Hubert, "Les banques d'affaires et la sortie de la crise," *Le Débat* (May–September 1986).

Boublil, Alain, *Le socialisme industriel* Paris: Presses Universitaires de France, 1977.

Bourdieu, Pierre, *La noblesse de l'état: Grandes écoles et esprit de corps* Paris: Editions de Minuit, 1989.

Boyer, Robert, *The Regulation School: A Critical Introduction* New York: Columbia University Press, 1990.

Boyer, Robert, "The Current Economic Crisis: Its Dynamics and Its Implications for France," in *The Mitterrand Experiment: Continuity and Change in Modern France,* ed. George Ross et al. Oxford: Polity Press, 1987.

Cameron, David, "Exchange Rate Politics in France: The Regime-Defining Choices of the Mitterrand Presidency," in *The Mitterrand Era: Policy Alternatives and Political Mobilization in France,* ed. Anthony Daley. New York: Macmillan and NYU Press, forthcoming.

Cerny, Philip, "The 'Little Big Bang' in Paris: Financial Market Deregulation in a *Dirigiste* System," *European Journal of Political Research* no. 17 (1989).

Chenot, Bernard, "Philosophie des nationalisations françaises," *Revue Française d'Administration Publique* no. 15 (July–September 1980).

Cohen, Elie, *Le colbertisme "high tech": Économies des Télécom et du Grand Projet* Paris: Hachette, 1992.

Cohen, Elie, "Dirigisme, politique industrielle et rhétorique industrialiste," *Revue Française de Science Politique* vol. 42, no. 2 (April 1992).

Cohen, Elie, *L'état brancardier: Politiques du déclin industriel (1974–1984)* Paris: Calmann-Lévy, 1989.

Cohen, Elie, "L'état Socialiste en industries: Volontarisme politique et changement socio-économique," in *Les élites Socialistes au pouvoir (1981–1985)* Paris: Presses Universitaires de France, 1985.

Cohen, Elie, and Bauer, Michel, *Les grandes manoeuvres industrielles* Paris: P. Belford, 1985.

Cohen, Stephen S., "Informed Bewilderment: French Economic Strategy and the Crisis," in *France in the Troubled World Economy,* ed. Stephen S. Cohen and Peter A. Gourevitch. London: Butterworths, 1982.

Cohen, Stephen S., *Modern Capitalist Planning: The French Model* Berkeley: University of California Press, 1977.

Cohen, Stephen S., Galbraith, James, and Zysman, John, "Rehabbing the Labyrinth: The Financial System and Industrial Policy in France," in *France in the*

Troubled World Economy, ed. Stephen S. Cohen and Peter A. Gourevitch. London: Butterworths, 1982.

Coleman, William D., "Reforming Corporatism: The French Banking Policy Community, 1941–1990," *West European Politics* vol. 16, no. 2 (April 1993).

Commission Général du Plan, *La France et l'Europe d'ici 2010,* ed. Jean-Baptiste de Foucauld. Paris: Documentation française, 1993.

Couroux, Bernard, *De la faculté d'adaptation d'un établissement public à son milieu: l'exemple d'EDF,* Ph.D. dissertation (Faculty of Law, Economic Sciences, and Management, University of Nice, January 11, 1991).

Crozier, Michel, *L'entreprise à l'écoute* Paris: Interéditions, 1989.

Crozier, Michel, "Pour une analyse sociologique de la planification française," *Revue Française de Sociologie* vol. 6, no. 2 (June 1965).

Dacier, Pierre, Jean-Louis Levet, and Jean-Claude Tourret, *Les dossiers noirs de l'industrie française* Paris: Fayard, 1985.

de Boissière, Jean-Baptiste, and Warusfeld, Bertrand, *La nouvelle frontière de la technologie européene* Paris: Calmann-Lévy, 1991.

de Boissieu, Christian, "Recent Developments in the French Financial System: An Overview," in *Banking in France,* ed. Christian de Boissieu. London: Routledge, 1990.

Delion, André, "Le contrôle des entreprises publiques," *Cahiers Français* no. 214 (January–February 1984).

Delion, André, *L'état et les entreprises publiques* Paris: Sirey, 1959.

Delion, André, and Durupty, Michel, *Les nationalisations* Paris: Economica, 1982.

Delmas, Philippe, *Le maître des horloges* Paris: Odile Jacob, 1991.

Derivry, Daniel, "The Managers of Public Enterprises in France," in *The Mandarins of Western Europe,* ed. Mattei Dogan. New York: John Wiley, 1975.

d'Iribarne, Philippe, *La logique de l'honneur: Gestion des entreprises et traditions nationales* Paris: Seuil, 1989.

Dubois, Pierre, *Mort de l'état-patron* Paris: Editions Ouvrières, 1974.

Dumez, Hervé, and Jeunemaître, Alain, "L'état et le marché en Europe: Vers un état de droit economique?" *Revue Française de Science Politique* vol. 42, no. 2 (April 1992).

Dumez, Hervé, and Jeunemaître, Alain, "La France, l'Europe et la concurrence: Enseignements de l'affaire A.T.R./De Havilland," *Commentaire* no. 57 (spring 1992).

Durand, Claude, Durand, Michelle, and VerVaeke, Monique, "Dirigisme et libéralisme: L'état dans l'industrie," *Sociologie du Travail* vol. 27 (March 1985).

Durupty, Michel, *Les privatisations* Paris: Documentation Française, 1988.

Estrin, Saul, and Holmes, Peter, *French Planning in Theory and Practice* London: George Allen & Unwin, 1983.

Feigenbaum, Harvey, *The Politics of Public Enterprise: Oil and the French State* Princeton: Princeton University Press, 1985.

Fontaneau, A., and Muet, P.-A., eds., *La gauche face à la crise* Paris: Presse de la Fondation Nationale des Sciences Politiques, 1985.

François-Poncet, Jean, and Barbier, Bernard, *1992: Les conséquences pour l'économie française du marché intérieur européen* Paris: Economica, 1989.

Freyssenet, Michel, *La sidérurgie française, 1945–79: L'histoire d'une faillite. Les solutions qui s'affrontent* Paris: Salvelli, 1979.

Fridenson, Patrick, "Atouts et limites de la modernisation par en haut: Les en-

treprises publiques face à leurs critiques (1944–1986)," in *Le capitalisme français 19e–20e siècle: Blocages et dynamismes d'une croissance,* ed. Patrick Fridenson and André Straus. Paris: Fayard, 1989.

Gabriel, Pierre Dupont, *L'état patron c'est moi* Paris: Flammarion, 1985.

Gélédan, Alain, *Le bilan économique des années Mitterrand 1981–1993* Paris:
Le Monde Editions, 1993.

Green, D., "Strategic Management and the State: France," in *Industrial Crisis: A
Comparative Study of the State and Industry* Oxford: Martin Robertson, 1983.

Hafsi, Taïeb, *Entreprise publique et politique industrielle* Paris: McGraw-Hill,
1984.

Hafsi, Taïeb, and Keonig, Christian, "The State–SOE Relationship: Some Patterns," in *Strategic Issues in State-Controlled Enterprises* Greenwich, CT, and
London: JAI Press, 1989.

Hafsi, Taïeb, and Thomas, Howard, "Managing in Ambiguous and Uncertain
Conditions: The Case of State-Controlled Firms in France," in *Strategic Issues
in State-Controlled Enterprises,* ed. Taïeb Hafsi. Greenwich, CT: JAI Press,
1989.

Hall, Peter A., "The State and the Market," *Developments in French Politics,* ed.
Peter A. Hall, Jack Hayward, and Howard Machin. New York: St. Martin's
Press, 1990.

Hall, Peter A., *Governing the Economy: The Politics of State Intervention in
Britain and France* New York: Oxford University Press, 1986.

Hall, Peter A., "Socialism in One Country: Mitterrand and the Struggle to Define
a New Economic Policy for France," in *Socialism, the State and Public Policy in
France,* ed. P. Cerny and M. Schain. London: Frances Pinter, 1985.

Harris, André, and De Sédouy, Alain, *Les patrons* Paris: Seuil, 1977.

Hayward, Jack, *The State and the Market Economy: Industrial Patriotism and
Economic Intervention in France* New York: New York University Press, 1986.

Hayward, Jack, "Institutional Inertia and Political Impetus in France and Great
Britain," *European Journal of Political Research* vol. 4 (1976).

Hayward, Jack, "National Aptitudes for Planning in Britain, France, and Italy,"
Government and Opposition vol. 9, no. 4 (1973).

Henry-Meininger, Marie-Christine, "La réforme du statut de la communication
audiovisuelle (lois du 30 septembre et du 27 novembre 1986)," *La Revue
Française d'Administration Publique* no. 41 (January–March, 1987).

Holton, Richard, "Industrial Politics in France: Nationalisation under Mitterrand," *West European Politics* vol. 1, no. 1 (January 1986).

Howell, Chris, "The Dilemmas of Post-Fordism: Socialists, Flexibility, and Labor
Market Deregulation in France," *Politics and Society* vol. 20, no. 1 (March
1992).

Howell, Chris, *Regulating Labor: The State and Industrial Relations Reform in
Postwar France* Princeton: Princeton University Press, 1992.

Kemp, Tom, *Economic Forces in French History* London: Denis Dobson, 1971.

Kesselman, Mark, "The New Shape of French Industrial Relations: Ce n'est plus
la même chose," in *Policymaking in France: From de Gaulle to Mitterrand,* ed.
Paul Godt. London: Pinter, 1989.

Kindleberger, Charles P., "The Postwar Resurgence of the French Economy," in *In
Search of France,* ed. Stanley Hoffmann et al. New York: Harper and Row,
1962.

Kuisel, Richard, *Capitalism and the State in Modern France* New York: Cambridge University Press, 1981.

464

Bibliography

Ladrech, Robert, "Europeanization of Domestic Politics and Institutions: The Case of France," in *Journal of Common Market Studies* (March 1994).

Le Bolloc'h-Puges, Chantal, *La politique industrielle française dans l'électronique* Paris: L'Harmattan, 1991.

Levet, Jean-Louis, "Réindustrialiser la France," *Politique Industrielle* no. 19 (spring 1990).

Levet, Jean-Louis, *Une France sans complexes* Paris: Economica, 1990.

Levet, Jean-Louis, *Une France sans usines?*, 2d ed. Paris: Economica, 1989.

Levy, Jonah, "Tocqueville's Revenge: The Decline of *Dirigisme* and Evolution of France's Political Economy." Ph.D. dissertation (Political Science, Massachusetts Institute of Technology, 1993).

Lipietz, Alain, "Governing the Economy in the Face of International Challenge: From National Developmentalism to National Crisis," in *Searching for the New France,* ed. James Hollifield and George Ross. New York: Routledge, 1991.

Lipietz, Alain, *L'audace ou l'enlisement: Sur les politiques économiques de la gauche* Paris: La Découverte, 1984.

Long, Marceau, "La diversification des entreprises publiques françaises," *Revue Française d'Administration Publique* no. 15 (July–September 1980).

Loriaux, Michael, *France after Hegemony: International Change and Financial Reform* Ithaca, NY: Cornell University Press, 1991.

Lucas, N. J. D., *Energy in France: Planning, Politics, and Policy* London: Europa Publications, 1979.

Lutz, Vera, *Central Planning for the Market Economy* London: Longmans, 1969.

Machin, Howard, and Wright, Vincent, eds., *Economic Policy and Policy-Making under the Mitterrand Presidency* London: Pinter, 1985.

Maurice, M., Sellier, F., and Silvestre, J.-J., *Production de la hiérarchie dans l'entreprise: Recherche d'un effet sociétal* Aix-en-Provence: LEST, 1980.

McArthur, John H., and Scott, Bruce R., *Industrial Planning in France* Cambridge, MA: Harvard Business School, 1969.

McCormick, Janice, and Stone, Nan, "From National Champion to Global Competitor: An Interview with Thomson's Alain Gomez," *Harvard Business Review* (May–June 1990): 127–135.

Merlin, Albert, "Réponse aux Cassandres industriels," *Politique Industriel* no. 18 (winter 1990).

Michalet, Charles-Albert, *Le capitalisme mondial* Paris: Presses Universitaires de France, 1976.

Millot, Michèle, and Roulleau, Jean-Pol, *L'entreprise face aux lois Auroux* Paris: Les Editions d'Organisation, 1984.

Ministère de la Recherche et de l'Industrie, *Une politique industrielle pour la France: Actes des journées de travail des 15 et 16 Novembre 1982* Paris: Documentation française, 1982.

Mioche, Philippe, "Le financement public de la sidérurgie: Réalité ou illusion d'un contrôle par l'état?" in *Le capitalisme français 19e–20e siècle,* ed. Fridenson and Straus.

Morin, François, *La structure financière du capitalisme français* Paris: Calmann-Levy, 1974.

Mouriaux, René, "Trade Unions, Unemployment, and Regulation: 1962–1986," in *Searching for the New France,* ed. Hollifield and Ross.

Mytelka, Lynne Krieger, "In Search of a Partner: The State and the Textile Industry in France," in *France in the Troubled World Economy,* ed. Cohen and Gourevitch.

Bibliography

Nora, Simon, and Groupe de Travail du Comité Interministériel des Entreprises Publiques, *Rapport sur les entreprises publiques* Paris: Documentation Française, 1967.

Observatoire des Entreprises Nationales, *Le secteur public industriel en 1985* Paris: Ministère de l'Industrie, des P. et T. et du Tourisme, 1986.

Padioleau, Jean G., *Quand la France s'enfrerre: La politique sidérurgique de la France depuis 1945* Paris: Presses Universitaires de France, 1981.

Palloix, Christian, *L'économie mondiale capitaliste et les firmes multinationales* Paris: Maspero, 1975.

Pastré, Olivier, *La stratégie internationale des groupes financiers américains* Paris: Economica, 1979.

Pébereau, Michel, "Les promesses de la privatisation," *Projet* (January–February, 1987).

Priouret, Roger, *La France et le management* Paris: Denoël, 1977.

Rapport de la Commission d'Enquête sur les conditions dans lesquelles ont été effectuées les opérations de privatisation d'entreprises et de banques appartenant au secteur public depuis le 6 août 1986, Assemblée Nationale no. 969, 3 vols., *Journal Officiel*, October 29, 1989.

Rapport 1986 du Haut Conseil du Secteur Public Paris: Documentation Française, 1988.

Rapport Raynaud Paris: Documentation Française, 1993.

Riboud, Antoine, *Modernisation, mode d'emploi* Paris: Union Générale d'Editions, 1987.

Rose, Michael Jehan, "Les syndicats français, le jacobinisme économique et 1992," *Sociologie du Travail* vol. 31, no. 1 (1989).

Ross, George, "French Labor and the 1992 Process," *French Politics and Society* vol. 8, no. 3 (summer 1990).

Sainsaulieu, Renaud, ed., *L'entreprise, une affaire de société* Paris: Presses de la Fondation Nationale des Sciences Politiques, 1990.

Sauzay, Michel, "Le rôle moteur du secteur public," in *Une politique industrielle pour la France*, ed. Ministère de la Recherche et de l'Industrie. Paris: Documentation Française, 1983.

Savage, Dean, *Founders, Heirs, and Managers* Beverly Hills, CA: Sage, 1979.

Seidentopf, Heinrich, and Ziller, Jacques, eds. *Making European Policies Work: The Implementation of Community Legislation in the Member States* London: Sage, 1988.

Smith, W. Rand, "Nationalizations for What? Capitalist Power and Public Enterprise in Mitterrand's France," *Politics and Society* vol. 18, no. 1 (1990).

Smith, W. Rand, "We Can Make the Ariane but We Can't Make Washing Machines: The State and Industrial Performance in Postwar France," in *Contemporary France: A Review of Interdisciplinary Studies*, ed. Jolyon Howorth and George Ross. London and New York: Pinter, 1989.

Smith, W. Rand, "Towards *Autogestion* in Socialist France: The Impact of Industrial Relations Reform," *West European Politics* vol. 10, no. 1 (January 1987).

Stoffaës, Christian, *La grande menace industrielle* Paris: Calmann-Lévy, 1978.

Taddei, Dominique, and Coriat, Benjamin, "Spécial: Made in France," *Industries*, special ed. (September 1992).

Thoenig, Jean-Claude, *L'ère des technocrates* Paris: Editions d'Organisations, 1973.

Ullmo, Yves, *La planification française* Paris: Dunod, 1974.

Vasseur, Philippe, *Patrons de gauche* Paris: Lattès, 1979.

466

Vickers, John, and Wright, Vincent, "The Politics of Industrial Privatisation in Western Europe: An Overview," *West European Politics* vol. 11, no. 4 (October 1988).

Vickery, L., "France" in *Small Business in Europe* London: Macmillan, 1986.

Wilsford, David, "Facing European Economic Integration: The French Pharmaceutical Industry," *French Politics and Society* vol. 8, no. 3 (summer 1990).

Wilson, Frank L., "Democracy in the Workplace: The French Experience," *Politics and Society* vol. 19, no. 4 (December 1991).

Wright, Vincent, "Industrial Policy-Making under the Mitterrand Presidency," *Government and Opposition,* vol. 19, no. 3 (summer 1984).

Xardel, Dominique, *Les managers* Paris: Grasset, 1978.

Zahariadis, Nikolaos, "The Political Economy of Privatization in Britain and France." Ph.D. dissertation (University of Georgia, Athens, 1992).

Ziegler, Jonathan Nicholas, "Reshaping the Industrial Plant," in "The State and Technological Advance: Political Efforts for Industrial Change in France and the Federal Republic of Germany, 1972–1986." Ph.D. dissertation (Government Department, Harvard University, 1989).

Zinsou, Lionel, *Le fer de lance* Paris: Olivier Orban, 1985.

Zysman, John, *Political Strategies for Industrial Order: State, Market, and Industry in France* Berkeley: University of California Press, 1977.

Zysman, John, "The French State in the International Economy," in *Between Power and Plenty,* ed. Katzenstein.

Index

Index

Index

Peyrelevade, Jean, 116, 153, 211, 303, 304, 305, 306, 312, 313, 329, 387, 398
pharmaceuticals industry, 64, 270, 364–5
Piette, J., 100
Pineau-Valencienne, Didier, 329, 342
Plan Calcul, 55, 206, 261
Plan: Second, 253; Third, 207; Sixth, 81, 253; Seventh Plan, 81; Ninth, 10
planning: pre-1981, 52, 76–9, 81–2, 86–9, 250, 251, 252–5; post-1981, 101, 139, 146–7; contracts, 209, 223–7; and corporatism, 36; process, 52–3, 61, 63–4; sectoral, 63–4, 255–62; and socialist economic project, 98, 99, 101
Planning Commission, 41–2, 200, 204, 206–9,
pluralist model, 15, 17–29, 35–6, 50–1, 58, 69; and the EU, 67, 243
policy communities model, 16, 17, 42–5
politique de créneaux, 53, 82, 93
politique de filières, 53, 93, 98, 118–19
Polytechnique, see X
Pompidou, Georges, 83
Ponts, École des, 286, 287, 297; corps des, 408, 412–13
presidential powers, 50–1, 200–1, 203
prime ministerial powers, 50–1, 200–1, 203–4; see also executive power
private enterprises, appointments of CEOs, 307–8,
privatization: pre-1981, 82; from 1981 to 1986, 128–130, 270; from 1986 to 1988, 130, 147, 153–63, 211–12, 271–6, 371–7; from 1988 to 1993, 186, 187, 276–7, 377–81; from 1993 to 1995, 191–2, 195, 281–2, 381–6; attitudes towards, 147–50, 168–9, 393, 404; policymaking process, 51–2, 56, 150–3
privatized enterprises, 219; appointments of CEOs, 306–8; see also privatization
protected capitalism, 370, 372, 391
PTT, 75, 145–6, 268, 399
public sector democratization law, 101–2, 310, 317, 402; see also Auroux laws; autogestion
public service enterprises, 64, 80, 90–1, 180–1, 262, 270–1
PUK, 80, 82, 116, 117; see also Péchiney

Quilès, Paul, 172, 174, 279, 290

RATP, 123
regulatory model, European Union, 67, 245–8

Renault, 77, 79, 80, 91, 115, 124, 125, 127, 129, 142, 179, 192, 193, 220, 258–9, 265, 277, 278, 281, 361, 363, 372, 374, 388, 398, 415
Rhône-Poulenc, 64, 82, 115, 116, 118, 122, 125, 126, 129, 180, 187, 192, 240, 260–1, 267, 277, 281, 361, 363, 372, 374, 378, 382, 383, 397, 404, 415
Riboud, Antoine, 233, 329, 398
Riboud, Jean, 110
Rocard, Michel, 68n, 116, 117, 142, 169, 176, 177–83, 209, 226, 289
Rothschild, David, 155n, 329
Rothschild bank, 82, 117, 122, 150n
Roussel-Uclaf, 117, 118, 180, 277, 278
Rousselet, André, 129–30, 297
Roux, Ambroise, 124, 267, 289, 301
Royer law, 80, 112–13
RPR, 135

Sacilor, 116, 119, 121, 127; see also Usinor-Sacilor
Saint-Geours, Frédéric, 330
Saint-Gobain, 64, 115, 116, 119, 124, 125, 126, 127, 129, 149, 157, 158, 160, 226, 265–6, 269, 271, 361, 365, 372, 374, 375, 376, 378, 382, 383, 384, 397, 398, 403, 404, 414–15, 434
Saint-Louis, 361, 378
scandals, 194–5, 440, 446
Schneider, 265, 361, 375
Schweitzer, Louis, 174, 192, 263, 277, 278, 305, 309, 374, 398, 402, 415
Séguin, Philippe, 137
SEITA, 80, 91, 281
SFPI, 125, 160–1
Shell, 104, 114
shipbuilding industry, 121
small European countries, 29, 33, 51
SMEs (small and medium-sized enterprises), 80–1, 351–2
SNCF, 60, 80, 89, 91, 123, 144, 192, 260, 262, 413
SNECMA, 190, 192, 222, 265, 397–8, 414, 431
Socialists: break with socialism, 95–6, 99–104, 105, 111; economic project, 96–103; and elite recruitment, 316–17, 320, 321–2, 327–8, 331–3, 338; and the state, 338–9
Société Générale, 115, 117, 122, 153, 161, 274, 367, 372, 375, 377, 378, 382, 383, 384, 386
Société Générale de Belgique, 372, 375, 378, 383
Sogenal, 154, 273

475

Index

standard-setting bodies, 235–6
Stasse, F. X., 116
state: aid, 143, 189–90; concept of, 15–17, 20–9; crisis of, 68, 194–5, 244–5, 342–3, 440–1; culture of, 315, 337–41; interventionism, 19, 24–5, 27; *see also dirigisme*
state-centered model, 16, 38–42
statist model, 26, 46–70, 88, 199–200, 249–50, 441–2; and European integration, 66–8
steel industry, 63, 64, 75, 81, 92–3, 119, 120, 121, 123, 124, 125, 126, 171, 256–7, 264–5, 365
Stern, Jacques, 305
Strauss-Kahn, Dominique, 100, 173, 178, 185, 186–7, 210, 217–18, 262, 330, 402, 421–2, 423, 425, 429, 433
students, 57, 59
Suard, Pierre, 173, 275, 304, 306, 342, 365, 390
Suez, 82, 117, 122, 129, 149, 153, 265, 274, 281, 370, 372, 374, 375, 376, 378, 383, 390
Sweden, 26, 29, 169
Syrota, Jean, 279

Tapie, Bernard, 194, 422
taxe professionelle, 83
Tchuruk, Serge, 413
teachers, 36, 41; and educational policy-making, 50, 57
telecommunications industry, 268–9
textile industry, 55, 75, 88, 120, 171, 260, 364
TF1, 130, 144, 153, 154, 157–8, 161, 178, 211, 247
Thatcher, Margaret, 141, 239
Thomas, René, 297, 305, 306
Thomson, 63, 82, 115, 116, 119, 122, 125, 126, 128, 129, 158, 180, 192, 193, 222, 258, 261, 268, 279–80, 281, 361, 366, 372, 374, 378–9, 434
Tocqueville, Aléxis de, 20, 58, 133, 341
Total, 186, 221, 257, 266, 267, 277, 364, 372, 375, 378, 383, 413
training, 351

transportation industry, 259–60
Treasury, 207, 209–10, 211, 219–20, 262, 273; *see also* Ministry of Finance
Trichet, Jean-Claude, 152, 279

U-turn, Great, 54, 95, 111, 112, 120, 211
UAP, 122, 162–3, 180, 192, 272, 281, 372, 374, 378, 383, 384, 387, 390
UDF, 24, 135
United States: business environment, 141, 169, 222; and corporatism, 34–5; industrial policy, 28, 53–4, 56–7, 88, 170; management culture, 400; management education and career path, 406, 409–10; pluralist policymaking process, 16–17, 21, 47, 48, 57, 62, 69, 199, 201, 246; and the state, 21, 28–9, 49; and the state-centered approach, 38–9; women managers, 430
university education, 407, 429–30
Usinor, 116, 119, 121, 127, 378; *see also* Usinor-Sacilor
Usinor-Sacilor, 115, 186, 279, 361, 365
UTA, 144, 276

Vernes, Jean-Marc, 381
Vernes bank, 117, 122
Victoire, 376
Vienot, Marc, 115, 274, 306, 329
Vincent, Claude, 330
volontarisme, 25, 73, 176, 184, 185, 186; *see also colbertisme*; *dirigisme*; state: interventionism
Volvo, 179, 192, 277, 278, 361, 362, 363

Weber, Henri, 11, 333
Wissocq, François de, 213, 341, 413, 426
wood industry, 55, 120, 171
workplace democracy, 31, 101–2, 177–8, 401, 403; *see also* Auroux laws; *autogestion*; public sector democratization law
Worms, Gérard, 329

X (École Polytechnique), 26, 43, 286, 287, 297, 322–5, 330, 406–7, 408, 412–14, 419, 433

476